ETHICS AND THE MULTINATIONAL ENTERPRISE

Proceedings of the
Sixth National Conference
on Business Ethics

"National Conference on Business Ethics (6th: 1985: Waltham, Mass.)"

WITHDRAWN

ETHICS AND THE MULTINATIONAL ENTERPRISE

Proceedings of the
Sixth National Conference
on Business Ethics
October 10 and 11, 1985

Sponsored by
Center for Business Ethics
Bentley College
Waltham, Massachusetts

Edited by

W. Michael Hoffman
Director
Center for Business Ethics

Ann E. Lange
Research Associate
Center for Business Ethics

David A. Fedo
Associate Undergraduate Dean and
Business Ethics Conference Chairperson
Bentley College

UNIVERSITY PRESS OF AMERICA

LANHAM • NEW YORK • LONDON

Copyright © 1986 by

University Press of America,® Inc.

4720 Boston Way
Lanham, MD 20706

3 Henrietta Street
London WC2E 8LU England

All rights reserved

Printed in the United States of America

Co-published by arrangement with the
Center for Business Ethics, Bentley College

Library of Congress Cataloging in Publication Data

National Conference on Business Ethics (6th : 1985 :
   Waltham, Mass.)
   Ethics and the multinational enterprise.

   Bibliography: p.
   1. International business enterprises—Moral and
ethical aspects—Congresses.   2. Business ethics—
Congresses.   I. Hoffman, W. Michael.   II. Lange, Ann E.
III. Fedo, David A.   IV. Bentley College.   Center for
Business Ethics.   V. Title.
HD2711.N38   1985   174'.4   86-19038
ISBN 0-8191-5654-X (alk. paper)
ISBN 0-8191-5655-8 (pbk. : alk. paper)

All University Press of America books are produced on acid-free
paper which exceeds the minimum standards set by the National
Historical Publications and Records Commission.

HD
2711
.N38
1985

CONTENTS

Foreword   Gregory H. Adamian   xiii
Preface   W. Michael Hoffman   xvii
Introduction   Ann E. Lange   xix

CHAPTER ONE: THE ISSUES AND THEIR CONTEXT: SOME
PERSPECTIVES ON THE SOURCES OF ETHICAL DILEMMAS FOR
THE MULTINATIONAL CORPORATION

Changing Rules of International Corporate Behavior -
  S. Prakash Sethi, Professor of Management and
  Director of the Research Program in Business and
  Public Policy, Baruch College (CUNY)   3

Ethical Dilemmas of Multinational Enterprise: An
  Historical Perspective - Mira Wilkins, Professor
  of Economics, Florida International University   25

Social Responsibility of the Multinational
  Corporation - Charles P. Kindleberger, Visiting
  Professor of Economics, Brandeis University   31

Ethical Dilemmas for Multinational Enterprise: A
  Philosophical Overview - Richard T. De George,
  Distinguished Professor of Philosophy, University
  of Kansas   39

Using Macroeconomic Theory to Anchor Problems: Ethical
  Issues and Multinationals - Karen Paul, Associate
  Professor of Management, Rochester Institute of
  Technology, and Otto A. Bremer, Director of Laity
  Programs, Vesper Society, and Lecturer, Graduate
  Theological Union   47

CHAPTER TWO: INTERNATIONAL ACCORDS AS TOOLS FOR
PROBLEM SOLVING

Ethics and the Multinational Enterprise - Raymond
  Vernon, Clarence Dillon Professor of
  International Affairs Emeritus, Harvard
  University   61

Defining the Ethical Obligations of the Multinational
  Enterprise - Duane Windsor, Associate Professor
  of Administrative Science and Assistant Dean, The

v

Jesse Jones Graduate School of Administration,
Rice University ... 71

Multinational Corporations: Ethics or Self-Interest? - Hans J. Spiller, Director, Berlin Economic Development Corporation ... 87

CHAPTER THREE: CORPORATE MODELS FOR ETHICAL DECISION MAKING

Ethics at Honeywell: Wrestling with the Horns of Dilemma - Joe E. Chenoweth, Executive Vice President - International, Honeywell, Inc. ... 95

Ethics as a Way of Life - Robert Gunts, Vice President, International Division, Whirlpool Corporation ... 101

Ethics, Capitalism, and Multinationals - E.F. Andrews, Vice President (Retired), Materials and Services, Alleghney International ... 107

Every Cloud has a Zip-Out Lining - Robert McClements, Jr., Chief Executive Officer, Sun Company, Inc. ... 113

Ethics and the Scientist: Common Sense or Camelot - Etcyl H. Blair, Vice President and Director of Health and Environmental Science, Dow Chemical U.S.A. ... 121

CHAPTER FOUR: CONSULTING STRATEGIES FOR DEALING WITH MULTINATIONAL BUSINESS ETHICAL DILEMMAS

Ethical Issues in the Multinational Environment - David Nosnik, Partner, Deloitte Haskins & Sells ... 129

Ethical Criteria for Multinational Consulting - Verne E. Henderson, Ethics Consultant and Professor of Ethics and Social Issues, Arthur D. Little Management Education Institute ... 133

An Ethical Dilemma for Multinational Consulting - William W. Bain, Jr., President, Bain and Company ... 143

CHAPTER FIVE: CHURCH ACTIVISM AND THE MULTINATIONAL CORPORATION

The Church Corporate Responsibility Movement: Fifteen
    Years Later - Timothy H. Smith, Executive
    Director, Interfaith Center on Corporate
    Responsibility   151

Reflections on Church Activism and Transnational
    Corporations - J. Philip Wogaman, Professor of
    Christian Social Ethics, Wesley Theological
    Seminary   159

Business Ethics and the Churches - Rafael D. Pagan,
    President, Nestle Coordination Center for
    Nutrition, Inc., and Chairman, Pagan International   163

Activism, Religion, and Economic Justice - James
    Armstrong, Senior Vice President, Pagan
    International   169

Theological Ethics and the Multinational: Diverse
    Assessments - Oliver F. Williams, Associate
    Professor in Management and Co-Director, Center
    for Ethics and Religious Values in Business,
    University of Notre Dame   175

CHAPTER SIX: POVERTY IN THE THIRD WORLD: SOURCES AND SOLUTIONS

Poverty: A Condition of Life for Most of the World's
    People - Lee A. Tavis, C.R. Smith Professor of
    Business Administration, University of Notre Dame   189

Creating Wealth, or Causing Poverty? - Denis Goulet,
    O'Neill Professor of Education for Justice,
    University of Notre Dame   197

Multinational Companies and World Poverty - John B.
    Caron, President, Caron International   209

Foreign Equity Investment and Economic Development:
    Four Ethical Dilemmas of Multinational
    Enterprise - Lawrence G. Franko, Professor of
    International Business Relations, Fletcher School
    of Law and Diplomacy, Tufts University   215

Poverty - Jean Wilkowski, Chairperson of the Board,
    Volunteers in Technical Assistance   223

CHAPTER SEVEN: INVESTING IN DEVELOPMENT: THE PROMISE AND THE PROBLEMS

**The Role of the Private Sector in Developing
    Countries: A World Bank Perspective** - Marjorie
    K. Sheen, Public Affairs Advisor, The World Bank   231

**Environmental Concerns Associated with Multilateral
    Development Bank Activity** - Barbara Bramble,
    Director, International Division National
    Wildlife Federation, and Sheila Harty, Director,
    Corporate Initiatives Division, National Wildlife
    Federation   239

CHAPTER EIGHT: THE IMPACT OF MULTINATIONAL BUSINESS ACTIVITY ON WOMEN IN THE THIRD WORLD

**Multinational Enterprises, Development, and Women: An
    Overview** - Anita Anand, Professional Consultant,
    International Development   251

Transnational Corporations and Women's Health - Luisa
    M. Rivera Izabal, Social Worker, SEDEPAC
    (Service, Development, and Peace)   257

**Women Factory Workers in Asian Developing Countries:
    Some Dilemmas for Multinational Employees** -
    Linda Y.C. Lim, Assistant Professor and Research
    Director, Southeast Asia Business Education and
    Resource Program, University of Michigan   263

CHAPTER NINE: ETHICAL DILEMMAS INVOLVED IN THE MARKETING AND SALE OF PRODUCTS IN LESS DEVELOPED COUNTRIES

**Ethical Dilemmas of Multinational Enterprises: An
    Analysis of Nestle's Traumatic Experience with
    the Infant Formula Controversy** - James E. Post,
    Professor of Management, Boston University   285

The Infant Formula Controversy: Everybody's Ethics -
    Carol Adelman, Professional Consultant,
    International Health and Nutrition   299

Note on the Export of Pesticides from the United
   States to Developing Nations - Kenneth E.
   Goodpaster, Associate Professor, Graduate School
   of Business Administration, Harvard University
   and David E. Whiteside, Former Associate in
   Research, Harvard Business School   305

The Principles of Pesticides: A Moral Dialogue - Scott
   Cook, Associate in Research, Harvard Business
   School   335

CHAPTER TEN: BHOPAL

The Bhopal Tragedy: The Failure of Corporate
   Responsibility - A. Karim Ahmed, Research
   Director, Natural Resources Defense Council   345

Unethical Fallout From Technical Decisions - Paul
   Shrivastava, Associate Professor of Management,
   New York University   349

The Bhopal Tragedy: Some Implications and Guidelines
   for Multinational Business - Gary Edwards,
   Executive Director, Ethics Resource Center   357

Chemical Industry Accidents, Liability, and Community
   Right to Know - Michael S. Baram, Professor of
   Health Law, School of Public Health, Boston
   University   363

CHAPTER ELEVEN: SOUTH AFRICA

The Role of Multinational Coporations in Helping to
   Bring About Change in South Africa - Leon H.
   Sullivan, Pastor, Zion Baptist Church   379

A Case for Sanctions Against South Africa - Kenneth
   N. Carstens, Executive Director, International
   Aid and Defense Fund for Southern Africa   387

South Africa: Time Has Run Out - Howard Wolpe, U.S.
   Congressman, Michigan   401

Some Personal Observations Regarding South Africa -
   Harry Johnson, Manager, Public Relations,
   Polaroid Corporation   409

Multinational Enterprises, Sanctions, and South Africa: A Host Country Perspective - D.G.M. Fourie, Deputy Consul-General, South African Consulate-General ... 411

The American Multinational Enterprise and South Africa: Maintaining the Proper Balance - David M. Ludington, Associate Professor of Marketing Saint Mary's College ... 419

Moral Justifications for Doing Business in South Africa - Patricia H. Werhane, Associate Professor of Philosophy, Loyola University of Chicago ... 435

United States Corporations in South Africa: A Case for Staying - Wilfred D. Koplowitz, Vice President and Director, International Public Affairs, Citibank, N.A. ... 443

CHAPTER TWELVE: BRIBERY AND THE FOREIGN CORRUPT PRACTICES ACT

A Selective Review of the Criminal Prosecutions Under the Foreign Corrupt Practices Act of 1977 - Kevin F. Wall, Assistant Professor of Accountancy, Bentley College ... 451

Managing the Rules of Conflict -- International Bribery - Mark Pastin, Professor of Management and Director, Center for Private and Public Sector Ethics, Arizona State University ... 463

Ethics in the FCPA Debate: Some Public Policy Lessons - John M. Kline, Deputy Director, Karl F. Landegger Program in International Business Policy, School of Foreign Service, Georgetown University ... 477

CHAPTER THIRTEEN: JOBS, INFORMATION TECHNOLOGY, AND MULTINATIONAL BUSINESS

The Foreign Direct Investment Decision and Job Export as an Ethical Dilemma for the Multinational Corporation - Marjorie Thines Stanley, Professor of Finance and Chairperson, Department of Finance and Decision Sciences, Texas Christian University ... 493

Ethical Dimensions of Information Technology in Global Business - Abbe Mowshowitz, Professor of Computer Science, The City College (CUNY) 511

FOREWORD

The marriage of business and ethics, though a solid partnership of long standing, has regularly been confronted with innate conflict situations. It was a union formed originally in the marketplace of ancient Greece, during the time of Socrates, when democracy was a wonderful new idea that no one was quite sure how to implement. The earliest attempts to apply ethical standards to the daily transactions of busy Greek merchants were fraught with the complexity of real life wheeling and dealing, a far cry from the isolated serenity of an idealistic ivory tower.

Human progress during the past twenty-five hundred years owes much to the fact that this durable marriage of business and ethics has consistently weathered the strain of daily crisis. However, in more recent years, as popular reaction to big business has taken a decidedly negative turn, the level of tension and uncertainty has escalated to new heights of moral confusion. Today's large business enterprise is forced to confront deeply disturbing ethical issues.

When we turn to the special case of the multinational corporation, the situation pushes complexity to its breaking point. Intense Third World economic and social distress, ongoing tensions with the Soviet Union and China, continuing balance of payments problems, unending anxiety about the Middle East, South Africa, Central and South America, and the constant threat of terrorism combined with the inevitable clashes of differing cultural values suggest that the transactions of large scale international business would be hopelessly obstructed by seemingly insurmountable obstacles.

And yet multinational enterprises survive, and they will continue to survive, because the relationship between the multinational and host country is symbiotic: the multinational needs raw materials, affordable labor and new markets, but the developing country needs know-how, technology, affordable products, and infusions of capital. They really cannot exist without each other. And this, I suggest, is precisely the situation between business and ethics.

No business that consistently disregards the moral and cultural views of the public it serves will ever thrive, and no attempt to establish ethical standards can afford to ignore the economic realities that underlie both personal and corporate interactions. No matter how rocky their relationship, business and ethics <u>need</u> each other, and so the marriage endures.

However, some regular recourse to outside counseling and inside soul-searching would certainly ease the tension and maybe even offer hope of smoother sailing in the future. This brings us to the reason for this collection of essays presented at the Sixth National Conference on Business Ethics. Representatives from both sides of the family share their concerns and their insights in an attempt to strengthen the bond between the real and the ideal, between what <u>is</u> and what <u>should be</u>. Our goal is to narrow the gap that we know we can never breach entirely. If we can better define the nature of the complexity that is our given, we will have made a major contribution.

I am personally optimistic that there is real potential for concrete progress. The phenomenon of multinationals is still in infancy; there remain so many untried possibilities for using corporate mechanisms to make life better for countless individuals worldwide. As Thomas Donaldson has pointed out, the sorry record of political programs in curing human misery leaves plenty of room for improvement. Multinationals offer hope for international cooperation based not on unstable political emotions, but on the proven human propensity for trade and commerce.

In fact, experts have suggested that in the coming years more and more people will look to the corporation as a visible, powerful institution to help resolve tensions and avoid conflicts. Although the primary role of the corporation will continue to be the process of producing quality goods and services while earning an acceptable profit for its shareholders, it is clear that this creation of wealth must go hand in hand with some measure of social responsibility, especially in the case of troubled developing nations. This is no easy task, even on a local level. When today's multinationals are forced daily to confront pressing global concerns, the problem magnifies exponentially.

There is no doubt that the spirit of internationalism is the trend of our times. We at Bentley College are convinced that the study of business must henceforth involve a respect and appreciation for the wealth of cultural diversity that affects so many vital business decisions. The brash, and often narrow-minded, American chauvinism that propelled so many of our captains of industry earlier in the century is no longer appropriate. It simply won't work in an era when national pride is asserted with such ferocity by citizens of even the smallest and youngest of emerging nations. If moral conflicts are inevitable in an interdependent world, this is probably because systems of law and morality are not as interdependent as economic activities.

The litany of accusations against the activities of United States corporations abroad demands case-by-case intelligent judgment. No doubt multinationals have often been unprepared for the endless ambiguities of their interactions with host cultures.

The contrast between modern and traditional societies would generate profound moral conflict even under the best of circumstances. When well-meaning companies operate with the handicap of widespread popular mistrust of big business, along with all too frequent anti-Americanism, then their task of defining an appropriate ethical code is fraught with an overpowering complexity.

If we can combine all the best wisdom and experience of representatives from the fields of business, higher education, government and the public sector, we will maximize our chances of creating some much needed order in the midst of what sometimes seems like moral chaos. That, at least, is the contention of our Center for Business Ethics here at Bentley.

                                      Gregory H. Adamian
                                      President
                                      Bentley College
                                      June, 1986

PREFACE

The Center for Business Ethics at Bentley College, in Waltham, Massachusetts, was founded in 1976 to provide a nonpartisan forum for exchanging ideas on business ethics in an industrial society, in relation to the activities of corporations, labor, government, special interest groups, and the professions. The Center thus far has sponsored six National Conferences on Business Ethics. It is hoped that these conferences have fostered and will continue to foster greater awareness and understanding of moral issues within the business world from diverse perspectives.

The Center has published the proceedings of the six conferences in book form. They are: <u>The Proceedings of the First National Conference on Business Ethics: Business Values and Social Justice</u> (1977); <u>The Proceedings of the Second National Conference on Business Ethics: Power and Responsibility in the American Business System</u> (1979); <u>The Work Ethic in Business: Proceedings of the Third National Conference on Business Ethics</u> (1981); <u>Ethics and the Management of Computer Technology: Proceedings of the Fourth National Conference on Business Ethics</u> (1982); <u>Corporate Governance and Institutionalizing Ethics: Proceedings of the Fifth National Conference on Business Ethics</u> (1984), and now this book <u>Ethics and the Multinational Enterprise: Proceedings of the Sixth National Conference on Business Ethics</u> (1986).

In addition to the conferences and <u>Proceedings</u>, the Center publishes the <u>Business Ethics Report</u>, which describes the highlights of the conferences; various bibliographies on business ethics; collections of syllabi of business ethics courses; and data gained from national surveys of business ethics. It also videotapes the proceedings of the conferences and makes these tapes available for sale or rental. Furthermore, the Center serves as a general clearinghouse for ideas and information concerning the field of business ethics studies and moral issues connected to business activities. As a result of this work, the Center has helped to create a climate of greater understanding and trust among various constituencies and has furthered its ultimate aim of establishing a better ethical framework within which to conduct business in general.

The Sixth National Conference, held October 10 and 11, 1985, at Bentley College, and other activities of the Center for Business Ethics were made possible in part from grants from the following: Arvin Industries; Robert W. Brown, M.D.; the Council for Philosophical Studies (sponsored by the National Endowment for the Humanities); Exxon Education Foundation; the General Mills Foundation; General Motors Corporation; Midland-Ross, Inc.; the Motorola Foundation; Rexnord, Inc.; Richardson-Merrill, Inc.; the Rockefeller Foundation; Semline, Inc.; Stop and Shop Manufacturing Companies; and F.W. Woolworth Company. We would like to give special recognition to Raytheon Company for its most generous contribution toward this past Sixth National Conference. On behalf of the Center, I thank all of these contributors and all of the participants of the Sixth National Conference for sharing their support and ideas.

I am also pleased to express our appreciation to the following session moderators at the conference: Jane H. Ives, Assistant Professor of Management, Suffolk University; Jennifer Mills Moore, Research Associate, Bentley College; William K. O'Brien, Managing Partner, Coopers & Lybrand; Walter H. Palmer, Director of Public Affairs and Community Relations, Raytheon Company; Dharmendra T. Verma, Professor of Marketing, Bentley College; Arnold Weinstein, Dean of the College of Management, University of Massachusetts/Boston; and Alexander Zampieron, Professor of Economics, Bentley College. Thanks should go to the following members of Bentley's conference program committee: Norman M. Bryden, Anthony F. Buono, Steven G. Grubaugh, Jeremiah J. O'Connell, Walter H. Palmer, Herbert L. Sawyer, and Thomas F. Slaughter. Our appreciation goes to all the faculty, staff, and students at Bentley College whose support continues to make our conferences a success, with special thanks this year to Margo Amoroso, Janice Corcoran, Ruth G. Horowitz, Jeffrey Kelly, Aileene McDonagh, Alan S. Morris, and Paulette Mungillo. Finally, we would like to acknowledge the tremendous help received from S. Prakash Sethi in suggesting topics and obtaining speakers for the Conference.

> W. Michael Hoffman
> Director
> Center for Business Ethics
> June, 1986

INTRODUCTION

A multinational corporation (MNC) can be defined as a business whose operations extend beyond the boundries of one nation. Such a business, then, most likely will have one or more branches or subsidiaries somewhere other than in the nation in which it is legally chartered (its home country). Both the scope and the nature of American-based MNCs have changed significantly since the early 1900s when the United Fruit Company was growing bananas in Central America and gaining some notoriety for its "invasion" of Honduras. No longer are American MNCs primarily to be found among extractive industries as they were then. Financial institutions, drug, chemical, auto, and other manufacturers, agricultural firms, service industries, and other types of enterprises can all be found operating as multinational concerns. In fact, in just the past 30 or so years, investment by American firms in foreign operations has risen from around $20 billion to nearly $250 billion.

The incentives for corporations to move into the international business arena are many and clear. Businesses obviously are in existence to make a profit. Among other benefits, expansion into foreign countries, and especially into so-called "emerging nations" or less developed countries (LDCs), can often offer new markets, lower labor costs, access to raw materials that might be scarce and more expensive at home, and greater returns on investment than would be possible at home. Obviously, any or all of these would help a corporation's overall position. In fact, it is often suggested that large corporations can no longer afford to ignore the potential offered by foreign expansion if they are to survive.

However, with this expansion come a number of ethical dilemmas unique to such operations. That such dilemmas do exist and create problems for the MNC is certainly evident given even a superficial glance at the events of the past 15 years. The infant formula controversy, the Lockheed Aircraft payments to Japanese government officials, the continuing social and political turmoil in South Africa, the involvement of ITT in the overthrow of the government of Salvador Allende in Chile, the "exporting" of jobs to Third World countries, and the tragic accident at a Union Carbide plant in Bhopal, India, have all, at one point or another, been front page news, and all have provided both the critics and the defenders of MNC activity with enough material for seemingly endless debate.

What, if any, special obligations does a corporation have when marketing a product in a country where many people might be likely to use it incorrectly? How far should a company go in pursuing profits when the means of doing so clash with what is considered to be accepted practice in the home country, but are well within the standards of the host country? Should a corporation do business with a country whose political processes and social policies are judged by many to be abhorrent? How far should a corporation go in attempting to influence political processes in its host country in order to protect its interests there? Is it ethical to shift production to another country to avoid dealing with labor problems and/or environmental controls at home? How should plants producing potentially hazardous products be run in a country whose laws and safety standards are considerably more lax than those of the home country and whose officials demand some local control of the facilities? How should the claims of countries with differing cultures and customs be weighed in corporate decision making? Should corporations even be involved in trying to deal with any of these questions or should answers be left to legal institutions, agreements between countries, and the forces of the marketplace?

The cases mentioned earlier do not have easily identifiable villians or heroes, and the questions they raise do not admit to some simple analysis that will rid them of all ambiguities. There are no easy solutions to the dilemmas the cases embody. Rather, they need to be examined both in themselves and in the broader context of the complexities that beset multinational corporate decision making in its ethical dimension. And methods need to be devised to deal with some of those dilemmas so that the possibility of the occurrence of problems arising out of them can be minimized.

Written in conjunction with Bentley College's Sixth National Conference on Business Ethics, the papers in this volume present a number of perspectives on all of these points. Included in the first chapter are some general overviews of the context and nature of the dilemmas facing the MNC; the next four chapters outline various models and strategies for dealing with these dilemmas; and the final chapters discuss some specific cases and issues involving the dilemmas.

S. Prakash Sethi begins Chapter One by presenting an extensive overview of both the changing socio-political environment of the MNC and the various pressures on the MNC to respond to issues and conditions in certain ways. This context, he argues, must be clarified because it establishes the limits within which multinational corporate power can be exercised. An understanding of it is crucial to all parties involved in attempting to devise strategies to aid MNC decision-making processes. Failure to grasp the changing context in which these decisions must be made, he feels, can lead only to unfortunate consequences.

He identifies what he sees as important new elements in the "emerging international environment" of multinational businesses. Prior to the 1960s, he states, "the primary elements of the MNC's external environment ... were host country and home country governments." But, more and more, international organizations such as the United Nations and private voluntary organizations such as consumer advocates, church groups, and representatives of varying ideologies are emerging as "non-market intervenors" with which the MNC must also deal directly. Both often challenge MNC activity (especially in less developed countries), and their potential influence can be seen in examples such as the World Health Organization's Code to regulate infant formula marketing practices and in efforts to influence American firms with holdings in South Africa to abide by the Sullivan Principles or even to disinvest. Sethi suggests that a failure to recognize the influence and strength of such groups could have serious effects on corporate "survival, profitability, and growth."

He also discusses recent changes in the technologies involved in manufacturing and production processes as well as the entrance of businesses from countries like Japan into multinational ventures. All of those elements, as well as certain factors relating to the traditional role of the MNC in the host country, must be appreciated and taken into consideration in order to ensure the viability of the MNC.

Both Mira Wilkins and Charles P. Kindleberger see the great number of potentially conflicting influences in the environment of the MNC as setting the stage for multiple and complex ethical dilemmas, and neither one thinks that easy solutions to the dilemmas are available. Wilkins presents an historical overview of the MNC in order to show that the problems faced by modern MNCs are not much different than those that were faced by such enterprises in the past. When "rules, regulations, and goals" of sovereign states conflict "and the conflict effects the business of the multinational enterprise, the institution is by definition caught in a quandry." An essential question becomes that of how managers of MNCs should deal with such quandries. Another related and equally crucial question is if they should be involved in the transmission of any ethical or political values or systems to the host country and, if so, which ones.

Kindleberger echoes Wilkins' concerns, presenting a number of questions about such issues as bribery, Italian tax reporting practices, the infant formula controversy, South Africa, and Bhopal to illustrate his point that dilemmas confronted by MNCs operating in differing cultures afford no simple anaylses and that degrees and distinctions tend to be murky. But the problems must be grappled with, and the one thing that he feels is totally unjustified is for the MNC to switch "between two positions continuously on an ad hoc basis determined by the bottom line on each separate issue."

While he agrees with both Wilkins and Kindleberger that "conflicting demands made from opposing, often ideologically based, points of view" are the source of the ethical dilemmas of MNCs. Richard T. De George also suggests that there are some ways to constructively approach the problem. In the first place, some dilemmas can be identified as being false (and can thus be dissolved) if it is recognized that regulatory standards used in the United States are not necessarily morally mandatory for the entire world.

Moreover, he feels that there are seven moral "norms" that MNCs should follow no matter what conflicting demands exist. MNCs (specifically those operating in Third World countries) should: (1) "do no intentional direct harm"; (2) "produce more good than bad for the host country"; (3) "contribute ... to the host country's development"; (4) "respect the human rights of its employees"; (5) "pay their fair share of taxes"; (6) respect the local culture and work with it" (given that the local culture adheres to moral norms); and (7) "cooperate with the local government on the development and enforcement of just background institutions." These rules will not put an end to all dilemmas, but following them will certainly put the MNC beyond reproach.

To end the chapter, Karen Paul and Otto Bremer suggest that it is useful to look at ethical issues through a system or social analysis. Such an approach does two things: (1) it enables the problems to be viewed as "part of systems functioning, rather than as a result of individual error, or ignorance, or wickedness"; and (2) it makes it possible to see relations between particular cases rather than just a series of unconnected unique events. Accordingly, Paul and Bremer present four sets of macroeconomic theories which they think give a conceptual framework that will help to both clarify and analyze the nature of ethical dilemmas faced by MNCs. The four theories -- Rostow's economic development theory, the North/South approach, the rise and fall of nations approach, and the limits of growth approach -- all offer differing perspectives on the benefits and the harms that accrue to both the MNC and the host country (in this paper assumed to be a less developed country) as a result of their relationship. Taken together, Paul and Bremer claim, the four perspectives can provide a useful framework for sorting ethical issues confronted by MNCs into groups and systematically analyzing them.

De George's suggestion that there is a set of ethical guidelines that can be used by MNCs in approaching decision making leads to another concern: how can the MNC best deal with the dilemmas it faces? In the next four chapters, a variety of strategies and models are presented as potential answers to the question. In Chapter Two, Raymond Vernon, Duane Windsor, and Hans J. Spiller all suggest that the best and most effective strategy is one that primarily relies on international codes and agreements for its direction. Vernon, in fact, suggests that the only ethical question unique to the multinational enterprise is that of whether it is "ethical for such enterprises to resist the formulation of international agreements when they are designed to create workable arrangements among governments to deal with conflicts in national values and objectives."

MNCs, he suggests, are often singled out in connection with ethical issues because of their size, high visibility, and foreignness. In fact, however, national enterprises often have problems similar to those faced by MNCs. The difference lies in the fact that MNCs must deal with the often conflicting demands not only of shareholders, employees, and the community but also of differing national interests and ideologies.

Echoing a point made earlier by De George, he says that "ethical behavior commonly entails avoiding use of power that might be hurtful to others." But what nation or group's demands should take precedence? None? Is the MNC then only to take its own interests into consideration? He mentions Bhopal and South Africa as cases in point. In that problems unique to MNCs do not, according to Vernon, stem from MNCs themselves, but rather from the conflicting and inconsistent values of various countries and given that there is no easy way to calibrate ethical superiority, he suggests that there is a pressing "need for some agreed set of rules that would mediate national clashes and would formulate the obligations that multinational enterprises should assume to the world economy at large."

Windsor also thinks that the development of international codes and agreements is critical for the decision-making dilemmas facing multinational business. He reiterates a point made by Vernon and many authors in this volume: MNCs face many difficult problems because of their very nature. Potential conflicts "among economic performances, legal compliance, moral conduct, and social responsibility" that plague national businesses are exacerbated in the case of the MNC by the myriad of differing customs, laws, and standards in the various areas in which they operate. The situation is difficult at best.

Windsor claims that the most difficult ethical issues facing MNCs do not lie in "ethical diagnosis," but in "moral prescription" or in figuring out how to right that which is seen to be wrong. For instance, almost everyone is uncomfortable with bribery and apartheid and everyone agrees that the Bhopal incident was a tragedy. The problem lies in devising proper responses to such issues. He suggests that while businesses in general are simply not well equipped to deal with such conflict resolution, possible strategies for dealing with the problems are to be found in three areas: (1) internal corporate codes which reflect "externally defined standards" need to be devised; (2) international agreements need to be formulated through organizations such as the United Nations to guide these internal codes; and (3) individual countries need to review their particular laws governing MNC activity.

In the final paper in this chapter, Spiller suggests that for a corporation "ethics" usually means obeying rules in order to stay out of trouble and benefit itself. Using a number of examples including environmental concerns, the exporting of hazardous materials, and product safety, he contrasts the self-interest approach with the idea of an "ethical conscience" or doing the good simply because it is good. The implication of his presentation is that for corporations "ethics" is a direct result of social approval or disapproval or of morality translated into law. He bluntly states that "...it is my contention that corporations do not act 'ethically'. They simply obey laws." A well-articulated legal framework, then, is essential to the ethical functioning of the MNC.

Chapter Three presents a number of corporate perspectives on possible strategies in dealing with ethical issues in multinational business dealings. Joe E. Chenoweth and Robert F. Gunts both suggest that models that rely on law and international codes provide an inadequate approach to the problems. Corporations themselves must somehow deal with the ethical dimensions of their decision making.

Chenoweth sees two levels of behavior operative in any corporation: that defined by law and that defined by what he terms the "corporate culture." There is a limit to the guidance that laws can give, and they are often open to interpretation. That is why the development of corporate ethics is so important -- they fill gaps and "create a base from which to do business." Especially in a decentralized MNC setting, Chenoweth feels, the corporation must have a strong ethical framework which communicates corporate standards openly and vigorously. Such a framework should be devised by the input of all, put in writing, and instilled by example from the top on a day to day basis and not so much prohibit certain actions as promote certain goals. He points to the Honeywell Principles as an example of such a code. Dilemmas will still arise, but a strong corporate culture will minimize them as much as possible.

Gunts also speaks of the need for a corporate culture and of a "charter in the community" which demands of the corporation "the highest ethical standards and practices." Certain activities may vary depending on local customs and laws, but if certain basic ethical principles are articulated clearly enough, they can be taken anywhere in the world. Whirlpool, he says, tries to do just this and backs its commitment to ethical standards by employing 15 internal auditors charged with investigating "any aspect of corporate life." Their board of directors (of its 13 members, 10 are outsiders) also has an audit committee assigned the same function.

E.F. Andrews and Robert McClements, Jr. have a different approach in that they both stress what Andrews terms "the positive ethical consequences of capitalism." Andrews feels that the economic freedom promoted by capitalism is the only assurance of political freedom. Moreover, the literacy and skill levels capitalism demands and the economic well-being it brings directly militate against "serfdom." As such, MNCs should be given free reign to invest and to expand their activities no matter what the political climate of the host country.

He is aware that, on the international level, values can often conflict and decision-making processes are often more ambiguous and difficult than when a shared, understood tradition exists, but too much emphasis on such problems tends, he thinks, to obscure his main point about capitalism. As such, he strongly objects to what he terms the "selective morality" that leads to sanctions against business activities in certain countries with whose ideologies we do not agree. In the first place, he regards such sanctions as political expediency rather than morality and, in second place, he feels that the presence of MNCs can only help to better things. Their absence, on the other hand, is an open invitation to manipulation by forces that usually bring agony to the indigenous population.

McClements calls for an "ethics of balance" that will provide an unbiased look at business and the market system. Such a look can only, he thinks, lead to the conclusion that the market-based economy on which business is built is the best hope for creating an economic and ethical balance in all parts of the world. MNCs help to alleviate poverty in less developed countries by investing in them, building houses and schools, and creating a demand for literacy. Thus the activity of multinational business tends to balance what we in the developed world have with what they in the underdeveloped world have. Capitalism also leads to a healthy separation and balance between the power of government and the power of the marketplace. Business, in short, cannot do all, but it can do much if we are willing to see the good that it does and stress its possibilities.

Finally, Etcyl H. Blair suggests that for any model or strategy to be effective in dealing with ethical dilemmas faced by the MNC, two conditions must be met: (1) businesspeople and scientists need more training in the liberal arts and especially more formal training in ethics; and (2) almost everyone needs more training in science so that scientific literacy can be achieved. An "infusion of ethical thought" is needed to counter post World War II societal changes which led to a demphasis on religion and family as the places where values were learned. And scientific literacy is needed to avoid being overwhelmed by what he terms the "factoid" or "a bit of information, presented as fact, which has no reality outside of its use in the news." It is impossible, that is, to devise adequate and workable strategies and models for dealing with ethical dilemmas faced by the MNC without some knowledge of ethics and without some way of validly assessing the factual information at hand.

In Chapter Four, David Nosnik, Verne E. Henderson, and William Bain continue the discussion about methods for dealing with ethical dilemmas of MNCs from their perspectives as members of the consulting profession. Nosnik reiterates some of the concerns and suggestions presented by Joe Chenoweth and Robert Gunts in Chapter Three and anticipates some of the comments made by John M. Kline about the Foreign Corrupt Practices Act in Chapter Twelve. MNCs, Nosnik claims, need to look for ethical codes that somehow will mediate between all concerned parties, and this is no easy task. For the most part, managers of United States' firms have tried to accomplish this by looking to the law and to corporate legal departments to provide an ethical framework to guide their actions. He thinks that the approach taken to the issue of bribery illustrates this point well. The Foreign Corrupt Practices Act was signed into law by President Carter in 1977, and corporations responded by instituting a series of structural changes to assure compliance with it. Internal auditing departments were created, external ones increased in scope, "conflict of interest" statements were promulgated, and law staffs and audit committees designed numerous codes in reaction to the new law.

Nosnik sees this kind of a reactive approach as being too limited and quite unsatisfactory. He suggests that the ethical dimension of decision making should not be relegated to the legal department and should not focus on structural design and change or on, that is, "looking for the right formal structure." Developing an ethical framework has nothing to do with rigid structures. Instead, it is a dynamic process to which flexibility is the key. What is needed is to "focus on the challenge of developing and maintaining a complex decision-making process." According to Nosnik, the MNC can best accomplish this by devising new management perspectives that reflect the complex demands of multiple markets, languages, and cultures and by giving "underrepresented" management groups a voice in decisions and allowing representatives of different viewpoints access to the decision-making process. Finally, he suggests that corporate views should be disseminated by a precise communication of strategies and norms, and there should be strong role model behavior and rewards for compliance. Positive thought-out action, not simply reaction, is a must for the MNC in dealing with the dilemmas it faces.

Henderson also feels that there are a number of things that MNCs can do to help themselves in dealing with the ethical dilemmas that they might face, although there will always be decisions that are difficult to make and differing interpretations of what is right in any given situation. After providing some introductory comments on the nature of MNCs and discussing the role of the consultant, he comments that there are "five major areas in which corporate ethical issues emerge today -- human investment, ecology, consumer welfare, political relationships, [and] corporate responsiveness..." For the MNC, any attempt to deal with these issues is "compounded by culture and value clashes." He then develops a conceptual framework which illustrates just how complex ethical dilemmas can become because of those clashes, coupled with the pluralism of our own society.

Finally, he presents what he terms an "ethical algorithm" or formula that he has devised as a tool to use in analyzing what has gone wrong in past decisions and in anticipating consequences of future decisions so that "catastrophes" can be avoided. The formula consists of (1) examining the business and ethical goals of a corporation in order to clarify each and make sure that they are compatible; (2) checking methods in areas such as marketing to see how various constituents will be effected; (3) becoming clear about motives behind actions; and (4) learning to calculate ethical as well as business bottom lines or learning to anticipate consequences. Following these guidelines and affirming that there is "an ethical side of enterprise," he believes, can be invaluable to the MNC.

To end this chapter, Bain mentions an ethical dilemma in the area of consulting itself. In the last 20 years, consulting firms have become more and more involved in advising MNCs on key strategic decisions. Such "strategic consulting" deals with "highly leveraged resource allocation decisions that are nearly irreversible in the short term" and have a major impact on the corporation's performance. The ethical problem emerges when one consulting firm attempts to do strategy consulting for two competing firms. A serious conflict of interest question arises in that the point of strategy consulting is to give the client an advantage at least in part by putting the client's competitor at a permanent disadvantage.

Bain feels that the market system will ultimately solve the problem in one of two ways. Either a large number of firms will opt for total commitment to clients that hire them and this will become the dominant standard in the industry or more and more potential clients will become aware of the problem and, when looking for strategy consulting, insist on a firm where such a conflict will not arise.

In Chapter Five, a final and quite different strategy for dealing with some of the ethical dilemmas posed for multinational businesses is explored. Timothy H. Smith, J. Philip Wogaman, Rafael D. Pagan, James Armstrong, and Oliver Williams all write about church activism, its rationale, and its impact on MNCs. Smith shows how the last 15 years have witnessed a tremendous growth in the active involvement of the churches in a number of multinational business issues such as investments in South Africa and the infant formula controversy. This new advocacy approach is marked by such strategies as shareholder resolutions, the leading of consumer boycotts, divestment of stocks, the petitioning of investors, and attempts to establish a dialogue with management. The goal of such activism is to bring into the open certain matters pertaining to social justice or, as he states, "to ask human questions of economic decisions."

Such an approach is, he feels, justified for two reasons. In the first place, "economic decisions have a tremendous impact on all our lives. It is an obligation of the church to raise social and ethical questions concerning business decisions that further or retard the movement toward greater social and economic justice." Secondly, the churches themselves are investors and, as such, have a responsibility to monitor the use of their investments. He outlines a number of lessons learned over the past years, and stresses that church activism complements corporate attempts to create strategies to deal with ethical issues in that it provides a method of cooperative conflict resolution, helps in the early identification of potential problem areas, and can aid in the development of a sense of social responsibility. In short, businesses and churches working together can defuse some dilemmas before they have the chance to develop into serious problems.

Wogaman stresses a rationale similar to that of Smith in defense of church activism stating that "whatever contributes to human good is a part of the church's mission; whatever diminishes human life is to be resisted." MNCs often do good, but when their power is perceived as being used in ways antithetical to human good, the church is obligated to try to intervene. Moreover, again echoing the claims of Smith, Wogaman states that the relationship between churches and corporations can be valuable. He identifies three specific benefits that accrue from the relationship: (1) the church can provide a disinterested perspective on economic questions "amended by a bias for the poorest, most vulnerable members of society"; (2) in that it is worldwide, the church can provide corporations with knowledge of many local customs and practices; and (3) church activism can help to regulate the market so that unjust and unethical practices do not lead to market advantages. This can be done, among other ways, through efforts to change the corporate culture and through efforts to secure the adoption of certain legal frameworks. He closes by cautioning that activists who attempt such interaction with business must themselves be accountable, honest, and understanding of the difficulties and dilemmas facing the businessperson.

Pagan focuses on one particular issue, the position of the Nestle Corporation in the infant formula controversy, in his discussion of church activism in relation to multinational business. In the early 1970s, infant formula manufacturers became the focal point of a dispute about their methods of marketing breastmilk substitutes in the Third World. They were accused of aggressively and deceptively marketing an inappropriate product in cultures where, it was claimed, serious problems resulting from its use often caused malnutrition in infants and even resulted in the death of some infants to whom it was fed. Among the manufacturers, Nestle was singled out and, with the active backing of various church groups, boycotts were instituted against its products. The dispute lasted some 11 years before an International Marketing Code for Breastmilk Substitutes was accepted by the World Health Assembly, the governing body of the World Health Organization. It was another three years before the Nestle boycott was suspended.

In the process of the dispute, Pagan says, both businesses and churches were hurt, many resources were used, and little help was given to the children who needed it. But he sees a number of valuable lessons emerging from the experience. First, in such situations, boycotts alone are too confrontational;

dialogue is critical. Second, the tactic of "setting an example" of one company in order to pressure and humble others does not work. Finally, corporations need to learn that legal compliance is not enough when introducing new products, technologies and advertising to large masses of poor illiterate people where "there is no developed and effective health and social infrastructure or control." Business leaders, he suggests, are for the most part quite ethical and will work with churches and others. Church and business cooperation is both possible and essential in dealing with future ethical dilemmas -- and in even perhaps avoiding them.

Armstrong and Williams close this chapter with a discussion of underlying conceptual clashes between MNCs and certain church activists and between church activists themselves. Armstrong traces the history of church activism, showing that, far from being a recent phenomenon, it can be traced back to early experiences of the Hebrews and is evident in many movements in American history.

He then turns to a discussion of institutional activism which he sees as being rooted in and defined by "conceptual activism." That is, every issue-oriented body or institution grows out of some concept of reality and how things should be. It is in this context that he mentions Liberation Theology, a conceptual activism that has as its basis two central themes: (1) God's bias for the poor; and (2) a mandate to enter solidarity with the poor. Unfortunately, proponents of it tend to see MNCs as exploitative and evil, and MNCs tend to see its proponents as Marxist and evil. Armstrong calls for a reconciliation and a synthesis which would stress "that the creation and equitable distribution of wealth are not contradictory economic processes, but rather are desireable complementary processes."

Williams, on the other hand, does not have such an optimistic view of the possibilities of reconciliation between the MNC and Liberation Theology. In fact, he suggests that there is little use in trying to mediate the views and form a consensus. In general, he states, church activists see their goal as that of shaping and transforming the world in terms of the life of Christ, but they are divided as to what model of change they support. One group calls for evolutionary reform within the system, while the other presses for radical revolution against the system.

Each model grows out of what he terms different "middle axioms" which provide a view of the world that should be created and a content for concrete problem solving. Each model also presents MNCs in a very different light, as he shows through various examples. The reform model sees them as instruments of development which can help alleviate problems in the Third World, while the revolutionary model sees them as instruments of oppression and dependence. Liberation Theology, as Williams interprets it, adheres to the revolutionary model which has among its middle axioms that of the abolition of the private ownership of the means of production. Thus, MNCs tend to be able to do no good at all in the eyes of its advocates. Ultimately, dialogue among all parties on strategies, he says, must be supported by empirical research" and "must focus on the likely consequences of the various scenarios.

The two primary models for action and change that church activists advocate may, indeed, have some important conceptual differences that lead to disparate ways of identifying and trying to deal with the ethical dilemmas that beset multinational enterprises. But, both approaches are rooted in concern for the hungry, the illiterate, and the powerless. As such, church activists tend to be especially attentive to potential issues arising out of the presence of MNCs in less developed or Third World countries. This focus does not seem to be misplaced. The number of articles in this book that deal wholly or in part with issues and cases relating to MNC operations in such areas attests both to the primacy of concern about this subject on the part of all parties involved and to the very real problems that can arise out of such business ventures. The next five chapters in this volume deal directly with a number of these problems.

In Chapter Six, Lee A. Tavis, Denis Goulet, John B. Caron, Jean Wilkowski, and Lawrence G. Franko focus on a concern common to many discussions about the expansion of businesses into less developed countries -- poverty. The statistics pertaining to gross national products, infant mortality and life expectancy rates, the presence of malnutrition, and expected population growth that Tavis presents and on which he comments clearly reveal two things: the extreme poverty of many of the people in the less developed countries in which MNCs operate; and the disparity in the conditions in which the people of First and Third World countries live. But, given that MNCs are business operations, should they even concern themselves with such an issue? If so, why? And just how should they address it?

Tavis suggests that MNCs have contributed to the economic growth of the less developed countries in which they operate and have certain unique capabilities which make them especially suited to the task of development in such areas. But, at the same time, he thinks that MNCs are "part of the problems" that such nations face. "The dramatic worldwide growth of the past quarter century has not reached the lives of those millions of people in urban and rural areas living at the boundries of physical existence ... As a component of national development patterns, multinationals share in the persistent maldistribution of resources." Given their "linkages" to the poor through direct contacts with and involvement in the communities in which they operate, MNCs have what he thinks is a "unique" social responsibility" to aid in development in such a way that it is advantageous to the poorest.

Goulet expands on this position, posing the question as to whether the primary emphasis of the MNC on the pursuit of wealth has as a necessary effect of the creation of poverty. Such a question, he suggests, cannot even be approached until some other, more fundamental issues concerning the purpose of human existence are addressed. He identifies the three most essential of these questions as having to do with: (1) the nature of "genuine" wealth and poverty (are they to be measured solely or primarily in terms of material goods?); (2) the kind of wealth that ought to be created and whom it should benefit; and (3) the principles that should govern the distribution, appropriation, and uses of wealth. After these questions are dealt with, certain policy issues must be raised such as what economic system best satisfies the ethical obligation to eliminate poverty and whether MNCs can promote the acquisition of wealth without at the same time perpetuating poverty.

Goulet proposes answers to some of these questions. In the first place, profit should be "optimized, not maximized." MNCs must internalize a lot of values such as environmental concerns, racial and sexual justice, the impact of corporate decisions on society, and the "equity in the availibility of goods and services produced" that were once considered to be externalities. In the second place, such "optimization" or internalization of values requires that MNCs cooperate and consult with citizens and local governments in the process of decision making. Finally, he states that corporations must go beyond "mere wealth creation" to a broader vision of the purposes of production: "...optimum life-sustenance, esteem, and freedom." "Corporate decision makers," he concludes, "like technical or political leaders, must be held to a standard higher than Machiavellian logic in the pursuit of their peculiar goals." When wealth creation, that is, is pursued as a purely self-interested and singular goal, it only leads to pain for many in less developed countries, and it ignores certain ethical obligations that should define any activities undertaken by human beings.

Offering a somewhat different viewpoint, Caron suggests that MNCs do not hurt Third World countries at all, but instead help them considerably. Many criticisms of MNC activity in less developed countries, he claims, are based much more on emotion than on logic and are simply unfounded. Echoing the comments made by E.F. Andrews and Robert McClements in Chapter Three, Caron says that MNCs, among other things, build schools, provide health care centers, pay decent wages, and contribute to the balance of payments in the countries in which they operate. Some countries, for reasons that Lawrence G. Franko will discuss later in this chapter, are now even actively seeking MNC investments to offset the debt problems that they face.

Caron, commenting that "in many countries, the vast majority of the poor live mostly outside the economy," admits that there is a gap between the extent of poverty in many of the less developed countries and what the MNCs can do. However, he feels that multinationals themselves are not necessarily responsible for filling that gap. What should be done? The rest of his article deals with some strategies for dealing with the problem. He presents these through a discussion of Technoserve, an agricultural-based organization which promotes enterprise development in Third World countries. "The Technoserve approach is a concentration on very basic food production and better methods of distribution." Among other things, it trains local managers to run operations, creates indigenous operations to do the work it is doing, and develops technology that directly addresses the problems of the local people. The presence of both traditional MNCs and enterprises such as Technoserve, Caron thinks, offers the most hope for alleviating poverty in less developed nations.

Providing support for some of the points made by Caron, Franko suggests that asking what effects MNCs have on the development of Third World countries is a bit like asking what is the sound of one hand clapping. MNCs do not exist by themselves. They exist in political and policy contexts, and their effects can only be understood in terms of those contexts. Given such an understanding, he claims, it can be seen that poverty is often directly caused not by the presence of MNCs, but by host country policies that restrict such businesses and interfere with market economies.

Largely as a result of fears of dependence, nations in Africa and Latin America chose in the 1960s and 1970s to strictly limit and control MNC investment. Their resulting reliance on state-owned enterprises as well as their institution of permit systems and various other controls led to corruption, overvalued currencies, staggering debt, an increase in the wealth of a very few at the expense of the vast majority, the exit of vast amounts of money from the host countries, and various dilemmas for the few MNCs trying to operate in such environments.

Two major points emerge from Franko's comments. The first, an implication drawn in part from his observation that the poorest countries are also the countries with few or no MNCs operating in them, is that there is a relationship between the lack of MNC activity and the lack of development in Third World countries. The second is his conviction that market economies provide a sound basis for economic policies in any country, whether it be developed or less developed. Along with Andrews and McClements, he would contend that interferences with the market system, not the market system itself, play a large part in the poverty problem.

To close the chapter, Wilkowski presents an overview of the United States Agency for International Development (AID), a government agency charged with promoting growth and development in Third World countries in order to further certain foreign policy objectives. She points out that, from the time of its inception, there has been a great amount of criticism of the program. The charge is often made that the agency's efforts neither focus on the poorest countries nor effect the poor majority in the countries in which it is most operative. Part of the problem, according to Wilkowski, is that the foreign assistance program has a number of potentially conflicting goals which often shift in priority depending on the political perspectives of those in power. Along with the mandate to deal with poverty, the program is also supposed to meet the emergency needs of poverty-stricken people, promote the strategic and political influence of the United States, and foster the expansion of United States commerce.

Recent government efforts have tried to approach the poverty problems facing less developed countries by associating AID more closely with "private sector initiatives." Attempts have been made to encourage Third World entrepeneurship, facilitate loans for small businesses, and involve American corporations in development projects with such private voluntary organizations as Volunteers in Technical Assistance. Wilkowski suggests that these efforts are "disappointingly modest" and "need to be monitored to be certain they do not distract AID from its primary purpose of helping the poorest people in the Third World, rather than serving business interests." They also need to be seen for what they are: part of the overall foreign policy objectives of the United States. But she remains optimistic about them, offering the opinion that both long-term business and government interests clearly include concern about poverty "not only on ethical and humanitarian grounds, but for sound economic reasons as well."

In Chapter Seven, Marjorie Sheen and Barbara Bramble and Sheila Harty discuss the role of multi-lateral banks in the development of the Third World. Established by international convention and funded by various governments, such banks, as Bramble and Harty state, "make loans at preferential rates for projects intended to gradually improve the standard of living of people in developing nations." One of the largest and most influential of these institutions, The World Bank, is the subject of Sheen's paper. She gives an overview of the purposes of each of its three parts: the International Reconstruction and Development Bank (IRDB) lends money and provides technical assistance for certain economic development programs and projects of its Third World members; the International Development Association (IDA) does the same for poorer members ("those nations with a per capita GNP of less than $140 per year") at less cost; and the International Finance Corporation (IFC) promotes the growth of the private sector, encourages the development of local markets, and promotes foreign private investment in less developed countries.

Sheen discusses specific ways in which each organization attempts to accomplish its goals and makes an overall observation quite similar to Wilkowski's: in the case of the promotion of Third World development, the goals of ethics, of businesspeople, and of government tend to be complementary. Economic growth in less developed countries can only increase the well-being both of the poor and of "the global economy in which industrialized nations must compete."

While not disputing the goals and the good intentions of multi-lateral development banks, Bramble and Harty claim that sometimes the unintended consequences of the projects that they fund make situations worse for the very people they are supposed to help. To support their contentions, they give examples of irrigation projects, cattle projects, and transmigration schemes funded in the past that have tended to be counterproductive to indigenous populations and harmful to the environment. Such problems have occurred, they claim, because institutions such as The World Bank are entrenched in traditional ways of thinking and, as a result, often lack understanding of how natural systems work. Efforts must be made to change this situation because multi-lateral development banks wield a great deal of influence. The ideas they have about growth and development, Bramble and Harty point out, are often adopted by local governments for use as their own major planning tools and often become the basis of other investment decisions by commercial banks.

But "ethical responsibility," they suggest, "may be a learned capacity." Such banks have only had around 30 years of experience in effecting change and have much to learn. More environmental information and planning is needed early in the development of projects, and the environmental office of The World Bank needs to be restructured with this in mind. They propose four guidelines, gleaned from past experiences, which they feel must be followed if any lending institution is to fulfill its ethical responsibilities to the people and the environment of the Third World: (1) "environmental planning and sustainable natural resource management must be part of overall analysis and strategic economic planning"; (2) local people must be involved in planning; (3) environmental impact assessments must be made both before a project is undertaken and after it is completed; and (4) all studies must be made public. After making a number of recommendations for changes in specific procedures in the operations of multi-lateral development banks that would help in implementing these guidelines, they conclude that "...the trade-off is not between environment and development, or between saving trees and saving people. Responsible and sustainable economic development requires sound management of natural resources."

In Chapter Eight, Anita Anand, Luisa M. Rivera Izabal, and Linda Lim discuss the effects that the development models brought by MNCs to less developed countries have on one particular group of people -- women. Although Anand says that the jobs that are made available to women by MNCs provide some income and self-worth, she claims that the trade-offs are not worth the small gains. Corporations literally reshape in their own images the countries which they enter. Industrialization becomes the norm, and the agrarian lifestyle common to the majority is altered, sometimes fairly quickly, to conform to a development model that is based on the production of goods for export.

As women become wage laborers in this setting, and as a cash economy becomes predominant, the power that they once held as transmitters of culture and tradition and the control they once had over local resources are eroded. Moreover, women become targeted as consumers, often of goods that have little or nothing to do with the traditional culture. Finally, Anand suggests that their work is tedious, the hours are long, the pay is low, and health conditions are questionable at best.

All in all, she charges that MNCs have a management style that is "patriarchal, hierarchial, and elitist" in that they tend to listen to none of the locals in less developed countries -- and especially not to women. Given the increasing activism of women's (and other) groups and the growing "sophistication" of host countries, if MNCs do not begin to examine and reevaluate their own tendency to exclude from decision making the people who are most effected by the process, the dilemmas they face in their Third World operations will only increase and eventually become detrimental to their well-being.

Expanding on Anand's comments about the poor working conditions faced by women employed by MNCs, Rivera examines the situation of women who work in Mexico's electronic and electrical assembly plants. The transfer by MNCs of such assembly plants to Mexico, she suggests, is in part caused by "relaxed applications of environmental protective measures" and a general lack of concern about health hazards on the part of the host country. This leads to a number of problems in for the 63% of Mexican women laborers who are employed the industry and who have little knowledge of labor laws, workplace rights, or health regulations.

After sketching some of the physical ailments suffered by the women who do this kind of work and pointing out that it simply does not pay for corporations to research the health and safety aspects of production in such settings, she concludes that "national and international laws should be designed to control the export of dangerous working conditions and also to prosecute those who are responsible for destroying health and life."

Lim, on the other hand, simply does not see the presence of multinational enterprises in less developed countries as being in any fundamental way detrimental to the condition of women. The accusations that corporations exploit, morally corrupt, culturally disrupt, and inhibit the free labor organization of women are simply unfounded. Women working for such enterprises often earn the highest income in their family, their work is fairly stable, and working conditions tend to be better and safer than those in any occupation available. In fact, she feels that employment opportunities offered by MNCs do much to help women in the Third World to escape the terrible poverty in which so many of them and their families seem so hopelessly trapped.

Further, she insists that "the multinational does not function as a primary cause of cultural disruption and moral corruption among women factory workers, either by inducing migration or by factory cultural practices..." Claims that it does are made either by those who fail to see clearly the cultural conditions of women in the Third World or by host country males whose authority, control, and status are weakened and threatened by the emerging economic independence of women.

Finally, Lim claims that multinationals are more highly unionized than local enterprises, and "many are also more willing to be unionized in developing countries than in their home countries..." After examining some of the policy implications resulting from these observations, she concludes that "for the women workers themselves, multinationals are only one, and not necessarily a very important, influence on their lives, and an influence which is as likely to be positive as negative."

Some of the most perplexing ethical dilemmas faced by MNCs arise in conjunction with the marketing and sale of certain products in less developed countries. In Chapter Nine, some of these dilemmas are presented and discussed in conjunction with two issues: the infant formula case and the exporting of pesticides to developing countries. James Post begins the chapter by reviewing the history of the emergence and development of the controversy over the marketing and sale of breastmilk substitute to Third World countries, an issue discussed earlier in this introduction in conjunction with the paper of Rafael Pagan. He then turns to the ethical issues and lessons that he thinks can be learned from it.

Certain products "which are appropriate and acceptable in one social environment may be inappropriate in the social environment of another nation." Breastmilk substitute, he suggests, is just such a product. For it to be used safely, there must be clean water and refrigeration available, and potential customers must be able to read instructions pertaining to its use. It simply should not have been advertised or marketed in the Third World where these conditions could not be readily met.

He also states his conviction that corporations should undertake post-marketing reviews "to determine who is actually using the product" and how it is being used. If it is found that an already-marketed product cannot be used safely in a certain area, the product should be demarketed. Finally, he is critical of the use that manufacturers made of people dressed as nurses who visited new mothers in Third World countries and encouraged them to discontinue breastfeeding and use the formula instead.

He does not claim that any harm was intended by the companies that advertised and marketed the formula in less developed nations. Rather he feels that, in the process of doing business, they simply overlooked some important issues concerning the ethical obligations involved in the introduction of new products or new technology to Third World markets -- or, for that matter, to any market.

Carol Adelman, on the other hand, claims that many of the problems that led to the controversy and to the ultimate development by the World Health Organization of a Code for the marketing of breastmilk substitutes simply did not clearly exist at all. She feels that shoddy statistics, poor research methods, and emotional reactions, not factual data, were the basis of many of the complaints against MNC activities. There is no substantiation of a dramatic decline in breastfeeding among poor women, no proven correlation between the formula and high disease and death rates of infants in less developed countries, and no evidence that the promotional practices of manufacturers led to either a decline in breastfeeding or a rise in deaths in the areas in question. In the final analysis, Adelman is convinced, too much time and money was spent developing the Code and, in the long run, the controversy over the issue diverted attention and resources from the crucial problem which is "quite simply to use the knowledge we have accumulated in our scientific research and field work to help the malnourished children of the world."

In an article prepared under the supervision of Kenneth E. Goodpaster, David E. Whiteside presents the context of the debate over the morality of exporting to less developed countries various pesticides which do not meet human and environmental safety standards in the United States. In the process, he provides a great amount of information about pesticides and their benefits and dangers, as well as about the pesticide industry and attempts to regulate it. He also presents specific arguments on both sides of the issue. Among the charges made by the critics of pesticide exporting are: (1) the practice presents unacceptable hazards to both the people and the environment in less developed countries; (2) corporations who engage in "dumping" such dangerous chemicals in countries whose governments do not have the experience, the ability, or, in some cases, the desire to regulate such activities are acting unethically; and (3) the practice shows that MNCs place profits above Third World lives. On the other hand, those who defend the sales claim that (1) harm comes only from the misuse of the products; (2) the United States' regulatory standards are too strict and should not be imposed on other countries; and (3) the pesticides are useful and quite beneficial in the less developed agriculture-intensive countries to which they are exported.

The issue, as is also pointed out in Scott Cook's report on a discussion of it led by Goodpaster at the Conference, raises a number of difficult questions and involves a number of stakeholders with varying values and interests. Goodpaster suggests that both an understanding of those various perspectives and attention on the part of the multinational enterprise itself to the ethical dimensions of the problem are crucial to arriving at any satisfactory solutions.

The chemical industry faces other dilemmas relating to its operations in less developed countries. On December 3, 1984 in Bhopal, India, toxic fumes wafting through slum neighborhoods killed over 2,000 people and injured more than 50,000 others. The source of the fumes was leaking methyl isocyanate, a chemical used in the manufacture of pesticides at a plant owned by Union Carbide India, Ltd., a subsidiary of the Union Carbide Corporation.

In the aftermath of the accident, a number of questions have arisen about such multinational production facilities in less developed countries. It is argued in many places in this volume that MNCs bring needed jobs, housing, and health care to poverty-striken areas. But when building and operating a plant that handles potentially lethal chemicals, what are the special ethical obligations, if any, that the corporation has to employees and to the surrounding environment? What should be its legal obligations? In that such facilities are often located in less developed countries because environmental and safety laws are not as strict as in the home country, how much responsibility for such accidents should be placed on the host country government? What can and should be done to avoid future problems? Chapter Ten deals with these and other issues of concern that have grown out of the Bhopal tragedy.

A. Karim Ahmed puts the blame for the accident completely on Union Carbide, arguing that it resulted from "failures of corporate policy and management neglect." He is especially critical of what he terms the "management by exception" approach that the company takes to its foreign operations. Instead of monitoring facilities on a regular basis, he suggests, Union Carbide issues directives and enforces existing codes only when problems arise. This policy, plus the facts that the Bhopal plant was "undersigned in safety features and devices," had been allowed to deteriorate, was subject to recurring safety problems, and had a host country management which tended to ignore operational procedures led, in Ahmed's opinion, to the accident.

There are, he suggests, ways of avoiding such tragedies in the future: (1) safety should be considered first; (2) the Board of Directors of a corporation should be fully accountable for health and safety matters; and (3) uniform international health and safety standards should be devised. He concludes by commenting that "if important changes are not made soon and implemented quickly, the [chemical] industry's ... role in national economies around the world will diminish or even fade away in the next few decades."

Paul Shrivastava approaches the Bhopal issue a bit differently, assessing it in light of his contention that routine technical decisions can have what he calls "unethical fallout" because "they are based on technical rationality alone." In complex technological endeavors, he suggessts, decisions are often made taking nothing but their technical feasibility into consideration. Each decision taken by itself can make perfect production and technical sense, but when put together the result can be disastrous. In the case of Bhopal, there were many different decisions made over the course of the years about plant design, procedures, maintenance, location, raw materials, and personnel. Even though each was perfectly rational, combined they led to the accident and the problems resulting from it.

He urges that, to avoid such ancidents, steps must be taken to "incorporate ethical concerns into technical decisions." Among other things, the potential social impact of decisions should be looked at carefully, ethical criteria should be considered along with technical and economic ones in all areas of business enterprise, health and safety concerns relating to specific decisions should be addressed, and if critical information is absent, decisions should be postponed until it can be obtained.

Gary Edwards suggests that the tragedy has raised certain complex ethical issues in ways that may lead to dramatic changes in the international business environment. Further, he is convinced that the development and implications of international codes, with all of the time-consuming problems that such a process entails, simply cannot be depended on to deal with the issues. Corporations themselves must become actively involved in self-regulation. He presents some positive steps that he thinks corporations can take now "to reduce the danger of future Bhopals," protect their investments, and see that their ethical obligations are carried out. Included are reviews of corporate policies about health and safety standards, the development of codes of conduct, the meeting or exceeding of all host country regulations, the assessment of environmental, health, and safety standards in foreign operations, and the careful choosing and training of personnel and managers in those operations.

In the final contribution to the chapter, Michael S. Baram brings a very different perspective to the issue. He discusses various courses of legal action that individuals and local communities have undertaken to try to insure that the chances of a similar disaster are minimized. Because of accidents such as the one in Bhopal, he suggests, people have lost confidence in the ability of both the chemical industry and government regulative processes to provide them with any protection from such events. They have turned instead to strategies such as suits and threats of suits under state tort laws and the enactment of right to know laws which can be used as a basis for controlling and curbing industrial activities and developing emergency response systems. He goes on to compare American and European models for giving some authority to these initiatives and concludes by indicating his belief that individuals and communities exercising their rights under such laws can put much pressure on industries and agencies to comply with their duties to identify hazards, warn about them, and act to reduce or control them. Such "self-help" strategies can be valuable in both developed and less developed countries.

Doing business in South Africa presents a different sort of dilemma for the MNC. Through its constitution and legal system, the white supremacist government enforces the policy known as apartheid. This policy effectively segregates society along racial lines, systematically oppressing the 24 million black South Africans to the advantage of the 4 million whites. Adopted as an official policy in 1948, apartheid effectively confines blacks to 13% of the land in separate residential areas known as "bantustans" or homelands. Further, both the occupations and the movement of blacks are severely restricted, blacks may neither vote nor run for public office, and they receive lower pay than whites even when the jobs are similar. On the other hand, the economy is well-developed and the land is rich in resources, and certain MNCs are well-entrenched there.

A number of pressing questions arise as a result of this situation. Given that businesses operating in South Africa inevitably (whether intentionally or not) strengthen the existing regime by strengthening the economy, it is often asked whether MNCs can maintain a presence is South Africa and still be considered to be acting ethically or whether they must withdraw. Involved in a system most people find totally abhorrent, what exactly are their responsibilities? How do they weigh the claims of host county, home county, shareholders, and those who insist that for them to align themselves in any way with the current regime is indefensible?

The Sullivan Principles were devised by the Rev. Leon Sullivan in 1977 in an attempt to address this dilemma. As a member of the board of directors of General Motors, Sullivan was concerned with drawing up a set of guidelines which would enable corporations to stay in South Africa, while at the same time working for changes in the system. Among other things, the Principles call for American companies operating in South Africa to grant equal pay for equal work; to desegregate all work facilities; to train blacks for and place them in management and supervisory roles; to recognize black unions; to support black businesses; and to work toward improving the living conditions, schooling, and health facilities for the black population.

In the paper that begins Chapter Eleven, Sullivan defends his Principles and states his conviction that corporations "can and should play the major role in helping to bring an end to racial injustices, because more than others, the companies have been the beneficiaries of cheap labor and inhumane practices." In fact, he claims that corporations unwilling to work for change have no right to be there and should be compelled to leave. MNCs that want to continue operating in South Africa should be required, he suggests, to comply with his Principles and to publicly disclose their equal rights efforts there.

But in this presentation he goes beyond the scope of the original Principles and calls on businesses not just to be concerned with job and wage issues, but also to actively work to end all apartheid laws and to become part of the liberation movement. Moreover, he feels that there should be no new expansion of business and no new loans allowed until "full and equal" participation for blacks is achieved. Finally, he calls for a total embargo if the system of apartheid has not been ended by May of 1987.

But do the Principles work and can their implementation justify doing business in South Africa? Kenneth N. Carstens, Howard Wolpe, and Harry Johnson think not. Carstens' contention is that "every investment in or loan to South Africa and every business deal with South Africa is an explicit moral and political statement. Disinvestment and refusal to do business with South Africa are equally explicit moral and political statements. One course of action is morally wrong. The other is morally right. There is no neutral ground." To support this claim, he traces the history of the system of apartheid and counters what he sees to be two central arguments against disinvesting: (1) that apartheid is dying; and (2) that the investments of American coporations moderate its effects. In fact, he claims that power has become even more entrenched in recent years and that our investments have only helped to perpetuate the system. As our investments have grown, the system has gotten worse, not better. Businesses operating in South Africa give symbolic support to the existing power structure simply by being there, and they give economic support whether they want to or not in the form of taxes and other contributions that result from host country regulation of sales and services. The South African government has passed extensive legislation to guarantee that "the investor's interest in apartheid is given full force and effect." There is no choice, and whatever benefit accrues to the blacks by the presence of United States business interests is far outweighed by these factors. Divestment, disinvestment, and sanctions, he argues, are the only ethical options.

Wolpe agrees with Carstens and points out that, even if the Sullivan Principles do help, only 70,000 blacks (less than 1% of the entire labor force) are employed by American firms, and firms adhering to the Principles employ only about 2/3 of those workers. So the United States business presence helps very few blacks. He further suggests that our conceptions of the South African situation are based on three myths. The first is that the South African situation is analogous to our own experiences with racial problems; the second is that "economic change is inevitably linked to the process of political liberalization and democratization"; and the third is that our own inherent racism has had nothing to do with our position toward South Africa. Wolpe counters each of these myths and points out how they have led to policies such as Constructive Engagement which in turn, have led to even more repression of blacks. Echoing Carstens' claim that business involvement only strengthens the government, he calls for a "distancing" of the United States from South Africa and says that "...there may be a decision to stay in South Africa made for narrow corporate profit reasons, but...such a decision does not facilitate the process of change. It sustains Afrikaners in the belief that theirs is a system that is economically viable over the long haul."

Johnson concurs with the assesments of Wolpe and Carstens. Referring to the 50% infant mortality rate in the bantustans, the absence of franchise for 73% of the population, and the forced separation of members of families, he writes, "...when I accept generous economic returns on South African investments, I am obligated to accept as well the dehumanizing ethical returns of apartheid..." This trade-off he finds morally reprehensible and inexcusable.

On the other hand, D.G.M. Fourie, David Ludington, Patricia Werhane, and Wilfred D. Koplowitz offer support for the position that the only ethical response for business is to stay in South Africa, and each one feels that the Sullivan Principles are an effective way of dealing with the corporate dilemmas involved in maintaining a presence there.

Fourie mentions the great economic power that MNCs wield, but states that the power is somewhat mitigated by the understanding that the MNC must respect the laws and customs of the host country and not interfere in the political process if it is to be allowed to remain there. Thus, the relation between the host country and the MNC becomes mutually beneficial and is based on principles of fairness and justice. Such principles can and should include the "concept of corporate-sponsored betterment and other socially beneficial programs." In the case of South Africa, however, he sees the issue of corporate social responsibility being carried into the area of foreign policy and moving away from fairness toward double standards based on "the causes of ideologues and vested interests."

In the past, the Sullivan Principles have led to many positive results for blacks including training, schooling, housing, unions, upward mobility, and the emergence of a black middle class. Countering the claims of Carstens and Wolpe, he says that the resulting "economic clout" has led to a rethinking of the political structure and laid the groundwork for a process of reform. American businesses, that is, have directly contributed to a change in the policies and attitudes of the South African government. In support of this claim, Fourie lists numerous laws that have been repealed or are under revision.

On the other hand, sanctions and divestment would only create a number of serious problems. The process of reform would be hurt, as would the black middle class and the agenda of moderates and reformists. Moreover, the rest of the African continent would inevitably suffer from such sanctions. South Africa accounts for 86% of the region's GNP, employs neighboring workers, is an import-export conduit, supplies electricity for neighboring nations, and is a creditor for subsaharan Africa. Fourie, citing recent events in Iran, also points out that such pressure can often be counterproductive. Finally, he sees such policies as unethical because they are inconsistent and based on a double standard. The United States and United States businesses pay no attention at all to some regimes that are much worse than the South African one and are not even trying to reform.

He concludes that the only ethical approach is for MNCs to "continue to play a vital role through providing employment and equal opportunity and by utilizing their influence to create a climate conducive to negotiations between the various groups in order to achieve a solution which is acceptable to all."

In general, Ludington's assessment is similar to that of Fourie. He points out that there is a definite political-ethical dilemma in the maintaining of a "proper balance between the interests of the American multinational in a foreign country and the various political interventions of the government of the host country, the government of the home country, and the various political interest groups in both countries." He further argues that any model for decision making created by an MNC must take into account a variety of factors including fiduciary responsibility to stockholders, the host country culture and environment, current established norms for the activities of industry, current home country foreign policy, and short- and long-term risk assessment.

Relating all of these factors to the South African issue, Ludington concludes that sanctions and disinvestment would answer the demands of only some very narrow special interest groups which "do not have the best interests of American multinational enterprises in mind." Nor, he indicates, do they really have the interests of any other elements in South Africa in mind. For the MNC to "walk away from this problem" would simply be wrong. The Sullivan Principles, on the other hand, offer a way to successfully balance all of the factors and provide an effective strategic framework to guide business in dealing with the dilemma at hand.

Werhane approaches the dilemma in a slightly different way. For businesses currently operating in South Africa to simply leave for the reasons that Carstens, Wolpe, and Johnson suggest would, according to Werhane, violate certain other moral claims such as fiduciary responsibility, providing needed jobs for blacks, and doing positive good by providing a model for efficient and just business operations. But for a business to stay and operate as a South African firm would operate, even if it follows the "Negative Harm Principle" of "not intentionally or deliberately causing harm," would also be wrong because of the support of apartheid that would ensue or the contribution to positive harm that would result. The situation is at best ambiguous and fraught with what she terms "moral risk." Companies already there must approach the dilemma with care and work out guidelines for their actions.

She identifies the Sullivan Principles as the best way to deal with the various elements of this dilemma in that they (1) contribute "positively to the moral involvement of nonwhite South Africans"; (2) allow the companies to "engage in economically successful operations"; and (3) do not "blatantly insult the South African government." The difficult decision of choosing to remain in South Africa with a specific moral agenda, then, is ethically risky but not a wrong as it may seem."

Koplowitz, too, supports remaining and working within the framework of the Sullivan Principles. He observes that operating in a global market often means dealing with standards different than ours. Echoing Andrews' contentions in Chapter Three, he critiques selective morality and asserts that a consistent application of sanctions and disinvestment against all regimes with whom we have moral differences would have catastrophic economic results. Moreover, staying is not immoral if it helps blacks to gain freedom and puts pressure on white rule. In fact, he feels that investing will help the blacks, while leaving will only punish them. Finally, he insists that some interference in South African affairs is justifiable because corporations operating there have a stake in the country and are citizens in some sense of the word. In closing, he points to some of the work Citibank has done in South Africa and interjects a note of caution by reiterating a point that both Ludington and Werhane make: corporations have responsibilities to their shareholders. They must think of the "viability of their equities and investments." If the situation begins to look impossible, they should and will leave.

Bribery is another issue that poses dilemmas for MNCs. Strong arguments can be advanced to show that it is at least a questionable practice, if not morally wrong. It is seen to be at odds with the working of a fair free market system. Were bribery to be universalized, the entire system would, in fact, collapse. Further, it is argued that bribery readily leads to the purchase of inferior goods that are detrimental to society in general and that the price of the bribe most often is unjustly passed on to the users of the potentially inferior goods.

But the issue is not as simple as it might seem. What if bribery is condoned by the people of a country in which the MNC operates and is, moreover, a norm for business dealings there? Is a bribe a bribe if it is demanded or solicited by the host country? Should a home country impose its standards against bribery on MNCs under its jurisdiction? Such standards, it is often pointed out, could seriously interfere with the business opportunities of MNCs operating in foreign environments. This last question is the focus of the discussions in Chapter Twelve.

In the mid 1970s public shock over disclosures of bribery, kickbacks, and illegal campaign contributions by various corporations (the Lockheed involvement in payments to the Japanese in connection with the sale of its L1011 TriStar is a prime example) led to the development of the Foreign Corrupt Practices Act (FCPA) which was signed into law in 1977. The law basically applies United States bribery standards to the operations of United States firms in foreign countries. But, as can be seen in the discussions of Kevin F. Wall, Mark Pastin, and John M. Kline, the law is an extremely controversial one.

Wall gives a brief overview of injunctions and laws dealing with bribery and then traces the inception of the FCPA and various arguments both for and against it. The major portion of his paper is devoted to a selective review of FCPA cases. Given that: (1) only 50 injunctive and administrative proceedings have been initiated by the Securities and Exchange Commission since the inception of the law in 1977; (2) only 12 cases have been prosecuted by the Department of Justice; (3) no one has been imprisoned under the law; and (4) the fines assessed have been light, Wall concludes that the judicial system has been reluctant to impose penalties and the effectiveness of the FCPA is thus an open question.

Pastin would regard such reluctance as a proper response to a well-intentioned but essentially misguided law. The product of ethical and political motivations, the FCPA is, at best, a flawed piece of legislation. Pastin feels that neither utilitarian nor deontological principles offer any support for it. The rule "bribery is wrong" must be considered to be prima facie, not categorical. As such, some violations of the rule may be perfectly ethical. In fact, he insists that when such a rule is categorically applied, it becomes harmful and immoral. He comments that "the FCPA is our Prohibition," claiming that it increases bribes made by foreign firms, forces managers to violate obligations to employees and stockholders (jobs and sales are lost because of it), forces violations of government commitment to the well-being of the United States (our ability to compete in foreign market is reduced by it), and violates the "principle of tolerance" of others who permit bribes.

Kline also regards the law as flawed. It simply is poor public policy that is unwieldly, confusing, inefficient, and not thought through. The problems that it had led to, he claims, were forseeable and could have been avoided. In fact, the general aims of the FCPA could more successfully have been accomplished by the use of already existent legislation. Unilateral imposition of our moral standards concerning bribery has effectively acted as a disincentive for international discussions on the issue and has stopped any progress toward an international law. Moreover, bribery has become the focal point of the codes of United States MNCs at the expense of a host of other important issues. The issue has become so dominant that "...it preoccupies executives' thinking and distorts the development of a positive approach to defining international business ethics."

Although he does not favor repeal of the law, Kline finds in its example two major lessons for business to learn if it is to avoid similar public policy problems in the future. In the first place, business must anticipate the strength of such concerns and the direction they are likely to take. Secondly, business must participate fully in the public policy debate when such issues do arise. And to effectively do this, Kline feels that corporations must make a "more concerted effort than in the past to examine the application of ethical value concerns to their multinational business operations in advance of the time that such issues are drawn into the public policy arena."

The volume closes with the discussion in Chapter Thirteen of two quite diverse topics. Marjorie T. Stanley writes about a problem sometimes faced by those corporate managers who are responsible for making "direct foreign investment decisions." Opening production facilities in other countries often means closing similar ones at home. As a result, jobs are "exported." It is claimed by some that such moves are unethical because they displace United States' workers and are harmful to the communities which the corporations leave. More local investment, not less, it is argued, is the only ethical approach.

But what if, even though home country "financial and economic conditions are such that an acceptable ... level of profitability is attainable," a move to another country would maximize profits? Or what if "United States-based production is no longer competitive"? Or what if it is simply easier to move than to deal with unions and workers in attempting to make production at home more competitive? In short, Stanley suggests that a crucial question is that of just how the value of the retention of home country jobs and the support of local communities should be weighed against the value to the business of the move. The situation increases in complexity when issues relating to the creation of jobs in foreign markets are addressed.

She reviews a number of economic and ethical theories and tries to apply them to the issues, but finds that none of them can satisfactorily resolve the dilemmas. Nonetheless, she concludes that such questions must be addressed, just solutions sought, and ethical components introduced into decision making that will "foster greater managerial and corporate awareness of relevant ethical issues, in both the domestic and the international environment."

Ending both the chapter and the book, Abbe Mowshowitz examines the ethical issues raised by the use of "information technology" in multinational businesses. By enabling the centralized control of large enterprises spread out over vast areas, recently developed telecommunication and computer networks have directly led to the growth and proliferation of MNCs, allowing free enterprise to go where the most money can be made. But the "virtual organization" (the matching of needs with resources) made possible by technological advances, he suggests, also "militates against sensitivity to human problems and the needs of local communities." People and places become entities to be manipulated on a global scale for the purpose of the maximization of profits and, as such, become "footnotes to the balance sheet." Moreover, management control and the specialization of functions becomes central in day to day business operations.

The more such "quantification" and "abstractification" occurs, the more ethical problems surface. Thus, according to Mowshowitz, technology and the globalization of business together contribute to the creation of ethical dilemmas in that the environment they create tends to alienate people from themselves, from others as people, from communities, and from ethical decision-making capabilities. "Without," he states, "adjustments to organization and management, designed to compensate for the abstract treatment of human relationships and regional communities, the ethical dilemmas will persist and the controversies will intensify."

Concrete human concerns and the interests of business need to be recognized as being complementary, not antithetical. Hopefully, these essays written by the participants in the Sixth National Conference on Business Ethics will contribute both to that recognition and to the on-going dialogue between all who are involved in developing ways of identifying and dealing with the complex ethical issues that confront multinational corporations.

           Ann E. Lange
           Research Associate
           Center for Business Ethics
           June, 1986

CHAPTER ONE

THE ISSUES AND THEIR CONTEXT: SOME PERSPECTIVES ON THE SOURCES OF ETHICAL DILEMMAS FOR THE MULTINATIONAL CORPORATION

S. PRAKASH SETHI
Professor of Management and Director of
the Research Program in Business and Public Policy
Baruch College (CUNY)
New York City, New York

MIRA WILKINS
Professor of Economics
Florida International University
Miami, Florida

CHARLES P. KINDLEBERGER
Visiting Professor of Economics
Brandeis University
Waltham, Massachusetts

RICHARD T. DE GEORGE
Distinguished Professor of Philosophy
University of Kansas
Lawrence, Kansas

KAREN PAUL
Associate Professor of Management
Rochester Institute of Technology
Rochester, New York

OTTO A. BREMER
Director of Laity Programs
Vesper Society
San Leandro, California
and
Lecturer
Graduate Theological Union
Berkeley, California

CHANGING RULES OF INTERNATIONAL CORPORATE BEHAVIOR*

S. Prakash Sethi

The role of multinational corporations (MNCs), especially as regards to their operations in the Third World, has been a subject of long standing public policy debate and critical analysis. Like a tidal wave, this criticism has gone through many phases and has focused on different aspects of MNC operations, covering such issues as corporate control, cultural adaptability, profit repatriations, technology transfer, and interference in host countrys' internal affairs. This paper is not intended as an all-inclusive treatise on the historical critique of MNC behavior. Instead, I look at the changes that have more recently been taking place in the global economic and political environment. My objective is to evaluate the impact of the changes on MNC operations on the one hand, and the economies and policies of the countries where they operate, on the other hand.

I believe we have entered a new era of conflict surrounding MNC operations, especially as they pertain to the Third World countries. This era has been accompanied by a rather significant change in the socio-political global environment -- a change that would make the direction of future conflict qualitatively different and perhaps cause historical stereotypes to be irrelevant and lead to erroneous strategies with unfortunate consequences for all concerned. Therefore, in this paper, I focus attention primarily on the changing rules of international corporate behavior and the events that have led to these changes. Finally, I suggest some new issues that should concern us because they arise out of these new rules of the game, and have hitherto not been subjected to careful enquiry.

---

*The material presented in this paper is partially adapted by the author's forthcoming book, THE RIGHTEOUS AND THE POWERFUL: Corporations, Religious Institutions and International Social Activism -- The Case of the Infant Formula Controversy and the Nestle Boycott, to be published by Ballinger Publishing Company, Cambridge, MA. in late 1986.

No vision of the future is ever totally perfect, and only the passage of time and events will determine the impact of what has been wrought. We are captives of our imagination, which is constrained to a large extent by our living environment. Therefore, it would be presumptuous for someone who is so close to it to predict the precise direction of our odyssey. For this, we must await the objective judgment of history. Instant history, however, has its uses. For neither now nor in the future can we ignore the recent past. It provides us with a point of departure by which we can measure progress or deflection from it. We are encumbered by it in our perceptual biases about the behavior and motives of the people and institutions with which we must deal. And most importantly, it influences the goals we wish to achieve and the means we would like to employ. History repeats itself precisely because we have short memories.

Globalization of Business-Society Conflict -- Institutional and Structural Changes

Most observers of the international economic scene involving MNCs, international organizations, and the Third World countries are familiar with the controversy during the last few years pertaining to the marketing of the infant formula in the Third World countries -- a controversy which led to a worldwide boycott of Nestle products and the passage of an international marketing code under the aegis of the World Health Organization (WHO). What is not generally appreciated is the extent to which the controversy provides us with a mirror to see that our institutional stereotypes are no longer valid either as institutions themselves perceive them or as their opponents portray them.

The infant formula controversy, more so than any other event, has crystallized the growing internationalization of conflicts between corporations and host country governments, with the intervention of both international organizations and public interest groups representing different constituencies and viewpoints. For example, until recently social activism was a major force primarily in the United States, and an important influence in some Western European countries, at essentially a local level. It has now emerged as a significant element at the international level where social activists are building effective networks across national borders and coordinating their activities to confront MNCs in the international arena. In the process, social activists have escalated the level of conflict as to both its diversity and its magnitude; they have built alliances with different governments; and, above all, they have politicized many international organizations such as WHO, UNCTAD, UNICEF, UNESCO, and FAO that had previously been primarily technical or program-oriented agencies.

A somewhat simplified version of the new external environment of the MNC is presented in Exhibits 1 and 2.

Exhibit 1 shows that up until the sixties, the primary elements of the MNC's external environment, with a measure of direct control over the MNC's behavior, were host country and home country governments. International organizations -- both United Nations-based and others -- drew their resources, and authority to act, directly from their member states. The United Nations even then had become highly politicized and was losing its capacity for action. Nevertheless, most of the technical and program agencies were still devoting their energies to carrying out their program mandates in the areas of scientific research and information dissemination, and carrying out field programs of assistance in various countries needing help.

Of the four components of the external environment, i.e., non-market intervenors, the MNC has had a large measure of familiarity and experience in dealing with home country and host country governments. Hence, within the constraints of national sovereignty, MNCs have developed sophisticated coping mechanisms. They rely on the control of technological, financial, and marketing resources available to the MNC; the host country's needs for these resources; and the options available to MNCs for investing its resources among countries seeking such investments.

While there is a perception among the less developed countries (LDCs) that the balance of negotiating power, aided and abetted by MNCs' home country governments, has historically rested with the multinationals, this is not always the case. MNCs are not a homogeneous group and have different corporate goals and investment and marketing strategies that are based on their asset dispersion, market penetration, and propensity to take risk. Thus, in many cases, a lack of bargaining power on the part of a host country may be the outcome of insufficient interest for MNCs to invest in a particular nation because of poor investment opportunities commensurate with perceived risk. Where host countries offer desirable investment opportunities, even the poorest among the LDCs have been known to negotiate mutually satisfactory agreements.

Nor is the question of lack of negotiating skills or incomplete information totally sustainable. LDCs have available to them the resources of many international agencies such as The

EXHIBIT 1

INTERNATIONAL SOCIO-POLITICAL ENVIRONMENT OF
MULTINATIONAL CORPORATIONS - PRE 1970s

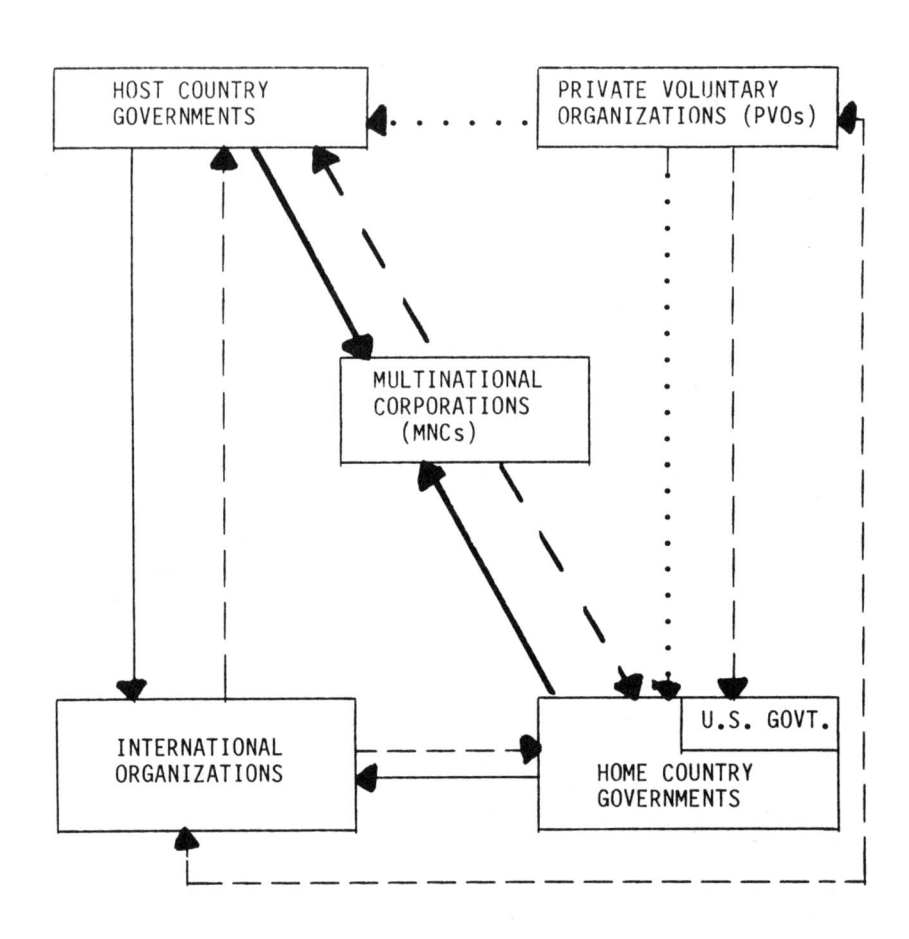

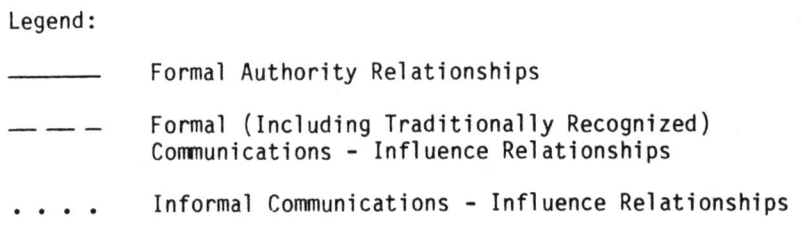

Legend:

——————— Formal Authority Relationships

— — — Formal (Including Traditionally Recognized)
Communications - Influence Relationships

. . . . Informal Communications - Influence Relationships

EXHIBIT 2

INTERNATIONAL SOCIO-POLITICAL ENVIRONMENT OF
MULTINATIONAL CORPORATIONS - POST 1970s

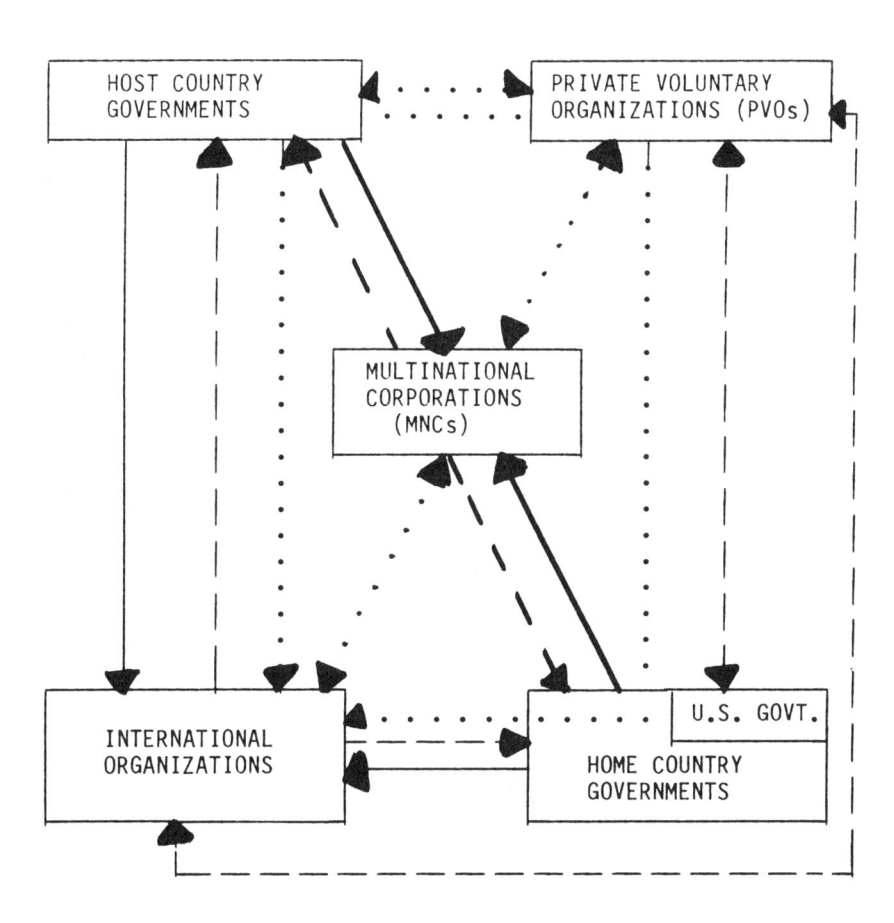

Legend:

——————— Formal Authority Relationships

— — — Formal (Including Traditionally Recognized)
Communications - Influence Relationships

. . . . Informal Communications - Influence Relationships

World Bank, and even private consulting firms of international repute, to provide legal and technical assistance in dealing with MNCs. Certainly the OPEC nations have lacked neither technical nor marketing skills in dealing with the MNCs and Western governments on their own terms. A growing number of multinational corporations based in developing countries such as South Korea, Taiwan, the Philippines, India, and Pakistan, and many of the OPEC-related Middle-Eastern nations, have been successfully competing in international markets with their Western counterparts. All this is not being stated to suggest that LDCs do not need help. However, we should also disabuse ourselves of the notion that these countries lie in a state of total helplessness and are easy prey to the greed and cunning of MNCs.

Non-Market Intervenors - International Organizations

The third type of non-market intervenors are various international organizations, notably United Nations' organizations and affiliated agencies. Until the beginning of the seventies, there was little formal direct contact between international organizations and MNCs. Nevertheless, industry was represented in many technical groups created for such purposes as standard-setting and information sharing, and working as part of, or in association with, international organizations. Since then there has been a significant change in the situation (Exhibit 2). The increasing number of newly-independent nations has altered the character of many of these organizations. Politically conscious, yet economically backward and sorely in need of technological and financial resources of the industrially advanced countries, the LDCs have used their numerical power in the UN organizations and agencies to redress the economic imbalance which they perceive to be existing in the marketplace where capitalistic countries and private enterprises are said to hold inherently advantageous positions. Working as political power blocs, less developed and newly developing countries have proclaimed the need for a New Industrial Economic Order (NIEO). It blames all problems of the LDCs on the exploitative policies -- both past and present -- of the Imperialist West. Even the repressive character of many of the LDC dictatorial governments and the poor management of their own economies are blamed on the Western governments and MNCs. The NIEO declares that LDCs have a right to a share of all the world's resources, and it demands that Western nations and MNCs must provide LDCs with technology as a matter of moral and historical right. At the same time, any excesses on the part of LDCs are justified as part of the effort to catch up with the Western World. When promoting these ends, the nations involved find that Soviet bloc countries readily become willing allies.

The issue is not solely that of the LDCs' legitimate and rightful expectations of economic assistance and cooperation from the Western World, but also that of reciprocal obligations and internal and external accountability to ensure efficient utilization of resources that are available to them.

The politicization of many international organizations has been one manifestation of this approach. Thus, these organizations are being increasingly driven by a political agenda, comprised as they are of member nations and, therefore, must reflect the emerging power alignments -- even when their mandates are primarily humanitarian and scientific-technical. Until recently, this process of politicization has progressed largely unabated because of the unwillingness or inability of the industrialized nations to confront the new reality in terms of its larger implications for democratic societies. In a world where many of the LDCs operate under dictatorial rule, and with little respect for basic human rights of their own people, their accusations of oppression against Western nations and foreign multinationals have begun to lose their biting edge. We are also beginning to see the development of a new and less acquiescing response pattern on the part of governments of many industrialized nations.

The WHO Code of infant formula marketing practices is one example of a more active and interventionist approach on the part of international organizations. Other examples can be found in the current efforts to develop a code of ethics for MNCs and international codes for marketing pesticides and pharmaceuticals. The changing role of international organizations raises the two important issues of process and of outcomes. The scientific character of these agencies called for a strong role to be vested in the organizations' bureaucracies because it was assumed that technical decisions were best made by scientists and professional experts who were shielded from undue political pressures. However, the political nature of intervention, both in terms of regulation formulation and implementation, calls for a closer scrutiny both of the "process" itself and of the role of the organizations' staffs. The modus operandi of these organizations as they affect the global operations of MNCs has not yet fully developed, and their future shape and success remain largely undetermined. Nor is it clear how their relationship with the industrialized nations of the free world will evolve in the long run.

Non-Market Intervenors - Private Voluntary Organizations (PVOs)

The fourth component, private voluntary organizations (PVOs) or, in the parlance of United Nations, non-governmental organizations (NGOs), represents one of the most significant changes in the MNC's external environment. At one end of the spectrum, PVOs include scientific and professional organizations with a legitimate stake in the deliberation on issues involving their respective professions or scientific expertise. Somewhere in the middle are institutions representing organized religion; consumer groups with long standing concern for the poor and under-represented; and other affiliated groups advocating causes and positions on humanitarian and ethical grounds. At the other end of the spectrum are special interest groups and social activists, whose socio-political and ideological orientations cover the entire spectrum of values and beliefs. These groups often do not represent constituencies of people in the conventional sense of the word, but instead represent constituences of ideas or a vision of a different, and what they perceive to be a better, world. They seek legitimacy and operate through other more established groups and, above all, are identified through a common adversary, e.g., the MNC. This is not necessarily the outcome of an ideological animosity against the capitalistic system or private enterprise; rather, it stems from the more obvious reason that most of the issues that are of concern to these groups are rooted in the behavior and activities of the MNCs. MNCs also offer the most fertile cachet of resources that are claimed and desired by their constituencies. Therefore, MNCs have become the focus of attention on the part of a large number of these activist groups.

The influence of these groups on domestic political decisions and national agenda in the United States has become amply manifest over the last two decades. American corporations have come to accept it as a fact of life. Consequently, an analysis of the role of PVOs is increasingly becoming an integral part of strategy development by the United States corporations. A failure to deal with PVOs can have a devastating effect on corporate survival, profitability, and growth. Exhibit 2 shows the changing role of these groups in impacting international political and public agenda. There has been a shift in the relative influence of different types of PVOs and NGOs. The scientific and professional groups are losing their former pre-eminent position, while non-scientific activist groups are gaining in ascendency.

The role of PVOs at the international level is more recent and not well understood. And yet their impact on MNC operations can be even more far reaching and traumatic. The most recent examples of these efforts can be seen in the successful enactment of the International Marketing Code for Breastmilk Substitutes (WHO's Infant Formula Code). In one single swoop, the PVOs accomplished on a worldwide basis what they had been unable to gain at the individual country level. In the process, they also handed MNCs a devastating defeat as to the latter's objectives and strategies for managing a corporation's external environment. Other ongoing efforts involving international organizations, Third World countries, and PVOs, include the Law of the Sea, technology transfer, international codes of conduct for multinational corporations, and efforts to enact an international code for the regulation of the pharmaceutical industry.

Therefore, it is of paramount importance that we understand the changing nature of our socio-political environment; its impact on the relative power and authority of various institutions in commanding a society's physical and human resources; and the constraints it imposes on institutions in the exercise of that power. At the micro level, a failure to perceive accurately the changing nature of these power relationships can cause us to react and repond incorrectly to external challenges, often with disastrous results for all concerned. Even more fundamentally, at the macro level, changing institutional power relationships will not only affect business-society conflicts, but also influence and shape the very character of international and national geopolitical arrangements and the nature of political order in democratic societies.

The Changing Role of Multinational Corporations

We must, therefore, begin to appreciate anew the changing role of private economic institutions, including MNCs, the uses of their economic resources, and their contribution to human welfare. We must also look at the adverse consequences that accrue both as a direct result of corporate activities and also as second-order effects of corporate actions that may expose people and communities to unnecessary harm, notwithstanding the fact that these harms were unintended and their impact unforeseen. Such an assessment is important. For regardless of our ability to control the activities of MNCs and redirect their resources, if we ignore the market constraints within which MNCs must operate, and without which they would cease to exist as viable economic entities, there would follow an inevitable loss in aggregate growth in the Third World, as well as in efficient production and even more in equitable distribution.

This assessment has two dimensions. The first one deals with the conventional aspects of multinational operations in the Third World and their effect on the welfare of people in these countries both as MNCs project it and these nations perceive it and experience it. It is this gap in the relative perception that perhaps accounts for greater antagonism between MNCs and LDCs than the purported harm caused by MNCs to Third World people through their sins of omission and commission. Our ultimate objective is to define a proper role for the multinational corporation and how one might maximize the Third World welfare without, at the same time, creating prohibitive and, therefore, self-defeating barriers to the MNC's overseas operations.

The second aspect of the new MNC reality has to do with the radical changes in manufacturing technology brought about by electronics, computers, and information processing. These changes have dramatically altered the ground rules of international competition by: 1) shifting emphasis in cost structure where traditional economies of scale have become less relevant; 2) bringing about a change in the competitor mix where multinational companies from Japan and newly industrializing countries of Asia are entering the international competitive arena; and 3) making the traditional sources of comparative advantage and cheap labor on the part of Third World countries less important.

The influence of these factors is twofold: the new MNCs have a different set of core values, ideologies, and operating philosophies which do not lend themselves to criticisms similar to those inflicted on Western-based MNCs; and by changing the notions of competition, these factors have also lessened the potential dependence of MNCs on LDCs either for the former's physical resources or for their inexpensive labor, thereby lessening the potential bargaining power of the Third World countries to influence MNC behavior.

The Traditional Role of Multinational Corporations in Less Developed Countries

One aspect of the role of MNCs has to do with their functioning in LDCs and the impact of their activities on local people and societies. At the aggregate level, the assumption that MNCs serve public interest in host countries through their activities in the private sector is largely supportable and easily defended. We have the example of such industrializing nations as South Korea, Taiwan, and Singapore. There is also strong evidence to suggest that in the Third World the countries that seem to have made the least progress in improving their people's economic and social welfare are also the countries that have restricted the growth of private enterprise -- domestic and foreign -- and have relied primarily on state-owned enterprise and government-to-government assistance.[1] Moreover, even China has more recently recognized the strength of private enterprise and foreign investments in improving its economy and its population's standard of living and welfare.

The munificence of the multinational corporation is not an unmixed blessing, however. At the aggregate level, problems arise simply because the objectives of privately-owned multinational corporations in investing abroad may not always agree with those of the host countries, especially the poor and less-developed ones. Nor do these countries always have the choice in terms of significant alternative sources of foreign capital and technology. Second, the host country may have built an unrealistic expectation of what it can expect, or extract, from the MNC within its borders. There is a whole body of scholarly literature and polemical-political publications listing the MNC's sins of omission and commission.[2] The movement for a New International Economic Order (NIEO) is, in fact, one response by the Third World nations to seek a larger, and what they consider to be a more equitable, share of the world's resources from the industrialized countries.[3]

There are also some other problems that arise at the level of a single company or industry in the Third World as a consequence of MNC operations. These may have to do with the inappropriate or ill-conceived transfer of technology or plant operations in less-developed countries. The most recent, and by far the most tragic example of this kind, occurred in December 1984 in Bhopal, India. The accident caused the death of over 2,000 people while injuring another 200,000. The specific causes of the gas leak, the exact nature and extent of Union Carbide's culpability, and the size of damage awards remain to be determined and may never be completely known. The important thing is to realize that the Bhopal accident was not a natural disaster which could not be foreseen and, therefore, not prevented. It was not the price of progress that must be paid. Nor, from all accounts, would it appear that the accident was caused by the unforeseen failure of some highly sophisticated and complex piece of machinery. It was instead a combination of small errors, postponed maintenance, and poorly trained personnel the cumulative effect of which resulted in the ensuing catastrophe. One should assume that the expected can be prevented. No responsible corporation would deliberately create systems that were prone to major failures. However, it is the unexpected, the small, the insignificant and therefore routine, that should be anticipated and taken into account in any prudent operational system.

None of the factors leading to the accident should have been a surprise to Union Carbide or for that matter any other MNC with operating experience in LDCs. The lack of an industrial culture, poor emphasis on preventive maintenance and training, and a general disregard for safety procedures are a fact of everyday life in these countries. Therefore, their presence cannot be used as an excuse for the accident, but should be considered proper grounds for demanding an explanation from the management for the lack of prior action.[4]

Therefore, while an MNC may not deliberately violate any laws, its normal business activities can and do sometimes have unintended, but nevertheless undesirable, social consequences. Each individual action, pursued in enlightened self-interest, does not always lead to collective good. In other words, rational micro-actions may and do cause irrational macro-outcomes. A single individual leaving an empty can on a vast beach may not consider his action particularly consequential, but when thousands of individuals do the same thing, we have dirty beaches with no one responsible for clean-up. Thus, rational individual actions lead to irrational collective outcomes which had we known before the fact, we would not have wanted to cause.[5] We become victims of the tragedy of the commons where collective responsibility becomes total irresponsibility.[6]

All marketing activities of individual firms have second order effects that extend far beyond the boundaries of the parties to their immediate exchange. Quite often, these effects are far more pervasive in their collectivity than visualized by individual firms when making simple transactions. The infant formula controversy is one such example. Other cases and industries involved in similar issues where their marketing practices are perceived to cause unnecessary harm include, among others, the pharmaceutical, processed foods, and agribusiness industries.[7] Thus, since the users of the product or those indirectly affected by it are unable to seek adequate remedy and relief in the marketplace, the cumulative effect of their dissatisfactions leads to transferring the issue from the private to the public domain. The resulting solutions are essentially political in nature; are externally imposed; may be quite inflexible to accommodate specific peculiarities of the individual MNC operations; and, in the long run, may not be the optimal solutions for the MNCs or the LDCs involved.

Once again, the infant formula controversy and the WHO Code provide us with a vivid illustration of the fallacy of the stereotype that protrays MNCs as economic behemoths whose enormous power makes them impervious to the needs of people in countries where they operate and makes host country governments -- notably those among the LDCs -- afraid of and unable to control them.[8] Having power alone is not enough, for its exercise rests largely on its political legitimacy. In a free society, this legitimacy accrues from the consent of people and social institutions which represent other spectrums of political will. Corporations are no exception. The degree to which they can exercise their economic power rests largely on society's judgment that its use is prudent and is directly related to its intended purpose, i.e., welfare of the owners of the corporation.

The power of the multinationals -- to the extent that it can be associated with their command of economic resources -- has to be exercised rationally, i.e., in response to market opportunities which are determined largely by people exercising free choice. It is unreasonable to blame the multinationals for all the economic and social ills of LDCs. To expect them to exercise their economic power in a manner that is radically different than the wish of political authority is impossible. The argument is based on inconsistent logic. To exercise such a power, MNCs must have political support, and yet, it is against the prevailing political will that we expect MNCs to assert their power. Economic power can be abused only when it is exercised irrationally, illegally, or under the aegis of political dictatorships and command economies where people's freedom to assert their economic will is subjugated to the dictates of centralized authority.

Therefore, the extent to which a corporation can and must deviate from this narrow mandate depends on society's changing expectations of the functions and performances of economic institutions. Democratic societies impose tremendous constraints on the use of economic and political power on the part of their holders. Therefore, it is not surprising that we impose strong procedural and review constraints on those we authorize to use power. Power also imposes its own discipline. It must be wielded in a restrained manner or the holder loses its legitimacy.

The New International Competitive Environment

In terms of market competition, the world has become truly a global village. The new entrants from the Asian countries, notably Japan, in the international competitive arena have radically altered the competitive equation. The new reality of a different competitive environment can be accounted for by two broad sets of factors: changes in production and manufacturing technologies, and changes in the composition of competitors.

Technological Changes

The intensification of global competition[9] has been brought about by a revolution in manufacturing processes that have radically changed the economics of manufacturing. Economies of scale, based on large production runs of standardized products, together with the use of low-skilled labor, no longer deliver lower product costs measured in terms of consumer-driven product attributes. Although the present system creates production economies through lower unit manufacturing costs, it also leads to greater specialization, longer production runs, and a certain rigidity in the types of products manufactured.

The emerging computer-integrated manufacturing technology, on the other hand, creates greater flexibility. It makes possible shorter production runs and facilitates the creation of more customized products. It offers faster responses to changes in market demand. It provides for greater control and accuracy of processes and reduced manufacturing in-process time. It requires greater emphasis on manufacturing engineering rather than operations management.[10] The new technology radically alters the terms of tradeoff between changeover and inventory costs in favor of the former, with profound implications for corporate strategy. By providing greater flexibility in creating product differentiation and shorter response times, it creates tremendous new marketing opportunities for the corporation.

The new international competition centers on manufacturing efficiency. There is tremendous emphasis on quality. In comparison with American companies, the foreign competitors have been able to deliver a higher quality/price ratio. The new technology also offers greater innovation and product variety. For example, one of the major strengths of the Japanese companies has been their emphasis on integrated manufacturing processes. They have exploited this advantage by building greater option -- added value -- into their production, thereby increasing product variety. When combined with better quality controls, the Japanese have been able to compete both at the lower and at the higher ends of consumer products markets and in many of the smokestack basic industries. The new competition of the 80's is not in mass produced and highly standardized products, but in more specialized goods available at reasonable prices to highly segmented markets. The result has been a secular decline in the comparative advantage of the United States in standardized products manufactured in highly capital-intensive plants, using relatively unskilled labor.

The miniaturization of products and automation of manufacturing has resulted in successively reduced use of commodities and minerals on the one hand and the number of workers required to produce a given amount of output on the other hand. Thus, the old notion of macro-level comparative advantage located in the Third World countries, and based on availability of raw materials and cheap labor, is becoming less important. Instead, the greatest source of value-added is increasingly coming from knowledge and knowledge-based skills which are traditionally in short supply in the Third World countries.

The New Competitors

Corporations from different countries bring with them their own "institutional baggage" in terms of philosophies of competition and cooperation, factor endowments, propensity for risk taking, desire for market entry, and corporate objectives as to pay-back periods and acceptable rate of financial rewards. At the same time, different tax systems and governmental supports for exports and overseas investments make them into competitors that are qualitatively different from competitors in one's own country. Consequently, they call for different strategic responses in the marketplace.

The Emerging International Environment

Not all the changing trends in the international economic and socio-political environment have stabilized to the extent that their mutual interaction and impact on MNC operations can be predicted with a high degree of certainty. Nevertheless, it is quite reasonable to expect that during the next ten years MNCs will be confronted with a large measure of turbulence in their socio-political environment that will call for the development of new rules of behavior on the part of various players in the international arena.

International Organizations

International organizations, both United Nations-affiliated and regional blocs, e.g., the Common Market, will continue to emphasize a greater monitoring role for themselves in the regulation and guidance of MNC activities. At last count, there were at least 30 codes of conduct at different stages of development and enforcement.[11] These codes generally fall into two categories. The first category of international codes deals with MNC operations that are primarily in the Third World, or where the Third World economic interests are pitted against those of the industrialized nations, e.g., the WHO Code on Marketing of Breastmilk Substitutes, the United Nations Code of Conduct for Transnational Corporations, and the Law of the Sea. The motivation behind these codes is not only economic, but also ideological and political. Therefore, their enactment, even by overwhelming majorities, may largely reflect political grandstanding and not necessarily be an indication of the prospect of their being implemented either by the host countries, or by MNCs and their home countries. Alternately, they may languish interminably in the corridors of international bureaucracies as hostages to one power bloc or another.[12]

Nevertheless, the very process of their formulation raises public awareness of the underlying issues. They also afford opportunities to various political groups to form coalitions and thereby develop joint strategies against MNCs and Western industrialized nations. Moreover, their propaganda value cannot be underestimated. Although the solutions advocated in these codes may not be totally inappropriate to the problem, they do indeed become a rallying point because MNCs in the past chose to ignore many of the legitimate complaints of the Third World that became the basis of early reform movements. While they may not have a seriously adverse impact on the interests of the MNCs in the short run, their long-term potential for damage to the freedom of MNCs cannot be ignored. Therefore, MNCs must become sensitive to the problems of their overseas operations as they emerge rather than wait for them to become acute. Otherwise, they run the danger of antagonizing public and political opinion not only in the Third World but also in their home countries, thereby inviting further regulation of their activities.

The second category of international regulation involves primarily industrially-advanced countries and relates to regulating behavior that impacts international investments and trade, e.g., the Common Market's regulations prohibiting anti-competitive behavior.[13] These codes are generally promulgated after long periods of negotiations and discussions and have had a higher degree of success in compliance. Moreover, these codes do not call for changes that are contrary to the precepts of free markets, international competitive behavior, or good business practices. In fact, in many cases they strengthen international commerce by harmonizing trade and investment practices in different countries of MNC operations.

Private Voluntary Organizations

It appears that the Reagan Administration has not seriously diminished the influence of private voluntary organizations (PVOs) in the United States. In fact PVOs have been quite successful in thwarting many of the Reagan Administration's initiatives in the areas of environment and conservation, such as off-shore leasing. PVOs have also been quite active in the worldwide anti-apartheid movement against South Africa. In the United States, they have consistently kept the issue in the limelight. Furthermore, in cooperation with a variety of state,

city, and labor pension funds, they have put pr
United States MNCs and banking institutions to
Sullivan Principles in their South African operatio
aggressive of these groups have also called for to
of United States companies from South Africa if that country's
government does not completely dismantle its apartheid structure
and grant full citizenship rights to its black majority in the
foreseeable future.[14]

Moreover, PVOs are also becoming more active and influential in countries such as the United Kingdom, Sweden, Denmark, Norway, and West Germany. Their influence is especially noticeable in areas of pharmaceuticals, chemicals, nuclear power, and other industries that adversely affect the earth's physical environment. In the international arena, activist groups have continued to form power coalitions with various Third World political blocs on issues of common interest. In this, they also find sympathy among the professionals of United Nations agencies who must depend for their political support on the growing voting power of the Third World countries and their allies.[15]

The success of PVOs, especially those affiliated with the organized church, has created its own backlash in the form of criticism from more conservative groups who have charged these groups with leftist orientation, selective moral outrage against social injustices, and undermining the values of capitalism and even democracy. To date, the influence of these groups in restraining the activities of PVOs has been, in my opinion, rather negligible, although it has raised public consciousness about the types of criticism that can be leveled against church-affiliated PVOs.[16]

The Less Developed Countries

LDCs are being buffeted by a variety of conflicting forces. At the ideological front, there is increasing emphasis on self-sufficiency and an aversion to dependence on foreign capital's unfettered operations. The ideological and political counterparts of the New Industrial Economic Order are liberation theology and the dependency theory. They argue that a dependence by the poor countries of the Third World on the capitalist countries and their agents, the MNCs, is both morally and politically unacceptable because it destroys the cultural underpinnings of those societies through the import of inappropriate, and culturally incompatible, technologies.[17] Liberation theology first found expression in Latin American countries where an activist Roman Catholic church sided with the poor and the oppressed against the atrocities and inequities of an authoritarian political order.

It is unfortunate that liberation theology arises in those countries where poverty is at its worst and political dictatorships are rife with corruption and prone to excesses in human rights violations. Since these regimes also control large economic enterprises and use them as vehicles of corruption and self-enrichment, capitalism has come to be viewed in these countries as a source of exploitation. This experience is historically at odds with that of the United States and Western Europe where democracy and individual freedoms are inextricably tied to private enterprise and capitalism. The authoritarian regimes also have provided a stable -- albeit a repressive and coercive -- political environment which appears less risky to many MNCs who have chosen to invest in these countries without adequate regard to future implications of such an association when there is a change in the political power in these countries. It is often argued that MNCs provide jobs and other benefits through their investments even under these repressive conditions. However, since these benefits are the secondary and not the primary motive for investment, these investments are viewed by MNC critics as merely after-the-fact rationalizations and, therefore, not highly credible. Thus, the poor masses and radicalized clergy see private enterprise in general and foreign private enterprise in particular as instruments of evil that must be banished if they are to achieve liberty from the tyranny of the military and their foreign allies.

Multinational Corporations

MNCs face an uncertain future in a changing socio-political international environment. However, this is not entirely without its positive aspects. There is growing awareness among many LDCs of the important role that private capitalism and MNCs can play in the development process. Evidence of this tendency can be seen in shifting trends in China, India, and Ceylon. At the same time, changing technology and manufacturing processes have made MNCs less dependent on cheap labor and mineral resources of the Third World. The mix of MNCs has also been changing, with more MNCs coming from Third World and Asian countries. These MNCs not only bring a different time perspective and risk orientation to their overseas investments, but also carry a different institutional baggage about the treatment of their overseas workers and the management of their enterprises.

At the same time, the LDCs are becoming more sophisticated about their economic and social needs and the variety of sources available to them to meet those needs. The challenge for the MNCs would be to find a role for themselves that would take into account these new realities. This would involve an awareness of the increased information and negotiating ability of LDCs and the growing power of these countries in the international arena to raise issues and exchange information that would make it all but impossible for the unscrupulous among the MNCs to hide behind legal or technical considerations or raise the flag of defense of free enterprise.

MNCs will have to become more sensitive to the entire spectrum of technology transfer that will not only take into account the profit maximization aspects of the MNC enterprise, but also, and more importantly, contribute to the stabiliby of the society and its cultural values and to a growth that is accompanied with more equitable distribution of income. It is only when the interests of the MNCs and the countries involved are in harmony and can stand the test of public scrutiny that the MNC will be able to survive and grow in the new international environment. Investments will have to be justified simultaneously for their economic efficiency, political legitimacy, and moral sufficiency. It is hoped the MNCs will indeed be able to rise to this challenge and develop new modi vivendi that will contribute to a better world for all concerned.

NOTES

1. P.T. Bauer, Equality, the Third World, and Economic Delusion (Cambridge, Mass.: Harvard University Press, 1981).

2. See for example, Richard J. Barnett and Ronald E. Muller, Global Reach: The Power of the Multinational Corporations (New York: Simon & Schuster, 1974); C. Tugendhat, The Multinationals (London: Penguin, 1973); Raymond Vernon, Storm Over the Multinationals: The Real Issues (Cambridge, Mass.: Harvard University Press, 1977); Kari Levitt, Silent Surrender: The Multinational Corporation in Canada (Toronto: Macmillan of Canada, 1970); F.G. Lavipour and Karl Sauvant (eds.), Controlling Multinational Enterprises: Problems, Strategies, Counterstrategies (Boulder, Colo: Westview Press, 1976); and Lee A. Tavis (ed.), Multinational Managers and Poverty in the Third World (Notre Dame University Press, 1982).

3. Willy Brandt, North-South: A Program for Survival (Cambridge, Mass.: The MIT Press, 1980); and Karl V. Sauvant and Hajo Hasenpflug, The New International Economic Order (Boulder, Colo: Westview Press, 1977).

4. S. Prakash Sethi, "The Inhuman Error - Lessons from the Union Carbide Plant Accident in Bhopal, India," The New Management (Summer 1985), pp. 41-45; Larry Everest, Behind the Poison Cloud: Union Carbide's Bhopal Massacre (Chicago, Illinois: Banner Press, 1985); Paul Shrivastava, Bhopal: Anatomy of a Crisis (Cambridge, Mass: Ballinger Publishing Co., in press); Alfred de Grazia, A Cloud Over Bhopal (New Delhi, India: Kalos Foundation, 1985); and, Ward Morehouse and M. Arun Subramaniam The Bhopal Tragedy (New York: Council on International and Public Affairs, 1986).

5. Thomas C. Schelling, "On the Ecology of Micromotives," The Public Interest, 25 (Fall 1971), pp. 59-98.

6. Garrett Hardin, "The Tragedy of the Commons," Science, 162 (December 13, 1968), pp. 1103-07.

7. Mike Muller, The Baby Killer, supra note 1. See also, Andy Chetley, The Baby Killer Scandal (London: War-on-Want, 1979); Andrew Chetley, Taming the Transnationals: The Experience of Baby Milks Campaigns (in press); Andrew Chetley, Cleared for Export: An Examination of the European Community's Pharmaceutical and Chemical Trade (London, England: Coalition Against Dangerous Exports, 1985); J. Braithwaite, Corporate Crime in the Pharmaceutical Industry (London: Routledge, Kegan Paul, 1984); Garry Gereffi, The Pharmaceutical Industry and Dependency in the Third World (Princeton, N.J.: Princeton University Press, 1983); Charles Medawar/Social Audit, The Wrong Kind of Medicine? (London: Consumers Association and Hodder & Stroughton, 1984); Diana Melrose, Bitter Pills (Oxford, England: OXFAM, 1982); and Mike Miller, The Health of Nations (Boston: Faber & Faber, 1982).

8. Bauer, Equality, the Third World, and Economic Delusion, and Vernon, Storm Over the Multinationals.

9. The discussion in this section is largely based on the ideas developed in S. Prakash Sethi, Nobuaki Namiki and Carl L. Swanson, The False Promise of the Japanese Miracle (Marshfield, MA: Pitman Publishing Co., 1984), pp. 281-297.

10. J.D. Goldhar and Mariann Jelinek, "Plan for Economies for Scope," Harvard Business Review 61, 6 (Nov.-Dec., 1983) pp. 141-148; see also Donald F. Barnett and Louis Schorsch, Steel: Upheaval in a Basic Industry (Cambridge, Mass.: Ballinger, 1983).

11. Mary A. Fejfar, *Regulation of Business By International Agencies*, Center for the Study of American Business (St. Louis, MO.: Washington University, 1983); "Current Status Report: Selected International Organization Activities Relating to Transnational Enterprises, 1984," Office of Investment Affairs, Department of State, Washington, D.C., 1984; Seymor J. Rubin, "Transnational Corporations and International Codes of Conduct: A Study of the Relationship Between International Legal Cooperation and Economic Development," *The American University Law Review*, 30, 4 (Summer, 1981), pp. 903-922; and, Servaas van Thiel, "U.N. Draft of Code of Conduct on Transnational Corporations," *Bulletin of International Fiscal Documentation*, 39 (January, 1985), pp.29-33.

12. S. Prakash Sethi, *The Righteous and the Powerful: Corporations, Religious Institutions and International Social Activism - The Case of the Infant Formula Controversy and the Nestle Boycott* (Cambridge, Mass.: Ballinger Publishing Co., in press); and Timothy W. Stanley, "International Codes of Conduct for MNCs: A Skeptical View of the Process," *The American University Law Review*, 30, 4 (Summer, 1981), pp. 973-1008.

13. Rubin, supra note 11, and Stanley, supra note 12.

14. There is a growing body of literature about the South Africa debate that is too voluminous to cite here. The reader's attention is directed to a special issue of *Business and Society Review* (Spring, 1986) which is entirely devoted to a discussion of the South African apartheid policies and the role international economic and political institutions can play in bringing about a change in those policies.

15. Sethi, *The Righteous and the Powerful*, supra note 12. See also: Burton Y. Pines (ed.), *A World Without U.N.* (Washington, D.C.: The Heritage Foundation, 1984); Tobi T. Gati (ed.), *The US, the UN and the Management of Social Change* (New York: New York University Press, 1983); Chetley, *Cleared for Exports*, supra note 2; Charles Medawar and Barbara Freese, *Drug Diplomacy* (London: Social Audit, 1982); and Dianna Melrose, *Bitter Pills: Medicines and the Third World* (Oxford, England: Oxfam, 1982).

16. Thomas C. Oden, *Conscience and Dividends: Churches and the Multinationals* (Washington, D.C.: Ethics and Public Policy Center, 1985); and Enrest Lefever, *Amsterdam to Nairobi: The World Council of Churches and the Third World*

(Washington, DC: Ethics and Public Policy Center, 1979).

17. For a better understanding of the ideas and concepts underlying liberation theology and dependency theory, the reader is directed to: Cornel West, "Religion and the West," Monthly Review, 36, 3 (July-August 1984), pp. 9-17; Phillip Berryman "Basic Christian Communities and the Future of Latin America," Monthly Review, 36, 3 (July-August 1984), pp. 27-40; Allan Boesak, "Black Theology and the Struggle for Liberation in South Africa," Monthly Review, 36, 3 (July-August 1984), pp. 127-137; Joel Kovel, "The Vatican Strikes Back," Monthly Review, 36, 11, (April 1985), pp. 14-27; Sol W. Sanders, "The Vatican Gets Tougher on Nicaragua's Liberation Theology," Business Week (August 27, 1984), p. 47; A.J. Conyers, "Liberation Theology: Whom Does it Liberate?" Modern Age, (Summer/Fall, 1983), pp. 303-308; George Hunsinger, "Karl Barth and Liberation Theology," The Journal of Religion, 63, 3 (July, 1983), pp. 247-263; Enrique Dussel, Ethics and the Theology of Liberation (Maryknoll, New York: Orbis Books, 1978); Gustavo Gutierrez, A Theology of Liberation, translated by Bernard F. McWilliams (Maryknoll, New York: Orbis Books, 1973); King Paul and Dave Woodyard, The Journey Toward Freedom: Economic Structures and Theological Perspectives (Rutherford, NJ: Fairleigh Dickinson University Press, 1982).

18. Peter Evans, Dependent Development (Princeton, N.J.: Princeton University Press, 1979); Andre Frank, Critique and Anti-Critique: Essays on Dependence and Reformism (New York: Praeger, 1984); Doran, et. al., North/South Relations: Studies of Dependency Reversal (New York: Praeger, 1983); Chilcote Johnson, Theories of Development (Beverly Hills, California: Sage Publications, 1983); Gary Gereffi, "Power and Dependency in an Interdependent World: A Guide to Understanding the Contemporary Global Crisis," International Journal of Comparative Sociology, XXV, 1-2 (1984), pp. 91-108; Adrienne Armstrong, "The Political Consequences of Economic Dependence," Journal of Conflict Resolution, 25, 3 (September 1981), pp. 401-428; Michael Timberlake and Kirk R. Williams, "Dependence, Political Exclusion and Government Repression: Some Cross-National Evidence," American Sociological Review, 49, (February, 1984), pp. 141-146; Volker Bornschier, "Dependent Industrialization in the World Economy," 25, 1, (September, 1981), pp. 371-400; Volker Bornschier, Christopher Chase-Dunne and Richard Robinson, "Cross-National Evidence of the Effects of Foreign Investment and Aid on Economic Growth and Inequality and Survey of Findings and a Reanalysis," American Journal of Sociology, 84, 3 (1984), pp. 651-683.

ETHICAL DILEMMAS OF MULTINATIONAL ENTERPRISE:
AN HISTORICAL PERSPECTIVE

Mira Wilkins

The essays in this collection address the dilemmas facing managers of the contemporary multinational enterprise. How are these dilemmas similar to or different from ones that faced managers in years past? The multinational enterprise is, after all, an institution with a long history. The modern multinational enterprise, as we know it today, came of age in the late ninteenth century. But the fundamental questions raised in these pages are not new ones, although the dimensions of some are unique: for example, on the issue of safety, the scale of the Union Carbide disaster in Bhopal has no historical precedent.

There is one broad and perennial difficulty for the multinational that I want to discuss; it is inherent in the naure of the institution and, as such, leads to a set of dilemmas that are special to this type of firm. By definition, a multinational enterprise operates over borders, under different national sovereignties. In its purely business operations, this should make no difference. Strategies of managers should be designed to meet the realities of factor and product markets. Yet, each sovereign state has rules, regulations, and goals, and a businessman operates under them. When such rules, regulations, and goals conflict, and the conflict affects the business of the multinational enterprise, the institution is by definition caught in a quandry. The conflict may be partial and easily resolvable through compromise. At the extreme, when home and host countries are at war, the dilemma can only be resolved by the dissolution of the multinational enterprise.

What makes a multinational enterprise viable is coordination and control. Raymond Vernon has often pointed out that a multinational enterprise is a cluster of companies, jointly coordinated. The ethical justification for a multinational enterprise is that it uses resources better, more efficiently, within the enterprise than would be the case with separate firms. A multinational enterprise does not make economic or social sense unless it substitutes efficiency for inefficiency.

But business is conducted under the rules of sovereign entities, and when two sovereign states are at war, business becomes transformed into an instrument for national security. Before World War I, for example, many German multinationals operated in the United States. When, after American entry into the war as a combatant, the Alien Property Custodian took over the German properties, the denunciation of the German companies was associated with the dilemma to which I have just referred. The Alien Property Custodian was not concerned with the business operations, but saw the German enterprises as agents of the German government or as German industrial army invading American soil. What about the managers of these German multinationals? The multinational enterprise fragmented on national lines. Naturalized Germans, who had become American citizens and who managed these German-controlled American properties, became caught in a dilemma. After America entered the war, most aligned themselves with the American cause.

War between the home and the host country of an enterprise usually breaks up the multinational enterprise, albeit sometimes temporarily (that is, for the war's duration). There are some cases, especially with European multinationals, of firms attempting at least for the first few months of war to do business as usual on both sides of war. It does not work. When home and host country are at war, the political takes precedence over the business activity, and the dilemma resolves itself in what for all practical purposes is the dissolution of the multinational.

The conflict dilemma is not as serious to the institution itself when there are wars between host countries in which the enterprise operates, or civil war within a particular host country. In these cases, often, the decision is not made for the manager by circumstance; managers have to make choices, as many have done over the years in relation to the Arab-Israeli conflicts and in circumstances such as Angola and more recently in the Sudan.

Political conflict involving the home nation and other countries often has ramifications in noncombatant countries. After war broke out in Europe in 1914 and before American entry, some German multinationals in the United States defaulted on their sterling borrowings from American banks rather than buying sterling at the extraordinarily high dollar price and thus giving aid to Britian.

A multinational enterprise sometimes has meaningless choices. Once it decides to operate within a sovereign state, it has to operate under the rules of that state. Yet, there are many circumstances of ambiguity that do involve options. A German multinational enterprise in the United States in 1914-1917, when America was not yet a combatant but was very sympathetic to Great Britain, faced four different possible options: (1) patriotism (not helping the American economy, which might well become embroiled in war and which was already aiding Germany's enemy); (2) preservation of enterprise (doing business, coordinated from abroad, where business was available to be done, irrespective of politics); (3) farsightedness (forecasting the potential conflict and protecting the enterprise by camouflaging ownership or transferring it into American hands -- but this of course involved risk to perserving the enterprise should war between America and Germany not break out); and (4) acceptance that when doing business in America, America took precedent over German "causes," and patriotism to the home country was not desirable. In the years 1914-1917, German companies in America solved their dilemma in different ways, and all four paths were taken by different companies.

Where there are laws (war is declared), there is the dilemma of conformity with those laws, or loyalty with an outside cause. Most companies operating under the rules of sovereign states conform; if, to repeat, there is war between home and host country, the enterprise usually fragments. The most serious dilemmas are in cases of ambiguity. When there is ambiguity and potential for choice, to what extent should political, ethical, and moral issues take precedence over business ones for the corporate executives?

I want to dwell on this for a moment because it seems to me that this is at the heart of many of the questions raised in the following essays. A modern multinational enterprise is exposed to the public at home and abroad; it is under a spotlight. It pays for the modern multinational enterprise to be a good citizen and to have a good image. Especially if the firm makes consumer goods, it does not want to have its name tarnished. Its name is a very important business asset. We are not talking about the world of little companies where cheating may pay. Top management in a modern multinational knows that antagonizing its public (shareholders, customers, employees) has negative effects on the performance of the firm. If we assume that large companies take into account public relations consequences of their strategies, then we must ask if there are higher, more important values.

I want to return again to the ultimate dilemma of political conflict. Where does patriotism fit? Is it a higher value? Does it depend on the war? Are there universal values that we should impose on managers of multinational enterprise?

Likewise, it seems to me that when we talk about the perennial dilemmas of multinational enterprise, we must ask which values are the relevant ones. Americans believe corruption is wrong. While there exists corruption in our society, we prosecute men who are found guilty of corrupting members of government. Let's take the case of a multinational enterprise that is operating and wants to continue profitable operations in a small sovereign state. The head of the state demands a payment as a condition of doing business. The payment is not public; it is out of channels; but it is not "illegal" since the recipient is the head of state. Essentially, he sets the rules in this undemocratic state. There is no violation of foreign law; there is, however, a violation of American values and were the transaction to take place in the United States it would be illegal. It is cultural or political imperialism to impose American values on other countries? Businessmen have argued over the years that that is the way business is done abroad, that American business will be at a disadvantage in world markets because French, German, British, and other businesses have no such scruples. Should multinational business be the conduit for the transference of what are clearly American values abroad? The dilemma arises where the interests of enterprise are in no corruption worldwide, but if <u>only</u> United States enterprise follows that rule, American enterprise will lose what is legal, profitable, business. Is opposition to corruption an eternal value?

Let me give you an historical case on the very same issue. In the 1880s, certain British companies investing in the United States faced taxes and regulations of various sorts imposed by state legislatures. The companies considered these prejudicial to their property rights. They went to the British government and asked it to go to Washington and arrange a treaty that would transcend the legislation put forth by "ignorant" (and corrupt) American state legislators. The British businesses thought they had a "moral" case; the state legislators were acting improperly. Yet, was this opposition legitimate? Neither the United States nor the British government thought so, and when the United States government told the British minister that such a treaty would abrogate states' rights, the British minister did not pursue the "moral" cause on behalf of British businessmen.

When, by contrast, in years past, a British multinational in China supported by the British government wanted to operate under British law rather than Chinese law and wanted to introduce order and stability and British values (which they saw as the right values), we labeled this extension of extraterritoriality "imperialism."

What distinguishes a multinational enterprise from a domestic one is that it operates under different national sovereignties. To what extent do and should moral, ethical, and political values accepted and enacted in legislation in the home country supersede laws in the host country abroad? Equality of opportunity is the law in the United States; it is contrary to the law in South Africa. Should a multinational enterprise be a transmitter of home country values that have been translated into law at home to other countries where laws are different? The multinational enterprise is clearly a transmitter of process and product, of technology, of mode of work, to foreign countries. It clearly competes with domestic enterprise, methods, products, and style. Obviously, by its very nature it standardizes culture. But, should it go further? Conversely, should a South African company operating in the United States carry South African law to America? Of course not, we reply. But why? Because their law is "wrong" and ours is right? Or because when in the United States, we expect South African companies to follow American Law? Are there values that transcend law, and if so, should the multinational enterprise be expected to be the conduit of such values? In the case of South Africa, these questions were being asked twenty years ago. They are still being asked. They are important ones, lying at the heart of any discussion on ethical dilemmas for multinational enterprises.

We all know we want managers of multinationals to transfer technology, products, and processes and to contribute to economic growth wherever they operate. How much do we also want them to be transmitters of ethical and political systems? How much should the home government support, or encourage them, in this transmission process? If we favor the values, we want them transferred; if we oppose the values, we argue national sovereignty. Are there universal values that transcend sovereign choice that we expect multinationals to transmit? These have long been open questions, with no easy answers.

SOCIAL RESPONSIBILITY OF THE MULTINATIONAL CORPORATION

Charles P. Kindleberger

The social responsibility of the domestic corporation raises all sorts of ethical dilemmas, but when one goes outside the country, these seem to multiply. The heart of the issue is the clash between "When in Rome, do as the Romans do," and "To thine own self be true," as Polonious, that old windbag, put it. When ethical standards differ, should one go with the local standard, or bring the (presumably) higher standard from home, at some cost in competitive ability? An economist is tempted to ask for cultural neutrality, as for tax neutrality. But where tax systems differ, we know all-around neutrality is impossible. Neutrality between the MNC and its local competition is one thing, but if that is achieved, there is violation between the MNC in its home country and other domestic companies. If in a mythical Rome, companies do not pay taxes, for an MNC to cheat on taxes which it would pay at home is to subsidize foreign investment and be non-neutral.

Let us take first domestic neutrality. In primitive societies, there is one standard of morality within the group and another outside. Margaret Meade observed that the injunction in rural Greece to be honest meant honesty only toward people in the village. It is thought that Moslems discriminate in their honesty between members of the faith and infidels. But within the group -- family, tribe, village, neighborhood, region, nation whatever it be -- what is the standard of responsibility? It has obviously changed as the group has widened. Nepotism made sense so long as one could not trust people outside the family. Bazaar trading gave way to fixed written prices when the store outgrew the size that could be run continuously in the family, and it was feared that a non-family employee would offer excessive bargains -- "give away the store," so to speak -- to members of his family. (The Quakers had agitated for fixed written prices a century before fixed pricing was adopted widely in the nineteenth century -- first with the department store of Aristide Bouricault in Paris in the 1840s -- so that children could be sent to shop and their parents would not fear that they would be cheated). The question whether employees can be trusted or not arises in economics today in the form of "agency problem." Everyone is supposed to be self-interested -- critics would say "motivated by greed" -- and the question arises whether the man hired by an employer will look after the employer's interest, as per his contractual arrangement, or his own when the two come into conflict. Cynical observers expect the agent to cheat on the principal, so that the latter is advised to monitor the agent's actions and to take insurance to cover defalcation, malfeasance, or subversion -- to use some big words for stealing.

A separate issue arises with dealings between two principals where there is inequality of information between them. The Chicago, hard-nosed school, tends to believe in <u>caveat emptor</u>, let the buyer beware, which can be extended to inviting the seller to beware if he has something that the buyer thinks is valuable on the basis of information not shared with the seller. One can perhaps distinguish between cases where the seller misleads the buyer and those where there is no deception, but abundant ignorance. Is the seller -- to deal with only one side of the bargain for expositional efficiency -- bound to educate the buyer? Or is it ethical to take advantage of inherent ignorance which the seller had no part in implanting? Most economists, I would judge, believe in deposit insurance for holders of bank deposits in small amounts -- though whether to draw the line at $2,500, or $10,000, $40,000 or $100,000 may be arguable -- on the gound that the ordinary person is not skilled in judging the soundness of a bank. The lemon law in automobiles protects the consumer when he or she buys an automobile which, let us assume, without the connivance of the factory workers, the manufacturer, or the dealer, unaccountably resists performing as a new car should. And we hold the producer, not the consumer accountable for design defects which prove dangerous, insisting on recall and correction. The Pure Food and Drug Administration has few adverse critics calling for its abolition, though it is sometimes chided for unduly drawn-out testing. Those like Milton Friedman who have advocated letting the market decide who is a good brain surgeon, and who a competent automobile driver, stripping society of all need for testing and licensing, are thought to be largely whimsical rather than serious. Most of us think that the state has the obligation to check yardsticks, as in the Middle Ages, or butchers' scales in poor neighborhoods today to assure honest weight, either because of consumer ignorance or to save on the transaction cost of each buyer testing weights and measures individually.

A line is sometimes drawn between actions that are approved between consenting arms-length adults -- I have in mind charging high interest, or what the market will bear -- and within the family, tribe, village, parish, or religious group. Albert Hirschman makes a distinction between "Exit" and "Voice." Exit is the economic response to dissatisfaction: quit the job, cease to buy the product. Voice, on the other hand, is the response to dissatisfaction within a group to which the actor is bound, speaking up as a voter, member of the family, urging a decision in the direction desired, but not leaving the group if outvoted. The line between exit and voice is shadowy. One does not sell heirlooms. A French observer of the American scene in the early nineteenth century was shocked that an American would sell a dog, a horse, the clothes of his father, "house first, and then the clothes," (Chevalier Lettres d'Amerique, II p. 128). The grants economy in which gifts, dowries, inheritances, and the like abound, differs from the market economy. A market differs from a budget, in that the market exchanges values, while a budget within a group raises funds to meet costs and deals out benefits on a sharing basis.

When we move from the domestic to the international scene, matters are more complex because the people dealt with are not (now) part of the empathetic unit. As the world gets smaller, the size of the unit one is bound to increases. The height of corruption was reached, in the eyes of a modern economic historian, in the East India Company. Not only did Clive and Hastings acquire large fortunes in India by special dealing with corrupt local rulers, but all those dealings with the company had their own rackets. The company's "writers" or clerks in India dealt for their own account on the side, and accumulated fortunes if they survived the rigors of climate, the Black Hole of Calcutta, and the pestilence. Ship captains were allotted a certain amount of cargo space to carry freight for their own profit, and took more. The directors of the company mostly had their own private companies which sold the East India Company provisions at exorbitant profit. The "rents" from dealing were enormous, like those in televising sports today, and all the elements in the operation competed freely for a share, without much regard to the letter of their contracts. There are similar actions that are clearly wrong: the gunboat of D'Arcy pointing at the Shah of Persia when the first oil concession was signed in 1902: did it protect D'Arcy or threaten the Shah, and was the contract invalid because it was made under duress? Or the cans full of damaging documents, covered over with a veneer of corned beef, smuggled out of Argentina by Armour and Swift in the early 20th century. ITT's record in Chile is difficult to defend. Amway was caught misrepresenting the value of equipment shipped to Canada so as not to pay heavy duties. The joint venture between Xerox and the British Rank organization started to unravel when Xerox learned that Rank was understating the valuation of leased equipment shipped to the Continent, so as to save on customs and duties. Differences in ethical standards can undo a joint venture.

It becomes more complex when trying to distinguish bribery from baksheesh. Some suggest that bribery is paying substantial sums to people to do things they should not do, such as buy the wrong kind of airplane in Japan, or military equipment in the Netherlands, and is different from small tips to officials to expedite what they are going to do in any case. The tyranny of the guichet or wicket is hard to overcome, and when natives grease the wheels with petty bribery, is it appropriate for foreign corporations to follow along? In taxation, I have heard the argument from a Milan accountant that it is important for foreign corporations to half the income they earned in the accounts submitted to the Italian tax authorities on the ground that everyone does it, and the authorities will double the tax, so that it all comes out about right. Some American companies find it difficult to adapt to local practice in such ways and form joint ventures, at least for a few years, in order to allow local partners to deal with authorities in ways that they morally or culturally cannot.

Is it appropriate to take advantage of the ignorance or inexperience of foreign government officials? The question arose primarily with the question of transfer pricing, with the prices of components shipped into, say, Colombia on pharmaceuticals allegedly from a Panamanian subsidiary but in actuality a tax shelter, vastly unstated so as to record no profits in Colombia on which income tax would have to be paid. Transfer prices within the firm must presumably be recorded at what arm's length prices in a competive market would have been. The Internal Revenue Service in the United States has power under the Internal Revenue Act of 1962 to deny the tax credit to tax shelters that produce less than 30 percent of the value added of a product, thus forestalling mere write-up, and to "construct" a profit on which income tax must be paid by its own determination of the appropriate transfer prices, thus seriously discouraging United States firms from attempting to understate United States profits. But the level of sophistication in these matters in developing countries has not been up to that here.

Where the unsophisticated persons who may be taken advantage of are consumers rather than government officials, the ethical question becomes murkier. The locus classicus here is the Nestle company's advertising of its baby formula, appropriate in the United States, where mothers of infants can decide for themselves whether to nurse or bottlefeed with full information on convenience, comparable sanitary conditions, health standards, and the like. It has been claimed by comsumer groups that the company used arguments in LDCs inappropriate to those countries where water was unsanitary and the conditions for sterilizing bottles and safely feeding infants were minimal. As a result of a world-wide boycott of its products, Nestle finally agreed to tone down its advertising and halt its attempts in hospitals to start babies off on formula. Other products appropriate to developed countries are objected to in other parts of the world, especially those subject to intensive advertising like soft drinks and breakfast foods. The convenience to the housewife is judged by critics to be worth less than the cost, and the advertising misleading.

Perhaps the most salient case of social responsibility of multinational corporations today turns on the political pressures on these corporations to boycott the Union of South Africa because of its stand on racial discrimination, or apartheid. Students and other groups are urging churches, universities, foundations, and others not to invest in companies that produce there. A General Motors director, the Reverend Leon Sullivan, has worked out a compromise position that accepts investments in companies that apply a set of principles resisting apartheid. Some companies make all but a few products that might be used by police in photographing, producing identity cards, and curbing unrest among blacks and colored. The pressures on companies against producing there, on banks against lending, and for interrupting all economic intercourse between the rest of the world and South Africa are powerful and mounting. But there are those who say that the issue is one for government and not private enterprise.

An objective economic observer -- one who, it should be stated, detests racial discrimination -- may perhaps usefully make three points: First, the record of boycotts in general has been poor. The Nestle boycott on a single company is a striking counterexample, but the record of economic sanctions by the Arabs against companies trading with Israel, by the League of Nations against Italy, and by the West against the Soviet Union, either in high-technology equipment in general or on grain at the time of the invasion of Afghanistan, is a poor one. The boycott is difficult or impossible to enforce in a world of many countries and many companies.

Secondly, a boycott of South Africa may be dysfunctional if the object of the exercise is to help the black peoples of that country. To assist the poorest paid members of the labor force, one needs not depression but inflation. Profits would accrue to the discriminating whites, to be sure, but what breaks discrimination is pressure for output. It is evident that the real breakthroughs of minorities against discrimination in the United States came in the First World War when black men moved north into factories as ordinary workers, and in the Second World War when black women broke out of restriction to servant occupations or teaching in black schools into general retail and office service jobs, and black men were upgraded to skilled jobs in the factory. It would go against one's instincts deliberately to buy more and more South African goods and gold to create inflation, and few would actually advocate such a course. But it must be recognized that putting South Africa into economic Coventry would be hardest on those we want to help.

Finally, on this issue I am unhappy about the pressures in today's world to convert economic transactions into moral judgments. Adam Smith suggested that the market-place allocated goods and services as if by an invisible hand, in which it was not necessary to know the identity, morality, life-style, etc., of the producers. With the development of software establishing a relationship between producer and the consumer, we have moved unhappily away from that day. It was important, beginning with the production of chemical fertilizer which had a tendency to explode if improperly handled, for the producer to be obligated to instruct the consumer in the use of his products, to provide spare parts for those that wore out, and to seek to build a reputation for high quality, fair dealing, and the like. The war on sweat-shops spread the union label. Cesar Chavez insisted that people contemplate the conditions of those who harvest lettuce and grapes and the morals of those who hire them. The age of innocence when the buyer could be ignorant of who producers where and how they worked has come to an end with the Ralph Naders. More is the pity. One must applaud the boycott on Nestle and its response to it while at the same time hoping that that is not the order of the day for the future.

I come at last to Union Carbide and the tragic event at Bhopal. The question of who was responsible for the disaster, the head office in Danbury, Connecticut, or the local officers and government inspectors in India is one that must be left to the courts to decide. Whom, however, would an ethical man or woman hold responsible? Is a multinational company a unit, where all responsibility for its operation everywhere devolves on the CEO wherever he is located, or is it an agglomeration of units, each tub on its own bottom, helped by central-staff services, but each an operating responsible entity? As in so many questions, where you stand depends on where you sit. In piercing the corporate veil in law suits, the United States pierces, except where its interests are strongly favored by the opposite position, whereas the British typically regard a corporation organized under the laws of a state as having that state's citizenship unless its interests favor the United States piercing positions. Many countries and most unions object to a corporation closing down an unprofitable subsidiary, arguing that it ought to be sustained by the profits of the complex as a whole. So passionately are such beliefs held that one American corporation withdrew in the middle of the night all the American personnel of its failing Madrid subsidiary which it was abandoning.

Clearly something like rule of reason is wanted here. One cannot approve corporations that move into an area for subsidies, tax, and other advantages for a limited period of time, and then move out when these have run out, as some American firms have done in Sicily and many have done in Puerto Rico. The inducements are offered and should be taken in expectation of a happy marriage lasting a long time. But if some aspect of the deal goes sour, without anticipation, some provision for divorce is called for. The Organization of Economic Cooperation and Development code calls for maintaining employment for a year after deciding to terminate operations. I do not know whether this is reasonable or not, but it sounds so. I have less sympathy with the union insistence that a company cannot expand operations in one country to offset a strike in another. This implies the opposite theory to the multinational corporation as a unit, the conditions of each subsidiary, and says each case must be decided on its own. But having one's cake and eating it too is unacceptable to the economists and, in the economist's view, should also be to the world as a whole. The ambiguity of behaving like Romans in Rome while staying true to one's own ethical standards is both inescapable and disturbing. But it does not justify the multinational corporation in switching between two positions continuously on an ad hoc basis determined by the bottom line on each separate issue.

ETHICAL DILEMMAS FOR MULTINATIONAL ENTERPRISE:
A PHILOSOPHICAL OVERVIEW

Richard T. De George

First World multinational corporations (MNCs) are both the hope of the Third World and the scourge of the Third World. The working out of this paradox poses moral dilemmas for many MNCs. I shall focus on some of the moral dilemmas that many American MNCs face.

Third World countries frequently seek to attract American multinationals for the jobs they provide and for the technological transfers they promise. Yet when American MNCs locate in Third World countries, many Americans condemn them for exploiting the resources and workers of the Third World. While MNCs are a means for improving the standard of living of the underdeveloped countries, MNCs are blamed for the poverty and starvation such countries suffer. Although MNCs provide jobs in the Third World, many criticize them for transferring these jobs from the United States. American MNCs usually pay at least as high wages as local industries, yet critics blame them for paying the workers in underdeveloped countries less than they pay American workers for comparable work. When American MNCs pay higher than local wages, local companies criticize them for skimming off all the best workers and for creating an internal brain-drain. Multinationals are presently the most effective vehicle available for the development of the Third World. At the same time, critics complain that the MNCs are destroying the local cultures and substituting for them the tinsel of American life and the worst aspects of its culture. American MNCs seek to protect the interests of their shareholders by locating in an environment in which their enterprise will be safe from destruction by revolutions and confiscation by socialist regimes. When they do so, critics complain that the MNCs thrive in countries with strong, often right-wing, governments.[1]

The dilemmas the American MNCs face arise from conflicting demands made from opposing, often ideologically based, points of view. Not all of the demands that lead to these dilemmas are equally justifiable, nor are they all morally mandatory. We can separate the MNCs that behave immorally and reprehensibly from those that do not by clarifying the true moral responsibility of MNCs in the Third World. To help do so, I shall state and briefly defend five theses.

THESIS I: MANY OF THE MORAL DILEMMAS MNCS FACE ARE FALSE DILEMMAS WHICH ARISE FROM EQUATING UNITED STATES STANDARDS WITH MORALLY NECESSARY STANDARDS.

Many American critics argue that American multinationals should live up to and implement the same standards abroad that they do in the United States and that United States mandated norms should be followed.[2] This broad claim confuses morally necessary ways of conducting a firm with United States government regulations. The FDA sets high standards that may be admirable. But they are not necessarily morally required. OSHA specifies a large number of rules which in general have as their aim the protection of the worker. However, these should not be equated with morally mandatory rules. United States wages are the highest in the world. These also should not be thought to be the morally necessary norms for the whole world or for United States firms abroad. Morally mandatory standards that no corporation -- United States or other -- should violate, and moral minima below which no firm can morally go, should not be confused either with standards appropriate to the United States or with standards set by the United States government. Some of the dilemmas of United States multinationals come from critics making such false equations.

This is true with respect to drugs and FDA standards, with respect to hazardous occupations and OSHA standards, with respect to pay, with respect to internalizing the costs of externalities, and with respect to foreign corrupt practices. By using United States standards as moral standards, critics pose false dilemmas for American MNCs. These false dilemmas in turn obfuscate the real moral responsibilities of MNCs.

THESIS II: DESPITE DIFFERENCES AMONG NATIONS IN CULTURE AND VALUES, WHICH SHOULD BE RESPECTED, THERE ARE MORAL NORMS THAT CAN BE APPLIED TO MULTINATIONALS.

I shall suggest seven moral guidelines that apply in general to any multinational operating in Third World countries and that can be used in morally evaluating the actions of MNCs. MNCs that respect these moral norms would escape the legitimate criticisms contained in the dilemmas they are said to face.

1. <u>MNCs should do no intentional direct harm.</u> This injunction is clearly not peculiar to multinational corporations. Yet it is a basic norm that can be usefully applied in evaluating the conduct of MNCs. Any company that does produce intentional direct harm clearly violates a basic moral norm.

2. **MNCs should produce more good than bad for the host country.** This is an implementation of a general utilitarian principle. But this norm restricts the extent of that principle by the corollary that, in general, more good will be done by helping those in most need, rather than by helping those in less need at the expense of those in greater need. Thus the utilitarian analysis in this case does not consider that more harm than good might justifiably be done to the host country if the harm is offset by greater benefits to others in developed countries. MNCs will do more good only if they help the host country more than they harm it.

3. **MNCs should contribute by their activities to the host country's development.** If the presence of an MNC does not help the host country's development, the MNC can be correctly charged with exploitation, or using the host country for its own purposes at the expense of the host country.

4. **MNCs should respect the human rights of its employees.** MNCs should do so whether or not local companies respect those rights. This injunction will preclude gross exploitation of workers, set minimum standards for pay, and prescribe minimum standards for health and safety measures.

5. **MNCs should pay their fair share of taxes.** Transfer pricing has as its aim taking advantage of different tax laws in different countries. To the extent that it involves deception, it is itself immoral. To the extent that it is engaged in to avoid legitimate taxes, it exploits the host country, and the MNC does not bear its fair share of the burden of operating in that country.

6. **To the extent that local culture does not violate moral norms, MNCs should respect the local culture and work with it, not against it.** MNCs cannot help but produce some changes in the cultures in which they operate. Yet, rather than simply transferring American ways into other lands, they can consider changes in operating procedures, plant planning, and the like, which take into account local needs and customs.

7. **MNCs should cooperate with the local government in the development and enforcement of just background institutions.** Instead of fighting a tax system that aims at appropriate redistribution of incomes, instead of preventing the organization of labor, and instead of resisting attempts at improving the health and safety standards of the host country, MNCs should be supportive of such measures.

THESIS III: WHOLESALE ATTACKS ON MULTINATIONALS ARE MOST OFTEN OVERGENERALIZATIONS. VALID MORAL EVALUATIONS CAN BE BEST MADE BY USING THE ABOVE MORAL CRITERIA FOR CONTEXT- AND-CORPORATION-SPECIFIC STUDIES AND ANALYSIS.

Broadside claims, such that all multinationals exploit underdeveloped countries or destroy their culture, are too vague to determine their accuracy. United States multinationals have in the past engaged -- and some continue to engage -- in immoral practices. A case by case study is the fairest way to make moral assessments. Yet we can distinguish five types of business operations that raise very different sorts of moral issues: 1) banks and financial institutions; 2) agricultural enterprises; 3) drug companies and hazardous industries; 4) extractive industries; and 5) other manufacturing and service industries.

If we were to apply our seven general criteria in each type of case, we would see some of the differences among them. Financial institutions do not generally employ many people. Their function is to provide loans for various types of development. In the case of South Africa they do not do much -- if anything -- to undermine apartheid, and by lending to the government they usually strengthen the government's policy of apartheid. In this case, an argument can be made that they do more harm than good -- an argument that several banks have seen to be valid, causing them to discontinue their South African operations even before it became financially dangerous to continue lending money to that government. Financial institutions can help and have helped development tremendously. Yet the servicing of debts that many Third World countries face condemns them to impoverishment for the foreseeable future. The role of financial institutions in this situation is crucial and raises special and difficult moral problems, if not dilemmas.

Agricultural enterprises face other demands. If agricultural multinationals buy the best lands and use them for export crops while insufficient arable land is left for the local population to grow enough to feed itself, then MNCs do more harm than good to the host country -- a violation of one of the norms I suggested above.

Drug companies and dangerous industries pose different and and special problems. I have suggested that FDA standards are not morally mandatory standards. This should not be taken to mean that drug companies are bound only by local laws, for the local laws may require less than morality requires in the way of supplying adequate information and of not producing intentional, direct harm. [3] The same type of observation applies to hazardous

42

industries. While an asbestos company will probably not be morally required to take all the measures mandated by OSHA regulations, it cannot morally leave its workers completely unprotected.[4]

Extractive industries, such as mining, which remove minerals from a country, are correctly open to the charge of exploitation unless they can show that they do more good than harm to the host country and that they do not benefit only either themselves or a repressive elite in the host country.

Other manufacturing industries vary greatly, but as a group they have come in for sustained charges of exploitation of workers and the undermining of the host country's culture. The above guidelines can serve as a means of sifting the valid from the invalid charges.

THESIS IV: ON THE INTERNATIONAL LEVEL AND ON THE NATIONAL LEVEL IN MANY THIRD WORLD COUNTRIES THE LACK OF ADEQUATE JUST BACKGROUND INSTITUTIONS MAKES THE USE OF CLEAR MORAL NORMS ALL THE MORE NECESSARY.

American multinational corporations operating in Germany and Japan, and German and Japanese multinational corporations operating in the United States, pose no special moral problems. Nor do the operations of Brazilian multinational corporations in the United States or Germany. Yet First World multinationals operating in Third World countries have come in for serious and sustained moral criticism. Why?

A major reason is that in the Third World the First World's MNCs operate without the types of constraints and in societies that do not have the same kinds of redistributive mechanisms as in the developed countries. There is no special difficulty in United States multinationals operating in other First World countries because in general these countries do have appropriate background institutions.[5]

More and more Third World countries are developing controls on multinationals that insure the companies do more good for the country than harm.[6] Authoritarian regimes that care more for their own wealth than for the good of their people pose difficult moral conditions under which to operate. In such instances, the guidelines above may prove helpful.

Just as in the nations of the developed, industrial world the labor movement serves as a counter to the dominance of big business, consumerism serves as a watchdog on practices harmful to the consumer, and big government serves as a restraint on each of the vested interest groups, so international structures are necessary to provide the proper background constraints on international corporations.

The existence of MNCs is a step forward in the unification of mankind and in the formation of a global community. They provide the economic base and substructure on which true international cooperation can be built. Because of their special position and the special opportunities they enjoy, they have a special responsibility to promote the cooperation that only they are able to accomplish in the present world.

Just background institutions would preclude any company's gaining a competitive advantage by engaging in immoral practices. This suggests that MNCs have more to gain than to lose by helping formulate voluntary, UN (such as the code governing infant forumulae)[7], and similar codes governing the conduct of all multinationals. A case can also be made that they have the moral obligation to do so.

THESIS V: THE MORAL BURDEN OF MNCs DO NOT EXONERATE LOCAL GOVERNMENTS FROM RESPONSIBILITY FOR WHAT HAPPENS IN AND TO THEIR COUNTRY. SINCE RESPONSIBILITY IS LINKED TO OWNERSHIP, GOVERNMENTS THAT INSIST ON PART OR MAJORITY OWNERSHIP INCUR PART OR MAJORITY RESPONSIBILITY.

The attempts by many underdeveloped countries to limit multinationals have shown that at least some governments have come to see that they can use multinationals to their own advantage. This may be done by restricting entry to those companies that produce only for local consumption, or that bring desired technology transfers with them. Some countries demand majority control and restrict the export of money from the country. Nonetheless, many MNCs have found it profitable to engage in production under the terms specified by the host country.

What host countries cannot expect is that they can demand control without accepting correlative responsibility. In general, majority control implies majority responsibility. An American MNC, such as Union Carbide, which had majority ownership of its Indian Bhopal plant, should have had primary control of the plant. Union Carbide, Inc. can be held liable for the damage the Bhopal plant caused because Union Carbide, Inc. did have majority ownership.[8] If Union Carbide did not have effective control, it is not relieved of its responsibility. If it could not exercise the control that its responsibility demanded, it should have withdrawn or sold off part of its holdings in that plant. If India had had majority ownership, then it would have had primary responsibility for the safe operation of the plant.

This is compatible with maintaining that if a company builds a hazardous plant, it has an obligation to make sure that the plant is safe and that those who run it are properly trained to run it safely. MNCs cannot simply transfer dangerous technologies without consideration of the people who will run them, the local culture, and similar factors. Unless MNCs can be reasonably sure that the plants they build will be run safely, they cannot morally build them. To do so would be to will intentional, direct harm.

The theses and guidelines that I have proposed are not a panacea. But they suggest how moral norms can be brought to bear on the dilemmas American multinationals face and they suggest ways out of apparent or false dilemmas. If MNCs observed those norms, they could properly avoid the moral sting of their critics' charges, even if their critics continued to level charges against them.

NOTES

1. The literature attacking American MNCs is extensive. Many of the charges mentioned in this paper are found in Richard J. Barnet and Ronald E. Muller, Global Reach: The Power of the Multinational Corporations, New York: Simon & Schuster, 1974, and in Pierre Jalee, The Pillage of the Third World, translated from the French by Mary Klopper, New York and London: Modern Reader Paperbacks, 1968.

2. The position I advocate does not entail moral relativism, as my third thesis shows. The point is that although moral norms apply uniformly across cultures, U.S. standards are not the same as moral standards, should themselves be morally evaluated, and are relative to American conditions, standard of living, interests, and history.

3. For a fuller discussion of multinational drug companies see Richard T. De George, Business Ethics, 2nd ed., New York: Macmillan, 1986, pp. 363-367.

4. For a more detailed analysis of the morality of exporting hazardous industries, see my Business Ethics, 367-372.

5. This position is consistent with that developed by John Rawls in his A Theory of Justice, Cambridge, Mass.: Harvard University Press, 1971, even though Rawls does not

extend his analysis to the international realm. The thesis does not deny that United States, German, or Japanese policies on trade restrictions, tariff levels, and the like can be morally evaluated.

6. See, for example, Theodore H. Moran, "Multinational Corporations: A Survey of Ten Years' Evidence," Georgetown School of Foreign Service, 1984.

7. For a general discussion of UN codes, see Wolfgang Fikentscher, "United Nations Codes of Conduct: New Paths in International Law," The American Journal of Comparative Law, 30 (1980), pp. 577-604.

8. The official Indian Government report on the Bhopal tragedy has not yet appeared. The Union Carbide report was partially reprinted in the New York Times, March 21, 1985, p. 48. The major New York Times reports appeared on December 9, 1984, January 28, 30, and 31, and February 3, 1985.

USING MACROECONOMIC THEORY TO ANCHOR PROBLEMS: ETHICAL ISSUES AND MULTINATIONALS

Karen Paul and Otto A. Bremer

The dominant Western approach to ethical questions tends to focus on the individual as the primary unit of analysis, the goal of personal responsibility for ethical choices, and the psychological aspects of moral development. This approach is consonant with the basic value structure of our own society as discussed by observers such as in de Tocqueville (1835-1840); Williams (1967), Bell (1976), Lasch (1978), MacIntyre (1984), and Bellah, et al. (1985). This emphasis on the individual, the role of personal choice, and the construction of collective action on the basis of democratic pluralism, dominates much of our analytical and moral thought not only in ethics, but also in other academic traditions such as psychology, political science, and economics. This theoretical perspective -- we might call it a microperspective -- sometimes obscures rather than illuminates important issues in ethics, particularly when the objects of analysis are collective entities such as multinational corporations (MNCs) and nation-states.

However, other theoretical traditions exist based more on collective units of society rather than on individuals. The sociological tradition is rooted in the analysis of collectivities. The history of Marxist-socialist thought revolves around class analysis. More recently, the development of liberation theology has made it necessary for Western theologians and philosophers to think more in terms of class-based groupings in society than has been the case in the dominant Western theological orientation which stresses individual responsibility and personal decision making. Parenthetically, we should note that Western thought tends to emphasize the individual as a unit of analysis more than do most Eastern philosophical traditions, where significance of the social collectivity is seen as having relatively greater importance. We might call the type of analysis which subsumes the individual to the social collective a macroperspective.

Use of a macroperspective to consider ethical issues involving MNCs has certain advantages over use of a microperspective. Problems can be seen in a more systematic way, i.e., as a part of systems functioning, rather than as a result of individual error, or ignorance, or wickedness.

We propose here to use a well developed set of macrotheoretical approaches to analyze ethical issues relating to MNCs in developed countries (DCs) and less developed countries (LDCs). Use of a macrotheoretical approach can lead to new insights precisely because it allows us to go beyond questions of individual choice and personal responsibility to questions of collective action. Judgments of rightness or wrongness rooted in individuals come to be superseded by assessments of impact on a societal level. True, the societal impacts of MNCs have consequences for individuals and at the same time are based on decisions and actions which in some sense can be traced to individuals. But there is a level of human choice and action which is more than the additive function -- the whole becomes more than the sum of the parts. Thus, macro-analysis becomes an appropriate perspective to use in problems involving MNCs and nation-states.

Macroeconomic theory provides a useful frame in which MNCs can be discussed. Economics is one social science in which collective units of analysis have been systematically analyzed and treated. The division between macroeconomics and microeconomics provides a neat delineation which, to some extent, isolates and spotlights the type of large-scale, societal theory needed for analyzing MNCs and their impact on societies.

The utility of this approach may not be immediately obvious to the managerial decision maker. Certainly, this approach provides no single set of guidelines for making ethical judgments or for inducing ethical behavior. Indeed, this approach makes judgments of rightness and wrongness complex and open to dispute. However, in the real world these decisions are frequently complex and open to dispute. A theoretical approach which acknowledges the richness of relevant considerations, the variety of impacts and effects, and the multiplicity of valid perspectives may contribute more to intelligent, responsible decision making and action than simple approaches do.

Moreover, the use of macroeconomic theory to frame ethical issues can be useful in providing a connecting framework into which various cases can be placed. Ethical issues involving MNCs tend to be considered as unique, isolated, topical events. Scholars have a tendency to adopt an attitude of outraged indignation when faced with the complex reality of situations like Union Carbide in Bhopal, or Nestle's marketing of infant formula in settings where proper use was nearly impossible. The ubiquitous use of the case method in business schools reinforces the tendency of scholars to consider such topics as unique events. Encapsulating each individual topic like Union Carbide, or Nestle, or bribery abroad, or apartheid, permits a fair degree of analysis and resolution and thus serves to further legitimate pedagogical purposes. However, the cost of such encapsulation is that we have difficulty in putting disparate events together in such a way as to allow us to formulate coherent guidelines for ethical conduct. Without an analyical framework, one has difficulty integrating new cases, making intelligent generalizations drawn from a body of old cases, and developing a theoretical tradition.

The Economic Development Approach

The economic development theory of Rostow (1960) suggests that investment of MNCs can "prime the pump" for the economic development of less developed nations, setting the stage for economic take-off. Five stages of economic growth are suggested: the preindustrial; the stage in which the preconditions for industrialization occur; economic take-off; the drive to economic and industrial maturity; and, finally, the mass consumption stage of modern society. The process of industrialization is thought to have a kind of historical inevitability, with various nations of the world moving through similar stages and eventually arriving at similar end-points, although the timing would vary considerably. From this perspective, MNCs are thought to have beneficial effects for both developed and less developed nations. Significant theoretical and empirical challenges to this perspective have been forthcoming (Paul and Barbato, 1985), yet most MNC managers implicitly operate using its assumptions.

Where the economic development approach is most useful is where benefits are observed or assumed to be occurring in both a developed nation or nations and a less developed nation or nations as a result of MNC activities. Ethical issues which are amenable to analysis using this model are those cases where some force or factor is interfering with free trade, the transfer of technology, or specialization among nations. This model takes as beneficial that the productive capacities of nations should become specialized along the lines of efficiency criteria developed by MNCs.

From this perspective, executives, labor union leaders, communities, or state governments who lobby for protection of established business interests like obsolete steel mills are engaged in perhaps well-meaning, but nevertheless wrongful actions. One who assumes the validity of economic development theory is likely to see interventionist trade policies as erroneous, motivated by selfish interests, and ethically indefensible.

The North-South Approach

Proponents of the North-South approach, sometimes called

dependencia theory, or the development of underdevelopment, assert that MNCs inevitably serve to benefit developed nations and to harm less developed nations (Chirot, 1977; Wallerstein, 1974). According to this school of thought, the MNC hinders rather than helps the economic development of less developed nations, draining them of their own domestic capital and human as well as physical resources. For example, Pinto and Knakel (1973) have shown that between 1960 and 1968 profit remittances by MNCs to the United States from Latin America exceeded new investment by $6.7 billion. Thus, investment previously available for locally owned and managed business enterprise is diverted to MNCs based in the developed nations.

North-South theory emphasizes the dislocations that occur in a traditional society when MNCs intrude. People in less developed countries are prematurely exposed to the promise of greater opportunities and a Western lifestyle, but the possibility of their realizing these opportunities is remote (Evans & Timberlake, 1980; Todaro, 1969). The result can be political and social breakdown in the less developed nation. Often customary forms of social integration are disrupted. Extended family networks, community leaders, and even religious leaders may lose influence, particularly among the young. Furthermore, the people of the less developed country may be inclined to abandon agriculture and to move to urban slums in the hope of acquiring a job in the modern, particularly the MNC, area of the economy.

But the opportunities engendered by the MNC go disproportionately to the elites rather than to the masses of the less developed countries. A considerable body of research has shown that, indeed, MNC investment has retarded rather than promoted economic development in less developed countries (Chase-Dunn, 1975; Bornschier & Ballmer-Cao, 1978; Evans & Timberlake, 1980; Symanski, 1976). Furthermore, MNC investment appears to exacerbate the amount of inequality among the population of the less developed country. Unemployment actually grows, bureaucracies become inflated in response to political pressure, and a large number of poorly paid people come to be employed in service jobs for the elite (Bornschier, Chase-Dunn, & Rubinson, 1978; Evans & Timberlake, 1980).

Where the North-South approach is most useful is where the operations of MNCs appear to be benefitting consumers or owners in developed countries, but exploiting workers in less developed countries. Also, cases where importing and using inappropriate technology causes hardship or perhaps disaster, as in the case of Union Carbide in Bhopal, can be analyzed within this framework. Finally, issues revolving around the marketing of inappropriate goods like Nestle's infant formula fit into this perspective.

The Rise and Fall of Nations Approach

Another macroeconomic perspective postulates that nations undergo a cyclical pattern of economic, social, and moral development and deterioration. We tend to associate this approach with Spengler (1926-28), but a long-standing theoretical tradition elaborates on this theme (Ibn Khaldun, 1958/1377; Sorokin, 1937-1941; Schumpeter, 1942). Using this perspective is appropriate where long-term benefits are thought to flow away from developed nations, and to less developed nations, as a result of their being linked together through international trade as well as political struggle. Although in today's world the usual form through which a transfer of wealth would occur would be the MNC, the basic reason postulated for the rise and fall of nations has more to do with the cultural, social, and moral attributes of the population, particularly the population of the developed nation, and especially the leadership class of the developed nation. Over time, this group is thought to tend to grow lazy, decadent, and obsessed with consumption. But the people in less wealthy nations are thought to be more oriented toward work and saving, more oriented toward the future, more inclined to sacrifice personal advantage for communal benefit, and more morally righteous. These cultural factors, together with the fact that the developed nation has a high cost of maintaining military strength adequate to be dominant, ensure that a cycle will occur and today's rich nations will become progressively more impoverished over time.

This type of grand theory is not much in vogue these days. Empirical tests are difficult, and the moral judgments implied are troubling to the thoughtful ethicist. Yet one has a sense that in certain circles, particularly with skilled and unskilled labor in developed countries, these ideas merit attention. Representatives of MNCs maintain that jobs established in other countries do not necessarily detract from the number of jobs available for workers in the United States or other developed nations (Kendall, 1973). Nevertheless, potent pressure for limiting the activities of MNCs is being exerted by organized labor in the developed nations (Phillips, 1984). Other issues where this approach provides a useful framework for analysis include questions relating to the capacity of MNCs to undermine fiscal and monetary policies of their home governments, trade deficit questions, the potential of MNCs to subvert the national interest in sensitive defense, communications, transportation, and energy policies, and the future consequences of technology transfer from developed countries to less developed countries

(Martin and Paul, 1979). In other words, wherever developed nations are thought to be experiencing harm from the activities of MNCs, and less developed nations are thought to be benefitting, the rise and fall of nations approach can be a useful analytical framework.

The Limits to Growth Approach

One final possibility remains concerning the impact of the MNCs on developed and less developed countries, and this approach involves the harm-harm combination. The effect of MNCs may be seen as negative for both types of nations. This suggestion has come forth from a number of sources, the most frequently cited being the Club of Rome which generated the elaborate computer simulation known as "The Limits of Growth" model (Meadows, et al., 1972).

The international team which included a heavy representation from the Massachusetts Institute of Technology used large scale computer modelling to generate alternative projections for world population growth, economic development, resource availability and cost, and the generation of environmental pollution as the industrialization process continues. Using various combinations of calculations and estimations, their outcomes all resulted in crises scenarios for the entire world, but with different projected times forecast for economic, social, and environmental disaster. Our purpose here is not to discuss the computational accuracy of this simulation, but rather to propose this model as a useful tool for understanding cases where MNCs appear to be benefitting no society in the long run. For example, cases involving the squandering of nonrenewable resources would fit into this category.

A related perspective which has passed into the popular consciousness via the phrase, "Small is beautiful," is the set of ideas contained in the book of that name by the British economist E.F. Schumacher (1973). A fundamental insight of his was to point out that the long-range consequences of dependence on a capital-intensive technology of the type promoted by MNCs. While this focus is on the social, cultural, moral and economic displacement caused by MNCs in less developed countries, we need not limit his observations to these nations exclusively. Indeed, since the oil crisis of the 1970's, developed nations such as the United States and Japan have become acutely aware of the possibility of system deterioration if natural resources are used unwisely.

Conclusion

Macroeconomic theory can provide a framework for the analysis of ethical issues involving MNCs. More particularly, these four macroeconomic perspectives on the functioning of MNCs in developed and less developed nations provide a set of frames into which ethical issues can be placed. The use of one or more of these perspectives should be determined by the harm or benefit being observed or assumed or attributed to the MNC in a given case. We can summarize these four perspectives with a model of theoretical traditions into which new issues and cases concerning MNCs can be placed. Thus, each new topic ceases to become a unique event and instead can be understood as a part of an analytical fabric. Issues of rightness and wrongness, of benefit and harm, can be analyzed in a comparative way using this model. Linkages can be seen, generalizations formulated, and the sense of theoretical wholeness more nearly achieved.

As the basis for our model we have taken four sets of macroeconomic theory, identifying assumptions of benefit and harm contained in each theoretical set. We have distinguished beneficial and harmful effects as to whether they are seen as flowing mainly to developed or to less developed nations. We achieved that classic tool of model-builders, the four-celled box. Then we showed how particular ethical issues involving MNCs can be understood in terms of their categorization within this model.

We present this model with the expectation that the use of this approach will serve to facilitate rational analysis of ethical issues involving MNCs in both developed and less developed nations. Once the usefulness of macroeconomic theory has been accepted, emerging ethical issues can be examined analytically using this scheme. The identification of a harm or a benefit will logically need examination and empirical evidence. What from the perspective of a developed nation may seem to be a benefit to a less developed country may be vigorously rejected by some of those in the less developed country. The ideological assumptions of a person doing ethical analysis can be identified and critically examined. As we contemplate the increasing influence of scientific analysis and technical planning, each of these four macroeconomic theories can provide a useful basis for the question of if and how the ethical dimension is to be included in the decision-making process of MNCs (Habermas, 1972). The presentation of these four macro-economic theories is especially useful because there is a tendency for many MNC managers to assume the legitimacy of economic development theory, an assumption not necessarily shared by government officials and private citizens of many host countries in which

MNCs are located (Bremer, 1978).

These macroeconomic perspectives can be useful when considering ethical issues involving MNCs. Identifying basic harms and benefits which are seen to flow from MNCs in developed and less developed countries enables one to conceptualize the type of issue under consideration in comparison to similar and dissimilar problems. Cases in which both developed and less developed countries are thought to be benefitting from MNC activities are amenable to analysis using the economic development approach. Cases where MNCs are thought to be doing harm to less developed nations, but benefitting developed nations, can be understood best with the North-South approach. Cases where developed nations are thought to be harmed by MNCs, but where less developed nations are thought to be the long-term beneficiaries of MNCs, can be analyzed with the rise and fall of nations approach. And finally, those issues which involve harm being done to both developed and less developed nations by MNCs can be understood in the context of the limits to growth approach. By the use of this categorization, specific cases cease to be disparate, isolated, unique topics. Both managerial and philosophical discussions can be logically grounded in these theoretical frameworks. This systematization enables us to make intelligent generalizations from old cases and to make a logical integration of new cases. In this way the development of a theoretical tradition can be furthered, a systematic body of knowledge can be created, and guidelines for ethical judgments may be developed.

Less Developed
Counties

		Positive Effects (Benefits)	Negative Effects (Harms)
Developed Countries	Positive Effects (Benefits)	Economic Development Approach	North-South Approach
	Negative Effects (Harms)	Rise and Fall of Nations Approach	Limits to Growth Approach

Figure 1. Model of Theoretical Approaches to Cases Involving MNCs and Their Positive and Negative Effects on Less Developed and Developed Countries.

REFERENCES

Bell, D., Cultural Contradictions of Capitalism. New York: Basic Books, 1976.

Bellah, R.N., Madsen, R., Sullivan, W.M., Swindler, A., and Tipton, S.M., Habits of the Heart: Individualism and Commitment in American Life. Berkeley: University of California, 1985.

Bornshier, V., & Ballmer-Cao, T., Multinational Corporations in the World Economy and National Development: An Empirical Study of Income Per Capita Growth from 1960-1975. Zurich: Sociological Institute of the University of Zurich, 1978.

Bornschier, V., and Chase-Dunn, C., and Robinson, R., "Crossnational Evidence of the Effects of Foreign Investment and Aid on Economic Growth and Inequality: A Survey of Findings and Reanalysis." American Journal of Socialogy, 1978, 84, 651-683.

Bremer, O.A., "Ethical Decisions in Capitalist Structures." The Forum, Association for Social Economics Journal, 1978, 34-55.

Chase-Dunn, C., "The Effects of International Economic Dependence on Development and Inequality. A Crossnational Study." American Sociological Review, 1975, 40, 720-738.

Chirot, D., Social Change in the Twentieth Century. New York: Harcourt Brace Jovanovich, 1977.

Evans, P.B & Timberlake, M., "Dependence, Inequality, and the Growth of the Tentiary: A Comparative Analysis of Less Developed Countries." American Sociological Review, 1980, 45, 531-552.

Habermas J., Wissenschaft und Technologie als Ideologie (Science and Technology as Ideology). Frankfort: Suhrkamp, 1972.

Khaldun, I., The Mugaddima: An Introduction to History Vol.1-3. Translated by Fraz Rosenthal. Princeton, NJ: Princeton University Press, 1958.

Kendall, D.M., "The Need for Multinationls." Columbia Journal of World Business, 1973, 8, 103-106.

Lasch, C., *The Culture of Narcissism*. New York: Norton, 1978.

MacIntyre, Alasdair, C., *After Virtue: A Study in Moral Theory*. Notre Dame, Indiana: Notre Dame Press, 1984.

Martin, W.C. and Paul, K.H., Social Control and the Multinational Corporation: Some Contemporary Concerns. In Raj P. Mohan (Ed.), *Management and Complex Organizations in Comparative Perspective*. Westport, CT: Greenwood Press, 1979, 223-247.

Meadows, D.H., Meadows, D.L., Rander, J., and Behrens, W.W., *The Limits to Growth*. New York: The New American Library, 1972.

Nozick, R., *Anarchy, State, and Utopia*. New York: Basic Books, 1974.

Paul, K., and Barbato, R., "The Multinational Corporation in the Less Developed Country: The Economic Development Model Versus the North-South Model." *Academy of Management Review*, 1985, 10, 8-14.

Phillips, K.P., *Staying on Top: The Business Case for a National Industrial Policy*. New York: Random House, 1984.

Pinto, A. and Knakel, J., "The Centre-Periphery System 20 Years Later." *Social and Economic Studies*, 1973, 22, 34-89.

Rawls, J., *A Theory of Justice*. Cambridge, MA: Harvard, 1971.

Rostow, W.W., *The Stages of Economic Growth*. Cambridge, England: Cambridge University Press, 1960.

Schumacher, E.F., *Small is Beautiful*. New York: Harper & Row, 1973.

Schumpeter, J.A., *Capitalism, Socialism, and Democracy*. New York: Harper, 1942.

Sorokin, P.A., *Social and Cultural Dynamics*, Vol. 1-4, New York: American Book Company, 1937-1941.

Spengler, O., *The Decline of the West*, Vol. 1-2, Translated by C.F. Atkinson. New York: Knopf, 1926-1928.

Symanski, A., "Dependence, Exploitation and Development." Journal of Military and Political Sociology, 1976, 4, 53-65.

Tocqueville, Alexis de, Democracy in America. Edited by J.P. Mayer and Max Lerner. New York: Harper & Row, 1966, (Originally published 1835-1840).

Todaro, M.A., "A Model of Labor Migration and Urban Development in Less Developed Countries." American Economic Review, 1969, 59, 138-148.

Wallerstein, I., The Modern World System. Orlando, FL: Academic Press, 1974.

William, R., Individual and Group Values. Annals of the American Academy of Political and Social Science. 1967, 20-37.

CHAPTER TWO

INTERNATIONAL ACCORDS AS TOOLS FOR PROBLEM SOLVING

RAYMOND VERNON
Clarence Dillon Professor of International Affairs Emeritus
Harvard University
Cambridge, Massachusetts

DUANE WINDSOR
Associate Professor of Administrative Science and
Assistant Dean
The Jesse Jones Graduate School of Administration
Rice University
Houston, Texas

HANS J. SPILLER
Director
Berlin Economic Development Corporation
Boston, Massachusetts

ETHICS AND THE MULTINATIONAL ENTERPRISE

Raymond Vernon

The Multinational Enterprise's Special Character

I have sometimes wondered why any discussion of multinational enterprise so readily evokes a discussion of ethics. A little reflection suggests some possible clues.

Multinational enterprises tend to be very large. They are characteristically found in industries in which high barriers exist to the entry of newcomers. Those barriers sometimes exist because very large plants are required for the particular product line, or because considerable technical and managerial skills are needed to enter the industry, or because a strong trade name is required for the successful marketing of the industry's product. where barriers of this sort exist, society cannot always rely upon competition to hold the economic power of the enterprise in check.

The history of world industry is rich with cases in which large enterprises have exercised their power in ways that seemed hurtful to others. For example, the history of chemicals, metals, and oil contain numerous examples in which a few large firms dominating the market have extracted a heavy rent from consumers. There have been cases, too, in which the power of the multinational enterprise has been manifested by its decisions to open or close plants, with powerful effects upon the communities in which such enterprises have operated. Still other cases, the most recent being that of Bhopal, have involved the pollution of the environment or the manufacture of harmful products. Finally, these enterprises have sometimes used their power in the political arena, helping to elect candidates, shape legislation, and influence the outcome of the regulatory process.

Yet, this litany of the exercise of power still does not quite explain why the multinational enterprise should so frequently figure as the centerpiece in discussions of ethics. The capacity to exact a monopoly rent, to pollute the environment, to plunge a city into depression, or to influence political processes is not confined to multinational enterprises. Large national enterprises also possess such powers. The history of British Steel, Petroleos Mexicanos, Electricite de France, Montedison, and dozens of other large national entities provide ample illustrations of the exercise of power in all of the dimensions that have so far been mentioned.

The fact that large corporations possess so much power creates some support for the view that they ought to take on special obligations as well. One could argue, for example, that such enterprises ought to be required to make elaborate disclosure of their corporate affairs, that they ought to provide plenty of warning regarding decisions to open and close their plants, and that they ought to be restrained by one means or another in the full exercise of any monopolistic market power they might possess. But these are requirements that might be relevant for all large enterprises, whether or not they are multinational.

Does it make any sense, then, to think of the multinational enterprise as generating some special set of ethical considerations? The answer is a qualified "yes." Multinational enterprises are usually distinguishable from national enterprises in two respects: First, some of their properties are located in foreign countries and, because they have the capacity for establishing production facilities in more than one country, they are presumed to be able to shift their production more readily from one country to the next. Secondly, because the international transactions between affiliates of a multinational network are transactions internal to the enterprise, the terms of those transfers are presumed to be much more under the control of the multinational enterprise than would be the case for national firms.

To be sure, even in these special dimensions, the multinational enterprise is not altogether unique. National industries will expand or contract according to their ability to compete in international markets, and the expansion or contraction will have effects similar to those created by a multinational enterprise that shifts the location of its production. Moreover, importers and exporters in any country may juggle the prices they report for the goods or services that they are moving across the national border. Nevertheless, the multinational enterprise will still be singled out for special attention because it characteristically combines three distinctive characteristics in a single firm: high visibility, large size, and identifiable foreignness. These characteristics in combination make the multinational enterprise inescapably a target for careful scrutiny.

Inescapable Vulnerability

Anyone who has followed carefully the experiences of multinational enterprises in their interactions with governments is tempted to draw the following general conclusion: Almost irrespective of the policies that they pursue, multinational enterprises will not escape being singled out for special criticism, especially in the foreign countries in which their subsidiaries are located.

The evidence in support of that generalization is compelling.

Consider the wage policies of multinational enterprises. Such enterprises have been criticized for paying wages that are too high, but they have also been criticized for paying wages that are too low. When multinational enterprises pay low wages, of course, they are seen as exploiting labor in the national economy, taking advantage of an overly abundant labor supply. In countries in which their wage patterns appear high, they are typically charged with attracting the best of the indigenous work force away from their domestic competitors in the national economy.

Multinational enterprises have been accused of raising too much of their capital in the foreign countries in which they operate, but they have also been accused of bringing in too much capital from abroad. When accused of using too much foreign capital, the complaint has been that the use of such capital has represented an unfair competitive advantage to the multinational enterprise. And when accused of using too much domestic capital, the complaint has been that such capital has been diverted away from domestic enterprises.

At times, the technology employed by the multinational enterprise has been at the heart of the complaint. Sometimes the complaint has been that the multinational enterprise has brought in technology inappropriate for a country and has not tried to adapt that technology to the special factor-cost conditions and demand conditions of the foreign country. But at other times, the complaint has been that the multinational enterprise has withheld the most advanced technology available to the enterprise, preferring instead to bring in processes or products of an earlier vintage that it had decided would be more approriate.

There have been times when the complaint has centered on the enterprise's policies in the recruitment of skilled labor. When enterprises have recruited skilled workers from the national work force, the complaint has been that such workers have been diverted from national enterprise, but when the multinational enterprise has sought to bring in skilled workers from abroad, the complaint has been that the enterprise was thereby denying the local work force an opportunity to fill the most attractive jobs.

Occassionally the complaint has centered on the participation of the multinational enterprise in national affairs. In some cases, the complaint has been that the enterprise, even though created as a national under national law, has remained aloof from involvement in the national life of the foreign country in which it operated. But, in other cases, the complaint has been that it was engaged in the political process in ways that were inappropriate for a foreigner.

The inference to be drawn from these examples is not that the complaints are unfair or irrational. Much more plausible is the assumption that some pervasive, deep-seated problems have troubled leaders in the countries in which multinational enterprises have operated and that the various particularized complaints have simply been surrogates for some deep-seated uneasiness that has been more difficult to articulate.

The Underlying Problem

The uneasiness, I believe, stems from the fact that national leaders in the countries in which multinational enterprises operate are fearful that such enterprises will escape the control mechanisms that the leaders have devised, and they are fearful that the enterprises will introduce elements into the national economy that will weaken the control of those national leaders. In order to appreciate the nature of that concern, it helps to distinguish between two kinds of external influences. One set of such influences originates with foreign governments who make demands on the multinational network that reverberate through the network into other countries. Another set of such influences is generated by the multinational enterprise itself, pursuing a global strategy that may be threatening to the objectives of some governments. Let me illustrate some of the issues that fall under each of these headings.

Governments are constantly seeking to promote policies through the medium of the multinational enterprise that could have adverse repercussions upon other governments. When, for example, a government demands of a multinational enterprise that the subsidiary located in its jurisdiction should export more and import less, the response of the multinational enterprise to that command characteristically is to require its affiliates in other countries to export less and import more. Accordingly, when Mexico commands the Dow Chemical Company to expand the exports of its Mexican subsidiary, the effects are likely to be felt in Sao Paulo, Brazil, or Seoul, Korea.

Governments use the sprawling networks of the multinational

enterprises to project their influence and support their goals in other ways as well. France and Japan, for instance, have encouraged the multinational enterprises based in their respective countries to develop raw materials abroad, primarily as a means of guaranteeing supplies for the home market in time of shortage. The United States government has used the foreign subsidiaries of United States based multinational enterprises to deny technology to communist countries, to promote United States antitrust objectives, to increase the security of bank deposits in the United States, to end apartheid in South Africa, and for various other purposes.

In some cases, the governments that have been affected by the outreach of other governments through the multinational enterprise network have chosen to ignore the foreign intrusion. The United States government, for instance, has for the most part disregarded the fact that other governments may have adversely affected the United States economy by commanding the foreign subsidiaries of United States based firms to export more or import less. By contrast, the efforts of the United States government to influence the behavior of such foreign subsidiaries in fields such as security, export controls, and antitrust have drawn bitter protests from governments in the countries in which those subsidiaries were located.

I suggested earlier that the influence that multinational enterprises exert on national economies through their existing networks sometimes is the result of initiatives taken by the multinational enterprise itself rather than by governments. The decision to shift a line of production from country A to country B would be decision of that sort, as would the various efforts of multinational enterprises to hold down their tax bills by arranging for their profits to arise in a low tax jurisdiction rather than a high one.

Whenever the actions of a multinational network can have consequences that reverberate across international borders, the multinational enterprise faces a profound problem: Is the enterprise to be responsive to the needs of country A, or to the desires of country B?

The problem of deciding whose desires ought to prevail is exacerbated by the fact that any given government commonly is promoting a number of different objectives with regard to the multinational enterprise, objectives that need not be altogether consistent. The existence of such a multiplicity of objectives is hardly surprising. Ministers of finance worry about exports and taxes; ministers of labor worry about empolyment; and ministers of foreign affairs worry about international relations.

And coordination among the ministries as a rule is less than perfect.

The problem of dealing with multiple objectives in a host country is graphically illustrated by the Bhopal case in India. One of the most powerful and enduring objectives of the Indian government has been to maintain its national autonomy and to control all enterprises that operate in its territory, even when relying upon those enterprises to provide foreign capital or technology needed for the country's development. Accordingly, the Indian government has consistently demanded of multinational enterprises that they provide the desired technology and capital with the smallest possible degree of control over the Indian subsidiaries of the enterprises. To the extent possible, plant designs have been drawn up by Indian architects and engineers, machinery and supplies have been obtained from Indian sources, and supervision and training have been the responsibility of Indian nationals. Once the subsidiary is in operation, the multinational enterprise is expected to conduct its supervisory responsibilities discreetly and with restraint, in the hope that Indians would as a result acquire technological and managerial capabilities more rapidly. At the same time, the Indian government has another objective -- one that is endemic to all governments. This is the desire to place the maximum responsibility for error on the foreigner rather than on the Indian government itself.

Obviously, these various objectives will sometimes work at cross-purposes. That possibility is greatly heightened by the fact that as the multinational enterprise gives up some of its control over a foreign subsidiary, local employees who are nationals in the country of the subsidiary are likely to acquire a certain amount of autonomy. The local managers may exercise that autonomy, however, in ways that have no relationship to the goals of their own government. For instance, as the parent relinquishes control over such problems as plant safety and environmental pollution, it does not follow that local managers will automatically step in to perform at the level desired by their government. In such settings, the ethical issue becomes extraordinarily complex. Where does the responsibility for ethical behavior reside, and how is it to be pursued? While it is too early to be sure if this kind of problem played a role in the Bhopal case, my present hunch is that it will eventually be seen to contribute substantially to the explanation of that disastrous episode.

Closely related to the kind of difficulties represented by Bhopal is another phenomenon that grossly complicates the issue of ethical behavior. Even with the best of intentions, governments are bound to have short memories; it is not surprising, therefore, to find them espousing mutually inconsistent principles at different points in time. Moreover, every country has a well-developed capability for finding the principle that happens to coincide with its interests, even when that principle is inconsistent with its position in other cases. In their policies toward multinational enterprises, governments have been known to move from one principle to another, according as their interests have changed.

Illustrations of this tendency of governments are provided by the history of the Calvo doctrine in Latin America. The doctrine, which takes its name from an Argentine prime minister of the nineteenth century, was intended to address a very real problem, namely, the conflicts that arise by reason of the dual character of any foreign-owned subsidiary -- that fact that it is both the property of a foreigner and the creation of the laws of the state in which it is doing business. According to the Calvo doctrine, such subsidiaries are normally viewed as enjoying the rights, privileges, and duties of nationals; if, however, such a subsidiary appeals to a foreign power for support, it loses all such rights. Having enunciated a doctrine that seems a reasonable way of cutting the Gordian knot, however, Latin American governments have frequently espoused other principles that are flatly at variance with the Calvo doctrine. Latin American governments have commonly imposed special requirements on these foreign-owned enterprises in disregard of the ordinary rights of nationals. And, in the many cases in which such governments see some advantage in reaching beyond the subsidiary to the foreign parent -- in "piercing the corporate veil" -- they have not hesitated to address their demands directly to the parent. The United States government has been equally inconsistent in its espousal of principles. It has demanded national treatment for the foreign subsidiaries of United States-based companies, while at the same time reserving the right to command those subsidiaries or support those subsidiaries as if they were under United States jurisdiction.

If the principles of governments are so eclectic and so ephemeral, one is hard put to know what principles multinational enterprises ought to pursue in determining their ethical responsibilities. Because the goals of governments are multiple at any moment, and variable over time, the problems of multinational enterprises in taking national goals into account are especially acute.

Consider, for instance, the enterprise that regards it as unethical to export products from the United States that the

United States government has determined to be dangerous, or to erect factories or build automobiles that do not conform to United States anti-pollution requirements. One might suppose that such decisions would be greeted with applause by countries that had failed to develop such restraints on their own initiative. But experience suggests that the actions of other countries in response to such an initiative would be far more equivocal. Some might take satisfaction from the decision of the multinational enterprise, but experience suggests that the reactions of most countries would be acutely ambivalent. The fact that United States standards had been used to determine what products might be available and what processes might be used would be seen in most countries as an impairement of the country's autonomy and a reflection on its ability to govern itself.

My assumption so far has been that the objectives of governments ought to have some influence in defining ethical behavior for the multinational enterprises. But how much influence? Was Ford Motor Company behaving ethically when it permitted its British subsidiary to build tanks for Britain during World War I, at a time when the United States was still a neutral? Was it ethical when it permitted its German subsidiary to produce tanks for Hitler in World War II? The contemporary case of multinational enterprises in South Africa also raises even more acutely the question whether and to what extent government policies ought to figure in determining what is ethical for multinational enterprises. If the views of the government of South Africa must be disregarded in defining such conduct, as surely they must, whose views should be taken into account, especially when men of good will are in deep disagreement? In the South African case, for instance, how is a multinational enterprise to choose between the views of Alan Paton and those of Bishop Tutu?

Groping for Guidelines

Philosophers and other scholars have given so much profound thought to the issue of ethics that those of us who devote most of our time to other subjects must approach ethical issues with diffidence and humility. I suppose it is safe for me to observe, nonetheless, that ethical behavior commonly entails avoiding the use of power that might be hurtful to others. If that observation is valid, then it is clear why the issue of ethics is commonly raised with respect to the multinational enterprise. Because such enterprises typically exercise considerable market power, they generate ethical issues with relative frequency.

The distinctive aspect of those issues is that they usually involve the interests of more than one country. Accordingly, the multinational enterprise cannot solve its problems simply by taking national objectives fully into account. Nor does it require much argument to dispose of the possibility that the multinational enterprise would satisfy its ethical requirements by disregarding national objectives and thinking only of the well-being of mankind at large. In refusing to serve any national interest, the multinational enterprise runs the risk of serving no interst at all other than its own.

Accordingly, as large powerful corporations wrestle with the problem of ethical behavior, I find it hard to define some special subset of ethical problems that stem out of their multinational structure. Problems there are, to be sure, but they appear to me problems that arise mainly out of conflicting and inconsistent national values, with no easy means for calibrating those values in terms of their ethical superiority. If two countries are in disagreement over whether competition is to be encouraged of suppressed, or whether the Soviet Union is to be denied technology, or whether automobiles should be equipped with anti-pollution equipment, I do not see this as a conflict in whose resolution ethical considerations can play much of a part.

Much more than the clarification of ethical behavior, therefore, is the need for some agreed set of rules that would mediate national clashes and would formulate the obligations that multinational enterprises should assume to the world economy at large. I have already mentioned a few areas in which such agreements are badly needed, including restrictive business practices, bank security, corporate financial disclosure, and trade in dangerous products. But I do not see these problems as susceptible of solution when defined as ethical issues. Indeed, as I grope for ethical questions that might be addressed uniquely to multinational enterprises, only one such question readily occurs to me: is it ethical for such enterprises to resist the formulation of international agreements when they are designed to create workable arrangements among governments to deal with conflicts in national values and objectives?

DEFINING THE ETHICAL OBLIGATIONS OF THE MULTINATIONAL ENTERPRISE

Duane Windsor

The evolving method for defining the ethical obligations of multinational enterprises is the adoption of both corporate and international codes of conduct. In the case of United States firms, use of corporate codes was greatly accelerated by the 1977 Foreign Corrupt Practices Act. The United Nations has adopted a Code of Conduct for Transnational Corporations, while the International Chamber of Commerce has formulated Rules of Conduct to Combat Extortion and Bribery. Such codes reveal that the basic problem lies not in ethical diagnosis of "right" and "wrong" (even without a general moral theory, we can usually establish some reasonable sense of right and wrong), but in the subsequent stage of moral prescription (how to "right" that which is judged to be "wrong"). It is here that most corporate and international codes sail into shoal waters.

There are three basic considerations which hamper the formulation and enforcement of effective corporate and international codes of conduct. First, we do not in fact possess a general moral theory by which firms can readily make ethical judgements independently of legal stipulations. Rather, corporate and international codes represent more a working out at a first level of the appropriate set of moral issues at stake in transnational business activities. Business entities are simply not good conflict-resolution or tradeoff devices: on the contrary, they operate by authority or consensus within legally enforceable constraints; face potential conflicts among several decision dimensions (economic performance, legal compliance, social responsibility, and moral conduct); and owe obligations to various internal and external constituencies.

Second, this problem is complicated by the operating environment of multinational corporations (MNCs). These firms face different circumstances, moral standards, and legal stipulations in home and host countries which require intimate working knowledge of country conditions not fully captured in codes of conduct. The ethical issues for trade within the Organization for Economic Cooperation and Development (OECD), between OECD and less developed countries (LDCs), and East-West business relations are often quite different in character.

Third, even legal sipulations, where definable and enforceable in principle, may be vitiated by lack of effective sovereignty over a business entity. We face different situations for domestic, multinational, and global firms. Fully domestic firms are the most easily controlled. Home country standards are fully determinative for these firms. MNCs owe primary legal and moral allegiance to a particular home coutry; moral obligation may depend on home-host country relations. The term "multinational" is misleading because firms doing transnational business are typically chartered, headquartered, managed, and owned in one home country. Union Carbide is a United States company, and the Indian government will be suing the parent company in the United States rather than its Indian affiliate. International guidance must be shaped within the context of defining MNC obligations to host countries. "Global" corporations are ethically and legally "footloose" by comparison.[1] A home country barely exists, host countries will find it difficult to regulate such firms, and formal multilateral agreements will have to replace international guidance. Such corporations would literally have no home base (other than a regulatory haven) or primary national allegiance for effective regulation.

This paper proposes a theory for: (1) understanding the ethical dilemmas of the multinational enterprise; and (2) providing a foundation for defining its ethical obligations. The ethical dilemmas are rooted in conflicts over values, beliefs, and interests exacerbated by differences in culture, political processes, and levels of economic development. As a result, the ethical obligations are strongly affected by variability in legal concepts which can only partially be offset by international and corporate codes of conduct -- the evolving methods for addressing definition of ethical duties. Rather than relieving MNCs from deciding ethical questions, the situation places a greater moral burden on transnational firms, while domestic activities in a developed country like the United States are probably more effectively regulated by law.

Problem of a General Moral Theory

At a previous meeting of this Conference in 1983, I presented a paper arguing two major points.[2] First, the fundamental problem confronting both the theory and practice of business ethics is the potential conflict among four principal dimensions of enterprise decision making: economic performance, legal compliance, social responsibility, and moral conduct. Moral choices with which business ethics is concerned arise from conflict or disagreement about values, beliefs, interests, and so on and focus on how to properly resolve such conflict through some method such as litigation, mutual consent, persuasion, or formal ethical analysis. Second, enterprises are most reliably guided socially to desired moral conduct through evolution of the legal system which can explicitly define restraints and penalties. The basic social function of law is, however rough and ready, to resolve conflicts over properties, rights, obligations, and values. I do not mean at all to relieve any enterprise or employee (any more than the rest of us in our daily lives) from their ethical duties -- which clearly exist. A delivery truck cannot simply run over a child or his pet and then speed away because it has a schedule to meet, even though the law makes mandatory the obligation to the child and more discretionary that to the pet. The problem is rather that the ethical duties of a business do not entirely admit of easy definition; life is a rough and tumble proposition of unhappy tradeoffs. (Suppose the incident involving a pet concerns an ambulance racing a heart attack victim to the hospital.) The present paper builds on these two points in order to tackle the ethical issues presented by transnational business operations.

By economic performance I mean profitability interpreted, not as maximization of owners' equity, but rather (and more properly) as a crude measure of relative efficiency of social resource allocation under conditions of consumer sovereignty exercised through reasonably competitive markets. Firms serve society in part through serving their customers. Owners come last after customers and employees and risk their capital in competitive opportunities.[3] Legal compliance connotes the moral obligation to obey the properly stipulated laws of the land, including public regulation of markets to ensure competitiveness, safety, non-pollution, equal opportunity, and so on. Monopoly power and anti-competitive moves have long been viewed as reductions in social welfare. Social responsibility implies the obligation or duty to look beyond profit and even compliance to a concern with the long-term viability and quality of society as a whole.[4] By moral conduct, I mean the various ethical obligations (some stated at law, others more vaguely defined) to honor contracts, treat employees fairly, trade value for value to customers, provide safe products, and so on. It must be remembered that business has some responsibility -- to society as well as to its employees and shareholders (ownership is more broadly diffused for public companies) -- to be profitable, as an index of economic performance. Failed enterprises contribute little or nothing to anyone. Nevertheless, profitability is not necessarily the overriding dimension.

The inherent difficulty in business ethics is rather that enterprises have a variety of different and potentially conflicting obligations to several constituencies: consumers, employees, shareholders, the public. The corporate governance process is not well suited to determining tradeoffs among its several constituencies or the four dimensions of decision making. Legislatures and courts can debate principles through adversarial methods; firms cannot function as debating societies. Business decisions are determined by authority or consensus. It is therefore difficult conceptually and practically for the enterprise to develop appropriate ethical standards internally. This difficulty clearly does not relieve any person or organization from ethical duties, but there is no point in pretending that moral obligation is always clearly defined and therefore readily determines action. Consider the following live domestic controversies: should there be capital punishment for heinous crimes; can abortion be legitimate? Our society is unable to resolve these issues precisely because strong disagreement is involved. Each side of the debate has at least an understandable viewpoint. The business enterprise is simply not a particularly good conflict-resolution system.

I argued in my earlier paper that external standards evolved at law are more readily useable (although certainly imperfect at best). The legal system is itself, of course, only a very rough and ready approach; but it is oriented toward conflict resolution. Corporations can readily adopt lip-service codes of conduct: "we will obey the laws, treat customers and employees fairly, etc." But the law provides the possibility of penalties and restraints translatable to the bottom-line. For the multinational enterprise, the conflicts, constituencies, and legal system are multiplied by transnational activity.

The Operating Environment of the MNC

For our purposes, we can define international trade relations affecting MNCs as illustrated in Figure 1. The debate over MNCs concerns essentially firms headquartered in the industrialized OECD countries. MNC ethical issues are at least partly shaped by the axis (North-South, East-West) and particular quadrant involved in decision making. The ethical debate over MNCs is in practice focused on trade relations between quadrants 1 (OECD) and 2 (LDCs), with certain narrower issues such as technology transfer and Cold War conflict affecting Western trade relations with the Societ bloc. The Western debate over MNCs hardly extends to Soviet relations with Eastern Europe or the Third World. MNC ethical issues thus fall concretely into three dimensions noted by number in Figure 1: (#1) among the industrialized democratic countries (OECD), which share reasonably comparable economies, moral and cultural standards, and politico-legal systems (within quadrant 1); (#2) between what Heath calls the industrialized economies of the "North" (OECD in quadrant 1) and the developing "South" (LDCs of the Third World), whose trade relations are dominated by essentially economic considerations as illustrated by OPEC; and (#3) between what Heath calls the industrialized policies of the "West" (OECD) and those of the "East" (the Soviet bloc organized economically as Comecon), whose trade relations are dominated by essentially political conflict.

Figure 1. Structure of MNC Trading Relationships

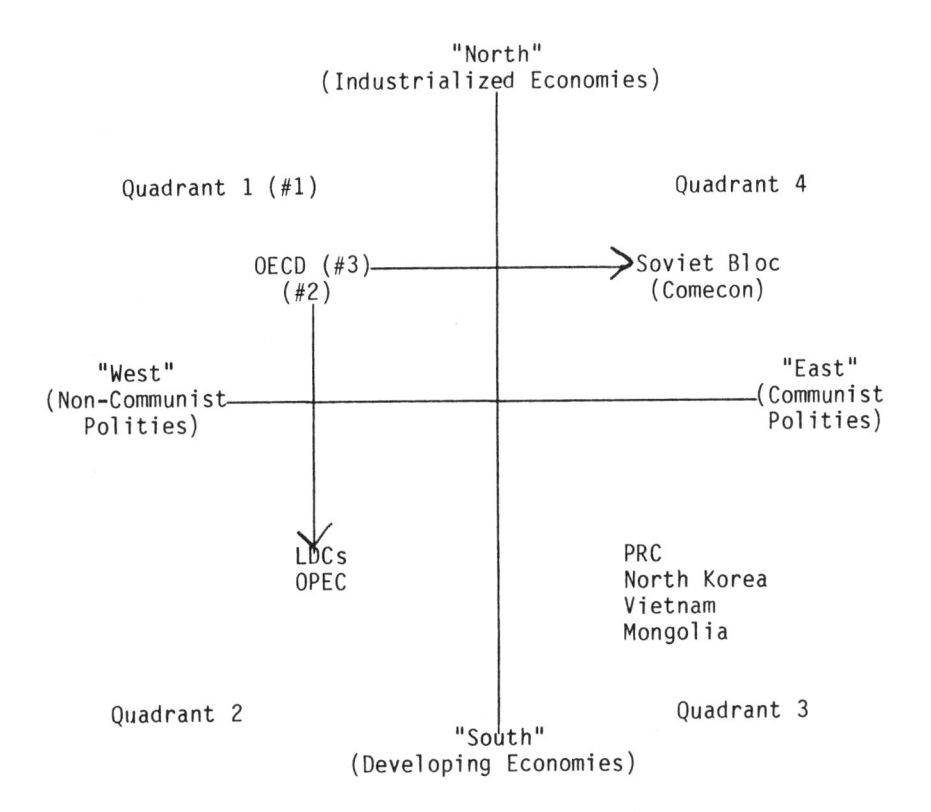

```
                        "North"
                (Industrialized Economies)

    Quadrant 1 (#1)         |         Quadrant 4
                            |
            OECD (#3)───────┼────────▶ Soviet Bloc
              (#2)          |           (Comecon)
                            |
  "West"                    |                    "East"
(Non-Communist──────────────┼──────────────────(Communist
  Polities)                 |                    Polities)
                            |
                            ▼
                          LDCs          PRC
                          OPEC          North Korea
                                        Vietnam
                                        Mongolia

    Quadrant 2              |          Quadrant 3
                         "South"
                (Developing Economies)
```

Source: Adapted from Edward Heath, "East-West and North-South Relations," 1984 David R. Calhoun, Jr. Memorial Lecture (St. Louis, Mo.: Washington University, Center for the Study of American Business).

The range of ethical issues invovled in MNC operations can best be indicated by a few examples drawn from the three basic types of problems delineated above. There are problems even within the OECD countries despite a comparable level of economic development and largely democratic politics. A classic illustration concerns Italian tax administration. In Italy, tax payments are quite literally negotiated; standard operating procedure for business is therefore to maintain two sets of books, so as deliberately to misstate taxable income, not for tax evasion as such, but rather as a basis for bargaining. Tax officials understand this game and proceed accordingly. An American bank newly established in Italy ignored, on moral grounds, advice by its local Italian attorneys to file a falsified return; the bank was eventually compelled to practice tax negotiation "Italian style" by the resulting tax bill which was declared "Italian style" despite its good-faith representations.[5]

Dresser Industries has found itself embroiled in two controversies concerning trade with the USSR. There was an unsuccessful effort to withhold a license sought by Dresser for export of deep-well rock bit technology.[6] On another occassion, Dresser received conflicting orders from the United States (to stop) and French (to proceed) governments in connection with construction of the Soviet natural-gas pipeline to Western Europe.[7]

In 1974, Nestle was accused by a British journalist of killing Third World babies through sale of infant formula that allegedly could not be properly used in LDCs. A boycott of all Nestle products in the United States was organized by an "Infant Formula Coalition Action" (1976-1984). In May of 1981, by a vote of 118 to 1 (the United States alone dissenting), the United Nations General Assembly adopted a WHO and UNICEF formulated International Code of Marketing Breast Milk Substitutes.

On December 3, 1984, an accidental leakage of methyl isocyanate gas killed some 2,500 and injured nearly 200,000 Indians at Bhopal. There is some indication that no laws of the state of Madhya Pradesh were violated,[8] indicating laxer standards for safety than in the United States where Union Carbide is headquartered. On the other hand, it has been alleged that the former managing director of Union Carbide India, Ltd., advised "only token storage" of the chemical at Bhopal in small individual containers for both "economic and safety considerations."[9] Union Carbide built large bulk storage tanks as at its West Virginia facility. Imposing stricter United States safety standards overseas would not have obviated this apparent error; storage tanks are used in the United States. The EPA authorized Union Carbide to resume production of methyl isocyanate in West Virginia.[10]

We are used to thinking of United States companies causing problems overseas in LDCs as the dominant example of the MNC issue. But the reality is more complicated because of the increased competition among European, Japanese, and even Third

World firms (Brazil is a major arms exporter and OPEC prices affect LDCs as well as the OECD). A good example is that of "all-terrain vehicles" (ATVs), as recently featured on a "20/20" television news story. ATVs are three-wheeled motor vehicles intended for both industrial and recreational use on non-road terrains. They are manufactured for sale in the United State by Japanese companies: Honda, Suzuki, Yamaha, Kawasaki. Increasing evidence alleges that ATVs are inherently unstable and therefore dangerous; but consumer demand is very strong. The United States Consumer Product Safety Commission is considering how to regulate the ATVs and their use. The manufacturers respond that injuries and deaths are associated with improper use and failure to wear appropriate protective gear. The equipment is specifically intended for off-road use. Does the solution lie in banning, restriction to adults, redesign, safety equipment, or instruction in proper use?

Analyzing Ethical Issues

Where home country and host country moral standards, legal concepts, or interests conflict (as is likely to be the case in practice), a variety of international arrangements might be tried for resolution. The Sullivan Principles require United States firms operating in South Africa to remove race designation signs, support the right of blacks to union representation, and review job descriptions. A determination that interaction with South Africa may help erode apartheid (the only proper reason for operating there), does not relieve the moral obligation to oppose apartheid. Bilateral and multilateral arrangements may afford scope for negotiation over proper standards of conduct and MNC obligations. International codes include the Sullivan Principles (South Africa), the United Nations Code of Conduct for Transnational Corporations, the United Nations International Standards of Accounting and Reporting, the WHO Code of Pharmaceuticals and Tobacco, the International Chamber of Commerce Rules of Conduct to Combat Extortion and Bribery, and the WHO-UNICEF International Code of Marketing Breast Milk Substitutes.[11]

Because of the diversity of home and host economies, our model of the typical MNC's operating environment must be extended in detail to "country analysis,"[12] by which I mean an intimate knowledge of the particular home or host country as illustrated in the Italian tax example cited above. The critical factors can be generally defined as local moral standards, level of economic development (including the capacity to absorb modern technology, products, and procedures), and critical social features (such as racism, corruption, instability, or dictatorship).

Local moral standards in both home and host countries are a compound of the formal legal framework, mores, and folkways. The legal system in all countries involves an evolutionary process as it encounters new problems. OECD countries have well established legal procedures for tackling conflicts; LDCs are not necessarily positioned (administratively or legally) to handle modern technologies and products, as revealed in the Bhopal, India chemical disaster. It is not clear that the Indian legal system can respond to this incident locally; suit is likely to be litigated against the Union Carbide parent company in the United States.

Folkways are traditional, widely practiced patterns of behavior which thus acquire informal or tacit social approval. Commercial and political graft is endemic in Mexico and other countries, for example. Mores are more formally articulated, prescriptive standards of conduct; they are usually stated as corporate codes of conduct. Folkways and mores may well diverge in a society, organization, or social groups. In this sense, commercial bribery and price collusion are folkways; corporate or international codes of conduct are mores (which may be embedded in the formal legal framework).

The principal moral issue for businesses in South Africa is apartheid. Is the best course of action for OECD countries modification by embargo or through interaction? It will be seen that the solution is not wholly ethical in character, but depends partly on an assessment of the strategy question just posed. If an embargo worsens apartheid, the advocates of this strategy have assumed an unanticipated moral burden; an empirical judgement is required. The nature of moral choice is that it is quite often uncomfortably difficult. The 1977 Foreign Corrupt Practices Act forbids bribery overseas by United States firms and imposes accounting responsibilities for detection of improper payments. But the statute explicitly permits "facilitating payments," because low-level corruption is endemic in LDCs and semi-officially condoned. American firms reported evidence as well of "extortion" overseas rather than "bribery".[13] Government contracts and prevailing laws regulating business activity are often the products of dictatorships. Much of Africa, the Middle East, and Latin America is dominated by military regimes which obtain large amounts of military supplies. Even reasonably democratic regimes may suffer from chronic instability and civil violence, as well as corruption. Difficult practical choices are posed for MNCs operating from home countries with relatively well defined legal, political, ethical, and business standards not applicable elsewhere.

Environmental analysis for home and host countries and formulation of international codes are reasonably empirical exercises in character. But to weigh particular decisions, we need something approaching a general moral theory which shows us (and MNCs) how to define ethical obligations as a basis for corporate and international codes of conduct. We do not have such a general theory at present.[14] I suggest the reason lies in the diversity of conflicting views. Consider the question of homicide within a given legal system. Killing is regarded as legally acceptable in cases of self-defense, criminal execution, or "just" wars fought for morally acceptable goals (such as bringing down fascism in World War II); even culpable homicide is divisible into murder, voluntary manslaughter, and involuntary manslaughter depending on the specific motives and circumstances involved. There is disagreement over the issues of capital punishment, abortion, and euthanasia. No general moral theory tells us how to resolve these debates, not even the Biblical commandment not to kill. The legal and moral system evolve by conflict.

It would be easy to caricature MNCs as caring for nothing but profits or driven by competitive pressures to provide mere lip service to other considerations. There is, of course, a very strong element of truth to this characterization. The Pinto decision, the Kepone story, the Dalkon shield, and other incidents are ample testimony of mistakes within the United States made by purely domestic firms. We have antitrust, securities, and pure food and drug legislation for a sound reason. But there is another side of the coin, illustrated in Johnson & Johnson's handling of the Tylenol problem. It is no more possible for firms than it is for people and governments to anticipate everything. They may naively misunderstand the impact of modern products and technologies in unfamiliar settings, and they vary in moral caliber.

Ethical analysis is complicated by the white heat level of political controversy over MNCs. While criticism of many incidents is of course justified, there is a deeper strain of emotionalism which clouds the debate. The problem ignored is that of differentiating intentions (or motives) from consequences. Business is driven by the profit motive, but consquences may be accidental or unexpected. Nestle's marketing of infant formula in Third World countries turned out to have substantial but probably unanticipated side effects. If anything, it can be argued that a (not the) motive behind such marketing was the assumption that child care would obviously be enhanced by modern products. Nestle was wrong, and insufficient consideration was given to the severe limitations on customer use. There are no doubt firms which find South Africa attractive because of lower labor costs and government control of unions. Nevertheless, the larger issue turns on whether embargo or interaction is the sounder strategy by which OECD countries can erode the aparteid system. Economic embargos have shown only limited effectiveness in past usage. What OECD needs is a concerted program for influencing South Africa; the problem is how to concert mutual action in a given direction. And countries are divided in their views, values, and interests, so that the United States is the only country both to enforce a foreign corrupt practices act and to vote against the infant formula code. The OECD countries are hard pressed to agree on a concerted policy for control of technology transfer to the USSR.

The lack of a general moral theory and the existence of significant political controversy over MNC obligations should not be regarded with despair. As argued at the beginning of this paper, the fundamental problem confronting business ethics is precisely the conflict over economic performance, legal compliance, social responsibility, and moral conduct. Firms should work for society through individual incentives; firms should strive for profitability, but not at the expense of other decision-making dimensions. The difficulty lies in determining the proper tradeoffs in each circumstance. At least in substantial part, existing international codes are the result of political controversies (particularly concerning North-South relations) rather than the application of a general moral theory.

Moral choice begins in disagreement. It is only by judging particular decisions and circumstances that we can develop a feel for how to proceed more generally. There are certainly three concrete steps for beginning to address the ethical dilemmas confronted by MNCs. First, corporations should develop internal codes of conduct covering both domestic and foreign activities. Given the lack of a general moral theory, such codes will necessarily be incomplete. Nevertheless, firms should grapple with the issues involved. How else can they realistically begin to develop a feel for the problems and controversies increasingly encountered in business? Second, internationally accepted codes of conduct should be articulated wherever feasible as guidelines to MNCs and national legal frameworks. All organizations are reactive in character, but United Nations and OECD working groups to tackle MNC problems are fully appropriate. Finally, OECD countries need to take the lead in reviewing their laws affecting MNC activities. The 1977 Foreign Corrupt Practices Act is an example not followed by the rest of the OECD. Footloose global enterprises will complicate this process, because multilateral agreements will need to be generated on top of international codes of conduct.

I do not believe that the fundamental problem lies in ethical analysis as such. The lack of a general moral theory is not an absolute barrier to reasonably proper diagnosis. I have no difficulty determining that South Africa is a police state, a dictatorship dominated by a white minority, or that apartheid is a corrupt system. I believe the weight of evidence indicated that Nestle made technical errors in marketing milk substitute, as did Union Carbide in storing large quantities of a dangerous chemical in Bhopal (apparently contrary to advice from its Indian subsidiary). Diagnosis can be reasonably successful; most of us believe in a common hierarchy of moral values that does not endorse profitability as more important than other competing values. The fundamental problem lies in proper prescription. What is the correct strategy for tackling apartheid: embargo or interaction? Do LDCs need to run greater risks for economic development? The Bhopal plant was engaged in manufacture of needed pesticides. Should Union Carbides be crippled financially by forced settlements to the victims of the disaster? Liability depends on whether the circumstances, errors of judgement, or negligence are at fault. The heat of political controversy tends to obscure the problem of prescription.

Foreign Corrupt Practices Act

The Foreign Corrupt Practices Act (FCPA), enacted in December 1977 largely but not exclusively as a series of amendments to the 1934 Securities Exchange Act (1934 Act), was adopted for the purpose of "prohibiting bribery of foreign government officials by United States companies." The statute was legislated in the wake of 1976 admissions to the SEC by more than 400 American corporations subject to the 1933 and 1934 securities acts, including 117 of the Fortune 500, that they or their foreign agents or affiliates had made illegal or questionable payments overseas exceeding a total of $300 million.

Many United States firms adopted internal codes of conduct following these revelations. The FCPA forbids direct or indirect (through intermediaries) bribery of foreign officials, political parties, party officials, or candidates for political office by all United States firms. The statute marked a major step forward in extraterritorializing American law; it was also a significant move by the United States towards unilateral definition of a code of business ethics (mores in my conceptual framework) in the international marketplace. Folkways approve commerical and political corruption in many countries, and that corruption is as much (perhaps more) extortion as bribery. Facilitating or "grease" payments are exempted for practical reasons of expediting commerce. To the same goal of prohibiting bribery, the FCPA imposes stringent requirements for internal-accounting controls on securities issuers and reporting companies subject to the 1934 Act. These requirements make such firms responsible for detecting violations of both the antibribery and accounting provisions by foreign agents and affiliates. The United States has acted alone in this prohibition mandated by the Foreign Corrupt Practice Act. President Carter subsequently instructed the Justice Department to establish a preclearance procedure for payments on which firms would like a judgement in advance.

Since enactment, the FCPA has been the subject of substantial criticism arguing that: (1) both the antibribery and accounting provisions are ambiguous, due particularly to the absence of explicit scienter and materiality standards; (2) dual enforcement by the SEC and Justice Department has been unpredictable; (3) the internal-accounting control requirements are excessively costly, especially for small exporters and domestic firms not involved in international operations; (4) the statute involves some uncertain degree of responsibility of foreign agents and affiliates through extraterritorial application; and (5) as a result of these other factors United States firms have suffered in international markets where foreign competitors are unfettered by any similar restrictions.[15] These critics conclude that the FCPA needs clarification of ambiguities in the antibribery and accounting provisions, simplification of enforcement, the addition of explicit compliance guidelines, and the creation of a multinational framework for solving the problem of foreign corrupt practices.

Facilitating or grease payments overseas results from three factors: (1) bureaucratic red tape which can be short-circuited by "gifts;" (2) prevailing low wages which result in gifts being regarded as "tips" for services performed; and (3) shortages of equipment and permits which are allocated in line with extra payments.[16] Under such conditions, it is difficult to distinguish a tip for ministerial service from outright bribery or extortion. Saudi Arabia and Kuwait require by law the use of local agents for all transactions by foreign companies. It has been suggested that most foreign political payments above low-level grease of this sort were in fact the result of extortion or solicited bribery. Some companies, like Lockheed, argued that payments were necessary for effective overseas competition. Generally this view has not been accepted, although the evidence is doubtful in either direction. The real problem -- the one identified as such by the SEC -- was not the payment per se, but the fact that the corporations which claimed that such payments were a practical necessity of doing business overseas (but did not go to the United States government for counsel) concealed those payments fraudulently.

At the root of the controversy over questionable payments overseas is the question of whether such payments are realistically necessary for the conduct of international business by American companies in a highly competitive global marketplace. It is perfectly clear that we can and should completely ban corrupt payments of any sort at home (for obvious reasons) as do virtually all countries. The problem is whether this moral standard can, or should, be imposed abroad with criminal enforcement by the United States. That problem decomposes into three related issues. First, what is the distinction, accepted in the FCPA, between bribery (or extortion) and facilitating payments (what should be our "mores")? Second, do foreign governments tacitly tolerate, or even encourage, extortion and bribery regardless of what their laws state formally (what are the host country "folkways")? Third, do foreign competitors engage in such practices with the tacit consent of their own governments, and thus operate overseas without the handicaps imposed on American companies by the FCPA? There is a legal difference, incorporated into the FCPA, between a bribe and a gift. Facilitating payments and middlemen ("agents") are a widespread phenomenon overseas, espeically in Asia, Latin America, and the Middle East.[17] An international framework is ultimately necessary but has not been forthcoming. No other country has adopted any such statute.

Summary and Conclusions

The reader should not assume that this paper is rooted in ethical relativism. It is perfectly clear that South Africa is a police state and apartheid is morally unacceptable; firms such as Nestle and Union Carbide made serious errors of judgement; and the Foreign Corrupt Practices Act tackled a rising tide of extortion and bribery in transnational business. But the political controversies over such issues have misdirected attention from prescription to diagnosis; the former is more difficult than the latter because tradeoffs are involved. In practice, MNCs cannot judge these tradeoffs (as in the cases of Nestle and Union Carbide) without more explicit external guidance on "right" and "wrong." External definition is especially difficult for MNCs because of international disagreements over principles and interests. Domestic firms have a difficult enough time trying to decide proper actions (as illustrated in the Ford Pinto case); MNCs have an even less well-defined legal framework and are more dependent on ethical judgements for which a general moral theory does not exist. The course of action dictated by these circumstances is to encourage corporate and international codes of conduct. As the Bhopal and FCPA examples show, home country legal standards are not necessarily a reliable guide to overseas conduct.

Notes

1. It has been argued that MNCs are now beginning to evolve into such truly global firms. Theodore Levitt, "The Globalization of Markets," Harvard Business School, vol. 61 (May-June 1983), pp. 92-102.

2. George Greanias and Duane Windsor, "Corporate Governance: The Legal Framework for Institutionalizing Ethical Responsibility," in W. M. Hoffman et al. (eds.), Corporate Governance and Institutionalizing Ethics: Proceedings of the Fifth National Conference on Business Ethics (Lexington, MA: Lexington Books, 1985), pp. 95-106.

3. See "Lincoln Electric Co.," Harvard Business School, Case No. 9-376-028.

4. See Richard T. Pascale and Anthony G. Athos, The Art of Japanese Management: Applications for American Executives (New York: Warner Books, 1981), ch. 2, "The Matsushita Example," pp. 37-86.

5. Arthur Kelly, "Italian Bank Mores," in Tom Donaldson (ed.), Case Studies in Business Ethics (Englewood Cliffs, NJ: Prentice-Hall, 1984); cited in Donaldson, "Multinational Decision Making: Reconciling International Norms," draft paper (Loyola University of Chicago).

6. Dresser Industries, Inc.," in S. P. Sethi (ed.), Up Against the Corporate Wall (Englewood Cliffs, NJ: Prentice-Hall, 1982 [4th ed.]), pp. 3-28.

7. "The Soviet Gas Pipeline," Harvard Business School, Case No. 9-384-007 (1984).

8. Houston Chronicle (February 18, 1985), quoting a spokesman for the state government.

9. Wall Street Journal (February 4, 1985).

10. Wall Street Journal (April, 17, 1985).

11. This list is taken from Donaldson, "Multinational Decision Making."

12. See Bruce R. Scott, et. al., "Country Analysis," in *Case Studies in Political Economy: Japan 1854-1977* (Cambridge, MA: Harvard Business School, 1980), pp. 7-17.

13. See George Greanias and Duane Windsor, *The Foreign Corrupt Practices Act: Anatomy of a Statute* (Lexington, MA: Lexington Books, 1982).

14. See Donaldson, "Multinational Decision Making."

15. U.S. Department of Labor, Office of Foreign Economic Research, *Report of the President on U.S. Competitiveness Together with the Study on U.S. Competitiveness* (Washington, D.C.: 1980).

16. James R. Basche, Jr., *Unusual Foreign Payments: A Survey of the Policies and Practices of U.S. Companies* (New York: The Conference Board, 1976), Report No. 682.

17. Ronald Wraith and Edgar Simkins, *Corruption in Developing Countries* (New York: W. W. Norton, 1964).

MULTINATIONAL CORPORATIONS: ETHICS OR SELF-INTEREST?

Hans J. Spiller

I come not from a Third World country but from a highly industrialized country which is host to a great number of multinational corporations. IBM, GM, Ford, UTC, and many other companies can be found in Germany. But when asked about any ethical dilemmas resulting specifically from the activities of these corporations, I have to declare that there are none. That does not mean that all such enterprises are so good and so decent that they are not causing any problems. Germany does have problems, but not specifically because of multinational or United States corporations.

Now why would that be? Maybe it is because United States companies started to invest in Germany years ago. In fact, they started to invest after the First World War, and many of the companies which are in Germany today (such as IBM and Gillette) have been around for more than 50 or 60 years.

The second reason might be that many of the American companies did not invest in Germany by buying a piece of land and building a factory, or buying land and raising bananas. In most instances, they bought a German company and turned it into an American company. For instance, GM bought Opel, IBM bought Hollerith, UTC bought Otis, and Otis bought Flohr. So, in the end, many of the large companies were basically German companies and, for the most part, they still are.

Another reason might be that multinational corporations are not among the largest companies in Germany. The largest companies in Germany are German companies. We have Volkswagen and Siemens and AEG and others. We have Gloeckner and Thyssen and Krupp and Flick, all brand names; all German names. In that sense, the multinational corporations are playing second fiddle. I do not mean that large companies do not pose problems, but I would say that in Germany the problems are not coming from the multinational companies; they are coming from large companies per se.

When I hear some of the very sympathetic remarks concerning large companies, I tend to be a little bit skeptical. I have a different theory or feeling or experience. I think the Christian Ethic, about which we could speak for hours, is not what we talk about when we talk about the behavior of large companies. It is my belief that companies follow rules. If there are no rules, then companies will behave differently than if rules are present. If companies have the power to change rules, they will change the rules to their benefit. In Germany, we have rather strict rules for everything. We are raised to follow these rules and to obey the law, so for any good company in Germany there is no other choice: it also has to follow the rules and the law. Therefore, it is my contention that corporations do not act "ethically." They simply obey laws. If there are no rules, then companies will primarily do what benefits them.

I will give you some examples. In Germany, there was much use of a herbicide called DDT. After years of testing that proved how deadly the chemical was, the government finally decided it must be abolished. So now it is against the law to use or sell DDT in Germany. The same companies that supplied DDT in Germany follow the rules and do not sell it anymore in Germany; otherwise, they would end up somewhere where they do not want to be. However, they did not stop producing DDT and selling to other countries. Now, in the Christian sense of ethical behavior, if I find out that what I am doing is wrong and I decide that I should stop doing it, I would not look at where I am doing it, I would just stop doing it altogether.

There is another German product called Xylamon which is used to preserve wood. It had been used for many years when it was found that there is a great danger involved in using it: it causes cancer. They outlawed Xylamon in Germany, but the same companies still sell Xylamon in other places.

I will give another example. In the United States you have very tough environmental controls regarding cars. Every car has a catalytic converter. Every car has reinforced bumpers and doors in order to protect the driver and the other persons riding in the car. In Germany, we do not have any of that. If you had followed a little bit of the debate over such issues in Germany, you would know that for two years there has been a large discussion going on as to whether we should or should not have any of those things. If yes, when and why and how much would it cost? Big German car manufacturing companies are fighting this law because they are afraid they might lose business or competitive edge or whatever.

The same companies (which are very successful in this country), the Mercedes and the BMWs and the Volkswagens, send cars to America with perfectly designed catalytic converters, very nicely reinforced doors, and very strong bumpers. Looking at the statistics, you will note that the ratio of death and injured per million kilometers or miles driven is much lower in the United States than in Europe and Germany. Therefore, chances are that these bumpers and reinforced doors help. You will also note that the air pollution in big cities in Germany is much worse than in the United States, so chances are that the catalytic converter plays a major health and environmental role. Would it not be ethical to produce <u>only</u> these kinds of cars not only for the United States where you cannot sell a car without a catalytic converter, but also for Germany where it is not mandatory?

There are other little examples to prove my point that companies are doing what is in their best interest and, if it is in their best interest to be ethical, then they will do it -- little examples which do not mean much but which just show this attitude. You know that German companies are used to a very good and successful way of dealing with employees and unions based on the principle of codetermination which is specified by law. Looking at the frequency of strikes and looking at the days lost because of strikes, I can state very honestly that it is a very good principle, and it works very nicely.

Now I deal with a lot of German companies because I am a businessman. When I talk to German companies who have had success with the codetermination principle and with cooperating with unions and who want to come to the United States to build a subsidiary, the first question they will ask me is if they can find a location where there are no unions. Would not one expect those companies to continue with the just and ethical principle of close cooperation between management and owners on one side and workers and unions on the other?

Not to be biased, my last example regards American companies. We who represent the Berlin Economic Development Corporation deal with American companies who come to Europe from the United States where the environmental laws regarding emissions, waste water, and solid waste are pretty stiff. When we talk to these companies about environmental laws, which might be more or less the same as they are in the United States, the same American companies will ask if there is not some place where they could go without having to follow these laws or if there would be a way of finding a personalized solution for this environmental question. So again, they would like to avoid such regulations in spite of the fact that it is well known that the environment is suffering.

I am not saying that any country or any multinational company is worse than any other. You have your E.F. Huttons and Banks of Boston, we have our Flicks and our wine scandals, so I do not think we have to talk about that. But what we might have to talk about is the ethical conscience. Is that developing for the better? Everyone says it is, but I do not believe that it is because I think a company, much like any human being, behaves differently if they see that they cannot go on doing what they are doing. They will react to certain pressures, either peer-group pressure or outside pressure. My theory is that with the information age we are in, with telecommunications expanding and improving all the time, there is little place to hide. Everything you do is apt to be known someday somewhere by somebody; so maybe it is better not to do it, not because you are a believer, but just because you do not want to be caught. I think this may be the reason why the behavior of companies is changing -- not because companies are becoming more ethical.

When I was preparing this, I was looking at the material pertaining to the topics covered by this collection of essays. There were ethical questions regarding everything: shareholders' rights, workers' rights, energy, bribes, subsidies, etc. Now maybe I did not find it, but I did not read anything about the question: Is it ethical to produce whatever the market wants or should there be some kind of limit? Is it ethical to produce agent orange? Is it ethical to produce valium? Valium is a drug produced by a Swiss company, and everyone knows people become addicted to this kind of drug. Is it ethical to produce all kinds of detergents which do nothing but wash dirty linen and, at the same time, are dangerous to plant life and to the water supply?

In light of my point of view, the main question resulting from such a consideration has to do with whether it is ethical to produce weapons. I very pointedly ask this question because I am in a very good position to ask it. I represent Berlin, and Berlin is the only state in this world where it is against the law to produce anything for the military. When Berlin was divided between the four major powers, and you know that Berlin is still under the Four Power Agreement, it was part of the convention that Berlin should be allowed to survive economically, but it should not supply weapons or any components for weapons. So, in Berlin, it is against the law to produce weapons, and you end up in prison for life if you do so.

This is why I am in a very good position to raise this point and also to say that it is not only good for the conscience, but also good for business. Right now Berlin, which is a large city with a GNP of about half that of Austria and twice that of the Republic of Ireland, is doing very nicely not producing weapons. Our productivity and investment per capita is higher than that of the Federal Republic. Our unemployment figure is shrinking faster than that of the Federal Republic. Berlin is the only city that started growing again after a certain period where it was very difficult. I am not saying that you stop manufacturing weapons, and you start growing economically. What I am saying is that this might be one of the problems that should be discussed because it is a major ethical question. In fact, I end with this question and my good conscience because maybe Berlin is the only ethical city in this world after all. Can you imagine?

CHAPTER THREE

CORPORATE MODELS FOR ETHICAL DECISION MAKING

JOE E. CHENOWETH
Executive Vice President - International
Honeywell, Inc.
Minneapolis, Minnesota

ROBERT GUNTS
Vice President
International Division
Whirlpool Corporation
Benton Harbor, Michigan

E.F. ANDREWS
Vice President (Retired)
Materials and Services
Allegheny International
Pittsburgh, Pennsylvania

ROBERT McCLEMENTS, JR.
Chief Executive Officer
Sun Company, Inc.
Radnor, Pennsylvania

ETCYL H. BLAIR
Vice President and Director of Health
and Environmental Science
Dow Chemical U.S.A.
Midland, Michigan

ETHICS AT HONEYWELL:
WRESTLING WITH THE HORNS OF DILEMMA

Joe E. Chenoweth

The subject of business ethics is one of great importance to us at Honeywell, and I welcome the chance to share some of the ways ethical issues affect our decision-making process.

Recently, we conducted a survey of our employees and customers to better understand how our company is perceived. Overall, we learned that we have a good reputation for providing reliable products and dependable service and support. In addition, the survey showed that Honeywell is considered a high-integrity company. To quote a respondent, "Honeywell is a good company to do business with. They don't pull any funny stuff." This response was especially gratifying since we feel that a high level of integrity is crucial to the success of our business.

Honeywell, as a $6 billion-a-year international company, has more than 94,000 employees in 42 different countries. We have been in operation for 100 years and have come to see two levels of behavior operating in the business community: behavior as defined by the laws throughout the world and behavior as defined by the values of a corporation's culture.

Everyone here is aware of the law because we all spend an enormous amount of time keeping up with the regulations it brings. Nevertheless, the law does go a long way toward regulating behavior. If a company obeys the law, it is legally trustworthy; if it breaks the law, it is punished.

Ethical problems arise when the law isn't as clear as it might be. There are often gaps, popularly called loopholes, through which people and organizations can slip. Snaking through loopholes, however, is no way to run a business. Just try to develop honesty and loyalty in your workers when legal corner-cutting is encouraged, or even tolerated. How can you earn the trust of your customers when cheating, even legal cheating, is promoted? It is impossible.

That is why the corporate ethic is so important. It fills the gaps in the law left open to interpretation. It transcends the letter and intent of the law to a more complete understanding of how we should act. Most important, it creates a solid ethical base from which to do business.

Our corporate ethic, embodied in the Honeywell Principles, is designed to exceed the requirements of the law. Because our company is so large and its operations relatively decentralized, we cannot efficiently check the legality of every decision. Our employees need to make business decisions quickly and naturally, without a team of lawyers scrutinizing every decision or government regulations dictating solutions to problems.

Because our corporate ethic anticipates many significant decision-making issues such as integrity, customer relations, employee satisfaction, and quality, to name only a few, we can minimize crisis decision making, which keeps us out of the legal department and the CEO's office. Moreover, the operations of the company run more smoothly because our employees understand what is valued most in the organization. Our people make better decisions more naturally and have confidence that top management will support those decisions.

Any company that presses the letter of the law to find the loopholes should remember that it takes years of hard work to build a good business reputation and only one false move to destroy it. Obviously, from time to time there will be employees who violate the company's ethical standards, but this shouldn't result from a failure to articulate the company's policies and standards. Strong ethical practices require a strong corporate framework. The company must communicate its standards openly and vigorously.

As I mentioned before, we place at the center of our corporate culture the Honeywell Principles. The Principles express our commitment to profits, integrity, customers, people, quality, decision making, and citizenship. They were distilled from 26 operating and employee-relations guidelines, involving input from top Honeywell executives, general managers from around the world, and all levels of employee representatives, including labor unions and directors of human resources.

The Honeywell Principles put into writing our ideal, our aspirations, what we want to be as a company. But there is a catch, a dilemma of sorts. By the very act of defining the ideal, we admit, by virtue of being human, our inadequacy. We do not make the right decisions every time, and it would be self-righteous to claim otherwise. But we sure try to put our best judgment behind what is right. Said another way, the Honeywell Principles are used, not so much to avoid mistakes, but to help us achieve our goals.

Let me give you an example. Our commitment to profits, the first principle, reflects our need to prosper and grow. A business is, first and foremost, an economic endeavor, and profits are a measure of its success. That is why Honeywell is committed to achieving profits that equal or exceed those of other leading international companies.

But we can not expect long-term profitability if we are not equally committed to our other principles, namely, promoting individual development and accomplishment in our employees, working together with our customers, ensuring the quality of our products and services, and encouraging well-managed innovation and risk-taking. These other principles work together with the first to contribute to our overall prosperity and growth. Again, ethics at Honeywell does not so much prohibit behavior; it promotes the values that help us achieve our goals.

No talk on ethics would be complete without a quote from a famous philosopher. This one is from one of our truly great contemporary thinkers, Woody Allen. "The future holds great opportunity. It also holds pitfalls. The trick is to avoid the pitfalls, seize the opportunity, and get back home by six o'clock."

Woody's quote describes business life. We are all trying to avoid the pitfalls and seize the opportunity. Even more so, the quote acknowledges that dilemmas and conflict can be expected at every turn. Let us take another look at profits, for example. Of course profits are crucial to a company's success, but doesn't business also have a responsiblity to the society in which it operates?

Since the equal employment opportunity push of the mid-1960s, business has been expected to play a larger role in the improvement of society. Today, ethical consideration relating to neighbors, cities, and even nations are a part of many companies' decisions.

But what happens if a company lays off a thousand workers in the same year it donates a half-million dollars to local food shelves? Couldn't that money have been used to save jobs? Then again, maybe there is no conflict if the money was donated for the right reason, namely, to help the poor, rather than to improve the company image.

It is easy to see how sharp the horns can get. Here is another example. Last September, in anticipation of President Reagan's sanctions against South Africa, a company in South Africa suggested that we place in escrow some designs for our industrial-control technology. Under the plan, the designs could be released when United States sanctions were initiated, thereby enabling the South African company to build the equipment we could no longer sell.

This plan brought several of the Honeywell Principles into conflict. First, we are committed to finding answers to our customer's problems, but we are also committed to integrity and good citizenship in host countries. The plan, although legal, would have compromised one principle to serve another.

As it turned out, we declined to go ahead with the plan because we felt it would not serve the long-term interests of our customers or employees in South Africa and would undermine several of our programs there. Honeywell, one of the original signatories of the Sullivan Principles, is working to achieve a racially balanced workforce that reflects the demographics of the country overall. In fact, we have just received the top rating given by the Sullivan organization in this regard. We are investing a half-million dollars over the next four years in education, training, and community development programs to prepare blacks in South Africa for management and technical positions. We feel this initiative responds to the needs of our employees there, as well as to the concerns that our shareholders have expressed.

I have tried to show that Honeywell, like many of the other companies represented here, has ethical policies and standards that help guide decision making. But having policies and making them work are two separate matters. The values of a company become part of the culture only after hard work and aggressive support. First, as I've already discussed, the corporate ethic must be written out and openly and vigorously communicated to everyone in the organization. There is no substitute for putting the standards in print; it reinforces their legitimacy. Interview the senior management, review their recommendations with general managers and employee representatives, and come to a consensus about what the company stands for. Then put the results in writing and get the word out.

Statements of ethics do not guarantee ethical behavior, however; they merely inform. If executives do not demonstrate the company's values in every decision they make, the values become meaningless. An executive who cuts a corner to secure a contract sends a resounding message throughout the organization: "In this shop, profits come before principles." If this message is reaffirmed over time, dishonesty becomes the norm.

But what about employees throughout the organization? How can they be encouraged to make ethics a part of their decision making? First, read the culture. Find out what behavior is being rewarded. Is advancement in the organization linked strictly to performance, regardless of the methods used? Is the bottom line discussed daily, whereas ethics is reserved for the quarterly pep talk? Are ethical issues overlooked when the pressures to meet plan are strongest?

If a company's ethical principles are to become more than a few lofty statements, they must be rewarded equally along with efficiency, innovation, and profitability. Without this firm commitment to supporting and promoting ethical practices, I believe the long-term result is that, and Woody Allen would agree with me, nobody gets back home before six o'clock.

ETHICS AS A WAY OF LIFE

Robert Gunts

I have been asked to address a point of ethics from a somewhat unique point of view: What are the ethical considerations of a company that is looking to grow internationally? One of Whirlpool Corporation's most important business goals today is to become a larger, stronger international company with more sales and profits coming from foreign markets. So addressing this question is very timely for our company as well.

While we are not a big player in the <u>international</u> arena, we are one of the larger <u>American</u> companies with the resources to become a factor world-wide. We are a 75-year old, $3 billion company that is a leading manufacturers of major home appliances for the United States market.

Internationally, to round out the Whirlpool picture, we export brand products to independently-owned distributors in 39 countries and to United States military exchanges around the world. We license foreign manufacturers and own a substantial equity interest in three Brazilian companies which produce components and finished appliances for the Brazilian as well as export markets.

As further evidence of our new international thrust, last year we created the Whirlpool Trading Company of which I am President. International growth is essential if we are to meet our very ambitious corporate objectives. The United States appliance market, as strong as it is, does not offer the potential to meet our ambitious goals. Hence our need to look internationally.

Fortunately, our products serve common global needs. Everywhere in the world, people want appliances to store and cook food, clean clothes, and clean their homes. In the industrialized countries, appliances mean more convenience, more freedom, and enhanced lifestyle. In developing nations, expanding economies and improving infrastructures are making it possible for people to purchase their first major appliances for better health, nutrition, and sanitation.

The potential for Whirlpool's growth and participation in this expanding world market is mind-boggling. China and India's combined population of nearly two billion people is almost one-half of the world's populace. Both nations are virtually untapped as markets for home appliances. We plan to share in those market opportunities.

Even though our international business has been modest compared to some other United States corporations, we are by no means neophytes to world trade or to the economic and ethical pressures American companies must face in the world economy.

Prior to my current position, I was President of Whirlpool's subsidiary Thomas International Corporation, a builder and marketer of electronic organs and musical instruments. We also had an electronic subsidiary in Italy serving the European market and trading companies in Holland and England.

Our Thomas International manufacturing and assembly plant was near Los Angeles, while two of our feeder plants were located in Mexico. Shipments of our integrated circuit boards and other component parts moved continually across Mexican border points into the United States. As such, they were subject to Mexican inspections and demands for grease money if we did not want them delayed at the border.

Long before we established our plants in Mexico, we were advised by other businesses that our shipments would likely be delayed at border points if we did not meet demands for "mordida." To us, such demands were extortion, and we would have no part of it. The demands, always veiled, never outright, normally come from lower-level border officials, many underpaid and living locally. Mexican officials at the state level were opposed to these payments and, in our meetings with them, they expressed their willingness and full cooperation to stamp out the practice. With that agreement, we established our two Mexican operations.

I wish I could say that our agreement solved the problem; but it did not. Shortly after we initiated our first shipments to Los Angeles, some Mexican border agents made it abundantly clear that payment of "mordida" was necessary to guarantee swift passage of our trucks across the border. We refused, and our trucks were moved to the sidelines for time-consuming and total, and I mean piece-by-piece, inspection. We immediately complained to higher level Mexican officials. True to their agreement, they demanded an explanation by border agents, and our shipments were processed without undue delay. I can say that we never, to my knowledge, succumbed to border extortion.

We were not alone in our effort. We worked closely with a number of other United States companies that faced similar harassment. As a group we brought pressure to bear on an intolerable situation. We could not have achieved this result without the full cooperation and aid of the Mexican government.

I'm not sure at this point if our Mexican experience is transferable elsewhere. But, unless my experience as a business executive has been totally misapplied, I believe that most business practices are fairly uniform around the world.

However, what is <u>legal</u> and what is <u>ethical</u> is <u>not</u> necessarily uniform worldwide. For example, in several countries payments of grease money to high-level military officials to sell weaponry to their governments is not <u>illegal</u>. In fact, it is a common practice. But to <u>our</u> way of thinking, it is <u>unethical</u> as well as illegal. Payoffs like these feed on themselves, and there is no end in sight once the word is out that a company will barter on its principles.

At Whirlpool, we don't place a lot of ceremony on maintaining some lofty ethical standard. It is just part of our corporate culture. We expect our managers and employees to live by those standards and to perpetuate that culture to our future managers. As a corporate citizen, we believe our charter in the community demands of us the highest ethical standards and practices. In the final analysis, ethical behavior should be an integral part of the organization, a way of life that is deeply engrained in the collective corporate body.

If we cave in to demands for payoffs, we compromise our ethical standards. We have an analogous situation at the national level. Secretary of State George Shultz has affirmed our national policy that we will not yield to international blackmail or negotiate with terrorists for American hostages still in Lebanon. To do so, he said, would send a loud message to every terrorist organization around the world that the high principles for which America stands can be manipulated like some stringed puppet by amoral international thugs.

Let me say unequivocally here: Whirlpool will forego business opportunities if it takes unethical payments to acquire new business. We make that commitment with eyes wide open, knowing full well that we will lose some business opportunities, particularly when competing against business from nations that do not subscribe to our principles.

At Whirlpool we have a basic statement of ethics which places the ultimate responsibility for ethical behavior precisely where it belongs in any organization - on the shoulders of the person in charge. That statement reads: "No employee of this company will ever be called upon to do anything in the line of duty that is morally, ethically, or legally wrong. Furthermore, if in the operation of this complex enterprise, an employee should come upon circumstances of which he or she cannot be personally proud, it should be that person's duty to bring it to the attention of top management if unable to correct the matter in any other way." That obligation applies to the chairman as well as the employee on the product line. Adherence to that basic philosophy has kept us in good stead throughout our company's history.

Back in the early 1900's, Lou Upton, co-founder of Upton Machine Company, our predecessor company, received a whopping order for 100 of his new-fangled electronic wringer-washers from a subsidiary of Commonwealth Edison in Chicago. When the washers were delivered, a cast iron gear in every single washer failed. This could have been the death knell for a company with only six employees, where neither Lou nor his brother Fred were receiving a salary and there was no cash on reserve. Rather than desert his customer, Lou and his people found a way to repair the defect and fixed all 100 units. There is another happy ending to the story: in the process, he gained an order for 100 more washers. Maintaining product quality is as much a matter of business ethics to consumers as any other issue. It is also a basic business fact that if a company offers a slip-shod product or service its longevity is in serious doubt. We at Whirlpool firmly believe in this principle. Part of our corporate mission statement reads, and I quote, "We promise to build, and sell only good quality, honest appliances designed to give you your money's worth, and we promise to stand behind them."

A question for today is: Should our ethical principles at home be transferred to the international business community? I believe the answer is "yes." I feel we can take them with us anywhere in the world. We may alter our actions or practices as local customs and law require, but we will never adopt business practices in violation of legal and moral principles.

Having said this, we are not naive. There are no safeguards that Whirlpool employees will not act foolishly or out of greed, even in spite of our corporate guidelines. If a violation occurs, the parties will be acting for themselves, not on behalf of the company demands. But we will take corrective action to remedy the matter and to protect the good name of Whirpool.

Just to let our employees know we mean buisness and that we will tolerate no breach of conduct, we employ some 15 internal auditors who, along with their other duties, have free reign to probe any aspect of our corporate life. To assure independence, the audit function reports to the chief financial officer. Our Board of Directors, of whom 10 of 13 are outsiders, also maintains an audit committee to investigate any company function.

There is another dimension to this matter of ethics not often discussed. Most laws are written to make <u>unethical</u> practices illegal. But occasionally the reverse occurs, and a law can make a normally <u>ethical</u> practice illegal. One of these United States laws is the Export Administration Act of 1979. In its present form, this law makes it extremely difficult for us to achieve our goals for international growth in the Middle East. Here is a little history.

In 1944, several Arab nations formed what is known as the Arab League. Its purpose was, and still is, essentially to identify and to boycott nations from the Arab world who also have trade relations with Israel. In the mid-50's, Whirlpool, to our utter surprise, was placed on the boycott list. It resulted from our former association with the RCA Corporation.

Back then, Whirlpool's trade name was not well-known. To increase our name recognition, we reached a very important marketing agreement with RCA to create the RCA-Whirlpool brand name. However, the two companies were independent and, as some of you may know, the agreement no longer exists. At the time our agreement was in force, RCA began a record pressing business in Israel. Soon after, it was on the Arab boycott list. Because of our marketing association with RCA, Whirlpool's name was also added. Our products are still boycotted, even if unfairly so.

Passage of the Export Administration Act was, at least in part, United States retaliation to the Arab League boycott. Because of its "eye-for-an-eye" mentality, it doesn't represent a high water mark in United States legislative history. The law places extremely controlled restrictions on how United States companies can petition the Arab Boycott League to remove their name from the list. Even minor unintentional infractions are punishable by imprisonment, fines, or both.

Whirlpool will comply with the Export Administration Act. To do so takes an army of attorneys to study and advise our top management on how to comply with 69 pages of "do's" and "don'ts" contained just in section 369 of the Act. This law makes no sense. Its moral and ethical justification is nothing more than an economic "quid pro quo" which punishes United States firms for the Arab League's actions.

Companies like Whirlpool who are not a party to the Middle East political rift are being made economic captives for something beyond their control. I remind you, this law applies <u>only</u> to United States companies on the Arab League boycott list. The company down the street from you, which is <u>not</u> on the list, is not subject to the law. This law penalizes business actions that we feel are neither unethical nor immoral. We believe that it is high time to reassess the need and legitimacy of this law.

In these pages, I have highlighted what ethics means at Whirlpool. I have touched only the tip of the iceberg. In closing, I would compress my remarks into one sentence: Ethics is nothing more than, in the words of one man, the obligations of morality. Business <u>must</u> subscribe to a high code of civil and ethical behavior. To accept less is a violation of a public trust.

ETHICS, CAPITALISM, AND MULTINATIONALS

E.F. Andrews

My topic today deals with "Ethics, Capitalism, and Multinationals." It is a big topic, one where mere mortals might fear to tread. But it is a vital subject.

On this question of ethics, George Bernard Shaw wrote a play called Major Barbara. In it, a businessman named Andrew Undershaft is concerned that his 24-year old son has not settled on a career. He asks the boy if he has any interest in literature or philosophy or business or the military or the church or the legal profession. The young man confesses he has no knowledge or interest in any of these areas. Finally, the exasperated father asks: "Well come, is there anything you know or care for?" The boy replies: "I know the difference between right and wrong." To which the father replies: "You don't say! What, no capacity for business, no knowledge of law, no sympathy with art, no pretension to philosophy. Only a simple knowledge of the secret that has puzzled all the philosophers, baffled all the lawyers, muddled all the men of business, and ruined most of the artists. The secret of right and wrong -- at 24 no less!"

I think we would all grant Shaw's general point. In complex areas, it is hard to act with complete certainty on moral questions. And yet, moral questions have to be faced. Corporate executives, like anyone else, have to look at themselves in the mirror every morning and have to live with themselves.

For example, when I first entered the purchasing profession after World War II, the receiving of gifts, gratuities, and excessive entertainment was commonplace. As the son of a country preacher, it did not take me long to see that this was a practice that was wrong. I set about immediately establishing policies prohibiting such practices in my own organization, and I joined with other purchasing organizations to help rewrite the book on purchasing ethics. Later, as President of the National Association of Purchasing Management, I brought about the first disaffiliation of two local associations because of their questionable practices.

All of this was fairly easy. It was black and white, right and wrong. We are all living under the same rules. We all came from the same general Judeo-Christian background. It was clear cut in an ethical sense. Beyond that, it was good business because the foundation of doing business lies in fair, honest, and ethical behavior.

But later, when I began working for a large multinational corporation, I started travelling internationally. I found out that not everyone in the world agreed with my version of what was right and what was wrong. These were not cheating, conniving people. In many cases, they were people who were devoted to their families, their countries, and their religious beliefs. But they just did not believe what I did. In some cases, they regarded our views as naive, even childish.

For example, in many foreign countries into which we went, we found that what in this country would be considered to be commercial bribery was considered there merely to be <u>commissions</u>. In fact, such payments were part of the system of compensation. What's more, as you know, our government even changed the Foreign Corrupt Practices Act to allow for "grease."

Doing buisiness in countries with such different heritages, different cultures, and different standards presents a real challenge to people trying to remain true to their consciences. Let me stress that it goes without saying that we do not break the law. We might disagree with the law, but if it is illegal, it is not up for debate. The law is the law.

That said, it is still true that the representative of a multinational corporation serves many masters. He must at all times try to remain true to the values and culture of his own country, but he cannot ignore the values and the cultures of the host country. Sometimes the balancing act can be extremely difficult.

My question is this: how far should we go in forcing traditional backgrounds out of the way to make room for what we believe is right? Let me give you an example.

Many years ago, before passage of the Foreign Currupt Practices Act, I was involved in a consortium to develop a nickel mine in a certain Pan American country that I will leave unnamed. We were joined by the Japanese, the Germans, and the Swiss. There was a good opportunity. The country needed the jobs as well as the income for taxes. When we got to a certain stage in those negotiations, I was advised that we would be expected to put one million dollars in the Swiss bank account for the highest government official with whom we were dealing.

I pulled out. It was not against the law here or there then. It was against my ethics, and I pulled out. Those Germans and Japanese and Swiss were livid. They had actually budgeted two million dollars and thought we had a bargain. They went ahead with the deal and developed that mine.

Six years later, during the year-long nickel strike in Canada, I was laying people off and shutting down furnaces and paying the Russians $5 a pound for nickel when it was coming out of that mine to their countries at 90 cents.

In this case, did we serve well our stockholders, our employees, our customers, and indeed, the American economy? Who was right? Who was wrong? It is all very well to pose philosophically sound answers to hypothetical questions. But it is the real-life situations that cause us trouble.

I would like to make two points: first, all too many times what passes for ethics in today's world actually turns out to be based on selective morality and expediency. Second, in concentrating on precise points of multinational morality, we tend to ignore the positive ethical consequences of capitalism itself. In today's world, capitalism is the engine of modernization and progress.

First, the matter of selective morality. A personal reminiscence will show what I mean. During the early 1960's, I represented Allegheny Ludlum, a steel company, at a hearing in Washington. The question was whether the United States should impose economic sanctions on Cuba. At the time, Cuba supplied about 50 percent of the nickel used in this country. I argued against sanctions. My point was that sanctions would drive Cuba to Moscow, that they would not bring positive political change to Cuba, that they would not be supported by anyone else in the world, and that they would hurt most our industries and employment. Sanctions would be the economic equivalent of cutting off our noses to spite our faces.

One Senator described me as a "left-wing pinko."

My question is this: if we had retained a business presence in Cuba, would Cuba have become so slavishly dependent upon Moscow? In fact, would there have been a Cuban missile crisis?

A decade after I had made my remarks on Cuba, and obviously being a glutton for punishment, I was back before the same Congressional committee. This time the issue was sanctions against Rhodesia, forbidding United States companies from buying chromium, an essential ingredient in stainless steel, from that country. The point made in Congress was that we should get our chromium from the only two other sources in the world, those notable humanitarians, the Soviet Union and South Africa.

This time, when I argued the exact same points in opposition to sanctions as I had in the case of Cuba, they did not call me a left-winger. Instead, I was called a "right-wing racist." It is like the old story about the left-wing extremist, the right-wing extremist, and the moderate. The leftist lights the fire under the pot. The rightist stirs the pot. And where is the moderate? Why, he is the one in the pot.

In my two appearances before the committee, what had changed? Not my position, which has not changed to this day. In the matter of sanctions, when we take our ball and go home, we lose every chance to influence the outcome of the game. Inevitably, our places on the field are taken by new players -- largely from the Communist bloc.

In what kind of countries should we do business? Should we do business in nations that oppress their people on the grounds of political beliefs or on the grounds of race or tribal affiliation or on the grounds of religion? We might feel more comfortable, morally speaking, if we avoided such nations. But if we did so, we would not do business many places in the world.

For example, should we do business with the Soviet Union? That nation's discrimination against Jews, against fundamentalist Christians, and against its own Muslim minorities is well documented. How much political freedom exists in the Soviet Union? How much freedom of the press? We all know the answer. And yet how is the course of peace, understanding, and our own economic progress served by turning our backs, in a business sense, on that resource-rich and strategically crucial nation?

Or take the continent of Africa. After centuries of colonial rule, Africa is struggling to find its place in the economic and political sun. Should we refrain from participating economically in countries that do not fit our standards of morality? Much is now heard on the subject of sanctions against South Africa. But why not apply sanctions against Burundi? Twelve percent of the population enslaves eighty-eight percent of the population. Up to 100,000 people are killed a year. But have you ever heard about it? And no one says not to go there. Or how about Mozambique? There have been 300,000 people there in concentration camps for ten years. They call them re-education centers. That is not what most Africans mean by <u>independence</u>. But we do not hear much about not going there.

The proponents of sanctions trace their stand to morality. But in many cases, their actions seem to have their source in political expediency and public opinion polls or in misinformed notions about countries and continents. The proponents of sanctions talk about ethics. But what they offer us are flexible, political guidelines. Selective morality is, per se, hyprocrisy and its application in an imperfect world won't stand. We really have to stop kidding ourselves about the nature of the world we live in. If our actions are political, expedient, even cynical, let's not call them moral.

Morality, for us as individuals and as businesspeople, is certainly not what makes us feel warm and cozy, no matter what the consequences. As businesspeople and as Americans, we need to ensure that our actions do not lead to one dictatorship being replaced by another. Our goal should be to encourage respect for the legitimate rights and aspirations of all people.

Two wrongs do not make a right. But selective morality does not make ethical sense. Ethical action means applying our principles in the light of the knowledge that we live in an imperfect world. I am not saying we should leave our principles at home. What I am saying is that we need to apply our principles with the recognition that Cuba is not Connecticut and Burundi is not Boston, and we need to constantly ask how, if multinationals stay away, will situations ever change? How will the economic growth and industrialization that nations need ever take place? Of course, the Marxists are not squeamish about entering an economic and political vacuum. But their presence hurts a lot more than it helps.

This brings me to my second main point: in the long run, the greatest enemy of economic and political liberty in the less-developed countries is Marxism. The greatest friend of that economic and political liberty is capitalism, as practiced by indigenous businesses and as practiced by indigenous corporations and multinationals.

Those corporations are staffed by fallible human beings who do make mistakes and, from time to time, violate ethical norms. But on balance, they are great forces for progress in the developing world. They bring technology, capital, jobs, hope, and dignity to people. They help awaken the desire for a better, freer life for the citizens of the host countries.

I can assure you that no businessman in his right mind cares whether he sells cereal or steel or small appliances to a black person or a white person, to a Muslim, a Christian, or a Jew. We should not underestimate the ethical dynamism of capitalism and its capacity to undermine artificial distinctions. As Paul Johnson, former editor of the journal New

Statesman, put it, "Capitalism...cannot coexist with a social and political system based on inherited racial caste, which forbids freedom of movement and a free market in labor, and subordinates all business decisions to the needs of a primitive world view."

The motive force behind capitalism is to generate a rising tide of economic opportunity for all those willing to work. If a country wants to stop its economic development and put up a roadblock on the road to change, personal development, and political liberty, let it choose Marxism, that graveyard of broken hopes and dreams. Political liberty cannot flower in the soil of economic despotism.

Capitalism <u>works</u>. It is the engine of progress in the United States, in Europe, in Asia, and in Africa. It also works to remove artificial distinctions in race and social class. It undermines these distinctions by its insatiable need to expand the education, the skills, and the earning power of all consumers. Capitalism begins to falter and fail when large numbers of people are kept in a state of serfdom.

Rather than restricting the activities of multinational corporations, we should be encouraging them to expand their scope of activities. That is the way to speed up the process of positive change throughout the world. Finally, let's recognize the direct connection between the economic liberty represented by those capitalists in the multinational corporations and the political freedom that goes hand in hand with economic freedom.

EVERY CLOUD HAS A ZIP-OUT LINING

Robert McClements

Bhopal, pesticides, poverty, South Africa -- all of these issues and many more concern those people examining ethical dilemmas for the multinational enterprise. It is at times like this that I wish I were someone else. If I were a comedian, I could make people forget all these troubles. If I were a teenager, I could give them all the answers. If I were a politician, I could run for office on them.

Instead I am a businessman who really tries to conduct his company in the fair and balanced best interests of all parties, but I am also one who recognizes the first law of reality: whatever it is that hits the fan will not be evenly distributed. In the following pages, I am going to talk about balance and about optimism. An optimist is a person who falls out of a 13th floor window and, as he passes each floor on the way down, shouts: "I'm all right so far!" I happen to be among those who feel they have read and heard enough gloom about America's mistakes.

Our Gross National Guilt is at an all-time high. Now we have built in a distribution system for it, as we almost seek the blame for every problem on this planet, no matter how remote. It seems the only certain things anymore are death, taxes, and if there is a problem anywhere in the world, America will find a way to get blamed for it. But if America was wrong at one time to believe that we could be the solution to all the world's problems, we are just as wrong now to believe that we are the cause of all of them.

Think for a moment of Christopher Columbus whom we honor every year. He went in the wrong direction from Spain looking for India. He landed in the Bahamas and decided he had discovered America. If he were alive today, he would be a government economist. The serious side of that turning-point voyage illustrates to me the "ethics of balance." Had Columbus and all other adventurers stayed home to weigh the ethics of what they were doing, the world might be quite different today. Imagine a world without the experiment of America having taken place. But because that experiment did take place, you and I have had an opportunity to participate in the great American success story. It is a political success story and an economic one.

The economic success comes out of a system we call

capitalism. Lately, though, we have gotten shy about using that term because its critics make it sound like a synonym for greed. So we call the system free enterprise, or a market-based economy. No matter what label you put on it, it has some vociferous critics around the world. What our economic system could use is a few more outspoken friends. So I have decided here to be one of them. I am going to ask that we consider the "ethics of balance." We hear enough about what business does wrong. I intend to focus briefly on what business does right. I go so far as to suggest that a healthy, market-based economic system may be this world's best hope of bringing economic balance to the people of the earth.

Last year we had a chance to witness how destitute life is for some people on this planet. We had been reading about the famine in sub-Saharan Africa for well over a year. But when television showed us pictures of the suffering, the shock and impact became dramatic. And Americans responded. We are a generous people, and we gave. My point here is this: we gave not because we _had_ to give, but because we _had it to give_. And we _had_ it because our economic system works.

The theory of the system is not too complicated. We exchange goods and services based on market factors. But the dynamics of a market-based economy keep balancing a number of factors: what people want to buy, what they are willing to pay for it, what the goods cost to produce, and how much there is to go around.

The system also works to balance some more elevated, more ethical considerations. I am going to mention three examples of how the "ethics of balance" operates in business.

In the first place, our system helps to balance _what we have_ with _what they have_.

Right now we share this earth with about five billion other people. And if you think it has been getting more crowded here lately, you are right. World population grew by 84 million last year. By the year 2000, human population is expected to be growing by 100 million a year. I like the comment that by the year 2000 there will be 300 million cars in the United States of America, so if you want to cross the street, you had better do it now.

What is critical about that world population acceleration is that 90 percent of that growth will take place in poor countries and in the spreading urban slums of the world. Poverty and malnutrition and ignorance still hold multitudes in their grip. Millions still live in mud huts, or worse, and feed themselves through primitive agricultural methods. Medical care and education are luxuries.

Now enter on this scene, not a white knight, no champion, not even a John Wayne. Just call it a step forward. I am talking about businesses that stimulate the economies of the Third World that must be built on a growing base of educated people, highways, dams, irrigation projects, and industries. For every case study cited about the bungling and exploitation of American business, we can cite many more illustrations about how business has improved the life of the local people:

-Ford Motor Company has built 128 schools in Mexico.

-Champion International subsidizes 13,000 meals a day for its workers in Brazil and offers a low-price co-op supermarket to employees.

-When Bechtel built a 500-mile pipeline in Peru, it also built communities along the line to make sure workers had clean housing, adequate food, and decent public health facilities.

-Caltex constructed 50 schools in Indonesia, with enrollments of over 15,000 children. It also built 2,600 kilometers of roads and maintains them at a cost of one million dollars a year.

-Goodyear Tire and Rubber built a mosque near its rubber plantations to make it easier for workers to worship.

-IBM has opened 13 agricultural research centers in its Third World locations.

-DelMonte Corporation's food processing plant in Nairobi employs 6,500 Kenyans, and another 5,000 jobs have been created to support the plant. DelMonte has built housing in Nairobi for 12,000 people.

There are hundreds more stories like these. Jobs in multinational corporations do in fact promote a better life for people in less developed countries, and that is why these jobs are so highly prized. No one claims that the motivation here is altruistic. Corporations are not charitable organizations. The principle of capitalism is that it mobilizes one of the most basic human instincts, self-interest, in a way that promotes the well being of others. The fact is that corporations have to have a healthy, intelligent work force, and those people must be able to get to work every day. In nations where people are hungry and lack housing, companies have to intervene to make sure these basic needs are met.

Multinationals are not the whole solution to Third World needs, but surely they are part of the solution. Success in this endeavor will not be spectacular. It will be a daily, weekly, monthly process, gradually changing opinions, overcoming barriers, and building new bridges of understanding among people. A worthwhile goal is to help individuals structure their pride and self-confidence. We should force them neither to become something they are not nor to be carbon copies of Americans, but we should strive to give individual human beings the opportunity to be measured for their achievements and to be rewarded for their contributions.

One thing is clear, the solutions to the economic distress of many Third World people requires more than charity and good intentions. The proof of that is the fact that developing countries outside OPEC now earn twice as much from their exports to the United States as they gain in direct aid from all the countries of the industrialized world.

Does business treat its employees fairly? What are the possible hazards of the workplace? What are the side effects of government-approved pharmaceutical products? Who should be punished for overcharging on government contracts? These are fair and important questions. But while we ask them, we should also recognize certain facts telling us that people in less developed countries account for three-quarters of the world's population, but they consume only one-quarter of its resources. In the Third World, 700 million people are classified as destitute. Seventy percent of the children there suffer from malnutrition. Three hundred million are physically or mentally impaired because they do not get enough to eat.

When we nit-pick the flaws of capitalism, let us also consider how vigorous business activity can alleviate some of these conditions. In effect, the corporation becomes a way of helping to redistribute the world's resources. We will not eradicate poverty. But that is no excuse not to try. We are talking here about adjusting the balance between what we have and what they have. That is not a job for charity alone. It is a job that will have to call on business, because business has the jobs. And jobs are where a decent living begins.

The second way our economic system can help to bring balance to life is by balancing the <u>power of government</u> with the <u>power of the marketplace.</u>

The popular argument is that corporations are powerhouses in American life. They say we mold public opinion and influence government. I admit we would like to see pro-business policies understood and accepted, but the record simply does not show that what business wants, business gets.

They also say that corporations are powerful because they set prices. That is news to us in the oil business. In the oil industry, we have almost no control over prices. Prices used to be in the hands of OPEC ministers. Now, since the use of oil is declining and non-OPEC nations are finding more oil, price is set by the market. And right now, price is falling. Once again, the market works. When there is more of a product available than people need, the seller has to take what price the market is willing to pay.

The only real power of business is in the marketplace. If we read the markets right, if we respond quickly and with quality goods and services, and if we price our products competitively, then we are successful. We are employing people, producing goods and services, and rewarding investors. And that is our power. If we do not do those things well, we are a rusty, creaking obsolete enterprise that can easily turn into another shutdown plant.

As long as American business remains successful, it is an effective counterbalance to the role of government in the life of our nation. When we stop doing our job well, that is the day that government starts doing it for us. And one important freedom, economic freedom, is lost. Do not be too sure that could not happen. First, we should not assume that business can adapt to any climate just by being nimble and smart. This capitalistic system and its private, voluntary corporations have only been around for some 200 years, and in only a few countries.

Internationally, the "ethics of balance" requires us to consider how American business feels when after investing time, talent, and money into a foreign project, the enterprise is taken over by the host government with little notice and less compensation. The tendency is to pull back from the next opportunity and to entertain an instinct for isolationism. Business cannot stand up indefinitely under the weight of an unfriendly culture.

That is why when I hear that self-interest is evil, that ambition is dangerous, that profits are dishonorable, I get uneasy. Challenge those traditional attitudes. See if they are not the very attitudes that are holding back progress in the developing nations.

Now I am not silly enough to think that self-interest always leads to harmonious results. It does not. Greed, corruption, and pure selfishness will always threaten and weaken our system. That is why our system requires, more than any other, self-restraint and respect for the public good. These are not just pleasant virtues to practice on the Sabbath. They are critical policies in the daily operation of a business.

In business, we try to keep our own conscience on those virtues. When we do not, we have backup consciences: the public, the press, and our national leaders. I do not deny we need that backup. I simply ask that we also keep in mind the basics here. The basics are that we need business. We need its jobs, its goods, and its services. And business needs something back. It needs the confidence and support of the public, because it is not indestructible.

The third, and last, way that business lends balance to our lives is by reminding us that we must always weigh <u>what is ideal</u> against <u>what is possible.</u>

Some say the real mark of maturity is the ability to live with ambiguity. If that is so, our system is a real test of maturity for our citizens. It abounds with ambiguity and especially in the area of ethics. Consider a few propositions:

-In a recession, is it more ethical for an executive to keep everyone on the payroll and all go under together; or is it better to lay off some people so the business can survive and possibly rehire later?

-For an American company, is it better not to do business in countries that trade through a system of what we call bribes? Take the case of a few years back of the aircraft company that got into trouble for paying a fee to a Middle Eastern agent to get a defense contract. As outraged as the general public and press seemed to be about that incident, might we not have gotten a different view of "ethics" from one of the 10,000 Americans who would keep their jobs because it happened? What would those individuals and their families have considered the ethical thing to do?

-Management is responsible for the health of the corporation, we all know that. What is not so clear is whether it is more ethical to make decisions that serve the short-term profitability of the company today, rewarding today's shareholders, or whether it is better to invest in the long-term life of the corporation, building it for future generations.

We all know that decisions about our personal lives are complex enough. The ethics of running a business is far more nuanced. What we decide affects thousands of employees and stockholders and often millions of other people, either as users of our products or residents of our community. And always our best aspirations have costs as well as benefits.

Our system provides us all with the freedom to make our own decisions. Businessmen in Moscow do not have ethical dilemmas because they do not have choices. The state makes their decisions for them. In this country, we accept that no ruling body has a corner on economic wisdom. Here we believe that the best test of the value of a decision is in the marketplace of life.

And while we are free to make choices in our international ventures, we are not always free to choose the nature of the consequences. Our soul-searching, our fears, our doubts, and our mistakes merely illustrate that we are imperfect. But if mankind had waited until it was sure it could create a Camelot on earth before launching great ventures, we would still be in a cave.

What is important is to weave a pattern of progress from the circumstances of our times. I am fascinated by the United Nations. A lot of nations knock it. But they go to it for the same reasons people go to the senior prom -- to make contacts, to eye the competition, and to avoid the risk of not being there.

We are involved in a race between common sense and catastrophe. Realism warns us that we cannot do everything. Common sense tells us that we can do a great deal. Every cloud has a zip-out lining. In dealing with our problems, foreign and domestic, we can insert a negative lining and dwell on our limitations, or we can insert a lining of optimism to help us pursue our possibilities.

I think we owe it to future generations to come out on the optimistic side of that question. The most creative and forward moving actions in any society are taken not by those who doubt, because those people never leave home. The new worlds are created by men and women who have faith in human possibilities. We can leave that task to others; or we can choose to be among them.

ETHICS AND THE SCIENTIST: COMMON SENSE OR CAMELOT?

Etcyl H. Blair

I suppose that many a businessman has opened a Bentley Conference speech with the observation that he feels out of place, totally inadequate to the task he has accepted. At least that is the inclination I fought off as I prepared this.

Why is that? Why is it that so many businessmen and businesswomen find the topic of ethics so unfamiliar? Why do they experience such discomfort when a discussion of ethics becomes a part of their agenda?

I am aware that there are those among you who have a quick, simple answer to those questions. "Easy," you would say. "Businesspeople have problems with ethical concepts because they don't have any ethics."

I utterly reject that, of course, or else I would not be presenting this. I don't know any businessman or businesswomen who wouldn't; most of them possess varying degrees of certainty that they are scrupulously ethical.

I do have some answers to my own questions. They may be as quick and simple as the cynical answer I already rejected. For that reason, I have some hesitation in offering them. I am going to do so, however, because as simple as they are, they may have a profound significance.

Before I present them, I would like to enter one disclaimer. For purposes of the general observations I am making, I do not really consider myself a businessman. I am a vice president of the largest purely chemical company in the United States, and I could not live without being a proponent of the profit motive. But I am a scientist, a researcher, and I have spent my entire career without business, commercial, or marketing-management experience. I am not trying to distance myself from businessmen. I am trying to speak for them, after all, but I think it is important that you should understand I am doing so from the vantage point and perspective of a scientist, a chemist.

There are observations from that particular perspective which can be applied to the scientist as a businessperson, and I will draw on those observations later to reinforce my conclusions on business ethics.

My first observation is that very few businessmen or businesswomen have ever spent much time contemplating the subject of ethics per se. That clearly distinguishes them from ethicists, clergymen, philosophers, and maybe journalists. But it leaves them, I would observe, in the company of politicians, truckdrivers, lumberjacks, farmers, labor union leaders, and fishermen, all of whom clearly must exercise ethical standards from time to time in the ordinary course of events.

It may be that this is especially true in the chemical industry, which tends to be peopled more heavily by chemical engineers than by Harvard MBA's, who would have had more classroom occasion to contemplate the subject. However, I strongly suspect that the situation would not be too much different in any basic industry, which, until the last couple of decades, has tended to make managers and operating officers out of bright technically-trained employees.

My second observation is that very few businessmen, and few other people without some theological training, have any inkling that the work they do was not very respectable at all until the 19th century. There is simply very little realization on the part of the average businessperson that his or her position in society throughout most of recorded history was comparable to that of farmers and common laborers, little better than serfs.

From my observation, he or she has very little awareness of what Aristotle or Thomas Aquinas thought about the profit motive. If businesspeople knew that, they would be surprised to learn that Martin Luther agreed with them and would be puzzled by the idea that John Calvin was the first important theological figure to judge this behavior as acceptable. Do you mean to say that market society capitalism, which so pervades our lives from the moment the clock radio snaps on in the morning unitl Ted Koppel is done with us, did not always exist?

This may or may not come as a surpise to those of you who teach business or philosophy or theory, but it cannot be very encouraging. The captains of industry assume that it has always been this way, or at least they do not accord very much importance to an understanding of their heritage.

My third observation is that a company like Dow can and does observe extremely high ethical standards, even with little influence from employees who have had exposure to academic training with components of ethics and business history.

How can that be the case?

About 10 years ago, the sociologist Morris Massey made a very big splash in American business circles with his ideas about the character formation of American youth. Massey packaged his arguments into a rapid-fire delivery of "pop" sociology which he called "You Are What You Were When." It had serious shortcomings, but his central argument was difficult to refute. He argued that value systems were firmly implanted by the age of 12 or 13, and that events subsequent to that merely put a veneer on hardwood. One could explain institutional trends and phenomena at any given time, he contended, by subtracting 40 or 50 years from the date and then examining the socioeconomic events which dominated the headlines for the answer. That gives one telltale evidence of the character and values of the leaders of American institutions, as of the original date.

I mention this to point out that men in charge of America, including its corporations, had their value systems firmly in place around 1940, give or take a couple of years. They come from an era in which religious teachings were an important ingredient in the educational process, and not a whole lot of people thought you needed much more than the Three R's, the Ten Commandments, and the Golden Rule to succeed in America.

My simple conclusion is that, on a day-to-day basis, the ethical considerations that go into the decision-making process at a fairly typical Fortune 500 company have their genesis in religious experience. I am sure you have heard such a conclusion in many forms before today. Probably this is not even the first time you have heard it from a Kansas farm boy, whose profile would pretty much match Massey's pattern. So I want to take this one step further. I want to ask: Is that sufficient? Is it acceptable that the conscience of American industry be built on Biblical admonitions which so many people violate so freely and frequently?

I don't think so.

I say that not because I think the commandments are outmoded and not becaue I think they have served poorly. I say that because I think the transformation of American society following World War II brought about a rapid change in value systems. The society became more mobile, less rooted. The importance of religion in American life faded, as did the importance and authority of many other institutions. Change was gradual and probably fairly healthy for a generation, but it certainly became radical and much harder to understand and accept by the 1960's.

If you follow Massey's timetable, perhaps you will guess what I'm thinking: America's institutional leaders by the year 2000 will be those people who were conditioned by the troubled sixties. Massey didn't think so, by the way. He thought leadership would bypass a generation and the result would be a younger generation in authority at the turn of the century.

I am neither convinced of that nor do I believe it would necessarily be desirable for a generation to be that grossly disenfranchised. I do judge that the Judeo-Christian ethic did not fare well in that era and, from my perspectives, the most reasonable way to give an industry and other American institutions an infusion of ethical thought is through the formal education process.

I am of the opinion that the circumstances call for more academic training in the liberal arts, including philosophy, history, literature, and sociology. I recognize that a great many disciplines which have not been strongly represented in American business must be drawn into its mainstream. It would be helpful to find more chemical engineers with strong exposure to the arts, and it would be heartening to encounter liberal arts graduates with some exposure to science, especially its methodology. It is probably not enought to stop there; I am inclined to think that a baccalaureate degree ought to require a five year curriculum, which I understand is becoming the norm in some places.

I confess that my desire to elevate the level of scientific literacy is at the top of my mind for somewhat self-serving reasons. I told you earlier that my perspective is that of a scientist. Some of you may be familiar with James B. Conant's tightly reasoned Arthur Stanley Eddington Lecture at Princeton in 1966. In it, he reached the conclusion that there is no such thing as "the scientific method," only advances in science, which come about because scientists are engaged in the extension of the commonsense world, and that ethics therefore cannot be based on science.

Were I to subscribe unreservedly to Conant's line of reasoning, it seems to me I would have little ground to argue the case of scientific literacy. I depart from him because he would leave me no room to rationalize my perspective of the scientist as a businessman.

To demonstrate that our system is in desperate need of more scientific literacy, I want to look no further than the disturbing phenomenon of the factoid. A factoid is a bit of information, presented as fact, which has no reality outside of its use in the news. "Deep Throat," the name Woodward and Bernstein coined to protect their unidentified sources in Watergate, is perhaps the best-known factoid. The accuracy of their information is not at question, and I do not propose to rekindle the debate within the journalistic fraternity about the propriety or ethical grounds for "Deep Throat." The point is, "Deep Throat" was a factoid.

Factoids abound.

A few months back, an outfit in Washington called the World Resources Institute released a study which said that 300,000 farm workers are victims annually of pesticide poisoning in the United States. The study got a lot of newspaper space and television time and whipped up a great deal of concern. Some people wondered about the 300,000 figure, though. Where did that come from?

Well, it turns out that in 1978, in an article in the Journal of Occupational Medicine, an author ventured the opinion that California doctors report only about one percent of the pesticide poisonings in that state. The author of that article subsequently changed his mind and estimated that 80 percent of the California cases are reported. Nevertheless, the World Resources Institute took the 235 cases reported in California in 1982, multiplied by 100, figured that the answer, 23,500, was 7.8 percent of the California farmworker population, and multiplied the national farmworker population (4 million) by 7.8 per cent. Presto! 312,000 and a factoid.

A statistician at the EPA's Pesticide Response Center has taken California figures and estimated that the outside number of pesticide poisonings in the nation annually is 10,500. The real truth of the matter is that EPA has received 56,000 reports of these incidents in the 15 years of its existence -- an average of 3,733 a year. Unfortunately, that is not the figure you are likely to hear or read if that sort of story comes to your attention in the next few months.

A couple of weeks ago, the EPA announced that it intends to classify chloroform as a cancer-causing air pollutant under the Clean Air Act. At least one major metropolitan newspaper said the average person has one chance in a hundred of contracting cancer from chloroform and that the total national risk is about 13 cases annually. The numbers, of course, are mutually refutable. If the risk is 13 cases annually, that means less than a thousand cases in 70 years, which, placed over the population base, makes the chance of contracting cancer from chloroform about one in 235,000. If the risk is one in a hundred, that means 2.35 million cases in 70 years, or about 33,500 cases annually. That is simplified statistical analysis, you understand, but a decent ballpark basis. A lack of scientific literacy caused the factoids in the reporting, and it will cause them to be repeated many times over in the months ahead.

I could go on for some time. The point, of course, is that a scientifically unprepared population has no basis whatsoever for recognizing factoids, let alone putting them in perspective. Perspective -- that is what I think is sadly lacking and could represent an important gain, if we could do a better job of preparing tomorrow's graduates for the roles they're going to fulfill.

So I say we need to broaden our educational programs, to provide our young scientists, engineers and business leaders with more understanding of the liberal arts. Likewise, we need to expand the role of the physical sciences in the schools of philosophy, history, literacy, and journalism. The more people we have who can differentiate between facts and factoids, the better off we all are.

CHAPTER FOUR

CONSULTING STRATEGIES FOR DEALING WITH MULTINATIONAL
BUSINESS ETHICAL DILEMMAS

DAVID NOSNIK
Partner
Deloitte Haskins & Sells
Boston, Massachusetts

VERNE E. HENDERSON
Ethics Consultant and Professor of Ethics and Social Issues
Arthur D. Little Management Education Institute
Cambridge, Massachusetts

WILLIAM W. BAIN, JR.
President
Bain and Company
Boston, Massachusetts

ETHICAL ISSUES IN THE MULTINATIONAL ENVIRONMENT

David Nosnik

Ever since it was first published in late 1982, In Search of Excellence has been read by more than five million people, in fifteen different languages, who are desperately seeking excellence in business. Don V. Siebert, CEO and Chairman of J.C. Penny Co., was once quoted as saying:"...in the long run, the best business decision is that which is founded on the most ethical judgments." Furthermore, in the preface of their book It's Good Business, Solomon and Hanson state flatly that "The search for excellence, whatever else it may be, begins with ethics..."

But what is ethics? What represents the most ethical judgments? In today's highly uncertain and rapidly changing environment, the manager of any business, let alone a multinational corporation, would be hard pressed to articulate a code of ethics that would satisfy all of the interested parties he must interact with on a day-to-day basis.

In the United States, where many ethical issues effecting business, including product liability and questionable payments, are settled through litigation, many American managers look toward the law to provide the ethical framework in which to operate. The repository of this ethical framework is an army of corporate lawyers. When faced with questionable transactions, managers turn to legal counsel for the final decision making. This, of course, is when senior management is likely to become aware of questionable transactions before they have been executed.

Since the passage in 1977 of the Foreign Corrupt Practices Act, theoretical ethical issues have taken a more pragmatic legal focus for managers of United States-based multinational corporations. The sections of the Act specifically dealing with foreign corrupt practices are quite limited in scope, but violation can result in a company being fined up to $1 million. Moreover, managers face possible fines of up to $10,000 and imprisonment of up to 10 years. Furthermore, the act provides for accurate and fair recordkeeping of transactions, as well as the maintenance of adequate systems of internal accounting controls. In short, the law requires managers to fully document instances when they are breaking the law.

As a result, managers have carefully read the provisions of the Act and have sought advice from lawyers and independent auditors covering the means and ways to ensure compliance with the Act throughout their organizations. Again, for many managers, the law represents an ethical operating framework. After passage of the Act, many structural changes were implemented by both multinational and domestic SEC registrants to assure compliance with this newly-devised ethical framework.

Compliance with the Act took the form of larger international internal auditing departments and an increased scope for external audits, as well as dissemination of "conflict of interest" statements to managers in offices and plants throughout the world. Yet, barriers of distance, language, and culture presented some multinational companies with unanticipated burdens in implementing these compliance programs.

Take the case of a large midwest industrial company with operations in Europe and Latin America. A corporate "Code of Ethics" and a "Conflict of Interest" Statement was approved by the Board of Directors after endless drafting sessions between lawyers and members of the Audit Committee. Upon approval, the statement was translated by staff in the International Department and disseminated to plant managers throughout the world.

A section of the statement originally reading, "We do not condone corrupt practices..." was translated to "We no longer condone corrupt practices " in the Spanish version. Two months later, an internal auditor from the home office paid a visit to the company's Piedras Negras, Mexico Plant. This was the first visit of an internal auditor in 20 years and came as a result of the newly-implemented compliance program. Upon arrival at his hotel, the auditor found an anonymous note advising him to leave town immediately. Not knowing how to react, he decided to consult with the manager at the plant. He left the hotel, walked to his rented car and realized that the four tires had been slashed flat. Within two hours he was on the next flight back home.

At about this time, the legal department of the same company received a confidential note from a country manager in South America. He explained in his letter that about seven months previously the mailman in a remote plant, who diligently delivered the mail daily, announced that he would have to take a second job because his wife had just had their sixth child and his salary from the post office was not enough. Of course, if the company would agree to help him out, he would not have to take this job. And, the manager continued, the plant had been contributing to the mailman's family welfare ever since. He wanted to know if this was a corrupt practice that needed to be stopped, according to the home office memo.

For managers like Mr. Siebert at J.C. Penny, who do believe in the need for a sound ethical framework to provide for firm business decisions, the challenge goes beyond the legal department. Looking to develop a worldwide framework of shared values and ensuring compliance with it, international organizations operating in a myriad of markets, languages, and cultures must focus on the challenge of developing and maintaining a complex decision-making process, rather than looking for the right formal structure. This challenge requires the development of new management perspectives, attitudes, and processes which reflect and respond to the complex demands faced by companies with international strategies.

The development of a worldwide corporate framework of shared values has to be, by definition, sensitive to all of the actions and cultures where the organization operates. Further, because pressures in the international operating environment are diverse and rapidly changing, this framework should be based on a dynamic internal management environment which is able to respond quickly to these external demands and opportunities.

Rigid organizational structures, either by country subsidiary or product line, foster a one-dimensional decision-making process. In order to develop multiple management perspectives, staff groups should be given increased responsibility for monitoring and control. Roles must be redefined and information systems redesigned to provide both line-and-staff personnel with information which is carefully tailored to their newly defined responsibilities.

Senior management must communicate clearly the enhanced roles of staff personnel. Quality management will then be attracted to these newly-defined positions, rather than avoid transfers because of perceived lack of career enhancement, as can be the case today.

Currently, line personnel are the recipients of meaningful information for decision making. However, staff managers have traditionally been handicapped in this respect. Enhancement of the role should be followed by providing the proper tools.

Through this process, the company elevates previously underrepresented management groups, recognizes the need to monitor the environment from their perspective, acknowledges their competence to analyze the strategic implications of key issues, and accepts the legitimacy of representing such views in the overall corporate decision sequence.

Beyond developing a capable organization and analyzing issues from various perspectives, managers representing numerous points of view need to gain access to the decision-making processes.

To make the organization flexible, top management should ascertain that managers understand how their individual points of view fit in with corporate strategies. Thus, their understanding is reinforced with a culture supportive of cooperation and compromise. Development of the corporate ethical framework is a dynamic process. It feeds from enhanced, complex decision-making procedures where decision makers throughout the corporation are actively contributing to this evolving process.

Informal channels of communication should be encouraged to complement formal ones within the existing organizational structure. Corporate norms and values are then carefully disseminated throughout the organization by means of a variety of small actions and decisions such as:

- Precise communication of corporate strategies and behavioral norms;

- Implementation of systems that evaluate and reward compliance with these strategies and behavioral values;

- Senior management's words and actions which provide role models that strongly influence values and behavioral norms throughout the organization. Signals should be sent routinely encouraging behavior consistent with corporate ethics.

In summary, focusing on the decision-making process instead of on organizational structuring and restructuring will provide a gradual organizational evolution rather than a sudden structural change. Emphasizing changed behavior rather than structural design will provide a dynamic ethical framework instead of a static organizational chart.

ETHICAL CRITERIA FOR MULTINATIONAL CONSULTING

Verne E. Henderson

Introduction

In the following paper, I intend to introduce some new definitions and concepts which should help in understanding multinational corporations (MNCs). After a few introductory comments about MNCs themselves, I will discuss briefly how I function as a consultant, what I see as a necessary distinction between morals and ethics, what I define as the ethical side of enterprise and the spectrum of ethicality and, finally, I will present a conceptual framework and an ethical algorithm or decision making model that I developed approximately five years ago.

The Multinational Corporation

Size. MNCs are a growing and changing phenomenon in the world economy. Approximately three hundred corporations account for more than ninety percent of this global business. About two hundred are based in the United States. Despite the inordinate amount of media attention MNCs receive, they are relatively small when compared to a total of 2,500,000 corporations in the United States. MNCs account for approximately ten percent of the United States Gross National Product (GNP). While MNCs can boast of a history of more than a hundred years (Singer, 1867), the greatest growth followed World War II.

Some firms now receive more than fifty percent of their profits from overseas operations. Gillette, Mobil, Citicorp, IBM, Coca-Cola, and Pfizer are among the better known ones. On average, United States based MNCs achieved about thirteen percent of sales and twenty percent of profits overseas in the mid-1970s.

Definition. David Lilienthal is believed to have coined the term "multinational" in 1958. While scholars argue about the precise definition of an MNC, with some preferring the term "transnational," I use three characteristics to set them apart from firms which simply export products or services. Those three are:

1) the deployment of corporate assets in two or more countries;

2) direct foreign investment which might be subject to

expropriation; and

3) management from the parent company headquarters.

I reserve the term "transnational" for those firms that either simply export goods and services or do not require a parent country and can move quickly and easily to any country and continue business.

Controversies. Multinational corporations face a number of ethical controversies. The host countries sometimes accuse them of taking excessive profits, gobbling up precious local resources, failing to train indigenous employees, dominating the economic and political environments, contributing to inflation, restricting access to modern technology, staffing top management especially with expatriates, and sometimes affronting local customs. The parent countries accuse them of exporting jobs, contributing to a deleterious balance of payments, and exerting undue influence on foreign policy. In my ethical lexicon, such accusations fall into the category of **macroethical** considerations. They raise the question as to whether MNCs contribute positively to the human welfare of a nation's economy. At another level, we have **microethical** issues which arise when an MNC is perceived as not complying with known and acknowledged laws, rules, or customs. Both dimensions will be implied but not specifically addressed in the following pages.

The Role of Consultant

Consultant Not Conscience. I think of myself as a consultant to my clients, not their conscience. Those clients include a few MNCs, as well as students at Northeastern University and at the Arthur D. Little Management Education Institute (ADLMEI). The latter institution requires further explanation. ADLMEI bestows a Master's of Science in Management degree upon those who successfully complete the eleven month program. The course in business ethics is required of all graduates. The average class size is about sixty-five students, most of whom are already middle managers with a decade or more of work experience. A typical class is ninety percent foreign born with English as a second language, represents twenty or more less developed countries, and all six major religions (plus a sprinkling of atheists). Six years at ADLMEI has altered my approach to business ethics, MNCs or otherwise. Class discussions, for instance, reveal heated value conflicts which cannot be resolved by simplistic application of Western laws or ethics. New definitions and distinctions emerged.

Ethics Not Morals. Morals is the term I now use to

describe what I expect of myself; not what I believe, but how I behave. Ethics, in contrast, is what I expect of others and what I perceive they expect of me; a kind of social contract, if you will. Morally speaking, I expect to behave ethically in the eyes of others. I cannot satisfy all those expectations of others, partly because there are so many and some are either mutually exclusive or contradictory. So, I must decide whose expectations, or which constituency, I most want to satisfy. This, I submit, is the same kind of choice every business decision maker and every MNC must also make. The difference here between individual choice and corporate choice is only a matter of magnitude. Being ethical, then, means trying to fulfill the behavioral expectations of those whom you believe to be your most valued constituency, which is often a vaguely perceived dominant culture. Let me hasten to add that satisfying a constituency, valued by me or not, does NOT always mean doing what they expect behaviorally. Satisfying a constituency can take a lot of different forms, as we shall see. With corporate clients this means that if they do not possess the moral imperative to behave ethically, there is relatively little I can do **as a consultant** to help them. When a business executive seeks my services as an expression of his moral conviction to satisfy ethical expectations of one or more of the corporation's constituents, I can help.

The Ethical Side of Enterprise. As consultant or teacher, I see my major role as one of clarifying issues. My client and I must first agree on the nature of reality before discussing how we might best react to it. Part of that reality is the recognition that business has an ethical side as well as a business side. The business side addresses such questions as "will it sell" and "for how much" and "to whom." The ethical side of enterprise asks, instead, "will my product or service be harmful to persons in some way" or "will my product or service promote some common good." To be sure, the value orientation of a pluralistic culture such as the United States provides a great variety of answers to the ethical questions. A need for one person is a luxury to another, and so forth.

A Spectrum of Ethicality. Corporations, in my experience, are also arranged along a "spectrum of ethicality." Some are content to "do no harm" (e.g., Milton Friedman), while others aspire to provide only the most worthy and beneficial goods (e.g., Kenneth Dayton). For example, any number of firms may be equally dedicated to affirmative action, some satisfied to fulfill the letter of the law, others to reverse what they perceive as decades of economic injustice. What I am outlining here is a situational ethic. Namely, there is no single or perfect ethical behavior or principle that can be mandated for every corporation in every case. Each firm must find its own answers, wrung out from a myriad of considerations unique to itself. Moreover, in today's dynamic business environment, those answers change with time and the extension of technology. The five major areas in which corporate ethical issues emerge today -- human investment, ecology, consumer welfare, political relationships, corporate responsiveness -- can trace their alarming growth to four relatively recent developments: population growth, affluence, technology, and the institutionalizing of our major social tasks. For the MNC, the issues are compounded by culture and value clashes. Tough decisions follow.

Additional concepts and definitions are needed in order to bring some coherence to an increasingly complex world. You will not find this distinction between morals and ethics in the textbooks, for instance. I have simply found it helpful to my clients. I would now like to introduce two major concepts that can help MNC decision makers. I hesitate to call them "ethical criteria." Rather, they are guidelines or checkpoints.

The Conceptual Framework

Let us assume that most corporate decisions yield products or services deemed legal and ethical. But in these changing times they do not always stay that way. What has become a classical example is the manufacture and use of asbestos, possibly disastrous for the Manville Corporation. Pesticides and herbicides fall into a similar category, effecting Dow Chemical and Union Carbide, particularly. Because of subsequent technological research years after their appearance in the marketplace, all were found to be toxic, one way or another, and labeled "unethical." Laws were then written or changed to reflect this new status.

Another example is found in questions surrounding business activity in South Africa. To date, it is still legal to be doing business there but it is perceived as unethical by a growing segment of our population. Eighty-seven major United States corporations are involved in this dilemma.

Reversing the field as to legal versus ethical, bribes (or "commissions," whichever term you prefer) are now illegal, according to the Foreign Corrupt Practices Act. Lockheed and Gulf were prominent corporate actors here. Yet there are plenty of business persons who consider them ethical. "When in Rome, do as the Romans do," is the unspoken justification. How can we conceptualize these differences? (See Figure 1, next page.)

A CONCEPTUAL FRAMEWORK

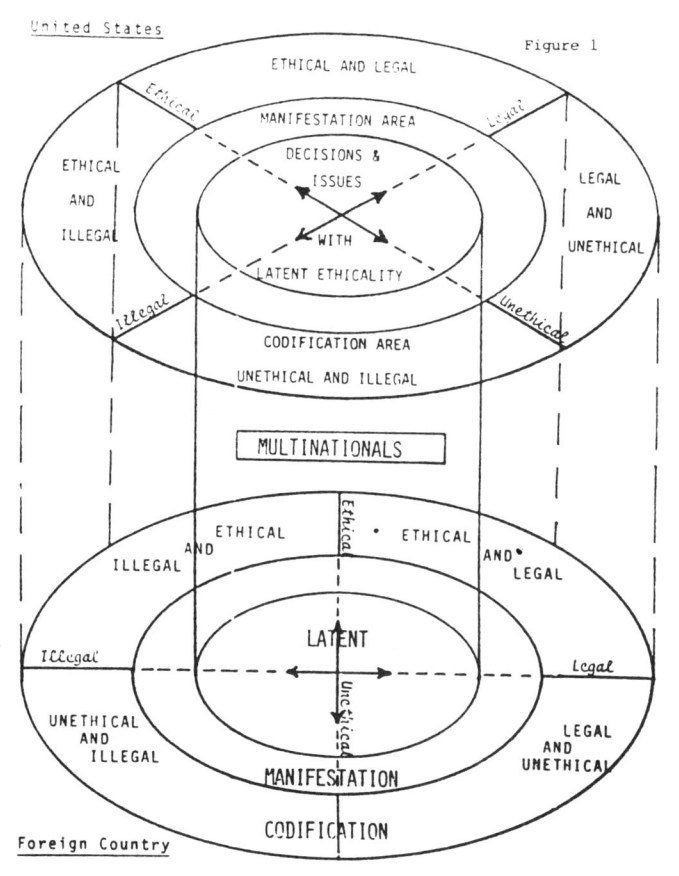

Figure 1

Picture, if you will, a circle divided into four quadrants such as we often drew in high school math class. The upper right hand quadrant (I), valued as + + to identify a coordinate within its area, corresponds to corporate decisions which are and remain legal and ethical. The lower left quadrant (IV), in contrast and valued as - -, we can label illegal and unethical. The other two quadrants, upper left (III) and lower right (II), provide an interesting mixture, - + and + -. These decision areas involving products and services of MNCs translate as illegal but ethical and legal but unethical. Such graphics characterize the complexity of our time. Unfortunately, for the multinational that is only the beginning.

Picture now, if you can, two such circles with their accompanying quadrants, each representing a different culture or nation. Pivot them from their centers such that the quadrants do not match, meaning that what is legal and ethical in one nation does not coincide with what is in another. Now, position the MNC between the circles. That is how many of them experience life today; caught in the middle! (See Figure 1.) The current unitary tax battle between Britain and the United States is a case in point. Two nations with a shared language and culture have conflicting laws regarding corporate income taxes. While the respective governments delay and argue, corporations are stalled in current operations, let alone future planning. The significance of the Framework for the business executive is that his or her decisions must survive in a turbulent environment. It is not just what you do but how you are perceived in the long term that determines your ethicality. Moreover, given our pluralistic society, some degree of social conflict is inevitable. Perhaps the nature of this conflict will become clearer as we move to the algorithm and illustrate with specific corporations.

The Ethical Algorithm

The algorithm, or formula, can be used as an analytical tool to look back on previous corporate action to possibly determine what went wrong, as we do with case studies. It can also be used as a forecasting device to look ahead, to anticipate consequences and avoid the catastrophes. We will use it to look backwards on corporate action already taken. The four calculations in the algorithm involve looking at GOALS, METHODS, MOTIVES, and CONSEQUENCES of corporate decisions. Some of the corporate examples will be of firms that are only marginally multinational, but they provide the richest and perhaps most widely known illustrations.

Goals. The Polaroid Corporation was on record as having a business goal of making some money in South Africa and an ethical goal of "doing something about apartheid." These worthy goals proved to be incompatible. The camera was perceived as a Nazi-like device used by the government to enforce apartheid. Regardless of the percentage of Polaroid cameras actually used for this purpose, it was highly unlikely that Polaroid could ever be perceived as functioning ethically by any constituency except the South African government. Moreover, Polaroid sold their product through a distributor there; they did not have any "direct investments," such as a manufacturing plant. They had little leverage, in other words, to do something about apartheid, except what they finally did -- withdraw in public protest. In sum, in order to achieve their ethical goal, they sacrificed their business goal. Obviously, corporations are limited as to the number of times and circumstances they can make such sacrifices.

It has been estimated that Polaroid's revenue from South Africa comprised less than one-half of one percent of total global sales. It is safe to assume that corporations facing similar dilemmas, coupled with survival instead of marginal revenue percentages at stake, will most likely sacrifice the ethical goal. It is a fact of business life. Even so, corporate decision makers are not entirely powerless in this regard.

It has become increasingly important for MNCs to look at their goal structure very carefully, insuring clarity on both their business goal and an ethical goal. An ethical goal should be something a firm is trying to achieve, not simply a legal or ethical constraint it is willing to accept or abide by in order to conduct business. (Signatory corporations to the Sullivan Principles vary in the degree to which they adopt an ethical goal versus acknowledge an ethical constraint.) In most developing nations, the ethical goal -- doing something to enhance the social good -- is stronger than it is in the United States. Goals should also be checked for compatibility: Is it reasonable to assume that both can be accomplished? What alternatives are available if conflicts between the two should arise? Who are the principal constituents associated with those goals? Such questions, of course, are best asked before a product or service is marketed.

Methods. The sale of an infant feeding formula in less developed countries is also a celebrated controversy, the principal firms being Nestle, Bristol-Myers (specifically, its Mead Johnson Division), and Abbott Laboratories (specifically Ross Laboratories). After more than a decade of expensive and heated opposition, some of which was deemed "unethical" by more than one critic, a "peace treaty" was signed early in 1985. While it was never made sufficiently clear, the issue, in algorithmic terms, was one of METHODS rather than GOALS. The business goal of selling the formula in less developed countries was clearly legal and, on the face of it, ethical. But the marketing methods selected ignored local customs, educational levels, income factors, and political realities. True, the CONSEQUENCES of selling the formula were also debated: infant deaths, lost resources (mother's milk). But these consequences resulted from the methods used to market the product. The MOTIVES of corporate executives were also questioned -- "greedy capitalists" was the implication. Yet, the action of Ross Labs in forming a "Third World Team" suggests an honest and costly effort to satisfy its most critical constituents and be deemed ethical.

Ideally, MNCs should anticipate how their methods will effect their various constituents before they launch a new product or service. It is likely that profits cannot be maximized if major ethical dimensions exist. Finally, corporations can too easily assume that there is only one method available. They can be more creative, more ethical (i.e., sensitive to the welfare of a larger constituency), and perhaps surprisingly enough, more successful in the long term.

Motives. Following the debacle in India at the Union Carbide plant, Chief Executive Officer Warren Anderson boarded an airplane the next day and flew to the site of the tragedy. He was widely cheered for this action, except by the Indian authorities, who put him in jail, and the firm's attorneys who evidently muzzled him, fearing that public displays of sympathy were tantamount to admissions of legal or financial liability. In a follow-up story in the Sunday New York Times business section (dubbed "only a story" by corporate insiders), it appeared that Warren Anderson was one CEO willing to let his deeper motives of human compassion be on public display. Mr. Anderson had little visibility beyond those first few days. Why? Legal ramifications, most likely. Litigation might become more complicated and costly.

Public exposure for corporate executives is risky from several perspectives. Few are trained in public speaking, let alone legal matters. It is all too easy to say the wrong thing, even a "no comment." Bodily harm to themselves or family members is also a danger. In Europe, more than the United States, major executives must guard their private lives, telephone numbers, home addresses, and even friendships very carefully.

Nevertheless, whether it is a Warren Anderson flying off to India or a John Akers of IBM saying that corporate America must help solve society's problems, it is sometimes necessary for CEOs to reveal a bit of their motives, unmasking those driving egos that manage thousands of employees and billions of dollars. It is important, and again especially so in less developed countries, to possess and reveal a humanness of global dimensions. Above all, top executives should know what motivates them, even if it is plain old greed, which they might be wise NOT to share publicly. It has been said that Warren Anderson surprised even himself in his demonstration of compassion. Whether or not Mr. Anderson did indeed discover through Bhopal a new dimension to his character, top executives ought to possess some self insight, and be cognizant of what drives them and, therefore, less vulnerable to discovering who they are in the midst of a crisis.

Consequences. It is standing practice among MNCs to calculate a business bottom line. The ethical bottom line can also be calculated, and needs to be. Sometimes, real dilemmas emerge in these calculations, visited upon a corporation by factors beyond its control.

Johnson & Johnson, makers of the pain killer Tylenol through its subsidiary McNeil Labs, was such a victim. Most of America knows this sad tale: some unknown person injected a lethal dose of cyanide into several Tylenol extra-strength capsules. For decades, Johnson & Johnson had affirmed both an ethical goal ("The Credo") and a business goal, naming its consumers and its stockholders, respectively, as its prime constituents. The Tylenol scare brought these goals and constituents into conflict. (Exogenous factors introduced this goal incompatibility.) During the course of several agonizing weeks, Johnson & Johnson developed what proved to be a costly but effective strategy designed to satisfy both. (They were caught in a conflict of obligation, rather than a conflict of interest, making compromise possible.) Among other things, they openly affirmed their ethical goal of consumer welfare, they sacrificed profits along with market share and ordered the removal of $100 million worth of products from the drug shelves. The paper loss of Johnson & Johnson stock exceeded $650 million within weeks. They paid for their ethics.

Market share, in addition to profits, was an important economic goal for Johnson & Johnson. They were locked in an intense competition with Bristol-Myers' Datril. Two changes in marketing methods were introduced during the heat of this competition: using capsules instead of pills and marketing directly to the consumer rather than through doctors, both of which made the injecting of the poison easier. It would have been difficult, but not entirely impossible, to anticipate the consequences of these two new methods.

The Tylenol story illustrates how difficult yet how necessary it is for corporations to spend some time anticipating the consequences of their decisions, whether how to market a product or what to do about unanticipated consequences. Interestingly enough, this story has a happy ending. Early in 1985, Tylenol regained the market share it enjoyed prior to the tragedy, suggesting that they must have handled the issue of public trust rather well.

Consequences must be anticipated in both the long term and the short term. Ask, from an ethical perspective, what is the worst possible consequence; what is its probability; what can we do if Murphy's Law prevails; are there factors or forces beyond our control; and what or who are they? In sum, there is an ethical bottom line. It, too, can be calculated.

Summary

In these rapidly changing times, characterized by global competition, rising expectations, and unprecedented social problems, it is too much to expect that MNCs or the business community in general will make all the right decisions all the time. If, however, business executives let it be known that they affirm the ethical side of enterprise and demonstrate some effort to achieve it, they might at least be awarded an "A" for effort. There is a joke attributed to physicians: "The operation was a success, but the patient died." Similarly, corporate executives might be measured by the **process followed** rather than the undesirable **consequence suffered.**

AN ETHICAL DILEMMA FOR MULTINATIONAL CONSULTING

William W. Bain, Jr.

I believe that a large segment of the management consulting industry is in the midst of an ethical dilemma. This dilemma was created by the emergence, during the last couple of decades, of the kind of practice called strategy consulting. The dilemma becomes even more intense as strategic consulting becomes more and more a multinational business.

Before these developments, management consulting firms were rarely called on by their corporate clients to be directly involved in their key strategic decisions. They might do market studies, or studies of compensation, or assessments to predict where a certain technology was headed, or even recommendations on organizational structure. But although these studies can be very useful to clients, they do not have a clear, significant impact on strategic actions and decisions.

Let me take a minute to explain why I say that. Of all the options open to a corporation, maybe 10 percent of them will have 90 percent of the impact on a company's performance. In my view, an action or decision has to fall within that 10 percent to be called strategic. Strategic decisions also normally involve a significant commitment of resources -- for example, investment in a new plant, entry into a new business, or sale of a division of a company. And once that major allocation of resources has been made, you cannot just turn around and undo the decision. That is how strategy is usually defined: highly leveraged resource allocation decisions that are nearly irreversible in the short term.

Management consulting firms were rarely involved in these kinds of strategic actions until a couple of firms showed that there were some valuable analytical techniques and business principles that could be consistently applied when you develop strategy. Because these methods were so effective, client companies began to realize that outside consultants could, under certain circumstances, make valuable contributions in the strategy development process.

For consulting firms, strategy consulting became a very attractive business because, obviously, the fees that clients will pay for work that has strategic impact on their company are significantly higher than the fees they will pay for consulting services that have much less leveraged influence on their performance.

So, with the creation of this new, more lucrative kind of consulting, it was only natural that virtually every consulting firm in the business, and some who were not in the business, decided they would be strategy consultants. Of course, some of these firms were really doing strategic consulting, and some of the firms just renamed the kind of work they were already doing.

Obviously, the popularity of strategy consulting did not wipe out the more traditional kind of management consulting. In a traditional practice, most consulting firms build their reputations and their client bases on the strength of their industry expertise. The normal course is for a firm to become highly knowledgeable about various industries -- the more, the better. This knowledge base is constantly being expanded and updated as a normal result of the work being done for clients in these industries. The firm is then able to attract other clients because of its experience and sell those clients the expertise it has built up through previous client work.

Now that may sound like the perfect perpetual motion money machine -- the more clients you have, the more you learn about their industries, and the more you learn about their industries, the more clients in that industry you can attract. And, in fact, the management consulting industry overall has done very well following this practice.

But when this approach is used in <u>strategy</u> consulting, a serious problem develops because the traditional consulting approach and strategy consulting do not, in my opinion, make a good ethical mix.

The reason is that the heart of any effective strategy has to be a proprietary <u>competitive</u> strategy, in other words, a strategy that is designed to give your client a sustainable competitive <u>advantage</u>. You are trying to devise ways to put his competitors at a permanent <u>disadvantage</u>. This always reminds me of the Oscar Wilde quote: "It isn't enough that I succeed; my enemies must fail."

The reason you want to give your client an improved competitive advantage is that it has been shown beyond a doubt that the long-term profitability of a company is determined <u>primarily</u> by its relative competitive performance; that is, how it satisfies the needs of its customers, as defined by those customers, <u>relative</u> to how its competitors satisfy those needs. So if a so-called strategy study or assignment does not have as one of its principal objectives leaving the client with a sustained, competitive advantage over particular competitors in particular markets, then one of the central ingredients of strategy is missing.

Of course, this is much easier said than done. In fact, effective, proprietary competitive strategies are hard to find, and one of the main reasons is the lack of sufficient commitment by the management consulting firms who are supposed to be developing them or, that is, who are supposedly helping their clients gain permanent advantage over their competitors. I believe that commitment must be nothing less than total.

Let me give you a simple analogy. Suppose you have been done a grievous wrong by someone and, in fact, that person has it in his power to completely wipe you out financially. But you do have a way to protect yourself, and that is to sue. So you hire the best law firm you can find to represent you, and you proceed to file suit. But as the case progresses, you discover that, lo and behold, your own law firm is also representing that scoundrel you are suing. The firm may give you all kinds of assurances, but I wonder if you would feel that this firm is doing absolutely everything it can to press your case, represent your interests, and defeat your opponent. I do not think I would feel very confident of that. Of course, that is a situation that should never arise under the ethical standards of the legal profession.

That is not the case in management consulting. In our profession, we have firms that attempt to do strategy work for their clients, but that still follow the traditional approach of building industry expertise by working for many competing clients. I believe a firm cannot have the partisan attitude necessary to give one client a sustainable advantage over one of its competitors when the same consulting firm is working equally hard for the <u>competitor</u> trying to put the first client at a competitive <u>disadvantage</u>. In the business of developing proprietary competitive strategies, you cannot sit on both sides of the same table.

At this point you are probably wondering how, as a member of a strategy consulting firm, I can cast stones at my profession. Well, in the first place, I am trying not to cast stones. I may have some critical things to say, but I also am fully aware that many of the firms in my profession have been in this business much longer than we have, and they would not have survived and prospered all those years if they had not been following practices that were essentially ethical -- and practices that were of value to their clients.

At the same time, I do feel that the emerging importance of strategy consulting has raised a very clear conflict of interest question. In many ways, it has been a simple question for our firm to answer because we faced it at the time we were founded and before we were committed to the conventional approach. We started our firm 12 years ago to provide our clients with proprietary competitive strategies. So we decided from the very beginning to follow what, in the consulting industry, is a radical policy: we would not work for directly competing companies. This was one of our founding principles, and today, with approximately one thousand people working for us worldwide, we are still the only major consulting firm that does not work with competing clients.

Over the past few years, the ethical dilemma I have described has become more acute. That is because the consulting profession was put under real economic pressure during the recession of the early 1980's. People were scrambling for business, and it was natural for the industry specialist firms to go to their strength, which was selling a potential client a demonstrated solution to a problem, a solution they knew would work because they had used it with some of his or her competitors. As a result of this trend, one observer of the profession has found that the title "industry specialist" is the fastest growing title in consulting. But at the same time these firms were intensifying their industry specialization approach, they also were attempting to move into the attractive, high-margin segment of the business called strategy consulting. I do not envy them the problems they face in doing both.

I do, however, see two possible options for resolving such problems. One option would be to take the total commitment approach and make the decision not to work for directly competing companies.

The other would involve appropriate disclosure, just as you should have in any dealing with a client or customer. By appropriate disclosure, I mean that as a consulting firm, you have a major responsibility for shaping the expectations of your client and making sure he understands what he is getting and what he is not getting from his association with you.

Some firms attempt to do this. For example, here is a quote from the literature of a large consulting firm that has been in the business many years and has built an extensive practice around the world. At the end of a passage describing the benefits of their industry expertise and the communications network among their offices, it says, "Thus there is a constant interchange of information, experience, and personnel among our offices. A major exception to the foregoing practice arises because we do not decline to serve a new or existing client simply because that organization competes with another client of ours. In those circumstances, we follow well established procedures designed to ensure that the interests of all clients involved are fully protected. Thus, we hold in strict confidence any proprietary information that has been developed specifically for a given client, and that could be detrimental to that client if used or known by others."

It seems to me this firm faces a big task in attempting to compartmentalize and keep confidential a vast amount of data developed by a great number of consulting studies. But that problem is not the point anyway. It is not an information issue. That is a straw man. Approproate disclosure, in my opinion, would be: 1) We would be glad to work on a strategy for you, but it cannot include competitive strategy because we cannot be totally committed to your competitive success in this industry. This is because we also have to protect the interests of your competitors; or 2) We can help you develop a competitive strategy, but you have to understand it is not in our firm's best interest for you to really gain a permanent advantage over your competitors, who are also our clients. You should also know that after having done a competitive strategy for you, we will, if we can, develop a competitive strategy for the company that is your most serious competitor. When we do, we will have more experience than when we did it for you. Therefore, it is only fair for you to know the odds are that it will be a better strategy than the one we did for you, and we will help him more in defeating you than we helped you in defeating him.

That is a clear communication. At that point, the client understands what he is getting as well as you do.

I realize that the conflict of interest policy I am talking about still represents a radical departure from the accepted norms in our industry, and the appropriate disclosure I have suggested would hardly be a realistic sales pitch for a consulting firm to adopt. In fact, I do not think my suggestions in themselves are going to bring about any revolution in our profession. I do count on the forces of the marketplace, however, to make the ultimate judgment on the proper standard of conduct. I believe the free market will probably cause one of two things to happen. A large enough number of firms will adopt the exclusive commitment approach to their clients that this will become the dominant ethical standard of the industry. That is one possibility.

The other possibility , which I believe is more likely, is that some firms will not be able to adjust to the change in the industry -- maybe because they are so inextricably committed to some aspect of their current practice. They will avoid the dilemma which the change poses by not incorporating the change into their practices and by not doing proprietary competitive strategy and, therefore, not really practicing strategy consulting. As a result, you will gradually see two distinctly different segments of the industry emerging, if not two different industries.

I believe this is more likely to happen because there is a large and valuable consulting practice which benefits from industry specialization and, therefore, will not be abandoned. At the same time, it does not comfortably exist side by side with strategy consulting in the same firm. As potential clients understand this distinction more and more clearly, they will discriminate among firms on this basis. This will create a new segmentation in the consulting industry and eventually eliminate the dilemma for us.

CHAPTER FIVE

CHURCH ACTIVISM AND THE MULTINATIONAL CORPORATION

TIMOTHY H. SMITH
Executive Director
Interfaith Center on Corporate Responsibility
New York City, New York

J. PHILIP WOGAMAN
Professor of Christian Social Ethics
Wesley Theological Seminary
Washington, DC

RAFAEL D. PAGAN
President
Nestle Coordination Center for Nutrition, Inc.
and
Chairman
Pagan International
Washington, DC

JAMES ARMSTRONG
Senior Vice President
Pagan International
Washington, DC

OLIVER F. WILLIAMS
Associate Professor in Management and Co-Director
Center for Ethics and Religious Values in Business
Department of Management
University of Notre Dame
Notre Dame, Indiana

THE CHURCH CORPORATE RESPONSIBILITY MOVEMENT: FIFTEEN YEARS LATER

Timothy H. Smith

For decades the public has focused on the responsibilities and abuses of America's corporations. Whether years ago and about child labor or working conditions in the meat packing industry or the right to organize collectively and bargain with management, or more recent and about equal employment opportunities and environmental issues, discussions concerning the role and responsibilities of the business community have a long history. In the last twenty years, the transnational corporation has been "discovered," and its impact has been under careful scrutiny.

However, since 1970, there has been a new and active voice advocating corporate social responsibility on the part of America's business, the voice of the religious community. America's churches, which had played an important role in other struggles for social justice, began to raise very specific social justice issues with corporations. These churches did so as religious institutions concerned about the impact of business on society and the need for a new brand of ethics in business life. Moreover, they also entered this area as stockholders, as investors with literally billions of dollars of stocks and bonds in pension funds and endowments. As participants in the economy and owners of a "piece of the rock," churches felt the responsibility of being faithful stewards of this invested wealth. Churches realized the obligation to study the ways in which they made profits from their investments and the need to put their social values and pronouncements on the same table as their stock portfolio. In 1971, the Episcopal church introduced the first church-sponsored shareholder resolution. GM was challenged regarding its South African investments.

Over the fifteen year period from 1970 to 1985, there has been a tremendous growth in church advocacy with corporations. The issues have ranged from South Africa to toxic waste disposal, from infant formula abuse to equal employment opportunity, from corporate involvement in the nuclear arms race to plant closings. The approaches include dialogue with management, research, shareholder resolutions, petitioning institutional investors for support, divestment of securities, and on rare occasions, consumer boycotts. Fifteen years ago the discussion about the role of the church in business life would have been a theoretical discussion. Today the church is attempting to be a very real factor, an interest group, impacting business decisions.

This is a new reality for business leaders -- a reality some welcome, others are confounded by, and still others vigorously oppose. Yet it is one of the forces and trends that deserves the attention and understanding of business, for the churches have shown they will be involved over a long, long term.

Why has church involvement in the economic arena grown so substantially? The recent draft of the Roman Catholic Bishops' Pastoral Letter on the Economy describes the thinking clearly and rationally. Economic decisions have a tremendous impact on all of our lives. It is an obligation of the church to raise social and ethical questions concerning business decisions that further or retard the movement toward greater social and economic justice. Moreover, the church as investor participates in the profits made by the business community, and thus has an obligation to monitor the important decisions made by companies in which they invest.

The Reaction

Business reactions to church corporate responsibility activity vary widely. Chemical Bank, Johnson & Johnson, Bank of America, Bristol-Myers, GM, or Exxon would characterize our relationship as open, helpful, and something from which both groups learn. One company described the church as its social and ethical early warning system. In the case of Nestle, a formerly confrontational style has now turned to a creative working partnership, as church and company work together on the application of the Code of Conduct for Infant Formula. Other companies might well decry the unfairness of the pressure, criticize the self-righteousness of the church, and characterize the pressure as a nuisance rather than an asset. A very few companies might echo the 1970's charges of Castle & Cook that the Interfaith Center for Corporate Responsibility (ICCR) was a Marxist-Leninist front organization. However, nearly all of the companies with which we have dealt understand that the voice of the church is a new and continuing reality in their lives.

The Maturing of Church Corporate Responsibility Advocacy

Church involvement in shareholder advocacy is over 15 years old now. What are the lessons learned and the wisdom that has evolved over this fifteen-year period? What has been the impact of this religious advocacy in economic life? Has it been necessary for the conscience of the church but relatively ineffective in impacting business decisions? Or is the church advocacy having an effect in the boardrooms of America's corporations? How has that advocacy changed, become more publicly accepted?

There are myriads of lessons that have been learned over the last two decades, and each of the lessons and observations is worthy of a chapter. Let me provide them in headline form:

1. It is important for the church to continue to use a balanced combination of persuasion and pressure, appeals to virtue and appeals to self-interest, quiet petitioning and vigorous advocacy. The door always needs to be open for quiet diplomacy and conversation, but the influence of those conversations is considerably more if a company knows public pressure waits in the wings. Many people in business have explained to us that they are often unable to make a decision solely on the basis that it is ethically right if it cannot also be argued that it is in the company's long-term self-interest.

2. It is important to be committed to this advocacy for the long term. The church, the company, and the public all need to know that business is not just experiencing the latest fad. For example, churches have worked on the infant formula issue for almost a decade and on South Africa for twenty years. In some cases that has meant that a relationship established with a company on a given issue has endured for over a decade and has gone through a variety of phases.

3. Careful, documented research is vital. To be credible with business and the public, the church has to have done its homework and speak with specific expertise on an issue. The church sometimes has an image problem of being a well-intentioned do-gooder. This image is dispelled and our effectiveness enhanced if we speak with knowledge and authority.

4. One of the real strengths the church contributes to the public debate is an ethical awareness, an ability to ask human questions of economic decisions. The Roman Catholic Bishops' <u>Pastoral Letter on the Economy</u> is an excellent example of the necessity of raising ethical questions in economic life. Whom does an economic decision benefit, whom does it hurt?

5. The church has learned how to negotiate more effectively with business, to press toward a central goal, but be willing to compromise when necessary. In the early years, church representatives were adept at describing the social

issue facing the company. Over the years we have become more experienced in being more precise in what we wanted the company to do and in bargaining with management. For example, between one-fourth and one-third of the church shareholder resolutions now filed are withdrawn when negotiated agreements are made. When church representatives participated in the negotiations with Nestle for days, we sat and reviewed literally scores of details related to Nestle marketing practices in the Third World. The end result was a compromise agreement that had numerous parts, dealing with samples, gifts to doctors, advertising, etc.

6. It is important for the church to be a leader and in the forefront, but not at the expense of alienation from our own constituencies. We speak with a much stronger voice when, for example:

> the bishops receive feedback all around the country on the draft of the pastoral letter;
>
> a boycott of a company's products is not led by church headquarters, but has hundreds of thousands of local church-goers involved; and
>
> a church's pension fund divestment of stock because a company makes nuclear weapons is repeated by numerous local churches.

7. It is important to celebrate our achievements. There have been numerous 'success stories' when the church's voice made a significant difference in corporate decisions. These deserve to be celebrated. For example, churches have successfully petitioned scores of banks to stop lending to the South African government. Nestle, American Home Products, Abbott, and Bristol-Myers have all agreed to work within the WHO/UNICEF Code related to infant formula. We believe compliance with the Code will protect the health and lives of hundreds of thousands of infants. In response to church shareholder initiatives, scores of companies have agreed to report their statistics and progress on equal employment opportunity. These are but a few examples of the many that deserve to be celebrated.

8. Perhaps one of the most encouraging signs of the maturity of church corporate responsibility work has been the outpouring of interest and support by so many institutional investors. In the early 1970's, it was considered controversial for a university, foundation or pension fund to vote their proxies. The church was a voice in the wilderness. Now

hundreds of institutuions regularly review, study, and vote on church-sponsored shareholder resolutions. This is considered a necessity by any socially responsible investor. In fact, it is now considered inadequate by many investors to simply react to shareholder resolutions. More and more universities, foundations, insurance companies, state and city pension funds, and trade unions are writing companies, meeting with top management, publicly announcing their positions, or divesting of securities. In 1985, the New York City Employees Retirement System (with $8.5 billion in investments) filed shareholder resolutions with 20 companies and solicited the voting support of the pension funds of other cities and states. Many resolutions this year received over 10% of the vote, and one by New York City received 23%. It is no exaggeration to say that institutional investors worth over $200 billion are expressing corporate responsibility concerns with companies in which they invest. The funds of TIAA-CREF, the State of California, and the City of New York alone own over $100 billion in their portfolios. In the 1970's, investor activism was considered a questionable departure from the Wall Street Rule (sell your stock if you do not like a management decision). In 1985, it is an accepted mainstream fact of life. In fact, institutions with tens of billions of dollars in investments are taking the even stronger step of divesting securities in companies which support apartheid in South Africa. This list is impressive and shows the depth of feelings on the South African issue. In short, the voice of the church represented in the 1970's has now been joined by a chorus asking banks and companies to act responsibly. These are also numerous new allies with which the churches can make common cause.

9. It is important to commend corporations which take leadership and act responsibly. ICCR members try to let companies know when we appreciate the action they have taken. On occasion, churches have even filed shareholder resolutions commending companies. The corporate responsibility movement is not anti-corporate or anti-business. It is calling on business to act with the public's interest in mind, and we must commend those decisions that display that sensitivity.

10. Churches have learned to work in partnership with business on particular issues. For example, we are looking for investment opportunities with insurance companies to rebuild our cities. We are working together with the infant formula industry to encourage implementation of the baby formula code. We are looking at Third World health needs with pharmaceutical companies and finding ways to work together

to provide better health care.

These reflections on the past fifteen years attempt to describe a church movement learning from its experience, committed to increased research and action, surrounded by new investor support, more experienced in campaigning and negotiating, and with an impressive track record of achievements.

Implications for the Company

There are many ways in which companies can react to and utilize the process of church advocacy:

* as an opportunity for joint learning, constructive action, and solving problems together. For example, recently church representatives met with the top management of a major bank to discuss ways in which human rights criteria would be taken into account in international loan decisions;

* as an early warning system which can be used internally to interpret some of society's new issues and to accelerate action within the company;

* to show how a company has a new set of expectations itself -- that it wants to minimize social injury and maximize its positive social contribution and supports the concept that management will be graded on a social bottom line as well as financial returns; and/or

* to show corporate leadership. This is an opportunity for business leaders to develop new models to deal creatively with social issues such as South Africa or comparable worth, and not simply have to react to issues put before them. For example, some members of the pharmaceutical industry are now developing guidelines about marketing and promotion in Third World countries. Their action is a wise one, for they know that dependence on the status quo may well lead to an international code passed by the World Health Organization.

Should there be a separation of church and business as there is separation of church and state? No! We need each other too much and have too much to learn from each other. Our free enterprise system needs creative ideas and checks and balances on corporations too much. The church cannot retreat on this issue as is witnessed to in the Bishops' <u>Pastoral Letter</u>. And as shareholders, churches have an obligation to look at the social bottom line as well as the financial return provided by our investments. We hope that church advocacy with corporations has matured and become more effective, responsible, and seasoned. Certainly, it has shown its staying power, its ability to continue faithfully over the long haul. And just as certainly, the activities of the church signal new expectations of business from the public and institutional investors. We believe it also provides an opportunity for business to show leadership on the critical social issues of our times.

REFLECTIONS ON CHURCH ACTIVISM AND TRANSNATIONAL CORPORATIONS

J. Philip Wogaman

Sometimes, when church activists and corporate representatives find themselves in an adversarial relationship, there is a lack of mutual understanding of one another's basic motivations. Sometimes it takes a long time to get beyond fundamental misperceptions. Sometimes we are reminded of the truth of Fr. John Courtney Murray's observation that genuine disagreement is a rare achievement!

Despite occasional impressions to the contrary, church activists are not basically motivated by ideologies that are foreign to the faith they profess. They are not covert Marxists. The church exists by virtue of its faith in God as center and source of all being, whose love for humanity is deeper than all human caring, and whose intention it is that people should relate to one another as a family of love and justice. On the basis of this faith, the church has to be passionately and actively involved in the economic and political life of the world if it is to be true to the faith. Whatever contributes to human good is a part of the church's mission; whatever diminishes human life is to be resisted. The church can be mistaken -- I am sure it often is. But it cannot be aloof from the world's troubles without denying its very reason for existence. When they perceive that workers are being exploited, that Third World babies are suffering because of excessive marketing of infant formula, that people are dying prematurely because of lax standards of occupational safety or a casual attitude toward the processing, transportation, or use of dangerous chemicals, or that racial oppression is buttressed directly or indirectly by business firms in South Africa, church activists can be expected to speak and act, sometimes in very controversial ways.

Business leaders, on the other hand, do not think of themselves as cold, heartless Ebenezer Scrooges, out to squeeze the last penny out of the market, with no thought for human good. Doubtless there are businesspeople like that. But businesspeople are also creative and involved directly in producing and distributing the things people need. No doubt, most think of themselves as facilitating economic processes on a world scale in such a way as to build up the sum total of human good.

There is no question that transnational corporations are a major force in the world today and that their role is likely to continue and to expand for the foreseeable future. Undoubtedly, transnational corporations have done both helpful and harmful things. They have helped facilitate trade and development in many parts of the world. Most of their products are useful, some indispensable. They have also contributed their share of evil -- with stories to be catalogued from Bhopal, India to Santiago, Chile to Pretoria, South Africa. They can expect an alert world church to be "on their case" when their immense and growing power is registered against and not for human good. They will not always hear applause for positive accomplishments, although the church needs to be aware of their need for appreciation as well as for criticism.

Ethically sensitive leaders of transnational corporations can expect church activists to make three very special contributions to corporate social responsibility.

First, the church can contribute a largely disinterested perspective on economic questions. Of course, nobody's perspective is entirely disinterested. Individual church members have concrete economic interests they often have difficulty placing in perspective, and churches, as institutions, also have material interests. But the raison d'etre of churches transcends even their own institutional interests, and individual Christians, when they act in behalf of the church, are challenged to rise above their own self-interest. The true interest of the churches is the well-being of the world's people. If they have a bias, it is toward the poor, who often are forgotten when practical people set about to conduct the world's business. The disinterested perspective, amended by a bias for the poorest, most vulnerable members of society, is a perspective that is badly needed.

Second, the church exists worldwide. It has direct access to people in almost every nook and cranny of this globe. Through mission activity and ecumenical relationships, Christians of every land are linked to Christians of every other land. Consequently, the churches sometimes know more about how given practices and policies affect people in remote areas than do those who make policies in corporate boardrooms.

Third, the church, through selective use of its own economic power and through advocacy in political arenas, can help to remove the market advantages of unethical practices wherever these occur. That point needs to be understood very carefully. Transnational corporations, powerful though they doubtless are, are also subject to the disciplines of the market. They are competing with similar enterprises for sources of materials, for skilled labor and brainpower, for technologies, for a share of the market. Competition in the marketplace is never as perfect as some businesspeople would have you think. But it is very real all the same, and insofar as it <u>is</u> a reality, the market rewards unethical, unjust conduct whenever it helps increase sales or cut costs. That point was brought home to me through intense invlovement in the infant formula controversy. I was very actively engaged in seeking commitment by the Nestle Corporation to the World Health Organization Code of Marketing of Breastmilk Substitutes. The company made that commitment, and through service of the Muskie Commission, I found myself in a position to monitor the company's performance personally. They have done rather well, everything considered. But since so much of the world's attention had been focused on that one company, its competitors were able to take advantage of Nestle's new marketing restraints. The ending of exploitative marketing practices needed to be throughout the whole industry -- the whole market -- not just one company.

Corporate executives are not always receptive to this point, but I am pleased to note a recent comment by Elmer W. Johnson, general counsel and vice president of General Motors. He wrote that:

> The competitive market system very promptly penalizes and ultimately bankrupts the firm that would go very far in promoting social goals at the expense of private profit. Thus, when there are important social interests that the market fails to protect, even with the application of long-term enlightened corporate self-interest, management may have an obligation to support efficient government intervention or to cooperate with church and other groups to advance particular social reforms such as those embodied in the Sullivan Principles. Management should then utilize its experience and judgment in suggesting the best means for removing or overcoming competitive impediments to corporate social responsibility.

Doubtless the Sullivan principles do not go far enough, but Mr. Johnson's main point is valid and wise: those who really care about corporate social responsibility will be the first to want some constraints, some guidelines, some regulations to govern the market. Otherwise, unethical behavior will be rewarded by the market.

Mr. Johnson is also perceptive in noting the contribution of the churches. At their best, the corporate responsibility campaigns by the churches have sought to mobilize grassroots Christian involvement in market regulation. Sometimes that has gone as far as use of boycotts; more often, it has been a serious moral pressure. Sometimes churches flirt with inviting companies in the United States to violate laws prohibiting "combinations in restraint of trade" -- or so the lawyers contend. But antitrust laws were neither established to shield unethical practices nor to make it difficult for companies to agree not to do together what none can do alone to protect the wider public good.

Sometimes just by changing the climate of customs and values in which business is conducted, churches can be a potent catalyst for the right kind of industry-wide agreements or understandings. At other times, churches may need to actively seek legal regulation. I should think transnational corporations would be the first to seek effective regulation, both at national and international levels.

Corporations are not, of course, the only kinds of institutions that are capable of sin in this "fallen" world. Even churches, even church leaders and church activists, can be less than true to the implications of their faith. Don't we all fail to live up even to the good that we know to be good?

In their interactions with corporations, church activists must also be held accountable to high standards of integrity. They must be honest. They must avoid self-righteousness. They must do their homework or acknowledge the full ranges of their ignorance. They must relate to corporate representatives as human beings who are also the children of God. They should use raw power and coercive tactics sparingly, even though it is sometimes necessary for them to resist evils forcefully and directly. I believe they should use persuasion first, while remaining open to a deeper understanding of the dilemmas business representatives may face. Their mobilization of the power of the church in adversarial action should be as a last resort. When pushed to this last resort, the church's actions should be aimed toward the concrete removal of the corporate offense and toward a kind of reconciliation. Corporate leaders should not be in doubt as to the fundamental good will of church leaders, just as they should be clear about the church's intention to stay with an issue until it can be resolved on an ethical basis.

BUSINESS ETHICS AND THE CHURCHES

Rafael D. Pagan

When I was called by Nestle, early in 1981, to develop and manage an ethical strategy that would bridge the gap created by hostility, lack of trust, and ideological paranoia on both sides of the infant formula issue, there seemed to be little hope for an amiable, fair end to the controversy. The facts had been obscured by emotion and anecdotes by the more radical, politically-oriented critics; while the company was not listening to the main concerns of the more moderate, church-oriented critics of conscience.

After several early public relations disasters, Nestle was acting with timidity towards the media and the public. It thus became viewed as devious and deceitful. Its refusal to establish constructive dialogue with the more responsible church critics made the company's motivations and goals questionable in the eyes of the public.

The company believed, moreover, that its critics were operating from a flexible base of standards that could never be satisfied. Some in Nestle viewed the issue as a public relations nuisance, rather than as a public policy question with profound ethical roots. Attempts by two of the world's largest public relations firms to "solve" the problem with public relations palliatives seemed to backfire.

A new approach to the problem was needed. A bridge had to be built between the antagonists.

Nestle's problem had been primarily one of style rather than substance. It had seen the potential danger in advertising infant formula through mass media in the Third World and had changed its advertising policy before the boycott started. It thus had begun to revise its infant formula marketing policies. But there was a feeling among some in management that to make those changes known would be seen as an admission that something had gone wrong with the product. Later, it was felt that the announcement of further changes, while the boycott was still on, would be seen as yielding under pressure.

I believe the United Methodist Church sensed the situation. Even though some in that Church were already boycotting Nestle, it appointed a Task Force under Dr. Philip Wogaman to ascertain the facts on the issue and to seek, if possible, a constructive resolution of the conflict.

We in Nestle felt that, with the approval by the World Health Organization (WHO) of a Recommended Code on Marketing of Breastmilk Substitutes and the appointment of task forces by the Methodists, the Episcopalians, the Baptists, and the Lutherans to study the problem, a bridge over the moat was possible.

Three ethical principles guided our public policy in dealing with the issue:

First, Nestle had to show openness. We had to open windows for the public to peer inside the company and watch the evolution of a changing marketing policy for infant formula. At the same time, Nestle had to listen attentively to its critics.

Second, the evolution of that policy could be accomplished only through dialogue with those church groups that were willing to listen and to work with the company in a joint effort on behalf of improved infant formula nutrition and health and toward the resolution of the confrontation.

Finally, a unique system of public accountability establishing basic standards and rules of right conduct and practices for the company to follow had to be developed, along with an independent mechanism to monitor compliance with those practices. To this end, the Nestle Infant Formula Audit Commission under Senator Edmund Muskie was conceived and created. This pioneer concept in social audit was developed in close consultation with church leaders, ethicists, the United Methodist Task Force, academicians, and others.

Moreover, this system of corporate accountability demanded an equal degree of responsibility and facts from the critics.

The conflict ended in a satisfactory manner for both sides, and a cooperative effort was initiated with the churches to see that the WHO Code was implemented in all countries in the Third World. We were happy when Douglas Johnson, the leader of the Nestle Boycott, stated on January 24, 1985 at a news conference announcing the suspension of the boycott that, "Nestle has moved forward to become a model for the whole industry, a model which creates a new standard for corporate behavior."

In retrospect, there are several points I want to make on the issue of business ethics and the churches, for there are lessons to be learned that we must face honestly and with understanding.

I believe that engaging in a prolonged acrimonious public polemic costs both business and churches their credibility, and costs churches their mystic aura and their charitable image. Both church and corporate leaders sometimes find themselves poorly advised. Public blunders are made that prove costly on both sides. Deception and zealotry are present. Truth, tolerance, and civility are lost in the turmoil. I still believe that, despite its constructive settlements, the infant formula conflict was a very costly struggle in terms of time and resources and resulted in little benefit to the children of the world.

Those in the churches who opted for constructive dialogue helped build the foundation for precedent-setting conflict resolution between business and churches. The boycott alone could not have ended the controversy without such dialogue. Indeed, some in the company considered the boycott merely a bothersome nuisance that eventually would peter out. And to some of the critics, the boycott was a rallying cry for the "people of the world." Under these circumstances, it took rare courage and a respect for moral and ethical principles for senior church leadership and the company's top management to reach an agreement.

I also question the wisdom and the ethical principles involved in "setting an example" with just one company in the industry. The critics felt that once they had humbled one company, the other companies would cave in. Events have proven them wrong.

Finally, I hope that business is learning that, even though management in a company may believe that its marketing practices are based on sound science and are in strict compliance with the law of the land, its failure to listen to the world around it can be a critical mistake. The way to the mind of the people is through the heart. Understanding public perceptions and sensitivity to their perceived needs is a necessary attribute for today's top management.

By concentrating on confrontation for so long -- from 1970 to 1981 -- the infant formula industry, as well as its most obstinate critics, lost a tremendous opportunity and much time to really work together with the mainline churches and the world's health and nutrition institutions to develop joint, positive programs of action. Moreover, concentrating on the United Nations code approach has not served humanity well. The ideal ends envisioned by the WHO in dealing with infant nutrition and health education have been badly diluted. Some saw in the Code the beginning of a new era of responsibility. But only a handful of countries are following the WHO Code. Many who provided loud and insistent support are virtually ignoring the Code. The record is not a happy one. The Code's guidelines can come alive only through the cooperative efforts of responsible business firms and responsible critics alike.

I fear that the same mistakes that were made by the infant formula manufacturers and their critics are in danger of being made in other areas of potential conflict. As an immediate example, must the pharmaceutical industry and its critics go through yet another struggle over a WHO Code? Such a struggle only obscures the realities of the far more important daily struggle to bring health services to rural and village areas of the Third World.

Vaccines arrive and sit in the mid-day sun until they are useless; power outages destroy refrigerated drugs; a necessary warehouse that was promised is never built; health workers lose village confidence because they have no supplies; gasoline is lacking to get health services to the poor; transport breaks down and turns to rust for want of spare parts or a mechanic. These are the everyday health problems of the Third World. It is they that should be faced and resolved by ethical people.

Within this complex system of disease and health, the availability and utilization of pharmaceuticals plays a major role. They provide a mobile, cost-effective means of curing many diseases that affect the Third World. Indeed, because of the large capital expenditures required to develop extensive health care facilities and manpower for the secondary and tertiary levels of health systems, pharmaceuticals may be the only possible method of intervention for some time to come. Pharmaceuticals are essential in improving health in the developing world. Both private and public sectors are essential in achieving this goal.

The public/private cooperation required in health care systems is threatened, however, by the current acrimonious debate, both on the conduct of the pharmaceutical corporations in the Third World and on the economics of drug research and production. The debate has been fueled by charges and counter-charges from both sides of the issue. Industry and its critics have each produced a "pharmaceutical code" to throw at each other.

There have been no systematic programs on the part of the United States government, academic research centers, industry, churches, or other private institutions to develop and disseminate a factual base of information regarding these issues. Will these institutions live up to the moral challenge? Some of us who dealt with the most heated phases of the infant formula conflict until its resolution have an eerie feeling of hopelessness. We are haunted by deja vu images.

However, the United States government has a unique opportunity to offer positive alternatives to the regulatory approach of the UN to the world's problems. The health issue is an extremely important one where our government could take the lead in initiating an "Entente for Peace" with the Third World -- an Entente that could begin looking at, among other things, health issues of the poor countries. A comprehensive examination of their health systems would provide a timely and appropriate beginning for such an Entente where the private and the public sector, churches, academia, ethical institutions, and corporations could work together for the benefit of the poor of the Third World and for their own interests.

Corporations cannot be successful unless they are ethical. What that means to me is if corporations are to be accepted in the Third World, they must earn the right to operate in those societies and their communities. They must be sensitive to other cultures and traditions but, most importantly, they must see the inherent dangers involved in the introduction of modern technologies, new products, modern advertising, and product promotion techniques to societies with large masses of poor, illiterate people or where there is no developed and effective health and social infrastructure or control. Under those conditions, the safest products available to the public in the First World could be harmful to those who struggle for subsistence in the steamy jungles of Africa and of Latin America or in the refugee camps bordering Cambodia.

I have faith in the best that the free enterprise system can offer and in the institutions of our society -- businesses, churches, academia. Despite abuses of corporate power by some business leaders as reported recently in the media, I know that business leaders do not get to lead major corporations unless they have a strong sense of values and principles and unless they are open and fair-minded. That is why there is no difficulty in their understanding and working well with church leaders and the leaders of other ethical institutions. They are involved in the boards of churches, academia, foundations, and many other high-principled institutions. A recent book on corporate ethics suggested that business is involved in all aspects of the American society in a positive way and that the founding fathers were neither saints nor professional soldiers -- they were businessmen, lawyers, and landowners. I think we all agree that they did a pretty good job in starting this new nation.

In the Nestle experience, as well as in my experience with large agribusinesses or mining companies, companies have not hesitated to establish independent social audit systems to deal with serious ethical questions. We in business are used to accountability to various constituencies. Perhaps one of the main problems business has in its relations with critic groups is that the accountability of those groups to their ethical constituencies is not clearly perceived. This has resulted in suspicion by business on the motives of those groups that purport to represent churches. Independent audit systems that impartially hold both sides of a business-critic conflict equally accountable to a standard set of values and principles have proven to be a sound method of conflict resolution. There is a need for similar and other creative approaches in solving the conflict between the pharmaceutical, pesticide, chemical, and other industries and the groups who are attacking them. Both churches and businesses can work together to protect the best interests of the public and of the poor of the world. This is a call to fairness and to the higher values that motivate both institutions and that must be addressed on behalf of the human family.

I believe that discussions of ethics are meaningful only insofar as they lead to effective, cooperative action -- not action that makes us feel good about ourselves, but action that really helps those who most need it: the three billion people who live in poor areas of the Third World and, for that matter, in poor areas of our own country.

ACTIVISM, RELIGION, AND ECONOMIC JUSTICE

James Armstrong

Many have viewed church activism as being born in the 1950s and 1960s. During that time we witnessed the civil rights movement and the peace movement, the "new politics," the "greening of America," Father Groppi's march in Milwaukee, Martin Luther King, Jr.'s burst across the conscience of the South, and Cesar Chavez' gathering of forces in California. Wherever those persons and movements appeared, there seemed to be clerical collars present. There was a religious thread that was woven through much that was happening during that period. Many of those who looked on said, "Suddenly, religion is becoming involved." Not so. As Professor Prakash Sethi has suggested, that "suddenly" goes back generations, centuries, millennia.

In 1620, a group of people gathered on these shores and penned the Mayflower compact. It was an activist document. They were attempting to frame a community in the New World based on religious principles.

During America's pre-revolutionary days, historians suggest that colonial preachers stood in their pulpits with John Locke in one hand and the Bible in the other sowing seeds that led to independence. John Witherspoon, a prominent Presbyterian clergyman, signed the Declaration of Independence. The Abolition and Temperance movements of the nineteenth century were "religious" movements.

Late in that same century, the so-called "Social Gospel" emerged. One of the Social Gospel's leading preachers, Washington Gladden, spoke from his Columbus, Ohio pulpit about the "tainted money" of Standard Oil. He asked, "Should the church accept Standard Oil's funds for missionary purposes?" He, Josiah Strong, Charles Parkhurst, Shailer Mathews, and a handful of significant others became the Social Gospel's strong voices.

Walter Rauschenbusch, in many respects the spiritual father of the Social Gospel, wrote <u>Christianizing the Social Order</u>, <u>Christianity and the Social Crisis</u>, <u>A Theology for the Social Gospel</u>, and <u>Prayers of the Social Awakening</u>. Rauschenbusch took sharp exception to the "laissez-faire" theory of the economists. He came to the attention of President Theodore Roosevelt who read his works and invited him to the White House.

Yet, activism did not begin on the Mayflower, in colonial

America, during the Abolition and Temperance movements, or with the Social Gospel. In fact, each of these phenomena would trace its beginning back to the Scriptures, to the early experience of the Hebrew people. They appealed to the authority of Moses who felt called upon by God to identify with a people in bondage. Moses challenged the mightiest monarch of his time and pled for the slaves' freedom. The Pharoah ignored his plea, so Moses returned to those in bondage, identified with them, organized them, and led them on their march to freedom while being pursued by troops bearing the flag of Moses' own country. Activism.

There was a prophet named Elijah who considered his king utterly immoral and who called his queen a "whore" -- a relatively controversial public comment. Activism.

Amos, an unlettered but remarkably well informed herdsman of Tekoa, with trip-hammer effectiveness, talked about the transgressions of the nations surrounding Judea and Israel. They were guilty of war crimes and atrocities, of violating national borders and human rights, of social injustices and economic injustices. Amos zeroed in on his own people and accused them of selling the poor for a pair of shoes and trampling on the heads of the innocent. Activism.

There was Isaiah, a court chaplain of sorts, who identified with what was called by the Chronicler the "good reign of King Hezekiah." Hezekiah was a youthful King who opened the doors of the Temple, brushed down the cobwebs, re-lit the sacred lamps, and reconsecrated the Levites, the religious leaders of the people. Standing at his elbow, prodding, aiding, abetting through the entire process was Isaiah. A different kind of activism.

There was Jeremiah who was publicly ridiculed and later imprisoned because he dared criticize the foreign policy of his country. And there would follow Paul who was imprisoned for civil disobedience and Jesus who, according to liberation theologians, was killed as a political prisoner.

So you see, those who came to be associated with social change in this country drew their inspiration from the religious experience of an ancient people who gave them, they would say, their identity and much of their motivation.

All of this may seem planets and eons removed from those of us contemplating ethical dilemmas for multinational enterprises. Not so. In fact, there are many forms of activism finding expression today. Young people stretch their bodies across railroad tracks to stop the flow of nuclear waste in box cars;

others are arrested outside South African embassies and consulates; there are confrontations at shareholder's meetings; abortion clinics are bombed; hundreds of volunteers participate in voter registration campaigns in Mississippi's Delta or Fundamentalism's South; and there are always the idealists who picket grocery stores and banks and "defense" plants. In fact, I would guess that most of us have been and continue to be activists of one sort or another. We may try to manuever persons and programs in university senate meetings, influence school boards or city halls, or pull strings with our PAC contributions. We may take active leads in election campaigns. Apart from formal protestations and official postures, most of us are activists in our own rights.

Recently, I wrote an article for the Business and Society Review, in which I discussed the distinction between, and the importance of, institutional and conceptual activism. Institutional activism is that activism which is expressed through institutional structures -- through an agency, a board, some sort of official body. It finds its identity on the basis of a social problem, a pressing cultural issue, or its response to geo-political or socio-economic realities.

There are many such institutional expressions of activism. Perhaps the most respected body is the Department of Social Development and World Peace of the United States Catholic Conference. This particular department has wide influence and played a prominent part in the evolution of the Catholic Bishops' Pastoral Letter on Nuclear Disarmament. Now, it is deeply involved in the Pastoral Letter on Economic Justice. In the United Methodist Church there is the Board of Church and Society. In fact, all the mainline religious denominations have their own social action agencies that are designed to respond to crisis and to need.

The Interfaith Center of Corporate Responsibility (ICCR) and the Institute on Religion and Democracy (IRD), representing opposite ends of the spectrum, are well-funded and remarkably influential in the United States. The ICCR sees itself as "an organization of Church and religious investors concerned about the social impact of corporations and the application of social criteria to investments." The IRD sees itself as a necessary corrective to groups like ICCR and Clergy and Laity Concerned. It champions what it calls "democratic capitalism" and tends to walk in lock step with the Reagan administration's foreign policy while echoing its anti-Soviet rhetoric. Jerry Falwell's Moral Majority, with its strange support of Presidents Botha and Marcos, is an even more extreme expression of institutionalized activism.

It is not just the religious community, however, that has these issue-oriented bodies. There are secular groups as well: Bread for the World, La Raza, the National Committee of Right to Life, Nader's Raiders, the Sierra Club, PUSH, and the Ethics and Public Policy Center. All of these groups find their identities by making particular contributions to the development of a conscience that will somehow impact on the basis of a specific issue at a particular time thus helping direct the flow of history.

But behind the institutions, more important than the institutions, are the concepts. They become the flesh. It is the word, the idea, the commitment, the concept, that gives rise to structure. Adam Smith's Wealth of Nations in 1776: a concept. In 1848, the Communist Manifesto: a concept.

The creeds of the Church, from the early Apostles and Nicene to the modern Korean, have conceptualized those things considered central in the Christian tradition. There are particular "theologies" that appear to address specific constituencies or needs, e.g., black theology, feminist theology, liberation theology. Liberation theology -- conceptualized activism -- is viewed with suspicion if not downright hostility by the business community in the Western world.

To begin with liberation theology is not a monolithic school of thought. It comes in many shades, with many nuances and emphases. A wide variety of names, some Protestant, most Roman Catholic, are associated with it: Gutierrez, Sobrino, Segundo, Leonardo Boff, Jose Miguez-Bonino, and Rubem Alves to mention only a few. Prominent churchmen, like Cardinal Arns of Sao Paulo and Dom Helder Camara of Recife, have been associated with it. These are persons who have been influenced, in some measure, by Marxist analysis, but who draw their inspiration and authority from the messages of the Bible: God's preferential bias for the poor, the story of Exodus, the witness of the Prophets, the compassionate ministry of Jesus of Nazareth, and the significance of the cross and resurrection for the life-weary and oppressed.

Two major themes run through liberation theology: (1) God's bias on behalf of the poor as it is underscored from the Deuteronomic Code through the New Covenant; and (2) the mandate given the Church, because of God's nature and disposition, to enter into "solidarity with the poor" (a phrase that frequently falls from the lips of Pope John Paul II).

Liberation theology has tended to label capitalism in

general and transnational corporations in particular as enemies of genuine human development in the Third World. They are viewed as instruments of exploitation and greed. On the other hand, many corporate interests have come to see liberation theology as a tool in the hands of Marxist revolutionaries. The mythology is false. The stereotypes are terribly unfair and damaging. And the primary victims of the stand-off are the poor of the Third World. Somehow thoughtful persons in both camps -- that of Christian activism and that of corporate reality -- must come to see that the creation and equitable distribution of wealth are not contradictory economic processes, but rather are desirable complementary possibilities. Bridges must be built between the two worlds.

Dr. Emilio Castro, a liberation theologian in his own right, a Uruguayan who views the world from its "underside," is the newly elected general secretary of the World Council of Churches. The WCC is often accused of being a captive of liberation theology. Castro, however, has seized a series of refreshing initiatives since assuming his executive responsibilities nine months ago. He has entered into significant discussions with the chief executive officers of Nestle, S.A., concerning infant formula marketing practices in the Third World and corporate ethics in South Africa. He has visited the chief executives of GMC and Ford in Detroit and participated in cordial and constructive conversations related to the international debt crisis and corporate responsibility in South Africa. He continues to be available, opening doors, encouraging a long neglected dialogue and, where possible, building bridges.

A remarkable new chemistry is becoming evident. Fair-minded, committed activists in the religious realm and fair-minded, committed executives in the business world are moving beyond old antagonisms and are beginning to share a vision. Perhaps each group, "in solidarity with the poor," can help fulfill that vision, a vision of universal <u>human</u> development.

THEOLOGICAL ETHICS AND THE MULTINATIONAL: DIVERSE ASSESSMENTS

Oliver F. Williams

Can Multinational Businesses Alleviate Poverty in the Third World?

Academics, multinational business managers, and religious activists began discussing multinationals and poverty in the Third World under the auspices of a special seminar at the University of Notre Dame in October 1978. After six sessions, it was clear that at least one theme persisted: There is no commonagreement on what actions will actually be helpful to the truly needy of the Third World. While all would agree that no one ought to be hungry or illiterate, or die before their time, the means of achieving these important goods for the poor of the Third World are in dispute.

At root, there are dichotomous perspectives from theological ethics on the multinational, some seeing it as primarily an instrument of dependence, others envisioning it as an instrument of development. For example, Father Arthur McCormack, M.H.M., describes the multinational as "an institution which has shown outstanding capabilities in the past" and which must play a major part in solving the "vast problems that face the world for the rest of the century..."[1] Father Peter Henriot, S.J., on the other hand, is much less sanguine: "I personally am not yet convinced that the multinationals as now constituted and operating can in fact be a major force in meeting the challenge of Third World poverty."[2] He would advocate at least a partial adoption of the United Nations plan, a New International Economic Order (NIEO).

Considering multinationals as part of a global economic system, three major criticisms emerged: 1) Although most would agree that MNC's do contribute to economic growth in the Third World, critics focus on the inequitable distribution of resources which often leaves the poor without basic needs while an elite group lives in luxury. 2) Regulation, both local and national, was criticized as inadequate. Multinational advocates generally saw present regulation as inefficient, while critics argued for more government intervention. 3) An issue considered important by critics is that the poor of the Third World have no voice in the decision-making process. Participation by those who will be affected by decisions is considered crucial.[3]

A key insight from the Proceedings of the first three years of the seminar is that "a person's observation about the proper role of the multinationals may well differ depending upon the level of analysis one chooses." Three levels of analysis are evident: 1) The examination of the individual firm or enterprise (microeconomic level); 2) An analysis of multinationalsas a group (categorical level); and 3) The consideration of the multinational in the context of a global economy (systemic level).[4] The level of analysis tends to shape one's thinking. Most participants tend to see multinational corporate activity from one dominant point of view, and this point of view influences the level at which analysis takes place as well as the sort of remedies that seem appropriate to correct perceived deficiencies.

For example, consider a multinational manager who views the firm primarily from the micro point of view. This manager will perceive his world in terms of the constituencies for whom and to whom he is accountable. He comes to see things from the various stakeholders' perspectives and assumes that he has ample flexibility for responding on the local level to most problems.

Consider another person, a religious activist, for example, who views the significant unit of analysis to be the global system. This person would see problems as solved primarily through systemic change--national regulations, codes of conduct, NIEO, and so on. The firm is seen as relatively powerless to deal adequately with perceived deficiencies, and efforts are directed to broader structural change. Although direct pressure may be applied to a multinational business in some dramatic form, this strategy may be only a means of raising public consciousness so that new public policy might finally be enacted.

The experience of the seminar has been that discussion most often reaches an impasse at the point of assessing the "success" of multinational corporate activity in Third World countries. There are at least two distinct sets of criteria employed for evaluating multinationals, one set from the micro point of view, and one from the macro or systemic level of analysis.

An example from my experience independent of the seminar may illustrate how the horizon or context for judgment influences the criteria for judgment and hence the judgment itself. After spending a week visiting a number of sites at a multinational agricultural operation in a Third World country, I was impressed with the remarkable efforts being made to improve the lot of the black employees, most of whom were very poor. This MNC employed almost 30,000 workers and had made dramatic strides in housing, health care, nutrition, and wages. While there was still much to be done, I judged that, relative to others in the country, the MMC's employees were living adequately. Basic needs were being met.

While in the country, I also visited some missionaries from United States-based churches and was most impressed with their dedication to helping the poor. In relating the facts about the MNC's social programs, I had anticipated a positive response. However, I was told by a long-time missionary that she could not share my enthusiasm, for while the MNC's efforts were indeed helping some of the poor, in the long run they did more harm than good, for they only delayed the inevitable socialist revolution that would finally meet the needs of <u>all</u> of the poor.

What became clear was that I was speaking from a micro point of view in one theory of political economy, and she was speaking from quite another theory. From a systemic perspective, she had already decided that the only hope for the Third World nation was to break the economic dependence on the United States and begin to form a new socialist society. The facts that I was enthusiastically relating about an MNC's social programs served as a sad reminder for her that the key instrument of dependence was still in the land. In our discussions, we passed like ships in the night, generating more heat than light. I argued that my "micro" analysis was in the context of a development theory of political economy. Must one always begin with a systemic analysis? How bad must things be before moving from a micro point of view to a systemic analysis? Can revolutionary socialism really deliver all that it promises? Is there really any quick fix for Third World poverty?

It is a safe assumption that in any cross section of academics and multinational managers there will be some who see things primarily from a micro point of view and others from a macro or systemic point of view. It is also true that even if all perceive an issue from a systemic point of view, they may not all be seeing it from the same system. The two dominant theories of political economy of our time, Smithian and Marxian, both are likely to have adherents. Each of these theory-laden perspectives offers divergent interpretations of the same facts. Before reflecting on the import of perspectives on several important issues today, it may be helpful to review the crucial role of theologies in shaping interpretive schemes.

The Sort of World Mandated by the Christian Gospel

Whether a person looks at the MNC from a micro or macro point of view, it is helpful to call to mind that often a religious outlook shapes how managers and activists alike envision the world as it ought to be.

The Roman Catholic Church and mainline Protestant churches see their congregations as being called by God to transform the world and shape it along the lines of the way of life outlined by Christ. In his classic <u>Christ and Culture</u>, H. Richard Niebuhr calls this appropriation of the Gospel the "Christ the transformer of culture" model.[5] The theological conviction is that God's incarnate Son is present in creation sustaining it and drawing it to its fulfillment, as well as present in redemption as the one who died and rose again. History is not the arena to form a new counter-culture as the Amish might hold, or the encounter with the spirit in nature as in Hegelian philosophy, or simply a period of preparation for the final glory in heaven. Rather history is the arena where the drama of God's great deeds and peoples' responses are played out. One encounters Christ in the challenge of the situation and in history, as well as in the church and the quiet of one's own conscience.

Augustine and John Calvin stress that the gospel must influence the whole fabric of life, and in this sense they are pioneers in the transformationist mentality. The twentieth century Roman Catholic theologian Karl Rahner, S.J., writes in this transformationist vein when he sees the redemptive work of Christ actually present in individuals, cultures, and society where persons are following their best lights in leading a moral life. For Rahner, Christ is present, and God's intentions are discerned, through human reason; this knowledge is deepened and broadened with the life of the gospels. Salvation in this view is not a completely other-worldly transaction, but rather Christ (or grace) is active in converting the person in the present culture and society.

Mainline Protestant churches and the Catholic church see their mission as both ministering to the individual -- nurturing, developing character and virtue -- and transforming the world -- improving social structures to enhance social, political, and economic life.[6] This mission is achieved primarily through teaching, preaching, and the liturgy, although direct social action strategies are sometimes employed. For the churches to be effective in speaking about questions of justice in Third World countries, it is crucial that they maintain unity in the moral advice offered. This, unfortunately, has not been the case in regard to the Christian social teaching. There are two quite different approaches to change advocated by theologians and activists today: a gradual or evolutionary approach and a revolutionary approach.[7]

Theologian Gregory Baum employs the terms "radical" and "reformed" to refer to the two broad categories of activists in the churches. According to Baum, the radical envisions "a repudiation of capitalism and a struggle for a radical reconstruction of society."[8] Radical Christians "experience themselves as strangers in their own country. Faithful to Jesus and his message of justice and grace, they form spiritual counter-cultures..." "They are willing to live on the fringes of society, waiting for the moment when America will be more profoundly shaken and workers will organize their movement for socialism."[9]

When this sort of person is involved in the various strategies to apply pressure to corporations, managers might just as well face up to the fact that "no good deed will go unpunished." With the "radical" type, it is difficult to imagine how a manager could "win"; for if the ultimate goal is the downfall of the free enterprise system, no reform of that system, no matter how drastic, is likely to be satisfactory.

In contrast to the radical approach, the reformist critics will work in whatever ways possible to promote and protect human dignity, for "as disciples of Jesus they want to incarnate their spiritual vision in some concrete action."[10] To the radical, the reformist seems to have sold out to the establishment, for he or she is willing to work with the system and cooperate with its managers to advance a vision.

It may be helpful to explore some of the theological roots of the radical approach by examining the work of one of the most popular liberation theologians, Gustavo Gutierrez.[11] Father Gutierrez, writing in the context of Latin America, has been profoundly influenced by the widespread misery of his people. On a continent where military tyranny, torture, and manifold violations of human rights are common place, he calls for a new movement of social justice, liberation.

In reading the work of a religious social ethicist, the key feature to discern is how he relates the ultimate concepts to the real world he is addressing; that is, what sort of world he advocates as the vision for the faithful Christian. In the technical language of ethics, "middle axioms" mediate between ultimate concepts (liberation, salvation) and present empirical realities. What are the middle axioms of Gutierrez?

Several quotes from Gutierrez lay bare his vision of the sort of world that Christians should be striving for.

Paradoxically, what the groups in power call "advocating"

class struggle is really an expression of a will to abolish its causes, to abolish them, not cover them over, to eliminate the appropriation by a few of the wealth created by the work of the many and not to make lyrical calls to social harmony. It is a will to build a socialist society, more just, free, and human, and not a society of superficial and false reconciliation and equality.[12]

To participate in class struggle not only is not opposed to universal love; this commitment is today the necessary and inescapable means of making this love concrete. For this participation is what leads to a classless society without owners and dispossessed, without oppressors and oppressed.[13]

Focusing on the biblical mandate to build a just society that is truly human, that is, in accord with the Creator's intention, Gutierrez singles out private property as the basic impediment. The structural reform advocated by Gutierrez might be summarized by the following middle axioms:

1) Abolish private ownership of the means of production.
2) Redistribute wealth according to needs.
3) Fashion a socialist society.
4) Champion class struggle.

In Peru, Gutierrez's home, the activist priest leads a study group (Bartolome de Las Casas) and several members of that group are leaders of the Marxist coalition party known as Izquierda Unida (IU). The IU or United Left Party is widely supported by many of the poor in the urban ghettos, and the alliance came in second in the April, 1985, presidential and congressional elections. The New York Times (April 15, 1985, p. 6), reported that the private sector and middle classes of Peru view a United Left victory "with horror." It should be noted that, although a Roman Catholic, Gutierrez advocates a social vision that, in my judgment, is out of step with the teaching of the social encyclicals of the Catholic church and most mainline Protestant thinking as well. The sort of world suggested by Catholic social teaching is most often discussed under the rubric of the common good. Rather than identifying the common good with a socialist society, its middle axioms stress achieving a society where freedom and creativity flourish. Catholic social teaching portrays a vision of society that might be captured with the following middle axioms:

1) Private property is an important means for ensuring human development, but private property always has a social dimension which requires owners to consider the

best interests of the community.

2) Society ought to be structured so that those who are able might provide for themselves and their loved ones by freely employing their talents. Those who are unable to provide for their own basic needs are to be treated with full dignity and cared for by appropriate groupings of society determined by public policy.

These sort of middle axioms do not endorse any particular system of government, but allow for a wide variety of applications in different contexts and historical situations.[14]

The Relevance of the Vision of Middle Axioms

A set of middle axioms provides the social goal, the vision of the sort of world we should try to create. This vision also provides the backdrop or context for particular judgments. For instance, the missionary I encountered in the earlier example evaluated the facts on the multinationals' improvement of health care, housing, and salary in light of her social goal of transforming the society to a socialist one. She quite correctly perceived that raising that standard of living, even for a distinct minority of the population, would alleviate some of the pressure for revolution. In fact, our moral disagreement in that example was not so much on the level of an ethical assessment of the particular situation as on the level of the context for the judgment. All ethical judgments are made presupposing some context.

It may be interesting to reflect on how a religious activist's middle axioms influence the approach to concrete problems. For example, consider two controversial issues of our time: the ethics of United States investment in South Africa and the role of pharmaceuticals in Third World countries.

The Ethics of United States Investment in South Africa

There is no doubt that apartheid is wrong. It is a gross violation of human rights, and it is also harmful to society in that criteria other than competence are employed in awarding jobs and promotions. In the face of this evil, there are at least two responses, roughly parelleling the reformist and radical positions discussed above. The reformist would see United States investment as a way to dismantle apartheid, although a gradual way. Through the "progressive" Sullivan Principles and other similar measures, the blacks will gradually emerge as full citizens with rights and dignity.

The radical or revisionist scenario calls for a fundamental change in society, the abandonment of capitalism, and the creation of a new order. Apartheid in this perspective demands a quick fix, and disinvestment is a first step.

For the reformist to make a compelling argument that indeed United States investment in South Africa is moral, there must be some conclusive "evidence" that the lot of the blacks is improving. The trick, however, may be in getting a consensus with the radical position on what would count as "evidence." A radical/revisionist context would seem to allow little of the reformist "evidence" to count. Is there a way through this apparent impasse?

Third World Health Problems and the Role of Pharmaceuticals

Experience from past conflict on health related issues between industry and religious activists would seem to indicate two sorts of serious errors. On the one hand, industry should not assume all critics are Marxist seeking a revolutionary socialistic system. Critics should be listened to and their remarks carefully assessed. On the other hand, critics should be straightforward with the goals they are seeking. No matter how good the end, a less than forthright means is beneath the dignity of church representatives. The church as a moral leader ought to insure that its representatives are beyond reproach. In this light, consider the strategy on infant formula summarized by James Post in a recent article.

> Societies often have difficulties in shaping "sensible" policy solutions to complex policy issues. The reason that children die in developing nations is not because infant formula is a bad product. Rather, there is an environment of poverty, illiteracy, inadequate sanitation, unhealthy water, and limited health services that create dangerous conditions for the use of formula. Marketing did not create these conditions, but marketing was a more <u>actionable</u> aspect of the problem than poverty, water, or education... Because business corporations are responsive to external pressure, action targeted at them has a better chance of producing change than actions aimed at such underlying conditions as poverty and illiteracy. A marketing code will not alleviate the problems of poverty, illiteracy, and poor sanitation, but it can help to insure that companies do not exploit such conditions to their own advantage.[15]

While this may be acceptable strategy for some consumer groups, is it the most appropriate one for the church, the model of what human community ought to be like? The church must indeed be concerned to better the lot of the poor, but are not straightforward attempts to influence public policy much more fruitful? Should not the churches' major effort be directed at securing public policy aimed at improving the underlying condition of poverty, illiteracy, and so on? Is settling for a marketing code settling for too little?

Again, the radical and the reformist would have different responses to the query. The radical, already convinced that the status quo is evil, would see any strategy likely to diminish the influence of multinationals as the lesser of evils. The radical would see no utility in trying to reform the present system.

The reformist, however, would likely take quite another tack. Trying not only to reform the system, but also to be a model of integrity in the process, the reformer would actively pursue all avenues to bring justice to the oppressed.

The radical and the reformist positions are well represented whenever religious activists from around the globe are involved with multinational corporations. If it be true that multinational leaders and the critics speak from different levels of analysis and systems that are unlikely to converge, what is a reasonable goal at this stage? My contention is that a reasonable goal is <u>not</u> to form a consensus on fundamental perspectives and consequent decisions. At this point, probably the only way that sort of consensus could be achieved is by artifically suppressing differences. Rather, a more realistic objective of the dialogue is TO CLARIFY THE CONSEQUENCES OF OUR DIFFERENT PERSPECTIVES AND INTERPRETATIONS. Much more serious discussions, supported by empirical research, must focus on the likely consequences of the various scenarios.

NOTES

1. Arthur McCormack, M.H.M., "Poverty and Population," in <u>Multinational Managers and Poverty in the Third World</u>, edited by Lee Tavis (Notre Dame, Indiana: University of Notre Dame Press, 1982), p. 25.

2. Peter J. Henriot, S.J., "Restructuring the International Economic Order," in <u>Multinational Managers</u>, p. 49. For the economic perspectives, a good summary is presented in Karen Paul and Robert Barbato, "The Multinational Corporation in the Less Developed Country: The Economic Development Model Versus the North-South Model," <u>The Academy of Management</u>

Review 10 (January 1985), pp. 8-14.

3. Donald McNeill, C.S.C. and Lee A. Tavis, "The Nature of the Debate," in Multinational Managers, pp. 258-59.

4. William P. Glade, "Multinational Firms and National Economies," in Multinational Managers, pp. 102-12.

5. H. Richard Niebuhr, Christ and Culture (New York: Harper & Row, 1951).

6. For an elaboration of the social dimensions of the mission of the church, see O. Williams, "Introduction," The Judeo-Christian Vision and the Modern Corporation, eds., O. F. Williams, C.S.C. and J. W. Houck (Notre Dame, Indiana: University of Notre Dame Press, 1982), pp. 1-21. See also O. Williams, "Being a Christian in the Business World," Horizons 11 (2): 383-392, 1984.

7. Peter Drucker argues against the "revolutionary" approach to business ethics in "What is Business Ethics?" The Public Interest 63: 18-36, 1981. For my response to Drucker, see O. Williams, "Business Ethics: A Trojan Horse?" California Management Review 24 (4): 14-24, 1982.

8. Gregory Baum, The Priority of Labor (New York: Paulist Press, 1982), p. 44.

9. Ibid., p. 87.

10. Ibid.

11. For further discussion of this theme, see O. Williams, "Religion: The Spirit or Enemy of Capitalism, "Business Horizons 26 (6): 6-13, 1983; and O. Williams, "Who Cast the First Stone?" Harvard Business Review 62 (5): 151-160, 1984.

12. Gustavo Gutierrez, A Theology of Liberation, translated by Sister Caridad Inda and John Eagleston (Maryknoll, New York: Orbis Books, 1973), p.274.

13. Ibid., p. 276.

14. For extended discussions of the middle axioms appropriate for the United States, see Catholic Social Teaching and the U.S. Economy: Working Papers for a Bishops' Pastoral, eds., J. W. Houck and O. F. Williams, C.S.C. (Washington, DC: University Press of America, 1984).

15. James E. Post, "Assessing the Nestle Boycott: Corporate Accountability and Human Rights," *California Management Review* 27 (1985), p. 128.

CHAPTER SIX

POVERTY IN THE THIRD WORLD: SOURCES AND SOLUTIONS

LEE A. TAVIS
C.R. Smith Professor of Business Administration
University of Notre Dame
Notre Dame, Indiana

DENIS GOULET
O'Neill Professor of Education for Justice
University of Notre Dame
Notre Dame, Indiana

JOHN B. CARON
President
Caron International
Greenwich, Connecticut

LAWRENCE G. FRANKO
Professor of International Business Relations
Fletcher School of Law and Diplomacy
Tufts University
Medford, Massachusetts

JEAN WILKOWSKI
Chairperson of the Board
Volunteers in Technical Assistance
Arlington, Virginia

POVERTY: A CONDITION OF LIFE FOR MOST OF THE WORLD'S PEOPLE

Lee A. Tavis

When one looks at data on the allocation of resources across our globe, the pattern is striking. Differences among country groups as measured by statistics such as gross national product (GNP) are dramatic. In Table 1, population and GNP are compared on an aggregate, per capita, and real per capita basis for four groups of countries.[1] The picture is clear. Less than one third of the world's population in the high-income countries is consuming the overwhelming share of global resources as measured by gross national product. The good news is that GNP growth rates particularly for a number of middle-income countries in Latin America have been favorable. In spite of continuing increases in population and the disrupting effects of inflation, growth in real GNP per capita has been holding its own. The tragic news in Table 1 is the crushing poverty and the slow, slow rate of progress for the 1.3 billion people in the low-income countries.

The future holds little encouragement for a change in this pattern. Past growth, especially in the middle-income countries, was fueled by favorable economic conditions in the developed world and the recycling of petrodollars by private multinational banks. The channeling of these loans to so many nonproductive uses within the less-developed countries, combined with the external pressures of recession in the North, high interest rates, and changing oil prices have left the industrializing countries steeped in hard currency debt and battling one another for exports. The debt crisis and its associated austerity measures have been devastating to many of the poor.

There is little give in our present global economic system. An international financial crisis has been postponed only because of favorable developed country economic conditions and a willingness of the parties to work together. The full economic and political implications of the debt problem have yet to be worked out.

While GNP statistics outline the economic conditions, other measures such as infant mortality, life expectancy, and literacy rates touch people's lives more closely. The Overseas Development Council has combined these measures to form a Physical Quality of Life Index (PQLI). The PQLI and its components for the same country groups is presented in Table 2.[2]

The variation in life expectancy and literacy rates is

striking. Differences in infant mortality are unnerving. The Disparity Reduction Rate is an attempt to measure the progress of these countries in improving their physical quality of life. Here, the ordering from high-income to low-income is clear. The low-income countries, starting from abysmal conditions, are making litle progress.

Other data outlines the severity of life for these people. The numbers of hungry and malnourished are greater now than ever before in history, except in time of famine. The International Labour Office has estimated that 39 percent of the population in Asia, Latin America, and Africa is destitute -- living on annual incomes of $90 or less.[3] The number is growing. As many as 70 percent of the children in these countries suffer from malnourishment.[4] Inadequate diets have led to the mental or physical retardation of as many as 300 million people. When he was chairman of The World Bank, Robert McNamara described the plight of the poor:

> The word (poverty) itself has become almost incapable of communicating the harshness of the reality. Poverty at the absolute level -- which is what literally hundreds of millions of men, women, and most particularly, children are suffering from in these countries -- is life at the very margin of physical existence.
>
> The absolute poor are severely deprived human beings struggling to survive in a set of squalid and degraded circumstances almost beyond the power of our sophisticated imaginations and privileged circumstances to conceive.[5]

The poverty problem has many dimensions. Population growth absorbs much of the increased economic output. By the year 2000, world population is expected to grow from the present 4 billion to 5.8 - 6.3 billion with Third World growth far outpacing that of the developed countries. In fact, by the end of the century, 90 percent of the world population will live in the poor countries. Urbanization is growing even faster. Mexico City, for example, is expected to expand from its present population of 11 million to 30 million people by 2000 A.D. Fortunately, food availability is presently more a problem of distribution than of production. Production increases have outpaced population growth, but most of the increases have been in the developed world.[6]

These dimensions of the poverty problem are all interrelated and tied to other major world issues. Population growth is a function of economic development in that improved living conditions tend to be associated with moderated population growth; food production depends on fertilizers; and so forth. Meaningful solutions must deal with these interrelationships.

Moreover, increasing global scarcities further complicate the problem of these persistent imbalances. No matter where one stands on the Club of Rome initiated debates on growth, we all recognize that humankind has used up a great deal of our readily available resources.[7]

Multinational Involvement in Development

Multinational corporations are a component of development in these countries and are a part of the progress, but they are also a part of the problems. These firms have contributed in a major way to economic growth in both developed and less-developed countries in the past quarter century. Their technological capabilities, their ability to convert technology to productivity through the organization of complex productive systems and to marshal financial and other resources on a worldwide scale to support this production, have been a cornerstone of worldwide economic growth. At this point in time, I am convinced that multinational manufacturers, agribusinesses, resource firms, and banks must be a component of any successful transition to the rekindling of economic development.

In this process, however, multinationals tie nations closely together and to a market-driven international economic order. This system has often not worked so well. The dramatic worldwide economic growth of the past quarter century has not touched the lives of those millions of people in urban and rural areas living at the boundaries of physical existence. For many of them, economic development has not paralleled economic growth. As a component of national development patterns, multinationals share in the persistent maldistribution of resources.

Multinationals do have linkages to poverty in those less-developed countries where they operate. As an integral component of a host country's pattern of development, the multinational is tied to the poor, perhaps unwillingly or indirectly, through (1) the products they produce, (2) the people they employ, (3) the local supplies they use, and (4) their involvement in community development.

The specific linkages, of course, depend upon the country and the firm. A firm producing medical supplies or drugs in a less-developed African country, for example, would have close linkages. Their products are a necessary consumption item for the poor and must be usable under the most squalid, unsanitary conditions. The relationships associated with the local production of these goods would also create employment, training, financial, and other ties to the poor directly or indirectly through the country's development process. A firm buying from agricultural cooperatives or a bank lending to them is closely linked to rural living standards. Other kinds of multinationals, such as firms extracting minerals for export, would be a major factor in a country's balance of payments, but have fewer direct ties to the internal sector. The variety of linkages derives from the diversity among multinational firms and national patterns of development.

If the involvement of multinationals is a necessary condition for the rekindling of economic development in the Third World, then these firms have a responsibility to respond to these needs. Multinationals have a unique social responsibility -- a "development responsibility."[8] And there are many committed people working at various levels of this multinational involvement in the poor countries. Some work at the operational level, trying to forge linkages with the poor and make the international system work better. Others are concerned with the ethical dimensions of the system and believe that the system must be changed in some basic way. But all share the determination to somehow reduce the dehumanizing conditions in the poor countries of Asia, Africa, and Latin America.

TABLE 1
GROSS NATIONAL PRODUCT STATISTICS*

Country Classification[a]	Population Millions (1984)	GNP as % of Total (1982)	GNP[b] Per Capita (1982)	GNP Annual Growth (1970-1982)	Real GNP Growth Rate Per Capita Annual (1960-1982)
High-Income	1,183.9	85.4%	$9,364	2.8%	3.4%
Upper-Middle	620.1	8.2%	2,058	5.4%	3.6%
Lower-Middle	548.9	3.8%	714	5.3%	3.3%
Low Income	1,330.7	2.6%	250	3.4%	1.2%

*Excluding China

(See Footnote 1 for a and b and a more complete enumeration of countries, measurement decriptions, and sources.)

TABLE 2
PHYSICAL QUALITY OF LIFE (PQLI) STATISTICS*

Country Classification	PQLI[a] (1981)	Infant Mortality per 1,000 Live Births[b]	Life Expectancy at Birth[c]	Literacy Rate[d] (%)	Disparity Reduction Rate (%)[e]
High-Income	95	17	74	97%	3.3%
Upper Middle	74	69	64	73%	2.6%
Lower Middle	57	94	55	55%	1.7%
Low Income	46	121	52	37%	1.1%

*Excluding China

(See Footnote 2 for a, b, c, d, and e.)

Notes

1. Data for Table 1 were prepared as follows:

    a. Countries classified according to Per Capita GNP as follows:

High-Income	$3,700 and greater (e.g., Austria, Democratic Republic of Germany, Federal Republic of Germany, France, Hong Kong, Israel, Japan, Libya, Saudi Arabia, United States, USSR, Venezuela)
Upper Middle-Income	$1,070 - $3,699 (e.g., Algeria, Argentina, Brazil, Congo, Democratic People's Republic of Korea, Iran, Mexico, Republic of Korea, South Africa, Taiwan, Turkey, Yugoslavia)
Lower Middle-Income	$420 - 1,060 (e.g., Albania, Angola, Bolivia, Cuba, Egypt, El Salvador, Indonesia, Nigeria, Papua New Guinea, Philippines, Thailand, Zimbabwe)

       Low-Income $420 and less (e.g., Afghanistan, Bangladesh, Chad, Ethiopia, Gambia, Haiti, India, Kenya, Laos, Niger, Sri Lanka, Vietnam)

  b. Sources: <u>U.S. Foreign Policy and the Third World Agenda, 1985-86</u>, John W. Sewell, Richard E. Feinberg, and Valeriana Kallab, Editors.

    <u>World Development Report</u>, 1984, The World Bank.

2. Data for Table 2 were prepared as follows:

  a. The Physical Quality of Life Index is based on an average of life expectancy at age one, infant mortality, and literacy. This index was developed by the Overseas Development Council as a non-income measure of well-being.

    The scale is defined as "0" indicating the most unfavorable performance in 1950 to 100 indicating the best performance expected by the year 2000. For life expectancy at age one, the most favorable experience anticipated to be achieved by any one country by the year 2000 is 77 years. This would thus be set at 100 for the index. The most unfavorable performance registered in 1950 was 38 years in Guinea-Bissau. This becomes the zero index point. For infant mortality, the best performance expected by the year 2000 is 7 deaths per 1,000 live births (index of 100), and the poorest performance in 1950 was 229 deaths per 1,000 live births in Gabon (index base of zero). The literacy index is the percentage of the population over 15 years of age who can read and write. The three indexes are averaged together giving equal weight to each. The PQLI numbers presented here measure the physical quality of life as of 1981.

  b. Infant mortality data are drawn primarily from The World Bank, World Tables (Third Edition), supplemented by data from UNESCO Population and Vital Statistics (April 1984), "1984 World Population Data Sheet," and unpublished data from the U.S. Bureau of Census.

  c. Life expectancy at birth data are drawn primarily from The World Bank, World Tables, Third Edition, Volume II, supplemented by data from the "1984 World Population Data Sheet," United Nations, U.N. Demographic Yearbook (1982), The World Bank, World Development Report

(1984), and unpublished data from the U.S. Bureau of the Census. (Note that this is a slightly different measure than that included in the PQLI.)

d. That proportion of the population 15 years or older, able to read or write.

e. The Disparity Reduction rate is designed to measure a country's progress in meeting basic human needs. More specifically, it is the annual rate at which the gap between a country's level of performance in these social indicators and the best performance anywhere in the year 2000 is being closed. Data is from 1960-1982.

3. International Labour Office, Employment, Growth, and Basic Needs: A One-World Problem (New York: Praeger Publishers, 1977).

4. North-South: A Program for Survival, Report of the Independent Commission on International Development Issues, Willie Brandt, Chairman (Cambridge, MA: The MIT Press, 1980), pp. 90-104.

5. Robert S. McNamara, Address to the Board of Governors 1976 (Washington, DC: The World Bank, 1976).

6. Rev. Arthur McCormack, M.H.M., Multinational Investment: Boon or Burden for the Developing Countries? (New York and London: Arthur McCormack, 1980).

7. Jan Tinbergen, Reshaping the International Order: A Report to the Club of Rome (New York: Dutton and Company, Inc., 1976).

8. For a further discussion of developmental responsibility, see Lee A. Tavis, "Developmental Responsibility," in Multinational Managers and Poverty in the Third World, Lee A. Tavis, editor (University of Notre Dame Press, 1982), pp. 127-139.

CREATING WEALTH, OR CAUSING POVERTY?

Denis Goulet

THE ISSUE

The most basic ethical dilemma faced by transnational corporations (TNCs) can be framed as a brief question: "Does creating wealth cause poverty?" To pose the question in a more qualified and precise fashion: Does pursuing economic wealth as an exclusive and formally explicit institutional activity entail a necessary complicity in the creation or perpetuation of poverty? Or, at the very least, does it constitute a sin of omission by failing to work directly to eliminate poverty?

PRIOR QUESTIONS: TO CLARIFY ASSUMPTIONS

Before this ethical dilemma can be unraveled, three prior questions need to be answered. For TNCs the quandary is an acute one because they face repeated charges of cynical indifference to the lot of the poor, or of insincerity in their belief that the wealth they create can trickle down to the poor.

Prior Question Number One

What makes for genuine wealth or poverty? The following thematic statements on the question suggest possible answers.

A first text is drawn from Carolina Maria de Jesus, a black Brazilian slum dweller. Her diary, written on scraps of paper as an exercise in fantasizing to escape the unbearable drabness of her life in Sao Paulo's Caninde slum, was accidentally discovered by a journalist in 1958 and became an instant best seller. Carolina states simply that "(T)he basic necessities must be within reach of everyone."[1]

The next three texts paraphrase statements repeatedly made by Gandhi as he defined the type of development he sought for India:

- There are enough goods in the poorest Indian village to meet the needs of all; there are not enough goods in all of India to satisfy the wants of each one.

- I prefer production by the masses, which brings dignity and livelihood to all, over mass production, which is production by a few for the masses, who are reduced to being mere consumers of others' profit-making activities.

- Misery is a special kind of hell.

Barry Lopez, a student of Native American societies, observes that: "A psychiatrist who for the past several years has worked with Navajo singers (medicine men) claims that their medicine is more complex than any of ours -- with the possible exception of open-heart surgery -- and as efficacious in many instances.

"Some native ideas could serve us well in this historical moment: that a concept of wealth should be founded in physical health and spiritual well-being, not material possessions; that to be "poor" is to be without family, without a tribe -- without people who care deeply for you."[2]

The French writer Georges Perec is the author of Les choses (Things), a novel about the good life as seen by a modern consumerist French couple. They "make it" at the age of thirty. Yet the book ends with a bit of philosophic, and symbolic, musing by the author: "They will be well-housed, well-fed, well-clothed. They will have nothing to regret ... [it is] the prelude to a sumptuous feast. Yet the meal which will be served to them will be frankly insipid."[3]

Early Fathers of the Christian Church -- notably John Chrysostom, Gregory of Nyssa, and Basil the Great -- repeatedly preached on the difference between material and spiritual goods.[4] According to them, only spiritual goods such as virtue, friendship, truth, and beauty constitute genuine wealth. Material goods are by nature limited and cannot be shared without diminishing the advantages derived from them by some, whereas in contrast spiritual goods grow in intensity and in their capacity to satisfy as they are shared. True wealth, they conclude, resides in the internal freedom which makes one use material goods instrumentally to meet needs and as a springboard to cultivating those higher goods which alone bring deeper satisfaction. One finds a remarkable similarity here to the classical Buddhist doctrine of the alienating effects of "tanha," untrammelled desire. For both the Christian Fathers and the Buddhist sages, the road to happiness, as to virtue, lies in triumphing over desire.

These thematic reflections suggest two cautionary notes regarding mainstream capitalist conceptions of wealth: the purely instrumental, or relative, nature of material goods; and their potential illusory, or idolatrous nature, insofar as these relative goods easily tempt us to treat them as absolutes.

Clearly there is a lesson to be learned here; namely, that ethical judgments about institutions devoted to the pursuit of wealth need to be anchored in broader philosophical conceptions regarding the purpose of human existence.

Lewis Mumford warns us that: "real values do not derive from either rarity or crude manpower. It is not rarity that gives the air its power to sustain life, nor is it the human work done that gives milk or bananas their nourishment. In comparison with the effects of chemical action and the sun's rays the human contribution is a small one. Genuine value lies in the power to sustain or enrich life ... the juice of a lemon may be more valuable on a long ocean voyage than a hundred pounds of meat without it. The value lies directly in the life-function: not in its origin, its rarity, or in the work done by human agents."[5]

The recognition of this larger dimension of the economic value question led Adolf Berle, as early as in 1954, to write that: "The really great corporation managements have reached a position for the first time in their history in which they must consciously take account of philosophical considerations. They must consider the kind of community in which they have faith, and which they will serve ... In a word, they must consider at least in its more elementary phases the ancient problem of the 'good life,' and how their operations in the community can be adapted to affording or fostering it."[6]

Prior Question Number Two

What kind of wealth ought to be produced?

For Galbraith, "[T]he final requirement of modern development planning is that it have a theory of consumption...a view of what the production is ultimately for -- has been surprisingly little discussed and has been too little missed ... More important, what kind of consumption should be planned?"[7]

The Brazilian economist Celso Furtado judges that the question is answered when policy makers decide which precise "basket of consumer goods" they will provide to their respective nations. He argues that TNCs produce a basket designed to satisfy the wants of the middle and upper classes, not to meet the needs of the poor.

One readily understands why TNCs produce certain categories of goods and not others: they produce only what they expect to sell. They produce for those who have purchasing power, not for those in greatest need but who lack such power. In order to understand, if not to justify, this behavior, one has only to recall what a corporation is. A corporation is an artificial entity upon which the state confers juridical personality for the purpose of pursuing profit. A corporate charter is, in effect, a hunting license authorizing its holder to make money. When early corporations received their charters, the conditions imposed upon them by society were few and simple; they had only to obey the laws of the land and pay their taxes. Today's requirements have become far more stringent: chartered corporations must avoid practices such as racism or sexual discrimination and contribute positively to "development." No longer can they plausibly claim, as did their forbears, that the mere making of profit was itself tantamount to contributing positively to development. This is why the composition of the "basket of goods" produced by corporations centrally affects judgments made regarding their social utility. What kind of wealth corporations produce, and in whose benefit, thus become decisive questions.

Prior Question Number Three

A third preliminary question to be asked is: what principles ought to govern the distribution of wealth, its appropriation, and the uses to which it is put?

First, the principle that "needs have priority over wants" prescribes that scarce resources be used to satisfy the first-order essential needs of a society's citizens before being diverted to production aimed merely at meeting the wants of those who enjoy purchasing power. Eliminating absolute poverty, and perhaps certain elements of relative poverty as well, must take precedence over producing luxury goods or low priority utility goods. At issue here is, obviously, some explicit theory of needs and the policy implications which flow from it.[8]

Second, the question arises as to whether equality of opportunity or equality of benefits is to be observed. Equal opportunity may not suffice to meet vital needs: the requirement may be equal results. When the "cards are stacked" against certain categories of people, equal opportunity to compete in the market place guarantees nothing more than the perpetuation of initial inequalities. As numerous studies suggest, economic mobility may be a sham and equal opportunity may mask unequal selection of those who can truly benefit from that opportunity.[9]

Corporate decision makers in growing numbers now acknowledge the need to "internalize the externalities" which they had previously, and with tranquil conscience, omitted from their benefit-cost calculations. In Kenneth Goodpaster's lapidary phase, executives must add value to their value added.[10]

As such, and third, profits are to be optimized, not maximized. Optimizing profits entails internalizing the externalities and relinquishing partial control over what is produced and who benefits. Among the numerous contemporary "externalities" to be internalized by corporate decision makers are values pertaining to: distributive justice, absolute needs and relative needs, ecological wisdom, human rights/political freedom, cultural survival and diversity, and open-ness to transcendence.

SECOND LEVEL QUESTIONS: TO GUIDE POLICY

Once these prior questions have been answered, three derivative policy questions impose themselves.

Policy Question Number One

Which economic system, alone, or best, satisfies ethical imperatives governing the production of wealth and the abolition of poverty?

Henry Wallich, an economist at Yale University until named by Richard Nixon to the Federal Reserve Board, enjoins United States business executives to drop their old-fashioned stereotypes about capitalism and socialism. He urges them to look at the real world and discover that the survival of capitalism and the continued profitability of the firm, especially in Third World countries, do not depend on the private ownership of the means of production.[11] Consequently, the nationalization of mines or factories by governments need not be viewed as sounding the death-knell of capitalism.

Karl Mannheim explained that any system of economic activity is defined by the organizing principle it adopts.[12] Market competition is the organizing principle of capitalism, politically-guided state planning that of socialism. In addition to its organizing principle, however, any system may use various regulatory mechanisms in order to correct distortions arising from the untrammelled workings of its dominant, or organizing, principle. Hence, it is no evidence of "creeping socialism" for the United States government to lend money to Lockheed or Chrysler; those are but instances of government intervention used as a regulatory, or compensatory, mechanism. Conversely, it was no sign of backsliding toward capitalism for managers greater plant autonomy, or to instruct Gosplan central planners to utilize price signals as guides to what kind of goods final consumers wanted. Kruschev was simply invoking regulatory mechanisms ordinarily associated with capitalism in order to smooth out the workings of an economy still firmly wedded to the socialist organizing principle.

Development theorists grow periodically enamored of "third ways" which avoid the exaggerated individualism of capitalism while simultaneously escaping the collectivism of classical socialism. These attempts at hybrid third ways have usually failed, however.[13] Instead of getting the best of both systems, they end up getting the worst of each.

Policy Question Number Two

What lessons have been learned in efforts to wipe out poverty by deliberate policy measures?

First of all, people are the primary resource in any are society; they are of greater importance than money, technology, or material facilities. But if people are to become dynamic agents in the struggle to eradicate poverty, they need to be motivated and organized. Moreover, the organizations and movements they create must receive breathing room and respect from government and society at large -- this quite apart from any resources which may need to be transferred their way.

Second, micro-arena actors must gain entry into macro-arenas of decision making.[14] The qualitatively humane development paradigm successfully realized in small-scale experiments must find a way to shape the criteria of decision making in macro-arenas. The critical mass concept requires freedom for many communities of need to experiment with ways of satisfying those needs. Within corporations, this may mean allowing workers to have a true managerial voice. The precise modalities are obviously the subject of further experimentation.

Policy Question Number Three

Can TNCs create wealth without causing, or perpetuating, poverty?

The French theologian Pierre Antoine explains the difference between guilt and responsibility in these terms: "individuals, groups, and nations which, even by ethical means, have secured themselves an advantageous, strong and prosperous position in the world, and by so doing have impeded (even if it is only indirectly because goods available on this planet are limited) the economic development or the social promotion of other individuals or other peoples, are responsible to the latter for their deprivation and they ought to remedy it, by making use of the very possibilities which better position confers on them ... an obligation rooted in justice can exist, as a consequence of our acts, even when no fault of injustice has been committed."[15]

Corporations have sometimes muzzled claims in justice made upon them by invoking their practice of philanthropy, which they view as charity or something optional. But corporations, no more than individuals, can flee their duties in justice by practicing charity. Yet it must be conceded that TNCs have nowhere to turn for guidance in these matters. As Mumford writes, "there is no capitalist theory of non-profit making enterprises and non-consumable goods. These functions exist accidentally, by the grace of the philanthropist: they have no real place in the system."[16]

What is being asked of corporate decision makers is that they adhere to multiple loyalty systems, giving their allegiance to corporate objectives, to larger societal goals, to the well-being of the Third World, and to the improvement of humankind.[17]

One must go beyond the societal impact of individual corporations viewed separately, however, in order to determine whether TNCs help or hinder development. As I have written elsewhere in debating the duties of Christian corporate leaders to behave ethically: "Discussions of ethical responsibility in corporate personnel can be conducted in four distinct normative arenas.

"The first domain is that of personal and professional behavior within the context of presently accepted ethical ground rules and organizational values. Examples are such issues as truthfulness and honesty in handling expense accounts, the avoidance of illegal bribes or favors in order to win a contract, and the delivery of stipulated model and quality of goods purchased by a customer and not some slightly different and cheaper substitute.

"A second realm bears on corporate policy decisions, usually pertaining to complex issues of societal justice. Examples include such questions as investment in South Africa. (Does corporate investment help oppressed blacks or buttress the unjust apartheid system?) Another issue is whether corporations may responsibly 'export pollution' to a Third World site, thereby creating environmental damage even though host country laws may allow pollution. Still another instance is the choice of not making an otherwise desirable investment lest it wipe out local employment opportunities, etc.

"The third arena of ethical conflict deals with the over-all systemic effects (good and bad) of corporate activity in the world. Here the moral issues are whether, on balance, corporate activities benefit poor countries or poor populations, or whether, as some argue, they make things worse by widening gaps between privileged and deprived groups, by reinforcing technical and economic dependency, and by destroying vulnerable cultural values.

"A fourth and final level of ethical conflict focuses on competing images and standards of success operative in business circles, on the one hand, and in the Christian religion, on the other. Expressed in stark biblical terms, the question is whether one can be faithful to both God and Mammon.

"Most writings on corporate ethics concentrate heavily on levels (1) and (2) ... In this author's view, the moral responsibilities of Christian corporate personnel are not adequately discharged unless they make sound value decisions in all four domains just listed."[18]

Many individual pathways have been trod by conscientious executives in their quest for societal justice. It lies beyond the scope of this paper to analyze these multiple pathways to justice.[19]

CONCLUSION

One may now return to the basic question posed initially: "Does creating wealth cause poverty?"

If a corporation is to pursue wealth in an ethically acceptable manner, it must earn anew -- as it were -- its charter or hunting license by proving that it operates in ways consonant with today's conditions. Quite apart from initial normative judgments as to the authentic or spurious quality of the wealth it creates, several rules must be observed.

1. Profit must be optimized, not maximized. To optimize means to seek some best level, relative to another value or goal. Many values and goals which, in the past, could be treated as externalities must now make their way internally into corporate calculations of benefits and costs. These values include racial and sexual justice in the recruitment and

promotion of personnel, care for the environment, regard for equity in the availability of goods and services produced, the larger impact of corporate actions upon society at large in domains of national sovereignty, democracy, human rights, and so on. (This list is indicative, not exhaustive.)

2. The optimization of profits in ways which internalize essential social and political values will require that corporations accept processes of joint decision making in cooperation with other actors: local governments, national governments of host and home countries, citizens' groups of various sorts, and institutions serving as stewards of certain ethical values like human rights, just wages, non-discrimination, and ecological responsibility. Andre Van Dam,[20] for many years the chief economic planner for the Latin American division of Corn Products, has taken the lead in advocating new models of joint planning.

3. A third normative principle is the subordination of profit seeking by corporations to a higher vision of what production is for. Authentic development is measured on three scales: its contribution to optimum life-sustenance, esteem, and freedom.[21]

Keynes himself acknowledged the instrumental nature of all wealth-getting enterprises when, shortly before his death, he declared: "I give you the toast of the Royal Economic Society, of economics and economists, who are the trustees not of civilization, but of the possibility of civilization."[22]

During China's Cultural Revolution, Mao Dze Dong was fond of repeating the slogan: "Values command politics, politics command economics, economics command technique." Mao's name, like the Cultural Revolution itself, is now discredited in China. But the dictum remains valid. Neither technology nor economics -- and a fortiori mere corporate profit-seeking -- must be allowed by any society to assume primacy over the higher demands of politics, charged with the common good and, in turn, over the values to which politics itself must be subordinated: the inviolability of the person, and open-ness to transcendence or ultimate meanings.

At stake, ultimately, is something of far greater importance than the mere validation of wealth creation. It is the possibility of creating a new model of decision making which harmonizes the demands of three conflicting rationalities -- the technical, the political, and the ethical.[23]

Corporate decision makers, like technical or political leaders, must be held to a standard higher than Machiavellian logic in the pursuit of their peculiar goals.

NOTES

1. Carolina Maria De Jesus, *Child of the Dark*, New York: Mentor Books, 1962, p. 39.

2. The American Indian Mind, *Quest/78*, September-October, 1978, p. 109.

3. George Perec, *Les choses*, Paris: Les Lettres nouvelles, 1965, pp. 128, 130.

4. On this see Charles Avila, *Ownership, Early Christian Teaching*, Maryknoll, NY: Orbis Books, 1983.

5. Lewis Mumford, *Technics and Civilization*, New York: Harcourt, Brace and Co., 1934, p. 76.

6. Adolf A. Berle, Jr., *The 20th Century Capitalist Revolution*, New York: Harcourt, Brace and Co., 1954, p. 166.

7. John Kenneth Galbraith, *Economic Development in Perspective*, Cambridge, MA: Harvard University Press, 1962, p. 43. Italics are Galbraith's.

8. For further discussion see Denis Goulet, *The Cruel Choice*, New York: Atheneum, 1971, pp. 236-249.

9. On this see Charles Elliott, *Patterns of Poverty in the Third World*, New York: Praeger, 1975. Cf. Edgar Z. Friendenberg, *The Disposal of Liberty and Other Industrial Wastes*, Garden City, NY: Doubleday & Co., Inc., 1975, and Denis Goulet, Steven H. Arnold, and Adele K. Levine, "The Limits of Abundance: Dominant Myths, Competing Values, and a Search for Alternatives in the Unites States," *Overseas Development Council Working Papers*," July, 1982, 50 pages.

10. Kenneth Goodpaster, "Adding Value to Value Added: The Moral Agenda of Corporate Leadership," *Working Paper No. 9-786-003* (1985) of Harvard Business School, Division of Research.

11. "The Future of Capitalism," *Newsweek*, January 22, 1973, p. 62.

12. K. Mannhein, *Freedom, Power and Democratic Planning*, London: Routledge & Kegan Paul, 1951, p. 191.

13. Denis Goulet, "Economic Systems, Middle Way Theories, and Third World Realities," in *Co-Creation and Capitalism: John Paul II's Laborem Exercens*, John W. Houck and Oliver F. Williams, C.S.C., editors, Washington, DC: University of Washington Press, 1983, pp. 141-169.

14. On micro-macro linkages, see Denis Goulet, "The Relationship Between Rich Nations and Poor," in James A. Devereux, editor, *The Moral Dimensions of International Conduct*, Washington, DC: Georgetown University Press, 1983, pp. 49ff.

15. "Qui Est Coupable?" *Revue de l'action populaire*, No. 32, November 1959, pp. 1055-65.

16. L. Mumford, *Technics and Civilization*, New York: Harcourt, Brace and Co., 1934, p. 377.

17. On plural loyalties and identities, see Denis Goulet, "Socialization and Cultural Development," *Interchange*, Vol. 10, No. 3 (1979-80), pp. 1-9.

18. Denis Goulet, "Goals in Conflict," in *The Judeo-Christian Vision and the Modern Corporation*, Oliver F. Williams and John W. Houch, editors, Notre Dame, IN: University of Notre Dame Press, 1982, pp 220-221.

19. See Denis Goulet, *Pathways to Justice*, Inaugural lecture for the William and Dorothy O'Neill Chair in Education for Justice, University of Notre Dame, 29 April 1980, 24 pages.

20. Andre Van Dam, "Recursos Globales, En las Visperas de una negociacion planetaria," *Compentencia*, No. 165, pp. 98-104; Andre Van Dam, "The Management of Global Resources," *Industrial*, April 1978, pp. 10-13; Andre Van Dam, "The Third World: Poised to Become A Partner in World Commerce," *Industrial Development*, March/April, pp. 18-22; Andre Van Dam, "Global Development: From Confrontation to Cooperation?" *Planning Review*, Vol 2, No. 5, August/September, 1974, pp. 1-4, 20-23; Andre Van Dam, "Cooperation for All Seasons," *JCI World*, July/September, 1981, pp. 4-5; Andre Van Dam, "Renewable Energy: Renewable Hope?" *Intercinecia*, Vol. 7, No. 1, Jan./Feb., 1982, pp. 47-48; Andre Van Dam, "Pulling those Policies Back to the People," *Asiaweek*, August 10, 1979, pp. 29-30.

21. On this see Denis Goulet, *The Cruel Choice*, New York: Atheneum, 1971, pp. 85-95.

22. Benjaman Higgins, *Economic Development, Problems, Principles and Policies*, revised edition, New York: W. W. Norton, 1968, p. 3.

23. On this see Denis Goulet, "Three Rationalities in Development Decisions," *Working Paper #42*, Notre Dame, IN: The Helen Kellogg Institute for International Studies, June 1985, 34 pages.

MULTINATIONAL COMPANIES AND WORLD POVERTY

John B. Caron

What effect does or can a multinational company have on poverty in the Third World?

Some people say a corporation's sole purpose is to make a profit, and there is something to say for this in that without profit the corporation ceases to exist. With low profit it suffers a slow death because it is not able to keep up to date with its research and development, technology, and market development. However, corporations are made up of individuals who for the most part have a conscience and want to do what is right. The existence of poverty bothers most people. They would like to be able to do something about it. But, what can a corporate executive do, especially one working for a multinational company?

Six years ago, Father Hesburgh, president of the University of Notre Dame, asked Professor Lee Tavis to get together a group of corporate executives and academics to address the problem of how multinational companies could have a favorable impact on solving the problem of poverty in the Third World. Father Hesburgh felt that these companies had the resources, trained people, finances, know how, and management skills. They had the markets. They could provide jobs and transfer skills. Lee Tavis was given the responsibility to see how these resources could be harnessed to help solve the problem of Third World poverty.

In the course of studies arising from these meetings, we have found much criticism of multinational companies. Any self-respecting conference on the Third World must pass a resolution condemning multinationals. Some people even feel that multinationals are the cause of poverty in the Third World. Our initial inquiry focused on answering the question of why there is this criticism of multinational companies.

An in-depth study of the Dole Pineapple operation in the Philippines was undertaken, which subsequently resulted in a book. This comany was chosen for the study because the parent company, Castle and Cook, had been under considerable fire. The Philippines had a great gap between poverty and wealth. There had been considerable criticism of the Dole operations by church groups in the Philippines.

On the surface, Dole did everything right. They paid the

highest wages. They created infrastructure such as schools, health care, and transportation. They developed land that was not being used for farming. They contributed to the balance of payments. On top of all this, it was not a very profitable operation. Why then all the criticism?

It seemed primarily a problem of nationalism. Dole got preferential tax treatment, but inducements are common throughout the world. There was resentment that the markets were controlled by a foreign company. There was a fear that the company would close, suddenly leaving their very substantial investment behind. Criticism seemed more emotionally based than logically based.

The criticism of multinationals continues, so a more basic question we needed to answer was: "Is a Third World country better with or without multinational companies?" Cardinal Arns of Sao Paulo, Brazil is a critic of the whole industrialization process which has brought urbanization and materialism. However, most people do not seem to aspire to the small is beautiful, simple agrarian life. They aspire to a life of consumption, televisions, refrigerators, cars, travel. Whether Cardinal Arns or the Aspiring Consumer is right is not the question we are trying to address here. We are recognizing the reality of human nature as we know it today. I feel it is unrealistic to say that these aspirations are caused by the advertising campaigns of multinational companies. We have had acquisitive societies throughout the ages and well before advertising was developed. Furthermore, if multinational companies did not exist, then national companies would fill the gap.

So let us get back to the key question: "Is a Third World country better with or without multinational companies?" I feel there is a preponderance of evidence pointing to a net beneficial effect of multinational companies. The Dole Pineapple operation mentioned previously is an example. The United Fruit Company banana operation in Honduras is another example. This company was very much in the news because of its bribery of Honduran government officials and its chairman Eli Black committing suicide by jumping out the window of his Pan American Building office. Despite all the negatives, the people working for the United Fruit Company in Honduras are better off than most other people in that country. They have better housing, health care, education, and benefits. The marketing of fresh fruit such as bananas is complex. There are only a few companies that can do it. These exports provide a needed source of foreign exchange. It is interesting to note that with the current problem of foreign debt many Third World countries are now seeking multinational company investments, especially considering the ineffectiveness and losses of state-owned companies.

The Notre Dame program is exploring the question of what else multinational companies can do in cooperative efforts with local industry and agriculture. We find that many multinational companies are receptive to ideas which could help low income people in the countries in which they are operating.

A very interesting study was done of Standard Fruit Company's banana operation in Honduras. There, Standard Fruit is not raising their own bananas, but is working with a local cooperative. Standard Fruit controls all conditions of planting, cultivating, and harvesting and buys the bananas at a pre-agreed upon price. The study compared this cooperative with another, and the results were dramatic. The other cooperative was barely beyond subsistence while this one was extremely profitable. The cooperative even got to the point where they were playing one American banana company off against another to see where they could get the best deal.

The problem is that most multinationals affect only a small percentage of the population. In many countries, the vast majority of poor live mostly outside the economy. They subsistence farm, and they receive few services from their government -- sometimes some education and minimal health care. They are drawn to the big cities with the hope of bettering their lives, but it is a slow trickle down process that often is negated by rapid population growth.

The basic problem of world poverty still exists and, even if we accept that multinational companies have had an overall positive impact due to providing jobs, transferring skills, developing resources, and contributing to balance of payments, there remains an obvious huge gap between the effect a multinational company can have and the extent of the poverty that exists.

How can this gap be filled? I have been working with Technoserve almost since its inception 18 years ago. Ed Bullard went to Ghana as a lay missionary to work in a hospital as an administrator. Many missionaries felt that the country needed more than the schools and hospitals that the missionaries provided. Job creation was needed to improve standards of living, and often the missionaries got involved in enterprise development. The problem was almost all failed, usually because they were not financially feasible. Ed Bullard formed Technoserve to do feasibility studies for these projects that had been identified by missionaries. Most of the projects after preliminary study were considered nonfeasible. Those that were feasible usually failed because of lack of managerial skills. Technoserve's next step then was to provide volunteer advisory people for these enterprises. The problem here was as soon as the volunteers left, the enterprises usually failed. Then Technoserve set up offices in the countries in which they were operating to provide ongoing help. This was still not enough because most enterprises still failed. Eventually a process developed where Technoserve put their own management in to actually run the operation and train the management and gradually withdraw as the enterprise managers developed their skills. A further step is to train indigenous organizations to do the work Technoserve is doing. The process is working. It is mostly agriculture-based with some savings and loan institutions providing credit to small farmers.

The Technoserve approach is a concentration on very basic food production and better methods of distribution. The technology is simple. In Ghana, government price controls on sugar were such that the cane growers could not afford to truck their sugar cane to the sugar mills. On the other hand, the sugar mills were partially shut down because of the lack of cane, and the tragic conclusion was that the country imported about half of its sugar. Technoserve developed some simple technology to produce sugar syrup, not refined sugar, that was sold to local bakeries and soft drink manufacturers.

In El Salvador, cattle routinely died and milk production drastically declined during the annual dry season. Technoserve developed a system of small catchment ponds to hold water for the dry season. They developed small cooperative feed mills that used locally available materials, such as waste from a brewery, to provide nutrious feed supplement during the dry season. The results were a substantial increase in income for these small farmers.

In Panama, a system was developed to get onions planted approximately six weeks before the normal time and which got them to the market when prices were high. Normally, onions were not planted until the rainy season was over. But Technoserve devised a system of planting the onions in diked areas to get them started and replanting them in the normal fields as soon as it was dry enough. These farmers got almost four times the usual price for onions. For the first time in their lives they had cash income.

Technoserve is now trying this process in some very tough countries. We are now operating in Rwanda, which in a recent book on Africa was described as one of the world's "hopeless countries." We are operating in Zaire which is widely considered to have the most corrupt leadership in the world. Zaire has great resources but cannot feed its own people.

Poverty in the Third World is an overwhelming problem, and there is obviously no quick fix. But I wanted to make a point in this brief paper that multinational companies can and do have a net positive impact on helping solve the problem. But this is a trickle down effect. The Technoserve approach affects the poorest end of the population -- and it is working. We need both approaches to help solve this problem of world poverty.

FOREIGN EQUITY INVESTMENT AND ECONOMIC DEVELOPMENT: FOUR ETHICAL DILEMMAS OF MULTINATIONAL ENTERPRISE

Lawrence G. Franko

Four years ago, when I was living and working in Geneva, Switzerland, I was head of a team for the International Labor Organization which reviewed the role of multinational companies in job creation and employment, first in industrialized countries, and then in less industrialized countries. We noticed something that in retrospect seems very obvious. It was that rich countries had a lot of their own multinationals. Rich countries also had a lot of employment concentrated in their own multinational firms. Rich countries, countries like the United States, Switzerland, Germany, and increasingly Japan as it joined the ranks of the wealthier nations, spawned large numbers of multinational firms or, that is, firms with production locations in many places around the world.

While rich nations had a lot of their own multinationals, semi-rich nations, nations that were almost as rich, had other people's multinationals. Canada is host to many American multinational investments. Belgium has many American and European multinational investments, as do Ireland, Italy, Singapore, Taiwan, Hong Kong, and South Korea. These last four countries are considered among the growth and income distribution success stories in the lesser-developed world.

The stark conclusion was that the rich countries had their own multinationals, the medium level countries had other people's multinationals, and poor countries had no or very few multinationals of their own or of others. Poor countries also had a much lower proportion of their total labor force employed in multinationals. Thus, the role of multinational companies by number, volume of investment, or employment was much smaller in the poorest countries than it was in the wealthier countries.

For many of the poorer countries, the limitation of multinational investment had been a matter of conscious choice. Many countries, particularly in Latin America and Africa, adopted very restrictive laws on foreign equity investment. Those laws have, in fact, limited foreign equity investment. Argentina for instance has had a series of laws limiting or forbidding foreign equity investment in the petroleum sector, with the result naturally being that there has been virtually no foreign investment or other activity in the petroleum sector in Argentina. Restrictive investment laws really did restrict.

A third set of observations is more recent. The countries that had neither multinationals of their own nor those of other countries, and restricted other people's multinationals, are now typically at the the top of the list of countries that have debt problems. They are the countries currently going through austerity programs. They are the countries that borrowed a great deal of money at short maturities and at high interest rates. Mexico is but one example. Even before the earthquake, it was clear that Mexico was going to have a very, very difficult problem coping with its debt burden. Mexico and a number of other countries with restrictions on multinationals have gotten themselves not just into a poverty problem, but also into a reversal of expectations problem, an increasing austerity problem. The primary cause is the inability of their economies to earn foreign exchange with which to service debt. More specifically, since <u>firms</u> and <u>businesses</u>, rather than abstractions like "economies" or "countries," actually earn foreign exchange, the cause of debt problems is the inability of <u>firms</u> located in places like Mexico to earn sufficient foreign exchange.

Personally, I think that there is a link between the debt and foreign investment issues. The developing countries with the restrictive equity investment laws are precisely those that have run into debt problems. Statistically, this can be demonstrated. The developing countries of Asia have allowed considerable foreign equity investment. They have not had debt problems. People talk about the "developing country debt problem." I think one might more accurately term it a "Latin American and African debt problem" not a "developing country debt problem." Furthermore, I do not believe that the term "debt problem" tells the whole story at all. One might also call it -- at least in part -- a "developing-country-refusal-of-equity-investment problem."

The intellectual history of the "refusal of equity problem" takes us back to the days when I was a student in Professor Kindleberger's class. Some people in the 1950s and 1960s, not Professor Kindleberger as I remember, made a great effort to sell developing country economic policy makers on something which came to be called "unbundling." The "package" of skills and technologies of the multinationals was to be unbundled from their equity ownership. The idea was that you did not want to accept these horrible, big, usually American multinational companies as investors in your developing country, not only because they might "control" or "exploit," but also because if they made foreign equity investments in your country, this would result in a perpetual claim on your economy in the form of dividends. This was said to be bad because it gave rise to a permanent claim on scarce foreign exchange. (The idea that foreign exchange need not be permanently scarce for a developing country apparently did not occur to the proponents of this view!) In addition, back in those days at least, debt looked awfully cheap. I am old enough to remember that many people were shocked in the late 1960s when interest rates started to move slightly above six percent. I even recall a "credit crunch" back in the late 1960s when the prime rate went from 6.25 percent to 6.5 percent! So there was a whole school of "development economics" that said that foreign investment was <u>prima facie</u> suspect because it was big, American, and oligopolistic and/or monopolistic, but it was even worse because it gave rise to a permanent claim and of course debt was cheaper, and if we financed development by debt financing rather then foreign equity financing, we, the developing countries, would then end up owning it on our own and controlling this.

This philosophy of "unbundling," of refusal or limitation on foreign investment, was most frequently propounded by Latin American officials and economists. They were usually the same people advocating other so-called "development" policies. "Unbundling" was to be, and in practice most typically was, combined with a set of economic policies which were inward-looking and focused on import-substitution. The idea was that you put up a trade barrier wall around your economy, and you stimulated fully or partly locally-owned, often state-owned, infant industries behind these barriers. You did not worry too much about exports, in part because there was yet another "theory" of development which had to do with political relationships. The so-called "dependency theory" stated that the developing countries had been exploited mercilessly by the advanced countries of the "center" and that the "peripheral" countries would only do themselves a disservice by being linked by exports to yet more "dependency" on the international capitalist system.

Not only were these policies inward-looking and oriented toward import-substitution, but they tended to glorify the role of the state. Economic development was something that was done by people who were "development economists," or by people who were bureaucrats trained in "development economics." It certainly was not something done by firms, much less by foreign firms. Everybody knew not only that foreign multinationals were motivated by a rather dirty thing called "profit," but also that domestic entrepreneurs -- especially those outside currently established elites -- might be motivated in a similar suspect way. The ideal, in addition to the infant-industry tariff, import-substituting mode of development, consisted of state companies. After all, who would be more socially responsible to the development imperatives of the state than companies owned by the state? One therefore soon found that large sections of the economies of Argentina, Mexico, Brazil, Peru, Venezuela, and many African countries were, or became, reserved to the state. The state was to be the driving force of development. Where state firms -- "para-statals" in the jargon -- were not owners of the means of production, state bureaucrats were the controllers. "Permits everywhere," was one result. "Bureaucrats everywhere," was another result.

Partly because overvalued exchange rates allowed the appearance of maintaining low, local currency prices for imported goods, the bureaucratic-statist regimes maintained overvalued currencies as well. In other words, fewer Mexican or Argentinian pesos per dollar were required to pay for imported goods when imports were permitted at all. A free market economy would have allowed currency rates to be set by relative inflation rates.

Overvalued exchange rates, of course, required yet more important permits and currency controls, and yet more direct "gatekeeping" of private transactions by bureaucrats. Intellectual rationales for this state of affairs were fabricated. Bureaucrats argued that keeping currencies in line with market equilibria and relative inflation rates would not further development by reducing foreign exchange shortages because their countries would not be able to export more anyway. The whole idea of a devaluation is to encourage more exports and fewer imports. This is why the United States in 1985 began intervening to get the United States dollar down so the United States would have more exports and fewer imports. But a lot of the developing countries' policy-makers said, "Devaluation won't help, because no matter how cheap our coffee beans or our copper are, we're not going to be able to export more, so why bother?" They did not notice, or course, that by doing this they were discouraging non-traditional exports, and they were creating a situation of encouraging imports -- and of the employment of controllers of imports. How does one reconcile an overvalued currency with an inward-looking import-substitution development policy and a shortage of foreign exchange? There have to be many permits and a lot of bureaucrats who give licenses for imports.

Another part of this so-called development policy was in fact yet another way to abort development. When foreign investment <u>was</u> allowed, it was allowed not in the form of 100 percent ownership, because multinational companies might "control" things if they had 100 percent ownership. They might choose which managers to hire and fire. They might chose to remit 100 percent of the profits in dividends. And, indeed, if the MNE subsidiaries were producing in protected, controlled "markets" they would be earning supra-normal profits or what economists call monopoly rents of protection. So these countries imposed local joint-venture partners on foreign investors. All too often, these local partners became tax farmers -- collectors of the rents of protection "on behalf of" the country, not entrepeneurs actively involved in management. They also became vigorous lobbyists for continued, permanent protection.

This is some of the not-too-often told background of what occurred in many of the Latin American and African countries that are now in deep economic trouble. It may be harsh, but it is unfortunately accurate.

The state of affairs portrayed above led directly to four ethical dilemmas of multinational enterprise. First, there was, and is, the ethical dilemma of rentier, tax-farmer, joint-venture partners. The countries that closed their domestic markets by persuing import-substituting development policies, typically reserved their domestic markets to selectively chosen infants. In contrast to Japan's "infant industry" developmental history, there was very little competition behind trade barriers among the putative "infants" in most LDCs. As such, the question arose concerning who would get the monopoly rent: Would it be the foreign company, the domestic joint-venture partner, or the government? Many governments, rather than altering their general tax laws, said to foreign companies: "Take-on Mr. So and So as your joint-venture partner." One finds "Mr. So and So's," or "Mr. Big's" all around the world of the developing countries: in the Philippines, in Peru, in Brazil, in Mexico. These "Mr. Big's" end up having 50 percent or 51 percent of a lot of different affiliates of foreign companies -- those that are allowed in at all -- and they do not seem to be terribly interested in absorbing foreign technology or learning how to do the foreigners' business. They collect dividend payments. They are rentiers, and their status hardly improves the income distribution/distortions in many developing countries. If government "development" policy creates a rentier class, one can be pretty sure there is going to be something wrong with the income distribution. And MNEs that cooperate in such protected joint-ventures are tarred with the association.

A second ethical dilemma is the elimination or distraction of entrepreneurship. If a government creates a rentier class, it can rationalize the fact by arguing that it is giving some people an opportunity to accumulate capital. But what do these people do with it? If the natural outlets for capital accumulation are forbidden because the government reserves large swaths of the economy to public sector, paristatal enterprises, and the government has an overvalued exchange rate policy, we know what they do with it. They turn it into dollars. They bring it to the United States and keep it in United States banks or in United States treasury bills and finance the United States budget deficit -- or they purchase American real estate. Argentina's external debt is estimated at something over 40 billion dollars. Argentinian individuals' holdings of dollars are estimated at something over 40 billion dollars, but these holdings are not being used to pay back the debts to the foreign banks.

A third ethical dilemma arises over the appropriation of monopoly rents of protection through transfer pricing. Many problems of transfer pricing between multinational companies and host governments and local partners over who gets what, and what imported inputs should be priced at, would probably not exist were it not for the artificially protected markets that give the multinational firm an incentive to try to move money out of the country by means other than (usually controlled) dividend payments.

A fourth ethical dilemma is that of bribery and corruption. My suspicion is that if one looks very carefully at the issue of bribery and corruption, the nature of the economic system has much to do with it. In a market system, if you as a manager want to influence a customer to be favorably disposed to your product, you can either make a better product or offer it at a cheaper price. It is very hard to "bribe" a customer in a sense of giving a customer a highly privileged price for very long, partly because word gets around, and partly because under market-competitive conditions it is neither possible nor much in your interest to do so. If you want to move more product, you give <u>everybody</u> a cheaper price, not just the person who might want to purchase your product today. However, if you have a state-dominated, bureaucratic system, built up along the import-substituting, excess-import-demand, bureaucratic, state-controlled model, you have a very different animal. There are a lot of privileged gate-keepers. The multinational firm, indeed any firm, cannot operate unless it gets a permit, contract, or license from some government official. Opportunities abound for personal 'toll-taking' where location-permits, import licenses, non-publicly-tendered state company contracts and the like are the norm. Non-market rationing is easily bent to favor the rationer. Is it not interesting that bribery and corruption in the United States are virtually synonymous with bribery and corruption of government officials in the context of solicitation of government contracts? The more market-oriented the system, the less bribery and corruption by definition.

The above is a sketch both of what I think has gone wrong with many of the "growth models" in developing countries and of the circumstances that have plunged multinational companies frequently -- and often quite unknowingly, unwillingly, or even beyond their comprehension -- into at least four ethical dilemmas.

I would like to close by making two final observations. First, is it not time that we stop asking the Zen-Buddhist question of "What is the sound of one hand clapping?" For many years, many people have been preoccupied by the question: "What is the effect of multinational companies on economic development?" But multinationals are only one hand clapping. Multinationals operate in, and have very different effects in, different government policy contexts. If one listens for the sound of two hands clapping, one becomes aware of countries where multinationals have clearly had a very positive impact. These countries include Singapore, Hong Kong, Taiwan, and South Korea, not to mention a Japan over parts of its development history. The policy environment was such as to allow multinational companies to operate productively in a competitive, not overprotected, context as exporters and foreign exchange earners who contribute greatly to employment, tax revenue, and even the encouragement (via suppliers and departures of trained personnel) of local entrepreneurship. Ethical dilemmas were not totally absent -- they never are -- but they were many fewer, and development was vastly greater.

My second observation is partly historical. Gottfried Habeler, a former professor of International Economics at Harvard with whom I once studied, gave a lecture in 1956 at the National Bank of Egypt which was read by students during the 1960s -- and disagreed with by most. In this lecture, he said that for the life of him, he could not see why there should be two branches of economics, one called "development economics" and one called "market economics." He felt that there was one valid view of policy economics: market economics, and that sooner or later there would be evidence to show that good economic policies were good economic policies whether they were pursued in developed or less-developed countries. If one looks at what has happened in terms of the developing country success stories versus the development failures, I think we now know that Habeler was right.

POVERTY

Jean Wilkowski

The subject of poverty is a difficult one to get a grip on, unless, of course, you are poor. Then it envelopes your entire being and completely undermines any hope of genuinely human existence. There is a moral imperative here, but also an economic imperative, which other humans on this globe cannot ignore. Those of us who are fortunate enough not to be poor are always ready to deal with poverty in the abstract and from any number of perspectives.

My perspective on poverty is that of a person who has spent a lifetime in government as a professional diplomat. Half of that career was in the poor, developing countries of the Caribbean, Latin America, and Africa or talking about the developing countries (and how we talk!) at the United Nations. My perspective also draws on my current experience, both as director of a private voluntary organization which implements government programs in developing countries, and as a director of a multinational food corporation which operates in 47 countries, including developing countries in Asia, Africa, and Latin America.

In this presentation I have four objectives:

1. To explain how the United States Agency for International Development (AID) interprets its mandate from Congress to help the poor of the world;

2. To review some shifts in AID's policies and programs under the Reagan Administration;

3. To look more specifically at the Reagan Administration's policies and programs to engage the private sector and to promote private enterprise in development; and

4. To urge better understanding of why it should be in United States corporate and national interests to be concerned with and active in policies and programs for dealing with poverty in the Third World.

Agency for International Development

As its name implies, AID is a government development agency whose purpose is to promote long-range foreign policy objectives of the United States, a factor sometimes overlooked or forgotten. AID's basic purpose is a foreign policy objective: to promote growth and development in the Third World. Congress, which created AID, provides funding on an annual basis. This currently runs at around 18.7 billion dollars. Only about one-third of this is labeled development assistance.

Since the start up of the program under President Truman's Point Four, AID's history has been fraught with frustration and criticism. While there has been growth in the developing countries, and remarkable growth at that for countries such as Korea and Taiwan, the benefits have not always "trickled down" to the poor majority of these countries. Nor have the low income countries been a priority focus. Determined to reverse these trends, Congress in 1973 amended the Foreign Assistance Act and called for "New Directions." The law states that the poor majority of the people within developing countries should be helped to participate in a process of equitable growth, with emphasis on the last two words.

Yet Congressional criticism and public dissatisfaction have continued. In December, 1982, Congress inserted a Targeted Aid Amendment calling for no less than 40 percent of development assistance funds to finance productive facilities, goods, and services which would expeditiously and directly benefit those living in absolute poverty (based on World Bank standards). In its required report back to Congress, AID asserted that 100 percent of its projects and programs are directly or indirectly targeted to benefit the poor majority. AID admitted that it could not assign an exact percentage of benefit to those in absolute poverty. But AID felt that its required report to Congress had helped the agency focus more on who received what.

Dealing with poverty is only one of several conflicting goals of the foreign assistance program. Another goal is to meet emergency needs of the poorest people suffering from natural disasters, such as famine, drought, floods, and earthquakes. A third and important goal to the present administration is to satisfy United States strategic and political interests. A fourth goal is to expand United States commerce. It is understandable why these goals compete with the basic goal on poverty and why priorities sometimes become skewed, depending on political interests. Indeed, the Reagan Administration has been taken to task for tending to down-play the poverty goal, while favoring the political and security aspects of foreign assistance, most notably in Central America but also in the Middle East.

However, it is a mark of the Reagan Administration's

political wisdom not to have contested the basic human needs legislation of 1973. Instead it chose the administrative route of aligning the foreign assistance program more closely with its own ideology and economics. Not incorrectly, it blamed the world economic recession for inhibiting the basic poverty goal of the program. And it rightly recognized that two other factors were hampering foreign assistance: the absence of strong, indigenous institutions and effective economic policies in many Third World nations. The Reagan Administration then designed its own four point AID policy, calling it "four pillars." These are: 1) policy dialogue with AID-recipient countries; 2) private sector initiatives; 3) technology research, development, and transfer; and 4) institution building. These four themes run throughout AID's attack on inadequate income growth, health deficiencies, illiteracy, and population pressures.

It needs saying that there is little that is genuinely new in these four policy pillars. Each has been tried in varying degrees by previous administrations. It is the manner of emphasis and ideological content which gives newness to these policy directions.

Time does not permit full examination of how each of the four policies impacts on the poor majorities in developing countries. Let us examine the most relevant for this conference -- private sector initiatives -- which some regard as controversial.

AID's Private Sector Initiatives

A new bureau, that of Private Enterprise, was created in AID to administer this program. Its present assistant administrator, Neal Peden, explained that the Reagan Administration discovered that most of this country's foreign aid was government-to-government with private enterprise tending to be overlooked. Especially out of the picture, it was thought, were Third World entrepreneurs who could help move their countries from dependency to self-sufficiency.

Relying for counsel and advice mainly on private sector collaborators such as the International Executive Service Corps, the Young President's Organization, Business International, and the National Council of International Health, the bureau sent out teams with a mix of experts from government, corporations, and banks to study, prescribe, and assist. In two countries, Kenya and Thailand, loan pools were created with local banks so as to provide more opportunities for small businesses, especially in agriculture where the poor are concentrated. In two years time, the bureau claims that 50 small business borrowers were served and 1,600 jobs were created in these two countries.

The bureau is particularly proud of its "satellite farming" concept and program. One example is a start-up loan granted to a joint venture in Thailand to build that country's first modern meat processing plant. The company now buys livestock from 2,000 independent producers, while offering them extension services to improve their herds. The bureau also reports it is forging new relationships with private commercial banks, leasing companies, and venture capital firms, and reorienting their lending policies toward small enterprise development. A major operation is the 17.8 million dollar revolving fund to fill loan gaps in indigenous capital markets. The fund makes loans at market or near market rates. Finally, the bureau is spreading private sector philosophy and methods not only in Third World countries but within AID's own bureaucracy through seminars and training led by United States business advisory teams.

The Overseas Development Council, a Washington study group now under the chairmanship of Robert McNamara, regards AID's private sector emphasis as useful in certain circumstances, but finds it "disturbingly unclear" as to who is benefiting, or even if the approach has been clearly defined. ODC notes that AID's focus on small farmers remained a constant theme of the government agency throughout the 70's. While the President has solid faith in the "magic of the marketplace," ODC and others fear that AID's private sector focus may be primarily promoting American commercial interests.

This judgment may be both hasty and harsh, given the short time the program has been in operation and the limited resources available to it. On the other hand, the critics recognize that there is not necessarily a conflict between poverty-oriented development and projects focusing on the indigenous private sector. It also recognizes that the private sector can help meet basic human needs in ways that over-extended (and one might add, inefficient) public sectors cannot. Also, AID can enjoy credit for some success in creating and expanding intermediate financial institutions and making credit available to groups previously excluded, especially small farmers.

AID's Bureau of Private Enterprise is essentially catalytic in its activity. Its annual budget of around $30 million dollars for such an ambitious and lightly publicized program is remarkably small. But the bureau is only one part of the picture. AID's regional bureaus are investing around $200 million annually in private sector projects. PRE provides them with policy guidance. Who can say what precise level of financial support is just right for this or that program? Doubters can say that whatever the level, resources are being diverted from important public sector infrastructure projects, such as roads, schools, and health care.

Certainly I would agree that the private sector AID program should be closely monitored to obtain reliable data on its developmental impact among low-income countries and the poorest of the poor.

Yet the program has had other benefits of development education and consciousness-raising about the poor majority which are certainly needed. The program's timing is also good. It comes at a point when a number of developing countries, especially in Africa, have come to recognize the shortcomings of centrally-controlled economies and parastatal companies.

The program also seems to have helped create a climate which has caused a trend of greater corporate involvement in foreign assistance programs. Corporations now seem more receptive to approaches from private voluntary organizations, partly because such organizations are learning how to sell their services to corporations, rather than looking mainly for grant assistance for their development work. Under the Reagan Administration's policies, AID's Bureau of Food for Peace and Voluntary Assistance had been catalytic in this regard, sponsoring a number of training sessions for private voluntary organizations on developing marketing concepts for consideration by corporations. A few examples come to mind to illustrate the point. Volunteers in Technical Assistance, or VITA, which I represent, has been counseled by AID-sponsored business advisors on a joint venture proposal to Control Data and also on a deforestation project for Philip Morris. This training has also helped VITA to conclude development project contracts with Hershey Food Corporation in a cacao production scheme for poor farmers in Belize and a similar one in Honduras. In addition, VITA has established its own Venture Service and is actively bringing small firms in the United States together with small firms in India, China, and elsewhere in joint ventures or licensing arrangements.

Technoserve has also benefited from AID's enterprise training and advice to private voluntary organizations, specifically on a joint venture with IBEC involving corporations serving parastatal companies.

What conclusions can be drawn from this brief sketch of AID's new policy emphasis on private enterprise efforts such as

AID's new policy emphasis on private enterprise efforts such as linkages between the private sectors in the United States and developing countries, credit facilities for small businesses, and closer collaboration between corporations and private voluntary organizations in Third World development?

While AID has probably involved the private sector in foreign assistance more deeply than in the past, the total amount of resources dedicated to the program, including credit for productive enterprise and the number of jobs created is still miniscule. In sum, the results are disappointingly modest within the total foreign assistance picture. Moreover, United States development assistance still runs a poor second to political and security assistance, but that is a subject for separate discussion.

It needs emphasizing that the private enterprise programs need to be closely monitored to be certain they do not distract AID from its primary purpose of helping the poorest people in the Third World, rather than serving business interests.

Something additional needs to be said on the distinctions between United States corporations and United States national interests. Let us not forget that AID was formed to promote long-range foreign policy objectives. Humanitarian interest and concern for the poor are a sub-set of these objectives. But international economic interests are another and very important part of these objectives. Many economic changes have taken place in United States - Third World relations in the past three decades. Third World Countries have become major markets for United States exports and increasingly significant suppliers of low-cost goods. They are also major customers (and profit centers) for United States banks, as well as the locus for a considerable amount of American private investment. United States Corporations and banks are thus already deeply involved in the Third World through trade and investment. While profit is their primary motive, corporations can afford to and do get involved in non-profit developmental activities as well. Such activities obviously help protect their investment stake and build customers for the future. So much for corporate interests.

In the area of national interests, the United States seeks to enjoy full and sustained economic recovery from the world recession. But it cannot hope to achieve this by domestic policies and programs alone. There must be growth in developing countries where there are many customers for United States exports. Therefore, American business and the government must be concerned about poverty not only on ethical and humanitarian grounds, but for sound economic reasons as well.

CHAPTER SEVEN

INVESTING IN DEVELOPMENT: THE PROMISE AND THE PROBLEMS

MARJORIE K. SHEEN
Public Affairs Advisor
The World Bank
Washington, DC

BARBARA BRAMBLE
Director
International Division
National Wildlife Federation
Washington, DC

SHEILA HARTY
Director
Corporate Initiatives Division
National Wildlife Federation
Washington, DC

THE ROLE OF THE PRIVATE SECTOR IN DEVELOPING COUNTRIES: A WORLD BANK PERSPECTIVE

Marjorie K. Sheen

Moral or ethical objectives and the goals of profitmaking organizations have often been seen as antithetical. But I would propose they can be complementary. This is perhaps not always true, but when private enterprise is specifically harnessed to the achievement of economic development in the Third World, then ethical standards and business objectives can have a common purpose: economic growth in the developing nations and the betterment of the lives of the struggling poor of the Third World. The path to that goal, however, is not always smooth, direct, or free of conflicts. In fact, in the current international economic arena, we see a wide array of conflicting goals, and nowhere are they more dramatic than in the relationship between the United States and Latin American economies.

In the struggle to repay foreign debt, Latin American countries have dramatically increased their export earnings, which may hearten the United States banks which are their lenders, but also creates some of the current trade problems in the United States. In the interest of servicing that dept and reducing expenditures, Latin American countries have drastically reduced their imports from the United States, creating a sizeable loss to United States laborers and economic hardships in many American communities dependent on Latin American purchase of their products.

During the last Annual Meeting of the International Monetary Fund and The World Bank, there was a growing recognition that Latin American countries and other Third World nations must be given the opportunity to grow and must have the necessary tools to achieve that growth if they are to honor their debt commitments, strengthen their economies, and provide opportunities for their people in their struggle for a better life.

The tools needed to accomplish that growth include continued capital flows and investment from the industrialized countries. Unfortunately, in recent years, there has been a serious fall-off in commercial lending, direct private investment, and multinational enterprise activity in developing countries. There has been great hesitancy on the part of multinationals and investors to take on new activities in the Third World, where political instability and fragile economies have discouraged private sector initiatives. Hesitancy on the part of foreign investors has been matched in many developing countries by host-country fears of foreign domination and control. This has led to restrictions which have unintentionally affected the flow of foreign portfolio investment.

Attitudes may now be changing on both sides. Debt problems have focused the attention of many developing countries on the rigidities of repayment schedules and on the "crowding out" of international capital markets as governments compete for funds. On the other side, institutional investors from industrialized countries, who have been limiting their foreign portfolio investment, are now looking for additional opportunities. There are now several regional investment funds, for example, for the Asian-Pacific area, and individual country funds have been organized for a number of countries including Mexico, Korea, and India.

In many developing countries, the burden of external debt and the demand for credit have been important causes of economic difficulties. With domestic and external resources currently constrained, the pursuit of efficiency and domestic resource mobilization is more critical than ever. The most rapid economic growth in the developing world has been achieved in countries where governments have recognized that private enterprise has a critical role to play. Therefore, there is an urgent need to expand and release the energies of the private sector. Foreign investment is critically important to the developing nations and should be encouraged, not discouraged, by those whose interests it can clearly serve.

This can be done only if the chronic lack of mutual confidence between developing country governments and business is reduced, if not completely eliminated. Governments and businessmen must work together to establish mutual trust and cooperation, because the participation of the private sector in the development process is not an option; it is an absolute essential.

The World Bank and its affiliate, the International Finance Corporation, see for themselves a significant role in, on the one hand, helping governments create an environment in which private enterprise can flourish and, on the other, working with the private sector as a catalyst or, in some cases, as a partner, to further economic development in the Third World.

The role of governments in the developing nations is the starting point. Governments need to adopt and adhere to coherent economic ground rules, establishing a framework in which private enterprise can operate both effectively in the sense of generating high returns to both the country and the investors, and in a manner responsive to the needs of society. The economic framework which could provide a supportive environment for private enterprise would, ideally, include the following characteristics:

- Adequate physical infrastructure such as roads, ports, and power;

- Minimal market distortions and rigidities, so that the prices of capital, labor, foreign exchange, and products reflect their relative scarcity;

- Support for research and for its wide dissemination;

- Relatively unrestricted entry into a particular industry;

- Extension of considerable autonomy to entrepreneurs in their investment and managerial decisions;

- Protection by law of property rights, including intellectual property;

- Consistent and uniform application of government policies, including nondiscrimination between foreign and nationally-owned enterprises, and the right of foreign investors to remit capital and earnings; and

- Adherence to agreements ensuring independent arbitration of the provision of insurance coverage against political risks.

These characteristics represent valid goals to be pursued in national development strategies and are no less valid individually, being difficult to attain in their totality.

Before addressing the question of how The World Bank, and particularly the International Finance Corporation, view their roles in the stimulation of private enterprise in the Third World, perhaps I should first explain the organization and functions of the institutions called The World Bank.

The World Bank is actually a group of three institutions: the International Bank for Reconstruction and Development (IBRD), the International Development Association (IDA), and the International Finance Corporation (IFC). Each of these institutions is designed to help the developing countries of the world in a particular way.

The IBRD lends money to the more creditworthy developing countries, at near commercial rates. Currently, the IBRD lending rate, which is adjusted every six months, is 8.82 percent. Last year, IBRD provided over $11 billion to 43 countries in the form of 15-to-20-year loans.

The International Development Association is the Bank's affiliate for less creditworthy borrowers -- those nations with a per capita GNP of less than $410 per year. IDA loans carry no interest and only a small service charge. As an IDA country's economy grows out of the low-income category and becomes creditworthy, it graduates to IBRD. Twenty-seven countries are now in this category of IDA graduates.

Loans from IBRD and IDA are primarily for specific projects and programs in developing countries. They must be economically viable; that is, they must yield economic rates of return of at least 10 percent per annum. Our projects cover not only agriculture and rural development, energy, and industry, but education, population, health, and nutrition as well.

The Bank's third affiliate is the International Finance Corporation. The IFC is our merchant bank, working with the private sector in developing countries to promote the growth of productive private investment and to assist enterprises that will contribute to the economic development of its Third World member countries. The IFC makes both equity investments and loans without government guarantees. Its principal tasks are to provide and bring together the financing, technical assistance, and management needed to develop productive investment opportunities.

Let us return now to the question of how The World Bank seeks to strengthen private sectors of developing countries.

First, The World Bank can provide advice and a measure of finance in support of a government's efforts to create the conditions conducive to productive private sector activity. Indeed, the Bank's charter lists as the second of its purposes the promotion of foreign private investment through the variaous instruments at its disposal. With its advice and a measure of finance, the International Finance Corporation also can help the private sector entrepreneur turn his or her creativity and drive to good account in circumstances where, without IFC support, that would not happen.

The International Finance Corporation has the specific

responsibility within the World Bank family for the promotion and support of private enterprise in the developing countries. Its activities are therefore crucial to an agenda for action to strengthen foreign private investment in the Third World.

Its distinctive role is to bring together foreign or domestic capital, technology, and managerial know-how for productive development endeavors. It provides on its own account, and mobilizes elsewhere, funds for promising private sector ventures in its developing member countries. The form its own financing takes is flexible; it is one of the very few official international organizations which can provide risk capital as well as long-term loans without government guarantee. It attracts additional funds in the international capital markets by syndicating loans and by underwriting and standby financing.

The recent decline in foreign investment and the slowdown in foreign commercial bank lending have prompted developing countries to place more emphasis on strengthening their domestic financial markets. For its part, the IFC will assist the process by expanding its already extensive technical assistance to financial markets and its institution-building activities in that sector.

The IFC's Board recently recommended to its member governments that they approve a doubling of its authorized capital, from $650 million to $1.3 billion. This will enable the Corporation to implement a new Five-Year Program. Under this program, the IFC plans to make gross investments of $7.5 billion (in current dollars), of which some $3 billion will be syndicated to banks. The total investment associated with these IFC investments will be in the region of $30 billion.

In discussing the role of the International Finance Corporation in developing greater private sector activity in the Third World, I do not want to give the impression that we believe direct foreign private investment to be some kind of panacea. It is not. There are limits to what it can do. It is linked to specific investment projects and cannot be used flexibly to finance the broad needs of development. It tends to concentrate in the few sectors of interest to multinational corporations, which fall, for the most part, in the process industries and in heavy durable goods. It also tends to concentrate in a small number of host countries, mostly those with large internal markets or those with special advantages for exports. Given such limitations, direct foreign investment must always be seen as complementary to other sources of development finance.

While the IFC moves ahead with its agenda, the IBRD and IDA continue to play important, complementary roles in support of private sector development. Their commitment to the strengthening of institutions in the economic sectors helps create a better environment for private enterprise activity.

The Bank will continue to do all that it can to help strengthen the incentive framework for private investors throughout the developing world. One important initiative we have recently taken is to develop a new plan for the establishment of a Multilateral Investment Guarantee Agency that would guarantee against non-commercial risks. Much of its business would be coverage against the risk of currency situations that would keep foreign investors from repatriating profits. But the agency would also provide guarantees against the risks of political violence and expropriation.

Four categories of non-commercial risks will be covered:

- First, the transfer risk resulting from host government restrictions on conversion and transfer;

- Second, the risk of loss resulting from actions or omissions of the host government which would have the effect of depriving the investor of ownership, control, or substantial benefit from investment;

- Third, the risk resulting from the repudiation of a contract by the host government, when the investor has no access to a competent forum, faces unreasonable delays, or is unable to enforce a final judgment; and

- Fourth, war and civil disturbance risk.

Apart from the Multilateral Investment Guarantee Agency, which we hope to see approved at our Annual Meeting in Seoul, there are three areas of World Bank activity in which we are looking increasingly to the private sector as a partner.

The first is in the area of energy resource development. The World Bank devotes a quarter of its lending to the energy sector as part of its diverse program to provide resources and technical assistance. Playing its catalytic role and, when appropriate, putting up its own funds, the Bank is making a major effort to bring private sector interests and developing country governments into fruitful partnerships to promote the development of oil and gas resources.

A second area concerns the involvement of commercial

banks. We are working hard to revive the confidence of commercial banks in Third World lending. We have fashioned a range of cofinancing instruments already attracting commercial banks into cofinancing highly-supervised, soundly-designed projects, providing the banks with the assurance of association with the World Bank in their Third World lending.

The third area is in the agricultural sector. We are looking to the private sector for increased support in the particularly vital area of agricultural research. The agricultural sector is crucial to the development of both the public and private sectors of developing economies. Generous support for agricultural research is therefore in the interests of all of us. Devising the technology to stimulate higher agricultural productivity is a top priority throughout the developing world. Nowhere is it more important than in Sub-Saharan Africa, where drought and famine have led to tragic health and environmental conditions.

The contribution that the private sector can make to development is still too little understood, and the potential too little harnessed. But vital as the role of the private sector may be, private enterprise alone cannot set the developing countries back on the path of sustained economic growth and social progress. How effectively governments perform in the overall management of their economies is the truly critical factor.

There is a risk that the total development effort may end in failure if we do not help mobilize more fully the entrepreneurial spirit of the developing nations. A more active partnership between business, governments, and institutions such as the World Bank and the IFC can help smooth the path and shorten the length of the long and challenging journey to prosperity.

The path of economic development is a difficult one, a path for which we do not always have a clearly-defined map. Economic development in the Third World has a short history, and the industrialized countries, with only four decades of experience in aiding Third World nations, still have much to learn about helping to improve living standards in developing countries -- countries with vastly different historical experiences, extremely varied and dissimilar cultural and social systems, and far more fragile human, institutional, and financial resources.

Not only are their societal structures quite different, but the scope of their challenges is far more enormous. Crippling external debt, unsustainable population growth, deteriorating ecological environments, rampant malnourishment compounded by declining agricultural independence, insufficient water supplies and medical care, and unstable political and economic structures threaten the viability of too many Third World countries.

These crises are matched only by the compelling incentives industrialized countries have in working with Third World nations to surmount their challenges. In the global economy in which industrialized nations must compete, the greatest potential for economic growth lies in the export markets of developing nations, but only if those nations can afford to purchase its products -- and they will not be able to do so if protectionist barriers are erected against their exports. The financial institutions of the First World are faced with the inescapable reality that their long-term clients reside in the Third World. Surely our historical perspective, our economic vitality, and our ethical commitment compel us not only to work, each at our own individual endeavors, but also to work together, in common cause, towards the enrichment of all mankind.

ENVIRONMENTAL CONCERNS ASSOCIATED WITH MULTILATERAL DEVELOPMENT BANK ACTIVITY

Barbara Bramble and Sheila Harty

This paper shifts gears from the focus on private enterprise to consider similar ethical dilemmas of influential public institutions which have a profound impact on the course of development in the Third World. We are referring to multi-lateral banks, such as The World Bank and the Inter-American Development Bank (IDB), which are established by international convention and receive their capital as contributions from governments.

The role of multi-lateral development banks (MDBs) is somewhat schizoid -- to assist poor nations and people, and to make money. MBDs make loans at preferential rates for projects intended to gradually improve the standard of living of people in developing nations. Our conclusion is that, unfortunately, sometimes the unintended consequences of these projects actually make the situation worse for the very people supposedly being helped.

One of the reasons for the difficulties and failures of many development projects is the lack of understanding among planners of how natural systems function. In many instances, the planners apparently fail to recognize the ecological opportunities and constraints in which the projects must operate.

Building awareness of the key role of natural resource management in economic development is a slow process. It is complicated by the sheer size of the development assistance organizations and the weight of traditional, entrenched, development thinking. Nevertheless, it is worth trying because of the disproportionate influence of some of these institutions. For example, The World Bank's country economic memoranda may be used by borrowing governments as their own development strategy and major planning tool.

The decisions of the MBDs also pave the way for other, perhaps even larger, investments by commercial banks in the same or related projects. Consequently, the influence of MBDs on development thinking and on natural resources goes far beyond the dollar amounts actually invested by them. Yet important decisions are being made without necessary information about consequences which adversely affect millions of people, as well as the natural environment.

There is an opportunity here for ethical leadership to ensure the consideration of consequences prior to commitment of finances for allegedly beneficial purposes. Recent changes in some MBD policies and programs seem to indicate a new willingness to address this problem. Under pressure from non-governmental organizations, The World Bank and the IDB appear to be developing a more ecologically sound approach to project planning. Yet, despite improvements, the banks continue to fund projects which seriously degrade the natural environment and which reduce the productive capacity of resources such as water, forests, and soil.

Water Projects

One category of projects which has caused serious problems is large scale water reservoirs for irrigation and/or hydroelectric power productions. These projects have been and still are conceived and implemented without full appreciation of the constraints of the predominantly tropical ecosystems in which they are located. Moreover, by their nature, dams and reservoirs interrupt the seasonal pattern of river flooding in which rich silts are deposited to renew the lands' fertility. Often thousands of people are forcibly moved to less productive land to continue subsistence farming, while the better land is converted to mechanized monocultures. Several projects have flooded major parts of the homelands of entire tribes of indigenous peoples, as did the Bayano Dam in Panama.

If an irrigation scheme is designed for the production of export crops instead of food, the net nutritional status of the region may actually decrease. In addition, conversion of subsistence farms to monocultures is not sustainable. Since the crops will be more vulnerable to pests, this initiates the treadmill of mass applications of pesticides.

In the Gezira irrigation scheme in the Sudan, widespread pesticide use to protect the cotton crop brought serious imbalance to the natural system of insect predators. As a result, increasingly sophisticated and expensive chemicals, such as the highly toxic aldicarb, are now needed. Such experiences have recently convinced The World Bank to turn to "integrated pest management" as a matter of policy. But we still await concrete changes in actual field projects.

In India and Pakistan, hundreds of thousands of irrigated acres are losing productivity due to waterlogging and salinization because of inadequate drainage. Downstream water quality may be reduced due to lack of dissolved oxygen, pesticide contamination, and lower flows. This adversely affects river and coastal fisheries which are often principal sources of protein.

The Volta River project in Ghana flooded 80,000 people from their homes to produce electricity for an aluminum plant, producing for export, which did not even make use of local labor or local bauxite. A similar portion of the population was afflicted with a debilitating disease, called schistosomiasis, as a result of this project.

The reservoirs may also flood important tracts of tropical forests which contain potentially valuable species found nowhere else. Reservoirs covering tropical moist forests are prone to severe water quality degradation due to decay of the forest vegetation of a period of perhaps decades. Thus, reservoir fisheries may not develop as a source of protein to compensate for loss of the river fisheries which were inundated.

Shifting farmers out of the bottomlands or facilitating entry to an uninhabited area for the first time via new access roads to a project have common adverse effects on tropical forests. Farmers move up onto the surrounding hillsides to cut forests and grow crops as best they can. Hillside plots, bared of trees and subjected to tropical rain and sun, erode quickly and lose their fertility. The farmers then must move on, continuing the deforestation process.

Meanwhile, silt accumulates in the reservoirs and damages power generation machinery or irrigation works. The project's life may be shortened; the forest, fisheries, and soil resource base of the region is degraded; and the food-production potential for the people of that area does not improve, and may even decline.

The World Bank and the IDB have begun to consider these factors in project planning. Recently, each required setting aside watershed protection areas as national parks and forest reserves to reduce deforestation. But unless the end use of electricity or of the irrigation water is labor-intensive industry or agriculture, it is hard to see the benefits of such projects to justify the natural resource destruction. Often the result is mechanized monocultures of export crops or industries which can only employ trained, and often foreign, labor.

Cattle Ranching

The benefits of development loans are even more difficult to discern for cattle projects. Both The World Bank and the IDB have put considerable sums of money into cattle production, particularly in Central America and Brazil, and in some areas of Africa. They have made loans to finance cattle ranches, construct beef packing plants, and protect livestock against diseases.

Lending for livestock operations has been one of the most important types of credit activities in the agriculture sector. Most of the livestock loans have gone into the development of large ranches. This beef is produced for export, much of it to the United States. The environmental and social consequences of these projects are almost all adverse.

Much of the expansion has taken place on land that is not suitable for cattle grazing. In some areas, tropical forests are cut down, on a huge scale, and converted to grasslands for a short period of years. Tropical forest soils are, by and large, infertile. The nutrients reside principally in the tree cover itself, and are quickly recycled from fallen leaves and branches back into living trees.

When the forest is cut and burned, the nutrients in the ashes and the top inch or so of soil can be used only for a few years until they leach out or wash away in heavy rains. Consequently, many of these projects, which are not very productive at their best, must be abandoned within ten years. By contrast, intensive agro-forestry techniques could produce thousands of pounds of corn and vegetables per hectare per year on a sustainable basis.

In some cases, preferential credit for cattle operations has encouraged the conversion of limited supplies of fertile cropland to cattle production in Central America. The region's per capita beef consumption has been actually declining, so there is little benefit to the majority of the population.

Loans for cattle ranching ignore another unintended consequence. That is, cattle ranching requires very little labor and so it contributes to already massive unemployment or underemployment. Farmworkers, displaced as cropland is turned into pasture, must seek even more marginal lands, such as forested hillsides, on which to grow food.

In recent discussions with conservation organizations, the IDB appears to be de-emphasizing loans for livestock operations. The World Bank, on the other hand, has recently approved funding of a national livestock program in Botswana. Past experience suggests that it is not in the best interest of anyone, except the individual landowners, for these lending programs to be continued.

Transmigration Schemes

Another category of destructive bank lending is financial assistance to governments who wish to move millions of landless people into undeveloped tropical forest regions. The projects are advocated to relieve the population pressure in crowded areas and to open up vast undeveloped resources. Brazil and Indonesia are implementing two of the most grandiose of these schemes, with the assistance of The World Bank and the IDB.

The problems and impacts of these projects are strikingly similar. Hundreds of thousands of people are being moved into tropical forest regions. Tools, seeds, roads, and in some cases, housing, village centers, schools, and clinics are provided. Until recently, little thought was given to planning for a forest-based economy, and instead project proponents intended that the land be cleared for farming.

In Indonesia, the crowded island of Java has a rich volcanic soil and a successful system of intensive agro-forestry which supports sixty-five percent of Indonesia's population on seven percent of its land. The transmigration project is designed to move millions of people to tropical forest regions on the thinly populated outer islands.

Estimates vary, but even fair-quality soil probably accounts for less than five percent of the total land area of the outer islands. Good quality soil, defined as that which would still be fertile after twenty years of agricultural use, accounts for less than one percent of the area. Nevertheless, the plan is for the immigrants to grow upland rice which will require regular applications of fertilizer and water. Thus, to have any chance for success, these farmers must have access to reliable credit to buy fertilizer, as well as access to irrigation for water throughout the growing season. Neither is likely. In fact, the farmers' yields so far have been low, and in some areas the rodent population, having lost its forest habitat, is happily destroying the rest of the crop.

In Brazil, too, many of the forest settlements are failing. The reasons are similar: inadequate training in the task of farming the poor soils; high costs of agricultural outputs; and lack of education in integrated pest management techniques. The Polonoroeste project, typical of other capital-intensive and uneconomic resettlement schemes, is designed to settle Brazil's vast Northwest by clearing nearly 2 million hectares (mostly tropical moist forest) near the Bolivian border. Yet, in Brazil's earlier attempts to colonize the Amazon basin along the Transamazonica Highway, only seven percent of the settlements appear to be successful after several years, and the highway was largely abandoned.

The Polonoroeste project has endangered several indigenous tribes, some of whom have only recently been contacted by outsiders. The tribal people are vulnerable to decimation by diseases, such as influenza and measles, and loss of the land which sustains them. To its credit, The World Bank has tried to ameliorate some of the worst aspects of the Polonoroeste project by insisting that the Brazilian government demarcate substantial areas as national parks and tribal reserves, and imposing other conditions. The Bank actually suspended disbursements temporarily in order to force a response from Brasilia. Although the results of this unprecedented move are encouraging, there is much more that the Bank could, and should, be doing.

Meanwhile, valuable ecosystems are being destroyed, for unsustainable uses, in an attempt to relieve political pressures caused by overpopulation, unemployment, and inequitable land distribution. A resource with great potential for sustained management is being destroyed or permanently degraded for a short-term use.

Ironically, in Indonesia, the most ambitious transmigration plans would relocate less than Java's <u>annual</u> population increase of 2.6 million. Thus, each year the government must face the same pressures with less resources on which to rely. Clearly forestry-based alternative sources of income on the outer islands and labor-intensive industry on Java would be projects more in the long-term interest of Indonesia.

Lessons to be Learned

As with most ethical dilemmas, the choice is not between good and evil. One cannot easily impute malevolent intent. Rather, ethical responsibility may be a learned capacity. We certainly have sufficient error upon which to improve.

It is our belief that The World Bank has learned much from these past experiences, and its environmental staff is promoting environmentally sound policies and improved analytical techniques. However, a staff of four or five professionals at their Office of Environmental and Scientific Affairs cannot possibly accomplish what is needed. This staff is also responsible for analyzing individual projects and trying to cajole other development banks to follow their lead. In this way, they are up against thousands of development economists and engineers. The staff of that environmental office has held up several projects in order to force inclusion of environmental safeguards. Politically this is difficult, however, and they cannot get away with it often.

Appropriate environmental planning starts at project conception and continues through evaluation of alternatives, project design, and implementation. Catching a project at the end, just before approval, always means that the environmental factors are seen as expensive add-ons and delays. They will be resisted for that reason, more than for any objections to their value. Thus The World Bank's environmental office can improve a few disastrous projects but, as currently structured, it cannot effectively promote ecologically sustainable development.

To avoid ethical dilemmas involving adverse impacts on the health and welfare of people on the earth's resources, we must learn from what this past history demonstrates: (a) environmental planning and sustainable natural resource management must be part of overall analysis and strategic economic planning; (b) involvement of the local people in planning is essential, particularly local conservation groups and tribal peoples, if they are affected; (c) full assessments of the environmental impacts of development projects must be made prior to decisions; (d) evaluations of impacts must also be made <u>after</u> project completion; and (e) all of these studies must be <u>made</u> public with information widely distributed, especially in the borrowing countries.

Public disclosure of environmental assessments would permit the true costs and benefits of the projects to be evaluated. In our view, promoting such disclosure is an ethical responsibility of the United States directors on the banks' boards.

The National Wildlife Federation and other conservation organizations have been focusing attention on the link between conservation and development worldwide. We and our colleague groups do not oppose responsible development programs. We are concerned about those which are not consistent with sustainable economic development and natural resource management.

Over the past two and one-half years in several hearings before the United States Congress, in published articles, and in numerous conferences, we have built an alliance among those concerned with the environment, as well as advocates for the rights of tribal peoples and those who question the efficacy of the United States development aid contributions. In combination with similar alliances in other industrialized countries and borrowing nations, a strong public constituency is emerging for redirecting international aid toward sustainable development. The MDBs are beginning to respond, but the pace of change is slow.

From our studies we have distilled the following recommendations for change in the procedures of the MDBs:

   a) All the banks should create policy and evaluation offices similar to The World Bank's Office of Environmental and Scientific Affairs, and staff them adequately for their workload.

   b) These offices should supervise the implementation of procedures to incorporate environment and natural resource planning in all sector planning and country development strategies.

   c) Environmental planners should be added to all project evaluation teams so that environmental factors and appropriate analysis of alternatives are taken into account along with economic factors from the beginning of project analysis.

   d) In addition to financial planners and traditional development experts, officials responsible for natural resources management and conservation <u>in the borrowing countries</u> should be routinely included in discussions between the banks and the borrowing countries to plan future economic strategies. This will increase the clout of the natural resources agencies in the developing countries where ultimately the responsibility and the will to achieve sustainable development must reside.

These changes, along with innovative attempts to include local people in project decisions, should result in the selection of development strategies more suited to local natural resources, and therefore more likely to produce sustainable improvements in quality of life.

Development assistance and its accompanying ethical responsibilities are relatively new. They grew out of the destruction of Europe in World War II. In little over 30 years, the industrialized world has been trying to learn how to encourage a complicated process of change among other people, when we really do not yet fully understand that process ourselves. So far, development agencies have been only partially successful, in some places, yet at great cost in damage to the natural resource base.

Certainly, the ethical deliberations and initiatives of

multinational enterprises, including MDBs, are on a learning curve. The dilemmas often arise when the impacts on people and the environment are not weighed along with expected economic growth. But the trade-off is not between environment and development, or between saving trees and saving people. Responsible and sustainable economic development <u>requires</u> sound management of natural resources. Moreover, true national security for any country will depend upon improving the standard of living within the countries that are our neighbors and all around the globe that is our common home.

CHAPTER EIGHT

THE IMPACT OF MULTINATIONAL BUSINESS ACTIVITY ON WOMEN IN THE THIRD WORLD

ANITA ANAND
Professional Consultant
International Development
Washington, DC

LUISA M. RIVERA IZABAL
Social Worker
SEDEPAC
(Service, Development, and Peace)
Mexico City, Mexico

LINDA Y.C. LIM
Assistant Professor and Research Director
Southeast Asia Business Education and Resource Program
University of Michigan
Ann Arbor, Michigan

MULTINATIONAL ENTERPRISES, DEVELOPMENT, AND WOMEN: AN OVERVIEW

Anita Anand

Why consider the topic of women and multinationals? Women comprise almost 50 percent of the population in most nations. Multinational enterprises have different effects on women than on men for several reasons. First, the sexual division of labor and the roles ascribed to men and women create different circumstances for each of the sexes. In 1975, the United Nations declared a Decade of Women. During this decade, three international conferences have been held and a wealth of research and information has been generated on the status of women nationally and internationally. The clear conclusion resulting from investigations of the decade is that women have needs, experiences, and aspirations that are sometimes similar to men but also different, and that women deserve a separate look at their situation within the context of the community of which they are a part.

Analysis of multinational enterprises reveals that they have preferentially hired women in jobs that are "female prone," often reinforcing society's stereotypes of women. In 1980, there were one million women hired by multinational enterprises. Multinational enterprises prefer to hire women in that they perceive them as being more hard working, more reliable, and probably less likely to be organized into unions than men.

Multinational enterprises also affect women as consumers and transmitters of culture. Women are usually the decision makers of home care and maintenance, and the marketing of goods and services produced by multinational enterprises is often targeted at them. Availability of luxury items, often perceived necessary through aggressive marketing and changing social values, creates a climate of conspicuous consumption in which underlying norms go unquestioned. Moreover, traditionally, women were the transmitters of culture, orally transferring knowledge and know-how from one generation to another. Improved communication systems, education, and urban migration have usurped this role and provided little guidance to fill the void. While multinational enterprises do not deliberately propagate a particular "culture" as such, their very presence incites a desire for what they represent - westernization.

Multinational Enterprises As a Vehicle of Development

Multinational enterprises are essentially vehicles of

development. To understand the role they play in an economy, development has to be understood first. Development means different things to different people, based on what influences their thinking. It is helpful to look at the work of Karl Mannheim who defines two basic modes of thinking, ideological and utopian, that are based on one's class interest and shape one's perception of reality. Sheldon Gellar applies these two modes to the thinking that influences development theory and models.

Ideological thinking asserts the world views of ruling groups, supports the status quo, and sees change taking place largely within currently established structures. Most mainstream development models and work are based on the ideological mode of thinking. Models based on such thinking view development as an administrative problem, the solution to which lies in the transfer of vast amounts of capital and technological resources from the rich to the poor nations. Utopian thinking reflects the opinions of certain oppressed groups, believes in the transformation of the existing structures by overthrowing the status quo, and sees change through destruction of structures responsible for exploitation and oppression of the masses. Models based on the utopian modes are generally Marxist or nationalist in orientation, rejecting the existing power relationships between the 'haves' and 'have nots' and calling for basic change in the system. In these models, underdevelopment is not defined as a problem of lack of resources or technology, but one of exploitation and poverty caused by capitalistic expropriation.

Multinational enterprises perpetuate mainstream development, choosing to invest in developing nations where they are offered tax incentives, relatively cheap and unorganized labor, low-cost raw materials, and high profits, as well as to escape rising demands of labor in the industrial North. Most colonized countries of the developing South achieved independence between the 1950s and 1970s, searching for development models. The socialist and capitalist models available to them were both industrial based. Developing nations felt they had to become a part of the international economic system and choose export-oriented development models that would enable them to compete with developed nations. This entailed imports of technical and financial resources to produce goods and services that developing nations could sell in the international market, earning foreign exchange to buy imported good and services.

During this time, large amounts of foreign aid and loans were made to the developing nations for purposes of building the infrastructures necessary for development, and the gross national products of many developing nations rose. The oil crisis hit in the early seventies. Developing nations that had developed industries and adopted models of development based on fuel intensive imports began to feel the pinch. They had to pay valuable foreign exchange for imports of oil, for which they had to boost their export markets, often at the neglect of local industry. Facing an imbalance of trade and a balance of payments problem, these nations borrowed from international financial institutions such as the International Monetary Fund, as well as from private banks in North America and Europe. This cycle of poverty and debt has become more evident in the last few years as nations struggle to balance their economies.

The Costs of Multinational Enterprises and Development

As the economies of developing nations were shifting from the rural agrarian to the urban industrial, women were losing out. With the rise of the cash economy, women were displaced by men and middlemen. In the subsistence economy, women had a definite and powerful role. It provided them with the means of daily subsistence and better access to and control over local resources.

In some countries, multinational enterprises have provided a job market for many displaced women as well as for women who would be out of the paid wage labor force. However, there are benefits and pitfalls to this provision. Most of the opportunities offered have been in agribusiness, textiles, and electronics. While the work provides women with an income through which they develop a sense of self-worth, confidence, and independence, the hours are long, the work tedious and monotonous, the wages low for services performed, and women perform a "double day," or work in and outside the home. Problems related to poor working conditions affecting women's health are enormous, as women work with equipment and materials whose side effects are detrimental to their health. These conditions, it could be argued, are no worse than would exist in local industries. However, one expects better standards from multinational enterprises as they come from nations where there is awareness of and commitment to workers' rights and protective working conditions. Besides these problems, women in newly independent nations in multinational enterprises face additional social and cultural discrimination in their attempt to work outside the home.

Certain factors are endemic to multinational enterprises, and these create problems for them as institutions. First and foremost, multinational enterprises are outsiders, with little knowledge and understanding of the nation and culture in which they are operating. In spite of cultural differences, the tendency is to perceive development and change in standards of living based on experiences in the home countries. This influences manufacturing and marketing decisions made by multinational enterprises. Second, multinational enterprises are in business for profit. Whatever they may articulate, they are in competition with other multinational enterprises or local corporations, and this affects their behavior. Third, they are in the business of producing and marketing goods and services on which they can get a maximum return. Local needs are not a high priority and, as such, human, financial, raw material, and land resources tend to be utilized in ways not responsive to basic needs of the community. Fourth, the management style of multinational enterprises is patriarchal, hierarchical, and elitist, with major decisions still being made in boardrooms and with little or no input from people who will be effected by these decisions. Finally, multinational enterprises cannot always predict the ramifications of their investments, even though many have developed some expertise in this. Social, political, and economic conditions in most developing nations, unless controlled by orgainized force, are difficult to predict. This encourages multinational enterprises to adopt policies that keep their investments safe.

If multinational enterprises are basically incompatible with local development needs, as defined by local people keeping in balance proper uses of resources, can they be compatible with the needs of women? Probably not, at least not in the more long-term needs of women. For this, the multinational enterprise world view of development will have to shift to encompass local control, notions of self-reliance and self-sufficiency, marginal profits, profit sharing, and aspirations of the local people. There are too few women in management positions in multinational enterprises and, of those, few have sensitivity to the needs of women in different situations. As women's movements in various nations move forward, voicing their opinions in the ways they would like to be politically, socially, and economically involved, it would be wise for multinational enterprises to take into serious consideration the aspirations of these women.

Conclusion

The ethical dilemma of multinational enterprises is really the dilemma of development, due to differing world views and varied theories and models of development. For example, what should be the minimum standard of living, and who should define this? Who defines needs and luxuries? How are resources appropriated, developed, and used, and who decides this? While local, state, national, regional, and international mechanisms exist to promote decision making, some people are not being heard or having input into decision making. These are essentially the men and women whose lives will be affected by these decisions.

A major problem for multinational enterprises in home and host countries has been one of accountability. It might seem that their ultimate accountability is to the shareholder, but even some multinational enterprises are astute enough not to limit their horizons. The impact of multinational enterprises, like other institutions, is on all of society, and increasingly different sectors of society are calling the behavior of multinational enterprises into question. Norms of behavior have sometimes been established through bilateral agreements between nations. Yet, there are no multilateral guidelines that protect all parties -- multinational enterprises, host countries, workers, consumers, etc. At the United Nations, a multilateral Code of Conduct has been evolving for almost seven years. It is the first document that would set a minimum standard for corporate and government behavior. Those who oppose the document in reality oppose the idea of regulation out of arrogance and in fear of accountability to others. The Code gives all parties an opportunity to come together and make decisions and reach conclusions to solve problems that arise from multinational enterprise investment.

The long-term financial interest of multinational enterprises behooves these enterprises to re-think their development ideology. The challenge for multinational enterprises in the future is to use the advances of technology and capital and efficient production to aid low-cost, labor intensive, and sustainable models of development for production of goods and services that benefit and meet the needs of <u>local people</u>. If there is a surplus, it could be exported, thus meeting the needs of the multinational enterprises and the host country governments, as well as the international market. Unless the multinational enterprises reflect on their ideological bases, they will continue to face the many dliemmas they currently do, and more. The growing sophistication of host-country corporations, activist, and women's groups will pose a serious challenge to the multinational enterprises' business as usual mentality.

TRANSNATIONAL CORPORATIONS AND WOMEN'S HEALTH

Luisa M. Rivera Izabal

Launched in Mexico in 1965, the Border Industrialization Program was part of the worldwide trend of transnational corporations (TNCs) to transfer assembly operations from core to semiperipheral and peripheral countries. Thirteen plants were established in several cities along the Mexican-United States border. Today, twenty years later, there are 700 plants employing almost 200,000 workers in the border area and in other cities in the interior of the country. About 80 percent of the workers are women (with the percentage varying with different types of plants), whose median age fluctuates between 16 and 25. Sixty three percent are working in electronic and electrical assembly plants. Represented are many major corporations such as RCA, General Electric, Zenith Radio Corporation, Rockwell, General Motors, and Union Carbide and their subsidiaries.

Why has the maquiladora program (as it is called in Mexico) grown so fast? There are a variety of reasons including the successive devaluations of the peso relative to the United States dollar, a real gift to corporations eager to cut down production costs. Another, which will be the subject of this presentation, is the fact that countries like Mexico have a relaxed application of environmental protective measures, and local authorities have only modest concern about health hazards and working conditions in industry.

Women and Health

As stated earlier, most of the women employed by these electronics plants are quite young. This means that they have no previous job experience and no knowledge of labor laws, health regulations, risks they are running, or protective measures.

The women themselves, as well as some researchers, are impressed by the appearance of the plants in the electronics-electrical sector. They tend to have good lighting, dust-free rooms, air conditioning, even uniforms and hair nets. Many have said that they are one of the cleanest industries. This visual image makes it even more difficult for the workers to be aware of the health and safety risks they face. It is easy to see that losing a finger while at work is a clear case of an industrial hazard, but it is more difficult to see that a recurring sore throat, dizziness, or allergies are related to that "clean" room where they spend 46 hours each week.

"Elfreda Castellano was 19 years old when she was accepted in the tin-dip station, Plastic Division of her plant, near Manila, Philippines. It was her job to soak integrated circuits (IC's) in pots of chemicals which were specifically designed to strengthen and rust-proof these IC's. She had to fulfill the 22,000 IC's per day quota imposed by the management. In the tin-dip station, she worked with solders and fluxes which were never dissolved into a liquid organic solvent. After a year of service, Freda began to experience a general weakening of the body. She complained of headaches, nosebleeds, recurring colds, and worsening of her sinusitis. She requested a transfer from the supervisor but was denied it. Several months later, in December, 1981, she was admitted to the Philippine General Hospital with raging fever and dark spots on her legs. The initial diagnosis was aplastic anemia. In March of the next year (1982), she developed water-filled masses on her shins, appearance of reddish spots, fever and nodules in her groin. In July, it was hard to recognize Freda with her bloated face and bruised body. At this point, a lymph node biopsy revealed lymphoma or cancer of the lymph nodes. She died in the evening of November 22, 1982.[1]

Symptoms and Chemicals

In Mexico, as in the Philippines or any other developing country, research on the electronic industry hazards is just beginning. It is through direct contact with the workers and data collected by a Mexican university (Universidad Autonoma de Mexico-Maestria de Medicina Social) and two scholars living at the border area (Patricia Feranandez Kelly and Jorge Carrillo), as well as more in-depth research in other countries, that we are able today to answer two important questions:

1. What are the physical problems about which the women working in the electronics plants complain? and

2. What does the information available on the effects of chemicals being used in electronics plants say about the risks and dangers the workers are running?

1. The most common symptoms about which workers complain as part of their daily life are: eye problems such as burning sensations, loss of sharpness of vision, and weepy eyes; digestive problems such as nausea, vomiting, and abdominal cramps; respiratory problems such as cough, sore throat, and tight chest; skin irritation; loss of sexual drive; menstrual irregularities; anxiety; insomnia; drowsiness;

and fatigue.

> I used to work (explains Rosaura Andrade, a worker in one of the electronics plants at the border) with a chemical and my hands would get red and irritated, really ugly. I complained to the supervisor but he did nothing. So I went to see the Social Security Doctor. He examined me and said that the problem was not job related, that surely I was using a strong detergent for my laundry.
>
> He almost convinced me. You know how doctors are, they speak as if they know everything. But then I realized that I did not do any laundry at home; my mother does the washing. So I insisted and he finally gave me a paper to present to my supervisor. He changed me and you can see my hands are OK now. What worries me is the new worker that the supervisor put in my place.[2]

2. The misleading appearance of the electronics industry is due partially to the fact that most people do not know that this industry relies on the use of hundreds of potentially dangerous substances for the production of its miracle chips. Some examples of these chemicals will help us to clarify the relation between the symptoms mentioned above and the effects of these substances.

Soldering tiny wires with lead is one of the operations that women workers repeat constantly every day. The fumes resulting from the operation are almost invisible, and the amount of lead oxide that they contain is so small that no damage should result from breathing them. But it can be and is seriously dangerous if some security measures are not strictly followed. Care must be taken not to overheat the solder or use more than minimum amounts; otherwise, lead poisoning may result. In the beginning, lead poisoning can cause fatigue, irritability, headaches, insomnia, loss of appetite, and joint pains. If the exposure continues, it will cause anemia, brain damage, reproductive problems, and miscarriages. Children born to the workers may suffer learning disabilities.

The harm caused by excessive exposure to some solvents used as degreasers and cleaners can usually be detected more rapidly, since the symptoms usually appear right after direct handling. This is not always the case with Trichloroethylene (TCE), already banned in many United States factories because it is strongly suspected to be a carcinogen. Health effects of TCE are central nervous system depression, miscarriages, irregular heart beat, ventricular fibrillation, or even sudden death. Women who are breast feeding can pass the solvent to their babies.

Epoxy resins are commonly used to bond silicon chips to circuit boards and also to protect components from humidity. High temperatures, which change their composition, and direct prolonged handling can produce harmful effects. The most frequent problems are allergic reactions in different parts of the body, burns (if there has been prolonged contact with skin), and irritation of nose, eyes, and throat.

Finally, it is important to mention a health problem also related to the electronics industry: stress. Stress, of course, is part of the challenge of human existence. Coffins are the only places where we find people who suffer no stress. But lack of control is not part of the human condition. A University of Michigan study found that the stress producers were constant speed-ups, low utilization of abilities, lack of participation in decisions about how the job is to be performed, low work complexity, and little or no power over the conditions that would help to meet a rapid flow of demands. Maquiladora workers in Cd. Juarez who worked overlapping shifts were found to be twice as susceptible to gastrointestinal disorders and nervous ailments than the population at large.

Corporate Responsibility

In February, 1980, an incident occurred in the border city, Cd. Juarez. What happened there leads directly into the corporate responsibility question.

Thirty five workers employed at the subsidiary of Sylvania (Comunicaciones Banda Grande) had to be rushed to the local Social Security Clinic in the middle of their night shift. Early reports indicated that a malfunctioning 'cooking van' containing Trichloroethylene (TCE) had produced hydrochloric fumes which spread through the shop causing widespread nausea, vomiting, and loss of consciousness. At first the local newspapers confirmed the connection between the breakdown of the 'cooking' equipment and the symptoms experienced by workers. However, 24 hours later, the official joint report of the plant manager and the director of the Social Security Clinic where workers were treated differed greatly from the original interpretation. Large headlines on a news article citing the report now stated that the incident had been a 'hysterical reaction to an imaginary ailment.[3]

Hysterical reactions do occur in the maquiladoras. Women may start singing or crying out loud for no apparent reason. Chronic stress for long periods of time or no legitimate channels for expression or protest (as Linda Lim and others propose) are behind these reactions. But it is totally dishonest to discount or discredit as hysteria sudden illnesses of the women workers when they have had direct contact with hazardous substances.

Are all corporations aware of the risks women are running while working for them? We do not have all the necessary information to give a general answer. But we know that because of intense competition, companies develop new production techniques rather than invest time and money to research the health and safety aspects of the production process. Only one percent of all the chemicals available on the market have been adequately tested for their effects on humans.

Paying very low salaries to increase a corporation's profits may be wrong and immoral, but allowing working conditions that eventually will damage or destroy young women's health and perhaps also that of their offspring is criminal. National and international laws should be designed both to control the exports of dangerous working conditions and also to prosecute those who are responsible for destroying health and life.

NOTES

1. Taken from interviews taped by the author and a team of students of Social Medicine of the Universidad Autonoma Metropolitana, June 1983.

2. Ibid.

3. "El Fronterizo," Cd. Juarez, Mexico, February 19 and 20, 1980.

BIBLIOGRAPHY

Carrillo, Jorge. "Danos a la salud en plantas maquiladoras, algunas hipotesis interpretatives." Centro de Estudies Fronterizos del Norte de Mexico (CEFNOMEX). 1983.

Chavkin, Wendy. "Double Exposure-Women's Health Hazards on the Job and at Home." Monthly Review Press. 1984.

Gassert, Tom. "Workers Health and Chemical Hazard." AMPO. Volume 15. Number 15. 1983.

Fernandez Kelly, Patricia. "Women's Industrial Employment, Migration and Health Status Along the U.S.-Mexican Border." Working Paper. 1982.

Haddox, John. "Twin-Plants and Corporate Responsibilities." University of Texas at El Paso, TX.

Healthsharing, A Canadian Women's Health Quarterly. Toronto, Ontario. (Summer 1985.)

Howard, Robert. "Second Class in Silicon Valley." Working Papers. Sept.-Oct. 1981.

Institute for Labor and Mental Health. "The Inside Story: Occupational Stress." 1981.

Isis International. "La Salud de las Mujeres. La experiencia de Brasil." June 1985.

Lim, Linda. "Women Workers in Multinational Corporations: the Electronics Industry in Malaysia and Singapore." Michigan Occasional Papers. No. 9, Fall 1978.

Pacific Studies Center. "Silicon Valley: Paradise or Paradox." October 1977.

Talbot, Cindy and Andrea Hricko. "Special on Electronics Hazards." The Monitor. Special Edition of Labor Occupational Health Program. Berkley, CA.

Universidad Autonoma Metropolitana (UAM) Maestria de Medicina Social. "Determinacion y Distribucion de la Enfermedad en las trabajadoras de la Industria Maquiladora." Meixo, D.F. 1983.

WOMEN FACTORY WORKERS IN ASIAN DEVELOPING COUNTRIES: SOME DILEMMAS FOR MULTINATIONAL EMPLOYEES

Linda Y. C. Lim

Some of the most prominent, or at least attention-getting, conflicts produced by multinational enterprise operations in East and Southeast Asia have centered on the employment of women in labor-intensive, mostly export-oriented, factories. In part this reflects the sheer volume of multinational activity in offshore manufacturing in this region in female-intensive industries such as garments, footwear, electronics, toys, sporting goods, and other miscellaneous manufacturers. Yet these industries account for a relatively minor share of total multinational activity in most of these countries, which is concentrated on local raw material resources or the domestic markets of the host countries and is mostly male-intensive. With the notable exception of Singapore, offshore manufacturing by multinationals also does not account for the largest share of female employment in Asian countries. The absolute numbers employed may seem large -- for example, some 100,000 women are employed in the multinational-dominated electronics industry in Malaysia alone. But there are nearly two million employed women in Malaysia. In most Asian countries, the majority of employed women are found in the rural sector. Even in the modern urban sector, most women are employed by small local enterprises rather than by multinationals.

Why, then, is such a disproportionate amount of attention paid to the relatively few women employed by multinational factories not only by academics, but more importantly also by student, church, and labor activitist groups in both home and host countries of the multinationals, and by various political interest in home countries including the governments in host countries? The interest in home countries like the United States is readily explained: home country nationals are most interested in and likely to feel responsible for the activities of their national enterprises abroad; offshore employment has an impact on consumers and especially on workers competing for the same jobs at home, and criticism of it thus finds ready support among popular protectionist coalitions; and feminist activism and the burgeoning academic interest in women's studies spill over into the international arena, where many international agencies have had an active interest in women and development, especially during the United Nations' Decade of Women which ended this year.

This home country interest spills over into host countries

as well, but the interests in the latter are somewhat more complex. I shall focus on them by discussing three major areas of conflict arising from the employment of women by multinational enterprises in developing countries in Asia. These are concerns, firstly, about exploitation; secondly, about cultural disruption and moral corruption; and thirdly, about labor organization.[1] My discussion will focus on isolating the variable of multinationality in what is obviously a multivariate situation. To do this, I will compare multinationals' behavior in host developing countries with their behavior in their home countries and compare multinationals with other employers in the host countries. If multinationality <u>per se</u> is an important real, as distinct from perceived, cause of these conflicts, then the multinationals should behave differently in host and home countries, and differently from non-multinationals in the host countries. This paper will thus provide a relative rather than an absolute evaluation of multinational behavior in the employment of women in developing countries.[2]

Exploitation

Criticism of multinationals in developing countries most frequently focuses on charges of exploitation. In female-intensive industries, the charge is that multinationals take advantage of women's weak labor market position by paying them extremely low, often below subsistence, wages which are only a fraction of wages paid for the same work in home countries. This international wage differential is considered a measure of multinational "exploitation" or "super-exploitation." There are many theoretical problems with such a measure which I shall not go into here.[3] The important thing is that it leads workers in the home country to complain about "unfair competition" from "sweated labor" in developing countries and to demand "protection," while workers in the host country are dissatisfied that the multinationals pay them much lower wages than they pay workers in their home countries.

The dilemma for the multinational is that it invests in these kinds of industries in developing countries precisely to take advantage of lower labor costs in order to maintain competitiveness in its home market or in third-country markets. Offshore manufacturing is often a defensive move against competition from cheap labor imports originating from local firms in these same countries. For example, in the consumer electronics industry, the United States firms which had not already been destroyed by import competition from national firms in Japan, South Korea, Taiwan, and Hong Kong had to move to Asia in the late 1960s and early 1970s to ensure their very survival. In the host country, these multinationals typically pay wages at or above the local market rate, sometimes running into criticism from local employers that they are "spoiling the (labor) market" and raising labor costs by charging wages which are "too high." This is true even where multinationals pay only the legislated minimum wage because the vast majority of workers in other enterprises in the host country earn less, often much less, than the minimum wage. For example, in Thailand and the Philippines, only 10 percent of urban wage workers receive the minimum wage or more, as compared with nearly all the women employed by multinationals from developed countries.[4]

In many Asian countries, the women who work in multinational factories are considered to be extremely fortunate, and their jobs are especially desired because of the higher incomes earned in them than in alternative local occupations, including factory work in local enterprises which more truly approximate the familiar "sweatshop" stereotype. Large-scale surveys which have been conducted of thousands of workers in different countries yield little evidence of below-subsistence wages or the familiar "super-exploitation" thesis. In most cases, the wages paid to women production workers are sufficient to cover not only their individual living expenses and some personal luxuries, but also often generous contributions to their families. Family contributions sometimes account for as much as two-thirds of a migrant worker's disposable wages and may amount to the largest single contribution to total family income. In countries like the Philippines and Thailand, for example, the woman working in a multinational factory is often the highest income earner in her family, earning wages which exceed those earned by her husband, brother, or father in unskilled or semi-skilled male labor.[5] Among other things, this shows that it is wrong to regard women as only "secondary" wage-earners for their families in poor developing countries.[6]

Besides low wages, complaints are often raised about the terms and conditions of employment for women in multinational factories. In particular, multinationals are accused of being "footloose," i.e., quick to lay off workers in one location to take advantage of lower wages in another. So far the evidence from Asia indicates that, given their potential mobility, multinationals in labor-intensive industries have proven to be remarkably stable presences in their chosen host countries.[7] They do lay off workers periodically, but this is largely in response to cyclical market downturns which would occasion the layoff of workers even in their home countries. Indeed, some multinationals, notably Japanese companies and American "model employer" firms like Hewlett-Packard, have a remarkable record of <u>not</u> laying off workers in recessions (because, for example, of the considerable costs of rehiring and training new workers in subsequent upturns). Given their greater market strength, multinationals are likely to be more stable employers than local enterprises, whose lower profit margins make them less able to sustain a full wage-bill in market downturns, when they are also more likely to go out of business altogether.

Employment in multinational factories is also likely to be more stable than employment in many other local occupations such as work in export-oriented agriculture or in small-scale local service industries and self-employment. Workers in large-scale modern factories, both foreign and local, are the best protected by government labor legislation which sets the terms and conditions of employment. For example, whether unionized or not, they typically receive annual wage increments based on seniority and are entitled to various benefits such as overtime payments, sick leave, and annual leave. (Women in Indonesia and South Korea are further entitled to one day's menstruation leave a month.) Laid off workers usually receive retrenchment benefits, which can accumulate with seniority to considerable sums.

In Singapore recently, for example, women workers readily responded to calls by multinational employers for voluntary layoffs because they received "small windfalls" (their union's term) in retrenchment benefits. Many reported that they were not taking advantage of their employers' and unions' formalized attempts to find them new jobs because they wanted to enjoy a "holiday" first and did not anticipate difficulty in eventually getting re-employed.[8] The Singapore case points out a very important factor that is often overlooked in developed and developing countries alike: it is not layoffs per se which are necessarily the problem, but the ease or difficulty of finding re-employment. In any dynamic economy, jobs are continually being lost and new jobs created. Where domestic full employment exists, as in Singapore, workers, including women workers, do not necessarily fear layoffs as they can easily get new, and often better, jobs. In addition, in a situation where men have high- paying and secure jobs, voluntary quits are especially high for married women. Many even reported to researchers that they were tired of working, but were holding on in the hope of being laid off so that they could get lucrative retrenchment benefits. During the recent years when the labor market in Singapore was very tight, multinational employers in fact sought to discourage women workers from quitting and were known to send representatives to the homes of those who had quit to persuade them to return.

In other words, though multinationals may be responsible for layoffs of women workers in developing countries, they are not necessarily responsible for their unemployment. This is a function of conditions in the host country economy in general. In places such as Singapore where there are many multinational employers, demand for labor is strong relative to other countries where there are only a few multinationals. Even in Singapore's current recession, with the economy showing a low or negative growth rate for the first time in 20 years and with widespread layoffs for the first time in 10 years, some multinationals are expanding and hiring the experienced women workers laid off by other multinationals.

Hours and conditions of work in multinationals are also often better than in local enterprises and other local occupations. Most multinationals from developed countries conform to host government regulations on hours of work. Multinationals from other developing countries (in Asia, from Hong Kong, Taiwan, and India, for example) are more like smaller local firms and often do not observe these regulations. It is reports of long hours and poor, often hazardous, working conditions in these "Third World multinationals" (most especially, in the Philippines' export processing zone) which have given rise to widespread impressions that this is the typical behavior of all multinationals in developing countries. Studies in Thailand and the Philippines have shown that women employed in multinational factories not only earn much more, but also work much shorter hours then women employed in small-scale local commercial enterprises and in domestic service.[9] The only common occupation for low-skilled women which pays more than multinational factory employment is prostitution. (Small-scale entrepreneurial activities are also very lucrative, but they have a high failure rate.)

In Malaysia, one study showed that even when multinational factory employment paid less than plantation labor, women preferred it because of better and safer working conditions. Machine work in a clean air-conditioned factory environment was strongly preferred to manual labor in the hot sun (as required by rice farming) or the dangerous dark early hours of the morning (as required by rubber tapping). Multinational factory environments are often more comfortable than the poor, overcrowded, unsanitary homes where the women workers live, for example, in urban squatter communities. Poor working and living conditions are characteristic of most developing countries, and developed country multinationals often provide superior physical facilities. Consequently, employment in multinationals is often considered to be relatively high in status, attracting women who are much better-educated than even the average man in their societies.

This is not to suggest that working conditions in multinationals pose no problems at all for women workers in developing countries. There obviously are some problems,[10] but they are not necessarily worse than, though they may be different from, the problems found in other occupations. For example, multinationals in labor-intensive export industries in developing countries often require their women workers to work rotating shifts, including night shifts. But this is also required in many other famale occupations in developed as well as developing countries where multinationals are not the employers, such as the jobs of nurses, hospital orderlies, hotel clerks, and office cleaners. Conditions in multinational subsidiaries in developing countries may also not be very different from conditions in similar factories (whether operated by multinationals or non-multinationals) in the developed home countries. For example, complaints of unsafe working procedures and exposure to toxic chemicals have been made against electronics factories in the United States as well as in developing countries, where health hazards in local electronics enterprises are often even worse than in the multinationals. There are probably also cases where working conditions in multinationals and local enterprises in developing countries are better than in the developed countries. For example, big modern textile factories in Hong Kong and Singapore may have safer and healthier working environments than small garment sweatshops located in unsafe century-old factory buildings in the cities of the Northeastern United States.

But even where factory conditions are identical in both developed and developing countries, they may produce more health problems among developing country workers who, because of poverty, poor nutrition, lesser education, and experience, are likely to be more vulnerable to work-related physical and psychological disorders than their counterparts in developed countries. Within a given developing country and even within a given factory, some workers will be more vulnerable than others. For example, not all workers are allergic to chemicals or textile dust, and not all workers suffer from eyesight deterioration when performing needlework or microscope work. Individual constitutional predispositions reflecting both genetic and environmental factors are involved. Adverse health effects felt by women factory workers may also reflect their living conditions outside the factory as much as if not more than in-factory working conditions. Stress and fatigue experienced by women workers, for example, often result not from arduous factory work <u>per se</u>, but rather from factory work combined with long daily commutes (reflecting poor local public transportation systems) and/or housework and childcare duties which must be performed after working hours or, in short, from the familiar burden of women's double day, which has its roots in the sexual division of labor rather than in multinational employment.

Despite wages, terms, and conditions of employment which are superior to prevailing norms in developing host countries, multinationals continue to be accused of exploitation, largely because the comparisons made are always with prevailing norms in the developed home countries. In the host countries, even if the women workers themselves are satisfied with their employment, as many are, charges of exploitation tend to emanate from other politically-interested groups. These include labor unions whose organizational efforts are hampered by restrictive host government and multinational company policies; oposition parties eager to embarrass governments seen to have welcomed the multinationals; nationalists (including businessmen and academics) opposed to foreign participation in the economy; women's groups influenced by particular feminist ideologies transplanted uncritically from the developed home countries of multinationals, etc.[11] Some of these will be discussed in greater detail in the following sections.

Cultural Disruption and Moral Corruption

Critics charge that multinational enterprises have contributed to cultural disruption and moral corruption among their women employees in developing countries in at least two ways. First, it is argued that employment in multinationals requires women to migrate from their home communities and live independently from their families in the cities where they work. This disrupts family life and leaves the women unprotected and vulnerable to various forms of "moral corruption," specifically of a sexual nature. Second, it is argued that many multinationals, especially American multinationals, institute factory practices which are alien to host cultures and societies, thus causing tension and confusion among workers and host communities. Changes in the employed women's behavior as a result of these two factors makes them "misfits" in their home communities, disrupting traditional family and social relations.

Manifestations of these disruptive effects include the following observed behavioral changes among women factory workers: the wearing of cosmetics and fashionable (including body-revealing) Western dress; attendance at movies, discos, and dance parties; dating and sexual relationships with men, including cohabitation; increased incidence of unwanted pregnancies and illegal abortions; individual (rather than parental) choosing of spouse and delays in the age of marriage; increased frequency of divorce and single motherhood; refusal to return to live permanently in home communities; consumption of "inappropriate" Western-style luxury products; increased support of freedom for the individual and more independence for women than is allowed in traditional society; reduced religious observances and practices; incidents of "mass hysteria" among ethnic Malay workers in factories in Malaysia; derogatory sexually-tinged name-calling by local host communities; some "slippage" of the young women into prostitution; and so on. These are considered disruptive for host communities where the multinationals are located. Workers' families and home communities, in turn, suffer from labor shortages and losses in income due to female outmigration, or become excessively dependent on remittance income from female migrants, who no longer accept the authority of male family members and traditional patriarchs (including religious leaders).

Accepting for the moment that these disruptions do occur, are they the responsibility of multinational employers? Many women do migrate to take jobs in multinational factories, but many also work in these jobs while continuing to live at home with their families. Living at home actually predominates in the urban areas where most multinationals are concentrated. Multinational factories which are located in rural industrial estates or export processing zones usually provide transportation to and from the factory for women workers who live with their families as far as thirty or forty miles away.[12] Among the women who do migrate, many have migrated with their families (whether parents and siblings or spouses and children), and continue to live with them. In some cases (for example, in the Philippines export processing zone), families may migrate to the vicinity of factories specifically to seek employment for their daughters. Young single women who do migrate without their families often reside with relatives or other family associates in their destination location. Many factories provide hostels for migrant workers where they are strictly (sometimes too strictly) supervised, in part to satisfy conservative families and persuade them to send their daughters to work in the city (for example, in Malaysia).

Migration to urban areas is itself a common phenomenon in most developing countries, and in Thailand, the Philippines, and Malaysia women equal or outnumber men in rural-to-urban migration streams. They migrate to advance their education, to accompany migrating family members (parents, spouses), and to seek employment. The vast majority of young women who migrate specifically for employment do not end up in multinational factories. These highly desirable jobs are more likely to be the preserve of established urban residents (also women) who have better education and contacts. Domestic service, small-scale local enterprises, and in some countries, prostitution, all employ many more young women migrants than do multinational factories.

What about culturally inappropriate factory labor practices in multinationals? In many countries, multinationals do offer various fringe benefits and social activities to attract and retain women workers, which reflect home country practices. American companies, for example, often provide lessons in fashion and make-up, as well as company shops which sell these feminine items; mixed-sex picnics, parties and holiday trips; Western movies and Western-style magazines, including women's magazines which sell "romance;" and personnel counselors who purportedly encourage the women to be "independent," "modern," and "liberated." But the impact of such activities on women's behavior and values is likely to be marginal.

First of all, surveys show that most workers do not have the time and inclination to participate in such after-work factory social and cultural activities. If they do participate in factory extra-curricular activities, exercise and sports tend to be favored,[13] along with programs which help the women to upgrade their education. Second, these activities and the attitudes, habits, and tastes which they arguably foster are by no means peculiar to multinational factories or new to the young women they employ. In fact, they are freely available in most modern Asian cities, and even rural women are acquainted with them through television. Third, in many cases the workers themselves expect, request, select, and organize such activities, and prefer companies which offer them to those which do not. Japanese companies, for example, are less preferred although they offer social and cultural activities which are arguably more traditional and less disruptive, such as cooking, sewing, and flower-arrangement classes, and promote Japanese ideals of virtuous womanhood. These Japanese factory activities have been criticized by feminists for reinforcing cultural ideas of feminine passivity and subordination, just as American factory activities have been criticized for fostering "bourgeois consumerism," individualism, and competitiveness among women workers. It appears that the multinational is damned if it does, and damned if it does not, accommodate traditional cultural practices and ideals. Either course of action is, to critics, a form of "cultural imperialism."

If the multinational does not function as a primary cause of cultural disruption and moral corruption among women factory workers, either by inducing migration or by factory cultural practices, does such disruption and corruption nonetheless exist? The evidence from Asian countries suggests that this idea has been much exaggerated. In Malaysia, for example, large-scale surveys show that multinational factory workers are much more conservative than popular stereotypes suggest. Most of the Malay women migrants retain their traditional dress, behavior, and values, are conservative in their expenditures, and retain very close links with their families through remittances and frequent visits in both directions. It is true that most do not desire to return to their home communities, but this is true of rural-urban migrants in general, including young men. Divorce rates in the Islamic Malay community have traditionally been high, and factory work, rather than encouraging divorce, provides an opportunity for divorced women to support themselves and their children "respectably." (In Thailand and the Philippines, on the other hand, premarital sexual activity and cohabitation are not uncommon in the indigenous society and cannot be attributed to multinationalemployment or even to the wage employment in general. Factory employment in these societies is positively respectable compared to widespead prostitution.) In Malaysia, mass hysteria outbreaks are common in Malay society (in girls' schools and dormitories, for example) and are by no means peculiar to multinational factories. (Mass hysteria also does not affect women workers of other ethnic groups, Indians and Chinese, who work alongside the Malay women.) And I have argued elsewhere that the derogatory sexually-tinged name-calling to which Malay women factory workers are subject by urban males reflects not provocative dress or behavior on their part, but rather an urban, upper- and middle-class sexist prejudice against rural migrant working-class women which has existed in other (including Western) societies at a similar female-intensive stage of their industrial development.[14]

If the cultural disruption and moral corruption of women workers in multinational factories in developing countries is at best an exaggeration, what are the reasons for this? At the home country end, feminist critics have perhaps projected many of their own anxieties and preoccupations onto women in the developing countries. For example, the desire for physical attractiveness (fashionable dress, make-up) and for romance has sometimes been seen by Western feminists as an expression of women's sexual objectification, entrapment, and subordination, whereas in many developing countries it may be an expression of women's defiant individual "liberation" from patriarchal control and sexual subordination (which in these countries involves a suppression of female sexuality, reaching its extreme in feminine seclusion and body-concealing dress). Many indigenous cultures in developing countries also have traditional means of enhancing female sexual attractiveness, as well as indigenous concepts of "romance," which is far from a Western import via the multinational.

In the host country, on the other hand, any cultural disruption from multinational employment is felt most acutely by those who stand to lose by such disruption or employment, and they are likely to be members of the traditional patriarchal establishment. In Malaysia, for example, fundamentalist religious leaders and conservative rural landlords are among the strongest opponents to women's employment in multinational factories. They shout the loudest about exploitation, cultural disruption, and moral corruption. This is because they stand to lose not only the social but also the economic base of their power in indigenous society. Male authority over wives and daughters is weakened when the latter have economic independence and especially when they actually move away from the patriarchal household. The religious authority of male priests is diminished with the declining observance of religious practices. And rural landlords lose the cheap female labor which has previously worked their fields, now lying abandoned with the outmigration of young women to multinational (and local) factories. Land rents, the landlords' income, and the value of their landholdings (in other words, their wealth) correspondingly decline. The alternative to modern factory employment that these groups propose is home-based employment for women, which would restrict not only their freedom, but also their incomes. In this case, cultural disruption for some people (men) may as well be cultural liberation for others (women).[15]

This being the case, even if multinationals scrupulously attempted to avoid being exploitative, culturally disruptive, and morally corrupting of women workers, opposition to them would still exist and need to be dealt with, given their vulnerability as foreigners, especially to opposition from the local elite.

Labor Organization

Multinationals, especially American mutinationals, have been accused of inhibiting free labor organization among their women employees in developing countries. The tactics allegedly used include harassment of union officials, firing of union sympathizers and activists, refusal to recognise or negotiate with unions, and a variety of suspect personnel practices including ethnic and linguistic fragmentation of the labor force, frequent layoffs to ensure worker insecurity and prevent the development of worker cohesion and solidarity, paternalistic labor practices, high wages, and modern, welfare-oriented personnel policies to forestall organization. The employment of women who have "naturally" high turnover rates due to the competing demands of marriages and child-raising and are less committed to the labor force and therefore less likely to organize has itself been seen as a tactic to prevent labor organization. And in some Asian countries, multinationals put pressure on host governments to discourage or prohibit union organization in particular sectors or industries.

There is no doubt that many multinationals in Asian countries do engage in practices to discourage labor organization. American multinationals are particularly fearful of unions, compared with the Europeans and the Japanese, who are more used to unions in their own home countries and so less threatened by them in host countries. At the same time, however, multinationals are much more heavily unionized than other sectors of the economy. Becuase of their size, prominence, and presumed profitability, multinationals are a prime target for organization by local unions in search of membership. They are much easier to organize than scattered small local enterprises with only a few employees each, whose owners or managers are even more hostile to unions than multinationals. Thus the women who work in multinational factories in Asia are the most highly-unionized segment of the female labor force in their countries. They may even be more highly-unionized than male workers in some male-intensive industries.

Many multinationals are also more willing to be unionized in developing host countries than in their home countries because certain host governments require it, because the local unions are "cooperative" or controlled by the governments, or because they are a convenient means of communicating with a culturally and linguistically different labor force and of maintaining labor peace. Thus in the Philippines, for example, a much higher proportion of multinationals than of local firms is unionized, and they have much lower rates of labor unrest. Multinationals may also be more heavily unionized in developing host country subsidiaries than in home country plants. For example, only 6 percent of the United States electronics work force is unionized, as compared with most of the workforce in American electonics companies in Singapore. Government-supported or -controlled unions are also not necessarily weak unions. In fact, government backing may give them more bargaining power vis-a-vis their multinational employers. In other cases, even where multinational employers do not discourage unionization, developing country governments themselves may in order to inhibit the formation of organized interest groups which might challenge their domestic political control.

Labor unrest has forced a few American multinationals out of some Asian countries where they had employed mostly women (although other factors were probably also involved in these decisions).[16] But such unrest is often more common in unorganized than in unionized enterprises and sometimes reflects poor personnel management practices on the part of the multinational itself. Workers in unionized enterprises usually enjoy higher wages and more benefits and protection, and so are less dissatisfied with their lot than unorganized workers who might have to strike to make management take their grievances seriously or simply to be allowed to organize (this is particularly common in Indonesia). Unionized workers have the means to express their grievances and to communicate with management without engaging in disruptive labor action. Their lower rates of labor unrest strongly suggest that multinationals which seek to prevent their women workers from organizing are wrong to do so, even from the perspective of their own self-interest.

Conclusions and Policy Implications

Whether they are justified or not, concerns in home and host countries about exploitation, cultural disruption and moral corruption, and restrictions on the labor organization of women workers, pose problems for multinational employers in developing countries. These concerns make it politically difficult for host governments to encourage multinationals and may cause them to impose various restrictions on multinational activity, or to discourage sectors, such as labor-intensive export manufacturing, where multinationals are dominant. In Malaysia, for example, there has been a marked shift in government priorities away from labor-intensive export manufacturing which is dominated by multinationals and employs mainly women, to capital-intensive, heavy industry based on domestic resources or the domestic market which is dominated by state enterprises and employs mainly men.[17] Many male-dominated governments and local patriarchal elites already discount employment created for women, a politically weak and socially undervalued group.

In both host and home countries, labor and supporting human and civil rights activist groups oppose multinationals on the grounds of their exploitation of host country workers, including women, and their obstruction of labor organization. These "unfair labor practices" could be and have been used to provoke consumer boycotts and could make the host country vulnerable to trade restrictions on the grounds of violation of human and civil rights.[18] Obstruction of labor organization in particular creates the erroneous impression that labor repression is the sole or main reason for developing Asian countries' comparative advantage in exporting labor-intensive manufactures. This contributes to popular support in the home countries for protectionist measures which now threaten women's jobs, in both multinational and local enterprises, in these countries.

The dilemma for multinationals is that they really are much less powerful or influential in the Asian developing countries than their critics in both home and host countries expect them to be. Their effects on women workers, whether positive or negative, are probably more a function of individual host country conditions than of multinational corporate policy. For example, the low wages earned by women workers in multinationals in these countries largely reflect local labor market conditions, including the structural features such as lower education and skill levels, short working lives, occupational segregation and "overcrowding," and employer discrimination which cause women's earnings to be generally lower than men's. Terms and conditions of employment are also set by host government regulations and prevailing local norms.

Multinationals can offer better terms and conditions, and many do. But in general they try to behave as much like local enterprises as possible, varying their labor practices in different locations to accommodate to local conditions. But they are often expected to behave as they would in their home countries, offering significantly better terms and conditions of employment than purely local conditions dictate. Yet when they do this, they may be accused of transferring practices from their home countries which are not appropriate for the developing host countries (such as employing women in managerial positions, or using capital-intensive technology which improves working conditions but saves on the use of labor) and may be economically (for example, by undermining local competitors) as well as culturally disruptive. Where host governments discourage or forbid independent unions, for example, multinationals will be criticized by different groups whether they follow or go against this principle. Similarly, they will be criticized by different groups whether their activities preserve or undermine women's traditional (usually subordinate) position in host societies.

Can multinationals nonetheless use their influence on host country markets or governments to improve local terms and conditions of women's employment? This might be possible for some multinationls in some countries, but it is rarely the case for multinationals which may employ women in labor-intensive export industries. Typically, these multinationals account for such a small and often segregated (in export processing zones) segment of the host economy, and employ such a small and politically weak proportion of the labor force (young women), that they are marginal to the political as well as to the economic life of the host country and have little influence to exert. Export-oriented multinationals are usually 100 percent foreign-owned, import most of their inputs and export most of ther outputs. This limits their linkages with potentially politically powerful groups in the host society such as the state bureaucracy and political leaders, blue-collar male unions, and the local business community which includes partners, customers, suppliers, and agents of multinationals oriented to the domestic market or involved in the extraction and processing of local raw materials (which frequently require joint-venture operations with local companies or state enterprises).

The female-intensive industries are important providers of foreign exchange, and thus can win certain concessions, such as infrastructure construction and exemption from import and export duties, related to the earning of foreign exchange, as long as this does not directly deprive or undermine local competitors. Labor market actions, however, will affect the economy at large, at least by a demonstration effect if not by significantly affecting the supply of or demand for local labor. They will thus face some opposition from local interests, including multinationals in other sectors, who wish to preserve the status quo. As export industries, the female-intensive multinationals are also subject to the final discipline of the world market, and labor costs can be raised without jeopardizing international competitiveness only if there are commensurate increases in productivity, which depend as much on host country factors (such as educational and skill levels) as on firm operations.

As the analysis in this paper suggests, multinationality is not a very important factor in determining either multinational labor practices[19] or their impact on women workers in developing host countries. On the contrary, the same multinationals often behave very differently in different host country locations (for example, paying different wages for the same work; accepting unions in one location and opposing them in another, etc.) and may sometimes behave in particular host countries very much like they do in their home countries (for example, laying off workers in cyclical market downturns; having inadequate safety measures, etc.). Even where they have identical labor practices in different host locations, the effect of these practices may be very different depending on local conditions (for example, layoffs may have a devastating effect where unemployment is high but only a minimal effect where there is full employment; a factory beauty contest may be welcomed in one community but opposed in another, etc.). Multinationals also differ among themselves in their local labor practices even within the same industry and in the same host country location. They may or may not differ from local firms in a given location, and where their labor practices do differ, the multinational's are often better. Whether they are better or worse may not reflect the effects of multinationals per se, or deliberate and intentional multinational policies, but other factors such as firm characteristics (industry, technology, size, profitability, parent company policy, etc.) and host government policies. Developing countries are not homogeneous. They differ vastly from one another in their cultures and the state of their economies. Multinationals are also not homogeneous. It is only to be expected that their behavior towards and impact on women workers will differ greatly from place to place, and from company to company.

It is necessary to identify the relative significance of multinationality for the purpose of drawing policy implications. If multinationals' corporate practices are the main determinant of their women employees' welfare, then it is reasonable to propose changes in these practices as a means of improving the women's welfare. But if multinational corporate practices are only one variable among the many which affect their women employees, then the policy implications are more complex. In South Africa, it is generally accepted that host country conditions, in particular the system of apartheid, are far more important than even progressive multinational corporate policies in determining workers' welfare. The same conclusion must be reached in the case of women employed by multinationals in other developing countries. It is the economic and social policies, patriarchal cultures, etc., of the host country which must be changed in order to significantly improve the lot of women, including the women employed in multinationals. Multinationals may have a role in this process, but it will likely be marginal and subsidiary to the roles of indigenous actors in the host countries.

For multinationals, resolutions to the dilemmas resulting from their employment of women workers in developing countries will vary from situation to situation, depending on the particular host country as well as on the individual company. For host governments, actions to improve women workers' welfare must focus not just on policies to influence multinational behavior, but also and more importantly on developing the economy, providing attractive alternative employment opportunities, enhancing women's job skills, and reducing sex discrimination. For the women workers themselves, multinationals are only one, and not necessarily a very important, influence on their lives, and an influence which is as likely to be positive as negative.[20] Though these women may be the victims of exploitation (depending on one's definition of the term), they are also the beneficiaries of new opportunities, and cultural disruption may be as liberating for them as it is disruptive for some of their men. Though their employers and governments alike may seek to discourage it, multinational factories also offer many women workers their best hope of labor organization. In the end it may be that the best thing that both multinationals and host governments can do for women factory workers in the Asian developing countries is to refrain from inhibiting their attempts to organize. Labor organizations may be the best means for women workers to achieve improvements both in terms and conditions of their employment within multinational factories, and in their economic, social, and political status in the host country at large.[21]

NOTES

1. For specific case examples and the evidence supporting my arguments, see the references in Women Workers in Multinational Enterprises in Developing Countries, Geneva: International Labour Office and the United Nations Centre on Transnational Corporations of the United Nations Decade for Women, 1985, a report prepared by Linda Y.C. Lim.

2. The literature abounds with descriptive material on this subject (see, for example, ibid.) but is deficient in the kind of analysis that I will attempt. Note, however, that not all the generalizations I make will apply equally to all host countries. In fact, a central feature of my argument is that generalization about multinationals' behavior and impact is difficult if not impossible, because of different indigenous conditions in the host countries.

3. See, for example, the discussions of exploitation in Linda Y.C. Lim, "Women Workers in Multinational Corporations: The Case of the Electronics Industry in Malaysia and Singapore," Michigan Occasional Papers No. 9, Fall 1978, Women's Studies Program, University of Michigan, and "Multinational Export Factories and Women Workers in the Third World: A Review of Theory and Evidence" in Nagat M. El-Sanabary, comp., Women and Work in the Third World: The Impact of Industrialization and Global Economic Interdependence, University of California, Berkeley, June 1983, pp. 75-90.

4. For more on wages, see Women Workers in Multinational Enterprises, ILO, pp, 39-44.

5. This is also true of maquiladora workers in Mexico. See, for example, J.A. Bustamante, "Maquiladoras: A New Face of International Capitalism on Mexico's Northern Frontier," in

J. Nash and M.P. Fernandez-Kelly, eds., <u>Women, Men and the International Division of Labor</u>, Albany, New York, State University of New York Press, pp. 224-256.

6. It is true that the woman factory worker's wage is rarely sufficient to support an entire family, but this is the norm in developing countries where technology and productivity levels are low. Typically, every member of the family, including the children, must work (for example, on the family farm) in order to produce or procure enough food for subsistence. The average family size is also very large, with large numbers of children and multi-generational, extended households.

7. See, for example, the discussion in <u>Women Workers in Multinational Enterprises</u>, ILO, pp. 65-68.

8. This is not an irrational decision in a situation of full employment and high wages for both men and women, where the women's work is intrinsically unsatisfying, and children and household duties make competing demands on their time.

9. For references, see ibid.

10. See, for example, the discussion of health problems in ibid., pp. 52-56.

11. See, for example, Lim, "Multinational Export Factories."

12. Company-provided transportation is a particular feature of female-intensive industries in Asia because women are considered to be at greater risk of physical danger, including sexual assault, especially when night shifts are worked.

13. One multinational in Malaysia was severely criticized because its young women workers wore brief shorts when engaging in sports activities, just as school-girls do.

14. Linda Y.C. Lim, "Women Industrial Workers; The Specificities of the Malaysian Case," in Jamilah Ariffin and Wendy Smith, <u>Malaysian Women in the Labour Force</u> (tentative title), forthcoming, 1986.

15. It should be noted, however, that the traditional partiarchy does not necessarily behave in the same way in every country. For example, in Indonesia, which like Malaysia is an Islamic country, male village leaders, landlords, and religious authorities in the rural areas

encourage the employment of young women in mostly local labor-intensive factories. This is because they directly benefit from such employment. In other words, it is economics, not culture, which primarily determines male opposition to female factory employment. See the discussion in ibid.

16. Examples are Control Data in South Korea and Dakin in the Phillipines.

17. There are of course many other reasons for this shift besides disillusionment with export-oriented multinational manufacturing.

18. Although calls for a "social clause" in international trade have diminished in recent years, labor rights have been built into various international trade agreements, such as the United States Generalized System of Preferences (GSP).

19. It may, however, be very important in determining other aspects of multinationals' operations in developing host countries.

20. This paper has focused on the dilemmas posed for multinationals by their employment of women workers in developing countries. For a discussion of the dilemmas posed for the women themselves, see, for example, Linda Y.C. Lim, "Capitalism, Imperialism and Patriarchy: The Dilemma of Third World Women Workers in Multinational Factories," in Nash and Kelly (eds.), Women, Men and the International Division of Labor, pp. 70-93.

21. For example, negotiations with multinational employers at the plant level allow consideration of both host country and company-specific factors, of both domestic and international market forces, in the setting of terms and conditions of employment. Unions will also give women workers a power base from which to work for political and policy changes that will improve the lot of all women in the society.

CHAPTER NINE

ETHICAL DILEMMAS INVOLVED IN THE MARKETING AND SALE OF PRODUCTS IN LESS DEVELOPED COUNTRIES

JAMES E. POST
Professor of Management
Boston University
Boston, Massachusetts

CAROL ADELMAN
Professional Consultant
International Health and Nutrition
Arlington, Virginia

KENNETH E. GOODPASTER
Associate Professor
Graduate School of Business Administration
Harvard University
Boston, Massachusetts

DAVID E. WHITESIDE
Former Associate in Research
Harvard Business School
Boston, Massachusetts

SCOTT COOK
Associate in Research
Harvard Business School
Boston, Massachusetts

ETHICAL DILEMMAS OF MULTINATIONAL ENTERPRISES: AN ANALYSIS OF NESTLE'S TRAUMATIC EXPERIENCE WITH THE INFANT FORMULA CONTROVERSY

James E. Post

Introduction

Among the many different types of dilemmas faced by multinational enterprises are those related to its marketing of consumer products. It has now become apparent that the marketing of First World foods in Third World nations poses a special type of concern to the populations and governments of host nations, and to the would-be marketers themselves. While there are a number of products that one can cite as illustrative of the generic issue, none has so sharply and clearly defined it as the controversy surrounding the marketing and promotion of infant formula in the developing world.

My perspective on the infant formula controversy, industry, and on Nestle in particular, is derived from more than a decade of research. In addition to field research on infant formula marketing in Latin America, Africa, and Southern Asia, I have served as a consultant to the World Health Organization (WHO) in the development of the international marketing code, and testified at congressional and United States Senate hearings on these issues. Most recently, it has included about 18 months of service on the Nestle Infant Formula Audit Commission, which was created to monitor the company's compliance with marketing policies that were drafted for the purpose of implementing the WHO Code.

Rest assured, this is no apologia for Nestle. I know that some of their managers disagree with my interpretation of the evidence. That troubles me little, for I cannot think of an ethical dilemma that does not breed some disagreement among caring participants. Were it otherwise, I doubt it could be called a dilemma. Among the various types of ethical dilemmas confronting the managers of multinational enterprises (MNEs) are those tied to the introduction of products developed and used in one social environment into a significantly different environment. I prefer to term this the introduction of First World Products in Third World Markets.

Within this category are several critical questions. It is important that we think about the conditions in which the <u>marketing</u> of such products is:

1. desirable;

2. acceptable;

3. questionable; and

4. obviously unacceptable.

The infant formula situation involves a product which is not defective in itself. This distinguishes it from such cases as the dumping of products which are unsafe or deemed unacceptable for sale in the United States, but are accepted for sale in another nation (e.g., Tris-treated sleepwear).

Infant formula is also not harmful to the consumer (user) when used properly under appropriate conditions. This distinguishes it from products such as tobacco, which are, in the view of most health professionals, per se dangerous to all users.

Infant formula is the <u>definitive</u> example, however, of a First World product which is safe when used properly, but which is <u>demanding</u>. That is, when risk conditions are present, it can be -- and is -- potentially harmful to users.

The fundamental ethical dilemma for MNE managers, then, is whether such a product can be marketed when it cannot be guaranteed, or reasonably expected, that it will be used by people who meet the minimum conditions necessary for safe use.

Evolution of a Public Issue

A chronology of the infant formula controversy is provided in Table 1. The criticism of the infant formula manufacturers for their aggressive marketing behavior in developing nations became a serious issue in 1970. Prior to that time, individual physicians and health workers had criticized promotional practices, but there was nothing to suggest an organized campaign of criticism. In 1970, however, the Protein-Calorie Advisory Group (PAG) of the United Nations held a meeting in Bogota to discuss the problem of infant malnutrition and disease in developing nations. Participants pointed a finger of blame at the industry, charging that it pushed its products to mothers, many of whom lived in circumstances that made the use of such products a highly risky adventure. First, infant formula must be sold in powdered form in tropical environments, requiring that the mother mix the powder with locally available water. When water supplies are of poor quality, as so often is the case in the developing nations, infants are exposed to

TABLE 1

Key Dates In Infant Formula Controversy

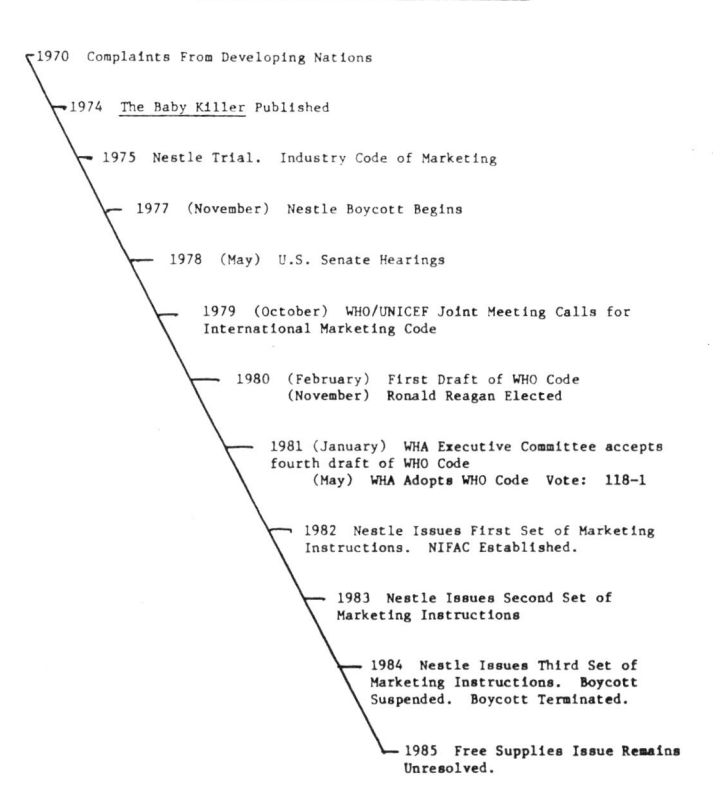

1970 Complaints From Developing Nations

1974 The Baby Killer Published

1975 Nestle Trial. Industry Code of Marketing

1977 (November) Nestle Boycott Begins

1978 (May) U.S. Senate Hearings

1979 (October) WHO/UNICEF Joint Meeting Calls for International Marketing Code

1980 (February) First Draft of WHO Code
(November) Ronald Reagan Elected

1981 (January) WHA Executive Committee accepts fourth draft of WHO Code
(May) WHA Adopts WHO Code Vote: 118-1

1982 Nestle Issues First Set of Marketing Instructions. NIFAC Established.

1983 Nestle Issues Second Set of Marketing Instructions

1984 Nestle Issues Third Set of Marketing Instructions. Boycott Suspended. Boycott Terminated.

1985 Free Supplies Issue Remains Unresolved.

FIGURE ONE
THE LIFE CYCLE OF PUBLIC ISSUES

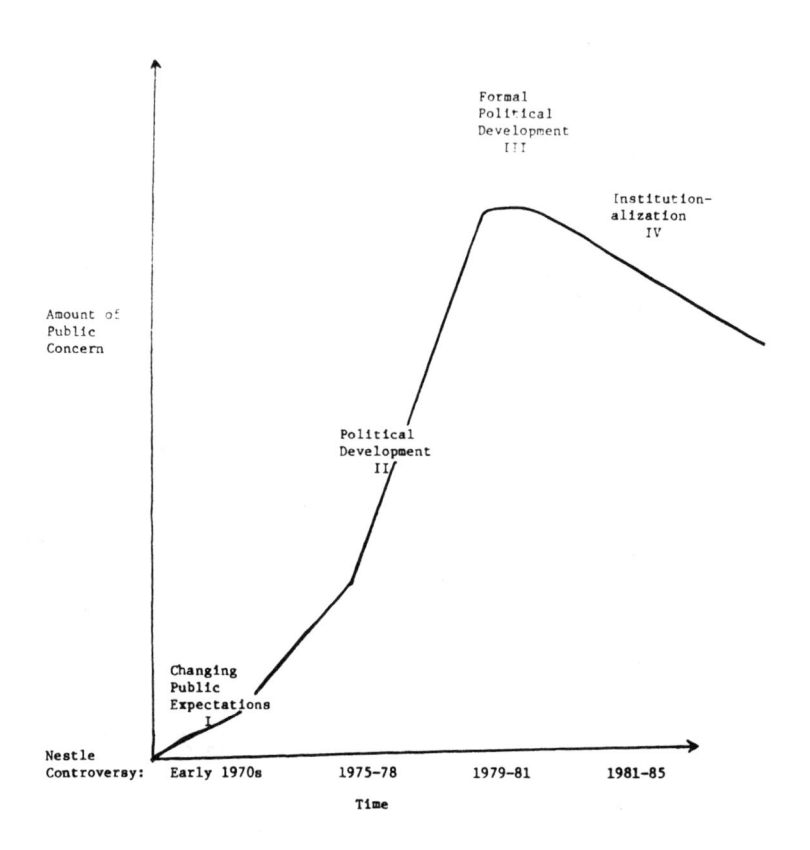

Amount of Public Concern

Formal Political Development III

Institution-alization IV

Political Development II

Changing Public Expectations I

Nestle Controversy: Early 1970s   1975-78   1979-81   1981-85

Time

disease. Second, since the product must be mixed, preparation instructions are important, and mothers must be able to read. Unfortunately, the rate of illiteracy is very high in many developing nations. Thirdly, since infant formulas are relatively expensive to purchase, there is a temptation to overdilute the powder with water. This effort to "stretch" its uses enables the mother to go a few extra days without buying a new supply. Unfortunately, overdiluted formula preparations provide very poor nutrition to the baby. Thus mothers who came to the health clinics with malnourished babies often reported that a five day supply of formula had been stretched to ten days or more. Having decided to bottlefeed their babies in order to improve their chances for a healthy life, many mothers discovered to their horror that they had actually been starving their little ones. Because corporate advertising by the infant formula companies had promoted the idea that bottlefeeding was better than breastfeeding, a view with which doctors disagreed, there was a sharp condemnation of the industry and its behavior at the Bogota meeting.

Management scholars now understand that public issues often proceed through a predictable series of phases in their evolution. Some refer to this as the "public issue life cycle," modelled after the product life cycle described in marketing research. The public issue life cycle can be thought of as a measure of continuing public concern about an underlying problem. In Figure One, the life cycle is drawn as consisting of four phases, each with a significantly different level of public concern -- especially active concern -- for the issue.

Phase I of the issue life cycle involved rising awareness and sensitivity to the facts of the issue. In the infant formula controversy, this phase began with the PAG Meeting in 1970 and continued for several years. An important element in the process of rising awareness was the activity of journalist Peter Muller who, with support from the British charity group, War on Want, travelled to Africa in the early 1970s to study allegations of marketing abuses. Muller wrote several articles and a pamphlet which War on Want published in 1974 under the title, The Baby Killer. These publications began to draw the attention of a broader public to the problem of sick and dying children, and the connection between commercial practices and this tragedy.

Because Nestle was, and still is, the industry's largest producer and seller of infant formula products, Muller encountered many examples of Nestle advertising and promotional practices in Africa. Indeed, Nestle employees were willing to speak with Muller, while those of other companies were often much less willing. Nor surprisingly, then, The Baby Killer pamphlet included Nestle actions as examples of unethical industry behavior. This became very important, because a Swiss public action group, Third World Action Group, reprinted the Muller pamphlet in Switzerland under the new title, Nestle Kills Babies!

Nestle immediately sued the group for defamation, and in 1975 the case came to trial in Switzerland. Because the trial involved several hearings, with experts from developing nations brought in to testify, the media began to show increasing interest in the story. It became quite clear that although the trial involved only Nestle and the defendants, the entire infant formula industry was being examined and criticized for their actions in the developing nations. Thus, the trial was a turning point in two important ways. First, public interest in the issue expanded greatly as the newspaper stories began to carry the details of what one doctor called "commerciogenic malnutrition" -- malnutrition brought about because of corporate commercial practices. Second, the infant formula industry began to respond as an industry, having formed an international association, known as the International Council of Infant Foods Industries (ICIFI). The council, whose existence was announced in Switzerland at the time of the trial, made an immediate effort to develop an international code of marketing which addressed some of the most criticized marketing practices. In this Phase II of the life cycle, both the critics, the media, and the industry recognized that the issue had become an important political matter, as well as a public health concern.

Between 1975 and 1978, the infant formula controversy became increasingly politicized. The media in Europe and the United States paid increasing attention to the conflict. Each newspaper or magazine story brought about more awareness in the general public. The critics highlighted the terrible tragedy of dying and sick children, while the companies, including Nestle, tried to respond to the criticism individually and through ICIFI. The political pressure mounted against the industry. In 1977, an official consumer boycott of Nestle and its products was begun in the United States. Interest in the boycott spread quickly, in part because many member churches of the National Council of Churches had been concerned about the problems of world hunger. The Nestle boycott gave church leaders an opportunity to educate their congregations about the problem of world hunger and suggest a practical course of action that would pressure companies to act responsibly in dealing with the poor and needy of the Third World. The National Council of Churches had been concerned about many corporate responsibility issues, and had a special research and action unit known as the

Interfaith Center on Corporate Responsibility (ICCR). ICCR became actively involved in the boycott campaign, and helped spread the message of consumer action to hundreds of thousands of people in the United States.

The high point of Phase II of the infant formula controversy occurred when boycott sponsors were able to convince the staff of United States Senator Edward Kennedy to hold hearings into the infant formula marketing controversy. These hearings were held in May, 1978 in Washington, DC, and occurred at a time when Senator Kennedy was widely rumored to be considering a campaign for the presidency against incumbent President Jimmy Carter. The media followed Kennedy's every action. On the day of the public hearing, every American television network had cameras in the hearing room, and many famous reporters sat at special tables to hear the testimony of witnesses. The witnesses were heard in three groups. First, people who had worked in developing nations told a tale of human tragedy and marketing abuses by the companies. The second panel consisted of experts in public health (Pan American Health Organization, World Health Organization), medicine, and the author of this paper, who was an expert on the industry. The third panel consisted of the company representatives. Nestle was represented by the head of its Brazilian operation, and the three American companies were represented by senior executives from their corporate headquarters.

The Kennedy hearings were a landmark in the history of this controversy. They represented the highest level of media attention and political attention that had been achieved in nearly eight years of conflict. Critics had to be pleased with their success. Moreover, Nestle behaved in a way that actually strengthened the claims of the boycott supporters and organizers. The company's representative charged that the consumer boycott was a conspiracy of church organizations and an indirect attack on the free enterprise system. Senator Kennedy exploded in anger at the charge that the churchmen and health workers were part of a conspiracy to undermine the free enterprise system. The Nestle statement was a political disaster. Every television program featured the testimony and the reaction from the political leaders in attendance. Nestle was denounced for its statement and its foolishness.

Phase III of an evolving public issue occurs when some governmental or other formal action begins to develop. In a single nation, this may take the form of a regulatory standard, a piece of legislation, or a government program. In the infant formula controversy, formal action took the form of an international code of marketing conduct which industry and national governments would support. Following the Kennedy hearings, the Director-General of the World Health Organization agreed to convene a meeting of interested parties to lay the groundwork for international action. An important meeting took place in 1979, with delegates calling upon WHO to draft an international marketing code. The code development process took several years, required extensive negotiation, and eventually produced a document that was adopted by the World Health Assembly (the governing body of WHO) in 1981. Throughout this process, Nestle and other industry members actively participated in the discussions and lobbied for particular terms and provisions. In advance of the World Health Assembly vote, Nestle was the only company to publicly state that it would follow the code if it was adopted.

Phase IV of a public issue involves the process of implementing the new policy throughout the organizations involved. This is called "institutionalizing" the policy action. Nestle considered how to implement the WHO Code's provisions following the World Health Assembly's adoption. But there existed a number of very serious obstacles. Many of the Code's terms were imprecise, leaving unanswered questions about the proper interpretations. WHO was reluctant to provide continuing interpretation and reinterpretation of the Code's terms, as this would require a staff of lawyers and a continuing commitment. In addition, the Nestle boycott continued in both the United States and Europe. Critics continued to pressure the company, and offered alternative interpretations of various code provisions. WHO had no desire to get further drawn into the dispute between the company and its adversaries. Thus, Nestle was left to negotiate proper interpretations with members of what was now called the International Nestle Boycott Committee (INBC).

Since 1981, Nestle has continued to pursue a process of institutionalizing the provisions of the WHO Code by transforming those requirements into policy instructions for its own sales and marketing personnel. A number of innovations have been created to assist this process. These will be discussed below. In early 1984, the international boycott group suspended the Nestle boycott, following extensive negotiations about such critical issues as product labelling, marketing in health facilities, gifts to medical personnel, and provisions of free supplies to health institutions. By October 1984, the INBC leaders had concluded that Nestle's commitment to implement the policies had proceeded well enough to permit them to terminate the boycott. Its conclusion was announced at a joint press conference attended by boycott leaders and senior Nestle managers. Nearly fifteen years after the first formal complaints began, Nestle had managed to close the controversy over its marketing activities.

Ethical Issues and Lessons

Throughout this long conflict, Nestle has faced a variety of difficult ethical issues. Some of the broad issues and lessons are summarized below.

All businesses which sell their products in developing nations must consider two basic questions: (1) Is the product an appropriate one for the people in that country? and (2) Are the proposed tactics for marketing the product proper for selling the products but not misleading consumers for whom the product is not appropriate? As Nestle discovered, both questions are easily overlooked by managers when they are concerned with sales and profits.

Managers should recognize the following points about the appropriateness of products in developing nation markets.

1. Products which are appropriate and acceptable in one social environment may be innappropriate in the social environment of another nation.

Infant formula products are demanding products. There must be pure water with which to prepare them, refrigeration to safely store unused prepared formula, and customers must be able to read instructions and have the income to purchase adequate quantities of the products. The greater the existence of these risk factors, the less appropriate the product becomes for marketing. This phenomenon applies to many other consumer products as well.

2. Good products, made without defects, may still be inappropriate because of the inherent riskiness of the environment in which those products are to be used.

Nestle and its competitors often stated that the market they sought to reach consisted only of those who could safely use the product, and who had adequate income. However, the evidence from many developing nations continuously showed that vast numbers of the population did not meet the necessary requirements for safe use of the product. By selling formula products to such people, managers could know with virtual certainty that there would be overdilution, improper mixing, or contamination with impure water. As Nestle discovered, many people would denounce and criticize any company that sought to sell its infant formula products under such conditions. When a large part of the population cannot safely use a product, and the company cannot effectively segment the market to ensure that only qualified consumers purchase and use it, there may be no choice for the business but to halt sales in that community.

> 3. Companies may not close their eyes once a product is sold. There is a continuing responsibility to monitor product use, resale, and consumption to determine who is actually using the product, and how. Post-marketing reviews are a necessary step in this process.

Repeatedly, Nestle and its industry colleagues claimed that they had no desire or intention to see unqualified consumers use their formula products. In 1978 at the United States Senate hearings, representatives from Nestle, Abbott Laboratories, American Home Products, and Bristol-Myers were asked whether they conducted any post-marketing research studies to determine who actually used their products. Each company representative answered that his company did no such research and did not know who actually used its products. Naturally, critics attacked the companies for such a careless attitude toward learning the true facts surrounding their products.

> 4. Products which have been sold to consumers who cannot safely use them must be demarketed. Demarketing may involve withdrawal or recall of products, limitations of the selling of the product, or even a halting of future sales.

The infant formula controversy raised the issue of whether, and when, companies should demarket products which have been commercially successful, but also harmful to innocent consumers. Nestle and its competitors gradually changed their marketing practices, and recognized that infant formula was not the same "mass market" product that it had once been. The World Health Organization Code specifically indicated that marketing had to be done in ways that guaranteed that the users of formula products had proper information to use the product safely, and to make an intelligent choice about whether or not infant formula was even an appropriate product for them to use. Much of this is to be done by insisting that companies not market directly to mothers, but channel product supplies and advice through health institutions which can ensure that unbiased health information is received by the mother.

> 5. Marketing strategies must be appropriate to the circumstances of consumers, the social and economic environment in which they live, and to political realities.

Consumer advertising to people for whom product use is highly risky is unacceptable and unethical marketing behavior. Critics of the infant formula industry continued to find evidence of highly aggressive and misleading advertising by companies for many years after the issue became well known. Mass marketing became an unacceptable and inappropriate marketing strategy for infant formula products. The companies, however, had difficulty segmenting their markets and drawing back from the mass market approach. It was only through an industry-wide effort, and then the WHO Code, that managers began to accept that it was more appropriate to focus marketing promotions through the health care system then to consumers directly.

6. Marketing techniques are inappropriate when they exploit a condition of consumer vulnerability.

Many firms in the industry used "milk nurses" during the 1960s and 1970s. These were sales personnel who dressed in nurses uniforms and visited new mothers in hospitals. They would try to encourage the mother to allow their babies to be fed formula, rather than breastfeed, in order to encourage formula adoptions. Since a mother loses the ability to breastfeed after several days of not doing so, such a decision would then require that the baby continue to be fed from a bottle for the next six months. This would be good for formula sales, if the mother could afford to buy it, but might be bad for the baby if the mother had to find a cheaper substitute product to put in the bottle. In South America, for example, members of my own research team saw mothers feeding a mixture of corn starch and water to babies because they had no money to buy formula. Mothers who have given birth are quite vulnerable, and the use of the milk nurses took advantage of that vulnerability in ways that were unethical and unfair. Actions which exploit consumer vulnerability and result in harm are inappropriate marketing tactics.

7. Marketing strategies should be formulated in such a way as to permit flexibility and adjustment to new circumstances.

In the early 1970s, Nestle management knew that critics had a legitimate concern for the sales practices of the industry, but were unable to change their marketing activities in response. The company seemed to be "locked in" to a strategy of resistance, denial, and anger at such charges. In retrospect, it seems that Nestle needed time to change its marketing strategy from a mass-market, consumer-advertising approach, to one which emphasized promotion through the medical and health care system. It took Nestle much longer to change its marketing strategy than it took many of its competitors. This may have been because of pressures from field managers or from the product marketing staff, which denied the truth of the critics' charges. Whatever the case, the company was injured by its slow response to criticism, and its seeming inability to find an alternative way to continue marketing its products. A company which can only market its products in one way is very vulnerable to public issues and political pressures.

Conclusion

Nestle's traumatic experience with the infant formula controversy has finally come to an end, but the impact is likely to last for many years. The company suffered a major blow to its reputation and to the morale of its people. It is traumatic and difficult for people to be told they are working for a company which "kills babies." Today, Nestle's senior management is again working to restore the company's economic and cultural fabric. Its future success will depend upon much more than sales and profits. Nestle has been a successful institution as well as a successful business. Institutions represent a structure of values, and it is this structure which was most sharply affected by the long controversy over infant formula.

If a historian writes the history of Nestle one hundred years from now, will he or she include a reference to the infant formula controversy? Very likely yes. The conflict continued for more than ten years, cost the company many millions of dollars of revenue, expenses, and profits, and damaged or destroyed the careers of a number of its promising managers. It is impossible to say how long it will take for the company to regain its good name and for the public to once again think of Nestle as a good corporate citizen.

Multinational corporations must learn to anticipate conflicts of the sort faced by Nestle, and be prepared to respond in ways that not only justify what the company is doing but also deal with the legitimate concerns of the critics. Union Carbide cannot forget its experience in Bhopal, India; Unilever cannot ignore its experience with Persil in England; Johnson & Johnson cannot forget its experience with Tylenol in the United States; and Nestle cannot forget its experience with infant formula. Each of these experiences involved a company with a good reputation, successful business strategies, and a major public credibility problem. The resolution of each dilemma required a careful integration of public affairs strategies with the business strategy for the company. And each situation demanded and required that the company's managers recognize the <u>common interest</u> that existed between the corporation and the public. In the long run, there is no other way to harmonize the legitimate interests of companies with the legitimate interests of the public.

THE INFANT FORMULA CONTROVERSY -- EVERYBODY'S ETHICS

Carol Adelman

I would like to talk about everybody's ethics, not just the ethics of multinational corporations. After all, we are all in this together -- industry, government, business, and public health schools; churches, consumer groups, and private consultants. Much has been said about ethics of corporations, but little about the ethics of any other participants in the now famous debate on infant formula. Since my experience with the infant formula controversy was primarily with the United States Government and the public health profession, I would like to address some of the ethical dilemmas in these institutions.

During my years of working in the government and now as I do consulting work with private voluntary and corporate organizations as well, I have learned that a very useful question to ask at the beginning of most meetings is: "What is the problem this program is designed to solve?" It is amazing what a conversation stopper this question can be. So I would like to pose this same question about the infant formula issue. What was the problem the World Health Organization Code was designed to solve? As with most issues, and especially ones with glaring moral overtones, the best and most ethical way to start, I believe, is with the facts.

The first alleged problem was that there had been a dramatic decline in breastfeeding among poor women in developing countries. As the Scottish judge says, "Not proven." The distinguished United States Government Task Force on the Assessment of the Scientific Evidence Relating to Infant-Feeding Practices and Infant Health conducted a thorough review of all the issues. Their results were published in Pediatrics one year ago. They analyzed the well known and frequently cited 1973 study by Mr. Alan Berg, currently senior nutrition advisor at the World Bank, which pointed to alarming declines in various developing countries. While there was evidence for one of the countries Mr. Berg cited, the analysis found "the source cited for the Chilean decline contains no mention of breast-feeding trends, the Mexican decline is based on data from a single village, and the Filipino trend is derived from two nonrepresentative and noncomparable studies."[1] The Task Force found that there were only a small number of countries (seven) in which a decline could even be adequately measured. They pointed out that this "is in no way representative of the entire developing world."[2] It is interesting to note that the decline was significant in only three countries - Taiwan, Malaysia, and

Singapore, countries which have some of the lowest infant mortality rates in the Third World.

Even the World Health Organization (WHO) survey completed at the height of the controversy showed that the vast majority of mothers in developing countries were breastfeeding. Those who were bottlefeeding were better educated and from upper middle income groups. Some scientists were reporting this but not many. For example, the Population Reference Bureau pointed out that breastfeeding was universal in the nineteen countries they had studied. Moreover, in countries where breastfeeding was the highest, infant mortality rates were also the highest. The University of Michigan's Dr. Knodel hypothesized that the lower rate of infant mortality in urban Thailand, where breastfeeding was also lower, was probably due to the compensating factors of general improvements in socio-economic status in urban areas. Such facts were simply disregarded by the breastfeeding activists in government and academia. The lack of data on breastfeeding declines, and even the contradictory evidence at the time, did not deter governments and public health professionals from making this "not proven" problem _the_ major reason for having a WHO Code.

The second alleged problem was that the use of infant formula in bottles in developing countries was a significant if not the sole cause of high disease and death rates among babies in developing countries. Again, "Not proven." The American Academy of Pediatrics points to the difficulties of assessing this issue: 1) obtaining comparable study groups is problematic since mothers who bottlefeed may also have other characteristics which effect health; 2) most healthy babies will continue to breastfeed and if they become ill they are more likely to be bottlefed; and 3) one rarely knows whether what is in the bottle is infant formula or non-nutritious food such as corn starch or even soda pop. The United States Government Task Force pointed out that the majority of studies on mortality and infectious disease had serious methodological limitations. Nevertheless, after a careful review they concluded that breastfeeding in developing countries has a beneficial effect on infant survival and gastrointestinal disease. Beneficial effects of breastfeeding on respiratory and urinary tract infections, meningitis, and sepsis were not found. This balanced review noted that the better studies "detected a positive association between the breast-feeding and infant survival, although they do not suggest that breast-feeding is the sole, or even necessarily the primary factor in infant survival."[3]

This analysis was in sharp contrast to the statements of

leading public health physician Dr. Derrick Jelliffe who attributed ten million cases a year of infant malnutrition and disease to improper bottlefeeding. Mr. James Grant, Director of UNICEF, offered a lower figure - one million deaths a year. When pressed, both later admitted that the figures were either "symbolic" or an "estimate," not a rigorous scientific assessment.

Everyone is entitled to their own opinions, but not to their own facts. We can all appreciate that for even a small percent of bottlefed babies from poor families, the risk of contamination, disease, and death is higher. Breastfeeding must be especially encouraged for these babies. But the emotionalism which clouded the pseudo-scientific debate on this issue obscured the much larger causes of infant mortality in the Third World - inadequate weaning foods, poor water and sanitation, and poor nutrition for breastfeeding mothers. And just what was a poor mother supposed to do who was ill, malnourished, or whose baby was born too weak to suckle or with a congenital defect? The Code failed to discuss what breastmilk substitutes these mothers could use. Indeed, it specifically banned the use of sweetened condensed milk, which, according to Dr. George Graham, may well be the safest and least expensive substitute for breastmilk because of its resistance to bacterial proliferation.

The third alleged problem was that infant formula company promotional practices were a major cause of this so-called dramatic decline in breastfeeding and thus a major cause of infant deaths. Once again, "Not proven." In 1978, Dr. Michael Latham stated categorically: "My interpretation of the scientific evidence leaves absolutely no doubt in my mind first that bottlefeeding is a major cause of morbidity and mortality in developing countries and secondly that the promotion of formulas by Corporations such as Nestle has contributed significantly to this most tragic problem."[4] The Task Force, however, found only one study which even specifically addressed this issue and concludes even with this that "...additional data and analysis are required to unravel these associations from potential confounding factors."[5] According to the Task Force, the other reports concerning the effect of marketing on infant feeding practices are "...either descriptive and anecdotal or are limited in scope and present potentially biased results."[6]

In testimony before the United States Senate Health and Scientific Research Subcommittee in 1978, Dr. Manuel Carballo discussed results of the WHO study on breastfeeding: "While no attempt has been made in this study to correlate patterns of breastfeeding with the type and degree of marketing of industrially processed infant foods, it appears significant that in two of the settings where mothers were provided with free samples of milk, there was also a marked low incidence of breastfeeding."[7] Yet in WHO's preliminary report on this same study, the following comments were made regarding the Philippines where a large proportion of mothers had been given free milk samples: "...although more than 40 percent of the 63 mothers delivered in hospital were given free milk, this did not appear to affect the prevalence of breastfeeding when these mothers are compared with other hospitalized mothers in the same study group. The custom of breastfeeding may still be sufficiently strong among these rural mothers that their behavior was not greatly influenced by commercial pressures."[8]

A charitable interpretation of the statements by scientists surrounding the above three "problems" which led to a WHO Code might be that they had ethical intentions even if they treated the issues either with no data, limited data, or contradictory data. For example, public health physician Dr. Stephen Joseph, who resigned from AID over the United States Government's "no" vote on the Code, put it this way: "It is probably fortunate (as well as necessary) that we do not wait until the data is all in before letting the political process drive policy decisions. It may not be so bad to stumble and lurch from one short term desicion to another -- providing that the longer range directions are shaped by what the evolving state of knowledge tells us."[9]

Fortunate for whom? Are mothers and babies best served by stumbling and lurching? Are they best served by UNICEF publications which state that 98 out of 100 mothers can successfully breastfeed when pediatricians have noted the common experience in all parts of the world of insufficient milk syndrome and breastfeeding failure? Indeed, the American Academy of Pediatrics Committee on Nutrition says that the vast majority of new mothers can breastfeed successfully, given adequate instruction, emotional support, and favorable circumstances. Can anyone who has worked in a developing country honestly say that all these conditions are met for the unfortunate mothers there? Are they best served by the tremendous diversion of time and resources focussed on bottlefeeding and company promotional practices? Indeed, the United States Pediatric organizations criticized the Code's overemphasis on the regulation of marketing practices to the exclusion of other aspects of the problem. The cost of one page of a United Nations General Assembly document after translation, transcribing, processing, and distribution is about $500, well over the per capita incomes of the poorest countries in the world. One United Nation General Assembly produced some 230 million pages. How many pages and at what cost did the infant formula controversy generate over some ten years, not to mention the salaries, travel, and overhead involved?

As scientists, our ethical standards should be guided by what is proven and what is not; what works and what does not -- not primarily by our intentions. A Third World Minister of Health who was both a pediatrician and nutritionist requested infant formula for mothers in his country who could not breast-feed because they were malnourished, were using contraceptives which reduced milk supply, or had to work outside the home. He was refused by the United States foreign aid program because of potential ill effects on babies and the torrent of criticism this could unleash. The United States Government began a thorough scientific review of the evidence surrounding the infant formula controversy six months after the vote on the Code. The WHO, the world's highest health body, passed a Code which after three years was adopted in its entirety by only four percent of its member countries who fought so adamantly for it. Only 20 percent of WHO's member countries had any kind of national code in force by the end of 1984. If we view results rather than intentions as important ethical criteria, then why hasn't the WHO evaluated the health effects of the Code? Writing in the Lancet, Australian physician Dr. A. E. Dugdale said that the test of the Code should be not the compliance of governments but its effects on infants.

There is a difference between the politics of breastfeeding and the science of infant nutrition. To this day, many of the key critics of infant formula have not acknowledged any contradictory evidence to their so-called scientific case. This is reminiscent of a story about Samuel Johnson who was asked one day by a friend how he could have written such a good review about somone's dreary novel. Dr. Johnson replied that he would much rather praise his books than ever read them. At least in the short term, we will continue to have health professionals and other experts who would rather emote over than learn about an issue. The ethical challenge before us is neither to "stumble and lurch from one short term decision to another" nor to pursue paths in international organizations that are evidently not working. Rather, the ethical challenge before us is quite simply to use the knowledge we have accumulated in our scientific research and field work to help the malnourished children of the world.

Notes

1. "Report of The Task Force on the Assessment of the Scientific Evidence Relating to Infant-Feeding Practices and Infant Health," *Pediatrics*, Vol. 74, Nos. 4, October 1984, p. 649.

2. *Ibid.*, p. 648.

3. *Ibid.*, p. 716.

4. Michael C. Latham, "The Case Against Nestle," Statement before The Governing Board National Council of Churches, New York, November 3, 1978.

5. "Report of the Task Force on the Assessment of the Scientific Evidence Relating to Infant-Feeding Practices and Infant Health," *op. cit.*, p. 692.

6. *Ibid.*, p. 692.

7. Manuel Carballo, Testimony, in "Marketing and Promotion of Infant Formula in the Developing Nations, 1978," Hearings before the Subcommittee on Health and Scientific Research of the Committee on Human Resources, U.S. Senate, 95th Congress, May 23, 1978.

8. World Health Organization, "WHO Collaborative Study on Breastfeeding," Methods and Main Results, Preliminary Report, World Health Organization, Geneva, 1979, p. 28.

9. Stephen C. Joseph, Commencement Address before Harvard School of Public Health, *Alumni Bulletin*, 1982, p. 40.

NOTE ON THE EXPORT OF PESTICIDES FROM THE UNITED STATES TO DEVELOPING NATIONS*

Kenneth E. Goodpaster and David E. Whiteside

The sale or distribution of any pesticide within the United States was prohibited by law unless it was registered with the Environmental Protection Agency (EPA). Registration required the submission of toxicity data showing that intended use of the pesticide posed no unreasonable risk to people or the environment. Each year, however, United States companies exported to developing countries millions of pounds of unregistered pesticides and pesticides whose registration had been cancelled or restricted. In 1976, for example, 25 percent of United States exports, or 140 million pounds, were unregistered and another 31 million pounds were pesticides whose registrations had been cancelled.[1] This practice was legal as long as these pesticides were manufactured only for export.

As concern about the environment increased in the 1970s, the morality of this practice, what to do about it, and who was responsible for changing it became widely debated. In Circle of Poison, David Weir and Mark Schapiro claimed that the export of these pesticides resulted in tens of thousands of poisonings and scores of fatalities in developing countries each year. Referring to the practice as an international scandal, they blamed the pesticide industry for dumping these pesticides in developing countries and argued that Americans were also harmed because imports treated with these pesticides contained toxic residues. The Christian Science Monitor called the situation morally indefensible and urged government intervention.[2] A main charge of critics was that the practice was based on a double standard -- the lives of people in developing countries were less valuable than the lives of Americans. Phillip Leakey, assistant minister of the environment in Keyna, asserted: "There is no question that the industrial nations and the companies which are manufacturing these things are guilty of promoting and sponsoring dangerous chemicals in countries where they think people don't care."[3] "What is at stake here is the integrity of the label 'Made in U.S.A.'," argued Rep. Michael D. Barnes (D-Md.), who introduced legislation in 1980 to limit the export of dangerous pesticides abroad.[4]

---

*Reprinted by permission of Harvard Business School Case Studies, Copyright 1983 by the President and Fellows of Harvard College. David E. Whiteside, research associate, prepared this note under the supervision of Kenneth E. Goodpaster.

The United States pesticide industry was opposed to more government regulation and countered that it, too, was concerned about the harm done by pesticides, but that this was largely a result of misuse. Spokespeople for the industry argued that they were making significant attempts on their own to reduce harm through education and by developing safer promotional and advertising methods. A principal argument of the industry was that each country had the right to make up its own mind about the risks and benefits of using a particular pesticide. Dr. Jack Early, president of the National Agricultural Chemicals Association (NACA), accused critics of elitism and asked: "Should we tell other countries on the basis of our affluent standards where the appropriate balance of benefits and risks should lie for them? What does the EPA know -- or care, for that matter -- about the strength of Brazil's desire to obtain a particular pesticide that has some undesirable ecological effect?"[5]

Key To Acronyms

ADI	acceptable daily intake
AID	Agency for International Development
Amvac	American Vanguard Corporation
EPA	Environmental Protection Agency
FAO	Food and Agricultural Organization
FDA	Food and Drug Administration
FFDCA	Federal Food, Drug, and Cosmetic Act
FIFRA	Federal Insecticide, Fungicide, and Rodenticide Act
GAO	General Accounting Office
GIFAP	Groupement International des Associations Nationales de Fabricants de Produit Agrochimiques
IPM	Integrated pest management
NACA	National Agricultural Chemicals Association
OSHA	Occupational Safety and Health Administration
OXFAM	Oxford Committee for the Relief of Famine
WHO	World Health Organization

Some Examples of Manufacturers and Pesticides

Velsicol and Phosvel

In 1971 Velsicol Chemical Company of Chicago began United States production of Phosvel, its trade name for the pesticide leptophos. The WHO classified leptophos as extremely hazardous due to its delayed neurotoxic effects -- it could cause paralysis for some time after exposure. Phosvel was not approved for sale in the United States by the EPA, although it was granted a temporary registration. Velsicol, however, sold it to developing countries where there were no restrictions on its importation.

Reports circulated in 1971 that Phosvel was involved in the deaths of water buffalo in Egypt.[6] Citing the report of the United States Pesticide Tolerance Commission, Velsicol contended that a conclusive determination of Phosvel's role in the incident could not be made because of incomplete facts. In 1973 and 1974 there were additional accounts of poisonings of animals and people.[7]

In 1976 OSHA revealed that workers at Velsicol's Bayport, Texas, plant which manufactured Phosvel had developed serious disorders of the nervous system. They vomited, complained of impotence, were fatigued and disoriented, and became paralyzed. Workers sued Velsicol, the EPA sued for pollution violations, and OSHA leveled fines. The company then withdrew its application for registration of Phosvel and closed its Bayport plant.

From 1971 to 1976, when Velsicol stopped manufacturing Phosvel, estimates were made that it exported between $10 - $18 million worth of Phosvel to developing countries. After the Bayport incident, several countries banned the import of Phosvel. Claiming that Phosvel was safe when used properly, Velsicol tried to sell its remaining stocks of Phosvel in developing countries.[8]

In 1978 Velsicol began reforms to change its environmental image. Responding to criticisms of the company, Richard Blewitt, vice president of corporate affairs, stated: "I'm sorry to say we don't have control over worldwide inventories of Phosvel. Velsicol has made an attempt ... to secure at our cost those inventories and make sure they are properly disposed of ... which far exceeds our obligation."[9] He observed, however, that some distributors were resisting efforts to buy back Phosvel inventories.

As of 1984, Velsicol also sold heptachlor, chlordane, and endrin to developing countries. Use of these pesticides had been canceled or restricted in the United States because they were suspected of being carcinogenic or mutagenic. Velsicol claimed there was no medical evidence that exposure to these chemicals had caused any case of cancer or birth defects in humans.

Amvac and DBCP

After workers at an Occidental plant in California were

found to be sterile in 1977, the state canceled the use of another pesticide, DBCP. At that time Dow, Occidental, and Shell stopped producing it. In 1979 the EPA canceled all uses of DBCP except for use on Hawaiian pineapples because it was suspected of being carcinogenic.

After the ban the American Vanguard Corporation (Amvac) could no longer sell DBCP directly to American companies, but it did continue exporting it. The company's 1979 10-K report stated: "Management believes that because of the extensive publicity and notoriety that has arisen over the sterility of workers and the suspected mutagenic and carcinogenic nature of DBCP, the principal manufacturers and distributors of the product (Dow, Occidental, and Shell Chemical) have, temporarily at least, decided to remove themselves from the domestic marketplace and possibly from the world marketplace." The report continued: "Notwithstanding all the publicity and notoriety surrounding DBCP it was [our] opinion that a vacuum existed in the marketplace that [we] could temporarily occupy. [We] further believe that with the addition of DBCP, sales might be sufficient to reach a profitable level." According to Weir and Schapiro, a former executive had stated: "Quite frankly, without DBCP, Amvac would go bankrupt."[10]

Dow Chemical and 2,4-D and 2,4,5-T
=====

2,4-D and 2,4,5-T were herbicides that often contained dioxin as a contaminant. These herbicides were probably best known as components of Agent Orange, one of the herbicides used as a defoliant by the United States during the war in Vietnam. A study done by Dr. Marco Micolta, director of the San Antonio Central Hospital in rural Colombia, claimed that 2,4-D and 2,4,5-T were responsible for the many miscarriages and birth defects -- usually harelip and cleft palate or both -- that occurred in the region.[11] In the United States 2,4-D and 2,4,5-T were manufactured and sold abroad by several companies, including Dow Chemical Company. All uses of these pesticides containing dioxin were illegal in the United States, and use of them without dioxin was restricted.

"Dioxin Reportedly Worst Cancer Causer" read the headline of an article in the Boston Globe. The article summarized a report by scientists for the EPA which concluded that dioxin was "the most potent cancer causing substance they have ever studied." It was further stated that dioxin probably caused cancer in humans and presented an unacceptable cancer risk when found in water in parts per quintillion. A trillionth of a gram of dioxin in a cubic meter of air would produce about nine additional cases of cancer for each 100,000 people, it was reported. The article pointed out that the conclusions in the report contrasted sharply with industry claims that "the most serious health effect caused by exposure to dioxin is a serious skin rash called chloracne."[12]

In testimony to Congress, a Dow vice president and toxicologist, Perry Gehring, stated that dioxin had "only mild effects on humans." Consistent with its policy of maintaining that 2,4-D and 2,4,5-T were safe when properly used, Dow had been lobbying to have restrictions of these pesticides eased. Robert Lundeen, chairman, said that Dow was trying to reverse the 1979 suspension of 2,4,5-T because "it was patently unsound and had no scientific merit. If we caved in on this one, we might lose the next one, when it was important." One study of the herbicide followed 121 workers in a Monsanto plant that produced 2,4,5-T. They had been accidently exposed to dioxin in 1949 and developed chloracne and other temporary symptoms. After 30 years of observation, the University of Cincinnati's Institute of Environmental Health reported that their death rate was below average and rates of cancer and other chronic diseases were at or below normal.[13]

What is a Pesticide?

Most pesticides were synthetic organic chemicals that were able to kill pests, including insects, weeds, fungi, rodents, and worms. (Clearly, people had different ideas as to what accounted as a pest. One survey in the Philippines found that farmers studied believed that any insect found in their fields should be killed by insecticides.) Pesticides were classified either by use or by chemical makeup. The three major kinds of pesticides by use were herbicides, insecticides, and fungicides. Classification by chemical makeup produced four major categories: organochlorines, organophosphates, carbamates, and pyrethroids. In addition to the generic names of the active ingredients (e.g., paraquat), pesticides also had been given brand names by the companies that produced them (e.g., Gramoxone).

In assessing the risks or hazards of using a pesticide, it was common to distinguish between the intrinsic properties of the chemical and aspects of risk that were under human control. Toxicity, persistence, and fat solubility were important innate characteristics to consider. Toxicity was measured in terms of the lethal dose (LD_{50}) required to kill 50 percent of the test animals -- usually rats. Acute toxic effects included nausea, dizziness, sweating, salivation, shortness of breath, unconsciousness, and possible death. Some commonly used pesticides, like parathion, could cause death by swallowing only a few drops or by skin contact with a teaspoon of the chemical. Chronic toxicity was produced by long-term, low-level exposure and was evidenced by infertility, nervous disorders, tumors, blood disorders, or abnormal offspring. A pesticide was considered persistent if it did not break down easily. Since persistent chemicals remained in the environment longer, they were more likely to affect organisms other than the target pest. The persistence of a chemical varied according to its interaction with the environment. For example, DDT had a half-life of 20 years in temperate climates but was reported in some studies to have a half-life of less than a year in the tropics as a result of increased sunlight, warmth, and moisture.[14] If a pesticide was fat soluble, it could bioaccumulate in the body and remain there. This accumulation might result in long-term harm. Although not acutely toxic, DDT was considered hazardous because of its persistence and fat solubility.

Controllable risk factors included the precautions taken in the manufacture, storage, and transport of a pesticide; the nature of the formulation of the active ingredients; the manner of application; the place used; and the amount of chemical applied.

The Pesticide Industry

The first step in producing a pesticide was synthesizing or creating thousands of chemicals and testing them for useful biological activity -- in this instance, the ability to kill pests. If the chemical passed this initial screen (and only 1 percent did in the first stage of development) then laboratory tests for acute toxicity began, along with a patent application. In the second stage of development, laboratory and green house tests continued. The chemical was tested for specificity of action -- did it kill only a few pests or a wide variety? An experimental permit was also applied for. In the final stage of testing, full registration was applied for, and final preparation for manufacturing and marketing began. (Figure A shows the process in more detail.) In 1981 it took six to seven years from the time of discovery of a chemical with biological efficacy to final registration with the EPA. A company might have screened 12,000 - 30,000 chemicals before it brought one to market. It was estimated that the research and development costs for a single pesticide averaged $20 million.

Major pesticide companies synthesized active ingredients and formulated them, or combined the active ingredients with inert substances to make them ready for application. United States production moved from the pesticide manufacturer to distributor, to dealer, to the farmer. Production in

Figure A
Pesticide R&D Process: Activities and Timing

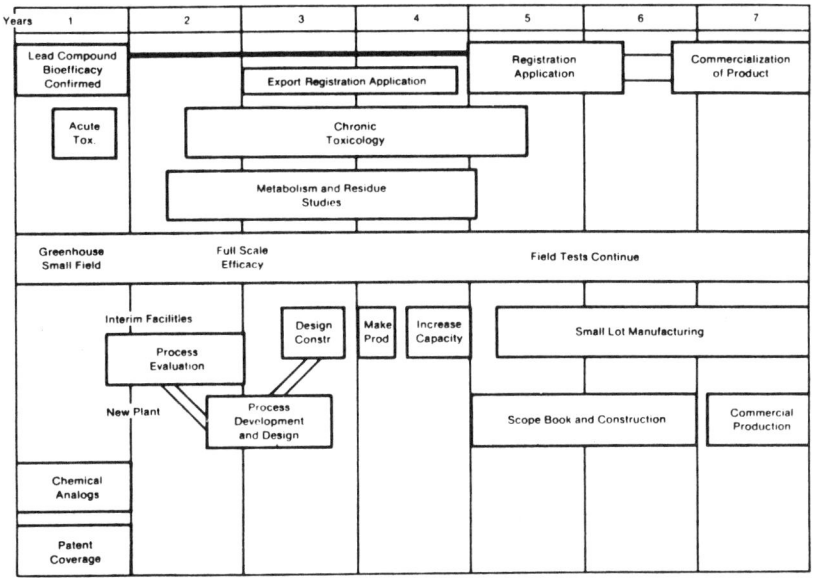

Years	1	2	3	4	5	6	7
Lead Compound Bioefficacy Confirmed		Export Registration Application			Registration Application		Commercialization of Product
	Acute Tox.	Chronic Toxicology					
		Metabolism and Residue Studies					
Greenhouse Small Field		Full Scale Efficacy		Field Tests Continue			
	Interim Facilities — Process Evaluation		Design Constr	Make Prod	Increase Capacity	Small Lot Manufacturing	
New Plant		Process Development and Design			Scope Book and Construction		Commercial Production
Chemical Analogs							
Patent Coverage							

Source: Data gathered by casewriter

311

developing countries was similar, except that dealers in the United States were often trained by pesticide companies and were knowledgeable about pesticide use, whereas in developing countries the user often bought pesticides from a small shopkeeper who was not well informed about pesticide use and toxicity. In addition, some large companies had established plants in developing countries that formulated the basic toxicants, which were then imported by the parent company. This enabled companies to decrease production costs due to lower labor costs and less government regulation. They also were able to take advantage of tax incentives offered to foreign investors in these countries. (Table A lists the top 10 producers of pesticides in 1980.)

From the 1940s to the late 1970s the pesticide industry, driven by the frequent introduction of new products, experienced rapid growth. Investment in R&D was high to sustain innovation and cheaper manufacturing processes. In 1981 R&D budgets were 8 percent of sales. The industry also required high capital investment because of the rapid obsolescence of plant and equipment; thus, capital expenditures were 7.2 percent of sales. These high technology costs, as well as high regulation and marketing costs, posed significant barriers to entry.

Table A
Top 10 Producers of Pesticides, 1980

Company	Value ($ mil.)	Production (mil. lb.)	% Market Share by Value	% Cumulative Market Share
Monsanto	$552–580	169–173	20%	20%
Ciba-Geigy	354–358	142–147	13	33
Stauffer	330	150–117	12	45
Eli Lilly	285–300	72– 82	10	55
DuPont	220	75– 99	8	63
Cyanamid	220	82	8	71
Union Carbide	150–160	57– 63	6	77
Shell	132–155	40– 55	5	82
FMC	135–140	55	5	87
Mobay	125–135	40– 45	5	92

Source: U.S. Pesticides Market (New York: Frost and Sullivan, Inc., 1981), p. 126.

Sales of United States producers steadily increased from $1.2 billion dollars in 1972 to $5.4 billion in 1982. (Figure B shows the increase in sales and exports of pesticides from 1960 to 1980.) Exports steadily rose from $220 million in 1970 to about $1.2 billion in 1980. Production of pesticides in the

United States rose from about 675 million pounds in 1960 to a peak of 1.7 billion pounds in 1975 and declined to 1.3 billion pounds in 1980.

Figure B
U.S. Sales of Pesticides, 1960–1980

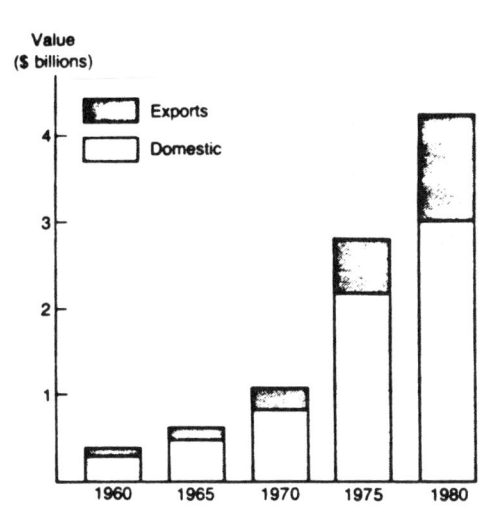

Source: Data gathered by casewriter

Prices and profits for pesticides depended largely on whether or not patents were involved. Pretax profit margins on proprietary products that had a market niche were about 48 percent. On older products, like DDT and 2,4-D, they functioned more like commodities and returned considerably less on investment. Even though a product was patented, competing companies often developed similar products not covered by the original patent. Prices of pesticides tripled between 1970 and 1980; in 1981 herbicides had the highest price and accounted for 60 percent of sales.

The pesticide industry was a mature industry and United States markets had become saturated. As demand in the United States slowed, exports increased. In 1978 exports were 621 million pounds and were 36 percent of total shipments. In 1990, it was predicted, exports would be 855 million pounds and would be 43 percent of total pesticide shipments. Dollar volume of United States exports was projected to reach $2.6 billion by 1990.[15]

Industry analysts agreed that exports would provide the fastest growth for United States producers, since the United

States markets were saturated. Farmers were also using fewer pesticides because of increased costs, declining acreage under cultivation, a slowing of growth in farm income, and increased use of integrated pest management (IPM) techniques which relied more on cultural and biological controls and less on pesticides.

There were 35 producers of pesticides worldwide with sales of more than $100 million per year. In 1982 total worldwide sales were $13.3 billion, up from $2.8 billion in 1972. Six countries -- United States, West Germany, France, Brazil, the USSR, and Japan -- accounted for 63 percent of worldwide sales. All of the developing countries combined accounted for 15 percent of the worldwide market in dollar volume. A report by the United States General Accounting Office (GAO) estimated that pesticide requirements in dollar value for these countries were expected to increase fivefold from 1979 to 1985.[16]

The Benefits of Pesticides

The pesticide industry and many agricultural scientists defended the sale of pesticides to developing countries, declaring that pesticides were necessary to feed an ever-increasing world population, most of it poor, and that pesticides were of great value in fighting diseases which primarily affected the poor. They also argued that there were important secondary benefits.

In 1979 the world population reached approximately 4.4 billion people. Using a minimum-intake level for survival, with no allowance for physical activity, the Food and Agricultural Organization (FAO) of the United Nations estimated that there were 450 million chronically malnourished people in the world. Using a higher standard, the International Food Policy Research Institute put the figure at 1.3 billion.[17]

World population doubled from 1 A.D. to 1650 A.D.; a second doubling occurred after 200 years; the next took 80 years; and the last doubling took place in 1975, requiring only 45 years. Given the 1980 worldwide birthrate of 2.05 percent, according to Norman Borlaug the next doubling would occur in 2015, when world population would total 8 billion. At that birthrate, 172 people would be born every minute, resulting in an additional 90 million people each year. David Hopper of The World Bank stated that developing countries accounted for 90% of this increase.[18]

In 1977, Borlaug noted, world food production totaled 3.5 billion tons, 98 percent of which came directly or indirectly from plants. Based on rates of population growth and projected income elasticities for food, Hopper emphasized the necessity for an increase in food availability of about 3 percent per year, requiring a doubling of world food production to 6.6 billion tons by 2015. Increasing demand for food by developing countries was reflected in the fact that imports of grains to these countries rose from 10 million tons in 1961 to 52 million tons in 1977, according to Maurice Williams, and food shortages were projected to reach 145 million tons by 1990, of which 80 million tons would be for the low-income countries of Asia and Africa.[19]

A major cause of these shortages was that food production in developing countries had not kept pace with the increased demand for food. While per capita production of food for developed countries had steadily increased since 1970, per capita production in developing countries decreased by an average of 50 percent, with the economies of Africa and Latin America showing the greatest drop.

Although experts agreed that it was important to attack the world food problem by lessening demand, they also concurred that deliberate efforts to slow population growth would not produce any significant decline in demand for food for the next decade or so. It was argued, then, that ameliorating the world food problem depended on increasing the food supply. Norman Borlaug, recipient of the 1971 Nobel Peace Prize for the development of the high-yield seeds that were the basis for the Green Revolution, argued that developed countries would not make significant additional increases in yields per acre and that developing countries had to increase their per capita food production. Due to the scarcity of easily developed new land, Borlaug concluded that increases in world food supply could only come from increased yields per acre in these countries, and that this required the widespread use of pesticides.[20]

There was little argument, even from critics, that pesticides increased food production. The technology of the Green Revolution, which depended on pesticides, had enabled scientists in the tropics to obtain yields of 440 bushels of corn per acre versus an average yield of 30 bushels per acre by traditional methods.[21] The International Rice Research Institute in the Philippines had shown that rice plots protected by insecticides yielded an average of 2.7 tons per hectare (2.47 acres) more than unprotected plots, an increase of almost 100 percent. They also found that the use of rodenticides resulted in rice yields up to three times higher than those of untreated plots.[22] (Only producing more food would not end world hunger. What kinds of foods people eat and the quantity are correlated with income. Thus, many experts maintain that economic development is equally important in eliminating world hunger.)

Even with the use of pesticides, worldwide crop losses because of pests before harvest averaged about 25 percent in developed countries and around 40 percent in undeveloped countries. In 1982, GIFAP estimated that total crop losses due to pests for rice, corn, wheat, sugar cane, and cotton were about $204 billion. Most experts (quoted in Ennis et al.) estimated an additional loss of 20-25 percent of food crops if pesticides were not used.[23]

Pesticides also contributed to reducing losses after harvesting. A National Academy of Sciences study identified most post harvest loss resulting from pests and observed that "conservative estimates indicate that a minimum of 107 million tons of food were lost in 1976; the amounts lost in cereal grains and legumes alone could produce more than the annual minimum caloric requirements of 168 million people." Post-harvest losses of crops and perishables through pests were estimated to range from 10 percent to 40 percent. Insects were a major problem, especially in the tropics, because environmental conditions produced rapid breeding. The National Academy of Sciences noted that "50 insects at harvest could multiply to become more than 312 million after four months." In India, in 1963 and 1964, insects and rodents attacked grain in the field and in storage and caused losses of 13 million tons. According to Ennis et al., this amount of wheat would have supplied 77 million families with one loaf of bread per day for a year.[24]

Many developing countries also relied on the sale of agricultural products for foreign exchange that they needed for development or to buy the commodities they could not produce. Cotton, for example, was an important cash crop for many of these countries. Several experimental studies in the United States had shown that untreated plots produced about 10 pounds of seed cotton per acre, but over 1,000 pounds were produced when insecticides were used.[25] It was estimated that 50 percent of the cotton produced by developing countries would be destroyed if pesticides were not used.

It was also argued that major indirect benefits resulted from the use of an agricultural technology that had pesticide use as an essential component. This "package" was more efficient not only because it increased yields per acre, but also because it decreased the amount of land and labor needed for food production. In 1970 American food production, for example, required 281 million acres. At 1940 yields per acre, which were generally less than half of 1970 yields, it would have taken 573 million acres to produce the 1970 crop. This was a savings of 292 million acres through increased crop yields.[26] The estimated 300 percent increase in per capita agricultural production from 1960 to 1980 also meant that labor resources could be used for other activities. Other experts estimated that without the use of pesticides in the United States, the price of farm products would probably increase by at least 50 percent and we would be forced to spend 25 percent or more of our income on food.[27] It was held that many of these same secondary benefits would accrue to developing countries through the use of pesticides.

Pesticides also contributed both directly and indirectly to combating disease; because of this, their use in developing countries had increased. Pesticides had been highly effective in reducing such diseases as malaria, yellow fever, elephantiasis, dengue, and filariasis. Malaria was a good example. In 1955, WHO initiated a global malaria eradication campaign based on the spraying of DDT. This effort greatly reduced the incidence of malaria. For example, in India there were approximately 75 million cases in the early 1950s. But in 1961 there were only 49,000 cases. David Bull estimated that by 1970 the campaign had prevented 2 billion cases and had saved 15 million lives. In 1979 Freed estimated that one-sixth of the world's population had some type of pest-borne disease.[28]

Risks to Humans

Reliable estimates of the number of pesticide poisonings worldwide were difficult to obtain because many countries did not gather such statistics. Using figures from WHO, Bull of the Oxford Committee for the Relief of Famine (OXFAM) calculated that in 1981 there were 750,000 cases of pesticide poisoning and about 14,000 deaths worldwide, with over half of the fatalities being children. OXFAM estimated that in developing countries there were 375,000 cases of poisoning with 10,000 deaths a year. Thus, developing countries, with 15 percent of pesticide consumption, suffered half of the accidental poisonings and three-fourths of the deaths. Another survey by Davies et al. estimated that in 1977, the annual worldwide mortality rate was over 20,000.[29]

Experts agreed that these estimates contained large margins for error, and they believe that the actual number of cases was substantially higher. Many countries did not collect statistics on pesticide poisonings. In addition, pesticides were often used in remote areas that lacked easy access to clinics or had physicians who were not trained to recognize the syptoms of pesticide poisoning.

Causes of Pesticide Poisoning in Developing Countries

Pesticide poisoning resulted from many causes in developing countries. Workers would remain in the fields when planes were spraying crops; they may not have left for fear that they would lose their jobs, or they may not have understood the risk. Much of the spray drifted through the area to cover homes, utensils, clothes hanging on lines, children playing, irrigation ditches, and animals. Sometimes workers too quickly entered a newly sprayed field; the pesticide, then still moist on the plant, rubbed off on their skin and clothing. Later, when they washed, they did so with what was available -- the pesticide-contaminated water in the irrigation ditches. This may also have been the source of their drinking water. Reports also surfaced of pilots dumping excess pesticide into lakes or rivers that were often vital food and water sources.

Another cause of pesticide misuse was the lack of education -- many of the people who used pesticides in developing countries were illiterate. In addition, they knew little or nothing about the dangers of pesticides and how they interacted with the environment. Developing countries did not have the elaborate agricultural extension services that existed in industrialized countries, especially in the United States. The farmers and laborers often did not know safe or effective methods for transporting, mixing, applying, storing, and disposing of pesticides.

Consider the example of one village on the shore of Lake Volta in Ghana. The fishermen began using Gammalin 20 (lindane) to catch fish. They would pour the pesticide into the lake and wait for the poisoned fish to float to the surface. The village depended on the lake for its food, income, drinking water, and water for cooking and washing. Soon the people around the lake complained of blurred vision, dizziness, and vomiting -- all symptoms of lindane poisoning. The number of fish in the lake declined 10-20 percent a year. The villagers initially did not connect their symptoms with the declining fish population. They believed that both were due to natural causes. When they did become aware that the fish were poisoned, they believed the poison remained in the fish's head and that cutting off the head made the fish safe to eat.[30]

Sometimes poisoning resulted because proper safety precautions were not taken when chemicals were mixed and applied. Often workers mixed the pesticide with their hands, or if in granular form, they sprinkled pesticides on the plants with their hands. The director of the National Biological Control Research Center in Thailand reported: "When mixing the formulation for spraying, the farmer may dip his finger into the mix and taste it by dabbing his finger to his tongue. If it gets numb it indicates the right concentration." Frequently, workers were not supplied with protective clothing, could not afford it, or chose not to wear it because of the heat. They also often had faulty equipment. If sprayers were carried on their backs, leaky valves allowed the pesticide to run down their shoulders. One survey done in the Philippines indicated that none of the farmers studied knew that a leaky valve could be fatal. Another survey in Gujarat, India, showed that none of the farm workers had face masks, only 50 percent covered their noses and mouths with a cloth, and 20 percent did not wash after spraying.[31]

Distribution methods in developing countries also caused problems. Pesticides were shipped in bulk containers and were then repackaged in smaller containers. Local merchants customarily sold the products in unlabeled bottles and kept them on shelves with other foodstuffs. Farmers relied on the local shop owner, often untrained, to advise them about what pesticide to use and how. For example, paraquat, which was dark in color, caused numerous poisonings because it was mistaken for coke, wine, or coffee.

The large drums in which pesticides were shipped were frequently used to hold drinking water and store food. Few understood that the residues of the pesticide on the walls of the drum might still be toxic. In one case 124 people were poisoned, eight fatally, after eating food prepared in the recycled pesticide drums.[32]

Critics contended that labels often failed to give the detailed information necessary for safety precautions and were sometimes not written in a language of the area in which they were distributed. Even when they were, however, many of the users could not read them because they were illiterate. According to Dr. Fred Whittemore, pest management specialist for AID, a check in Mexico found that 50 percent of the pesticides sold were incorrectly labeled. Labels usually did not state first-aid recommendations or contained recommendations that were unrealistic. In a remote part of India one pesticide label specified calling a physician and using atropine and 2 PAM as an antidote; however, the local clinic was hours away from home and, when checked, had never heard of 2 PAM.[33]

Critics charged that through promotion and advertising, companies encouraged farmers to view pesticides as panaceas. They emphasized that frequently the advertisements failed to mention the dangers of pesticides and created the impression that pesticides were safe to use. Critics also argued that companies occasionally encouraged overuse by advocating calendar spraying rather than spraying on the basis of the number of pests attacking a crop. They pointed out that many in developing countries trusted the goodwill of American companies. As Dr. Harold Alvo Nunez, former Colombian Minister of Health, put it: "You know, the label 'Made in U.S.A.' is very powerful here."[34]

Problems with pesticide overuse were particularly severe in developing countries. For example, Weir and Schapiro estimated that pesticide use was 40 percent higher in Central America than necessary to achieve optimal production. In 1975 El Salvador, with a population of 4.5 million people, was using 20 percent of the world production of parathion. This averaged out to 2,940 pounds per square mile, according to Woltering.[35]

In A Growing Problem, David Bull described the process by which farmers became hooked on using greater and greater quantities and more and more varieties of pesticides. He called this the "pesticide treadmill." When an insecticide was used, for example, not only did it kill the targeted insect but also other insects that were its natural enemies. These natural controls also kept in check other insects that potentially could become pests. Once the natural controls were killed, not only could there be an increase in the original target pests but also an increase in these secondary pests. Faced with an unexpected increase in pests, the farmer's typical response was to spray even more. Another result of repeated pesticide use was that pests developed a genetic resistance to them. Once this happened, the usual response again was to spray larger quantities and then to try another kind of pesticide. An additional reason for overuse was that formulation and methods of application for many chemicals had been developed for use in temperate climates. The more rapid breakdown of chemicals in tropical climates, however, required more frequent and larger applications.

The cultivation of cotton in Central America illustrated the pesticide treadmill at work. At the turn of the century, Central American farmers began growing cotton, which was native to the region, on a commercial scale. At that time, the boll weevil was cotton's only major pest and it was controlled by natural enemies and by hand removal from the cotton plants.

In the 1950s, as the amount of acreage under cultivation increased, mechanization and intensive use of pesticides began. Initially, insecticides were applied about eight times a year and resulted in improved yields. By the mid-1950s, three new pests were attacking cotton. During the 1960s insecticide use increased; as many as 50 different pesticides became available for a single pest. The number of applications increased to 28 per season. By 1970 there were eight pests causing serious damage to cotton. As new pests appeared the old ones became more resistant, and farmers applied more and more pesticides. By 1974, Central American growers were spraying up to 40 times a season. An average of 3,380 pounds of pesticide was being applied for every square mile.[36]

Food crops as well as cash crops were affected. Rice was the staple crop for hundreds of millions of people in Southeast Asia. One study reported that eight rice pests were resistant to at least one insecticide in 1965; 14 pests were resistant to pesticides by 1975.[37]

Pests worldwide have rapidly developed resistances to pesticides. In 1951 there were six species of pests of either medical or agricultural importance that were resistant. By 1961 Davies estimated that the number was 137 and in 1980 resistant pests increased to 414 species. An exacerbating factor was that sometimes pests developed multiple resistance to a whole group

**Figure C
Resistant Species of Arthropods and
New Insecticides, 1938–1980**

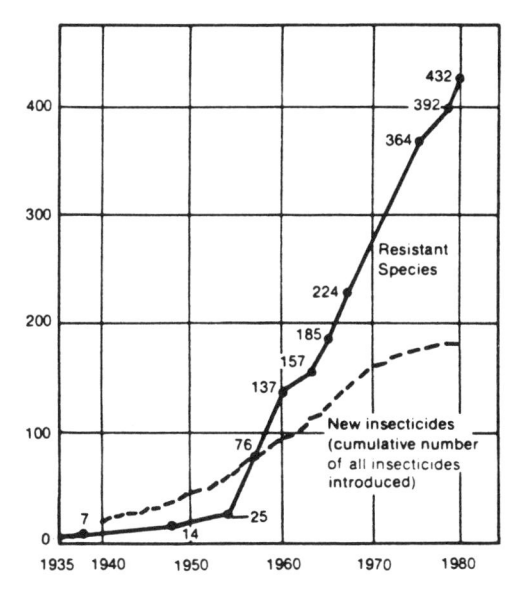

Source: David Bull, *A Growing Problem* (Oxford, England: OXFAM, 1982), p. 24. Reprinted by permission.

of chemicals in the same class. An example was the diamondback moth, which attacked cabbage in one region of the Malay peninsula. The moths become so resistant that farmers now sprayed three times a week, often using a "cocktail" made up of several insecticides. The diamondback moth, in turn, developed some degree of resistance to at least 11 insecticides. Bull estimated that in 1978 insecticides accounted for one-third of the production costs of cabbages. It was believed that soon it would no longer be profitable to grow cabbage in the region.[38]

In the 1970s a resurgence occured in the incidence of malaria. For example, in India, although the number of cases dropped from 75 million in the 1950s to 49,000 in 1961; the figure rose to 6.5 million in 1976. In Haiti there were 2,500 cases in 1968 but 26,000 in 1972. Worldwide the number of cases increased by over 230 percent between 1972 and 1976.[39] This increase was attributed to the disease-carrying mosquito's resistance to pesticides. (As Figure C indicates, the rate of introduction of new pesticides had not kept up with the rate at which pests were developing resistance.)

Industry Response

The pesticide industry argued that each country had the right to set its own policy based on its individual estimate of the risk/benefit ratio of using a particular pesticide, and that risk/benefit ratio for developing countries varied with economic and social conditions. A country with widespread malnutrition or insect-borne disease might be more willing to risk using a pesticide whose use had been canceled or restricted in the United States. Dr. William Upholt, consultant to the United States National Committee for Man and the Biosphere, stated: "Less industrial countries may consider a few cases of cancer in older people a small price to pay for increased yield of food crops. So it is reasonable to conclude that all nations do not need the same pesticide. There is an old saying that one man's food is another man's poison, and I guess that could be reversed."[40]

DDT was cited as an example of a pesticide whose registration had been canceled for use on food crops, but which was still produced in India and used by several developing countries. Robert Oldford, president of Union Carbide's Agricultural Products Division, said:

> How do some of the developing countries consider chemicals that have been banned or restricted here? Burma, for example, has stated that, "In many other countries the use of chlorinated hydrocarbons is being restricted because of

their persistent nature. The official position here is that these insecticides are effective, cheap, and, if used properly, are no more hazardous than other newer and more expensive insecticides."[41]

In developing the risk/benefit argument, Frederick J. Rarig, vice president and associate general counsel of Rohm and Haas Company, stated:

Margaret Mead taught us that morality is a relative, cultural concept. I have learned in 35 years of work in the field of hazard analysis that safety is similarly a relative, cultural concept. Safety is never an absolute. It is <u>not</u> an <u>absence</u> of hazard. Safety is an <u>acceptable level of hazard</u>.

Men will not forgo shelter simply because the only shelter they can build is combustible. Mothers will not leave their children naked and exposed to the elements because the only available cloth with which to clothe them is combustible cotton ... Men will not starve while insects and rodents flourish simply because there are risks connected with the poisoning of insects and rodents.[42]

Dr. William Hollis, science coordinator of NACA, also pointed out the toxicological risks from crops damaged by pests. He observed: "In this light, the risk versus benefit concept to evaluate pesticides is inappropriate. The ultimate evaluation to be made must consider risk versus risk. That is, the risk of using the pesticide versus the risk of not having optimum production and protection of food, thereby not preventing unnecessary human health hazards. Such health hazards include exposure to pest-induced toxins, carcinogens, mutagens, and allergens."[43]

NACA claimed that sometimes the EPA was out of step with other countries in its interpretation of toxicological data. For example, NACA pointed out that whereas the EPA suspended on-food uses of 2,4,5-T based on a study of its health effects, other countries -- including the United Kingdom, Canada, New Zealand, and Australia -- reviewed the same data and concluded it was acceptable to continue using the herbicide for such purposes.[44]

In trying to place the toxicity of certain pesticides in perspective, Dr. Ram Hamsager, chairman of Hindustan Insecticides Limited, compared the LD_{50} of DDT with nicotine. He indicated the LD_{50} for DDT was about 118 mg. per kilogram of body weight while the LD_{50} for nicotine was about 60 mg. per kilogram of body weight. He asserted: "This proves that nicotine is twice as poisonous as DDT. The toxicity level of some of the other naturally occurring chemicals which form part of our daily intake, like caffeine found in coffee and thiobromine found in tea, are comparable to safe pesticides like DDT, and BHC."[45]

Defending the export of pesticides that were not approved for use in the United States, Robert Oldford stated: "There are two fundamental reasons why such exports occur. First, products are not usually registered in the United States for an agricultural pest crop use which does not exist here -- coffee or bananas, for example. Second, developing countries have approval agencies that typically will require valid evidence of registration in a developed country in addition to other information needed to make a decision in the best interest of their citizens."[46]

The industry was trying to minimize pesticide misuse through education and had cooperated with several international organizations such as the FAO, AID, WHO, and The World Bank. Dow Chemical conducted over 400 agricultural chemicals meetings in South America in 1981, and Monsanto brought union officials of one developing country to the company's United States plants to learn of the safety procedures used there. Since 1978 NACA sponsored a series of international conferences between representatives of importing countries and United States manufacturers to harmonize registration requirements and develop safety training programs. As a result of a two-year consultation process with industry, consumer, church, and environmental representatives, NACA had adopted a product stewardship code containing voluntary guidelines for its 115 member companies.

It was argued that 1978 amendments to United States law greatly reduced the possibility of inadequate labeling, but that industry on its own was also trying to develop better labeling procedures. For example, Velsicol had developed a "One World Communication System," using pictographs adapted to different cultures to instruct users in safe handling techniques, supplementing the labels required by United States law. Manufacturers, however, had little control over how distributors in developing countries repackaged and labeled pesticides after removing them from bulk shipping containers.

The United States pesticide industry showed concern over the rise of thousands of small "pirate" manufacturers of chemicals that were imitations of proprietary pesticides produced in the United States. These companies, usually not closely regulated, sold products in developing countries that were less effective and more dangerous because of contaminants. They were often cheaper, however, than pesticides sold by quality-conscious United States companies.

Regulating Pesticides

Jacob Scherr of the Natural Resources Defense Council commented at the 1979 United States Strategy Conference on Pesticide Management: "Some developing countries have enacted virtually no legislation to govern the importation, domestic use, and disposal of potentially toxic chemicals. Few maintain any facilities for monitoring the effects of the products on health or the environment. Even where decent laws are on the books, many governments lack the technical and administrative capacity to implement them."[47]

Regulation in Developing Countries

An Agromedical Approach to Pesticide Management asserted that "a number of developing countries already have strong pesticide laws on their books, but in many cases efforts aimed at enforcing the laws are either negligble or non-existent."[48] Few countries, it was reported, had the necessary regulatory infrastructure for monitoring, testing, setting residue limits, enforcement, and so forth.

The FAO studied the extent of pesticide control among members. Of 144 countries surveyed, 31 had well-developed procedures and enforcement; 26 had well-developed procedures but the degree of enforcement was unknown; 6 were developing control procedures; and 81 had no control procedures or gave no information.[49]

Many developing countries asked the United States and other industrialized countries to help them develop adequate legislation, monitoring, and enforcement mechanisms. In particular, they requested the United States to share its knowledge of the harmful effects of the many chemicals already tested by the United States government or corporations. Many also wanted to be kept informed of changes in the status of pesticides registered in the United States.

The following comments made by Samuel Gitonga, agricultural expert for the National Irrigation Board of Kenya, were typical:

> We do not have the necessary machinery to go through an entire testing program to determine whether the product is safe or not. For these reasons, I believe that the United States and other developed countries have a responsibility

to ensure that the information they have painfully gathered is made available to as many people as possible in the developing world. I certainly reject the idea that the developing countries always know what they want or which pesticides are best to use. Information that a product is not allowed for use in a particular country would be a very useful starting point. The less developed countries must be made aware that there is a problem with using a particular product. These very real dangers of incompletely tested or banned products being used in the less developed countries should be strongly condemned by the international community.[50]

Regulation in the United States

A 1979 report by the General Accounting Office to Congress, entitled Better Regulation of Pesticide Exports and Pesticide Residues in Imported Food is Essential, contained the following pasage: "The Food and Drug Administration does not analyze imported food for many potential residues. It allows food to be marketed before testing it for illegal residues. Importers are not penalized if their imports later are determined to contain illegal residues. The safety and appropriateness of some residues allowed on imported food has not been determined." In 1977 the United States imported $13.4 billion of agricultural products. Most of these imports were from developing countries with less effective regulatory mechanisms than those in the United States -- 28 percent of United States pesticide exports went to Central American countries from which we obtain 38 percent of our imported agricultural commodities. The United States imported approximately 600 different food commodities from over 150 countries in 1979.[51]

United States pesticide exports and imports were regulated by the Federal Insecticide, Fungicide, and Rodenticide Act of 1947, as amended, and the Federal Food, Drug, and Cosmetic Act of 1938, as amended.

FIFRA required the EPA to register all pesticides before they were distributed, sold, or used in the United States. The EPA registered a pesticide when it determined that the pesticide, when used according to commonly recognized practice, could safely and effectively perform its intended function without unreasonable risk to humans or the environment. If a pesticide was produced for export only, however, it was not required to be registered by the EPA and could be exported regardless of its regulatory status or its intended use. FIFRA required that domestic producers maintain records of shipments and purchasers' specifications for packaging. Amendments made in 1978 required that unregistered pesticides produced solely for export be labeled "Not Registered for Use in the United States of America." Foreign purchasers of unregistered chemicals had to sign statements acknowledging their understanding that these pesticides were not allowed for United States use. Copies of foreign purchaser acknowledgements were then sent to the government officials of the importing countries. Labels for exports had to contain the same information as products intended for United States use. Among those requirements were the display of a skull and cross-bones if highly toxic and a statement of practical treatment, warning or caution statements, and no false representations.

FFDCA required that tolerances be established for pesticide residues. Any food was considered adulterated if it contained residues in excess of these tolerances or if it contained a residue for which the EPA had not established a tolerance.

The EPA and the Food and Drug Administration (FDA) administered these laws. The EPA established tolerances on the basis of the nature, amount, and toxicity of the residue of a pesticide. The FDA was responsible for assuring that all food marketed in the United States, either domestic or imported, met FFDCA residue requirements. The FDA monitored imported food for conformance with these requirements by chemically analyzing samples collected from individual shipments received at various United States entry points. Food that was adulterated was required to be denied entry and reexported or destroyed.

In its report, the GAO stated that "pesticide use patterns in foreign countries clearly indicate that a large portion of food imported into the United States may in fact contain unsafe pesticide residues."[52] For example, a 1978 study of coffee imported to the United States showed that 45 percent (25 out of 55) of the samples contained illegal residues. All of these residues were from pesticides whose use had been canceled or severely restricted in the United States. The cycle of food contaminated by United States pesticide exports being imported into the United States was referred to as the 'boomerang effect.'

The FDA estimated that approximately one-tenth of the food imported into the United States contained illegal residues. However, the GAO argued that this estimate was probably too low due to inadequacies in the FDA's analytical and sampling procedures. The two multiresidue tests used by the FDA could detect residues of only 73 of the 268 pesticides that had United States tolerances. The GAO studied the pesticides allowed, recommended, or used in developing countries on 10 major commodities: bananas, coffee, sugar, tomatoes, tea, cocoa, tapioca, stawberries, peppers, and olives. It found that an additional 130 pesticides used on these foods had no United States tolerances and could not be detected by the FDA's tests. Since the FDA did not know which pestides were used by other countries on food imported into the United States, it did not know which analytical test to use. This was one reason why the FDA used only two of the six multiresidue tests available and no single residue test. Without this knowledge, use of other tests would be too costly in terms of time and money. The GAO further concluded that the "anomalies" it found "do not inspire confidence in the validity of FDA's sampling program."[53]

The report also pointed out that "even when the pesticide residues on imported food are identified as being violative, the food will probably be marketed and consumed rather than detained or destroyed." For example, in Dallas Texas, Department of Agriculture personnel complained of an insecticide-like smell coming from a shipment of imported cabbage. Despite this complaint and the fact that the importer had a history of shipping adulterated products, the cabbage was allowed to be marketed. The GAO found that "half of the imported food that the Food and Drug Administration found to be adulterated during a 15-month period was marketed without penalty to importers and consumed by an unsuspecting American public."[54]

The Department of Health, Education and Welfare criticized the methodology of the GAO report and disagreed with several of its conclusions and recommendations:

> We believe this draft report neither accurately nor fairly reflects either the degree to which pesticide residues pose a risk to the U.S. consumer or the Food and Drug Administration's (FDA) program for identifying and detaining violative imported products. We recognize the need for improvements in FDA's coverage of imported food for pesticide residues, and several actions are well under way to accomplish these improvements. However, many of the criticisms of FDA programs and professional competence are based upon unsubstantiated conclusions. GAO has posed hypothetical situations without citing sufficent evidence to substantiate their occurrence and thereby may create unfounded apprehensions about the food supply and those charged with assuring its safety.[55]

NACA argued that the safety factor built into the setting of tolerance levels and the Market Basket Surveys carried out by the FDA since 1965 provided adequate safeguards for the American consumer. Tolerances were established by first determining a no-toxic-effect level for a pesticide on test animals and then increasing that many times over, usually by a factor of 100, to set the legal maximum for humans. As part of its yearly surveillance programs, the FDA examined 30 samples, each composed of 117 food items, from different regions and representing the diets of adults and children to determine the average daily intake of pesticide residues. These results were then compared with acceptable daily intake levels. Several studies had consistently shown that actual daily intake was less than ADI levels. For example, the average daily intake of parathion consumed in 1977 was $1/5000-1/1000$ of the ADI. In no instance was the actual intake of a pesticide as high as the ADI.[56]

NACA asserted that "we are being indicted in the so-called 'circle of poison issue' in spite of the basic fact that, according to the best experts, no one anywhere in the world has suffered illness from pesticide residues in or on food commodities."[57]

The pesticide industry was not in favor of increased government regulation of pesticide exports to alleviate the risks of pesticide use in developing countries and, indirectly, in the United States. About such a proposed change in 1980, Earl Spurrier, director of government relations for Monsanto, said that "the extra restrictions are unduly stringent and they are going to throw much of the export business to foreign competitors, who are not similarly restricted."[58] Instead, the industry favored voluntary efforts by companies to alter the pattern of pesticide misuse that existed worldwide.

Notes

1. <u>Better Regulation of Pesticide Exports and Pesticide Residues in Imported Foods is Essential</u> (Washington, DC: General Accounting Office, 1979), p. 3

2. "Exporting Poisons," <u>Christian Science Monitor</u>, February 13, 1980, p. 12.

3. "Kenya tries to put cap on imports of hazardous chemicals," <u>Christian Science Monitor</u>, May 3, 1983, p. 13.

4. "Hazards for Export," <u>Newsday</u>, December 1981, reprint, p. 14R.

5. Ibid. p. 13R.

6. Cited by Jacob Scherr, Proceedings of the U.S. Strategy Conference on Pesticide Management (Silver Springs, Maryland: Teknekron Research, Inc., 1979), p. 33.

7. David Bull, A Growing Problem (Oxford, England: OXFAM, 1982), p. 40.

8. David Weir and Mark Schapiro, Circle of Poison (San Francisco, CA: Institute for Food and Development Policy, 1981), p. 23.

9. Newsday, p. 11R.

10. Weir and Schapiro, p. 22.

11. Newsday, p. 11R.

12. The Boston Globe, July 24, 1983, p. 19.

13. "Dow vs. the Dioxin Monster," Fortune, May 30, 1983, pp. 84-85.

14. Ram S. Hamsagar, "Petrochemicals and the Environment." Paper published by Groupement International des Associations Nationales de Fabricants de Produit Agrochimiques (GIFAP), September 23, 1983, p. 4.

15. "Pesticides: $6 Billion by 1990," Chemical Week, May 7, 1980, p. 45.

16. Better Regulation, p. 1.

17. Maurice J. Williams, "The Nature of the World Food and Population Problem," in Future Dimensions of World Food Population, ed. by R. G. Woods (Boulder, Colorado: Westview Press, 1981), p. 20.

18. Norman Borlaug, "Using Plants to Meet World Food Needs," Future Dimensions, p. 180; David Hopper, "Recent Trends in World Food and Population," Future Dimensions, p. 37.

19. Borlaug, pp. 118, 128; Hopper, p. 39; and Williams p. 11.

20. Borlaug, p. 114 and pp. 129-134.

21. Hopper, p. 49.

22. Bull, p. 5.

23. GIFAP Directory 1982-1983, p. 10; W. B. Ennis, W. M. Dowler, W. Klassen, "Crop Protection to Increase Food Supplies," in Food: Politics, Economics, Nutrition, and Research, ed. P. Abelson (Washington, DC: American Association for the Advancement of Science, 1975), p. 113.

24. E. R. Pariser, et al., Post Harvest Food Losses in Developing Countries (Washington, DC: National Academy of Sciences, 1978), pp. 7, 53; Ennis, p. 110.

25. William Hollis, "The Realism of Integrated Pest Management as a Concept and in Practice -- with Social Overtures," paper presented at Annual Meeting of Entomological Society of America, in Washington, DC, December 1, 1977, p. 7.

26. Borlaug, p. 106.

27. Ennis, p. 113.

28. Bull, p. 30; Virgil Freed, Proceedings, p. 21.

29. Bull, p. 38; John Davies, et al., Agromedical Approach to Pesticide Management (Miami, FL: University of Miami, 1982), p. 9.

30. Ruth Norris, ed., Pills, Pesticides, and Profits (Croton-on-Hudson, NY: North River Press, 1982), p. 13.

31. Bull, p. 49.

32. Davies, p. 88.

33. Bull, p. 89.

34. Newsday, p. 11R.

35. Weir and Schapiro, p. 6; Martin Wolterding, "The Poisoning of Central America," Sierra, September-October 1981, p. 64.

36. Wolterding, p. 64.

37. Bull, p. 13.

38. Davies, p. 65; Bull, p. 18.

39. Bull, p. 30.

40. Upholt, P. 35.

41. Robert Oldford, Statement to the Subcommittee on Department Operations Research and Foreign Agriculture of the Committee on Agriculture, U.S. House of Representives, June 9, 1983, p. 13.

42. Proceedings, p. 29.

43. Hollis, p. 11. See Wendell Kilgore et al., "Toxic Plants as Possible Human Teratogens," California Agriculture, November-December 1981, p. 6; Garnett Wood, "Stress Metabolites of White Potatoes," Advances in Chemistry, p. 149, 1976, pp. 369-386; Bruce Ames, "Dietary Carcinogens and Anticarcinogens," Science, September 23, 1983, pp. 1256-1262.

44. Food, Health, Agricultural Chemicals and Developing Countries, published by NACA, May 1983, p. 4.

45. Hamsagar, p. 8.

46. Oldford, p. 13.

47. Proceedings, p. 32.

48. Davies, p. 238.

49. Bull, p. 144.

50. Proceedings, p. 41.

51. Better Regulation, cover page.

52. Ibid., p. 6.

53. Ibid., p. 14.

54. Ibid., p. 39-40.

55. Ibid., p. 70.

56. See the ongoing study of the dietary intake of pesticides in the United States in Pesticide Monitoring Journal, in Vols. 5, 8, and 9. See, also, J. Frawley and R. Duggan, "Techniques for Deriving Realistic Estimates of Pesticide Intakes," in Advances in Pesticide Science, Part III, ed., H. Geissbuhler (New York: Pergammon Press, 1979).

57. Jack Early, Remarks of the National Agricultural Chemicals

Association Before the Latin American Forum, May 4, 1982, p. 6.

58. "The Unpopular Curbs on Hazardous Exports," Business Week, September 1980.

THE PRINCIPLES OF PESTICIDES: A MORAL DIALOGUE

Scott Cook

Introduction

At Bentley's Sixth National Conference, participants of the session "Pesticides: Exporting Hazardous Products" were invited to read the Goodpaster and Whiteside "Note" in advance. At the session, Professor Goodpaster led a case method discussion of the pesticides export issue. In the discussion, five participants assumed the roles of an American consumer, a United States government official, a United States chemical export executive, a Third World government official and a Third World farmer. The session began with statements by each of the role players, then moved into an open discussion among all in attendance.

In an important sense, the session constituted an evolving moral dialogue. Opening with statements from seemingly disparate positions and concerns, the discussion progressed to the identification of underlying principles and ultimately ended with a measure of agreement concerning key moral issues and steps toward addressing them.

In what follows, the discussion is recounted and is presented as a moral dialogue on the pesticides export issue. In conclusion, an assessment of the dialogue is offered and some observations are made concerning how this sort of discussion can help illuminate the ethical dimensions of a complex dilemma of multinational enterprise.

The American Consumer

From the perspective of the American consumer, the pesticides issue presented three concerns. First, "as a consumer and particularly as a mother with children," she was worried about the "health hazards to Americans" posed by the reintroduction of presumably dangerous chemicals to America through imported food and other products. This concern was heightened by the increased attention to diet and health witnessed in the United States in recent years. In addressing this concern, she pointed to the efforts of consumer action groups in various areas, which have been effective both through publicity and by exerting influence on legislation.

A second concern was expressed by the consumer regarding long-term consequences of hazardous pesticides export and use.

There is clearly a need for agricultural chemicals, the consumer argued, but the benefits of their use need to be weighed against long-term risks and costs. And such costs apply to the Third World as much as to the American consumer. She felt that potential long-term consequences had not received the attention they deserved by either the exporters or the Third World users.

Lastly, she felt that "the term 'made in America' should inspire confidence, not terror in people in the rest of the world." American consumers, she argued, need to be concerned about and to take action against American products giving America and Americans a bad name in the Third World. "Publicity and legislative mobilization," she held, "can be useful avenues open to concerned American consumers."

The United States Chemical Exporter

As an executive from an American chemical producer, the exporter felt that others often "have difficulty identifying with the exporter's perspective." The decisions and balances which exporters must face, he argued, are difficult, complex, and must take into consideration several different perspectives and interests. His company exports a number of chemicals that are restricted or banned in the United States, and "I do so" he said, "with full knowledge, and I don't lose sleep at night." This is true, he held, because his company weighs all factors and has a commitment to act responsibly.

In the development of a product, the executive pointed out, his company typically "uses United States scientists, follows all United States laws, and does all the required registration and toxicology studies." Once a product is marketable, the company sells it in the importing country "through our subsidiary ... which we can control." Products are designed to be "safe when used as intended." And the company runs programs for distributors so that "they understand the safety and efficacy" of a product. All these things, the exporter maintained, contribute to the management and maintenance of responsible practice by his company in exporting products "that work and are desired."

As a specific example, he pointed to a rodenticide which his company successfully markets in a Third World country. The product is banned in the United States, he said, because government agencies do not consider it to be "child proof." However, he continued, the product was not designed to be child proof; it was "designed to be thrown into crop fields to kill rats," which it does safely when used as intended. And, in a country "where rats can destroy 40 percent of a crop," this is significant.

Pesticides, therefore, even ones banned in the United States, can be highly beneficial in the Third World when used correctly.

This does not mean, he strongly maintained, that the dangers and misuse of pesticides in the Third World are "a non-problem. There are serious problems." Yet, from a balanced perspective, he argued, one would have to say that "a lot has been done" already in addressing these issues "and a lot more needs to be done." Specifically, he suggested that areas for improvement included sharing of information, full disclosure about the nature and hazards of the chemicals, and labeling in local languages. Further, he pointed out, "international regulations are coming out every day."

The United States Government Official

The United States official was quick to agree with the export executive that the situation was far from one dimensional and that there are examples of "good and responsible companies" operating in this essentially problematic market. However, he just as quickly wished to voice three substantial concerns which he felt required particular attention from a legislative perspective.

First, he asserted that pesticides export was "an issue with significant foreign policy considerations." The market alone, this perspective suggests, is not sufficient to address or address adequately all the realities of the issue. "When there are major problems arising from the use of these products," he pointed out, "the United States as a nation is going to be blamed, even when the fault might lie in the user nation." And if the United States is blamed, the United States Government is expected to respond.

Second, he felt that in "fundamentally more important terms" a legislator has to consider "the human costs both in the less developed countries (LDCs) and in the United States." A government official "cannot say (as some voices in industry seem to say) that the evaluations of risks and benefits made by LDCs are not our concern. But, as a United States Government official, I certainly have major concerns" both in terms of human costs and in terms of implications for foreign policy.

Third, apart from these other matters, the issue is already one of concern for United States Government officials, he argued, for the very reason that "our counterparts, government officials in the LDCs, have already articulated what they feel are problems associated with the import and use of United States products in their countries. This calls for answers from us."

In view of these issues, he argued, "we have to come to grips with the cost/benefit analysis" in a way that addresses both the needs in the LDCs and the human risks and costs. Even if the benefits far outweigh the costs, he maintained, "it is this country's obligation to see that those costs in relative and absolute terms are minimized." As a legislator, he saw a need to foster educational programs on the safe use of these chemicals and to address the various issues associated with these products in collaboration with the governments of the user countries. "I do not feel" he concluded, "that relying on industry alone would be sufficient."

The Third World Farmer

"I don't know about people in other parts of the world," the role player began, "but I have a small farm. It is part of a larger farm my village owns. We grow corn. We've got good soil, but gophers eat our corn.

"A few years ago," he said, "some people came from America. Some must have been scientists, maybe from a university. Others were priests. They brought a poison we could use to kill the gophers. And they showed us how to use it. You use very little, very carefully, and it kills the gophers. Our yield has gone up, so we have more food to eat and more to sell to help our families and our village.

"Then someone said that people in America had problems with the poison. So we were told not to use it. They said in America the poison built up. That it hurt people. But I don't see any buildup here.

"There can be problems with anything. I know some people who work in a factory. It can be dangerous working in a factory. I want to grow corn. The people showed us how to use the poison and it works."

The farmer felt "the poison" addressed his immediate needs, that it helped him feed his family and improve his village. "It is important," he said, "to have people show you how to use these things." But as to long-term effects, he said, "I don't see them." He intended to continue using the poison, which was still available to him.

The Third World Government Official

The official described a tightly bound set of dilemmas. "We have to grow food, and we need pesticides," he said. "But we also see problems." He felt the problems of misuse were the result of multinational corporations too narrowly focused on short-term profit and a strong local need for the chemicals teamed with ignorance as to their proper use. Misuse cannot be controlled, he argued, because of corruption at various levels in some Third World governments and because of the absence of programs and policies among nations that would address the dangers inherent in the use of these chemicals.

There are many things which need to be done, he maintained. "Pesticides that are banned in the United States," he held, "should be banned in our country." He called for "strict control of labeling, which would inform users in their own language how to handle and use the products." Companies selling pesticides in the Third World, he held, should be "required to provide the training necessary for local people to be able to maintain the safe testing, use, storage, and disposal of these chemicals." Also, he felt that it was important for Third World countries to take "a unified position on these matters, perhaps through the United Nations," in order to be effective in being heard and in having the problems addressed.

Summary and Observations

Though the problems associated with pesticides often appear unbroachable and the interests of the different parties unbridgable, a significant amount of argeement was found to underlie the statements of the five role players. These points of agreement were highlighted in the open discussion led by Professor Goodpaster. All five parties agreed in some measure to the following.

* Pesticides are wanted, needed, and useful. The benefits associated with pesticides that the United States and other countries market in the Third World include higher crop yields, improved control of pest-born diseases, and contributions to the development of local economies.

* Pesticide-related problems nonetheless exist. The use of pesticides presents hazards to people and the environment, particularly when they are used in ways other than those intended. Risks of such hazards are particularly high in the Third World.

* Pesticide-related problems are significant. The costs of misuse, in both human and economic terms, deserve to be addressed.

* The situation entails several interested parties. Those who have a legitimate voice in defining the problems and

seeking avenues for addressing them include at least the five parties represented in the session.

* Different parties draw on different resources. The parties differ in the types and extent of resources they are able to bring to bear in addressing pesticide-related problems.

The latter point reflected both convergence and divergence of views among the role players as well as among members of the session as a whole. Whereas there was a common recognition that different parties had different resources open to them in addressing problems, there were varying views concerning how far responsibility to act was dependent upon the extent of a party's available resources. It was asked, for example, whether or not United States corporations, since they could be seen as having the most extensive resources, should thus assume responsibility for the largest role in addressing pesticide misuse. Though there was a great deal of sympathy with this equation at face value, it was observed that United States corporations may well be able to act in situations where they have no business doing so. At some point, it was argued, responsibility moves to the importing countries, local distributors, and users: American companies should not be expected to follow their products to every Third World farm in order to see to their safe use.

Discussion of the constraints on "total product liability" led to the examination of a related implication of United States corporate action in the Third World. Exporters should not be put in the position, it was argued, of making value choices for their clients. For United States corporations to insist that products be handled in a certain way or that American safety standards be met would constitute, in the view of several participants, a form of paternalism or moral imperialism. Exporting pesticides is one thing, it was observed, but exporting values is another. Importers ought to be free to decide for themselves what constitutes an acceptable or unacceptable risk from the perspective of their own needs and cultural values. On the other hand, some participants felt this argument could be used by United States exporters as a "rationalization" for shirking a more responsible (and more costly) role.

At the peak of the discussion of paternalism, the player assuming the role of the pesticides exporter offered a challenging example. "We market a fungicide in another country," he said, "the safe use of which, following our safety standards, requires that women of child-bearing years be kept from the fields for five days after its use. Now, the government of that country has given us their guarantee that that safety requirement, _our_ standard, will be met. So we sell the product to them. If they didn't give us their guarantee, we wouldn't sell. Is that paternalism? I don't know. But it's our policy."

The example suggested that even when we may wish to avoid imposing our values on others, we may still wish to impose them on ourselves. Thus, United States exporters face a complex situation in which they are called upon to assume a role of greater responsibility while both heeding their own values and respecting the differing values of customers from other cultures.

Professor Goodpaster closed the discussion by suggesting that the need to bridge the diverse values, interests, and resources among stakeholders in a multinational enterprise may be well served by undertaking the sort of discussion which had taken place in the session itself.

Goodpaster also noted that the session discussion had entailed three distinct types of moral reasoning. Two reflected traditional views as to how ethical matters ought to be addressed in business. The third suggested a different and rather new role for ethics in management. The first type Goodpaster described as appealing to free market principles, holding that economic forces themselves are sufficient to address the ethical dimensions of business. This form of reasoning Goodpaster saw in the discussion mainly in a negative or critical sense in the view among the participants that the problems of pesticide misuse call for deliberate actions by all parties, including and particularly by exporting corporations. The "invisible hand" of economic forces alone, the participants seemed to hold, was not sufficient to address the problems of pesticide misuse in the Third World.

The second form of moral reasoning Goodpaster saw was a call for the "visible hand" of regulation as a way to address the problems of pesticide export. This was evidenced in the recommendations of several participants for increased involvement by governments. This form of reasoning, Goodpaster noted, suggests that both economic forces and the hand of government are needed to meet the moral requirements raised by business activity.

Lastly, Professor Goodpaster saw a third form of moral reasoning, one which appeals to the notion that values and ethics deserve the attention of business in their own right. Goodpaster saw emerging through the course of the discussion the sense that the moral aspects of pesticide export deserve to be addressed by business not simply because hazards associated with

United States products might undermine the market or because certain actions may be required by government regulations, but because business should see itself as a moral actor within a moral context. This position, Goodpaster concluded, ignores neither the efficacy of regulation nor the importance of economic concerns, but it perhaps offers the best foothold for securing, along with these factors, an equal place on the corporate agenda for matters of moral concern.

CHAPTER TEN

BHOPAL

A. KARIM AHMED
Research Director
Natural Resources Defense Council
New York City, New York

PAUL SHRIVASTAVA
Associate Professor of Management
New York University
New York City, New York

GARY EDWARDS
Executive Director
Ethics Resource Center
Washington, DC

MICHAEL S. BARAM
Professor of Health Law
School of Public Health
Boston University
Boston, Massachusetts

THE BHOPAL TRAGEDY: THE FAILURE OF CORPORATE RESPONSIBILITY

A. Karim Ahmed

The tragedy in Bhopal, India was unprecedented in its magnitude. The worst industrial accident in modern history occurred on December 3, 1984, at a pesticide manufacturing plant on the outskirts of this central Indian city in the state of Madhya Pradesh. The plant was owned and operated by Union Carbide Corporation, a United States based multinational corporation. It is estimated conservatively that over 2,500 deaths and some 200,000 injuries resulted from the sudden accidental release from the plant of a highly toxic substance, methyl isocyanate, and its various breakdown products.

While the exact causes and full extent of this tragedy are still being pieced together, a number of key features of this accident can now be delineated. An examination of a number of preliminary independent scientific and medical studies, extensive interviews and investigative reports by the news media, and more detailed technical reports published to date by both Union Carbide and the government of India have made this possible.

In this paper, I will attempt to summarize briefly the principal failures of corporate policy and management neglect that led to the Bhopal disaster, and I will suggest means whereby these shortcomings should and must be overcome in order to avoid future Bhopals, both here and abroad.

To begin with, Union Carbide Corporation abided by what is believed to be a corporate policy of "management by exception." In past discussions with senior executives of Union Carbide, it was frequently stated that the corporation did not and could not manage the everyday implementation of its worldwide corporate policy, except when a plant or a foreign subsidiary failed to meet specific corporate objectives. Thus, it would appear that Union Carbide, as a corporate entity, did not closely police or monitor the performance of its affiliates or overseas operating facilities. Only when a major problem arose, or an important public issue surfaced, would the parent company step in and provide management directives or enforce existing corporate policies.

In the context of what occurred in Bhopal, it appears that in the operation of its Indian subsidiary's plant in Bhopal, Union Carbide not only managed "by exception" but also allowed its manufacturing plant to deteriorate through benign neglect.

Internal audit studies carried out by the parent company some two years before the accident indicated a number of serious operational deficiencies and high personnel turnover rates at the Bhopal plant. In spite of recognizing these shortcomings, the parent company let its subsidiary, Union Carbide India Limited, operate its plant by allowing:

- Severe lack of maintenance and repairs of process equipment and safety devices at the plant.

- Large cutbacks in maintenance and safety workers and supervisors at the plant.

- Dismantling of chemical storage cooling units and other safety devices, such as gas scrubbers and flares.

- Unsafe design changes, such as the use of "jumper lines" to connect process and gas vent units, that may have been a principal cause of the uncontrollable emission.

- No development of plans for emergency warning or evacuation of the surrounding community in the event of an uncontrollable emission.

It has been suggested by a number of safety experts that the above list of deficiencies, combined with the operating of the plant by poorly trained workers, had all the necessary ingredients for a major industrial disaster.

In addition to these management defects, the Union Carbide plant in Bhopal was not designed to avoid a major release of toxic material and was, from most accounts, considerably underdesigned in safety features and devices compared to a similar plant owned and operated by Union Carbide in Institute, West Virginia.

The next question that arises in the aftermath of Bhopal is whether such a catastrophic episode could occur in a more industrially sophisticated country such as the United States. Such an event is no longer considered a purely theoretical possibility. Since the accident in Bhopal, several industrial accidents in the United States have heightened concern about industrial plant safety domestically. Two episodes clearly stand out: the release of aldicarb oxime (and its heat-decomposed products) at Union Carbide's Institute, West Virginia plant last year, and the more recent releases of uranium compounds (and hydrofluoric acid) at the Kerr-McGee plant in Gore, Oklahoma. In both cases, a combination of equipment failure and management negligence led to the accidental releases of highly toxic gases into the surrounding community.

If one reviews accounts of major industrial accidents that have occurred during the past ten years in the United States, Europe, and certain less developed coutries such as Brazil and Mexico (where there is a national policy of accelerated industrialization), one important factor seems to be common in all cases: the failure of a corporation to manage its operating facility in a manner which optimizes plant (worker and public) safety. This failure in corporate responsibility begins with the plant design itself, i.e., the manner in which highly toxic materials are produced, used, stored, transported, and disposed of. It continues in the design (or even complete lack) of safety devices and measures used in the industrial facilities. Plants are not always equipped with state-of-the-art safeguard features and, if present, the safety systems are often woefully underdesigned and unable to contain or neutralize sudden, large releases of toxic materials. Finally, the lack of adequate safety maintenance and training of personnel compounds an already dangerous condition at many industrial facilities. Under production pressures or declining market share of company products, many corporations make severe cuts in safety programs and personnel -- a management policy that places economic welfare and production needs over safety and health considerations of both workers at the plant and the community in general.

In light of the above considerations, I would like to propose what I believe to be three fundamental corporate management principles that corporations engaged in the manufacturing or processing of highly toxic materials should consider adopting:

1. <u>Safety should come first</u>. Simply put, this principle states that the health and safety of workers and the community in which the plant is located have priority over any other consideration. This principle must be adhered to even at the expense of major economic losses. If there is any question that the industrial facility cannot be operated safely or has the potential to cause great harm to public health or the environment, the facility should be either redesigned and retrofitted with safety measures, or put out of operation altogether.

2. <u>The Board of Directors of a corporation has final accountability on all health and safety matters</u>. This principle squarely places direct legal, fiduciary, and moral responsibility on the governing bodies of each corporation. Such a policy

puts the top management of each corporation in full control in the development of health and safety policies. It makes them responsible for implementing and carrying out the enforcement of these policies and, most importantly, places the burden of any failure of health and safety measures on their shoulders. Under such a policy, no ultimate blame or legal liability can be assigned directly to the plant management or the supervisory middle managers of a corporate entity.

3. <u>Corporate standards on health and safety should be uniform worldwide and should not be based only on standards and norms of national governments.</u> Such a policy states that, regardless of government regulations or, more often, lack of regulations governing the field of industrial safety, the corporate body operating a domestic or overseas facility will adhere to the same standard on all health and safety standards. Differently put, it would state that no corporation would engage in a policy of double-standard on health and safety concerns when operating any facility over which they have a direct or indirect control. Under such a policy, local or national laws (unless they have a more stringent standard) cannot be used as a guide or regulatory least common denominator in the activities of a corporation in operating an industrial facility, whether at home or abroad.

In summary, there is much that the disaster in Bhopal can and must teach us. This unmitigated and continuing tragedy should serve as a warning sign that all is not well with the chemical industries around the world. These industries employ innately hazardous technologies and manufacture, use, transport, and dispose of highly toxic materials. The time for reassessing corporate responsibility in the field of industrial plant safety is long past. Unless the industry is willing to make sweeping management changes and adopt fundamentally different corporate policies in this field, the future and growth of this industry will continue to be a troubled one, at best.

It is not an exaggeration to state that if important changes are not made soon and implemented quickly, the industry's long term survival is doubtful and its role in national economies around the world will diminish or even fade away in the next few decades.

UNETHICAL FALLOUT FROM TECHNICAL DECISIONS

Paul Shrivastava

Professor Andrews in his last letter from the editor of the Harvard Business Review (Sept-Oct. 1985, p.2), writes,

> "Increased sensitivity to ethical dilemmas reveals that we walk among them everyday ... But sometimes somebody should identify them at the level at which routine activity is conducted -- lest the hidden unethical fallout from ordinary decision result in major breakdown."

The theme of this paper is close to Professor Andrews' insight that ethical analysis of corporate behavior needs to be conducted at a level of routine decisions. I am interested in understanding how technical decisions contribute to unethical and harmful outcomes. Since such decisions are almost completely under managerial control, understanding their unethical fallout can provide managers concrete means of reducing unethical behaviors.

Ethical analysis of corporate behavior can be done by focusing on concrete technical decisions. Every so-called 'technical' decision has an ethical component that gets ignored in routine decision making. Ignoring this ethical component does not affect the technical efficiency of decisions, but creates minor unethical fallout. This fallout is harmful for some stakeholders and is remedied on an ad hoc basis. Unethical fallout from decisions accumulate over time to the point of major breakdown. In this paper, I develop the above hypothesis and examine it empirically using data from the Union Carbide accident in Bhopal.

Technical decisions do not benefit from ethical and value considerations. They attempt to solve narrowly defined concrete context specific problems. These problems are technical, not in a narrow engineering sense, but in the sense that they deal with specialized areas of knowledge. Resolving these problems requires expertise and specialized analysis. Technical problems are solved on the basis of technical rationality of adopting the best means to achieve ends. The criteria used for evaluating solution alternatives include cost/benefit, technological efficiency, practical feasibility, and time/resource constraints. This may require substantive analysis of economic, engineering, financial, commercial, marketing, and other issues. Because of the predominantly technical nature of such decisions, ethics and values play minimal roles in making them.

Personal values enter such decisions as noise or nuisance. In fact, infusion of values into technical decisions is viewed as undesirable because it politicizes them.

This orientation towards technical decisions is consistent with the organizational context in which they are made. Managers have narrowly defined responsibilities and are rewarded for short term performance on technical criteria. They do not possess information necessary to understand the wider social and ethical ramifications of technical decisions.

However, since technical decisions are embedded in a social and cultural milieu, they necessarily possess ethical or value components. Ignoring ethical aspects technically simplifies decision making, but creates harmful fallouts. Managers deal with these fallouts as unintended consequences of decisions -as externalities. Organizations deal with such externalities by treating them as additional technical problems. They fail to recognize ethical components of technical decisions because these componants are small, indirect and hidden. (Kinghorn, 1985) For example, the potential for catastrophic accidents in a chemical plant is only indirectly and remotely related to decisions about personnel recruitment and training. Yet, under certain circumstances, such decisions can be pivotal factors in disastrous accidents. (Perrow, 1984)

Unethical fallout refers to harmful side effects of technical decisions. Individual decisions often have such small fallout that managers do not even have to deal with them. They just go away with time or are assimilated as part of other technical problems. But fallouts can accumulate silently to create explosive situations. Fallouts take a variety of forms. They may appear as problems of safe working conditions, product safety, accidents, environmental pollution, occupational health, worker alienation, work stress and mental health, absenteeism, etc. Often there is no single concept or set of problems to capture the unethical fallout of technical decisions. Hence, managers perceive them as unrelated fragmented problems unworthy of serious analysis. (Masuch, 1985)

An Illustration: The Bhopal Tragedy

The accident at the Union Carbide Plant in India on December 3rd, 1984, resulted in the deaths of over 2500 people and injured about 200,000 other. The accident has raised many very difficult and serious ethical questions about behavior of both government organizations and private sector organizations, about their roles in society and in economic development, and about their responsibilities towards workers and communities.

It raises ethical dilemmas for multinational corporations in general and Union Carbide in particular. These are large problems that cannot be settled in this paper.

Here, I simply want to show that at one level the Bhopal tragedy represents a corporate ethical dilemma caused by the cumulative unethical fallout from numerous technical decisions. These fallouts progressively increased the "hazardousness" of the plant. The concept of hazardousness captures the idea of harm in chemical plants. Harm caused by increased hazardousness is indirect and may be manifest in small accidents, worker illnesses, wastage, ineffeciency, etc. Over time, hazardousness built up to the point of major breakdown. Each technical decision that contributed to hazardousness of the Bhopal plant was made rationally, with adequate technical analysis, based on acceptable technical criteria. While many of these decisions seem wrong in hindsight, and some of them disregarded existing policies, they were technically justified at the time they were made. Their individual effects were not very alarming to local managers or technical experts from the parent company who conducted periodic operational safety surveys. (UCC, 1982)

Technical Decisions and Unethical Fallouts

1. <u>Plant Design Decisions</u>. Two decisions involving plant design are relevant here. The first involved design of MIC storage facility that permitted large volumes of the extremely toxic chemical to be stored in underground tanks. The alternative choices here included storage in small individual containers as done in Union Carbide's facility in Beziers, France, or avoiding storage of MIC altogether by using a closed system for production of SEVIN. The hazardous character of the large storage tank was identified by Mr. Edward Munoz, Managing Director of UC(1)L, but it was overruled on technical ground of <u>standardization.</u> Design of Bhopal plant storage tanks was made similar to tanks used in the company's Institute, W.Va. plant. The second alternative of avoiding the storage of MIC altogether was rejected because it would involve design of an entirely different and new production system which would not be cost effective. (Munoz, 1985)

The second design decision involved a design modification in the plant implemented a year before the accident. A jumper line was installed between the relief valve vent header and the process vent header. The jumper line allowed either header to be used as standby, when the other was under repair. This made <u>maintenance</u> of header pipes more convenient and economical and served as the technical justification for this design change. Unfortunately, by some accounts, this jumper connection allowed water to enter into the MIC storage tanks and cause a run away chemical reaction. (ICFTY-ICEF, 1985)

2. Procedural Decisions. Two decisions on plant operating procedures that contributed to hazardousness included: (a) shutting down the refrigeration unit; and (b) storage of excess quantities of MIC in storage tanks. Both these decisions were made on basis of explicit technical analysis. Both also represented depature from stated policies. It was decided to shut down the 30 ton refrigeration unit in June 1984. (UCC,1985) There were no mechanical problems with the system, but the coolant used in the system was drained off to be used in another part of the plant. This decision apparently involved <u>cost savings</u> on electricity and on use of coolant material.

The estimated amount of MIC in tank 610 at the time of the accident varies between 11,290 gallons (75% of capacity) to 13,000 gallons (87% of capacity). The decision to store these large volumes was a departure from safety policy stated in the MIC technical manual which suggests a limit of 50%. The technical justifications for this decision were <u>waste avoidance and safety</u>. When batch production runs resulted in production of larger quantities of MIC than needed, it made economic sense to over-fill storage tanks to higher limits, instead of simply throwing away the excess. Moreover, technical problems involved 'throwing away' a toxic chemical like MIC are not simple. Ways must be found to neutralize its toxicity before discarding it. This is expensive and cumbersome. Hence, the technically correct thing to do was to keep the material in storage.

These procedural decisions not only made the plant more hazardous, they created conditions in which runaway chemical reactions could not be mitigated. Large quantities of MIC served as the raw material for a violent and powerful chemical reaction. The lack of refrigeration facilities prevented operators from cooling the storage tank and thereby slowing down the accident and reducing damage.

3. Maintenance Decisions. Two technical decisions dealing with maintenance issues contributed directly to the accident. First was the decision to simultaneously shut down two safety devices for maintenance. The flare tower and the vent gas scrubber were both inoperational at the time of the accident. The flare tower was used for neutralizing toxic gases by burning them before they were released into the environment. This safety device was out of service for replacing a piece of corroded pipe leading to it. The vent gas scrubber had been removed from operating mode to standby mode on October 23, 1984, when the MIC unit was shut down after the production run.

Shutting down parts of any system for maintenance during periods when production is off is a <u>standard technical practice</u>. It allows maintenance to take place when the system is not in use. Supervisors decided to proceed with the maintenance because they thought it was unnecessary to keep the safety devices running when the plant itself was not running. (Bidwai, 1984)

The second decision related to maintenance was really a series of non-decisions that allowed the plant to operate in a 'rundown' condition. General maintenance of the plant was poor. Instruments were broken, measurement gauges were not working, indicator panels were malfunctioning, pipes and valves were corroded and leaking. (UCC, 1982) The plant had been loosing money for several years and a <u>cost cutting</u> program was being implemented. Non essential maintenance was kept down to a minimum as long as it did not hamper plant operation. (Diamond, 1985) While this decision in itself is not unusual or unethical, it did contribute to an increase in hazardousness of the plant. The lack of well functioning safety devices and gauges, in the presence of large inventories of MIC, made it impossible to detect leakages and control them in time. These created an environment in which the harm caused by an accident could not be controlled.

Several other decisions that could be technically justified contributed to plant hazardousness. I simply mention them to illustrate the variety of decisions that contributed to the disaster. First, the plant was located less than two miles from the Bhopal railway station and bus stand, which served as the hub of commercial activity. It was in one of the most densely populated residential centers of the city. The decision to locate the plant there was made on technical grounds of <u>transportation convenience</u>.

Second, raw materials indirectly affected safety of production processes. MIC that escaped from the storage tank was highly contaminated. It contained well over the specification maximum of 0.5 percent chloroform.

Third, two personnel decisions were made that reduced manning levels, and training of operators. At the time of the accident the MIC unit and the entire plant was working with reduced manpower. Personnel reductions were a part of the cost cutting measures. In the MIC plant, the production crew had been cut from twelve (eleven operators, one supervisor) to six (five operators, one supervisor), and maintenance crew reduced from six to two. Maintenance supervisor position on the second and third shifts was cut just one week before the accident.

Another personnel related decision that contributed to plant safety was the frequent change in Works Manager of the plant. In the period 1969-84, there were eight different executives who headed the plant.

Finally, failure to provide necessary safety information to relevant managers and community and local authorities contributed to the increase in plant hazardousness.

Incorporating Ethical Concerns into Technical Decisions

The need for making sound technical decisions has never been greater than in the current period of still international competition. Technical and economic efficiency are paramount concerns of managers who are under constant pressure to improve productivity of technical systems. Competitive pressures in hazard prone industries such as nuclear power and chemicals are bound to force organizations towards higher technical rationality and simultaneously towards more hazardous operations. It is therefore necessary to explore ways of making technical rationality sensitive to ethical concerns. Several positive actions can be taken to incorporate ethical concerns into technical decisions and to avoid unethical fallout. These actions involve procedural changes, managerial training, and reallocation of decision making authority.

Managers and researchers need to understand that all technical decisions have ethical aspects because these decisions are embedded in a social environment. Social impact of technical decisions is an under-explored area of organizational studies. These impacts can be surfaced by systematically analysing the harmful effects of decisions on stakeholders. A stakeholder analysis can be a useful starting point for organizations to explore ethical dimensions of decision making. (Freeman, 1984)

Technical decision making processes need to be modified to provide space for ethical criteria, alongside normally used technical and economic criteria. Organizations can develop ethical decision criteria, just as they are developing 'codes of conduct' for controversial social issues. These decision criteria would narrowly focus on specific decision dimensions in production, marketing, accounting, information systems, and other functional areas. This obviously means additional time and resource investment in modifying decision processes and requires support of top management.

Technical decisions that have serious harmful effects such as those dealing with occupational health and safety issues and community safety issues should be identified and dealt with at the strategic level, where ethical and value considerations are systematically integrated in decision processes. (McCoy, 1985).

In the absence of information about harmful effects of decisions, managers should abstain from making the decision. They should initiate search for new information. Managerial training can play an important role in providing more relevant information and frameworks for integrating ethical concerns into routine decisions.

These suggestions are intended only as points of departure for managers and researchers to develop detailed programs for their own organizations. Much more research is needed in understanding ethical aspects of technical decisions before use can prescribe specific changes. This problem is likely to become more strategic with the advent of more complex and hazardous technologies such as genetics research, laser and nuclear weaponry and space travel. We see this as a challenge facing managers and business ethicists.

REFERENCES

Anthony, Robert N. *Planning and Control Systems: A Framework for Analysis.* Boston: Division of Research, Graduate School Business Administration, Harvard University, 1965.

Bidwai, P. "Plant Design Badly Flawed." *The Times of India.* Dec. 27m 1984.

Blake and I. Maghsoodi, "Kinetics and Mechanism of Thermal Decomposition of Methyl Isocynate." *International Journal of Chemical Kinetics,* 1982, 14, pp 945-952.

Diamond, S. "The Bhopal Disaster: How it Happened." *New York Times* (Series of four articles), Jan. 1985, Fredericks, W. and Davis.

Freeman, R.E. *Strategic Management: A Stakeholder Approach.* New York: Pitman, 1984.

International Confederation of Free Trade Unions (ICFTU). *The Trade Union Report on Bhopal.* July 1985, ICFTU, Brussels, Belgium.

Kinghorn, Sandra N. "Corporate Harm -- An Analysis of Structure and Process." Paper presented at the conference on Critical Perspectives in Organizational Analysis, Baruch College, CUNY, Sept. 5-7, 1985.

McCoy, Charles S. *Management of Values: The Ethical Difference in Corporate Policy and Performance*. Boston: Pitman, 1985.

Shrivastava, P. *Bhopal: Anatomy of an Industrial Crisis*. 1986, (forthcoming) Cambridge, MA: Ballinger Publishing Company.

Starbuck, W.H. "Organizations as Action Generators." *American Sociological Review*, 1984.

Union Carbide Corporation, *Bhopal Methyl Isocyanate Incident Investigation Team Report*. March 1985, Union Carbide Corporation, Danbury, CT.

Union Carbide Corporation, *Operational Safety Survey*. October, 1982, Union Carbide Corporation, Danbury, CT.

THE BHOPAL TRAGEDY: SOME IMPLICATIONS AND GUIDELINES FOR MULTINATIONAL BUSINESS

Gary Edwards

My purpose in this paper is not to pass judgment on Union Carbide. Instead, I intend to address issues that many companies face in day-to-day operations and the relationship of some of those issues to the international business environment -- an environment that may be changing dramatically as a result of the tragedy of Bhopal.

This event has raised acutely public concern about the responsibilities of multinational corporations in developing countries. As more becomes known about the conditions and practices that led to the Bhopal disaster, and as the responsibilities and liabilities for it begin to be sorted out, some issues of policy and practice are beginning to emerge. They suggest that the public's concept of "corporate responsibility" may be going through yet another, very significant evolutionary stage.

Bhopal Raises Complex Issues

As exemplified by the Bhopal case, issues of ethics with which companies must deal are frequently intertwined with complex socio-economic and legal considerations. Among these issues of concern, I would like to identify and discuss three.

First, most developing nations, including India, both have a great need for and aggressively pursue the investments of multinational corporations. These firms are able to mobilize large amounts of capital, to create jobs, to produce consumer products and services, and to transfer technology and competencies to the businesses and the governments of host countries. It is thus socially desirable, and it may be politically necessary, for multinationals and developing nations to become partners in the drive to progress. However, attractiveness of rapid and expansive development may temper the desire -- or exceed the ability -- of host governments to develop, implement, and enforce policies and regulations necessary to protect employees, their communities, and the environment.

Additionally, some companies may have felt an obligation to their shareholders to invest in countries where regulations were the least intrusive and where compliance promised to be least expensive. Bhopal may have forever changed this assumption.

Second, when large companies expand into developing countries, they may be <u>required</u> to form partnerships with host country investors and to employ local managers. A reduction in the level of ownership and control of a company may bring with it a diminished sense of responsibility for local operations. While this is understandable, it will not relieve companies of their ethical responsibility, nor is it likely to exempt them from their legal liability.

Third, international law has allowed the separate incorporation of parent companies and their foreign subsidiaries, permitting some insulation of the parent firm from the liabilities of their subsidiaries. The Government of India, by entering United States courts on behalf of the victims of Bhopal, has challenged that principle, seeking to hold Union Carbide Corporation of New York accountable for the actions of its Indian subsidiary. Should India's challenge prove successful, not only will the principle of separate liability be breached, but the standard for recovery may be altered as well, exposing Union Carbide to punitive as well as compensatory damages. This could alter dramatically the risks for, and therefore the willingness of, multinationals to invest in developing countries.

Minimizing Risks for Multinationals and their Constituencies

As these issues of legal and ethical responsibility come into focus, what could minimize the risks for multinational companies operating in developing countries and ensure that multinationals fulfill obligations to their many constituencies -- to their employees, local communities, and host governments, as well as to shareholders?

External Regulation of Multinationals

One might look to international law and regulation, hoping that eventually legal standards would be provided that could be relied upon, but there is little historical evidence that such regulations will be developed quickly. Moreover, the regulations will only be as effective as their enforcement is consistent, and that will depend, in part, upon the resources and the commitment of host governments.

Voluntary guidelines might be developed by industry groups, international trade associations, or more broadly-based organizations. Indeed, several attempts have already begun: The Organization for Economic Development (OECD) has its "Declaration of OECD Member Governments on International Investment and Multinational Enterprises." It was adopted in

1976, revised in 1979, and revised again in 1984, yet there are no environmental guidelines provided in the OECD Declaration. There is an effort now to include new environmental guidelines in the Declaration, but it remains to be seen how soon those will be forthcoming.

The United Nations Commission on Transnational Corporations has a draft of guidelines for multinationals, which has been in preparation for a decade and is about two-thirds complete. It does include a section on environmental protection. It requires, for instance, that multinationals provide information, either "on request" or on a regular basis, regarding their activities and products that may be hazardous. It also requires that multinationals provide information concerning prohibitions of their products in other countries, and it seeks the cooperation of multinational corporations in developing uniform standards of corporate conduct.

The World Bank is presently developing guidelines for preventing and controlling industrial hazards. The guidelines, which in late 1985 were expected soon, may require detailed analyses of companies' accident prevention programs both in engineering and in management terms.

The International Chamber of Commerce has environmental guidelines for world industry, adopted in 1974 and revised in 1981. They attempt to balance the environmental responsibilities of companies and the financial constraints within which they operate.

Voluntary guidelines, however, are limited by their very nature. And they may tempt some companies to seek a competitive advantage by "free-riding" on the compliance of other companies while violating the guidelines themselves. Nonetheless, the size, complexity, and mobility of multinational corporations makes regulation at the national level extremely difficult; therefore, industry-wide, transnational standards are desirable. Such industry-wide standards could facilitate the transfer of technology and of managerial and technical expertise to developing countries. Although subject to "free-riding," especially by smaller local firms, the standards might lower competitive pressures among larger firms and encourage them to enforce more responsible environmental policies that could, over time, become the norm for smaller, indigenous firms as well.

Corporate Self-Regulation

Whatever the future of industry-wide or international standards of conduct, self-regulation by multinational corporations could begin, and begin now, to reduce the danger of future Bhopals. Ethically responsible multinational corporations must give priority to personal health and safety and to the protection of the environment. They should neither acquiesce in nor exploit any apparent disregard for human life and the environment in less affluent societies. There are some specific steps that multinational corporations should consider, not only to safeguard their investments in the Third World but also to fulfill their ethical responsibilities. Here, briefly, are twelve:

First, review corporate philosophy and policies regarding environmental health and safety risk management, setting standards at the highest level of the parent corporation.

Second, develop (or update) the code of conduct of the corporation, to be publicly endorsed by corporate leadership, disseminated throughout the corporation, and publicized in host countries as well.

Third, meet or exceed all host country laws and regulations. More may be required than mere compliance where regulations are inadequate for the risks that are posed.

Fourth, establish and enforce standards for foreign operations that are as rigorous as at home and are appropriately adapted to local conditions. For example, redundant backup safety measures should be implemented where local population concentrations heighten the potential risk from accidents.

Fifth, spell out in detail environmental goals and management tasks to be carried out by designated personnel with specific responsiblity for enforcement of the standards.

Sixth, undertake environmental, health, and safety assessments of overseas projects, reporting the resulting information promptly to host governments, and schedule continuing periodic audits and reports. In scheduling assessments and follow-up audits, companies should recognize that projects that may be relatively small in terms of investments and earnings may nonetheless pose major hazards.

Seventh, report to importing countries shipments of materials that may be hazardous and the nature of the potential hazard, including information on any bans and restrictions on the materials in the exporting country.

Eighth, negotiate explicit agreements with joint-venture partners, subcontractors, and distributors, requiring their compliance with the company's standards and practices.

Ninth, back up agreements with planning and support for necessary training of local personnel to deal with environmental problems and to ensure their compliance with corporate standards.

Tenth, exercise care in locating new plant facilities, with regard to available housing for employees and to other aspects of the surrounding environment, as well as the level of control that can be expected in joint ventures.

Eleventh, select overseas managers who not only are experienced in the area of the world to which they are to be assigned, but also are experts in the technology for which they will be responsible and well-trained in management functions and in home base standards of conduct and operations.

Twelfth, hold overseas management to corporate standards by requiring periodic signed assurances of their commitment and their compliance.

Conclusion

Multinationals can and do bring great economic and social benefits to the developing world. But to the extent that they contribute to the world's human and environmental problems, they must take a leadership role in solving those problems. Their greater technical and financial resources relative to those of the developing countries in which they operate impose on multinationals a commensurate responsibility to workers, to joint-venture partners, to subcontractors, and to host communities. As guests in developing countries, they have both ethical obligations and a pragmatic political need to earn and keep the confidence of host governments and peoples.

CHEMICAL INDUSTRY ACCIDENTS, LIABILITY, AND COMMUNITY RIGHT TO KNOW*

Michael S. Baram

The Bhopal tragedy and other industrial accidents (e.g., Seveso, Flixborough, Mexico City, Institute, W. Va.) have frightened the citizens of developed and undeveloped countries. These accidents, along with numerous hazardous waste problems, have led to a dramatic loss of public confidence in chemical industry management and their safety experts. The occurrence of such accidents also provides vivid evidence of the serious gap between government legislative promises and government performance in the actual control of industrial hazards.[1]

As a result, persons who believe they have been injured or put at risk by industry are now using tort law to secure private remedies in the courts, and are seeking increased information on industrial hazards from companies and agencies in order to develop new risk reduction measures. This public shift away from passive reliance on industry and government for protection to self-help strategies is most discernable in the United States, but is also taking place in the European Community.

Tort Liability

Over the past decade, workers suffering occupational disease have used dual strategies to secure compensation and other remedies. They have filed for and received the limited "benefits" available under state workers' compensation systems from their employer's insurer. And they have become increasingly successful in using tort law against the suppliers of injurious products, such as asbestos, to secure large awards of compensatory and punitive damages, by arguing that the supplier's failure to warn of product hazards constituted tortious conduct. The Occupational Safety and Health Administration has responded to these circumstances by enacting important regulations which impose affirmative duties on employers to warn workers of the hazards of chemicals in use, and which provide workers with rights of access to company medical and exposure records.[2]

---

*The author acknowledges National Science Foundation support in developing this paper, under NSF grant PRA 8212292, "Corporate Risk Management." This article also appears in the *American Journal of Public Health*, Spring, 1986.

Residents of communities with unusual clusters of disease are also filing tort actions against firms whose activities (routine emissions, accidents and spills, and waste management failures) have contaminated water supplies, crops, soil, and other features of the community environment, and put them at a risk of disease. In one well known case, <u>Ayers v. Jackson Township</u>, 350 residents sued the town for water supply contamination, emotional distress, and in the absence of any evidence of clinical illness, for being put at increased risk arising from improper management of hazardous wastes. They were initially awarded $16 million, of which $8.2 million was to be set aside for ongoing medical surveillance and testing of the population for disease symptoms over time, to facilitate medical intervention. On appeal, the award was reduced to $5 million for impairing their "quality of life" and water supply (eliminating the awards for medical surveillance and emotional distress).[3]

The threat of such suits brought under state tort law, which has been modified in recent years to the advantage of the victims, is now usually enough to compel industrial defendants and their insurers to quickly settle, rather than incur litigation costs, large damage awards, and adverse publicity.

Faced with numerous "toxic tort" actions by workers and community residents and evidence of wrongdoing by companies and other parties, state courts have sought to "do justice" -- to modify tort law and procedural requirements so that plaintiffs have a reasonable opportunity to secure compensation and other remedies from those at fault.[4] The major adaptations, which have invigorated the tort system and led to large jury awards, include:

* <u>modifying the statute of limitations</u> (the period during which a tort action can be brought) by holding that the state statute begins to run at the time the illness was discovered or reasonably ascertainable, rather than at the time of exposure, in recognition of the long latency period for chronic health hazards. (If left to run from the time of exposure, most toxic tort actions would be stifled.)

* <u>providing for strict liability theory</u> so that a plaintiff needs to prove injury and causation, but no longer need establish the defendant's negligence or lack of due care in order to prevail. (This eases the evidentiary requirements for plaintiffs.)

* <u>providing for imposition of liability on a "joint and</u>

several" basis under which one firm at fault can be held fully liable for the actions of all firms involved in causing harm, leaving it to this one firm to later file claims or other actions against the other firms to secure their respective shares of the liability. (This is another easing of the plaintiff's evidentiary burden.)

* permitting the introduction of circumstantial scientific evidence of causation (e.g., various epidemiological or toxicological studies of populations) as relevant to the particular victim's claim, and according substantial weight or significance to such evidence.

* expanding the "duty to warn" concept so that evidence of defendant's failure to warn serves as a basis for finding the defendant liable for the plaintiff's harm under strict product liability theory and negligence theory.

The insurers of the industrial firms being sued have borne much of this liability. Courts have consistently held that insurers have a "duty to defend" their insured against these claims (which is a costly proposition), and must provide compensation for most accident and pollution incidents, despite policy language used by insurers which had attempted to narrow insurance coverage only to "sudden and accidental occurences." As a result, property and casualty insurers and reinsurers in the United States and Europe, which are linked by "treaties" in order to provide coverage at high dollar levels for chemical firms, lost several billion dollars in 1985 (their worst loss year in 80 years), largely due to tort liability awards and settlements in the United States.[5]

Consequently, the insurance market for chemical industry coverage has "collapsed;" and chemical firms subject to the jurisdiction of American courts are finding it virtually impossible to obtain adequate insurance coverage at affordable prices.

Because of these new tort law developments and their extreme vulnerability to large economic losses without insurance, chemical firms are now pursuing several protective stategies. One is political and involves their lobbying for changes in the United States tort system (e.g., elimination of joint and several liability and contingent fees, and limits on the dollar levels of awards). This solution will not be completely successful, since the changes in the tort system have deep roots in the values of Americans and new scientific findings, and cannot now be easily discarded. Further, attorneys for plaintiffs are adept at devising innovative tort law strategies to overcome new obstacles.

The analytic solution involves the conduct of extensive in-house risk assessment and risk management initiatives by major chemical firms.[6] What these firms are finding is that risk assessment is fraught with difficulty since it is an art form not reduced to generic practice or confident results; that technical uncertainty prevails; that public values and attitudes about risk are shaping without apparent regard for probabilistic risk estimates by industry or experts; and that there is no "stopping point" at which a firm can determine with confidence that enough assessment and control measures have been undertaken. Since accident risks require both preventative measures as well as "post-loss" measures (to control losses after the accident), firms must cooperate with local officials, but encounter the further difficulty that the local government officials lack the necessary skills, authority, and resources to develop, test, and manage emergency response systems.

Community Right to Know

Given their mistrust of industry and government, citizens are now aggressively seeking risk information from these two sectors in order to take various self-protective actions, ranging from litigation to curb industrial activities to the design of emergency systems for responding to accidents. Laws in the United States and the European Community (E.C.) now require industry to communicate various types of risk information to government agencies at national, state, and local levels; and in some cases, they require industry and government agencies to disclose risk information to workers and community residents.[7] In the United States, laws establishing that persons at risk have a "right to know" certain information held by agencies and companies are based on at least three premises:

a. One who posseses information which can enable another to avoid harmful consequences arising from their relationship has a duty to disclose such information in timely fashion;

b. Risk management should be a joint enterprise which provides for the informed participation of persons at risk, along with the industrial risk generator, the government risk control agencies, and their various experts, since defining, measuring, and preventing risk is a complex problem which transcends the economic concerns of industrial firms and their insurers; and

c. Risk communication informs the public, and thereby promotes agency accountability.

For chemical industry accident hazards, a major concern since Bhopal, a multitude of old and new laws are now being used in the United States to promote the communication of relevant information about accident risk.

(a) State and Local Laws for "Community Right to Know" (CRTK).

Some 12 states and dozens of communities have recently enacted laws and ordinances requiring company communication of industrial accident hazard information to local officials, and in certain instances to the citizenry.[8] These laws vary considerably as to the chemical substances and industry installations covered, the information formats and communication processes to be used, and various disclosure and access requirements. A federal court has recently held that the CRTK provisions of New Jersey's law are not preempted or in conflict with the federal worker right to know rule promulgated by the Occupational Safety and Health Administration (OSHA) to inform workers.[9] Presumably, state laws with variable requirements for community right to know will now proliferate, but their implication will require the infusion of resources and skilled personnel, and sustained political support. Experience in Massachusetts and other states with these laws indicates that actual performance will fall far short of legislative promise without continuing public pressure.

(b) Federal Regulatory Requirements for Risk Communication between Industry, Federal Agencies, and Persons at Risk.

Numerous laws and regulations require firms to report risk information to federal agencies such as the Environmental Protection Agency (EPA), the Department of Transportation, and the Nuclear Regulatory Commission. For example, the Toxic Substance Control Act requires pre-manufacturing notice information and various health and safety findings on chemicals to be reported to the EPA, and federal pesticide laws require similar reporting of risk information. Other statutes and regulations dealing with hazardous waste management and cleanup, and with permits for the discharge of pollutants into air and water, also require the reporting of various risk information by firms to the EPA.[10] Once such risk information is acquired by an agency, it is subject to federal Freedom of Information law which provides for public access (discussed below).

Several OSHA rules go further in that they require

industrial communication of risk information to the agency and also to workers. As a practical matter, information provided workers can be expected to flow to members of the community as well. As noted earlier, OSHA's rules provide for worker access to their company-held medical and exposure records, and require manufacturers and importers of certain chemicals to provide material safety data sheets (MSDSs) and labels to their industrial customers, with all manufacturing firms involved in this "downstream" process of communication to then provide the MSDSs to workers at risk, together with education and safety programs.[11]

(c) Laws Guaranteeing Citizen Access to Agency-Held Information in General.

Federal and state Freedom of Information Acts (FOIA) provide citizens with the right of access to agency-held information, including information secured from industry, subject to various exceptions under which trade secrets and intra-agency memos can be withheld by the agencies. Other provisons confer on citizens rights of access to agency meetings and advisory committee activities.[12]

(d) Common Law Duty to Disclose and Warn.

State common law imposes on industry the duty to disclose risk information and warn those who are at risk from reasonably foreseable hazard circumstances. Well established for product hazards to consumers and workers, the duty to warn also applies to situations involving industrial hazards to community residents.[13] Failure to warn has had tragic health consequences for persons at risk (e.g., workers handling asbestos) and great economic impacts on the firms involved (e.g., punitive damages running into millions of dollars, which are not insurable in many states).

(e) Use of State Police Power to Protect Health and Safety.

Over the centuries, use of state "police power" has led to a multitude of state and local laws empowering state and local health and fire officials to control accident hazards. Although dormant for decades in many communities, such laws are now being used as authority for bold new actions by these officials, including the shutdown of industrial activities deemed to create health risks to community residents.[14] This local authority to regulate, site, inspect, and license dangerous activities, and to require industrial disclosures of risk information, is found in every state.

(f) Other Developments -- Since Bhopal.

Congressman Florio, Senator Lautenberg, and others in Congress have proposed sweeping new laws in 1985 for regulation of chemical industry accident hazards. Their bills essentially would require firms to inform state and local authorities about hazards, to permit evaluation of the internal activities of the firms, and to authorize these officials to develop local and regional emergency response plans across the nation.[15] Under the threat of Congressional action, industrial organizations (e.g., the Monsanto Company and the Chemical Manufacturing Association) have voluntarily proposed commuinity right to know initiatives whereby the material safety data sheets developed and used to inform workers under the OSHA "Hazard Communication Rule" would also be made available to state and local officials. In addition, unions have recommended new measures for the communication of industrial risk information to workers and communities.[16]

Thus, we now have in the United States a broad and growing array of legal authority for risk communication between industry and government, and in many instances between industry and citizens. Some of the new state right to know laws promote citizen access to industry-held information, without going through an agency intermediary, as noted earlier. And of course, once any litigation begins, there are pre-trial discovery procedures which enable plaintiffs' attorneys to secure many internal corporate risk studies and documents.[17]

There is no need in the United States for further legislative authorization of risk communication, from a legal perspective, since the authority needed is now in place. But the existing authority is difficult to use. The yields of information are fragmented and limited, and the authority now in place neither has much effect in forcing industry to cooperate with community officials and residents, nor does it impose emergency response plan requirements on local officials in most instances. As a result, new measures are being taken in the United States which are now discussed and compared to the approach being taken in the European Community.

The Environmental Protection Agency and European Initiatives

After considerable deliberation, the EPA published in late 1985 a set of materials to stimulate and guide state and local efforts at improved risk communication, accident hazard analysis and control, and the local development of emergency response systems.[18] The EPA materials consist of a "guidance package" for state and local officials as to how to establish an effective program for identifying the industrial hazards in their midst, and how to develop emergency response plans.

The EPA also promised to issue a list of some 400 substances with high propensity for accident hazards (e.g., due to their volatility, corrosivity, vaporization, flammability, and toxicity characteristics); and fact sheets for each of the 400 substances, providing basic information on their accident hazard characteristics and various self-help and emergency response options (e.g., first aid, evacuation, etc.). Neither the list nor fact sheets have been officially released to date.

This initiative will not be legally enforceable by the EPA. However, it does provide a set of principles about corporate responsibility to warn of certain chemical accident hazards and establishes a state of knowledge as to accident hazard prevention. Thus, if a company does not comply or act voluntarily by informing local officials, even if the officials do not actively seek the information, such a company becomes more vulnerable to punitive damages in tort actions which may be brought after an accident occurs, and to injunctive relief (e.g., stop work orders) before accident occurence.

The EPA initiative will do little to promote the uniformity of risk communication and accident control systems across the nation and will probably promote a multitude of new, highly variable state and local laws on industry accident hazards. Citizens will have access to much of the information communicated by firms to state and local officials under these new laws and other state FOIA-type laws, and this will lead to controversies at town meetings and litigation in state courts to shut down or otherwise restrict corporate activities involving designated toxic chemicals.

In addition, citizens will seek more information from companies than that contained in MSDSs, and companies will assert that such information is proprietary or protectable as trade secrets. This will lead to further litigation in state courts, since trade secret issues are matters of state law. Given the high potential for these controversies, industry has some hard choices to make about the information it will provide and the research and other information-generating activities it will conduct on safety matters.

In direct contrast to this tentative and non-regulatory EPA approach is the bold promise of the European Community's (E.C.) "Seveso Directive." By 1989, each of the ten European nations belonging to the E.C. and subject to the Directive is required to have in place an enforceable system for accident hazard control, risk communication, and emergency planning, authorized by national legislation.

Under Seveso, each firm handling any of some 178 chemicals in certain quantities is to develop an internal risk analysis or "safety case," which evaluates the storage and uses of the chemicals, potential accident hazards, existing systems to prevent accidents, events which can overwhelm the systems (internal malfunctions, external forces), and emergency response plans for workers. The safety case constitutes a package of company-developed information, much of which is proprietary and traditionally protectable as trade secrets. It is to be submitted to a designated public official in each nation for review, and this official can then act to force additional accident control measures to the extent provided by national law. The official must also act to establish community emergency plans.[19]

The Seveso system differs from the EPA guidance package and the existing legal mosaic in the United States in several respects:

a. it clearly imposes responsibility for accident risk analysis and disclosure on industry;

b. it requires government review at the national level, permits national controls and licensing programs for chemical industry facilities, and requires emergency planning by designated public officials;

c. it provides a blanket of trade secret protection by requiring that national officials withhold proprietary information from the public;

d. it affirms traditional European views that citizen access to risk information be limited to what citizens "need to know," e.g., under the British implementation plan being developed, citizens would learn only the accident warning signal, evacuation route, and recommended medical treatment;[20] and

e. it provides for accident reporting and analysis systems, a structured research program, and development of an automated "expert system" for accident control and emergency response programs.

The European chemical industry has voiced its concerns about the Seveso Directive, such as its potential for leakage of trade secrets, its extension of government authority into the management of chemical plants, and its mandate for a new licensing system to control chemical facilities. But the core issue for the managers of European firms is that of responsibility for plant accident hazards and control. If control over in-plant activities is now shared with government officials and their consultants, responsibility for control will also be diffused among several parties. As corporate autonomy and control are diminished, so is corporate responsibility. If an accident occurs, who will be at fault among the new trio of plant managers: industry, government, and/or independent consultants?[21]

American adoption of the Seveso model has been recommended by many who admire its explicitness as to duties and its systematic approach. But obviously, it has at least three major limitations as a model for the United States. First, its protection of trade secrets is more expansive than protection in the United States; second, its view of public access to information held by government officials on a "need to know" or other narrow basis conflicts with American "right to know" doctrine; third, its diffusion of management responsibility would blunt or reduce the risk deterrent effect of United States tort law on American firms, since responsibility is the basis for determining liability in the United States system.

If these three problems are carefully resolved, the Seveso model could become appropriate for American use. An American version would require a narrow definition of trade secrets and a careful limitation on public "right to know" so that industry willingness to disclose information on safety hazards to officials would not be chilled. Finally, it would have to address the allocation of liability in accordance with the actual exercise of responsibility. If these issues are appropriately addressed, American adoption of the Seveso model could lead to an acceptable and effective system for controlling chemical industry accident hazards.

Conclusions

The communication of hazard information is now recognized as a vital feature of the new self-help efforts being made by workers and community residents to prevent industrial risks and avoid harms. Legislation at state and federal levels, regulatory actions, and common law doctrines now impose on industry the duty to warn of hazards, and also provide persons at risk with the right to know hazard information. Thus, hazard communication is more than a theory or moral imperative, it is now rooted in explicit and enforceable legal doctrines.

Moreover, hazard communication is not an isolated development; it has broad implications for corporate management. The <u>duty to warn</u> imposed on industry carries with it two noncommittant duties for industrial officials: <u>the duty to identify</u> hazards through reasonable efforts and the use of expertise so that the duty to warn will be meaningful; and the <u>duty to act</u> diligently to control or reduce the hazards, once they have been identified, so that the duty to warn will not be dispositive on the matter of corporate responsibility. Thus, three corporate functions for risk management are inextricably linked.

Exercise of their rights under these doctrines, and of other authority for the right to know by persons who perceive they may be at risk, provides the continuing pressure on industry and agencies to comply with these duties and assures their accountability in carrying out the duties to identify, warn, and act. Thus, powerful tools are now available for use in the new self-help era of occupational and environmental protection.

NOTES

1. See M. Baram, "Regulatory Implementation," in <u>Managing Industrial Risk</u>, H. Otway ed., European Community Research Center, Butterworth Publishing Co., London, England (1985).

2. See P. Brodeur, "The Asbestos Industry on Trial," a four part series in the <u>New Yorker</u>, June, July 1985; and M. Baram, "The Right to Know and the Duty to Disclose Hazard Information," <u>American Journal of Public Health</u>, v. 74, n. 4 (1984) pp. 385-390.

3. <u>Ayers v. Jackson Township</u>, 189 N.J. Super. 561 (1983); ___ N.J. ___ (May 1985). (The award for impairing "quality of life" can be construed as liability for increased risk, a significantly new remedy under the tort system.)

4. See generally, G. Nothstein, <u>Toxic Torts</u>, McGraw-Hill Publishing Co., Colorado Springs, CO (1984); and M. Baram, "Chemical Industry Hazards: Liability, Insurance and the Role of Risk Anaysis," paper presented at Twelfth General Assembly of the Geneva Association, Oslo, Norway, June 14, 1985; and at the Joint Conference on Hazardous Materials, International Institute of Applied Systems Analysis and the Wharton Center for Risk and Decision Processes, Vienna, Austria, July 5, 1985 (to be published in IIASA-Wharton Conference Proceedings, spring 1986).

5. Id.

6. See M. Baram, "Charting the Future Course for Corporate Management of Health Risks," American Journal of Public Health, v. 74., n. 10 (October 1984) p. 1163.

7. See M. Baram, "Risk Communication and the Law," paper presented at Conference on Risk Communication sponsored by U.S. Environmental Protection Agency, Long Beach, California, Dec. 3, 1984 (to be published as EPA Conference Report, D. von Winterfeldt, V. Covello, P. Slovic, eds., 1986).

8. State laws recently enacted fall into two categories:

    (1) Comprehensive Community Right to Know Laws:
        (local official and individual person right to know)

    Iowa   Chapter 1085 of the Acts of 1984

    Massachusetts   Mass. Gen. Laws ch. 111E

    New Jersey   Worker and Community Right to Know Act, Chapter 315 of the Acts of 1983

    Pennsylvania   Act No. 159 of the Acts of 1984

    (2) Limited Community Right to Know Laws
        (local official right to know only)

    Connecticut   Conn. Gen. Stats. Ch. 557, 31-40c et seq.

    Delaware   Hazardous Chemical Information Act, Chapter 334 of the Acts of 1984

    Florida   Chapter 223 of the Acts of 1984

    Illinois   Chapter 240 of the Acts of 1983

    Maine   Chapter 823 of the Acts of 1984

    Maryland   Md Code Art. 89

    New Hampshire   N.H. Rev. Stat. Ch. 277A

    Rhode Island   Hazardous Substances Right to Know Act, Chapter 18 of the Acts of 1983

9. Manufacturer's Assoc. of Tri-Country v. Knepper, 12 OSHC 1553 (U.S.D.Ct., M.D. Pa., December 12, 1985); and New

Jersey State Chamber of Commerce v. Hughey, (Ct. App. 3d Cct., N.J., 1985), Nos. 85-5087, 5088, 5095; ___ F. 2d.___. Also see M. Baram, note 2 supra. State legislators are actively promoting new laws. See, for example, #A4145, the proposed "Toxic Catastrophe Prevention Act" of Assemblyman Bryon Baer, in New Jersey (September 9, 1985).

10. 5 U.S.C. 2601. Sections 5 and 8 of TSCA are of most relevance regarding risk communication. The pesticide law, 7 U.S.C. 136, also requires labelling and information for registration and approval procedures. The hazardous waste laws at 42 U.S.C. 6901 and 9601, and the air and water pollution control laws at 42 U.S.C. 7401 and 33 U.S.C. 1251, respectively, contain numerous reporting and inspection requirements which generate risk communications.

11. Worker access to medical and exposure records rule at 29 CFR 1910.20. Hazard communication rule at 29 CFR 1910.1200. See M. Baram, "The Right to Know and the Duty to Disclose Hazard Information," American Journal of Public Health, v. 74, n. 4 (April 1984) p. 385.

12. FOIA at 5 U.S.C. 552. See Litigation Under FOIA. Ctr. for National Security Studies, Washington, DC (annual reports).

13. Restatement of Torts, 2d at section 388.

14. See, for example, A.D. Little, Inc. v. Cambridge Commissioner of Health, 395 Mass. 535 (1985).

15. See Florio's proposed Chemical Manufacturing Safety Act of 1985, February 1985, for example.

16. See Chemical Week, Jan. 30, 1985, pp. 17 & 18, regarding industry initiatives. Also see The Trade Union Report on Bhopal, International. Confederation of Free Trade Unions, Geneva, Switzerland (1985), (which recommends that chemical manufacturers provide full information on hazardous chemicals and processes to workers, the public, and purchasers).

17. See P. Brodeur, note 2 supra, on the use of discovery techniques in litigation to acquire company-held information, such as the notorious Sumner Simpson file of memos evincing corporate activity to withhold risk information from asbestos workers, industrial customers, and the public.

18. See EPA Guidance, November 12, 1985, entitled "Acutely Toxic Chemical Substances: Guidance for Developing Community Awareness and Preparedness Programs."

19. Seveso Directive at 5 O.J. Eur. Comm. (No. L 230) 1 (1982). See A. Sheehan, "Chemical Plant Safety Regulation: The European Example," *Law and Policy in International Business*, v. 16 (1984) p. 621.

20. See *The Control of Major Hazards*, 3d Rpt., Advisory Committee on Major Hazards, U.K. Health and Safety Commission, London, U.K. (1984). A more expansive view has been drafted and may be recommended or required by the E.C. (Personal Communication, E.C. Staff, November 27, 1985).

21. Discussed in "CEFIC Colloquium on Seveso Directive," Conference Proceedings, CEFIC Brussels, Belgium (October 1982).

CHAPTER ELEVEN

SOUTH AFRICA

LEON H. SULLIVAN
Pastor
Zion Baptist Church
Philadelphia, Pennsylvania

KENNETH N. CARSTENS
Executive Director
International Aid and Defense Fund for Southern Africa
Cambridge, Massachusetts

HOWARD WOLPE
U.S. Congressman
Michigan

HARRY JOHNSON
Manager
Public Relations
Polaroid Corporation
Cambridge, Massachusetts

D.G.M. FOURIE
Deputy Consul-General
South African Consulate-General
New York City, New York

DAVID M. LUDINGTON
Associate Professor of Marketing
Saint Mary's College
Moraga, California

PATRICIA H. WERHANE
Associate Professor of Philosophy
Loyola University of Chicago
Chicago, Illinois

WILFRED D. KOPLOWITZ
Vice President and Director
International Public Affairs
Citibank, N.A.
New York City, New York

THE ROLE OF MULTINATIONAL CORPORATIONS IN HELPING TO BRING ABOUT CHANGE IN SOUTH AFRICA

Leon H. Sullivan

I want to address two compelling problems facing the world and suggest that we must find workable solutions to them if we expect to be able to adequately deal with barriers of fear and suspicion and hopelessness.

The first problem deals with the growing hunger, unemployment, and human deprivation in the developing nations of the world. In much of the world today, human needs are greater than they have ever been. The prospects for the world's masses are not bright. One of the greatest problems facing us today is the growing and deepening poverty in the world's developing nations. Estimates are that of the 4.7 billion persons in the world today, approximately one billion are now living between bare subsistence and disaster.

Developing countries of the world are in serious straits and, without extraordinary efforts, conditions are certain to get worse. This is particularly true in most of sub-Saharan Africa, southern and South East Asia, southern and Central America and in parts of the Caribbean. Looking ahead, the problem is further compounded as the world's population is expected to increase by 55 percent to 6.5 billion by the year 2000, with 80 percent of this growth in developing countries. While the world's food supply is expected to increase by over 90 percent between now and 2000, projections show an actual decrease in daily food consumption for developing nations.

If this trend continues, it will mean up to 2 billion people living in constant hunger by the year 2000 in developing countries, with hundreds of millions in a daily state of starvation. Projected still further to the year 2050, or within the lifespan of the average child born in so-called developed nations, the world population is expected to level off, barring extraordinary changes or nuclear holocaust, at 9 billion, with 5 billion in developing countries and with most of the people in the most destitute of human conditions.

Looking ahead into the next century, if new and effective ways are not found to alleviate hunger, poverty, unemployment, and ignorance among the masses of the world, the world can expect ever-increasing social and political upheval that, in time, will threaten the existence of democratic institutions. The question is what to do about the situation, because if we fail to find answers, all of our free enterprise and capitalistic theories and systems will go down the drain.

Indeed, some of us are trying to do something about it. In past years, I have initiated a self-help program called OIC, Opportunities Industrialization Center, that has spread across America and many parts of the developing world. OIC projects have been tremendous successes because they work with the grass-roots, and they develop the hands, the hearts, and the heads of the people, and they stress self-help. In America, these self-help OIC projects have trained and placed more than 600,000 people, most of whom were on welfare and who now are following a better and more productive way of life.

In Africa, these programs are spreading in eight nations and are developing skills centers and farms and reaching thousands and thousands of people every day. Hundreds and thousands of these kinds of programs must be initiated, stressing skills training, food production, literacy, self-help, and self sufficiency.

The people of the world are more concerned about their welfare than many in our governments and universities think. All that most people want is some hope and some help. For the most part, people have an inner self-pride and want to be able to stand on their own feet. What the masses of the world are looking for is a handup, not handouts, and we of the world, our resources more and more to respond to the human cries of the masses, and begin to help the people of the world who are struggling for survival to help themselves.

But remember, all cannot be left to the self-help of the people alone. Businesses, too, have a vital role to play in bringing about independence and self-sufficiency among the nations. The businesses of the world must cease their grasping for greedy profits and put some of the money back into the communities to help the people. The capitalistic businesses of the world have been too greedy. That is why the communists have taken over in so many places. The enemy of capitalism is not communism, but the selfishness of capitalism. If the businesses of the world would plough some of their profits back into communities to help the poor and use humanistic principles in dealing with their workers and nations, a revolution would begin to deal with poverty and need. Also, the Western businessmen must stop treating Americans, Asians, and Arabs as inferiors and begin to treat them as equals, or we will never get out of the problems of suspicion and fear in this world.

This leads me to the second problem that I want to mention,

and one that is immediately so close to my heart. It is the continuing existence of the evils of apartheid and the terrible racial injustices in the Republic of South Africa. We are all aware that the most racially segregated nation in the world today is the Republic of South Africa. The inhumanities practiced there against blacks and other non-whites are well known around the world. Apartheid and its policies of separate development, and all of the laws and regulations that follow from those policies, are a blight on civilization. The roots of 300 years of racial discrimination in South Africa go down so deep that one wonders if the only realistic answer might have to be a violent one involving massive human and property destruction. I hope not. And it is in the spirit of that hope that I stand here today reaching for another answer.

Somehow, through the help of God, there must be found a way to build a bridge between the white and non-white population in South Africa before havoc overtakes that country and further spills out over all of Africa and into the rest of the world. It was for this reason, looking for a peaceful solution, that my efforts with the multinational businesses were begun and the so-called Sullivan Principles were created. The Sullivan Principles must be viewed as a moral, humanistic, and economic effort to persuade companies of America, Europe, and other parts of the world with interest in South Africa to use their great resources, power, and influence for meaningful change in South Africa, and to help build a bridge of understanding, cooperation, and reconciliation between the races before it is too late.

I fully realize, and it must be made very clear, that the companies alone cannot solve the problem of apartheid. Even if all the companies of the world mounted a campaign against the system, more would be required than the efforts of the companies alone. For the roots of racial prejudice in South Africa are so deep in religious, cultural, and mental attitudes that the situation defies any one solution. But the companies can and should play the major role in helping to bring an end to the racial injustices, because more than any others, the companies have been the main beneficiaries of the cheap labor and the inhumane practices. Billions and billions of dollars of profits have been made on the agonies, torn families, and broken bodies of blacks and other non-white South Africans. Therefore, starting in the workplace and extending to the communities, the businesses must do all they can do to help change the inequalities of and injustices against black people. And the businesses must work to influence the government to rescind its unjust racial laws. Otherwise, the multinational companies have no moral justification for remaining in South Africa and should be compelled to leave the country.

I cannot emphasize enough that I am a minister of God looking for a peaceful solution to a problem. I am not a politician, not an educator, not a philosopher, not a businessman. I am first and foremost a clergyman and a Baptist preacher. Also, I am one of 700 million black people in the world, and we cannot permit a system that segregates and discriminates and humilitates us on the basis of the color of our skins to continue to exist on this earth. White men would not let it continue, and we cannot let it continue either. Apartheid must come to an end, one way or the other, and one way or the other it will come to an end, sooner than many think.

My aim with the multinational companies and the Principles has been to put a crack in the wall of apartheid and to be a catalyst for a change throughout South Africa. Working along with other forces, my goal is for the de-separation of the races, until the wall of apartheid comes down. The Principles were initiated in 1977 and signed by 12 American companies with subsidiaries in South Africa. The Principles are more than an academic response to a social problem. They are intended to be a massive effort of American companies, working with other companies of the world, for significant change.

Among other things, the Principles call for an end to all vestiges of discrimination in the work place for all companies operating in South Africa; equal pay for equal work; massive programs of education and skilled training; Blacks being uprated in all companies to management and supervisory jobs at all levels, including management of white workers; the recognition of representative black trade unions; support of black businesses in large numbers so Blacks will one day own shops, stores, factories, and mines; development of extensive housing schemes and health programs; and the lobbying of the South African government for an end to all apartheid laws, including influx control and separate development.

The Principles are working, frankly beyond my initial expectations, causing many changes in South Africa. Because of them, there has been the beginning of a revolution in industrial race relations in South Africa. Half of the American companies are signatories of the Principles and are being measured and graded with public disclosure. The other half are not yet cooperating.

In September of 1985, the United States Congress made an important move which I totally supported with testimonies and communications. It was to apply sanctions against the South

African government and to make the Sullivan Principles mandatory for all American companies in South Africa, backed up with loss of tax credits, embargoes, and heavy penalties against those who fail to fully comply with the Principles and who refuse to be measured and monitored. Unfortunately, that anti-apartheid act failed to pass the Senate and is now pigeon-holed and placed on the back burner by the Congress in lieu of other things. This is, indeed, regrettable. I had hoped that the anti-apartheid legislation would have passed and been signed into law. Instead, we got an Executive Order by the President that was far weaker than I had hoped to see coming out of Washington. But Americans must keep the pressure on Congress and on the President for sanctions and for anti-apartheid legislation. The Congress and the President must continue to be pushed and pushed and pushed for tougher efforts. Also, United States companies themselves must be pushed and pushed and pushed for greater results, and there must be standards applied to them, as well as requirements for full public disclosure of their equal rights efforts. Otherwise, the Sullivan Principles, and other codes that have followed in other parts of the world, will be used only as a camouflage for many companies to hide behind and an excuse for them to continue to do business as usual.

I have travelled across Europe trying to get the industrial nations of the world to put teeth into their equal rights codes and to push their companies along to stand up against the apartheid system in South Africa. In America and abroad, the pressure by investors, consumers, and governments must be put on the companies for greater and greater action in their compliance. If the Sullivan Principles and other equal rights codes that have followed are fully implemented and monitored, they will make a major contribution towards meaningful change in South Africa.

One thousand companies in South Africa from all over the world, desegregrating their facilities and ending all vestiges of discrimination among workers, will have to make a difference.

Hundreds of thousands of newly trained black and other non-white technicians will have to make a difference.

Hundreds of new technical schools, initiated and supported for training skilled black and other non-white workers, will have to make a difference.

Equal pay for equal work for millions of black and non-white workers, increasing their purchasing power by billions of rand a year, will have to make a difference.

A thousand schools adopted by companies, improving education for large numbers of black and non-white youth, until all education is unified, will have to make a difference.

Hundreds of thousands and millions, helped by companies with literacy education throughout the land, will have to make a difference.

Tens of thousands of scholarships from companies from around the world for black and non-white trainees in the arts, the sciences, and the professions, will have to make a difference.

Hundreds of black representative trade unions being recognized by companies, strengthening workers' rights, and providing the most hopeful sign for peaceful change in South Africa, along with the empowerment of the black worker, will have to make a difference.

Companies supporting the right of migrant workers to bring their families with them and the right to normal family life, and taking a stand against racial influx control laws, will have to make a difference.

Hundreds of executives of multinational companies lobbying the government to put an end to all discriminatory laws and the apartheid system will have to make a difference.

Growing numbers of blacks and whites, for the first time coming into contact with each other in plants and mines and other places, and the growth of human relationships, will have to make a difference.

My position goes beyond the Principles. I believe there should be no expansion of American businesses, and have long held there should be no new bank loans to the South African Government or its agencies by American banks or any other banks; there should be a halt to the sale of the Krugerrand in America; and there should be no sales to the South African police or military, or any other activities that can benefit oppression, until apartheid ends and there is full and equal participation for blacks in the political system of that country.

In a word, we need help all over the world to get companies to assume their social and moral responsibilities in the implementation of the fair employment principles and codes, with measurement, monitoring, and enforcement. But the efforts of the companies must go beyond fair employment and jobs. The urgent need in South Africa is not fair employment and jobs at this time, but freedom: freedom for the black masses that they might have equal status throughout South African society.

Therefore, in a recent amplification, an addition was made to the Principles that calls for American companies to actively work for an end to all apartheid laws. The Separate Amenities Act, the Population Restoration Act, the Group Area Act, and the Internal Securities Act must be abolished. Full citizenship rights for blacks and full and equal political rights for blacks must be established as determined by agreement with recognized black leaders in South Africa, such as Nelson Mandela, Desmond Tutu, Allan Boesak, Gatsha Buthelezi, and others. In a word, the latest amplification to the Principles requires that the companies challenge the South African Government to abolish apartheid and requires the companies to become part and parcel of the liberation movement for social, economic, and political justice.

An important step was taken several weeks ago when white South African Businessmen met with the leaders of the African National Congress, over the objection of President Botha, and called for an end to apartheid and for power sharing, politically, for the black population. This was a significant move, and I have asked American business leaders to make a united front with these South African business leaders and work with their counterparts in South Africa for the complete abolition of apartheid.

American companies must stand up and be counted. Now is the time. And they must be measured and judged by the extent to which they take a stand against that unjust system. But time is running out. People are being killed daily in South Africa, and South Africa does not have ten years, or six years, or four years to bring an end to its unjust system of government. Therefore, a deadline is necessary for decisive action to be taken. In this regard, as of May 7, 1985, I announced a 24-month deadline for United States Companies in South Africa, taking the position that if in 24 months apartheid is not actually and in fact abolished in South Africa as a system, all American companies should withdraw from South Africa, and there should be a total United States embargo against South Africa, including all exports and imports. And it is my hope other companies and other nations will do the same. The gauntlet must be laid. The evils of apartheid must come to an end.

This can be a bright day in the history of free enterprise. Historic world efforts for justice and freedom can be demonstrated now that will show a new face of America and Western business to the world. I am appealing this day to those who represent the multinational companies of the world to let the hammer of freedom ring on the anvil of international justice in South Africa. I am asking the businesses of the world, led the companies of America, to swing the hammer of freedom, and let it ring, let it ring, let it ring, until it is heard across South Africa and around the world and to help bring justice and freedom to the black people of the violence-ridden, destructive, and intolerably racist policies of the government of South Africa.

A CASE FOR SANCTIONS AGAINST SOUTH AFRICA*

Kenneth N. Carstens

Introduction

A sampling of recent reports in the Wall Street Journal and other similar sources suggests that a trend towards disinvestment from and other sanctions against South Africa may have begun.[1] The reasons cited by or attributed to United States firms that have disinvested from South Africa range from moral concern to political arm-twisting and what might politely be called prudential concern for the safety of and profits on capital invested in or loaned to South Africa. A persuasive case can be made for sanctions on both moral and pragmatic grounds, and this I will try to do in the following pages.

Preliminary to this, however, it seems necessary to present an approximately thirty-year perspective on apartheid and United States economic involvement in it. There are two reasons for this: first, there have been repeated but groundless announcements of the "death" of apartheid in recent years; and second, there is a deeply and persistently held article of faith that foreign investment in general and United States investment in particular has had and will continue to have moderating and benign effects on apartheid.

History and Foundations of Apartheid

In the 1950s, South Africa was neither a model democracy nor a paradise for blacks[2] -- in fact, this was true even before the pro-Nazi Afrikaner Nationalist Party (NP) came to power in 1948 on an overtly racist platform. The NP platform promised, in effect, to rationalize the disorderly patchwork quilt of racist laws and conventions into a smooth, efficient, and coherent system of white supremacy called "apartheid." Some of its essential foundation stones were already in place and merely required some reinforcement and alignment, while others had to be fashioned almost from scratch.

What emerged as -- and remain -- the main foundations of apartheid are the following: (1) The several hundred scraps of

---

*The views expressed in this paper are those of the author and do not necessarily reflect those of International Defense and Aid Fund.

impoverished rural ghettos or reservations, today's bantustans or "independent homelands" or "independent national states," had been established by the Land Acts of 1913 and 1936. (2) The existing Pass Laws which controlled the movement of African men were extended to African women and coordinated by the misleadingly entitled Bantu (Abolition of Passes and Co-ordination of Documents) Act of 1952. In accord with this Act, "passes" were euphemistically renamed "reference books." (3) The remnants of the black vote were removed by another misleadingly entitled law, the Promotion of Bantu Self-Government Act of 1959, and by the Separate Representation of Voters Amendment Act of 1968. (4) Basic to the operation of the whole system of apartheid was and is the need for racial classification, the central statute of which was created in the Population Registration Act of 1950. (5) Mandatory residential segregation was accomplished mainly on the basis of the Group Areas Act of 1950 as amended, especially in 1966. In the process of enforcing this and other laws requiring racial separation, more than 3,500,000 removals, most of them forced removals, have taken place since 1960, with another 1,800,000 people under threat of removal.

The grotesque edifice erected on these foundations was and still is considered to be in need of formidable buttresses to protect it against its enemies. Thus, in addition to the vast and intricate system of legislated racism, apartheid is propped up by an astonishing array of Draconian "security" legislation which has outlawed all serious political opposition and dissidence, but which has obviously failed to eliminate them. The human rights that still remained for the African majority thirty years ago either have been even more drastically reduced or have been completely removed -- some, such as political rights and freedom of movement, by such racist laws as those mentioned above; others, such as the right to life, liberty, and a secure family life and freedom of speech, association, assembly, and the press have been further curtailed or removed by theoretically non-racial security laws. Of the plethora of such laws, a couple of examples should suffice.

<u>Banning</u>, an extremely harsh form of restriction often amounting to house arrest, without charges, without trial or any hearing and without recourse to the courts, could be imposed only on African political dissidents under the Bantu Administration Act of 1927; however, the entirely arbitrary power of banning was vastly increased and extended to all races on even flimsier pretexts by a law passed in 1950 and now incorporated into the Internal Security Act of 1982.

<u>Detention without trial</u> was rarely used until 1960, although the NP Prime Minister for 1966 to 1978, B. J. Vorster,

was one of the more prominent people held without trial during World War II for his alleged pro-Nazi activities. The Public Safety Act of 1953 provided for detention without trial under a State of Emergency and was first invoked in 1960. Since then, detention without trial, usually incommunicado and accompanied by torture, has become a regular feature of South African life -- and scores of prisoners of conscience have met violent deaths while in police custody. Not only suspects, but also possible witnesses, may be and often are detained incommunicado and without trial. Moreover, the conditions for the existence of the power of detention without trial and other arbitrary restrictions are not related by statute to facts but only to the opinion of government officials ranging from Cabinet Ministers to police officers -- and indeed to any raw army or police recruit during a declared State of Emergency.

Foreign Investment and Apartheid: False Hopes

The sustained and systematic assault on blacks in order to consolidate the white monopoly on privilege and power was well under way in the 1950s, but its violent and homicidal operations were largely systemic and largely obscure to those, especially foreigners, who were not themselves the actual victims of apartheid. Nevertheless, foreign investors knew that the unusually high profits available in South Africa were not unrelated to the growing powerlessness, poverty, and suffering of blacks on whose exploitation and repression those profits depended. In the early 1950s, the United States financial stake in apartheid was less than $200 million and was unchallenged on moral and political grounds. In 1983, according to the columnist Jack Anderson, the United States Consulate in Johannesburg reported to the State Department that the United States stake in apartheid was over $14.6 billion. This includes loans, direct investment, and some but not all indirect investment.[3] Direct investment alone in 1985 was over $2 billion, a ten-fold increase over three decades.

The justification for this large (in South African terms) stake in apartheid is that prosperity in general and American business in particular has been and remains a positive force for change and exercises a moderating influence. Much is also made of the desirable changes promised by the apartheid government and already visible, if not to South African blacks, at least to some American business and political leaders who have a distinct interest in seeing such changes occur in order to justify their policies and profits. In trying to assess the changes during the period in which the United States financial stake has so vastly increased, as well as those currently under way, we should recognize that changes of great significance to right-wing white South Africans like State President P. W. Botha -- who defines change, controls it, and has instant access to the world's news media -- matter very little to the voiceless, voteless millions of Africans. For quite obvious reasons, they could not care less if the repeal of the Immorality Act now permits them to have sexual intercourse with the whites whose police shoot and kill four-year-old black children with impunity in soul-destroying ghettos.

What matters to the black majority is not that a few of the lucky ones have well-paid jobs, are sometimes called "Mrs." or "Mr." and use "whites-only" toilets; it is not even that black workers (and _not_ United States business interests, as is often asserted) forced the government by dint of repeated and dangerous strikes to "concede" the right of blacks to form their own trade unions which already existed in essence. What does matter to the blacks is that there are literally millions more of them living below the poverty level today than in the 1950s; that many more today than in the 1950s are dying of starvation and disease while whites live off the fat of the land; that 3.5 million blacks have been forcibly removed, many from ancestral lands and modest livelihoods to resettlement camps which have become death camps for thousands of them; that even those who cling to life are stripped of dignity and hope; that instead of seeing their children grow and learn like white children, they see their children arrested, whipped, beaten, and brutalized, if not killed, by savage white soldiers and police; that instead of children's laughter there is rage -- which this time, it seems, will not be quelled as in the children's uprising of 1976. Is this the utopia for which they must thank thirty years of benign American investment? Is this the change which two billion dollars will buy -- levels of fear, frustration, desperation, degradation, violence, and death beyond the worst nightmares of the 1950s?

There is an argument which emphasizes the _symbolic_ significance and potential for future progress in some changes which, in terms of their practical consequences, are purely rhetorical or cosmetic. It is a hopeful sign, it is argued, that whites now speak of a "non-racial society," "an end to discrimination," and "power-sharing," etc., even though white leaders do not really mean what they say in these terms. The argument suggests that if whites can utter today what was yesterday unthinkable, tomorrow they may be willing to do it. The fact is, however, that whites have been using euphemisms like "separate development" and telling each other and the world lies about apartheid for thirty years -- and look at the results. The extent to which language is misused and devalued by public figures is hardly a hopeful index to desirable change.

But the basic fallacy in this "let's be hopeful and upbeat" line of reasoning is the false premise that the government which invented and painstakingly built apartheid will now or soon begin to dismantle it. Has there ever been a class or group of people who have been persuaded by rational argument or moral insight to surrender their hold on privilege and power? Has it not always had to be taken from them by the application of some kind of force, whether military or economic? Was it morality, or economic pressure backed up with military force, that freed the slaves in the United States in the nineteenth century? Is it reasonable, in any event, to expect white South Africans (of whom I am one) to be the first in history to do the right thing solely because it is right or because reason reveals that there is no morally responsible alternative?

Those who continue to look to the architects and builders of apartheid to dismantle it are either deceived or trying to deceive; they are either ill-informed or they share P. W. Botha's definition of change, which is well exemplified in his "reform" Constitution of 1983.[4] This Constitution was framed under Botha's direction, and it made him both head of government and head of state, conferring on him as President powers so great that even his own right-wingers have correctly described them as dictatorial. His powers extend not only through the whole government bureaucracy, but also over Parliament, which he has the power to dissolve and whose legislative functions he can manipulate. The President is not elected by popular vote of the two minorities represented in Parliament (26.2% of the South African population), but by an electoral college dominated by Botha's own ruling white Nationalist Party.

Parliament consists of three houses: the white Assembly with 178 members, the Coloured House of Representatives with 85 members, and the Indian House of Delegates with 45 members. Legislation is divided into "general affairs" and "own affairs," the latter being defined as affairs relating only to the minority racial group concerned. It is the exclusive privilege of the President to decide which matters are of general concern and which are "own affairs," and his decision is final. An "own affairs" matter can be debated only in the house to which he assigns it. Matters which the President defines as "common concerns" go to all three houses. If there is disagreement between the three houses, the President's Council resolves the disagreement.

What of the Africans, who constitute, after all, 73.8% of the population? The "control and administration" of African affairs "shall vest in the State President." Along with the considerable diminution of the democratic powers of Parliament, this fact was one of the main reasons that the overwhelming majority of the South African population rejected the "reform" Constitution. Some 82% of the Coloured and Indian people, whom it is supposed to have enfranchised, rejected it. The depth of the reaction against it can also be gauged by the unprecedented intensity of the demonstrations and protests which began with the introduction of the new Constitution in September 1984. The often indiscriminate killing of both innocent bystanders and demonstrators by the hundreds has not yet suppressed the sustained, nation-wide black protests. The frequently understated official death toll after 18 months of protest is approaching 1,400, with many thousands wounded and tens of thousands detained. (The new Constitution was not the sole cause of the uprising of 1984, but it has become the symbolic focus of it.)

However, two out of three approved the Constitution. Voters representing little more that 10% of the population as a whole, therefore, approved the new constitution, which entrenches white power more deeply than either of the earlier South African constitutions and is the most racially divisive of them all -- and certainly the least democratic. That the United States State Department should have welcomed it as "a step in the right direction" is ironic, deplorable, and a clear indication of the kind of change United States policy is promoting in South Africa -- namely, new facades on the superstructure, but with the same foundations of apartheid, and with repressive laws and brutal actions still propping it up. This is also the kind of change in which United States businesses have been investing for thirty years. As the United States Senate Committee on Foreign Relations stated in a report entitled <u>United States Corporate Interests in South Africa</u>: "The net effect of American investment has been to strengthen the economic and military self-sufficiency of South Africa's apartheid regime."

Motives for Change

Real changes, however, may be under way in the United States if not in South Africa. Is it possible that a mixture of self-interest, political pressures, and perhaps even a grain or two of morality (one does not want to be too sanguine!) has persuaded United States businesses to pursue a more responsible policy than the United States government? On February 27, 1986, the <u>Wall Street Journal</u> reported that "blue-chip United States companies ... are pulling out (of South Africa) at an accelerating rate" due to "the twin pressures of unrest there and political harassment (sic) at home." The report added that "many large United States companies are developing contingency plans to get out." Figures cited in the report suggest the beginning of a trend: in 1983, six United States companies left and three started new businesses in South Africa; in 1984, seven left and two started new businesses in South Africa. These developments are taking place in a context of a growing national divestment movement in which hundreds, if not thousands, of divestment actions have been taken by groups ranging from national, regional, and local church bodies and trade unions to universities, journals, and family trusts. Moreover, by February 1986, some 90 state, county, city, and town authorities had committed themselves to divestment and/or selective purchasing actions which are exerting a very considerable financial and public relations pressure on corporations which might otherwise have less sensitive consciences on the matter.

While those departures from South Africa are to be most warmly welcomed as long overdue, the reasons cited for the exodus -- instability there and "political harassment here" -- lend support to the suspicion that a social conscience has not yet evolved in firms that do business with apartheid. Moral considerations remain absent from the plans, decisions, and actions of these firms even though the language of morality has found its way into their public relations statements and programs in South Africa and here.

Fear of lower profits and of being tarred with the apartheid brush are not ranked among the most noble motives for "pulling out." Better reasons for disinvestment and other sanctions against apartheid were being given thirty years ago by such leaders as South Africa's first Nobel Peace laureate, Albert Luthuli, President of the African National Congress of South Africa (ANC). As the non-violent campaigns for basic human rights were being suppressed with traditional white South African severity, Luthuli warned that soon the only recourse left to the black majority would be counterviolence. South Africa was set on a course leading inexorably towards a disastrous cycle of violence and counterviolence, he said, from which the black majority was vainly trying to steer South Africa. For decades, the Africans had sought to turn the government towards a rational solution, first by patient reasoning and then by boycotts, demonstrations, and campaigns of civil disobedience. The response had been whips, clubs, and guns wielded with brutal effect by the police, while racist and Draconian laws multiplied on the statute books, and torture became as routine as imprisonment. Why, asked Luthuli, did Britain and America misuse their moral authority and economic power in tacit approval of this disastrous road of violence and death? He pleaded with them to use their power for freedom and democracy instead by withdrawing investment and imposing sanctions. If the West did not end its de facto support of apartheid, Luthuli argued, they would in effect be endorsing counterviolence, which was a last resort the ANC had been struggling for years to avoid.

Luthuli's arguments were clinched by the police massacre of scores of African children, women, and men at Sharpeville in 1960 and the launching of the ANC's campaign of sabotage in 1961 -- the week after Luthuli had reiterated his plea and warning in his Nobel Peace Prize acceptance speech in Oslo. Three years later, Martin Luter King, Jr., on his way to Oslo to receive his own Nobel Peace Prize, stopped in London and in a powerful speech also advocated withdrawal of American investment from South Africa and economic sanctions as the one hope for achieving change non-violently.

Every credible black leader in South Africa has reiterated the pleas and the warnings of Luthuli and King: Mandela, Sobukwe, Biko, Boesak, Tutu, and Barayi -- the leader of the new and significant Congress of South African Trade Unions.[5] Their pleas for sanctions and their warnings of the dreadful alternatives to sanctions are more compelling and urgent now than when they were ignored thirty years ago. The facts of powerlessness, poverty, and repression speak for themselves, powerfully reinforced since 1960 by the initially low-level and sporadic counterviolence, which provoked disproportionate and brutal reprisals from the authorities, raising the level and intensity of the spiral. What particularly fuels and makes the escalation of the cycle of violence and counterviolence inexorable is the brutal way in which even non-violent protests and demonstrations are crushed. Early in March of 1986, Amnesty International charged that the South African government is "deliberately killing" people for taking part in anti-apartheid demonstrations and has "assassinated" opponents based in neighboring countries. Made in a letter to P.W. Botha, the charges were prompted by the killing by police in a ghetto near Cape Town of seven alleged ANC "guerrillas" who were trying to surrender or were wounded and defenseless.[6] There is every sign that the momentum which the cycle of violence is gaining will make the last nine months of 1986 even more blood-stained than the previous eighteen months have been. For the intransigence and brutality of the regime, its false promises of change, and its summary executions on ghetto streets have succeeded in replacing the patient endurance and persistent goodwill of the black people with rage and frustration fueled by fear -- and hope.

The Moral Argument for Divestment, Disinvestment, and Sanctions

There are more than 100 laws in South Africa which restrict the freedom of the press and distort the flow of news and information. Neverthless, on the basis of facts provided by the South African government itself, unaniminity as to the nature of the apartheid system has been reached by all reasonable people. I know of no American businessperson on public record who does not condemn apartheid as evil. Surely such people must also agree that it is morally indefensible to associate oneself individually, or collectively as a corporation, with evil. Obviously when one associates one's individual or corporate self with evil, one is associating one's name, one's reputation, one's values, one's religion, and one's nationality with that evil. The onus, therefore, is on business to justify associating itself with the unambiguous evil of apartheid; for to associate oneself in all one's public and private roles and identities -- which also means associating the traditional American values of freedom, justice, and democracy -- with a system which in theory and in practice is at best wholly unjust is not only to acquiesce in the injustice but also to aid it by lending it the respectability and legitimacy of the roles, identities, and values that one involuntarily represents. This would hold true even of a missionary who does not clearly and constantly identify with the victims rather than with the oppressors, an option which the business person does not and perhaps cannot choose without leaving commerce and going into religious or social service.

In addition to the acquiescence in and involuntary symbolic contributions to the system of injustice which simply <u>being there</u> entails, there is further moral blame in being there <u>for profit,</u> since the wealth of the few is related to the powerlessness and poverty of the many, and any investment gives the investor a tangible interest in this inequitable system and in its perpetuation in some form related to the present one. Many contribute involuntarily to the perpetuation of apartheid -- and those who might elect not to have no choice. The law sees to this. To ensure that the investor's interest in apartheid is given full force and effect, such laws as the Petroleum Producers Act of 1977, the National Supplies Procurement Act of 1977, the Official Secrets Act of 1956 as amended in 1972, and the Key Points Act of 1980 as amended in 1984 are on the statute books. Lest moral or other considerations should tempt a businessperson to act inconsistently with the <u>de facto</u> interest in the preservation of the status quo, these acts prohibit the following: (1) withholding supplies and services from the security forces; (2) shifting resources from such supplies or services to their more profitable lines or customers; (3) divulging information to an unauthorized person "in any manner or for any purpose prejudicial to the safety or interests of the Republic" of South Africa; and (4) not taking adequate steps to provide security in cooperation with the military authorities and under regulations drawn up by the Minister of Defense.

Thus, being there as an investor or trader, whether individual or corporate, not only becomes inseparable from *symbolic* support of apartheid, but also inevitably gives *material* support to the system in the form of taxes and the legal regulation of the sale of products and services. There simply is no choice in the matter. It is, after all, the government and not the black majority which sets the terms and conditions for investment and trade -- and much more so in South Africa's much-touted "free-market" economy than Americans suspect. Thus, one's identification with apatheid has gone beyond the vitally important realm of symbols to the equally important practical level of guns, butter, technology, skills, and taxes, all of which are vitally necessary to defend the system which those who invest in it deplore as evil.

As if to reinforce the logic of established facts and the moral logic of sanctions, as well as to underline the obviously desperate need apartheid has for all the taxes, all the computers, and all the bullets and biscuits and symbols of legitimacy which American businesses can provide, the apartheid government has fiercely opposed the sanctions movement in America and elsewhere by short-wave radio broadcasts, by glossy propaganda, by costly public relations firms and lobbyists, and by savage laws against its advocacy within South Africa. Could an impartial observer escape the conclusion that foreign investors are either suffering from self-delusion of pathological proportions or are in shameful collusion with the apartheid government if they try to deny such facts and such logic?

Nevertheless, some well-meaning people do still ask whether sanctions would not "hurt those we want to help." Albert Luthuli and the many who have echoed his arguments over the past thirty years concede that there *may* be some additional suffering for at least a few in the short term. After all, if an American factory closes down in Port Elizabeth, the few blacks employed there will obviously lose their jobs, even though the longer-term effect will in fact create more jobs as high-tech imports are replaced by cruder local goods and as the capital-intensive foreign investment is perforce replaced by labor-intensive enterprises. But Luthuli and the others who advocate sanctions have said: "Our people are suffering more than you can know at present. That suffering shows no sign of lessening and even less of ending. We are prepared to suffer a little more -- indeed, we are prepared to suffer a lot more in the short-term if we can see an end to the suffering. We would rather suffer far more now and have some hope for the future and for our children than keep our suffering at this level in perpetuity with no hope for the future."

For those concerned lest "we hurt those we want to help," the question is this: whom do you want to help? What is the normal, rational way of helping anyone other than infants and the insane? Is it not to give them that for which they themselves have asked? The apartheid government spends millions every year to ensure that you know what they are asking for, namely, more and more investments, loans, and trade. Genuine black South African leaders do not have the millions to ensure that you hear their requests, but you have nevertheless heard that both of South Africa's Nobel Peace laureates, Albert Luthuli and Desmond Tutu, have asked you to disinvest, as has every leader whom common sense and elementary facts would identify as credible.

In November 1985, three of South Africa's most renowned and genuine leaders, whom the overwhelming majority of South Africans of all races respect (even though one of them is white -- and an Afrikaner!), namely, Allen Boesak, Coloured Dutch Reformed Church minister and President of the World Alliance of Reformed Churches, C. F. Beyers Naude, white Dutch Reformed Church minister and General Secretary of the South African Council of Churches, and Desmond Tutu, Anglican bishop of Johannesburg and Nobel Peace laureate, called on United States and European creditor banks to demand the resignation of the South African government as a condition for rescheduling South Africa's $14 billion bank debt. The three leaders reiterated their call to the banks on February 19, 1986, pointing out that, far from dismantling apartheid, the South African government was more deeply entrenching it. The banks ignored the plea. The next day, a "partial agreement" on the rescheduling of the debt was announced, followed by a report on Radio South Africa three weeks later that a "full agreement" had been reached between the South African government and the American and European banks.

So the question is, Whom do you want to "help" or "hurt?" There is absolutely no way in which support for the evil system of apartheid can be defended on moral grounds. There is equally no way in which one can invest in South Africa, trade with South Africa, or make loans to South Africa without supporting apartheid -- and lest such a way should be found, the South African government has enacted statute after statute to ensure that support will be enacted. However, there is no law to compel anyone to invest there. That is a free choice, and with it it goes what cannot be bought or enacted by law, namely, the symbolic legitimation and moral support of an evil system.

Every investment in or loan to South Africa and every

business deal with South Africa is an explicit moral and political statement. Disinvestment and refusal to do business with South Africa are equally explicit moral and political statements. One course of action is morally wrong. The other is morally right. There is no neutral ground.

Notes

1. I use the term "sanctions" to denote all political and economic measures short of military action. Most often, I will use it to refer to economic measures such as boycotts, divestment (the selling of shares held in a company operating in South Africa) and, more especially, disinvestment (the withdrawal of a company or other investor from South Africa).

2. I use the term "blacks" to denote collectively Africans, Coloureds, and Asians. The official population estimates for mid-1984 were as follows (including the population of what South Africa but not a single other government calls the "independent" reservations or bantustans of Bophuthatswana, Ciskei, Transkei, and Venda):

African	24,103,458	73.8%
Coloured	2,830,301	8.7%
Asian	890,292	2.7%
Black Subtotal	27,824,051	85.2%
White	4,818,679	14.8%
Total	32,642,730	100.0%

3. Washington Post, 30 July 1983.

4. Republic of South Africa Constitution Act of 1983 and the Constitution Amendment Act of 1984.

5. As Americans discovered in their war of independence, every country has its collaborators, and South Africa is no exception. Bantustan leaders, despite impressive titles like "Chief Minister" and "President," are in fact civil servants of the South African government which controls every important aspect of even the four "independent" bantustans, both directly and by providing an average of 77% of their budgets. The bantustan leaders, together with their urban counterparts, are seen as second only to black police and informers among the collaborators. Paraded as the "real leaders," they are frequently quoted and interviewed on the state-controlled Radio South Africa

(which beams short-wave broadcasts to North America daily at 0200 G.M.T.) as well as on television. Their support of more foreign investment and trade is often highlighted during these broadcasts.

6. Manchester Guardian Weekly, 16 March 1986, p. 6.

SOUTH AFRICA: TIME HAS RUN OUT

HOWARD WOLPE

I always welcome opportunities to address the subject of Africa. As an Africanist professionally, it has been an unusual experience for me to find African issues very much at the center of the national political agenda. I confess that in Kalamazoo, Michigan, Africa is not the most salient subject of political interest, and it has been encouraging to me to find this country beginning to attend to the African continent. It is tragic that it has taken the human suffering that has characterized recent experience in Africa to focus American attention, but at least that has finally occurred.

In the following pages, I want to present some of the context of the debate on South Africa that has been going on for many years in this country.

It is no secret that Africa, for most Americans, is a very different and distant continent. I used to teach African politics, and the first day of every semester I would ask my students to take out a sheet of paper and put on that paper all of the images that they had of the African continent. We would assemble all of their perceptions on the blackboard and, when we were done, it was apparent that the images of my students (and I suspect they were really typical of Americans generally) were really framed by the most recent Tarzan movie or book.

That is not an exaggeration. There is a whole series of mythologies, stereotypes, feelings, and attitudes about race, about people of color that has very dramatically affected the way we have looked at Africa. It should be no surprise, then, that American foreign policy toward the African continent, not only in the Reagan years but literally for decades, has frequently been counterproductive. It has been based upon that mythology, that attitudinal set, we as a society have brought to our approach to the continent.

Three Myths

I want to identify three particular myths that I think have interfered with our objective exploration of the African continent, and particularly of the South African situation.

First of all, when people look at South Africa, they tend to project the American experience with race, with racism, and with the Civil Rights movement onto the South African scene.

The argument usually advanced in terms of facilitating non-violent, evolutionary change is a referencing of the American experience: it takes time, attitudes must change, there must be a process in the economy and the society that will eventually trigger political reform. But the important point to understand is that in two critical respects the South African experience is not like the American experience and, consequently, political stances and actions based on the assumption of similarities are doomed to boomerang and to be very counterproductive.

The first key distinction is that, unlike America, South Africa is, in fact, not a liberal democracy but a totalitarian police state -- one of the most brutal and most repressive in all the world.

I happened to have the opportunity to be in South Africa some years ago and spent one night in the black township of Soweto, right outside Johannesburg. This is an area of a very densely concentrated population of about 1-1/4 million people who are housed within 100,000 living units. Under South African law, it is illegal for a white person to live in a black area even for one night. (We did that thinking that they would allow certain privileges to a visiting Member of Congress.) I will never forget black Sowetans describing to me their perception that about one out of every ten of their neighbors was a police spy, the reason being that the women and children who are living in Soweto are, for the most part, there illegally. They have come to join their men who are working in the mines. They do not have work permits, and if they fail to cooperate with the police they are immediately subject to deportation to the so-called "homelands" or "bantustans."

You cannot comprehend the South African reality unless you understand the penetration by the police into every element of South African society, down to the neighborhood and the family. It creates levels of distress, disunity, suspicion, and paranoia that only that kind of police-state penetration could fuel. The fact of the matter is that to protest, to dissent, or to challenge the system of apartheid in any respect is literally to put one's life and liberty into jeopardy. That is why it sounds so ludicrous and absurd to the South African ear when well-intending Americans talk about evolutionary change occurring as more blacks receive education or employment.

Secondly, and equally critically, majority-minority relationships are reversed. In the United States, whites were the majority; the excluded were the black minority. The white majority could countenance full political rights for the black minority without ever fearing they would lose ultimate control of the national political system.

That is not so in South Africa. Clearly, political rights for the entire population will mean a loss of political control and of special economic privileges for the white minority. Political change need not mean the exclusion of whites from the political process any more than it has meant exclusion of blacks from the political process in the United States. However it will mean a loss of political control and a loss of special economic privilege. So the political dynamic in South Africa is very different and needs to be understood.

The second myth that has underpinned much of the debate occurring in this country about South Africa is that somehow economic change is inevitably linked to a process of political liberalization and democratization. Indeed, this is the argument of those who advocate that we should give great emphasis to the importance of the Sullivan Code and to American companies becoming signatories to that Code. The notion is that the presence of American companies constitutes a positive model of desegregation and that the skills that are being acquired by blacks in the industrial workplace will ultimately facilitate political change as well.

There is no question that in the limited respects I have just described, the Sullivan Code has been a positive force. Indeed, American Sullivan Code signatories have offered a different kind of model of labor-management relationships, desegregated workplaces, and for a very limited number of people, improved economic conditions. But there are no more than 70,000 blacks employed in American firms, which accounts for less than one percent of the entire black labor force. The "Sullivan" firms represent even less (about two-thirds) of that 70,000 population. Beyond this, there are 26 million non-whites in South Africa, and I think it should be apparent that to spend more than a minute discussing the fortunes of 70,000 workers at the expense of the 26 million would seem extraordinarily ludicrous from a South African vantage point. It misses the reality of what is South Africa is today.

Moreover, if we look at Nazi Germany or Stalinist Russia -- or indeed even South Africa itself -- there is clear evidence that economic change and industrialization need not be accompanied by increased democratization and liberalization, but may well be accompanied by increased repression. Over the past couple of decades, with all the industrialization and with all the economic change that has occurred in South Africa, repression has intensified. Apartheid has been consolidated. It has not been weakened in any respect.

Third, we need to understand clearly how racial considerations have distorted our perception and our understanding of the South African experience. If, in fact, the racial complexion of minority and majority were reversed in South Africa, and you had a black minority imposing this horrendous system of apartheid on a white majority, do you really think that, over the past several decades, this country would have engaged in a long and tortuous debate about the ethics or wisdom of the application of sanctions? Would we be engaging in a very involved discussion about the efficacy and morality of non-violence?

I think that if we are honest with ourselves the answer is clearly in the negative. Indeed, if we look at other somewhat similar situations -- the Soviet invasion of Afghanistan or the actions by the Polish state government in suppressing the Polish trade union movement, for instance -- we see clear instances not only of the United States responding instantly with sanctions, but also of the absence of almost any controversy about such sanctions within our own society, within the Congress, or within the executive branches of our government, no matter who was President at the time. We have even gone so far as to extend, in the case of Afghanistan, not only moral but also material support to people who are resisting Soviet oppression. We have characterized those who are engaged in the struggle for liberation in Afghanistan as "freedom fighters" and, in the Polish case, our President went on television calling upon all Americans to light a candle in our windows at night as a symbol of our solidarity with the Polish trade union movement.

How different our response has been when we have turned to South Africa! Not only is the subject of sanctions enormously emotive and controversial, but the whole texture of the language that we use in discussing the subject changes. Instead of talking about people fighting for liberation, suddenly you hear thrown into the discussion much about "terrorism" and the "terrorists" of the African National Congress.

The rest of the world understands very clearly that the United States is applying a double standard in its approach to South Africa when the double standard is so manifest, it clearly has important ramifications for American interests around the world.

The Failure of Constructive Engagement and the Sullivan Code

Now, the policies of Constructive Engagement and of the Sullivan Code flow directly from some of the mythologies that I have described. And because these policies are based upon myth, they have had some terribly counterproductive consequences both for the process of change in South Africa and for American national interests.

These initiatives have been justified as the means of facilitating non-violent, evolutionary change. Yet the principal consequence of the policy of Constructive Engagement has been to signal to the Afrikaner regime that it has a much freer hand to do what it will, both internally and within the region. What the policy has said, not only implicitly but also explicitly, is that no matter how repressive the regime is in its internal policies, no matter how much aggression it launches against neighboring states, there will be no cost imposed in terms of the South African-American relationship.

What has happened as a consequence is greater repression, more violence, and more bloodshed. In the past five years not only have we had a massive increase in police brutality in South Africa (and it was not just recently -- from 1981-1983 there was a doubling of arrests under the South African Pass Laws), but also a massive escalation of the forced removal of urban blacks to these so-called "homelands" or bantustans." Americans are suddenly seeing on the television screen only the most recent manifestation of a system that has been in place for decades now.

In addition, in the region itself, South Africa has occupied the neighboring country of Angola for most of the past five years. It has launched brutal raids, violating international law, into Mozambique, into Lesotho, and most recently into Botswana. It has attempted to overthrow the government of the Seychelles. It has sought to destabilize the government of Zimbabwe. These developments have flowed from the South African understanding -- made explicit in the policy of Constructive Engagement -- that there would be neither any penalty imposed nor any American reaction. Thus the United States is now implicated in both the extremism and the external aggression of the South African regime.

The abandonment of apartheid and a real commitment to negotiations will occur only when the white minority regime concludes that there are more costs than benefits to be derived from trying to maintain the system of apartheid. That calculation will be a product of both the internal pressures building within the country and the pressures from the international community.

Every time the United States, our international leaders, or the President engage in temporizing statements -- verbally condemning apartheid on the one hand, but allowing business as usual to flow on the other, or claiming that there is progress taking place when most reasonable people do not see progress taking place -- the Afrikaners are bolstered in their belief that they can maintain the system indefinitely without fundamental economic cost. The Afrikaners want to believe that the United States' current interest in South Africa is only a passing phenomenon. They desperately want to believe that the repression they are mounting now will eventually produce political quiescence within South Africa. When we reinforce them in the belief that they can hold on indefinitely without fundamental cost and without significant isolation, we only prolong the struggle, and delay the effort toward seeking a negotiated political solution.

Not only has Constructive Engagement encouraged greater repression and violence, but it has also alienated the black majority liberation movements within the region. We are told often that South Africa is anti-communist, and we therefore must be cautious in applying pressure for fear of losing an important ally in the struggle against communism. The reality is that South Africa itself is an open invitation to communism. As long as the system of apartheid is in place, as long as South Africa maintains its illegal occupation of the neighboring country of Namibia, there will be a struggle for liberation. If we do not want those who are struggling for their freedom to turn to the East, to the Soviets or others, then we had better well not be ambivalent or ambiguous in the way in which we identify ourselves with the process of liberation.

We simply cannot approach the rest of the Third World with credibility as long as we maintain the kind of double standard that we have applied in the South African case. Constructive Engagement not only has compromised American national values, but also has Significantly compromised American national interests.

Implications for Corporate Decision-Making

The questions that the corporate community is intimately concerned with are: What contribution can be made from within the private sector? What are the ethical and political implications of corporate decison-making in this situation?

One point that needs to be understood is that the American business community does have an enormous impact within the South African setting, not only economically but even more psychologically and politically. With the growing pressures in South Africa, with the decision by the United States to impose certain economic sanctions, and with the collapse of the rand and the extreme economic vulnerability of the South African economy, we have witnessed a sudden emergence of more pragmatic voices within the minority. Afrikans-speaking as well as English-speaking voices are now calling upon the government to abandon apartheid and to negotiate with the leadership of the African National Congress. None of that would have occurred without the various pressures and the economic, psychological, and political fragility of the regime.

The South African government likes to propagate the myth that it can go it alone; that there is nothing that we can do that would have any impact upon that society. Let me submit that the South Africans would not be investing the enormous sum of dollars that they do invest in America, in public relations and lobbying, if that were really a valid proposition. The Afrikaners care deeply about American public opinion and American political response.

That is not to say that application of economic sanctions by itself is going to bring down apartheid. It is not. It is to say, however, that we are into a process where the regime will, in the end, be responding to a combination of internal pressures and external pressures.

There may be a decision to stay in South Africa made for narrow corporate profit reasons, but please understand that such a decison does not facilitate the process of change; instead it sustains apartheid. It sustains Afrikaners in the belief that theirs is a system that is economically viable over the long haul.

When people argue that blacks would be hurt by sanctions, and that they are the people we are trying to help, let me suggest that it is the black response in South Africa that is the most eloquent rebuttal to that concern. Every day, blacks are not only exposing themselves to loss of jobs and enormous economic risks, but also to loss of life because of their participation in demonstrations and economic boycotts. Recently, the mine workers were called together by their leader who asked them to decide whether or not they wanted to support the Krugerrand import prohibition that was part of the Congressional sanctions legislation and which the President has recently imposed by executive order. These are the people most directly impacted by the Krugerrand legislation. If jobs are going to be lost, it is these people whose jobs are going to be lost. Yet, they voted unanimously to support the Krugerrand prohibition. That is not because they do not recognize there are not real short-term economic costs that might flow from the imposition of sanctions, but because they are persuaded that that is the only to avoid greater long-term costs, both economically and in terms of human dignity. It is the economic and diplomatic pressures, in combination, that represent the only alternatives we have to try to move the regime as quickly as possible to the point of negotiations with the black majority.

I do not recall a moment in our recent history when public opinion, generally, has had a more direct impact upon foreign policy. I think my proudest moment in the Congress in the past seven years occurred when we were able to negotiate a bipartisan agreement between the Senate and the House to impose economic sanctions against South Africa. Subsequently, Senator Lugar and Congressman Parren Mitchell of the Congressional Black Caucus and I were able to go in front of the cameras together in a united voice to indicate that we believe that our policy must change, that American values and American interests dictate an abandonment of the policy of Constructive Engagement. The next day the House of Representatives, on a bipartisan vote of 380 to 48, overwhelmingly approved this agreement that had been reached in conference committee.

This was an extraordinary moment and an extraordinary action, I think, not only for South Africa and the rest of the world but also for our country. But that would not have occurred if it were not for a vastly changed understanding on the part of the American public. The grass roots demonstrations in front of the South African Embassy, the divestment initiatives across this country the past several years, the media attention to Bishop Tutu's visit, the letter, signed by a number of my Republican colleagues, to the South African ambassador threatening to support sanctions if changes did not occur -- all of these wholly transformed the political climate of this issue within the Congress. Apartheid has become a national rather than a partisan question.

I believe that our traditions and our interests dictate that the United States must distance itself from the South African government and apply continuing pressure. It is my hope that the corporate community of the United States will recognize the very constructive role it can play in facilitating political change in South Africa.

SOME PERSONAL OBSERVATIONS REGARDING SOUTH AFRICA

Harry Johnson

At one point not too long ago, South Africa's State President, P. W. Botha, addressing the issue of racial reform before a Provincial Congress of the ruling National Party, claimed that his government and his party were committed in principle to the idea of a united South Africa, one citizenship, and universal franchise. He warned, however, that the universal franchise he spoke of does not mean one man, one vote, and declared that he would not turn South Africa over to a "dictatorship of the strongest black group" (which would, in his estimate, lead to greater struggle and more bloodshed).

Thus, South African rhetoric went through yet another mutation: from "separate development" to "cooperative coexistence" to "co-responsibility" to, now, "cooperative coexistence." Botha's latest comments are to me, simply another example of the deception and hypocrisy of Afrikaner rhetoric. In this case the message seems to be that racial groups should take care of matters relating to their own welfare, but national concerns are the domain of whites only.

What is most fascinating to me is Mr. Botha's fear of "dictatorship" of the strongest black group. Such dictatorship -- to use his term -- is obviously less desirable and more to be feared than the current dictatorship of the white minority. One's feelings about dictatorship, it is to be presumed, are determined by what position one occupies in the power equation. And, just as clearly, under Mr. Botha's system of logic, violence committed against one is inherently more evil than the violence that one commits. Certainly the letting of another's blood is much to be preferred over the letting of one's own blood.

More disturbing to me than any of Mr. Botha's logical misadventures, dictated as they are by his presumptive superiority, are the attitudes and behavior of many Americans doing business in South Africa, and the attitudes and behavior of many -- probably a majority -- of other Americans, including, but not limited to, the theological perambulations of -- it nearly chokes me to say the word -- the <u>Reverend</u> Jerry Falwell.

Perhaps my own blackness -- and thus my possible identification with the oppressed masses in South Africa -- colors my perception of the ethical implications of our presence in South Africa. I say "<u>our</u> presence in South Africa" because as a middle-class American citizen with a wife, two kids, two cars, two homes, and an appropriate level of indebtedness, I cannot escape, any more than you can, implications in this dilemma -- despite the fact that my wife owns no diamonds, and I eat no Granny Smith apples.

I declare to you, less in judgment than in wonderment, that I cannot, for the life of me, understand how persons reared in the Judeo-Christian tradition, weaned on the Bill of Rights, and nourished by two centuries of struggle to understand and embrace the essential dignity of all persons ... I cannot understand how such persons -- how we -- can reduce our concerns to what are, primarily, economic considerations. I cannot understand how we can sleep at night without first having struggled mightily with the demons that attend our presence in the company of the profit-merchants of apartheid.

Let me be very clear: I am no ethical virgin; my own skirts are unclean. And I do understand the obligations and implications of the "prudent man" rule. I have even danced, sometimes uncomfortably, to its demanding music. I am as greedy as most; and I want, as much as most, a maximum return on my investments. But, I submit, when I accept the generous economic returns on my South African investments, I am obliged to accept as well the dehumanizing ethical returns of apartheid -- including the thousands of black fathers forced to live apart from their families eleven months at a time, the fifty percent rate of infant mortality in many of the homelands, and the absence of a franchise and the consequent powerlessness of seventy-three percent of the South African populace.

For me to take comfort in the fact that the black employees of American companies in South Africa are treated well -- even equally -- without crying out in rage against the indecency, the inhumanity and yes, the obscenity of apartheid, is to suggest that my middle-class comfort in Brookline excuses me from any involvement in or concern for my black colleagues -- my brothers and sisters, if you will -- in Roxbury and Harlem and Liberty City.

I could make more money if I were a pimp in the Combat zone, but I do not consort with harlots. I could finance my daughter's college education more easily if I were a drug pusher, but I do not consort with hoodlums. I could get a better return on my investments if I were to do business in South Africa, but I do not consort with racist oppressors.

It is my profound hope that the call for divestment meets with overwhelming success.

MULTINATIONAL ENTERPRISES, SANCTIONS, AND SOUTH AFRICA: A HOST COUNTRY PERSPECTIVE

D. G. M. Fourie

With a few exceptions, most multinationals are located in First World countries and exist and do business as a part of a First World economic and financial order. When dealing with or in the Third World, multinationals assume a dimension that is unrelated to their relative standing within their own countries or areas.

This can be illustrated in the following way:

- Economically, South Africa is a giant in Africa, accounting for one-fifth of Africa's Gross National Product, and for 86.6 percent of the Gross National Product for the Southern Africa region (Angola Botswana, Lesotho, Malawi, Mozambique, Namibia, South Africa, Swaziland, Zambia, Zimbabwe), according to figures published in the 1985 World Bank Atlas.

- Relative to the world as a whole, South Africa's Gross National Product is surpassed by only 19 countries in the non-Communist world (1985 World Bank Atlas) and is higher than the Gross National Products of countries such a Norway, Nigeria, Denmark, and Austria.

These statistics have a totally different relevance however, when compared as follows:

- South Africa's national budget for 1985/1986, ($12.4 billion) was lower than New York City's budget for the same period ($20 billion).

- South Africa's Gross National Product ($60.4 billion in 1984) was lower than the total sales and revenue ("turnover") in 1984 of a large Multinational such as General Motors ($83.8 billion).

While the above-mentioned statistics are perhaps distorted to a degree by exchange rate imbalances which have resulted from the inordinate strength of the United States dollar, it is a fact that the total sales and revenues ("turnover") of a number of large multinationals exceed the Gross National Product of a significant proportion of the membership of the United Nations.

It is, therefore, clear that a multinational has economic

power which it could potentially wield with reference to a given host country, but practice has shown that it cannot always apply significant formal political pressure on the national level, except where a parent country may be prepared to intervene on its behalf.

Most host countries, moreover, normally view a multinational presence as providing the following benefits:

- a source of employment for its nationals;

- a purchaser of goods and services;

- a source of foreign exchange in the case where products or services are generated internally and sold outside of the host country; and

- a source of training and technological transfer.

Such countries also expect the multinational to respect the laws and customs of that state, and not to interfere in the internal political process, whatever that may be.

I think it is fair to say that this, on average, has been the basis of the relationship between multinationals and their host countries in the past, except where one of two factors has threatened such a relationship:

1) The multinational has openly exploited the host country or its nationals; and/or

2) The multinational has decided to take, or been coerced into, actions which have conflicted with the aims/policies of the host country.

There is much sensitivity among countries with a colonial past with regard to exploitation, since the colonial experience has so often been one of a parent country obtaining raw materials and products from the colony at the lowest price possible, refining and producing a finished product in the parent country in order to finally re-export the finished product to, among others, the original colony. It is also the case that currently a great deal of the "North-South Dialogue" between certain European and Third World countries is concerned with similar complaints by the Third World, particularly with regard to minerals.

Political interference in the internal affairs of a host country by multinationals is also an issue with the Third World, and the United Nations is currently considering a Code of Conduct for Transnational Corporations which would formally prohibit such interference.

Corporate responsibility programs have emerged for sound reasons, including abuses such as child-labor, inhuman conditions, and naked exploitation. Quite correctly too, the trend towards a corporate social conscience has been heavily influenced, if not led, by the churches.

There is nothing wrong per se with the concept of a socially responsible corporation, and I do not think that many Third World host countries would quarrel with the concept of corporate-sponsored betterment and other socially beneficial programs. Indeed, most could probably happily agree to the directing of a portion of corporate profits which may have occurred from investment in their countries toward programs which directly benefit the peoples who shared in creating those profits.

The issue of corporate ethics and social responsibility has, however, been driven into the arena of foreign policy, primarily over the question of South Africa, and it is here that I contend that double standards are rapidly resulting in a departure from the principles of justice and fairness in favour of the causes of ideologues and vested interests.

In the mid-1970's, a series of labour codes and principles were applied to multinationals operating South Africa. Rev. Leon Sullivan of Philadelphia has won increasing acceptance among United States corporations for the "Sullivan Principles," which consist of a six-point plan toward achieving the integration of company facilities, upward corporate mobility for black workers, and training and other social programs. The European Economic Community instituted an EEC Code of Conduct, and the South African Urban Foundation instituted its own Code of Conduct for South African Corporations. The effects over the ten years that followed have been dramatic:

- United State Companies have invested millions of dollars in social betterment programs, particularly in training, housing schemes, and schooling.

- The integration duly effected by the United States - owned subsidiaries has had a marked influence on the revision of South African labour legislation, the emergence of Trade Unions for blacks, the abolition of the reservation of categories of employment for certain race-groups and, in particular, the upward mobility of black workers within South African Corporations, to the extent that over 10,000 blacks now work in supervisory positions over whites in South Africa.

- The most inportant effect, in my opinion, has been the rapid emergence of a black middle class in South Africa. Since 1980, the purchasing power or "market-share" of South Africa's black population has exceeded that of the whites. This "economic clout" has not only shifted marketing strategies in the direction of the black community in terms of advertising, the selection of product ranges for production, etc., but also and most importantly led to a growing perception among the whites that it is necessary to re-think South Africa's political structure to accommodate the growing economic interdependence of the various groups and the political "clout" that axiomatically follows on economic "clout."

The process of Government reform which began tentatively in the mid-1970's accelerated markedly in the 1980's and particularly subsequent to the referendum of November 1983 in which two-thirds of South Africa's white population gave approval for a new (interim) constitution and mandated a process whereby political accommodations would be sought with regard to the black population on the basis of negotiation.

Corporations kept pace with this process. The United States corporations formed themselves into a lobby under the umbrella of the American Chamber of Commerce in South Africa and agreed to the adoption of no less than four amplifications of the Sullivan Principles. It is indeed the case that the South African business sector has mobilized in favor of change and is also exerting strong pressure and influence on the situation in general and attitudes in particular.

As matters stand now, the South African Government is committed to reform, but is being severely hampered in its endeavors by violent interplay between various ideologies and vested interests, particularly among the black community.

In the past, the rhetoric against South Africa has always included reference to the legislative "pillars of apartheid" -- the anti-miscegenation laws ("Immorality Act"), the Mixed Marriages Act, legislation on job-reservation, the "Pass-Laws," the Group Areas Act, segregation of facilities, restaurants, and hotels.

Currently the following laws have been systematically

repealed or are being substantially changed:

- the "immorality" or anti-miscegenation law (repealed);
- the law prohibiting mixed marriages (repealed);
- the political non-interference act which prohibited mixed-race political parties (repealed);
- the laws reserving specific employment for specific race groups (repealed);
- laws on land ownership in areas outside of the black homelands (revised to permit ownership and acknowledge permanence);
- laws on segregation of hotel and restaurant facilities (to be repealed - just announced);
- influx control or "Pass Laws" (to be revised drastically);
- provisions permitting immigration by whites only (repealed); and
- laws enforcing citizenship of homelands with resultant loss of South African Citizenship (to be repealed/amended to allow for common and universal South African Citizenship).

In the last-mentioned instance, it should be noted that the South African Government has also revised its policy of creating independent black homelands for the various groups in favor of the creation of a negotiated system which will simultaneously provide for minority interests while nevertheless permitting political participation at all levels by all groups.

Internationally, the South African Government is being subjected to severe pressure, particularly in the form of actual and threatened additional sanctions, which include pressure on United States corporations to withdraw or disinvest from South Africa, ostensibly on the grounds of moral and ethical considerations. There are a number of bitter ironies in this current severe pressure:

- The pressure is at its highest ever at the time when South Africa is reforming its internal policies voluntarily, systematically, and irrevocably.

- The sanctions and threatened additional sanctions being applied against South Africa will most directly affect the very forces which have created the South African reform process, viz., the black middle-class, who risk losing their employment, influence, and relevance; the transnational corporations whose influence on the reform-process has not been insignificant in the past and could be vital in the future; and the moderates and reformists within the South African political spectrum who can show no positive benefits from a policy of peaceful change based on negotiation, consultation, and a systematic correction of past and current wrongs.

There is another factor which should also be borne in mind, viz., regional interdependence in Southern Africa. Despite the formation of the Southern Africa Development Coordinating Council (SADCC) by South Africa's neighboring states, these states remain highly dependent on the South African economy. South Africa accounts for 86 percent of the region's Gross National Product, functions as a major conduit for the region's imports and exports, and employs large numbers of workers from neighboring states. Indeed, repatriated earnings of laborers from Lesotho accounted for 50 percent of that country's Gross National product in 1983. South Africa also supplies electricity to neighboring states, permits international telecommunications traffic from neighboring states to be routed through its facilities, and is a substantial creditor for Sub-Saharan Africa. A common customs union and Rand monetary area-arrangement functions with regard to South Africa's immediate neighbors, and South Africa also functions as a major regional exporter of food and primary products. Little consideration has been given to the potential repercussions for South Africa's neighboring states in the event that substantial damage should be inflicted on the South African economy by means of the kind of pressures and sanctions discussed with you today.

It was noted earlier that the notion of corporate ethics and responsibility is based on Christian principles and accepted social norms of justice and fairness. Implicit in the Christian faith are not only distancing, withdrawal, and condemnation, but also forgiveness, understanding, assistance, example, and patience. Moreover, United States corporations <u>have</u> highlighted and combatted inequities in South Africa and <u>have</u> played, and are still playing, an important and responsible role in moving the country in the direction of an acceptable and just dispensation.

It should be noted that there are finite limits to the ability of transnationals to positively influence a given situation in a foreign country:

- A "bottom line" situation can be reached where either the transnational corporation gives up due to the "hassle factor" or loss of reasonable profit, or where the economic benefit to the host country of the presence of the transnational corporation is outweighed by perceived national interest.

- As illustrated by the example of Iran where the excesses of the Shah were replaced by the inhuman rule of the Ayatollah Khomeini, even well-intentioned pressure can lead to undesirable results if this pressure is not applied wisely and fairly.

- The use of "corporate ethics" and transnational corporations as a vehicle of attack on governments with policies which are not acceptable to Americans could be counter productive in the long-term in a number of the following ways:
    -The Code of Conduct for Transnationals currently under discussion at the United Nations already attempts to prohibit such action (except in the case of South Africa).

    -Such actions can eventually be seen as a form of economic imperialism which seeks to impose United States' (and Western) norms and values on other societies and, thereby, lose all effectiveness in the long-term, as well as harming United States international trade in the process.

    -The precedent set in the case of South Africa can arguably be utilized by other similar vested interests to enforce similar action against countries such as the Philippines and El Salvador (human rights), Israel (occupation of the West Bank and the Palestinian issue), Britian (Northern Ireland and race-riots), and France (nuclear testing in the Pacific and the New Caledonia issue).

    -Such an approach is also flawed in the sense that it is not universally and fairly applied. South Africa may indeed have many faults in the field of human rights, but that country is at least attempting to address its problems, which is more than is being done by a host of other countries where conditions are markedly worse and where similar sanctions are not even being contemplated.

It can therefore be contended that corporate ethics, as defined in American terms, can be a useful instrument of American foreign policy only if they are applied in host countries in a subtle and educational manner. The current attempt to coerce transnationals into a crusading posture can be immensely counter productive with regard to long-term United States international trading interests and does not allow sufficiently for the powerful influence which such corporations can have in a given foreign market-place by being seen and heard giving support to the principles of freedom, equality, and opportunity which are so close to the American heart.

In the case of South Africa, transnationals can continue to play a vital role through providing employment and equal opportunity and by utilizing their influence to foster a climate conducive to negotiations between the various groups in order to achieve a solution which is acceptable to all. On the other hand, I find it difficult to see how a policy of economic destruction could be considered ethical or moral when, apart from also harming those it professes to help, such a policy can only result in increased frustration and unhappiness generally and thereby decrease the chances of a peaceful and negotiated transition to a more equitable dispensation. Violent options have been attempted before in South Africa's history, most notably by the British in wars against the Xhosas, the Zulus, and finally the Boer-republics. Not once has this option provided a lasting long-term solution, and I doubt that it ever will, given the unique composition and approach to life of South Africa's peoples.

I put it to you that only negotiation has been effective in the past, and that only negotiation will be effective in the long-term future. And my government is on record as stating that it is willing to negotiate on any topic, with any South African group, the only pre-condition being the renunciation of violence as a means of effecting change. Surely it would be morally and ethically responsible to actively strive for and encourage the peaceful option.

THE AMERICAN MULTINATIONAL ENTERPRISE AND SOUTH AFRICA: MAINTAINING THE PROPER BALANCE

David M. Ludington

Introduction

The world market is of strategic interest to most large American corporations. According to a recent study, 3,540 United States companies had over $200 billion invested in 24,666 foreign operations. This compares to 2,800 companies who had $25 billion invested abroad in the mid-1950s.[1] Strategic planning managers recognize that major United States companies cannot prosper into the 1990s unless their organizations develop and maintain a multinational orientation. According to international marketing expert Dr. Philip Cateora, this current interest in multinational marketing can be explained in terms of changing competitive structures combined with shifts in demand characteristics in markets throughout the world. Many United States firms have competition from domestic and foreign firms. They are now sharing the vast domestic market with other countries and must expand to foreign markets if they wish to grow or, in some cases, survive.[2] In addition, the returns on investment may well be greater from foreign operations than from domestic ones. The returns from these operations may also be keeping the domestic operations viable by providing needed capital and cash flow.

However, it is not always easy to enter and prosper in the world market. A multinational organization doing business in a country foreign to its base of operations must adapt to the culture and political climate of the host country. The firm's ability to adapt its marketing policies to the host country's culture and economic structure will probably determine the firm's ability to meet its sales and profit goals in that country.

Of even greater importance is that a foreign enterprise can only do business in a foreign country with the permission of the host government. The multinational, if it is to remain, must also be sensitive to the political concerns of that host country. If this host country has a political structure, policies, or practices that run counter to those of the various political interest groups in the home country, then the multinational can be caught between the conflicting philosophies of both nations. It must respect or at least obey the laws of the host country and be sensitive to its culture or risk being asked to leave. It also risks official and unofficial pressures from the home country if the domestic or foreign policies of the host country differ from those of the wishes of any one of a variety of political interest groups in the United States. The pressure may come from the United States federal government, but can also originate from state, county, or local governments. In addition, well organized political interest groups and the media are constantly attempting to regulate our multinational enterprises and to have an influence over their actions in other countries. Although this situation is a constant dilemma for multinationals in many settings, it is best illustrated by the current situation in South Africa where United States multinationals, although following the guidelines of the federal government, are increasingly being called to task by the media and a variety of leftist political interest groups.

Political Considerations in Assessing World Markets

According to Philip Cateora: "National environments differ widely ... of primary importance is that a government reacts to its environment by initiating and pursuing policies deemed necessary to solve the problems created by its particular environment ... the government is an integral part of every foreign business activity -- a silent partner who has nearly total control."[3] This 'silent partnership' also applies to the policies and practices of the home government. Our government, in the interests of expanding trade, building the economy, and promoting national aims, keeps a close control over the operations of American multinational enterprises. In addition, state and local governments, for economic and political reasons, are becoming involved in these operations. On the political front, five states and at least 20 cities and countries have passed anti-apartheid disinvestment legislation. In addition, some sort of similar legislation is pending in 20 other states and in at least nine major cities and countries.[4] This intervention into the overseas operations of United States multinationals by non-federal governmental units and political interest groups, especially when they are in conflict with the official positions of the United States State Department, clearly presents a political-ethical dilemma for the United States multinational.

In developing his model for the analysis of the political environment, Subhash C. Jain suggests that the sources of political problems can be divided into two main areas: political sovereignty and political conflict (turmoil, internal war, conspiracy). Political conflict can have direct effects (violence, strikes, etc.) and indirect effects (changes in economic policies). Jain also suggests that these problems and effects can have two bases of motivation: a motivation by real need to straighten things out and a motivation by the desire to divert public attention from other problems.[5]

Jain's suggestion that an analysis of the motivations of the people causing political risk is certainly germane to this discussion. In a pluralistic nation such as ours, multinationals must weigh the positions of the United States government as well as those of the various political interest groups. This can produce some very conflicting situations. For example, American multinationals have operations in many countries whose governments practice policies that are counter to those of the United States. They are encouraged to develop trade and multinational relationships with Russia and China, countries whose past and present human rights policies are certainly repugnant to most in the United States. Our multinationals trade with Poland where human rights are certainly in question. We provide food to Ethiopia although its tyrannical Marxist regime continues to starve thousands of political opponents and forces misery and death on rural people whom it is forcibly relocating despite horrible famine.[6] Our multinationals rarely receive any public criticism for doing business in these countries. However, for whatever reason the so-called progressives in our country have heated up the question of human rights in South Africa. The timing of this move is somewhat suspect in several quarters coming as it did right after the 1984 election of President Reagan. One author suggests that, after all, South Africa has been repugnant for years. These protests might have been raised in the 1960s or the 1970s. In fact, human rights in South Africa are probably better today than in previous years -- and they are certainly better than many other, including African nations where there exist brutal regimes more in need of the progressives' attention. Countries such as Iran, Vietnam, Angola, Mozambique, Zimbabwe, Cambodia, Laos, and Nicaragua have far more corruption and tyranny than South Africa -- and these are all countries who have 'benefitted' from changes in government brought on, in part, by the previous actions of many of these same progressives and their political interest groups.[7]

It is also quite possible that given the timing, coming as it does right after a major setback for these groups with the recent election of President Reagan, that the motivation may be more an effort by the progressives and their media to divert attention from their problems and to focus on an issue that will help them unite their followers for the 1986 elections. At least one black South African leader, Gatsha Buthelezi, the hereditary leader of the Zulu people, has suggested that "...apartheid had become an American football for party gain."[8] However, while it is important to recognize the motivations that might be at play in such a situation, it is also important, as Jain suggests, to recognize that these motivations present a variable that must be treated as a problem to be overcome rather than as a rationalization for not doing anything.

The Political-Ethical Dilemma in South Africa

There is little doubt that the continent of Africa is one of the most backward in the world. In economic and political terms it is on the verge of disaster. According to a recent Time Magazine article:

> It is increasingly evident that much of Africa is on the verge of economic and political collapse. Instability and repression are commonplace. The horror of famine grips Ethiopia and the Sahel. At least two-thirds of the continent's population live in extreme poverty, and these ranks are growing steadily. All the while, governments squander huge sums on pomp and prestige. Clearly, the rewards of independence seem to be enjoyed only by small, privileged groups at the top, while virtually everyone else suffers from extreme neglect. The World Bank reports that the continent's per capita income in 1983 was about 4 percent below the 1970 level. Gross domestic product has fallen every year since 1980 ... And markets for key revenue earners ... have plummeted, while more than 90 percent of the population exists on subsistence farming.[9]

This same article concludes that "For the future, unhappily, mere survival will be the biggest problem for many in Africa, and no amount of Western assistance may be enough."[10] One of the few positive exceptions to the general economic situation in Africa exists in South Africa -- even given their recent problems with inflation and a recession. Much of this difference is due to the involvement of multinationals -- especially American multinationals. Blacks and whites in South Africa enjoy some of the highest standards of living in the continent. There are no reports of people starving as is the norm in many African countries, and the country is experiencing great inflows of people rather than the outflows that are typical in many African countries.

Given South Africa's relative high standard of living, the political-ethical dilemma is pronounced for American multinationals. In 1983, United States investments accounted for approximately 23 percent ($10 billion) of all foreign investment in South Africa.[11] The Unites States is also South Africa's largest trading partner, supplying nearly 20 percent of its imports.[12] Some of the best known and most respected companies from the United States do business in South Africa and help contribute to its higher standard of living.[13] However, even companies who are following the United States government guidelines for doing business in South Africa and are subscribing to the Sullivan Principles[14] are being subjected to extreme pressure by the progressives and their disinvestment movement. Since the election of President Reagan in 1984, hardly a day has gone by without some media mention of the anti-apartheid movement. Because of this, companies must now develop political strategies that address the interests of the South African government and its people, those of the United States government(s), and those of United States leftist political interest groups who are not in agreement with official United States policy. The ethical dilemma is that there is no clear consensus among these various groups as to what actions are appropriate for the United States multinational. Thus, corporations need to develop a strategic framework to make these types of decisions without the common agreement among the other actors as to the proper courses of action.

The Clear Issue

The clear issue for multinationals in South Africa is apartheid. It is highly unlikely that any American multinational supports this form of government. There is every indication that these companies find this form of government to be as repugnant as those in Iran, Angola, Ethiopia, Nicaragua, Russia, and the other more repressive countries. What is less clear is how these companies should act in this situation. The opinions seem to be divided into two types of possible actions: American companies should divest their interests in South Africa and pull out to put economic pressure on the government and/or bring the current government down; or companies should stay in South Africa and do what they can to bring about change in the government.

According to The Economist, there are two kinds of commercial pressure being brought to bear on multinationals doing business in South Africa: disinvestment and the Sullivan Principles. It suggests that disinvestment is the stick while Sullivan is the carrot.[15] If American multinationals decide to keep their investments in South Africa, they will have to develop a position and strategy in these two areas.

Disinvestment

Net foreign investment in South African private companies has fallen since 1976; however, there is a net surplus of long-term capital inflows that is caused by increased borrowing by the govenment and nationalized industries. Some South African economists estimate that this real drop in foreign investment to private South African companies has accounted for a drop of at least one percent in the real gross domestic product growth during a year. However, this leaves South African black leaders, especially labor leaders, in a difficult position. While they want to end apartheid, they also want to bring down the unemployment rate of blacks, and with a population increasing at 2.6 percent a year, any drops in foreign investment will surely bring further increases in unemployment -- especially in the black sector.[16]

Mr. Prioshaw Camay, the Indian Head of the council of unions of South Africa, Bishop Tutu, and the American disinvestment movement all feel that 'selective' disinvestment is a positive way to put pressure on the government authorities. Anthony Lewis argues that, while American companies do a relatively small percentage of their worldwide business in South Africa, their mere presence gives the South African government an important symbol of legitimacy. It is his feeling that if American companies were to leave, they would be making a powerful statement against institutionalized racism and the force of this statement far overcomes any negative employment outcomes for the South African blacks.[17] It would seem that these people really do not want total disinvestment because of its negative impact on the black population; however, they do strongly feel that the threat of disinvestment and actual 'selective' disinvestment will go a long way in changing the policies of the South African government.

Not all agree. William Raspberry has written that to "...expect the white Africans to relinquish their awesome power to the black aborigines is no more realistic than expecting white Americans to hand control of this country over to the American Indians." However, he further states that "...rosy-eyed optimists are convinced that the white majority government can, by the prospect of some combination of economic pressure and international embarrassment, be nudged in the direction of racial justice.[18]

A similar view is that of Gatsha Buthelezi, leader of the Zulu people, who has "... concluded that disinvestment would be disastrous to millions of blacks and said: 'For Americans to hurt the growth rate of the South African economy through boycotts, sanctions, and disinvestment would demonstrate a callous disregard for ordinary people...'"[19]

A corporate view was expressed recently by John F. Akers, President and Chief Executive of International Business Machines:

Corporations have a choice. We can view South Africa as a tragedy, wash our hands of it and wait for the explosion that may or may not come, regardless of what we do. Or we can do business in a way that provides a model for a society in which black, white, Asian, and Colored might someday enjoy peace and freedom.[20]

There is also the view that while the white South Africa values American investment and American goodwill, they value more the political and economic control of a land they have ruled for almost as long as whites have ruled America. In addition, if black Africans really wanted disinvestment, they themselves could quickly effect it by simply walking off their jobs.[21] It has also been suggested that disinvestment by American firms of production facilities would probably have little positive effect since white South Africans would step in and take them over and probably return these operations to previous employment practices.

Secretary of State George Shultz has clearly stated the official United States position on disinvestment. He states that:

... apartheid must go, but the Reagan administration continues to oppose any economic sanctions against South Africa ... these measures, even the least punitive, would have the counterproductive effect of reducing United States influence on South African policy and of not helping the economically hard-hit blacks there. The only course consistent with American values is to engage ourselves as a force for constructive, peaceful change.[22]

However, there is increasing pressure, especially from our college radical groups and the media, for American firms to divest their interests in South Africa and if they do not, then institutions such as colleges and universities should divest their holdings in these companies as economic punishment. In addition, many state and local governments are now calling for a boycott of companies that do business in South Africa. This pressure from state and local governments, the political interest groups, and the media compound the political-ethical dilemma of disinvestment. In many ways, our multinationals are in a no-win situation. If they divest to appease the political interest groups, they risk losing their investments and possible profits and their influence with the Reagan Administration and the South African government. However, if they follow the official position of our federal government and the financial interests of their stockholders, they risk continued bad media coverage and economic boycotts.

Sullivan Principles

The Sullivan Principles, named after the United States Baptist minister and civil rights activist Leon Sullivan, were first drafted in 1977, and call for non-discriminatory practices by United States firms in South Africa. They require members to voluntarily:

1. desegregate eating, comfort, and work facilities;

2. provide equal pay for all employees doing equal or comparable work for the same period of time;

3. develop and initiate training programs that will prepare, in substantial numbers, blacks and other non-whites for supervisory, administrative, clerical, and technical jobs;

4. increase the number of blacks and non-whites in management and supervisory positions; and

5. improve the quality of employees' lives outside the work environment in such areas as housing, transportation, schooling, recreation, and health facilities.

Corporations in the Sullivan group must pay fees, determined by their annual revenues, to jointly monitor and rate company performance in meeting the principles' goals. At the end of April 1985, about 140 of the 284 United States companies with direct investments in South Africa had adopted these rules.[23] However, while these firms represent only 49 percent of the American firms doing business in South Africa, they represent 80 percent of the total American investments.[24]

Supporters of these principles claim they have made a real difference in bringing United States standards to South Africa and in improving the life of the black South African. Sullivan code participants are said to have put more than $100 million into education and community development. They also claim that over 20,000 blacks have received advanced training and good paying jobs, in unrestricted, integrated, work places.[25]

However, there are critics. Some claim that while the rules have helped raise the standards and quality of living for many black Africans, they tend to be too bureaucratic and rigid in their enforcement. One such critic cites the John Deere case in which the company wanted to spend money on retraining black workers during a slack period, but could only acquire "points" under the plan by laying them off and spending the money on workers' housing instead.[26] Other critics claim that companies that substantially comply with the principles have only about 22,000 black employees in a nation of 22 million blacks, and this modest improvement does not compare to the economic and image impact these companies could make if they divested themselves of South African operations.[27]

The Political-Economic Decision Framework

There is little doubt that American multinationals, long a favorite target of the leftist political interest groups, will be put into similar situations in other non-communist countries if the disinvestment movement is successful in South Africa. It is important for multinationals to consider a number of important issues in building a strategic decision model for action in South Africa and other areas. These decisions must take into consideration the following: stockholders' rights; whether the decision is ethical as defined by the current standards and norms; who determines American foreign policy; long-term and short-term risk assessment; the political role of the multinational in the host and home country; sensitivity to the host country culture and environment; and the extent to which the multinational is willing to treat the macroenvironment as a controllable or uncontrollable variable.

First and foremost, a multinational enterprise owes a fiduciary responsibility to its stockholders. Its main mission should be the long-term growth of the firm as measured by the value of a share of stock. In addition, there is a need for corporations to balance the desire for short-term profits at expense of the long-term growth of the firm. Short-term profits that come at the expense of longer-term gains are not prudent. Second, in today's environment, multinational firms must operate in a manner consistent with the established norms for that industry and society. Third, under our republic form of government, it is the duty of our elected federal officials to establish and promote American foreign policy. Fourth, multinational enterprises must be constantly engaging in political and economic risk assessment. Like the balance between short-term and long-term profits, they must weigh the effects of short-term risk against long-term risk. It may well be that the short-term, expedient solution may set precedent that causes longer-term, more dangerous risks to the enterprise or to multinationals in general. Fifth, American multinationals operate in host countries at the pleasure of established governments, and they should be sensitive to the political concerns of that government. At the same time, they must be ever mindful that the home government is a silent managing partner in any foreign operation. Sixth, the multinational must decide if the macro-environment is an uncontrollable variable to be considered in decision-making or a controllable variable to be manipulated. American multinationals have an obligation to manipulate the domestic policies of their home and host environments, within the legal frameworks of that country, to meet their ethical obligations to themselves, their stockholders, and to the people of the home and host countries.

An analysis of any political-ethical dilemma by an American multinational, using these criteria as a strategic decision framework, should produce a rational, ethical, and sound financial decision. The situation in South Africa presents an example for the application of this strategic framework. These criteria will be applied to the two kinds of economic pressure now being applied to American multinational enterprises who have operations in that country: disinvestment and the Sullivan Principles.

Balancing the Political-Ethical Issues -- Disinvestment

There is always a question in international marketing of the role a multinational should play in the host country system: should they become a part of the system, or should they attempt to change the system? This is the issue of disinvestment in South Africa. Is it better to be a part of the system and attempt to change the system, or is it better to walk away to either change the system or bring it down? There is a whole body of political science and public interest group literature that suggests that the best way to create change in a system is to join the system and work for change from within. Following this line of reasoning, it would seem that disinvestment is not the proper course. Multinationals have other considerations that need to be addressed, such as stockholder interests, and this is why the application of a more broad-based decision framework is helpful. If we apply the political-economic decision model, we would reject the idea of disinvestment in South Africa. Although there may be exceptions, an analysis would provide the following conclusions.

It is hard to imagine that a disinvestment based on the emotions of the leftist political interest groups would be in the best interests of the stockholders. Stockholders have the right to expect their management to set the long-term growth of the firm as their main objective. A decision to divest should be based on this criteria and not on the demands of political interest groups. Multinationals should also respect the Constitution of the United States and allow the federal government, through the elected president and his administration, to set

United States foreign policy. If they do, they can then work on change from a credible stance from within the system. This also suggests that it is a company's right and responsibility to treat the macroenvironment of the home or host country as a controllable variable. Disinvestment robs them of this right and responsibility. It would not speak well of our multinationals if they just walk away from this problem. It would certainly help to remove them from a position of influence in the host country. If they stay, they may have the 'ear' of the home country's current president and his administration. If they stay, they remain an important part of the host country, but if they leave, they forfeit that right. There is also a strong argument that the leftist political groups, based on their past actions, do not have the best interests of American multinational enterprises in mind and if they are successful in getting the United States and its multinationals to pull out, they will move on to the next target country. American multinationals must be proactive in defending their rights to do business in the world market. The very existence of the American economic system is at stake. If they were to stop doing business in every country that offends some United States political interest group, there would not be any market left -- including the domestic market.

Balancing the Political-Ethical Issues -- Sullivan Principles

So far the political boycotts, the calls for disinvestment, and other blackmail attempts have not caused one major firm to pull out of South Africa. However, if the media continues to heat up the disinvestment issue, it is clear that there will be greater pressure put on American multinational firms to give up their investments. It is for this reason that firms need to develop and articulate their stands on doing business in South Africa.

There is little doubt of the view of American multinationals on the ethical issue involved: apartheid. American multinational companies must refute the philosophy of this type of government at home. The adoption of the Sullivan Principles is a must. This will convey to the people in the United States and in South Africa that the companies are using the same working standards as they do at home. It is probably best for them to sign with the Sullivan people since this will give them a 'legitimizing' body to substantiate their actions.

There is nothing inherent in the application of the Sullivan Principles that should harm the stockholders' financial position. Their application helps support the United States position of anti-apartheid while providing the multinational the opportunity to provide an example in South Africa. They provide the framework for constructive action within the system and not a means to bring the system down. Much of Africa is now suffering heavily for its rush to independence and the revolution mentality. We do not need another Marxist state where millions of people are starving, as in the case in Ethiopia. The Sullivan principles also provide the American multinational with the means to treat the macroenvironment as a controllable variable while being responsive to the desires of the current host government.

To better position themselves in this environment, multinationals should make it a regular practice to inform the media of their positions as IBM's John Akers has done. It is clear, given the nature of our media and their reliance on their appointed black leader, Bishop Tutu, as spokesperson of all black Africans, that American multinationals will probably need to purchase media time and space to explain the corporate position. These advertisements should give the black leaders, who disagree with Bishop Tutu's views' of disinvestment, a voice to the American public. There are many black African leaders who hold views different from Tutu's, and they are not being regularly heard in the United States. Two such people are Zulu Chief Gatsha Buthelizi and Lucy Nvubelo, general secretary of the National Union of Clothing Workers, South Africa's largest union, who has said: "Remaining in South Africa and increasing your (United States) stake will be a boost to the evolutionary process which is now taking place."[28] This message could also be presented to the stockholders via a direct mail strategy.

Conclusions

The long-term role of the American multinational in the host country, South Africa, becomes less clear. Just what is the role of American multinationals in the political affairs of their host countries? What should it be? If they should, as some claim, take a proactive role in changing or bringing down governments that are not in favor with certain official or unofficial elements in the United States, might this not lead to some very dangerous precedents? If the multinationals impose economic sanctions on South Africa and withdraw their investments for human rights violations, should this apply to all other countries who practice some form of human rights violation that is vile to at least one of the variety of official and unofficial elements in our society? Might this application exclude our trading or setting up multinational operations in the vast majority of the world's countries? Even our neighbor Mexico and our ally Israel (for their treatment of the Palestineans) would probably have to be dropped if the criteria used to judge South Africa were applied to them.

And what of the applications of these same principles at home? Many of the very people and groups that insist that American multinationals take an active role in bringing down the host South African government are also strongly trying to limit corporations PAC contributions in an effort to control corporate influence with the United States elected officials. Is there not a dilemma of a political-ethical nature here for multinational enterprises? This then, is the balancing act. Our multinationals are being asked to take actions in a foreign country by people who reject those same types of actions at home. It suggests that American multinationals need to develop a unified and vocal approach to the increasing pressure being placed on them in the United States.

The American multinational needs to develop a strategic framework to guide it in dealing with situations, such as South Africa, if it is going to be able to balance the political-economic-ethical dilemmas that are bound to surface in a pluralistic nation such as ours. This situation in South Africa, while not unique, makes the balancing required by American multinationals more complex since most are following the general directions provided by our State Department for doing business in South Africa. Yet, they are still subjected to pickets, harassment, and economic boycott -- and not just by the usual leftist activists, but even by some state and local governments who have given in to the pressures of these political groups. It would probably be myopic to think that there is any action plan that American multinationals could take in this, or similar situations, that will leave them free from criticism. However, this does not mean that American multinationals should remain passive either. It is certain that multinationals can expect a greater use of these economic tactics in other countries should they be successful in South Africa. The development and implementation of a strategic framework and careful application of the sound principles of public relations and lobbying will assist them in meeting these dilemmas.

NOTES

1. "Companies Profit from Investments They Made Years Ago in Plants Overseas," The Wall Street Journal, March 11, 1981, p. 48.

2. Philip R. Cateroa, International Marketing, (Homewood, Illinois: Richard D. Irwin, Inc., 1983), p. 5.

3. Ibid., p. 151.

4. "Anti-Apartheid Movement Gains People and Sophistication," The San Francisco Examiner, April 17, 1985, p. 1.

5. Subhash C. Jain, *International Marketing Management*, (Boston: Kent Publishing Company, 1984), p. 220.

6. "South Africa," R. Emmett Tyrrell, The San Francisco Examiner, April 8, 1985.

7. Ibid.

8. "South Africa," Dan Walters, San Francisco Examiner, March 8, 1985.

9. "Africa: From Heady Hopes to a Dance of Death," Time, March 11, 1985, p. 16.

10. Ibid.

11. "Black Marks," The Economist, March 23, 1985, Vol 294, No. 7386, p. 81.

12. "U.S. Business and Apartheid," Anthony Lewis, Contra Costa Times, April 4, 1985.

13. General Motors, Caperpiller Tractor, Dow Chemical, Du Pont, Upjohn, Johnson & Johnson, General Electric, IBM, Hewlett-Packard, Xerox, Exxon, 3M, Coca-Cola, Revlon, Eastman Kodak, Bank of America, Citicorp, and First Interstate, to name just a few.

14. The Sullivan principles, named after the U.S. Baptist minister and civil rights activist, were first drafted in 1977, and call for non-discriminatory practices by U.S. firms in South Africa. Firms must pay Sullivan and his organization fees determined by annual revenues to jointly monitor and rate company performance in meeting the principles' goals.

15. "Black Marks," The Economist, March 23, 1985, Vol. 294, No. 7386, p. 81.

16. Ibid.

17. "U.S. Business and Apartheid," Anthony Lewis, The Contra Costa Times, April 4, 1985.

18. "Can't Get There," William Raspberry, <u>San Francisco Examiner</u>, March 29, 1985, p. B2.

19. "South Africa," Dan Walters, <u>San Francisco Examiner</u>, March 8, 1985.

20. "To Effect Change, IBM Must Stay in South Africa -- Not Cut and Run," <u>The Tribune</u>, March 29, 1985.

21. "Can't Get There," William Rasberry, <u>San Francisco Examiner</u>, March 29, 1985 p. B2.

22. "Shultz Decries Anti-South Africa Bills," <u>San Francisco Chronicle</u>, April 17, 1985, p. 13.

23. "More U.S. Firms Sign Anti-Apartheid Code," <u>San Francisco Examiner</u>, April 21, 1985. p. A12.

24. "Black Marks," <u>The Economist</u>, March 23, 1985, Vol 294, No. 7386, p. 82.

25. "More U.S. Firms Sign Anti-Apartheid Code," <u>San Francisco Examiner</u>, April 21, 1985, p. A12.

26. "Blunder by Conservatives," William Rusher, <u>Contra Costa Times</u>, March 14, 1985.

27. "U.S. Business and Apartheid," Anthony Lewis, <u>Contra Costa Times</u>, April 4, 1985.

28. "Disinvestment Would Hurt Black South Africans," Walter E. Williams, Heritage Features Syndicate, <u>The Tribune</u>, March 28, 1985.

BIBLIOGRAPHY

Ball, Donald A. & McCulloch, Wendell H. <u>International Business: Introduction and Essentials</u>. Plando, Texas: Business Publications, Inc., 1982.

Cateora, Philip R. <u>International Marketing</u>. Homewood, Illinois: Richard D. Irwin, Inc., 1983.

Jain, Subhash C. <u>International Marketing Management</u>. Boston: Kent Publishing, 1984.

Jain, Subhash C. & Tucker, Lewis R. <u>International Marketing: Managerial Perspectives</u>. Boston: Kent Publishing, 1979.

Kahler, Ruel. *International Marketing*. Chicago: South-Western Publishing Company, 1983.

Keegan, Warren J. *Multinational Marketing Management*. Englewood Cliffs, NJ: Prentice-Hall, 1984.

Kirpalani, V. H. *International Marketing*. New York: Random House, 1984.

Meredith, Martin. *The First Dance of Freedom: Black Africa in the Postwar Era*. Harper-Row, 1985.

Robock, Stefan H. & Simmonds, Kenneth. *International Business and Multinational Enterprises*. Homewood, Illinois: Irwin, 1983.

Salvatore, Dominick. *International Economics*. New York: MacMillian, 1983.

Terpstra, Vern. *International Marketing*. Chicago: The Dryden Press, 1983.

MORAL JUSTIFICATIONS FOR DOING BUSINESS IN SOUTH AFRICA

Patricia H. Werhane

Introduction

It is commonly argued that because of the abhorent nature of apartheid and other injustices committed by the South African government and South African law, it is morally objectionable to do business with or in South Africa. Indeed, according to this perspective, one is morally required <u>not</u> to do business with or in South Africa since to do so would appear to be in support of the principles of apartheid. Doing business with or in South Africa supports a government committed to injustices and provides it with financial and technical resources to strengthen its hold on South African nonwhite people. Thus businesses currently dealing with South Africa should withdraw their operations from that country.

On the other side, corporations doing business with and in South Africa argue that if they do not trade with this country, other nations will do so, thus depriving American business of profits while not depriving South Africa of industry. American corporations further point out that such businesses provide jobs for nonwhite South Africans, jobs they otherwise might have, but perhaps under less auspicious working conditions or poorer wages. Worse, it is very costly for shareholders if American companies withdraw from South Africa, because under South African law, companies can neither withdraw their assets nor expect any form of reparations when leaving that country.

American companies, then, appear to be faced with the dilemma of engaging in practices which are often questioned on ethical grounds by the American public and some of their shareholders, or sacrificing economic gains and thus not honoring their fiduciary commitments to the same shareholders. Note the schizophrenic position of transnational corporations vis-a-vis their shareholders. Some shareholders object on <u>moral</u> grounds to transnational South African operations, while others would object on fiscal ones to losses on major earnings which might be created by withdrawal. No wonder institutional shareholders have problems developing a policy toward owning shares in such corporations, and no wonder corporations have trouble deciding whether or not to leave South Africa!

In this paper I shall argue that this dilemma is misconstrued. What appears to be a clear-cut case of ethics versus economics is much more complicated in its implications.

While it may be ethically questionable to do business with South Africa, a question I shall not consider in this paper, businesses currently operating in that country can defend their existence there under certain ethically specified conditions. Such business operations might be justified if and where these companies engage in what I shall call moral risk in their business affairs in South Africa. Moral risk does not entail an ad hoc exportation of American customs and business practices nor does it require merely following the accepted practices of South African businesspersons and corporations. Rather, moral risk requires a careful analysis of what is not merely accepted practice, but also what is morally acceptable. And the business practices one adopts must also meet one's own moral standards and pass tests of ethical acceptability from a more universal perspective. It will turn out that in many instances one can continue to do business in South Africa without either sacrificing one's own principles or insulting the host nation.

Three Options for Multinational Enterprises in South Africa

Why is the case for or against doing business in South Africa so complex? Transnational corporations are faced with three kinds of choices, each of which has its positive and negative aspects. First, transnationals can simply remain in South Africa, doing business in the way that other white South African businesses do. This choice can be defended on a number of grounds. As I mentioned earlier, there are the obvious utilitarian arguments that American businesses profit from their South African operations, and since their operations would be replaced by businesses from South Africa or other countries if these corporations withdrew, the reasons for withdrawing are moot. Furthermore, following what I shall call the "Negative Harm Principle," the notion that a business dealing is morally permissible if it is not illegal so long as it does not deliberately or knowingly harm some person, some institution, or some nation, the operations of American transnational corporations are morally permissible. This is because (1) these corporations provide jobs, (2) they do not permit working conditions or wage scales which are worse than other South African companies, and (3) if these companies repatriated their operations, they would be replaced by other companies from other countries so that any positive benefit that might be accrued from their withdrawal is lost. Moreover, (4) since South Africa is a relatively wealthy "Westernized" country compared at least to other African nations, by and large transnational business operations in that country do not produce consequences often seen as heinous by critics of transnationals operating in the Third World. For example, there is little evidence that transnationals have imported radical economic, social, or cultural changes incompatible with the South African way of life. They have not exploited the agriculture of the country by replacing important food crops with exportable but locally useless products. They have not exploited the labor force with wages abnormally lower or higher than the South African norm or with temporary employment. At the same time, American transnationals have provided employment for decent wages and, with the exception of the mining industries, decent working conditions. In other words, American transnationals operating in South Africa have not aggravated or altered the social, psychological, economic, or ecological balance (or imbalance) of South Africa.[1]

This choice, to remain in South Africa under the status quo, however, has a number of difficulties including (1) moral objections of shareholders part of whom are institutional shareholders and (2) acquiescence to a system of apartheid neither approved nor practiced in the home country of the transnational. To support these objections, critics of transnational operations in South Africa argue that merely not deliberately creating cultural, economic, or physical harm is not enough justification for supporting any operation which cooperates with a government in a society which abets and aggrandises apartheid. To exist in South Africa and to contribute to its economy is to offer economic support for an inherently evil social and political structure and thereby to cause and to contribute positive harm. One cannot morally justify continuing to do business in South Africa on the basis of the Negative Harm Principle since merely not intentionally or deliberately causing harm is not enough in this case to prevent American transnationals from contributing to positive harm. It seems obvious, then, according to these critics, that doing business in South Africa is simply the wrong thing to do, and the alternate, withdrawing economic operations, is the right thing to do even though this creates economic hardships for some transnationals and their shareholders.

Aside from the deleterious economic effects of withdrawing from South Africa, a choice which itself has moral components, e.g., corporate fiduciary responsibility to shareholders, this choice is not a perfect one either. It is not a perfect decision first because American transnational corporations provide needed jobs for nonwhite South Africans. Now if other corporations take over American transnational operations when American companies leave, these jobs would continue, but under South African legal guidelines. Second, by withdrawing, American transnationals are giving up an opportunity to do positive good, not merely positive economic good, but also to serve as an example of how private enterprises can work efficiently and without deliberate injustice.

This brings us to the third most difficult choice: to stay in South Africa and not merely avoid deliberately causing harm, but also serve as a positive model for private enterprise at its most fair. This choice is the most interesting and the most challenging, and according to some critics, the least perfect, since it is, at best, a mixed moral action which cannot avoid the result of contributing economically to white South Africa.

Moral Risk

We must now ask why this third option is a viable option and perhaps even the best sort of choice, all things considered. Under what conditions could one continue to do business in South Africa without overwhelming moral impunity? The responses to these questions entail what I shall call "moral risk." Moral risk is entailed in any decision-making process in which one becomes engaged when the particular moral dilemma one faces (1) has neither a positive nor a negative alternative that is clearcut, (2) has no alternative that will produce a positive result (e.g., Sophie's Choice), (3) is characterized by the fact that not choosing itself is a contributory negative choice (German acquiescence to Nazism in World War II), and/or (4) results in any possible action having both contributory and deleterious effects. In these sorts of situations, because choosing not to choose (or simply, not choosing) is itself an effective choice, one needs to engage in serious moral deliberation. This deliberation calls for moral creativity and entails moral risk because of the ambiguous nature of any decision one is to make. Notice, again, that I have termed this "risk" in ethical decision making, because no choice one makes will be perfectly good. Since any choice one makes will have some negative consequences, how one chooses is of upmost importance. The structure of one's decision requires not merely drawing straws, but setting up guidelines, formal guidelines, for such decisions. These guidelines in turn must meet the following requirements: (1) universalizability, (2) respect for equal rights of all persons, (3) respect for individual, institutional, cultural, or national customs, mores, or ideologies, (4) respect for the Negative Harm Principle, and (5) when possible creation of positive benefits. Let us briefly discuss each of these.

The universalizability principle in these sorts of instances is to be interpreted as the evaluation of the decision in terms of whether I would expect others to make this sort of decision under these circumstances, all things considered. Without evaluating a choice by this principle, albeit qualified, the choice has no status as a moral choice since it cannot be justified except as my subjective preference. Yet the universalizability principle is a qualified principle, qualified by the particular situation and by the kind of decision to be made. Secondly, a decision, however universalizable, which does not respect persons and their rights and interests, has difficulty as a <u>moral</u> decision. The South African government, for example, appeals to the principle of universalizability in its governmental policies, since it advocates apartheid as the proper way for all nations to divide and govern races. Yet these policies fail on the grounds that they do not respect persons or respect persons equally. In much of moral decision making, of course, it is not simply the respect for persons which is at issue, but conflicts between rights or interests of persons or persons and institutions. Giving the benefit of the doubt, this is, in part, the issue in South Africa where there is a conflict between the rights of white and nonwhite South Africans. And a solution to apartheid which abrogates the rights of <u>white</u> South Africans would not be an acceptable one either.

Third, as Michael Walzer cogently argues, respect for individual and national autonomy is essential if one is to value human freedom. Therefore, such autonomy can be violated only where there is a clear-cut and radical violation of people's rights.[2] Fourth, a decision which creates harm to the present <u>status quo</u> is always questionable unless it can be demonstrated that violent and continued disrespect for persons requires it, or that in the long run positive benefits will accrue. Simply not creating harm may not, in every case, be the best choice. Fifth, any decision which produces positive benefits is more justified than one which does not, although I would place respect for persons as a more important criterion for a decision than the creation of positive benefits. South Africa claims to have the highest standard of living in Africa for blacks. Yet human rights are consistently and deliberately violated in such a way that the alleged economic benefits do not morally outweigh the violations of human rights.

Moral Risk and Multinationals in South Africa

Turning now to the choice of whether and how to continue to do business in South Africa, the criteria for this decision are complex, because individual, institutional, and national considerations must be taken into account. In criticizing South African apartheid policies, we can apply the principles of universalizability and respect for persons. Can these same principles be evoked and in what ways to <u>justify</u> doing business in South Africa? It would appear that <u>one can</u> justify such operations only if one can create a situation which improves the moral condition of black South Africans by enhancing their rights and interests in such a way that would be an acceptable practice in other similar business situations. At the same time, one cannot simply disregard the autonomy of South Africa as a nation, although its consistent practice of rights violations might warrant some sort of intervention at some point. But this is surely not the responsibility of a transnational corporation nor would we want to grant such corporations this power. Moreover, from a practical standpoint, no business will be allowed to engage in practices which are clearly antithetical to South African autonomy. Fourth, if doing business in South Africa does not improve the moral as well as the economic condition of black South Africans and indeed causes undue harm, one has no justification for remaining in that country since one is merely abetting apartheid without any balancing contribution.

The issue is, then, can one continue in South Africa while enhancing rights of nonwhite South Africans without alienating the South African government to the point of being expelled? Note that no business has the moral obligation to do more than it can -- its primary responsibilities are to its shareholders, its customers, and its employees. So if a corporation could create a nondiscriminatory climate within its corporation which enhanced the moral and working conditions of its employees and if it produces goods or provides services which are not harmful to blacks and the black economy, such a corporation would be making moral progress both on an individual level with its employees and as a model for morally decent private enterprise. It is obvious that American transnational corporations which actively endorse and practice the Sullivan Principles are engaging in moral creativity and contributing positively to the moral improvement of nonwhite South Africans. Such principles specify positive nondiscriminatory actions only within the corporation so that adopting them does not blatantly insult the South African government. These principles allow companies not to compromise their moral standards within the confines of the company, and at the same time allow them to engage in economically successful operations. Of course, putting these principles into practice uniformly and consistently is critical.

Merely adopting the Sullivan Principles, however, does not get a corporation off the "moral hook." For one may always ask whether these principles are adequate. What is the role of the transnational in a positive cultural change? Can a transnational do more, and should it? Moreover, no transnational corporation has adopted the Sullivan Principles solely because of their contribution to black South African life. The Sullivan Principles are adopted in large measure to protect transnationals from shareholder criticism and to respond to American public pressure without having to withdraw from that country.

And as we have repeatedly noted, these operations increase the GNP of South Africa and help to maintain it as perhaps the strongest and most stable country in Africa. So transnationals face two constant moral risks -- the risk of not doing enough, morally, and the risk of contributing more to apartheid than in helping its foes. Why, then, continue?

Although I cannot answer that question directly, I can illustrate what is at stake with another, more difficult example. During World War II, the German theologian Dietrich Bonhoeffer actively and publicly fought Nazism. According to a widespread but undocumented rumor, during the war Bonhoeffer's followers infiltrated concentration camps not as inmates but as guards. In trying to undermine the system, some of these followers were forced to participate in the actual deaths of inmates in order to protect their identity and continue with their mission. Were their actions good or evil? Was it better to do nothing than to engage in activities, some of which were abhorrent, that were aimed at creating changes? There is no simple answer. But if moral improvement of a society can take place best within that society, then it is not clear that Bonhoeffer's followers acted wrongly even though their individual actions contributed to evil. Perhaps it is an exaggerated analogy to compare the actions of Bonhoeffer and his followers to transnational operations in South Africa since the motives of the transnationals are not pure. Yet to withdraw from an opportunity to contribute to positive change in a situation as abhorrent as apartheid is perhaps not the best ethical decision either.

In conclusion, the Negative Harm Principle is not always enough to prevent harm from occurring as a result of one's well-intentioned actions. At the same time, positive moral action often requires making choices which are, at best, ambiguous. Doing business in South Africa in the way in which South Africans do embodies the Negative Harm Principle and contributes to positive harm. At the same time, withdrawing from South Africa makes no positive contribution in a situation where such a contribution is possible. The difficult decision of choosing to remain in South Africa with a specific moral agenda, then, is ethically risky but not as wrong as it may seem.

NOTES

1. For a discussion of the "traditional evils" often committed by transnationals see Richard J. Barnet and Ronald E. Muller, *Global Reach* (New York: Simon and Schuster, 1974), especially Chapter 13.

2. See Michael Walzer, *Just and Unjust Wars* (New York: Basic Books, 1977), especially pp. 88-106.

UNITED STATES CORPORATIONS IN SOUTH AFRICA: A CASE FOR STAYING

Wilfred D. Koplowitz

Mr. Carstens started with a description of entrenched racism and savage repression brought home to our television screens but not to the television screens of South Africa. I think he described those facts accurately. I do not think there is any argument about the nature of the regime fundamentally, philosophically, or in actuality. It is an evil regime in concept and in execution, and it is repressive. Even though some of the results, economically and in other respects, can be considered benign in a certain way for black South Africans and certainly for white South Africans, it is certainly beyond approval, and it must be eliminated. There is no argument about that. The argument is about how to do it, under what circumstances, and who can play what role and with what kind of ancillary consequences with regard to black South Africans particularly.

I have just returned from South Africa, and I might say, that although S.A.D.C. is not showing the same images that we're getting, there is an increasing amount of coverage of the violence from the print media, and the press there is very active. There is some self-censorship and some things they know they cannot print, but the week I was there there were calls in The Star and other important newspapers for President Botha's resignation and a gathering recognition in the media that apartheid simply had to go and reform had to be accelerated.

Both Mr. Carstens and Mr. Johnson take the position that it is immoral to be associated in any way with such a regime. Now, what constitutes association is, of course, at issue. Mr. Johnson thinks that deriving any profits from the economy of a regime of this kind, in which the political power is executed in the way it is, is immoral and unacceptable. I would think that Mr. Carstens would agree with that and also would consider that almost any presence in South Africa on the part of someone who did not have to be there was a kind of association because it is a tacit acceptance of the regime.

I do have problems with a couple of his assertions. In the first place, I do not think that to suggest there is a correlation between the growth of investment from 1950 to 1985, even discounted for inflation, and the increased repression through apartheid, is really quite fair. Second, the suggestion, by reference to Albert Luthuli and Bishop Tutu, that blacks want sanctions is also a little unfair. I think there are many black voices, many authentic voices among leadership elements in South Africa, and they do not always agree. Even Bishop Tutu has changed his mind several times, or at least varied what he has said, with regard to disinvestment and sanctions, sometimes outlining a timetable, sometimes insisting that we have to behave in a certain way in order to justify our presence. There is an honest disagreement, and there is good reason for there to be this disagreement. I happen to think that sanctions really will hurt black South Africans and not all want to be so hurt, and that it is somewhat presumptuous of us to take the position that most do while ignoring the fact that ultimately economic growth has been an engine of change.

Professor Werhane comes out on the other side, introducing a very interesting concept of moral risk. Certainly we do live with moral risk -- in our personal lives, in our national life, singularly and collectively -- and that is what the world is all about.

As Mr. Johnson said in his very eloquent presentation, he is not an ethical virgin. I doubt that there are any ethical virgins, and if there were any, or if there were a pristine, perfect, ethical mode of conduct for us as individuals or as corporations, or as countries and governments, or as churches or as political pressure groups, we would be living in a very different world. We probably would not be accomplishing many of the things that we do manage to accomplish in the kind of political and turbulent and imperfect world in which we do live. Because we cannot avoid moral risk, we cannot avoid moral dilemmas. It is a matter of doing what we think, on balance, is right and ultimately effective in good causes.

It is very difficult to reply to Mr. Johnson. Polaroid decided that what was happening to its product in South Africa was unacceptable, that its approach to South Africa was being abused in a virtually criminal way. They got out. Mr. Johnson personally has decided that to be deriving any profits from the economy of South Africa under any circumstances, regardless of the product and the services being rendered, or the relationship with the black labor force, or the rules under which it is done, or the social responsibility of the company, is not acceptable morally and to do so is to consort with harlots.

I do not happen to agree with that because I think that there are many extremely distinguished and worthwhile and freedom-loving, highly moral people of all races in South Africa, and they are in a fight for their lives and for their country, and if American corporations are on their side in that country, I would say that those corporations do not deserve that kind of denigration.

Professor Luddington, in an interesting six-point program, covered all the other points quite well and raised the point with which I, as a representative of a multinational or of a global financial institution, would have to agree. There are many regimes in the world that abuse human rights. Good, principled people live in those regimes. They all have economies. We cannot run them into the ground. We cannot apply sanctions to all of them. If we are going to be a global corporation, we must operate in the global market. We do not believe that operating in that global market implies acceptance or approval of the regime or of its social and political or even economic system. We simply cannot put ourselves in the position of passing these judgments. If we are to retreat to those countries where there is a democracy which is perhaps a mirror image of our own, we will not be in that global market, and of course there will be many other consequences in terms of tourism, diplomatic representation, and other things if we choose to accept that kind of constraint on economic activity.

The ethical dilemmas of the situation are very, very profound, and I do not deny them. One ethical dilemma is whether you demonstrate the rejection of an immoral system by withdrawal, or do so as a player participant, making very clear where you stand on the moral issue and using your moral, financial, and human resources in alliance with other forces fighting to end apartheid.

There is another moral dilemma. Do you invest in the country? Do you nourish its economy? Do you increase job opportunities for blacks? Do you work to build a black middle class? Do you work to help blacks aggregate and pursue their interests more effectively? Do you help blacks get ready to run the country by being sure that they have a job and some training and education? Or, do you punish South Africa and the blacks in South Africa in hopes of ending the system?

Here is where you get to the question of whether sanctions or punishments will, in fact, end the system. I think it is true that if you ask most black South Africans or anyone else who is in a prison (which is what South Africa is for whites, too, by the way) whether they would accept some transient pain, even extreme, in order to achieve freedom, they will say "yes." I submit to you that if you know the pattern of power and if you know the Afrikaners and how things are in South Africa, it is not certain by any means that we can promise the pain <u>will</u> be transient. I say it is somewhat presumptuous of Americans, thousands of miles away, with imperfect knowledge of the country (and I include myself in that very much, despite my trips there and familiarity with it), to make that kind of a decision and make that kind of an offer.

Third, there is the matter of interference in the internal affairs of another country. Professor Luddington alluded to this. There is a lot of double standard in that. We interfere where we do not like the regime. We do not dare to interfere where we find it congenial to our personal beliefs. I personally feel that, in this case, a certain amount of inteference is necessary and can only be justified by American subsidiaries and affiliates who are there. Because we are there, we have a stake; we are in a sense corporate citizens of that community even though we may be American-owned. We have a right to speak up because our interests are at stake.

Finally, there is the ultimate dilemma that we all face much of the time -- that of ends and means. In a way this is the cosmic moral dilemma. Is it right, in service of a glorious and moral objective, to use means or do things which make us uncomfortable and may be, by some measures, not precisely moral? I happen to think that being in South Africa is not an immoral act. I also happen to think that helping the South African economy is not an immoral act if it is quite clear that we are doing so in a way that helps South Africans gain their freedom and, at the same time, increases pressure on the South African white minority (and that is a generalization; I mean on the particular group that is running the country today) to end the system of apartheid.

Now, let me take just one minute to tell you about Citibank. We have ceased all lending to the South African government. We will make no new loans to the South African government or its agencies until apartheid is, in effect, dismantled. Ironically, however (and here we get into the political risk question and the way corporations and not just banks behave), the maximum pressure on the South African government that has occurred to date is coming from the banks because our assessment of the political risk, of the total country risk, has become increasingly negative.

While we do not think that time has run out, we are congnizant of the deterioration of the situation, the spreading violence, the likelihood of stay-aways or strikes, and of real difficulties in the economy. American companies and banks must think very carefully about the viability of their equities and investments and how long they can stay not because of what is happening in the United States in front of the South African

Embassy, but because of what is happening in South Africa -- cumulative rejection and hatred and the impossibility for black South Africans to live much longer under this regime.

The banks began to reduce their exposure dramatically in August of 1985. After the August 15th speech of President Botha, which certainly did not augur well for involving black South Africans in the negotiation process, we moved that up even more, refusing to roll over dollar loans, refusing to extend new credits.

The South African government imposed a freeze, a moratorium on repayment, and this is where we are today. I spent a week in South Africa with my vice chairman. We saw people at all levels of the government, and we made it very clear that there has been a loss of confidence in the financial market and the ability of the South African government to lead and manage a process of change and involve black South Africans in that process. That confidence will not be restored unless there is a change in that situation.

We think that the Afrikaners must now react positively to this and that there must be an acceleration of the process of reform. We will continue to comply with the Sullivan Principles. Reverend Sullivan is a remarkable man. We do not agree with him on ultimatums and timetables and a legislated mandatory Sullivan compliance, but the Sullivan Principles have had an impact in South Africa, and they will continue to do so. We have an unbroken record of top category ratings in compliance with the Sullivan Principles. We will increase the already substantial financial and humans resources we have devoted to social projects benefiting black South Africans in crucial areas such as small business development.

We think standing and fighting is better than cutting and running -- particularly right now. We are going to stay as long as we can. But, we do have a responsibility to the shareholders. No American company is going to stay if it looks like the country is absolutely going to go up in smoke.

The South African business community has never been more exercised than it is today. It is a powerful community. It has not flexed its muscles sufficiently in the past. It has begun to do so in the last 12 to 18 months. The Afrikaners are intensely concerned, obviously, about their massive investments and about their country. There is a great love of country in South Africa among all races, and there is still the possibility of their relating to each other in a sensible and comradely and common fashion because they love South Africa and they are all South Africans. I have not given up hope.

CHAPTER TWELVE

BRIBERY AND THE FOREIGN CORRUPT PRACTICES ACT

KEVIN F. WALL
Assistant Professor of Accountancy
Bentley College
Waltham, Massachusetts

MARK PASTIN
Professor of Management and Director
Center for Private and Public Sector Ethics
Arizona State University
Tempe, Arizona

JOHN M. KLINE
Deputy Director
Karl F. Landegger Program in International Business Policy
School of Foreign Service
Georgetown University
Washington, DC

A SELECTIVE REVIEW OF THE CRIMINAL PROSECUTIONS UNDER THE FOREIGN CORRUPT PRACTICES ACT OF 1977

Kevin F. Wall

Sir Robert Walpole is credited, back in the 1700s, with having coined a phrase that has found its way into the American business vernacular. That phrase is "All those men have their price." This is not to suggest that the issues of bribery or corruption are uniquely English. Nor are they uniquely American.

Early Akkadian literature details the plight of a citizen of Nippur in Mesopotamia in 1500 B.C.[1] Seeking to improve his lot in life, he offered the mayor of Nippur a goat, which was his only possession. The mayor accepted the goat but did not keep his part of the bargain. So, the citizen went to the king of the country and offered him one mina of gold in exchange for the use of the royal chariot for one day. Without inquiring as to the citizen's motivation, the king agreed.

The citizen then returned to Nippur where he was received by the mayor who thought that he was an official of the realm. Installed in the mayor's residence, the citizen opened a chest which he had brought with him and pretended the gold he said was in it had disappeared. The implication was that the gold was stolen by the mayor, who was then beaten three times for his crime. The mayor also tried to appease the citizen by giving him two minas of gold. The citizen had his revenge and also a very respectable return on his one mina investment.

Criticism of bribery is found in the Bible. The Hebrew term which expresses a disapproved payment or offering is "shohadh."[2] In the ninth century B.C., the first specific criticism of shohadh appears in the "Code of the Covenant." God is speaking to Moses on Mount Sinai, having just given him the Ten Commandments. He states: "You shall not take shohadh, which make the clear eyed blind and the words of the just crooked." (Exodus 23:6-8) Despite the ancient tales and biblical warnings of retribution and revenge exacted against those who give or receive "shohadh," corruption and bribery have continued.

Unfortunately, the United States cannot claim to be without stigma. Americans have had a certain historical curiosity about bribery. It is perhaps significant that one of the two crimes specifically mentioned in the Constitution which may cause removal of President, Vice President, or civil officers is bribery.[3] Allegations of corruption have decided elections. A president and vice president have resigned. Seven members of Congress have been convicted of bribery. Several governors and scores of public officials have been imprisoned during the last fifteen years for violating the laws against bribery. Not to be outdone by the public sector, several corporations have been involved in making bribes or other questionable payments.

With all of the foregoing, one might assume that the United States was void of laws forbidding bribery and corruption. Nothing could be further from the truth. In addition to the reference contained in the Constitution, various states and commonwealths including Maryland, Massachusetts, and Virginia prohibited "gift, fees, and rewards" shortly after the Revolutionary War.[4]

In addition, several major legislative enactments have dealt at least in part with bribery and corruption, particularly of a corporate nature. Included are the following Acts: Interstate Commerce; Meat Inspection; Grain Standards; Taft-Hartley; Federal Alcohol Administration; Federal Trade Commission; Anti-Kickback, and Interstate and Foreign Travel or Transportation in Aid of Racketeering Enterprises. Other laws which prohibit illegal foreign payments include the following Acts: Sherman Antitrust of 1890; Clayton Antitrust of 1914; Securities Act of 1933; Securities Exchange Act of 1934; Bank Secrecy and Reporting Act of 1970; International Security Assistance and Arms Control of 1976 and, finally, the Internal Revenue Code and its related revisions which deny a tax deduction for a payment considered to be unlawful.

In 1977, amidst the fallout of Watergate, Vietnam, and several major corporate scandals, however, a federal statute entitled the Foreign Corrupt Practices Act (FCPA) was enacted dealing specifically with corporate bribery.[5] The significance of the FCPA was that it was aimed specifically at extraterritorial corporate bribery. In this respect, it differed from the previous enactments which dealt with foreign corporate bribery as only one of several, and often times ancillary, sections of the respective law. Shortly after the passage of the FCPA, the American Bar Association described it as the most significant legislation effecting corporations since the 1933 and 1934 Securities Acts.[6] Actually, the FCPA was not completely new legislation, but was an amendment to a previously existing law, namely, the Securities Exchange Act of 1934.

There is a two-pronged approach to the FCPA. One (Accounting Provisions) requires issuers subject to regulation and the reporting provision of the Securities Exchange Act of 1934, among other things, to comply with certain accounting standards including record keeping, internal controls, and certain filing requirements. The provisions are contained in Section 102 of the FCPA.[7]

The other (Anti-Bribery Provisions) makes it unlawful to use any instrument of interstate commerce of any issuer or a domestic concern not subject to the Securities Exchange Act to offer, promise, pay, or give anything of value to foreign officials or certain other persons for any corrupt purposes. These provisions are contained in Sections 103 and 104 of the FCPA.[8] A significant aspect of the FCPA is that it has neither a scienter (i.e., intent) nor a materiality requirement.

Violations of the FCPA can be costly to both the issuer and any officer or director acting on behalf of an issuer. Issuers may be fined up to $1,000,000. Those acting on behalf of an issuer can be fined up to $10,000 and imprisoned for up to five years.[9]

Enforcement of the FCPA extends to two agencies, the Securities and Exchange Commission (SEC) and the Department of Justice (DOJ). The SEC conducts investigations, brings civil and administrative actions, and refers cases to the Department of Justice for criminal prosecution. This dual responsibility has created disagreements between the SEC, the DOJ, issuers, and the accounting and legal professions over the enforcement of the FCPA.

Needless to say, there has been tremendous controversy surrounding the FCPA. There are those who suggest maintaining the FCPA in its original (and largely unchanged) form. They state that it has stemmed the flow of questionable or illegal payments,[10] it has enhanced internal controls[11] and, since its passage, nonagricultural exports have actually increased.[12]

Others state that there is data which suggests that American companies have suffered a loss in sales because they are now at a competitive disadvantage,[13] that the FCPA is an instrument of foreign policy and not part of corporate governance,[14] that the dual enforcement is creating problems for issuers trying to develop a unified approach to dealing with the FCPA,[15] that it increases costs of internal control,[16] that many aspects of it are vague and ambiguous particularly in distinguishing so-called grease payments from bribery[17] and, finally, that under the Reagan administration, aggressive prosecutions of issuers or individuals have not taken place.[18]

Based on DOJ documents, one fact that is clear is that from 1978 through the spring of 1985 there have been approximately fifty SEC injunctive and administrative proceedings. During that time, there have been approximately one dozen prosecutions by the Justice Department. Some critics charge that the DOJ has not aggressively prosecuted violations of the FCPA.

The purpose of this paper is to selectively review certain key FCPA cases including the Pemex cases that have been brought by the DOJ. The sources of information for this review are many of the legal documents relating to these cases such as Indictments, Offers of Proof, Cooperative Agreements, and Plea Agreements.

The Early Cases

1. United States v. Carver & Holley, Civ. No. 79-1968 (S.D. Fla., 1979).

This is a one count complaint seeking a permanent injunction against co-defendants, Carver and Holley. Each owned fifty percent of the shares of Holcar Oil Corporation (Holcar) since its incorporation in the Caymen Islands in October of 1975. The corporation was formed to obtain an oil drilling concession from the Emirate of Qatar. After considerable negotiations and several trips to Qatar, it was determined that such a concession was obtainable if $1,500,000 was paid to Ali Jaidah, the country's director of petroleum affairs. The payment was made in January of 1976 from Carver's bank account in a Chicago bank to Jaidah's brother, using a Swiss bank account. Later that month, the concession agreement was completed between Holcar and Qatar.

In mid 1977, Holcar ran into financial difficulty and entered into a refinancing agreement with another company. The refinancing, however, was contingent upon the renewal of the concession agreement. Qatar was unwilling to renew because Holcar had not developed the fields as required by the original agreement.

At this point, in February of 1978, Holley sought the assistance of fellow Georgian, T. Bertram Lance, who was the former President of the National Bank of Georgia. Two years earlier, Holley had pledged portions of his stock in Holcar as collateral for a $200,000 loan from the bank.

Lance arranged an initial meeting which eventually led to two conferences in March of 1978 between the United States Ambassador, a foreign service officer, and the new Director of

Petroleum Affairs. At the second of these meetings, Carver revealed the $1,500,000 payment and stated that he thought the entire investment would be lost. He then asked the Ambassador, "Who do I go see now, how do I get it done?" At this point, all discussions were terminated.

This case was unique for several reasons: It was the first criminal prosecution under the FCPA; the crime itself took place prior to the passage of the FCPA; the nature of Carver's concession; the magnitude of the bribe; the inability of Holcar to use foreign corporations and banks in the furtherance of their scheme; and the use of a close personal friend of the President of the United States as a contact, who unwittingly led to the uncovering of the entire transaction.

2. United States v. Finbar v. Kenny et al. Civ. No. 79-2038 and U.S. v. Kenny International Corp., Civ. No. 79-372 (D.D.C., 1979)

Kenny International Corporation, a New York corporation, was charged with bribing a foreign official in violations of the FCPA. Kenny was a United States citizen and majority shareholder in the corporation. In addition to obtaining a guilty plea from the corporation, the DOJ obtained consent decrees against both the corporation and Kenny.

The corporation had obtained from the government of the Cook Islands (an independent South Pacific nation of 18,000 persons associated with New Zealand for purposes of external affairs and defense) exclusive rights to promote, distribute, and sell its stamps outside the islands for a period of ten years. Gross proceeds of $1,500,000 were reported by Kenny.

In 1978, in order to assure its continued exclusivity, the corporation agreed to assist the ruling political party, at its request, by subsidizing the air transportation miles for certain Cook Island voters who were now residing in New Zealand. Such a subsidy was illegal under Cook Island law.

It was agreed that the corporation would reduce "the stamp commissions" monies it would normally have paid the government for any "subsidies" it advanced the ruling party. The subsidy was approximately $337,000. The ruling party won the election as a direct result of the transported supporters, but the High Court of the Island disallowed the votes of those supporters whose travel had been subsidized as "unlawful votes tainted by bribery."

As was the case with Carver, it would have been difficult,

given the amount of the payment, for the DOJ not to prosecute the case. Kenny also clearly indicated that initiation of the bribe request by the foreign government would not be a defense to a prosecution brought under the FCPA.

The plea agreement between the DOJ and the corporation, as well as Kenny personally, provided for the following:

1. An agreement to voluntarily appear and plead guilty to all pending charges in the Cook Island Courts; and

2. Fines of $50,000 for the corporation and restitution to the Cook Islands by Kenny of $337,000.

The Pemex Cases

Summary

The next series of cases have been referred to, collectively, as the "Pemex Cases." The cases are as follows:

1. United States v. Crawford, Inc., Donald Crawford, et al., Crim. No. H-82-24

2. United States v. Ruston Gas Turbines Inc., Crim. No. H-82-207

3. United States v. C. E. Miller Inc. and Charles Miller, Crim. No. 82-788DW

4. United States v. Int'l. Harvester, Crim. No. H82-244

5. United States v. Gary Bateman and Applied Process Overseas Inc., Crim. No. 83-4 DC

6. United States v. McLean, Crim. No 83-2452

Petroleas Mexicanos, also known as Pemex, is the national oil company wholly owned by the government of Mexico and responsible for the exploration and production of all oil and gas resources in Mexico. Since 1977, Mexican oil production has tripled, and its gas reserves have increased tenfold. In order to achieve the mandated exploration, it was required to borrow heavily from The Export-Import Bank of the United States. Given the fact that Mexico was a country friendly to the United States and also had one of the few expanding economies in the West, the competition for sales of equipment to Pemex was tremendous. The common thread between the defendants was their interest in manufacturing, distributing, or marketing turbine compression systems to Pemex. Clearly the situation had all the makings of a disaster.

The result was a complex series of criminal activities including a conspiracy to violate the FCPA and bribery of senior Pemex officials, as well as aiding and abetting the various employees and agents in violating the FCPA. Included in the scenario was one of the original perpetrators, Gary Bateman, who eventually agreed to testify against his former employer, Donald Crawford. There was also a corporate parent, International Harvester, which was held liable for the acts of its subsidiary's (Solar) officer, George McLean, even though the parent had no knowledge of the payment. Furthermore, Harvester had had in place since 1961 a specific formal corporate policy forbidding any employee from making gifts or payments. For the calendar years 1977, 1978, 1979, and 1980, Harvester had obtained, through its annual audit, employee certification (including that of McLean) of knowledge and compliance with the FCPA.

When news of the alleged bribes became known to the President-elect of Mexico, Miguel de la Madrid Hurtado, he privately acknowledged that Pemex corruption had grown out of hand, and he promised an honest administration. A particular target of his eventual investigation was the former Director General of Pemex from 1976 to 1981, Jorge Diaz Serrano. Although Hurtado's administration was initially chided for having moved slowly against the widely-perceived corrupt administration of its predecessor, Jose Lopez Portillo, his critics were silenced in early 1983.

Former Director General Serrano was charged with corruption and defrauding Pemex of $34,000,000. Under Serrano's leadership, Pemex not only had become the world's fourth largest oil producer, but also had acquired a domestic and international reputation as a corporation where kickbacks were standard operating procedure. Serrano had been a former partner of Vice President George Bush and was once considered a possible successor to Portillo. A review of the DOJ documents indicates the following elaborate conspiracy by the defendants.

C. E. Miller (CEMCO) designed compression systems for the petroleum industry during the mid 1970s. It had performed subcontract work for the Solar Turbine division of International Harvester (Solar) which they, in turn, had sold to Pemex through its Mexican sales agent, Dyna Vulkano. The Vice President of Solar was George S. McLean.

During the fall of 1977, Crawford, William Hall, who was President of Crawford Enterprises Inc. (CEI), and Bateman, who at the time was employed by CEI, contacted Eyster and Smith, President and Vice President of Ruston Gas Turbines (Ruston) regarding "a joint venture" to sell the same type of compression system to Pemex that Solar was presently marketing. It was agreed that Ruston would use CEMCO as a subcontractor in its bid to Pemex. One of the components of the bid, which was alleged to have been known by all the parties of the Crawford/Ruston joint venture, was a five percent override which was to be paid ultimately to Jesse Chavairia and Nacho DeLeon. The payments were to be made through Crawford's Mexican "agent," Grupo Industrial Delta S. A. (Grupo). Andres Garcia was an official of Grupo. Chavairia and DeLeon were responsible at Pemex for the production and purchasing functions repectively. It was the intent that the venture would receive the five percent through bidding higher prices to Pemex.

Throughout the fall of 1977, Crawford, CEI, and Bateman "advised" Solar "if it wanted to continue to share in the Pemex business" it would need to deal with CEI. Solar resisted CEI, stating that it wished to continue selling directly to Pemex using its agent Vulkano. Crawford continued to assert that his company was a "power" to be reckoned with and told Solar's Vice-President McLean that its "power" originated from its connection with the "folks." In order to reinforce the point, McLean was told in late 1977, by Crawford, that the next Pemex order would be made to the Crawford/Ruston venture. On or about January 10, 1978, the bid was awarded to the venture. Solar saw the light and cast its lot with Crawford.

By the end of January 1978, Solar had conspired and participated in the bid preparation by Crawford, and both Crawford and Solar were awarded the bids by Pemex. Solar's sales after its agreement with Crawford amounted to $112,000,000. Crawford's sales were $225,000,000, including an $18,000,000 profit. Grupo was paid $10,000,000 for the "folks."

Indictments and Convictions

Clearly the primary indictment and conviction in the Pemex cases was the one obtained against Crawford. He was the instigator of the scheme that eventually involved several individuals and companies. After several years of investigation, indictments against the various defendants began being issued in the Fall of 1982.

The results of the indictments, convictions, and sentencing were the following:

1. Crawford Enterprises Inc. was found guilty of one act of conspiracy and 46 violations of the FCPA. Although it could have faced fines of $4,700,000, it was fined $3,450,000.

2. Donald Crawford was found guilty of similar charges that CEI faced. Possible penalties were 235 years in prison and fines of $470,000. He was fined $309,000.

3. William Hall was found guilty of one count of conspiracy and 35 counts of FCPA violations. Possible penalties were 180 years in prison and fines of $360,000. He was fined $150,000.

4. Andres Garcia was convicted of the same violations as CEI and Crawford. Facing similar fines and imprisonment, he was fined $75,000.

5. Eyster and Smith were convicted of one count of conspiracy and 44 violations of the FCPA. Fines of $5,000 were imposed.

The cases against the other defendants which were disposed of separately were as follows:

6. C. E. Miller Corporation and C. E. Miller pled guilty to aiding and abetting Crawford. Both were placed on probation.

7. Ruston Gas Turbines Inc. pled guilty to a one count felony information and was fined $750,000.

8. International Harvester (Solar) pled guilty to a one count felony information to violate the FCPA. It paid a criminal fine of $10,000 and civil reimbursement of $40,000 for the cost of prosecution.

9. In May 1981, Gary Bateman entered into a Cooperation Agreement with the DOJ. He became the government's primary witness in the Pemex cases. In exchange, he was charged only with currency violations. He paid fines of $229,512. In satisfaction of these fines, he also was required to pay the IRS $300,000 towards his civil tax liability arising from the Pemex cases. Finally, he paid $5,000 in civil reimbursement for the costs of litigation.

10. George S. McLean's acquittal of violating the FCPA was upheld by the United States Circuit Court of Appeals

for the Fifth Circuit. McLean argued that, since his employer had not been "convicted" but had entered into an "Agreement," he could not be convicted of a similar violation.

What We Have Learned

Several observations may be made by examining the cases that have been prosecuted to date, including those reviewed herein.

From Carver, it would appear that violations that predate the FCPA may be prosecuted; the use of foreign agents and banks may very well provide evidence sufficient to impute knowledge of a crime.

From Kenny, it can be determined that even if the foreign government initiates the bribe request, the company and its executives may be liable.

From the Pemex Cases, it can be seen that:

- The government can use a conspiracy theory. This may result in a conviction even if the underlying crime is not proven.

- Knowledge of the crime may be imputed based on a conscious disregard of the facts. Also subcontractors not dealing with all the parties may be liable. (The CEMCO decision.)

- A company may be guilty of violating the FCPA even though it does not make any payments directly to an official. (The Ruston decision.)

- A parent may have liability for the acts of a subsidiary even though it has well-documented procedures for reviewing compliance with the FCPA. This suggests that a parent which sees a dramatic increase in sales in a subsidiary in a foreign country must make a thorough investigation of the records of the subsidiary. (The International Harvester decision.)

- It may be unconstitutional to convict an employee of violating the FCPA if the employer is not first found guilty. (The McLean decision.)

Given the fact the no one has been imprisoned for violating the FCPA, it seems that the judical system is very reluctant to impose such penalties. This despite the DOJ recommendation for significant prison terms for Crawford in the Pemex Cases. Based on discussions with a DOJ prosecutor actively involved in the Pemex Cases, there was a clear sense of disappointment with the amount of the fines and the lack of prison terms.

Finally, there is a fitting postscript to the Pemex Cases from an interview with Jorge Diaz Serrano who is in a Mexican prison still awaiting judgment on charges of embezzlement. In concluding the interview, he points to an inmate who is serving tea and coffee in the prison cafeteria. He notes that inmate was a former waiter who was jailed for poisoning 25 people.

"They gave him a small tip, he says. He got angry."[19]

NOTES

1. See generally, J. Noonan, Bribes (1984), at 4-5.

2. Id. at 14.

3. United States Constitution. Article II, at 4.

4. See generally, J. Noonan, Bribes (1984), at 427-430.

5. Title I of Pub L. No. 95-213 (December 19,1977), codified as 15 U.S.C. 78 m(b), 78 dd-1, 78 dd-2, 78ff(c).

6. American Bar Association, Committee on Corp. Law and Accounting, "A Guide to the New Section (b)(2) Accounting Requirements of the Securities Exchange Act of 1934 (Section 102 of The Foreign Corrupt Practices Act of 1977)," The Business Lawyer, November 1978.

7. See, 15 U.S.C. 78m(b) and various sub-sections.

8. See, 15 U.S.C. 78dd-1 and 78dd-2 and various sub-sections.

9. 15 U.S.C. 78ff.

10. Maher, "Import of Regulation on Controls: Firms Response to the FCPA," Accounting Review, October 1981, at 751.

11. Aggarwal and Kim, "Should the FCPA be Abolished?" The Internal Auditor, April 1982, at 21.

12. Graham, "Foreign Corrupt Practices Act: A Manager's Guide," Columbia Journal of Business, Fall 1983, at 89;

also Aggarwal, Id.

13. Kaibati and Label, "The Foreign Anti-Bribery Law: Friend or Foe?" Columbia Journal of Business, Spring 1980, at 46; also Heine, "Curbs on Overseas Bribes are Hurting United States Business," Duns Review, September 1979, at 123.

14. Grenias and Windsor, The Foreign Corrupt Practices Act, Anatomy of a Statute (1982), at 4-5.

15. Kim, "On Repealing the Foreign Corrupt Practices Act: Survey and Assessment," Columbia Journal of Business, Fall 1981, at 16; also Aggarwal, supra note 11, at 20.

16. Aggarwal, supra note 11, at 20.

17. Bagby, "Enforcement of the Accounting Standards in the Foreign Corrupt Practices Act," 21 American Business Law Journal, 214.

18. Root, "Foreign Corrupt Practices Act, Where Do We Go From Here?" The Internal Auditor, April 1983, at 28; also Johnston," All in Favor of Bribery, Please Stand Up," Across the Board, June 1984.

19. Ibrahim, "Former Chief of Pemex Sits in Prison, But is He a Thief or Just a Scapegoat?" Wall Street Journal, October 9, 1985, at 26.

MANAGING THE RULES OF CONFLICT -- INTERNATIONAL BRIBERY*

Mark Pastin

All law is universal but about some things it is not possible to make a universal statement which shall be correct. Aristotle, (<u>Nichomachean Ethics</u>, Book V, Ch. 10, 1137b, lines 11-15.)

Conflict is a fact of life in business. But not all conflicts are conflicts of interests. Many of the most difficult issues in business involve conflicts of rules rather than, or in addition to, conflicts of interests. In the following pages, I concentrate on conflicts of rules -- conflicts between the rules of business or a particular business and the rules of different societies and cultures -- and how to manage them. One of the clearest examples of such a conflict is the conflict between the bribe-prohibitive ethics of most American corporations and the bribe-demanding climate in many countries where these corporations operate. This conflict clearly raises many of the facets of rule conflicts in general. But similar conflicts arise over different safety standards here and abroad (ours are more stringent), different trade practices (our arms-length business-government relationship versus the hands-on practice of other countries), different environmental standards (standards vary among regions within the United States and between countries), different attitudes towards nepotism, and different attitudes towards religion in the workplace.

To address conflicts of rules, I propose that we use an ethical tool, Rule Ethics. Rule Ethics will help us look at organizational actions and decisions and see the potential rule conflicts they raise. I also look at ways in which ethical rules are intentionally misinterpreted to the detriment of business. I use a case study of international bribery to illustrate these points.

Rule Ethics

Rule Ethics is simplicity itself. Rule Ethics states:

---

*Adapted by author from his book <u>Tackling the Hard Problems of Management: The Ethics Edge</u>, Jossey-Bass, 433 California Street, San Francisco, CA 94104, 1986.

A person or organization <u>should do</u> what is required by valid ethical principles. Further, a person or organization <u>should refrain from doing</u> anything contrary to valid ethical principles.

In short, Rule Ethics says that some actions are <u>obligatory</u> and some are <u>prohibited</u>. Actions which are neither obligatory nor prohibited are <u>permissible</u>. If you promise to repay a debt before a certain date, then you have an obligation to do so. On the other hand, you are prohibited from selling your children to raise money to pay your debt. You are not obligated to repay the debt before it is due, but you are permitted to do so.

Rule Ethics offers a reassuring categorization of right and wrong. An action is <u>right</u> if it is obligatory, or at least permissible. Otherwise, the action is <u>wrong</u>. At long last we have some clear ethical ground on which to stand. Rule Ethics is appealing to those who admire structure and legalism. This happy picture fades only when one asks to see the list of valid ethical principles separating right from wrong.

Background

The roots of Rule Ethics are ancient. Every religion proclaims a set of rules, such as the Ten Commandments, which embody that religion's understanding of right and wrong. (The terms "rule" and "principle" are interchangeable in ethics.) Thus, one rule frequently cited by rule ethicists is the Golden Rule, "Do unto others as you would have others do unto you." Non-religious ideologies also have sets of ethical rules. The Marxist maxim, "From each according to ability; to each according to need," is cited as frequently as the Golden Rule in Rule Ethical codes. The fact that the religions and ideologies of the world are far from agreeing about right and wrong underscores one feature of Rule Ethics: Rule Ethics, unlike End-Point Ethics, does not <u>by itself</u> answer any ethical questions.

It is tough to follow the rules if you are not told what the rules are. Further, you need rules specific enough not to leave everything open to interpretation. Thus, Rule Ethics must have a firm set of rules or principles to provide a genuine ethical perspective. There is no <u>one</u> Rule Ethics. Instead, there is a whole array of Rule Ethics corresponding to the many ethical codes adopted in the history of mankind. And that is a problem.

Whether or not one is convinced that there is one true ethical code -- supporters of Rule Ethics usually think there is -- one thing an ethical model should do is help us resolve conflicts among differing ethical perspectives. But Rule Ethics seems to offer little help in resolving conflicts. It is not too helpful to be told, "This is how it is according to my code; so line up!"

Supporters of Rule Ethics have responded to this problem. Defenders of religious versions of Rule Ethics try to resolve conflicts by insisting that their god(s) told them so, and trying to convert you. If that does not work, there is always holy war. If Marxists cannot convince you by appealing to their concept of justice, they annex and reeducate you. As long as the Rule Ethicist's fundamental appeal is to faith, force, or the "pure light of reason" (Kant, 1785), it is hard to establish even a starting place for discussion.

There are lessons to learn just from the problems that Rule Ethics has in resolving ethical conflicts. One of the reasons it is hard to resolve conflicts within Rule Ethics is that Rule Ethics pulls these conflicts to the surface, where the differences really show. We build on this feature of Rule Ethics in looking at the role of ethical codes in decision making and action.

Applying Rule Ethics in Decisions

Let us look at Rule Ethics in terms of ethical ground rules. A person or organization's ethics are no more or less than the ground rules of the person or organization. If you have ethics, you have ground rules. And those ground rules would seem to be your own Rule Ethics. But we are not so easily compelled to be Rule Ethicists.

Consider a process to uncover the ground rules of a person or organization. The idea is to look under actions for decisions and under decisions for ground rules. What you find at the core of a decision, once you uncover the alternatives and data considered, are ethical ground rules of value (what is desirable) and ethical ground rules of operation (what are acceptable/unacceptable ways of pursing what is desirable).

As the result of this reverse engineering of actions through decisions through alternatives/data through ground rules, you may find that your ethics, or an organization's ethics, is End-Point Ethics. In this case, you or the organization have essentially one rule of both value and operation: seek to maximize the balance of benefits over harms; operate in ways that do the same. But you may find that you or the organization have several distinct ground rules. Even this does not ensure that the ground rules are a form of Rule Ethics. For you must now ask: "Do these rules serve as the basis of my (the organization's) decisions and actions because they promote the greatest balance of benefit over harm?" If the answer is "Yes," the ground rules are still End-Point Ethics. If the answer is "No," the ground rules are genuinely a form of Rule Ethics.

Suppose that, through this reverse-engineering process, you find that you or an organization have ground rules which are a form of Rule Ethics. This leaves the question of to what particular Rule Ethics you or the organization subscribe. Knowing the specific code by which you and others act can help you better foresee what actions you and others are likely to take and to find approaches to problems which satisfy the ground rules of all involved.

In order to assess the Rule Ethics of a person or organization, we build on the stakeholder approach to decision making. In any key decision, identify the key groups having a significant stake in the decision. Then correlate with each group the ethical code, the specific Rule Ethics, of that group. This helps you spot points of resistance to your decision that will not be uncovered by simply specifying the interests of each group.

LESSON: IF YOU ARE DEALING WITH GROUPS, PARTICULARLY PUBLIC INTEREST GROUPS, WHOSE ACTIONS CANNOT BE FORESEEN OR UNDERSTOOD IN TERMS OF THEIR REASONABLE INTERESTS, DETERMINE THE SPECIFIC RULE ETHICS OF THE GROUPS. THEIR ACTIONS CAN BE BETTER FORESEEN AND UNDERSTOOD IN TERMS OF THEIR ETHICAL CODES THAN IN TERMS OF THEIR INTERESTS.

For example, if you are dealing with environmental groups, zoning boards, or the media, knowing the ethical codes (and I do not mean formal codes) of these groups will help you anticipate their responses to your initiatives. These groups often act in ways not easily viewed as self-interested. Thus, it is difficult to grasp the ethics of these groups in End-Point terms. But you can manage relations with such external groups by learning their basic ethical rules.

One area in which lack of understanding of conflicting ethical viewpoints is a daily hazard is international business. American executives often go to great lengths to understand the economic and technical conditions that prevail in a foreign market only to fail there for lack of understanding of the local ethics. One reason for this is that the ethical differences often seem so great that there is little hope of understanding the local ethics. But the prize is for those who succeed in finding enough common ground to allow for action that satisfies both one's own ethics and the local ethical viewpoint. Roger Fisher and William Ury base their "principled negotiation" process on essentially this Rule Ethical point (1981, pp. 17-40).

In the following case, a manager who did not concentrate only on differences but sought common ethical ground was able to create and sustain an important competitive advantage.

Trust Across Cultures

This case illustrates how finding common ethical ground can establish and stabilize good business relations across cultures. In the case, Mr. Jackson rose above the regular rules of business, and of his business, which insist on written contracts and documentation as a basis for service. Instead, Mr. Jackson met the customer more than halfway and did business in the way the customer expected -- based on undocumented trust. This opened a market for Mr. Jackson and allowed him to hold it.

Mr. Jackson is owner of one of the most successful Caterpillar Tractor dealerships in the United States. Mr. Jackson has succeeded by buffering his United States business from ups and downs through extensive participation in international markets. He illustrates why he has been so successful in international markets through the following story.

"In the early days of the dealership, I received an inquiry from Southeast Asia concerning an earthmoving machine. The fellow could only afford a very old, partly rebuilt machine, which I sold him. A few weeks after the machine was delivered, I received a panicked phone call from the guy saying that the machine broke down in the middle of a field. He was so busy telling me that he was going out of business and that he would come to the United States and kill me that I couldn't get a word in edgewise. I had no contractual obligation to repair this machine -- the machine was sold 'as is.' In fact, I had no contract at all with the guy, since we handled the entire deal by telephone. I finally found out where the machine was and had it repaired immediately. The fellow called me in shocked disbelief that he had been treated fairly, without a contract, <u>by an American</u>. He became a key source of my Southeast Asian business. We still move very little paper on business in that part of the world."

It is now over twenty years since the original incident. Mr. Jackson's dealership prospers in markets that his competitors regard as literally impenetrable. Mr. Jackson is aware that different people act from different ground rules and regularly teaches his representatives the art of finding an ethical common ground firm enough to provide a basis for doing business.

LESSON: WHEN DEALING WITH PEOPLE OR ORGANIZATIONS HAVING ETHICAL RULES WIDELY DIVERGENT FROM ONE'S OWN, REVERSE ENGINEER THEIR ACTIONS WITH AN EYE TO FINDING RULES THAT PROVIDE AN ETHICAL COMMON GROUND -- AND IGNORE THE DIVERGENT RULES SO FAR AS POSSIBLE.

Ethical Exceptions

One feature of ethical rules contributes so much to the misunderstanding of ethics and to the ethical indictment of business that we single it out for special attention. Ethical rules may be of one of two distinct kinds -- categorical or prima facie. Categorical rules allow absolutely no exceptions. Most ethical rules are not categorical. For example, the rule that one should keep promises has clear exceptions. In fact, sound ethics requires that this rule sometimes be broken. Suppose I promise to sell the rights to a patent to a friend. After making the promise, I learn that he is selling new technologies to the Soviet Union for military uses. He probably befriended me for no other reason than to find out what I know about missile guidance systems. I now think my "friend" wants to buy my patent to help the Soviets build an offensive missle. I am obligated to break my promise to him and, if possible, sell him a very misleading fake patent.

The rules that one should keep promises and tell the truth are not categorical. They are prima facie rules. These rules can, and sometimes must, be violated in favor of more pressing obligations, such as the obligation to help others avoid military domination. Prima facie rules have the form: other things being equal, one should keep promises, tell the truth, obey the law, and so on. The problem is, then, determining when other things are equal.

Review your ground rules and decide if there are any you will not violate under any circumstances. If there are, these are you categorical ground rules, and they take priority over all other rules. Very few managers will find that they have any categorical ground rules. The world of the manager is very complex, and circumstances require that one think twice before rigidly adhering to any rule. Think of H. Ross Perot's decision to rescue EDS employees held hostage in Iran. Perot had to violate many rules, including rules to respect our laws and the laws and customs of other countries, to make an ethical decision.

A common and effective strategy for ethically attacking business is to indict business, a specific firm, or an executive for violating a commonly accepted ethical rule. The trick is that although the rule is commonly accepted (do not lie, bribe, violate the law, etc.), it is a prima facie rule which sometimes must be violated to uphold ethics. And the complex circumstances of international business tend to produce just such situations which do not conform to simple maxims. Businesses and executives typically respond to such attacks in economic, legal, or other defensive terms, which suggests concession that they acted unethically. But once you realize that violating an ethical rule may be ethical, or even ethically required, you can take a positive stand without conceding ethics to the critic.

LESSON: IF YOU ARE CRITICIZED FOR VIOLATING AN ETHICAL RULE, DETERMINE WHETHER THE RULE IS A CATEGORICAL OR PRIMA FACIE RULE. IF IT IS A PRIMA FACIE RULE, MEET THE CRITICISM BY CITING THE ETHICAL RULES YOU UPHELD BY VIOLATING THE RULE AT ISSUE.

In the following case study of international bribery, we see how the strategy of confusing prima facie and categorical ethical rules was used to effectively attack business.

Bribery

According to a Louis Harris survey (September 19, 1983, p. 16), most Americans condemn businesses for bribing officials of foreign governments. The conviction that bribery is wrong is based on Rule Ethics. Paying bribes violates ethical rules or principles, such as the rules that one should not lie (as one surely must in covering bribes) and that one should not cheat (taking advantage of honest competitors). But the issue of bribery is not as ethically clear-cut as this observation suggests. And many businesses and some government officials know there is something suspicious about this easy indictment of a once-common business practice.

The issue of bribery in United States policy is a conflict among ethical views. The health of American businesses that engage in international trade and, thus, the overall health of our economy, depends on resolving this conflict. It is clear that the American public and most American businesses abhor bribery of domestic government officials and, by extension, of foreign government officials. The issue of bribing foreign officials came to a head in the aftermath of Watergate. Many of the corporate "slush funds" used to finance Watergate skulduggery existed primarily to provide funds to bribe foreign officials to gain or facilitate business. Battered by the public outrage about ethics in the superheated environment of the time, Congress did the only honorable thing: it regulated business and left itself untouched.

On December 20, 1977, President Carter signed into law S.305, the Foreign Corrupt Practices Act (FCPA). This act makes it a crime for American corporations to offer or provide payments to officials of foreign governments to obtain or retain business. Violators of the FCPA, both corporations and managers, face severe penalties. A company may be fined up to $1 million, while its officers who directly participate in violations of the Act <u>or have reason to know of such violations</u> face up to five years in prison and/or $10,000 in fines. The FCPA establishes extra-ordinarily stringent record-keeping requirements for publicly-held corporations to ensure that the proscribed payments, or knowledge of them, are not concealed.

The primary motivation for the FCPA was neither economic nor legal. The motivation was ethical and political. The ethical motivation stemmed from the fact that the public and Congress disapproved of corporations bribing foreign government officials. This disapproval was based on our strong prohibition of bribes of our own officials and the easy assumption that other governments work as ours does. The political motivation mixed the desire to comply with popular anti-bribery sentiment, the sense that attacking big business is politically advantageous, and the need to divert public attention from Congressional misdeeds. Given the important role of ethics in motivating the FCPA and the serious economic consequences of this law, it must be asked whether ethical disapproval of international bribery makes sense.

Are the proscribed payments really bribes? The willingness of the public to see these payments as bribes shows how business is losing the battle over ethics. A good case argues that the payments in question were, in many cases, extortion payments extracted from American corporations by corrupt foreign officials.

Carl Kotchian, President of Lockheed Aircraft Corporation during the period of the notorious Lockheed bribes to Japanese government officials, begins his memoir of the bribery scandal by saying, "My initiation into the chill realities of extortion, Japanese style, began in 1972" (1977, p. 6-12). Kotchian makes a convincing case that Lockheed had already won the competition on behalf of its Tristar passenger plane when he was informed he would have to pay "pledges" to high officials of the Japanese goverment or lose the sale. Kotchian strongly resisted paying the "pledges" but they were absolutely demanded.

Whether or not Kotchian should have complied (we are obligated to resist extortion if possible), the payments in question do not look like bribes. However, with so many dubious payments made in every part of the world, it is overwhelmingly likely that some American companies paid genuine bribes to foreign officials. The head of the legal department of a major oil company once showed me a list he developed to advise company representatives new to the Middle East on customary levels of bribes in each country. This leaves the question of whether such payments are ethical.

Opposition to international bribery cannot be based on End-Point Ethics. End-Point Ethics gives many secret payments and bribes a clean bill of ethical health. Suppose the Lockheed payments were out and out bribes. On End-Point Ethics, we weigh the benefits against the costs of the payments to determine whether they were ethical. The benefits are clear. The most important was selling the Tristar. This benefitted Lockheed management and stockholders, as well as Lockheed employees who would have lost their jobs without this sale. Kotchian offers the following assessment of Lockheed's stake in the Japanese market: "...Lockheed had nowhere else to go but Japan ... The bleak situation all but dictated a strong push for sales in the biggest untapped market left -- Japan. This push, if successful, might well bring in revenues upwards of $400 million. Such a cash flow would go a long way toward helping to restore Lockheed's fiscal health and it would, of course, save the jobs of thousands of the firm's employees" (p. 7). Kotchian's statement is accurate. Further benefits of Lockheed's payments include savings to American taxpayers from the revenues generated by this business and the unemployment benefits avoided. Finally, All-Nipon Airlines benefitted in acquiring what was, at the time, an outstanding airplane.

There are harms associated with secret payments to officials of foreign governments. First and foremost, these payments help corrupt officials maintain their positions, to the detriment of their local constituents. The cost of the payments must be passed along to consumers. In some cases, the payments may lead to the presence of inferior, possibly dangerous products on the market. In the Lockheed case, and in most reported cases of bribery by American companies, these harms were absent or minimal.

If Lockheed had not paid the officials in question, it is clear that somebody else would have paid them. The Japanese people were not made worse off. Their position was arguably improved, since the Tristar is a superior plane. On balance, there were substantive, otherwise unobtainable, benefits to the

Lockheed payments. There were few harms, and these harms could not have been avoided by a refusal to pay by Lockheed.

The End-Point view issues a favorable verdict on the Lockheed payments, and on analogous payments and bribes made by other American corporations. This does not mean all such payments are ethical on the End-Point view. It means that such payments are ethical if the product is good, the payment demanded, and others will pay if a particular firm does not. There are hardly grounds here for a blanket condemnation of bribes.

End-Point Ethics does not explain our blanket disapproval of international bribery. In fact, bribes may promote our individual or collective best interests. We oppose bribes because they violate our fundamental ethical principles. The grounds for condemning bribes must be sought in Rule Ethics.

The ethical codes of most American citizens and managers include a rule stating, "No person or organization should offer or pay a bribe or other secret payment to any legitimate government official." Even if the ethical codes of some countries tolerate bribery, ours clearly does not. The code of conduct for new employees of the Electronic Data Systems Corporation concisely summarizes the view typical of American business: "A determination that a payment or practice is not forbidden by law does not conclude the analysis ... It is always appropriate to make further inquiry into the ethics ... Could you do business with someone who acts the way you do? The answer must be YES." While some of us do not live up to the standard embodied in this code, it nonetheless is clearly a part of our ethics.

The fact that our ethics prohibits bribery does not close the case against bribes paid to foreign officials. The reasons for this are essential to understanding and intelligently applying any code of ethics -- and to meeting biased ethical attacks.

The rules proscribing bribes and other secret payments are prima facie rules having many exceptions. American pilots flying relief missions into Cambodia regularly bribed Cambodian officials to be permitted to unload critically needed food and medical supplies. It would have been morally degenerate for these pilots to refuse to pay bribes because this violated their ethical codes. Countless children would have died. The issue about payments to foreign government officials boils down, on Rule Ethics, to this question: Do American businesses have obligations that override our ethical prohibition of bribery?

Let us take a final look at the Lockheed case. Kotchian states that he felt obliged to Lockheed employees to promote their job security. Kotchian also had an obligation to Lockheed stockholders to earn a reasonable return on their investments. A less specific obligation on Kotchian was to promote economic well-being in the United States through the economic success of Lockheed. If these factors do not seem significant enough to override a general prohibition of bribery, you probably did not have twenty years service at Lockheed or a significant portion of your retirement fund committed to Lockheed stock.

Rule Ethics, which appeared to simply prohibit bribes at the outset, is not that simple at all. Kotchian's obligations to promote the well-being of Lockheed's employees and investors weigh heavily against the obligation not to pay bribes. Rule Ethics, despite any prohibition of bribery it may include, allows no blanket condemnation of payments like Lockheed's.

A Rule Ethics assessment of the FCPA is also not unequivocally supportive. While the FCPA reduces under-the-table payments to foreign officials by United States firms, it increases the number made by foreign firms. And it forces managers to violate obligations to employees and investors. If we assume the federal government is obligated to promote the interests of United States business and labor, then the FCPA requires that the federal government violate some of its obligations. Some versions of Rule Ethics include a "principle of tolerance" requiring that we respect the ethical views of others, even when they disagree with our own. The FCPA also requires violations of a principle of tolerance with respect to any country whose ethics permits officials to accept bribes. While the final reckoning of these conflicting obligations is unclear, it cannot result in unequivocal endorsement of the FCPA. At best, the FCPA is an ethically motivated piece of legislation in search of ethical justification.

Given the great costs that the FCPA imposes upon business and labor, and the lack of a clear ethical purpose for imposing these costs, it is depressing that we passed this law with little discussion of the ethical issues. Once a piece of legislation that purports to have the backing of ethics is put forward, it is hard to prevent passage. Once the law is passed, it is nearly impossible to rescind.

LESSON: ONCE LEGISLATION THAT IS SUPPOSEDLY ETHICALLY MOTIVATED IS PASSED, IT IS ALMOST IMPOSSIBLE TO RESCIND. THE TIME TO FORCEFULY PARTICIPATE IN DISCUSSION OF ETHICALLY MOTIVATED LEGISLATION IS BEFORE IT IS PASSED, NO MATTER HOW DIFFICULT THIS APPEARS AT THE TIME.

The FCPA is our Prohibition. There have been repeated attempts to modify the stringent accounting provisions of the FCPA. The intent of these efforts is to gut the law without repealing it. Executives and legislators have the courage to speak on behalf of gutting the law, but fear arguing for repeal. A Louis Harris poll revealed that 78 percent of United States executives view the law as a serious impediment to doing business in countries where bribery is an accepted practice. Sixty-eight percent favor gutting the law. Only a few endorse outright repeal (September 19, 1983, p. 16). Yet, off-the-record interviews with executives of multinational enterprises reveal almost universal scorn for the FCPA. In short, we painted ourselves into an ethical corner by passing the FCPA without thoroughly considering its ethical implications. (These issues are discussed in Pastin and Hooker, 1985, pp. 169-177.)

The Scarce Resource: Independent Thinking

When managers address ethics, they often think in terms of formal ethical codes or codes of conduct. When I receive something labeled "code of ethics" from an organization to which I belong or for whom I work, I promptly throw it out, or I initial it illegibly if absolutely required. My intelligence and integrity are insulted, ethics is associated with legalism and bureaucracy, and a lot of wastebaskets need emptying. No one earns the right to control anyone's ethics by employing them or by holding higher organizational office. The executive who promulgates such a code endorses the idea that ethical rules are categorical. He and the organization appear foolish and without integrity when the inevitable exceptions occur.

<u>The scarce resource in ethics is independent thinking -- not rule compliance.</u> Codes constrict thinking and reinforce the myth that the heart of ethics is compliance.

LESSON: TO GAIN ANYTHING BY HAVING A CODE OF ETHICS, MANAGEMENT MUST <u>RELENTLESSLY</u> EMPHASIZE THAT CODES ARE MERELY GUIDELINES, THAT THE RULES HAVE EXCEPTIONS, AND THAT THE ESSENCE OF ETHICS IS INDEPENDENT THINKING AND QUESTIONING.

This sort of responsible implementation of a code of ethics is virtually untested. My search of thousands of pages of management journals uncovered exactly no evidence that codes of ethics have a positive effect on conduct.

The thinking manager can learn by considering Rule Ethics and, particularly, its application to international bribery. End-Point Ethics asks the question, "What is in this course of action for me and for others who are affected?" Rule Ethics asks, "What set of rules are we playing by and who set the rules?" This question forces the manager to see his actions as instances of a code that he must either reinforce or oppose. Because ethical positions resist change, it is important to clearly grasp the accepted ethical code. Changing an organization is a long-term project. It requires that the manager be aware that he is trying to bring about a fundamental and lasting change and that he work consistently toward this change on every front.

The manager who turns his attention to the ethics of an organization will find conflicts among different sets of rules in different groups within the organization and more conflicts within each rule set. Because ethical rules are deeply felt and difficult to modify, attempted shifts should be framed in terms of the accepted code or codes as far as possible. For instance, once it is admitted that there is an ethical obligation to promote equity, one can argue for a balance of this obligation against other equally important obligations, such as keeping commitments to long-term employees and rewarding performance. A shift toward an ethics of performance may gradually result.

In public fora, it is particularly important to distinguish prima facie obligations, which include almost everything under the title of ethics, and categorical obligations. When business is attacked on ethical grounds, a standard strategy is to take a prima facie obligation and pretend it is a categorical obligation. Thus, critics might cite the obligation not to bribe other things being equal or the obligation to provide equal pay for equal work other things being equal, while ignoring obligations to employees and stockholders (bribery) or local pay standards (equal pay). Violators can then be characterized as unethical monsters. If one acknowledges the obligation without emphasizing its prima facie nature, one appears to plead for an exemption from ethics.

References

"Anti-Bribery Act Splits Executives." Business Week, September 19, 1983, p. 16.

Aristotle. Nichomachean Ethics. (M. Ostwald, Trans.) Indianapolis: Bobbs-Merrill, 1982.

Fisher, R. and Ury, W. Getting to Yes. Boston, MA: Houghton Mifflin, 1981.

Kotchian, A. C. "The Pay-Off: Lockheed's 70-day Mission to Tokyo." The Saturday Review, July 9, 1977, pp. 6-12.

Pastin, M. and Hooker, M. "Ethics and the Foreign Corrupt Practices Act." In K. D'Andrade and P. Werhane (Eds.), Profit and Responsibility. New York: Edwin Mellen Press, 1985.

ETHICS IN THE FCPA DEBATE: SOME PUBLIC POLICY LESSONS

John M. Kline

The Foreign Corrupt Practices Act (FCPA) is academically interesting, politically contentious, and commercially frustrating; it is also ethically important. The FCPA aims at reducing the use of bribery in international business transactions. Perhaps equally important, the Act may also teach us some political process lessons regarding how better to handle a direct appeal to ethical standards when setting United States policy on international commercial issues. Given the increasingly complex political and social environment within which international business must operate, such lessons cannot be learned too soon.

The FCPA was a political decision to enforce ethical standards on private economic actors. More than this, the Act used the extraterritorial application of United States law to apply ethical standards to international, cross-cultural situations where both American interpretation of ethical norms and the United States right to impose them in overseas political jurisdictions were called into question.

Nearly a decade has passed since this unique law was debated in the halls of Congress and in the pages of the public press. Several issues have already been extensively researched, if not fully resolved, such as the extent of the law's economic impact in the "real world" of business, and proposals to "reform" certain FCPA provisions. Indeed, the last several sessions of Congress have considered, but not yet passed, various modifications to the law. Important though these issues may be, I propose to leave their analysis to other commentators and concentrate instead on a retrospective look at the FCPA that will examine the role played by ethics in the law's passage, suggesting several lessons this historical experience may have for us in dealing with similar issues of business ethics today and in the future.

One clear impact of ethics in the FCPA debate is the final passage of the law itself. It is likely that no new legislation would have passed, and certainly no criminal statute with the FCPA's unique extraterritorial characteristics, without the influence of active appeals to prescriptive ethical values. Several other conclusions are less obvious, however. The role of ethics in the debate also can be said to have: (1) produced a complicated, unpolished, and largely inefficient law; (2) confused United States strategy for dealing with the international bribery problem; and (3) distorted the approach of United States companies to expressing ethical concerns on the international level.

The primary lesson to be drawn from an analysis of these conclusions is that policy leaders, perhaps especially those in the private business sector, must find better ways to prepare for and participate in the public policy-making process when issues arise that contain a highly emotive appeal to ethical standards. This challenge is particularly important since the incidence of such issues is likely to increase as international business continues to grow in importance and complexity.

Ethics and Law in the FCPA

Ideally we would all like to think that legal standards are at least based on, if not coterminous with, the ethical standards of a society. Often, however, one must strain hard to see the "ethical" components in a law-making process that is awash in political strategies and commercial impacts. This obversation is even more true when law-making involves setting policies for actions in the international arena, where preeminent concerns of national interest -- national security and global economic competitiveness -- seem to dictate a suspension of certain ethical norms that might be persuasive at the purely domestic level.

Without going into all of the historical details, it is possible to identify the FCPA as a notable exception to this general rule. Three driving forces provided the impetus behind the Act's passage -- foreign policy repercussions, economic competition impacts, and ethical value concerns. The foreign policy element arose from a perception that the questionable payments practices of private multinational corporations had created risks for United States political relations with important foreign countries, at times and in places outside the control of United States governmental authorities. Often cited as examples of this foreign policy concern are the complications that emerged in United States relations with implicated political leaders and parties in friendly governments in Japan, Italy, Korea, and the Netherlands.[1]

Economic factors also played a role in the development and passage of the FCPA. Bribery introduces inefficient, non-market distortions into sales considerations, raising the cost of transactions to the consumer, albeit usually indirectly through the mechanism of unnecessarily high government expenditures and subsequent taxation. This misallocation of resources is not only costly, but it is also considered unfair in the sense that it distorts the assumably unbiased system of marketplace competition.

The economic nature of this argument can be seen in its most telling use during the FCPA debate, which was the revelation that in one widely publicized case, an American aircraft manufacturer used bribery to secure a sale where the only real competitor was another American company. In other words, even the potentially overridding, or at least offsetting goal of securing a foreign sale for United States national companies was not at issue in this case; there were no foreign competitor firms using such "dirty tricks" and thereby forcing United States firms to compete on the same level. This example seemed to clarify a situation that otherwise could have become muddled in policy makers' minds. Concern over the use of bribery in international economic competition seemed amenable to the same standards of fairness used to judge domestic economic activity.

The link to notions of domestic economic unfairness points to a third and broader element of general ethical standards as an active influence in the policy-making process. In justifying the need for legislation, the Senate Banking Committee's report on the proposed FCPA noted both foreign policy problems and the misallocation of resources. The report made clear, however, that the fundamental issue was one of public morality, stating: "More importantly, bribery is simply unethical. It is counter to the moral expectations and values of the American public, and it erodes public confidence in the integrity of the free market system."[2]

This recourse to ideas of the nation's basic moral fiber -- the notion that bribery is just plain wrong -- played an enormously important role in the legislative outcome. First, the invocation of strong ethical norms helped shape the content of the legislation by justifying, even demanding, more extreme actions than would otherwise seem necessary. Yes, foreign policy complications had arisen and ecomomic distortions occurred, but existing regulatory remedies, or at most, a new statute with common civil penalties against offending companies, would normally have seemed in order.

Prior to the 1976 election, and even early into the new Carter Administration, the executive branch was arguing that the existing laws were, in fact, adequate and that an approach based on disclosure rather than new regulatory penalties was the appropriate solution. Such a bureaucratic proposal, however, did not embody a sufficient amount of penance to achieve the type of absolution from the sins of corporate bribery that was seemingly demanded by the American public. After months upon months of spiraling press revelations of corporate bribery that spanned the ranks of top industrial companies and reached into the multimillions of dollars, a more satisfying retribution had to be extracted. Indeed, even the executive branch experienced a policy reversal on the appropriateness of legislative remedies. The White House discovered that nothing less than support for a new law containing criminal sanctions against overseas corporate bribery would satisfy the requirements of the campaign promise-book that recorded positions taken by candidate Carter during his nationwide meetings with the American voter.

Not only did the invocation of ethical prescriptions seem to dictate more extreme forms of solutions, but the use made of ethical norms in the legislative debate circumscribed the balancing role that could be played by other political actors, particularly in the business community. The policy-making process in the United States is normally one of an open give-and-take between interested and affected parties. Proposals are formulated, adjusted, modified, and refined over an often protracted period of time. Competing and sometimes conflicting interests are balanced in an effort to meld the needs and desires of numerous groups into a beneficial and practical national policy. This congressional process does not always yield the most attractive results, but for all its warts, it is the expression of popular democracy in the United States. One sure way to distort the results, on any issue, is to eliminate from the process the effective representation of key affected parties. Clearly, the business community was eliminated from effective representation in the FCPA process when it voluntarily retired to the sidelines because it felt unable to participate within the heavily ethics-laden context of the debate.

The reluctance of individual business leaders to participate directly in the FCPA congressional process is understandable. Despite their obvious interest in the outcome, direct involvement in legislative advocacy could expose individual executives and corporations to the worst type of characterizations regarding unethical self-aggrandizement at public expense. Neither all businesses nor their executives were, in fact, guilty of the serious breaches of ethical behavior represented in the overseas bribery scandals. Still, a disturbingly large number of companies, nearly 500, ultimately disclosed instances of improper payments.

Furthermore, the congressional debate on the FCPA proposal occurred at the very same time that most United States multinational companies, on their own or under the Security and Exchange Commission's (SEC) voluntary disclosure program, were internally investigating their far-flung operations to determine just what their involvement might be in such payments schemes. There were very few business executives who felt confident enough to appear before Senator Proxmire's committee when there was a risk that corporate indiscretions abroad might surface under staff investigations and be laid out on the witness table for all to examine, including the news media covering the proceedings.

The prominent role played in the FCPA debate by appeals to standards of ethics and morality thus served to constrain effective opposition to the proposal for an extraterritorially applied criminal statute against overseas corporate bribery. Objections to the bill, particularly if they were voiced by corporate executives, were met by the skeptical retort: "Do you mean you want to continue bribing?" A public debate framed in these terms was not amenable to a serious discussion of the complexities of applying ethical notions to business operations in cross-cultural, multijurisdictional settings. This approach to policy-making yielded an unpolished law that has also unintentionally confused United States strategy on the international bribery issue and distorted the development of international business ethics within individual corporations.

The FCPA's Imprecise Standards

Passage of the FCPA in 1977 met the domestic political need for strong and timely action, but the law left unanswered many legal and ethical questions. Recognition of the legal ambiguities has come partly from the debate over the FCPA's accounting provisions, where somewhat unusual terms were used in drafting the law. Other concerns reflect problem areas in implementing the bribery prohibitions called for in the law. Among the more obvious issues are distinguishing between prohibited bribes and allowable facilitating payments, where both dollar amounts and a payment's purpose may be considered; determining when a corporation should have "reason to know" that funds are being used in a prohibited fashion, when intervening parties such as agents or dealers may be involved; knowing whether extortion is a legitimate defense (or an ethical excusing condition) where coercion is used to extract payments from a company; and overcoming problems of information-gathering and witness cooperation, for both prosecution and constitutionally-guaranteed defense purposes, where the locale of an alleged violation is in a sovereign foreign country and, by definition, involves political officials of that nation.

A full listing of the many important legal issues regarding FCPA interpretation and implementation is both beyond the scope of this paper and is unnecessary to make the point that what emerged from the congressional process was an unpolished law that has proven confusing, unwieldly, and inefficient in application. Neither the law's supporters nor its opponents are pleased with the results, although the opponents seem intent on revising the law while proponents more often question the nature of its implementation.[3] Greater attention to these difficulties, most of which were foreseeable during the FCPA formulation process, could have produced a more realistically usable instrument.

In the realm of ethical standards, the FCPA raises at least as many questions as it answers in terms of using United States law to enforce a standard of corporate ethics on international business operations. In distinguishing between bribery and facilitating payments, the FCPA follows a line of reasoning that the former is worse than the latter, a value orientation that emphasizes measuring the consequences of an action rather than the value content of the process or means by which the action takes place. Was this ethical judgment intended by United States political authorities, or does the outcome simply reflect a decision regarding which violations are more "reachable" by legal enforcement devices? Does the law's acceptance of facilitating payments constitute a judgment that these actions are ethically acceptable, at least in other countries where payments may be so prevalent as to appear culturally ingrained, thereby suggesting an approach of ethical relativism? If so, should it be United States law that determines the demarcation line between bribery and facilitating payments when they occur in a foreign nation?[4]

The FCPA outlaws only the bribery of foreign public officials by United States persons (including corporations). If these types of actions warrant the use of an extraterritorially applied United States law, should commercial bribery occurring between United States persons and foreign private sector individuals or corporations be considered equally unethical and deserving of United States legal sanctions? If the United States government accepts an obligation to enforce on United States companies anti-bribery standards that already appear in most foreign nations' legal statutes, does this country also accept a more general ethical obligation to make certain that United States companies do not engage in other practices that may violate foreign laws and would be illegal under United States laws if they occurred in this country? This question could arise, for example, in the related field of so-called "accommodation payments" that can assist violations of a nation's tax or foreign exchange regulation.

Again, without developing an exhaustive list of ethical issues, it is clear that the congressional debate over the FCPA, while intoning ethical precepts throughout the process, failed to address many key ethical issues relevant to the legislation directly and to the law as it constitutes a precedent for other potential United States actions.

The FCPA as Global Strategy

A 1979 article by Walter Surrey for the <u>Harvard International Law Journal</u> discusses many of the issues cited above regarding the FCPA's legal imprecision, but the author also raises a more fundamental question concerning the match between the policy objectives being sought and the choice of the FCPA as the means to attain those ends. As he put it:

> To return to the underlying question of the imposition of domestic concepts of morality in foreign transactions, it is important to inquire whether the purpose of the Act is to eliminate corruption throughout the world, or merely to eliminate corruption carried out by United States multinationals.[5]

He suggests that if the objective is the latter, increased disclosure requirements coupled with civil penalties would be a more appropriate and effective approach that would avoid many of the extraterritorial criminal liability problems created by the FCPA. On the other hand, if the policy objective is to seek to eliminate such bribery from international business transactions, this goal can only be reached with the active support and involvement of foreign governments and is not amenable to unilateral and extraterritorial United States enforcement.

Some individuals viewed the FCPA as compatible with a broader international move to prohibit such payments. Respected authorities such as George Bell suggested in congressional hearings that the passage of the FCPA would show other nations that the United States was serious about this issue, leading them to agree to an international accord outlawing such payments worldwide. This conclusion was obviously wrong. Other nations were reluctant to be drawn into potentially uncomfortable investigations or critical self-analysis in a public international forum and usually were under little domestic pressure to respond to the issue. Having seen the United States unilaterally constrain its multinational corporations in such an unusual fashion, these nations were content to let the matter die a quiet death. There was some concern that the extraterritorial application of the FCPA might create a few problems, but there was also the silent assumption abroad that some commercial benefits might accrue to competitors of the unilaterally self-restrained Americans.

The belief that passage of the FCPA would advance the negotiation of an international accord on bribery was an idea that grew within the ethically-charged atmosphere of the congressional debate. The moral outrage evident in the debate over the bribery scandals was easily imputed to exist at an equivalent level in the public and with political decision makers in other countries. The validity of this assumption was not sufficiently challenged because most critics, largely confined to business institutions, were too vulnerable to charges that they were simply trying to block or delay the adoption of an effective anti-bribery law by calling for priority to be given to the negotiation of bilateral or multilateral agreements. In the end, passage of the FCPA actually confused United States strategy for achieving international accords on the bribery issue and hampered the attainment of this goal.

The United States government initially developed a strategy on the bribery issue that placed a great deal of emphasis on international accords. Bilateral information-sharing agreements were negotiated with several countries. A segment of the 1976 voluntary Organization for Economic Cooperation and Development Guidelines for Multinational Enterprises condemned corporate bribery practices. A binding treaty was proposed by the United States at a meeting of the United Nations Economic and Social Council, which established a working group in 1976 and proceeded for several years to negotiate such an accord. Passage of the FCPA in 1977, however, provided no incentive to other countries to act on this issue and may have served as a disincentive to the extent that other nations perceived a possible commercial gain at the expense of unilaterally constrained United States companies. Once the FCPA was embedded in law, it also limited somewhat the flexibility of United States government negotiators seeking to draft an international accord.

The FCPA debate distorted the perception not only of what other nations really wanted, but also of how United States objectives might be obtained and at what potential cost. The United States could probably have forced international action on bribery standards if it had understood the lack of enthusiasm abroad and had been willing to pay the price for overcoming foreign reluctance. One avenue of approach was suggested by Senate Resolution 265, which called on the President to use General Agreement on Tariffs and Trade (GATT) mechanisms to develop a code prohibiting bribery in international trade transactions. That resolution pointed out that bribery can be considered an unfair trade practice of the type addressed in Section 301 of the Trade Act of 1974.[6]

While not suggested formally at the time, if progress were not made in achieving an acceptable GATT accord, the United States could apply pressure by moving unilaterally to apply Section 301 sanctions against countries that failed to control bribery practices by their firms and thereby engage in unfair trade practices that harm United States commerce. Such an action would have enormous implications for trade relations and would be likened by some to using a trade sanctions cannon to kill a pesky bribery fly. The point, however, is that the United States probably had the power to force greater multilateral action, but at some considerable risk. Listening to the FCPA debate over the immorality of bribery, one could assume that the elimination of this evil was worth the potential cost. This issue was never directly confronted in a cost/benefit fashion, however, due to the assumption that other nations held an equal interest in achieving stringent controls on bribery practices.

The FCPA debate confused United States strategy on seeking an international agreement, deluding policy makers on issues regarding the method and the cost of this goal's attainment. The interests and motivations of foreign actors were misinterpreted. Passage of the FCPA may have added a disincentive, rather than providing an incentive, for other nations to negotiate an international standard. Once in place, the law also limited United States negotiating flexibility in multilateral forums. As a result of these factors, the United States initiative seeking bilateral and multilateral accords on bribery was sidetracked, and the United States forfeited a chance to encourage and influence greater action at the international level.

The FCPA and International Business Ethics

The FCPA debate and resultant law also has distorted corporate views on the development of international business ethics. This conclusion emerges clearly in my study of individual corporate codes of conduct, now published in the book International Codes and Multinational Business[7], that examines particularly how firms address their international responsibilities. Passage of the FCPA is directly related to the growth of corporate codes, with most of them (90 percent of those examined in the study) originating only after the foreign payments controversy erupted, especially with the SEC's voluntary disclosure program acting as a stimulus. The FCPA is one of three topics consistently covered by nearly every corporate code, the other two subjects being antitrust and conflict of interest policies.

The most disturbing element in my findings was that the FCPA was often the only specific issue discussed in applying corporate policies to international business situations. The preoccupation with the FCPA is perhaps understandable from an historical perspective, but it is an unsatisfactory definition of the international responsibilities of a multinational enterprise. Multinational firms typically derive between 30 percent to 60 percent of their profits from international business operations, but what message is conveyed externally to foreign citizens, or even internally to a company's own employees, when the only international policy issue addressed in a firm's code of conduct is its responsiveness to an extraterritorially-applied United States law? A company's silence on the wide range of other important international business responsibility issues will speak loudly regarding the firm's priorities and its lack of an international, intercultural perspective.

Preoccupation with the FCPA has too often dominated the agenda of corporate concern on international business ethics, thereby biasing an understanding of global issues and distorting efforts to develop a more positive approach to defining corporate responsibilities. Too often international business ethics for United States companies is portrayed as engaging in philanthropic activities and not violating any laws, especially the FCPA! Doing good deeds is commendable and not violating the law certainly constitutes the floor of business ethics, but little attention has been given to addressing the particular ethical issues that arise when applying operational policies in the cross-cultural, multijurisdictional world of international business. The book suggests how such issues can be addressed in an individualized manner according to a specific firm's circumstances. The relevant point for the FCPA is that the bribery issue, and in particular the public debate and United States criminal law outcome, has so dominated the landscape of international corporate ethics that it preoccupies executives' thinking and distorts the development of a positive approach to defining international business ethics.

Unless a corporation addresses the relationship of ethics to the range of operational policies used in international business situations, the firm will not be approaching a serious application of international business ethics. Significantly, the company also will not be preparing itself to engage in public policy-making debates on such subjects. By analyzing and adjusting its own operations in an ethically-sensitive manner, corporations can act in advance of emerging public controversies, perhaps mitigating the need for regulatory action or, at the minimum, pre-positioning the firm to play a positive, active role in shaping the public debate's outcome.

The Shape of Future FCPAs

After reviewing all of the criticism of the FCPA contained in this paper, one might assume that the author favors repeal of the law -- but I do not. Some improvements in both content and administration are desirable, but repeal now would send the wrong signal to everyone involved, without recovering lost opportunities in terms of global strategy for dealing with the bribery issue or encouraging greater attention to international business ethics. The more important lessons to be learned from a retrospective look at the FCPA lie in the guidance it can provide for avoiding similar failings in future debates over public policy on FCPA-type issues.

In recent years, multinational corporations have not been subjected to the scale of broad and vigorous criticism that was directed at them throughout most of the 1970's. This relative lull is not likely to last. Stimulated by incidents such as the infant formula marketing controversy and the disaster in Bhopal, renewed activity is underway at the international level to address concerns about such issues as consumer rights, workplace safety, pharmaceutical research and marketing practices, and the transport and disposal of hazardous substances.

Further efforts should be expected that are aimed at achieving actions by home governments, particularly through public policy initiatives in the United States. The United States provides an exceedingly open policy-making structure with multiple points of access that can be reached by interest groups both directly and through a vigorous public media. Issues involving the operations of large United States companies, at home or abroad, can be carried easily onto the public agenda, particularly where intonations of unethical corporate conduct may accompany the challenge.

Ethical precepts can exert a powerful influence in open public debates about corporate regulation, or indeed on many other issues. Appeals to ethical prescriptions can be both used and abused. Normative language tends to force solutions toward the extreme, placing issues on a different level of public perception while driving them with the force of a moral imperative. A positive ethical role is best attained in a democratic policy process where all concerned parties are positioned to participate fully and effectively in the debate. For United States corporations, this requirement implies a more concerted effort than in the past to examine the application of ethical value concerns to their international business operations in advance of the time that such issues are drawn into the public policy arena.

Notes

1. For background reading on the overseas bribery controversy, see congressional hearings records for 1975-76 before the Senate Committee on Banking, Housing, and Urban Affairs and the Senate Foreign Relations Subcommittee on Multinational Corporations. An early summary book on the subject is *International Payoffs* by Yerachmiel Kugel and Gladys W. Gruenberg, Lexington Books, 1977.

2. U.S. Congress, Senate, Committee on Banking, Housing, and Urban Affairs "Corrupt Overseas Payments by U.S. Business Enterprises," Report No. 94-1031, 94th Congress, 2nd Session, p. 3.

3. Useful documentation on many FCPA legal issues and Justice Department enforcement procedures can be found in *The Enforcement of the Foreign Corrupt Practices Act by the Reagan Administration*, a report issued in the conjunction with an August 2, 1983 meeting of the American Bar Association, jointly sponsored by the Section on International Law and Practices and the Section on Corporations, Banking, and Business Law.

4. It is interesting to note that the business community, not normally given to moralistic language, speaks of the "evil" of extortion and bribery payments, even when involving minor amounts. Recommendations for action, however, concentrate on "the greater threat to competition" represented by large payments rather than instances of facilitating payments. See *Extortion and Bribery in Business Transactions*, report adopted by the 131st Session of the Council of the International Chamber of Commerce, November 29, 1977, p. 12.

5. Walter Sterling Surrey, "The Foreign Corrupt Practices Act; Let the Punishment Fit the Crime," *Harvard International Law Journal*, Vol. 20, No. 2, Spring 1979, p. 300.

6. U.S. Congress, Senate, Committees on Finance, Subcommittee on International Trade, "Protecting the Ability of the United States to Trade Abroad," Hearing on S. Res. 265, October 6, 1975.

7. John M. Kline, *International Codes and Multinational Business: Setting Guidelines for International Business Operations.* Quorum Books, Greenwood Press, 1985.

CHAPTER THIRTEEN

JOBS, INFORMATION TECHNOLOGY, AND MULTINATIONAL BUSINESS

MARJORIE THINES STANLEY
Professor of Finance and Chairperson
Department of Finance and Decision Sciences
Texas Christian University
Fort Worth, Texas

ABBE MOWSHOWITZ
Professor of Computer Science
The City College (CUNY)
New York City, New York

THE FOREIGN DIRECT INVESTMENT DECISION AND JOB EXPORT AS AN ETHICAL DILEMMA FOR THE MULTINATIONAL CORPORATION*

Marjorie Thines Stanley

Introduction

The subject of this conference, ethical dilemmas for the multinational corporation, involves an interesting formulation of the topic, because it does not speak of ethical dilemmas for the manager of the multinational corporation, but for the multinational corporation itself. Of course the corporation is a person, albeit an artificial person, a creation of law. The corporation as person can have intention, but that intention will have been defined by natural persons. The corporation as person can act, but it cannot act precisely as can a natural person. Rather, it must act through the acts of its directors, managers, and other employees. Ethical dilemmas of the multinational corporation thus involve an interesting combination of public ethics [26] and moral agency issues. They also involve ethical considerations at various levels. These range from the macro, in the sense of the multinational corporation as an institutional form, to the micro, in the sense of the multinational corporation as an individual firm, to the personal, in the sense of the role of the individual manager or other decision maker.

The specific ethical dilemma for the multinational corporation that I propose to address in this paper is the matter of ethical dilemmas involved in the foreign direct investment decision itself,[1] that is, dilemmas associated with the very decision by which the corporation becomes a multinational as opposed to a domestic corporation. As an example of one such dilemma, I will primarily focus on ethical considerations relevant to the effects of the foreign direct investment decision on domestic employment opportunities. Ethical considerations at the macro, micro, and personal levels are involved in this foreign direct investment decision.

On the macro level, despite a growing body of literature concerned with the role and scope of the multinational corporation [1, 5, 18, 29], we have not yet developed a philosophy that integrates the multinational corporation as an

*The support of an M. J. Neeley School of Business Summer Research Grant is gratefully acknowledged.

institutional form into the existing system of thought with regard to "capitalism" or "socialism," or into the evolving system of thought with regard to the role and function of the corporation not only in the domestic economy, but in the global economy. In the absence of such a philosophical system, a recognized ethical system of thought is also less likely to exist. Thus, value questions are constrained by and addressed within an implicitly domestic framework despite the multinational character of the institutions involved.

On the micro level, there is a substantial body of literature dealing with the foreign direct investment decision. This literature includes analyses of factors motivating the investment decision, analyses that stress economic, marketing, behavioral, or financial approaches. One can also find normative guides to decision making, such as the finance literature's analysis of the capital budgeting decision.

The individual manager, however, is likely to be aware of various pressures that make the decision something more than a purely financial one. To the extent that ethical issues are involved, the lack of a generally accepted macro system of thought reduces the likelihood that the individual firm will have delineated and adopted an ethical standard guiding the intent and constraining the actions of the multinational corporation in particularities. The value-pluralism of even our domestic society may tend to inhibit the adoption of ethical codes of conduct,[2] and the multinational corporation is faced with greater value pluralism than is the domestic firm. Thus, the managers who have the authority and bear the responsibility for the foreign direct investment decision may be aware that the decision has ethical dimensions, but lack a corporate-provided model for considering them.

One such ethical dimension associated with the foreign direct investment decision is the charge that multinational corporations, by investing abroad rather than at home, are exporting jobs, not products. This charge has been frequently voiced by organized labor over the past two decades, and has been taken up by "public interest" organizations. New attention has focused on the issue as a result of the impact of the dollar's strength in the foreign exchange markets of the 1980's [30]. The value judgment implicit in this charge is that jobs, indeed, particular jobs, have value in themselves; the corporation "should" therefore continue to produce at home; it "should not" produce abroad.

In response, defenders of foreign direct investment present an analysis which indicates that some United States domestically-produced goods are not globally competitive. Hence, they argue, the jobs would in any case be lost, if not to foreign workers producing for a foreign subsidiary of a United States-based multinational, then to foreign workers producing for a locally-based firm or for a subsidiary of a foreign-based multinational.

We can probably agree that displaced workers are reluctant to admit any individual or collective responsibility for the loss or absence of international competitiveness on the part of United States-produced goods. Workers naturally applaud their union's use of market pressure to gain "more" for the members; neither the workers nor their unions seem equally ready to acknowledge that these same market forces have now resulted in lost product markets and an associated induced loss of domestic employment opportunities. Rather, the multinational corporation is regarded as "at fault" for having made the foreign direct investment.

It is easy to see that the job-export problem has both economic and political dimensions;[3] it has been widely debated within both frameworks. Even the "fact" of job export is, itself, disputed. Various researchers, employing differing methodology, assumptions, and definitions of job export, and covering different time periods, have arrived at differing conclusions. These have ranged from substantial job export to job creation [11, especially Table 1, pp. 5-6; 15; 13, especially pp. 47, 88-89; 22]. For example, an AFL-CIO study proclaimed a net loss of 500,000 jobs between 1966 and 1969 [22, p. 40; 15, p. 151]. Other researchers have excluded from "job export" calculations the jobs associated with market-protecting shifts from United States to foreign production in response to competitive pressures (one form of so-called "defensive" foreign direct investment), and have counted as job exports only the job opportunities "lost" through <u>aggressive</u> profit-maximizing investment; the number of lost job opportunities is then greatly reduced. Other researchers have found not a job loss but a net job gain. This has been associated, for example, with exports of semi-finished goods to foreign affiliates and with the provision of managerial, technical, and professional services to these affiliates. In the latter case, there has been an upgrading of the skill composition as well as a net increase in the domestic job opportunities provided by the multinational corporation [13, pp. 66-70; 10, especially pp. 3-6; 15, p. 169]. Of course, these positive results for the economy as a whole do not necessarily directly benefit the workers who might have been employed in the absence of the foreign direct investment. In any case, the statistical studies must be interpreted with care; their message varies, depending upon the model employed.

For those who have voiced the job export charge, and requested changes in public policy so as to reduce its occurence and ameliorate its effects, any loss of domestic jobs associated with foreign direct investment is implicitly viewed as different from job loss associated with purely domestic economic change. There has been a corresponding tendency on the part of both parent and host countries to emphasize the home-country ties of the parent corporation, rather than its multinational nature. The distinction is important for ethical issues, because it establishes the framework within which one may apply ethical criteria to value questions. For the purposes of this paper, the issue is whether or not the foreign direct investment decision and the alleged associated loss of certain job opportunities present the multinational corporation with an ethical dilemma and, if so, the nature of this dilemma, and the applicability of various ethical criteria to it. In the following sections, this question as well as the ethical criteria presented by various ethical theories, including utilitarianism, the corporate social responsibility school, and Kant's categorical imperative, will be addressed.

The Foreign Direct Investment Decision and Induced Unemployment: Ethical Dilemma and Ethical Theory

As noted above, organized labor's charge that multinational corporations are exporting jobs, not products, involves a value judgment that the job opportunities have a value in themselves, and "should" be preserved. If doing so would entail financial loss for the corporation, the implicit argument is that job opportunities for workers "should" be valued more highly than profit opportunities for investors. A reader might conclude that this is either an example of class conscious union behavior and class conflict, or of job conscious union behavior focusing upon job security. The important thing for our purposes here is the value judgment with regard to retention of job opportunities, and the associated conclusions that: 1) the corporation "should" voluntarily behave so as to retain them; or 2) government policy "should" be changed so as to deter the foreign direct investment (e.g., by outright restriction of it, or by tax changes, export subsidies, import quotas, etc.); or 3) government policy "should" provide special aid and payment to the displaced workers. In other words, corporate policy and government policy would be determined by a judgment that specific jobs are the value to be preserved or purchased.

For the corporation and the individual corporate manager, governments may have defined away the ethical dilemma associated with the induced-unemployment issue. The Beveridge Commission, for example, in its 1942 recommendations with regard to the

British social security system [24, p. 538], identified the problem of unemployment as a macro one, and the solution of the problem as a socio-political responsibility, not the responsibility of the individual firm or of the individual manager. The United States recognized the social cost of unemployment, and instituted a system of unemployment compensation that shifted some of the social cost of unemployment from the workers to the corporation and its customers, via unemployment compensation premiums. In 1946, the United States adopted high-level employment as a goal of national economic policy. The individual manager/entrepreneur was thus correspondingly relieved of social responsibility for unemployment.

Indeed, to the extent that the individual firm and manager cannot really do anything about unemployment, it appears that the individual manager is also relieved of <u>ethical</u> responsibility for it. If one has an ethical dilemma only if one has the capability of taking action that will effect a solution of the dilemma, i.e., if "ought" implies "can" [27, pp. 165-166], one can argue that, for the individual manager, there is no ethical dilemma involved in unemployment induced by foreign direct investment in response to competitive pressures. Economic theory relieves the manager of ethical responsibility for unemployment by saying that the manager cannot do anything about it. Impersonal market forces dictate, or, less pejoratively, are the determinants of what "should" be done.

The Invisible Hand

The above position is consistent with "the invisible hand," which has long served as an approach to problems of business and economic ethics. This approach, which is consistent with utilitarianism, is a private enterprise, free market approach. It relies on the profit incentive and the invisible hand by whose operation the profit incentive serves to maximize welfare. Milton Friedman is a frequently cited spokesman for this approach, which is usually traced back to the work of Adam Smith [4, pp. 91-92; 9]. The following brief excerpts from this work illustrate Smith's position.

> Every individual is continually exerting himself to find out the most advantageous employment for whatever capital he can command. It is his own advantage, indeed, and not that of the society, which he has in view. But the study of his own advantage naturally, or rather necessarily, leads him to prefer that employment which is most advantageous to the society.

First, every individual endeavours to employ his capital as near home as he can, and consequently as much as he can in the support of domestic industry; provided always that he can thereby obtain the ordinary, or not a great deal less than the ordinary profits of stock.

. . . . . .

Secondly, every individual who employs his capital in the support of domestic industry, necessarily endeavors so to direct that industry, that its produce may be of the greatest value.

. . . . . .

. . . He generally, indeed, neither intends to promote the public interest, nor knows how much he is promoting it. By preferring the support of domestic to that of foreign industry, he intends only his own security; and by directing that industry in such a manner as its produce may be of greatest value, he intends only his own gain, and he is in this, as in many other cases, led by an invisible hand to promote an end which was no part of his intention. Nor is it always the worse for the society that it was not part of it. By pursuing his own interest he frequently promotes that of the society more effectually than when he really intends to promote it. I have never known much good done by those who affected to trade for the public good [28].

Note that Adam Smith was here contemplating an investment decision in favor of the home country, as opposed to a foreign investment decision, providing that the returns on capital were roughly equivalent. The "good" to be maximized was the value of the product; the value of jobs was not an issue. (Pre-Keynesian economists tended to assume full employment!)

Capital Budgeting Theory

A body of normative financial theory exists that is both relevant to the foreign direct investment/capital budgeting decision and consistent with the invisible-hand approach. Capital budgeting based on this theory employs discounted future cash flow techniques to allocate capital resources among alternative uses. In the multinational case, capital budgeting theory admits the existence of a number of ambiguities that do not exist in the domestic case (e.g., a given multinational corporation may have an investment opportunity which is profitable for it, but not necessarily the best use of resources from the point of view of the host country) [7, Chs. 7 and 9]. At the same time, however, the theory basically affirms the welfare-maximizing character of allocational decisions reached by the operation of the profit incentive, as postulated by the invisible-hand theory.

Unfortunately for the ethical peace of mind of the MNC manager, the multinational corporation may find itself operating or considering operations in geo-political parts of the globe where conditions prerequisite for the operation of the invisible hand do not exist. (Business, economic, and financial theorists in developed countries frequently assume the operation of market mechanisms and associated information systems and freedom of choice which are not a substantive reality in many parts of the world.) Then, neither the procedures nor the consequences of the market mechanism are those postulated by invisible hand theorists. Even in industrially developed countries, artificial incentives may be provided by tax holidays, low-interest loans, protected host-country markets, host-country export subsidies, and other similar measures. Such interferences with the market mechanism and market neutrality can be deliberately introduced by governments to affect allocation decisions. In performing a capital budgeting analysis, the analyst can specify and quantify these factors. They may distort, but they are designed to distort. They are recognized by knowledgeable market participants. Nevertheless, the invisible hand has been shackled.[4]

It is possible that international economic disparities are now so great that the invisible hand has outlived its usefulness. Governments, in both developed and developing countries, may be so unwilling and/or unable to establish political-economic environments requisite for the operation of the invisible hand that reliance on it may be misplaced. Or, despite its acknowledged weaknesses, the invisible hand may be preferable to currently visible alternatives, e.g., bureaucratically-managed economies. However, to the extent that the assumed conditions underlying its conclusions do not exist, neither the ethicist, the economist, nor the business manager can take the welfare-maximizing result of the invisible hand for granted.

The individual manager who can do nothing more than heighten corporate awareness of possible ethical issues has at least this much individual ethical responsibility. If the automatic operation of the invisible hand cannot be relied upon, the manager's area of ethical responsibility is enlarged.

In the case of unemployment induced by the foreign direct investment decision, both the individual manager and the corporation have ethical responsibility associated with the fact that they have some ability to affect the circumstances, although certainly the scope for action by the individual manager is narrow compared with that of the corporation. One wonders, however, to what extent it has simply seemed easier, as well as responsive to apparent profit incentives, to move production abroad rather than to take positive steps to improve the competitiveness of domestic plants. For example, it may be easier to move production abroad than to reshape and enrich job content in an attempt to improve worker job satisfaction and stimulate higher United States productivity. It may be easier to move production abroad than to cope with the resistance to change that would be involved in an attempt to improve the competitiveness of domestic plants by such measures as changes in sometimes outmoded work rules. Such conflict- and challenge-avoidance behavior itself introduces an ethical dimension into the foreign direct investment decision, which is no longer determined solely by financial factors within a capital budgeting model, or by impersonal market factors within an economic model; the managers have some ability to change these factors. Realistically speaking, however, the manager and the corporation may not be able to accomplish these changes without the cooperation of the union. Hence, a decision in favor of foreign direct investment would reflect an acknowledgement of their limited power to effect change, rather than a neglect of alternatives.

The ethical dilemma for the United States based multinational corporation is, however, broader than this. Jobs may be lost domestically, but the corporation may be creating jobs abroad. If these jobs are in a developing country, the dilemma associated with job export becomes part of a larger dilemma of the multinational corporation, as it establishes its policies in an environment in which it is alternatively viewed as an agent for development and for raising people from poverty, and as the exploiter of the human and natural resources and wealth of impoverished peoples.

Ethical Criteria Applicable to the Dilemma

The criteria provided by commonly enunciated ethical theories are not very helpful to the multinational corporate decision-maker concerned with the job export issue. A brief review of some individual theories and their possible application to the job shift problem will clarify why this is so.

Utilitarianism

Utilitarianism, specifically, "act utilitarianism," is a teleological theory whose ethical criterion is sometimes generalized as "the greatest good for the greatest number." This theory contributes little towards the ethical evaluation of foreign direct investment. How does one determine and measure what constitutes the greatest good for the greatest number when the choice involved is one of a shift of production by the multinational corporation from the parent country to a host country?

For example, let us look at a job lost in the United States as opposed to a job gained in Mexico. Suppose that, statistically, the Unites States worker supports a spouse and two children, while the Mexican worker supports a spouse and five children. Does the creation of a job in Mexico then have greater utility than the destruction of a job in the United States has disutility? Presumably, the United States worker will lose more income than the Mexican worker will gain (lower wage costs being one of the factors possibly motivating the foreign direct investment decision), but the loss may be greater than the gain even in the case of equivalent incomes. While psychologists tell us that all change is stressful, it seems probable that a change in income in an upward direction is less stressful than an equivalent change in a downward direction. The United States worker will also lose some human dignity, while the Mexican worker will presumably gain some. Human dignity is frequently cited as a "good" [see, e.g., 23, p. 147] to be maximized, but who can measure a relative loss or gain and the net result, or even determine whether it is positive or negative? And what are the alternatives facing each of these workers? Is there a value destroyed/created for society? United States society? Mexican society? World society? And what happens to this "calculus" if one considers factors other than the jobs?

On the one hand, multinational corporations are encouraged to take a global view [1, pp. 13, 14, 16]; on the other hand, they are exhorted to remember the displaced worker "at home" [1, Chapter 11]. Even if there were agreement on whether the multinational corporation should employ ethical criteria within a domestic or global framework, utilitarianism would provide an ambiguous answer to the job transfer issue.

Social Responsibility

Utilitarianism is consistent with the operation of the invisible hand, which is relied upon to provide the greatest good for the greatest number. An alternative approach, that of the social responsibility school, challenges the ability of the invisible hand to maximize welfare. This approach stresses the separation of corporate ownership and control. It emphasizes that the corporation is a creature of the state, created by the grant of a charter which explicitly or implicitly confers both privileges and responsibilities. This school of thought broadens the corporation's responsibilities, defining them to include social responsibility, rather than assuming that maximization of profits or shareholder wealth will automatically maximize welfare. Attempting to avoid domestic unemployment induced by a foreign direct investment decision might be one such social responsibility.

However, one must question whether the corporate social purpose implied by the term "social responsibility" is domestic or multinational. It is relatively easy to agree that the domestic corporation's social responsibility becomes geo-politically broader, e.g., with respect to such issues as corrupt practices and pollution, as it expands as a multinational corporation. Thus, it seems evident that social responsibility, if applicable at all, must be applicable in host societies, as well as in the home society.[5] But when we address the investment decision as a matter of choice between domestic and foreign production (and domestic and foreign job opportunities), the social responsibility approach fails to provide an unambiguous answer. In this instance, social responsibility inevitably entails conflict between mutually exclusive responsibilities.

The social responsibility approach to corporate ethics may be viewed as an attempt to resolve, for the individual manager, only some of the apparent ethical conflict between the pursuit of profit and values such as justice and love of neighbor. The social responsibility approach moderates, qualifies, and perhaps even subordinates the profit motive to societal motives. Those who defend the invisible hand argue that the attempt to practice social responsibility will produce less, not more, good for society, defining "good" in terms of economic welfare. The shortcomings of the invisible hand have already been examined.

Kant's Categorical Imperative

Alternatively, we can attempt to use a deontological approach. Consider the usefulness of Kant's propositions: 1) People should be considered as ends, not as means [3, p. 20]; and 2) "Act only on that maxim which you can at the same time will to be a universal law" [8, p. 30]. The multinational corporation is in a position to be particularly affected by this requirement of universality. (Its relevance to the Bhopal disaster was made almost immediately plain by the media's emphasis on the question of whether safety standards were the same in Union Carbide's Indian plant at Bhopal and in its United States plants.)

Applying Kant's categorical imperative that people should be considered as ends, not as means, to the issue of domestic unemployment induced by foreign direct investment, one might conclude that one "should not exploit" low-wage workers in less developed countries by employing them instead of domestic workers. Moreover, one "should not displace" high-cost domestic workers. All are ends in themselves, not means to production of goods. Thus, the immediate effects on persons, versus the effects on personal welfare inherent in the consumption of the goods, would be the ethical issue.

It would be easy to develop two correlative negative injunctions: 1) You shall not exploit low-wage workers; 2) You shall not displace domestic workers. It is, of course, too easy. In the case of foreign direct investment motivated by competitive pressures, the corporation's ability to dutifully maintain high-cost production and employees is limited; the corporation simply following such a route would sooner or later fail and be neither a producer nor an employer. Further, the "exploited" low-wage workers might experience their situation not as exploitation but as economic opportunity.

In this ethical dilemma, Kant's universality test also has interesting results. Could the corporate manager opt to make a foreign direct investment decision that would result in the hiring of foreign workers and the displacing of domestic workers, and will that all others in similar circumstances act the same way? In the case of competitively induced foreign direct investment, my answer would be a qualified "yes." But, from an economic standpoint, the employment effects of this category of investment do not qualify as "job export;" they do not qualify as such from an ethical standpoint unless the manager can indeed do something to change the competitive picture. Nevertheless, the qualification of the "yes" is there because so many questions with regard to justice come to mind (e.g., does the displaced employee have a right to the job, perhaps even a property right in the job?) and because the iron law of wages suddenly seems to have new life.

Consider, however, the alternative, that one not employ the low-wage workers but continue to employ the domestic workers as long as possible, i.e., until bankrupt. Can one will this to be a universal law? From an economic welfare point of view one cannot. The consumer is burdened with high-cost goods; the foreign worker is deprived of an opportunity to be economically productive and obtain a higher level of economic welfare; domestic structural adjustment is delayed; wealth is destroyed. In short, even displaced persons could not within this framework argue that the corporation acted unethically in displacing them.

A basic problem with the application of Kant's categorical imperative to the ethical dilemmas of the multinational corporation is of course the fact that corporations, even multinational corporations, are, at bottom, economic institutions, not humanistic development institutions, or social welfare institutions. As economic institutions, they have been motivated by economic incentives, directed toward economic goals, and valued on the basis of economic performance. If one's ethical system is not a teleological one that values the economic "good," one's ethical questions are no longer focused primarily on the multinational corporation as an economic institution. If one opts for alternatives such as a corporate social audit, or a behavioral theory of the firm, in which the goals of the firm's many constituencies or interest groups must be "satisfied," the ethical dilemma is rephrased or redefined, and, seemingly, made more ambiguous for the corporation, since no clear-cut decision model exists. However, some conflict may be resolved for the individual manager, since there is less inherent tension between financial/economic goals and other values.

Power as "Good"

Ambiguity could be resolved and we could reach a "solution" of the ethical dilemma for the multinational corporation as it is posed by the foreign direct investment decision that "exports" jobs, if we were to adopt a non-hedonist teleological theory identifying the "good" with power. Then, to the extent that the multinational corporation could expand and augment its geo-politico-economic power and the exercise of it via foreign direct investment and the employment of workers lacking a countervailing power base, the appropriate "ethical" decision would be to do so.

But surely someone would question what is entailed in the ethical use of power. Others would dispute the appropriateness of a value judgment identifying good with power. For many, an ethical dilemma would still exist. Nevertheless, our society no doubt contains individuals who would subscribe to the evaluation of power as good. While I do not recommend this approach, I have included it for the sake of argument.

The Ethical Dilemma: Corporate or Personal?

What then, of the ethical dilemma on a personal level? Can the corporation have an ethical dilemma that is not shared by the individual corporate manager? I think not. Similarly, publicly revealed unethical acts of the individual manager or other employee reflect back upon the corporation. While we can conceptually differentiate the corporate dilemma from the personal dilemma, for practical purposes the two are closely intertwined. The ethical criteria surveyed offer neither attractive solutions nor clear-cut decision rules. Thus, some writers have recommended an alternative approach stressing the importance of virtues or "character" possessed by the individual director or manager [6]. I believe that this alternative has a great deal of merit, but detailed discussion of it is beyond the scope of this paper.

Conclusions

The ethical dilemma discussed in this paper takes several forms. With regard to the kind of aggressive foreign direct investment that would be classified as "job exporting" in the purest sense, managers are faced with an ethical dilemma because the financial and economic conditions are such that an acceptable though not maximizing level of profitability is attainable from home-based production. Ethical factors, if part of the decision-making model, <u>might</u> swing a decision in favor of home-based production. However, the criteria provided by various ethical theories are of limited usefulness to decision making in such cases; much ambiguity remains.

With regard to defensive foreign investment when United States-based production is no longer competitive, one ethical dilemma for the manager is that of determining whether or not the retention of jobs in the United States is a value which should be sought at the expense of greater effort to improve the United States competitive position, perhaps entailing greater union/management conflict and/or cooperation. This involves an effort to determine what the manager and the corporation <u>can</u> do, as a prerequisite to determining what they <u>ought</u> to do.

In both of the above cases, the manager must recognize that unions do not represent all workers or even the interests of all workers. Yielding to the pressures of organized labor may not be ethical.

I conclude that there is no economic basis for a distinction between job loss which results from domestic economic, technological, and organizational change, and job loss associated with the same set of factors on an international scale. This is not to say that job export does not present the multinational corporation with an ethical dilemma. The charge of job export, by presenting the alleged loss of job opportunities as a problem for which something other than an economic solution was sought, has perhaps heightened awareness of the ethical dimension present in any employer-initiated job change, and may motivate a search for just solutions. From a domestic point of view, it should also cause United States corporations, managers, and labor to pay greater attention to positive and constructive efforts to improve the competitive position of United States industry. Such behavior would contrast with the multinational's alleged "flight" response, and labor's search for shelters.

A broader issue is the question of whether or not decision models should explicitly contain an ethics component. I believe that they should. While it would no doubt be extremely difficult to reach a consensus as to the details of such a decision-model component, a start could be made. This would acknowledge the limitations of the invisible hand, and foster greater managerial and corporate awareness of relevant ethical issues, in both the domestic and the international environment.

NOTES

1. Foreign direct investment is real investment in plant and equipment, i.e., ownership of physical assets in foreign countries.

2. Indeed, one writer has pointed out that the value-pluralism of our society "contributes to a situation in which the study of ethics as the enunciation of a set of universally shared agreements is impossible." See Long, A Survey of Recent Christian Ethics, p. 152.

3. Barnet and Muller spoke of "The Obsolescence of American Labor," in Chapter 11 of Global Reach, pp. 303-333.

4. Commenting on an early draft of this paper, one reviewer, John H. Stanley, suggested that the invisible hand has been replaced by sleight of hand; clearly, magic cannot be depended upon to produce the maximization of welfare that has been attributed to the operation of the invisible hand.

5. International codes of conduct for multinational corporations have been developed by agencies of the United Nations, the European Economic Community, the International Labor Office, and the Organization for Economic Cooperation and Development. See Kindleberger and Herrick, Economic Development, 3rd edition, p. 322. The very proliferation of such codes indicates that there was a perceived need for them, and that the concept of multinational corporate social responsibility was not operationally accepted.

REFERENCES

1. Richard J. Barnet and Ronald E. Muller, *Global Reach*, New York, NY: Touchstone Books, 1974.

2. Richard L. Barovick, "The Washington Struggle Over Multinationals," *Business and Society Review*, Vol. 18, Summer, 1976, pp. 12-19.

3. Tom L. Beauchamp and Norman E. Bowie, *Ethical Theory and Business*, Englewood Cliffs, NJ: Prentice Hall, Inc., 1979.

4. George C.S. Benson, *Business Ethics in America*, Lexington, MA: Lexington Books, 1982.

5. Peter J. Buckley and Mark Casson, *The Future of the Multinational Enterprise*, London: Macmillan, 1976.

6. Joseph Des Jardins, "Virtues and Corporate Responsibility," in *Corporate Governance and Institutionalizing Ethics*, edited by W. Michael Hoffman, Jennifer Mills Moore, and David A. Fedo, Lexington, MA and Toronto: Lexington Books, 1984, pp. 135-142.

7. David K. Eiteman and Arthur I. Stonehill, *Multinational Business Finance*, 3rd edition, Reading, MA: Addison-Wesley Publishing Company, 1982.

8. William K. Frankena, *Ethics*, 2nd edition, Englewood Cliffs, NJ: Prentice-Hall, Inc., 1973.

9. Peter A. French, "Corporate Moral Agency," in *Ethical Theory and Business*, edited by Tom L. Beauchamp and Norman E. Bowie, Englewood Cliffs, NJ: Prentice-Hall, Inc. 1979, pp. 175-186.

10. Milton Friedman, "The Social Responsibility of Business," in *Ethical Theory and Business*, edited by Tom L. Beauchamp and Norman E. Bowie, Englewood Cliffs, NJ: Prentice-Hall, Inc., 1979, pp. 136-138. Reprinted from Milton Friedman, *Capitalism and Freedom*: Chicago: University of Chicago Press, 1962, pp. 133-136.

11. Robert G. Hawkins, *Job Displacement and the Multinational Firm: A Methodological Review*, New York University, Center for Multinational Studies, Occassional Paper No. 3, June, 1972.

12. Robert G. Hawkins, *U.S. Multinational Investment in Manufacturing and Domestic Economic Performance*, New York University, Center for Multinational Studies, Occassional Paper No. 1, February, 1972.

13. Robert G. Hawkins and Michael Jay Jedel, "U.S. Jobs and Foreign Investment," in *International Labor and the Multinational Enterprise*, edited by Duane Kujawa, New York: Praeger Publishers, 1975, pp. 47-93.

14. W. Michael Hoffman, Jennifer Mills Moore and David A. Fedo, eds., *Corporate Governance and Institutionalizing Ethics*, Lexington, MA and Toronto: Lexington Books, 1984.

15. Michael Jay Jedel and John H. Stamm, "The Battle Over Jobs: An Appraisal of Recent Publications on the Employment Effect of U.S. Multinational Corporations," in *American Labor and the Multinational Corporation*, edited by Duane Kujawa, New York: Praeger Publishers, 1973, pp. 144-191.

16. Donald G. Jones, *Private and Public Ethics*, New York and Toronto: The Edwin Mellen Press, 1978.

17. Charles P. Kindleberger, editor, *The International Corporation*, Cambridge, MA: MIT Press, 1970.

18. Charles P. Kindleberger and Bruce Herrick, *Economic Development*, 3rd edition, New York: McGraw-Hill, 1977. See especially Chapter 19, "Foreign Investment and International Firms."

19. Thomas A. Klein, "Corporate Moral Responsibility: A Matter of Degree," *Business and Professional Ethics Journal*, Vol. 3, No. 2, Winter, 1984, pp. 70-71.

20. Duane Kujawa, editor, *American Labor and the Multinational Corporation*, New York: Praeger Publishers, 1973.

21. Duane Kujawa, editor, *International Labor and the Multinational Enterprise*, New York: Praeger Publishers, 1975.

22. Duane Kujawa, "U.S. Manufacturing Investment in the Developing Countries: American Labour's Concerns and the Enterprise Environment in the Decade Ahead," *British Journal of Industrial Relations*, Vol. 19, No. 1, March, 1981, pp. 38-48.

23. Edward LeRoy Long, Jr., *A Survey of Recent Christian Ethics*, New York and Oxford: Oxford University Press, 1982.

24. Lloyd G. Reynolds, *Labor Economics and Labor Relations*, NY: Prentice-Hall, Inc., 1949.

25. Barry M. Richman and Melvyn R. Copen, *International Management and Economic Development*, New York: McGraw-Hill, 1972.

26. James Sellers, *Public Ethics: American Morals and Manners*, New York, Evanston, and London: Harper and Row, 1970.

27. John G. Simon, Charles W. Powers, and Jon P. Gunnemann, "The Responsibilities of Corporations and Their Owners," in *Ethical Theory and Business*, edited by Tom L. Beauchamp and Norman E. Bowie, Englewood Cliffs, NJ: Prentice-Hall, Inc., 1979, pp. 160-168.

28. Adam Smith, "Of Systems of Political Economy," Book IV, Chapter 11 of *An Inquiry into the Nature and Causes of the Wealth of Nations*. See Vol. 39 of the Great Books, Chicago: The University of Chicago Press, 1952, pp. 193-194.

29. Raymond Vernon, *Storm Over the Multinationals: The Real Issues*, Cambridge, MA: Harvard University Press, 1977.

30. *Wall Street Journal*, April 9, 1985, p. 1.

31. Patricia H. Werhane, "Corporations, Collective Action, and Institutional Moral Agency," in *Corporate Governance and Institutionalizing Ethics*, edited by W. Michael Hoffman, Jennifer Mills Moore, and David A. Fedo, Lexington, MA and Toronto: Lexington Books, 1984, pp. 163-171.

ETHICAL DIMENSIONS OF INFORMATION TECHNOLOGY IN GLOBAL BUSINESS

Abbe Mowshowitz

Introduction

Information technology provides the global enterprise with a powerful set of organizational and managerial tools. In particular, this technology underwrites a form of organization -- called here <u>virtual organization</u> -- that has a systemic effect on ethical conduct in multinational corporations. The following is a discussion of the origins, evolutions, and consequences of the systemic effect of virtual organization on ethics in global firms.

After detailing the character and scope of globalized business, we examine the role of information technology in the globalization process. Then we introduce the notion of virtual organization and discuss its relationship to the anaylsis of human behavior in large organizations. This leads to a characterization of the ethical environment of organizations. The concept of <u>ethical space</u> defined here allows us to explain and trace the impact of the fundamental shift in the conditions of ethical conduct brought about by virtual organization. We conclude with an examination of contemporary ethical dilemmas faced by multinational corporations. These dilemmas are viewed in light of the systemic organizational change deriving from virtual organization.

Globalization of Business

The phenomenal growth of international trade and multinational enterprises since the end of World War II has been well documented. (Barnett and Muller, 1974; Reich, 1983; Vernon, 1977) In the mid-1960's, Perlmutter (1965) predicted that by 1988 most non-Communist world trade would be controlled by 300 companies. That prediction has since been echoed by many observers. Reich (1983, p. 266), for example, asserts that "By 1988, if present trends continue, 300 giant firms will produce half of the world's goods and services."

Statistics on international trade and investment and on the revenues of multinationals lend credence to these predictions. "In 1977, trade flows related to United States TNCs [transnational corporations] and affiliates of foreign firms located in the United States accounted for over 90 percent of total United States trade flows. During the same year, domestic and foreign TNCs were responsible for over 80 percent of total United Kingdom exports." (U.N. Centre on Transnational Corporations, 1984)

In 1983, the 100 largest United States multinationals had combined total revenues of $1.2 trillion (Forbes, 1984a), or 36 percent of the United States Gross National Product (GNP). The combined revenues of the 100 largest foreign companies totalled $1.6 trillion; and the top 200 largest foreign companies totalled $2.1 trillion. (Forbes, 1984b) Hence, this group of 300 multinationals had revenues totalling $3.3 trillion, an amount equal to the United States' 1983 GNP. The top 300 multinational companies may already be producing more than half of the world's goods and services.

Companies with international operations antedate the present era by several centuries. The East India Company and the Massachusetts Bay Colony were licensed by the British crown in the eighteenth century. During the nineteenth century, a number of international companies were formed to develop agricultural and mineral resources. In the early part of this century, American companies such as National Cash Register, Eastman Kodak, Singer, Coca-Cola, Quaker Oats, and Woolworth all operated outside of the United States. (Turner, 1970)

But the multinational corporations that emerged after World War II are radically different from their predecessors. The international activity of the earlier firms was almost exclusively importing and exporting. Today's multinationals embrace global production systems. Companies like IBM, General Motors, Toyota Motor, Unilever, Philips, and Siemens have production operations distributed across the globe. Specialized components are produced and assembled in dozens of locations. It is becoming increasingly difficult to find an "American" automobile or an "American" computer. Only certain parts are made in the United States and particular components assembled in this country. (Reich, 1983, p. 266)

The variety and complexity of global businesses are reflected in the various attempts to classify them. Robinson (1967) distinguished between international, multinational, transnational, and supranational firms. Permutter (1965) classified global enterprises as ethnocentric, polycentric, and geocentric. These schemes capture developmental rather than type differences, e.g., a firm that appears to be polycentric may be evolving into a geocentric organization. A more useful approach to classification would be to identify the principal attributes of globalization and characterize a given firm in terms of those attributes. Reich's (1983) dichotomy between pure and national multinationals comes closest to this approach by suggesting a spectrum of organizational arrangements.

The pure multinational owes allegiance to no particular country. Its managers, directors, creditors, shareholders, and employees are drawn from many countries. This international cast of characters helps to insure that global, corporate interests take precedence over the particular interests of the nations in which the firm operates. The pure multinational type is characteristic of a growing segment of American and British industry.

National multinationals resemble the pure ones in their global distribution of production, but they are oriented toward one country. This type of multinational aims to promote the welfare of its home country, and thus acts as an agent of a national economy. Much of Japanese industry and a portion of industry in continental Europe (e.g., Volvo and Airbus Industrie) fall into this category.

The critical attribute of the pure multinational is its exploitation of comparative economic advantage on a global basis. Reich (1983) illustrates this attribute by pointing to recent actions of some American-based firms including Hughes Tool, Dow, Exxon, Mobil, General Electric, RCA, Carlton Machine Tool, General Motors, McGraw-Hill, International Silver, Rockwell International, Samsonite, and most large American makers of consumer electronics products, textiles, footware, sporting goods, and toys. The actions described are the movement of production facilities out of the United States in order to reduce labor and other production costs, and to obtain advantageous financing.

Despite the success of some national multinationals -- especially the Japanese -- the future probably belongs to the pure multinational. It seems inevitable that global distribution of operations will lead to internationalization of management and, ultimately, to the weakening of national ties.

The globalization of production has been made possible by technological innovations in transportation, communications, and computing since the end of World War II. Barnet and Muller (1974) characterized the modern global corporation as the "child of the computer, the communications satellite, and the jet airplane." Containerized shipping, specialized tankers, bulk-cargo vessels, and jet air-cargo carriers have substantially reduced international shipping costs. (Reich, 1983, p. 123) Communications satellites provide reliable and relatively inexpensive channels for global communications.

Computers make it possible to process the enormous amounts of data required to coordinate production activities spread around the world.

In short, these new technologies "have enabled businesses efficiently to divide the production process into separate operations that can be performed across the globe at different production sites and then integrated into a single product." (Reich, 1983, p. 123)

Role of Information Technology

As Reich suggests, information technology allows for the integration of globally distributed production activities. It is now feasible to locate facilities in different parts of the world and to decentralize management functions without decentralizing control. Distribution without loss of central control is the foundation of efficient and effective global organization.

This enables multinational corporations to shift operations and production sites to exploit comparative, economic advantages such as cheap labor, proximity to resources and markets, political stability, abundant investment capital, low interest rates, etc. Shifts of this nature were possible in the past, but not with the level of integration that can now be achieved. With satellite communications and computers, sites that are remote from corporate headquarters and in a different country can be managed almost as effectively as if they were next door.

Corporate functions such as invoicing and paying, ordering and marketing, inventory control and product design, research and development, and payroll and personnel for one facility can all be performed at other locations. This is facilitated by the ability to transmit relevant data from one location to another. Telecommunications and computer networks support virtually instantaneous transfers of such data and thus make it possible to coordinate the geographically distributed activities of multinational corporations.

The importance of information technology to global business is evidenced by the growing dependence of multinational corporations on international data traffic. According to a report of the National Telecommunications and Information Administration (NTIA) to the Senate Committee on Commerce, Science, and Transportation: "International data communications have become crucial to the operation of United States multinational companies." (United States Congress, 1983, p. 168) In an extensive study of 89 companies in nine countries,

Business International concluded similarly that multinational companies "are dependent on computerized flows of information to conduct their business today -- and will be more so tomorrow." (Business International, 1983, p. 8) Table 1 shows the corporate functions supported by transborder data flows (TDF) currently and for the year 1988.

The results of major studies of the uses of TDF by the Organization for Economic Cooperation and Development (OECD), by the International Bureau for Informatics (IBI), and by Business International (BI) (cited above) are summarized in U.N. Centre on Transnational Corporations (1984, pp. 11-12). Among the major findings reported are the following:

1) 88 percent of the companies surveyed by BI indicated that TDF are now important or very important for at least one corporate function, and 90 percent stated that TDF would play an important role in 1988.

2) The main obstacle to the use of TDF is inadequate telecommunications networks, especially in developing countries. By contrast, laws and regulations in host countries appear to have little influence.

3) Financial management is the corporate activity most commonly supported by TDF. Next come marketing and distribution. These are followed by production (especially in extractive industries), management (including strategic planning), and research and development (especially in some manufacturing and extractive industries). TDF play less of a role in personnel and payroll management.

A key difference, alluded to earlier, between pre- and post-World War II multinational corporations is the latter's development of global systems of production. This difference is underscored by the rapid growth in the use of TDF to support global manufacturing, strategic planning, and computer-aided design, manufacturing, and engineering (CAD/CAM/CAE). Indeed, the last function showed the highest growth rate in the BI study.

Multinational corporations report three main benefits from their use of TDF:

1) increased corporate efficiency;

2) new business opportunities (e.g., in foreign exchange management and the creation and sale of database; and

Table 1. The importance of TDF by Corporate Activity and Region 1983 and 1988[a] (percentages unless otherwise noted)

Corporate Activity	1983 US	W.Eur.	Other	Total	1988 US	W.Eur.	Other	Total
Financial Functions								
Financial mgt.	63.5	57.7	45.4	59.6	71.2	80.7	63.6	73.0
Invoicing	30.8	34.6	27.3	31.5	34.6	46.2	36.4	38.2
Paying	28.8	30.8	18.2	28.1	30.8	38.5	27.3	32.6
Portfolio management[b]	15.4	23.1	--	15.7	23.1	26.9	--	21.4
Foreign exch. management[b]	13.5	7.7	5.1	11.2	17.3	15.4	9.1	15.7
Marketing and Distribution								
Ordering	36.5	30.8	45.4	36.0	42.3	34.6	45.4	40.4
Marketing and distribution	34.6	30.8	45.4	34.8	40.4	53.8	54.6	46.1
After-sales service	21.2	19.2	36.4	22.5	26.9	19.2	36.4	25.8
Cust. serv.[c]	11.5	23.1	18.2	15.7	11.5	23.1	18.2	15.7
Pricing infor.	3.8	3.8	--	3.4	3.8	11.5	--	5.6
Production								
Invent. cont.	38.5	26.9	27.3	33.7	44.2	46.2	36.4	43.8
Manufacturing	34.6	23.1	18.2	29.2	44.2	34.6	18.2	38.2
Sourcing	19.2	7.7	27.3	16.8	34.6	11.5	27.3	27.0
CAD/CAM/CAE	17.3	7.7	--	12.4	30.8	11.5	9.1	22.5
Product qual. testing	13.5	7.7	--	10.1	15.4	11.5	18.2	14.6
Management								
Str. planning	30.8	15.4	18.2	24.7	44.2	26.9	27.3	37.1
Mgt. infor.	15.4	26.9	18.2	19.1	25.0	30.8	18.2	25.8
Electr. mail	9.6	--	9.1	6.7	13.5	--	18.2	10.1
Research and Development								
R&D	23.1	26.9	9.1	22.5	32.7	38.5	18.2	32.6
Design engin.	21.2	7.7	--	14.6	25.0	11.5	--	15.0
Personnel								
Payroll, per.	23.1	11.5	9.1	18.0	28.8	15.4	9.1	22.5
Total # firms	52	26	11	89	52	26	11	89

Source: Business International, 1983.
[a] Percentage of companies viewing TDF important.
[b] Some companies lump foreign exchange in portfolio management.
[c] Applies to finance, transportation and data service firms.

3) opportunity to introduce new technologies into production. (United Nations Centre on Transnational Corporations, 1984, p. 12)

In sum, computer-communication supports greater integration of corporate activities, accelerates the diffusion of new technology, and improves financial management in multinational firms. Thus, information technology confers on the multinational greater flexibility in responding to changing economic conditions and helps the enterprise to maintain and sometimes to enhance its competitive position in the marketplace. Referring to the IBI study, Pipe (1984, p. 43) concludes: "The survey strongly suggests that computer-driven communication systems are in the process of becoming the lifeblood of international business."

Virtual Organization

The marriage of computers and telecommunications signals an order of magnitude jump in management's ability to use information technology as an instrument of coordination and control. Computer networks allow for the elaboration and refinement of rationalization and thus create the context of a higher level of integration. This means that physical facilities (e.g., plants, offices, agencies) and functions (e.g., accounting, marketing, claim or benefit assessment) can be decentralized without compromising central management control.

Studies of the impact of information technology on organizations confirm this observation. Most results indicate either an increase in the centralization of control (i.e., concentration of decision authority in a single person or small group) or reinforcement of existing control structures. The reinforcement effect is observed where the use of computer systems seems to have no correlation with centralization. Since organizations are almost always hierachically structured, such reinforcement contributes indirectly to a tightening of central control. (Mowshowitz, 1986)

The higher level of integration made possible by information technology suggests the emergence of a new principle that Mowshowitz (1986) calles <u>virtual organization</u>.

This principle is defined in relation to the idea of virtual memory in computer systems. In virtual memory, a distinction is made between physical and logical storage space. The relation between the two is recorded in a table that gives the current physical locations of items assigned logical space. Programmers using such a system need not concern themselves with the actual physical space assigned their programs. Indeed, virtual memory was developed in connection with time sharing so that the physical location of a program -- instructions, data, intermediate results, etc. -- may change from moment to moment under control of the operating system. The table of correspondences between physical and logical space keeps track of these changes.

The essence of virtual organization lies in this ever changing correspondence. Consider, for example, a company that makes a product consisting of parts a, b, c, d. Suppose that each of these four parts must be obtained from an outside supplier. The logical requirements of the company's final product are parts a, b, c, d; the actual resources that could be used are the potential suppliers of those parts. At any given time, the choice of suppliers defines a correspondence between logical requirements and actual resources.

The idea of matching needs with resources to achieve limited organizational objectives is, of course, standard practice. What is not standard practice is the extension of this idea to all aspects of management. The concept of virtual organization captures the centrality of this abstract matching in enterprises that have begun to make full use of the capabilities of information technology.

Virtual organization is a radical departure from traditional views of needs and resources that has profound social and economic implications. The key to these implications is the abstractification of temporal and spatial relations. Concretely, virtual organization implies management without allegiances, either to place or to origins. Pure multinational corporations already exhibit some of the features of virtual organization, notably the strategy of moving production facilities from one country to another in search of lower labor costs. But the concept applies to all kinds of enterprises. By operating without allegiance to place or history, business enterprises pose a major challenge to the nation state.

Like so many aspects of modern life, virtual organization has roots in the industrial revolution. The process of task resolution and replacement of craftsmen by man-machine systems may be analyzed as the virtual organization of time. Since the activitities occurring in the early factory were localized in space, we are justified in concentrating on the time dimension. The aim of task resolution is the elaboration of a temporal sequence of simple operations designed to produce a uniform result. Once the sequence has been determined, it is possible to treat the operations as abstract production requirements that can be mapped onto actual man-machine combinations in various ways.

Central to industrialization is the transformation of labor into a commodity. This transformation lies at the heart of the virtual organization of time. In the preindustrial period, when production was an integral part of family life, the treatment of labor as an abstract commodity was inconceivable. Likewise it would have been unthinkable to replace craft activity by sequences of abstract operations.

Information technology has made it possible to extend virtuality to space in an effective manner. Naturally, modern transportation systems -- railroads, automobiles, aircraft -- are indispensable to the movement of objects in space; but our focus here is on the management of needs and resources. Treatment of place -- localities, regions, countries -- as an abstract component of production systems is far from universal. The current stage of development is comparable to acceptance of the commoditization of labor in the nineteenth century.

With telecommunications -- telephone, cable, microwave, satellite and fiber optics -- linking all regions of the globe to each other, and computers to assist management in keeping track of geographically dispersed operations, it has become both feasible and attractive to embrace virtual organization of space. This extension of a development begun in the industrial revolution completes an organizational package that is reshaping the modern world in ways we can but dimly imagine.

Abstractification of Work and Management

Fromm (1955) described the fundamental economic features of Capitalism in terms of the process of __quantification__ and __abstractification.__ The organization of captitalist production centers on the balance sheet, and the essence of the balance sheet is the quantification of the costs, products, and profits of production. This quantification rests on a representation of costs (raw material, plant and equipment, energy, labor), products, and profits in terms of money. Expressed in money units, the elements of the production process become comparable quantities and can be incorporated into that abstract account known as the balance sheet.

The crux of the process of quantification and abstractification is the distancing of the producer from the concrete elements of production. Medieval artisans and peasants produced goods for a relatively small group of known customers. They followed traditional practices, were intimately familiar with every aspect of their business, and knew their costs from direct experience. Their profits were determined, not by what the market would bear, but according to what was necessary to maintain them in a traditionally defined social status. With rare exception, modern producers have only a fragmentary connection with the concrete elements of production. Division of labor and the formation of large-scale enterprises have defined highly specialized roles for workers and managers alike.

As Fromm (1955, p. 113) observes, "without quantification and abstractification modern mass production would be unthinkable. But in a society in which economic activities have become the main preoccupation of man, this process of quantification and abstractification has transcended the realm of economic production, and spread to the attitude of man to things, to people, and to himself."

The attitude of abstraction toward experience is what allows for the use of computer-communications to support virtual organization. Central to virtual organizations is the treatment of people and places as abstract components of production. Logical and actual business elements (i.e., needs and resources) must be clearly separated. Managers must be able to change the correspondences between logical and actual elements according to the principle of profit maximization. This mode of operating requires that one subordinate regional loyalties and human relationships to abstract organizational goals.

Abstractification of human attitudes is a <u>sine qua non</u> of virtually organized multinational companies. The institutionalized ability to close a plant in one country and open another in a different country bears witness to this abstractification. Such moves are made on the basis of balance sheet calculations: relative costs (labor, raw materials, shipping, etc.) in the different locations, capital and financial management considerations, distribution and marketing, adverse publicity, etc., are quantified in monetary units, and the path to higher profits is chosen.

The impact of a plant closure on its employees and the community enters the calculations primarily as a potential cost of adverse publicity. There may also be costs associated with relocating or retraining displaced employees. But none of these cost considerations have much to do with the concrete predicament of an unemployed worker or a community facing economic and social collapse. The standard capitalist justification for a move to reduce costs is that failure to do so would impair the company's ability to compete and, hence, market forces would eventually force it to close under less favorable circumstances. This argument is persuasive because managers and workers alike are loathe to challenge the authority of the balance sheet. The logic of money is the modern equivalent of fate.

Abstractification is reinforced in modern organizations by the use of information technology. Computer-based communications reduce the need and opportunity for face-to-face interaction. This effect is not entirely new since the post, telegraph, and telephone are also substitutes for direct interaction. Information technology extends and enlarges the realm of mediated communication.

Electronic mail is a real time version of the postal service. Message transmission is instantaneous as in telephony; but electronic mail is not subject to the simultaneity constraint of ordinary telephone communication, and thus does not incur the problem of "telephone tag." On the other hand, the absence of voice contact makes electronic mail more impersonal than the telephone.

Computerized conferencing -- tele-conferencing and computer conferencing -- offers a more sophisticated means of computer-mediated communication with special relevance for global business. Tele-conferencing is an extension of telephony that makes it possible for groups of people in different locations to hear and speak to each other as if they were in the same room. Video-conferencing enables the conferring parties to see as well as hear and speak to each other. These forms of remote conferencing can substitute for face-to-face meetings, thus reducing the need for travel. However, they do not appear to be adequate substitutes for direct interaction in cases involving complex or sensitive negotiations such as the exploratory phase of contract discussions.

Computer conferencing combines electronic mail with network facilities. (Hiltz and Turoff, 1978) It permits groups of conferees to communicate with each other without having to be in the same place at the same time. In addition, conference participants have access to a variety of network resources such as word processing and database management systems. Computer conferencing provides the means for multi-party discussions of complex issues over extended periods.

Computer-based communication is only the most obvious form of technological mediation of human interaction. Video Display Terminals (VDT) serving as gateways to intra- and inter-office networks make it possible for employees to complete many tasks by themselves that used to involve joint efforts with co-workers. (Zuboff, 1982) These applications of information technology reduce the occasions for human interaction at work and attenuate the social bonds between coworkers. The net result is greater fragmentation of the social environment of the workplace. In such work environments, the treatment of people and places as mere abstractions on a balance sheet seems perfectly normal. Managers are thus free to manipulate people as if they were nothing more than production resources, because abstractification in the workplace conditions employees to accept the legitimacy of virtual organization.

The Ethical Environment

Abstractification and virtual organization have far reaching consequences for ethical behavior in global organizations. They signal a fundamental change in the social context of ethical choice. This change goes beyond the challenges posed by specific normative issues such as corporate responsibility for product and process safety, for community programs, for training of displaced workers, etc. The basic change we are pointing to is a systemic one that affects the way in which people internalize ethical norms, the means by which they form judgments, and the conditions under which they are called upon to make such judgments.

Computer-related crime in large organizations is evidence for this basic, systemic change. Before arguing the case, let us consider the extent and significance of such crime. In a recent study, the American Bar Association (ABA) concluded "that computer crime is today a large and significant problem with enormous potential for becoming even larger and more significant." (ABA, 1984, p. 40) As part of its study, the ABA distributed a survey questionnaire to one-thousand private organizations and public agencies throughout the United States. The results reported by the ABA are based on the responses of the 283 survey respondents.

More than 25 percent of the survey respondents reported known and verifiable losses from computer crime. The total annual losses reportedly incurred by this group were between $145 million and $730 million. This means that the average loss was between $2 million and just over $10 million. Reliable extrapolations to the United States as a whole are impossible, but the ABA's sample clearly reveals major financial losses from computer crime.

In addition to the risk of financial losses, public and private computer-using organizations are vulnerable to a variety of injuries from criminal acts involving the computer as object or instrument. This is especially significant for sensitive, private databases (e.g., medical records) and public agency files such as intelligence and social welfare record-systems.

The ABA found that 77 percent of the perpetrators of computer crimes reported in their survey were organizational insiders. Coupled with other findings about perpetrators (discussed below), this strongly suggests that something is amiss within the organization apparently victimized by computer crime. That something is the failure to maintain organization environments in which ethical conduct can flourish. Virtual organization and abstractification take their toll in impaired ethical skills.

Crozier (1964) has observed a vicious cycle in the organization of work. It goes something like this: management perceives a need to tighten work discipline to achieve higher productivity, improve quality control, etc.; workers respond by taking less interest and pride in their work; management perceives workers' reactions as a signal to tighten discipline even more; and around it goes. Such vicious cycles are probably not rare; but in the present climate of the search for excellence, with its emphasis on sensitivity to "human resources" (Peters and Waterman, 1983; Reich, 1983), a vicious cycle in the blatant form described would be taken as a sign of bad management. However, if the cycle occurs over a relatively long period, it is likely to escape notice. This is the more common form of what Crozier observed.

Excessive management control is not conducive to ethical conduct in an organization since it weakens the social foundations of such conduct. The making of ethical judgments is a skill that needs to be kept in good working order through practice, just like any other skill. Ethical behavior is more than being able to recite the rules of a code; values are not acquired once for all in a person's life -- they must be rehearsed, relearned, and reinforced continually through participation in a community. Tight management control, effected through fragmentation of work and employee surveillance -- seemingly natural consequences of virtual organization and abstractification -- reduces opportunities for practicing ethical skills.

If employees are not trusted by management, they will become untrustworthy. There is an apt analogy with child rearing: a child's willingness to accept responsibility is ultimately commensurate with the parent's willingness to delegate responsibility to the child. Moreover, formal supervision of employees, like law enforcement in cities, works best when disaffection is at a minimum. No social order -- corporation, city, nation -- can long endure if a large proportion of its people reject its claim to legitimacy. Under such conditions, obedience can only be assured through the exercise of naked power.

Mowshowitz (1978) introduced the concept of ethical space to study the effects of technology on ethical judgment. Ethical space refers to the arena in which individuals make ethical decisions and may be analyzed in terms of autonomy, opportunity, and rectitude. Autonomy signifies relative freedom to initiate action; opportunity means occasions for exercising ethical judgment in situations with real consequences for real actors; and rectitude refers to ethical performance, i.e., the degree to which an individual acts in accordance with generally accepted ethical norms and precepts. These primary features of ethical space depend on a number of secondary characteristics including: prerogatives, scope, internal influence, external influence, access to information and resources, responsibilities, allegiances, accountability, ethos, and personal morality.

The concept of ethical space provides a framework for analyzing unethical behavior in organizations. In particular, it can help to interpret and perhaps remove the root causes of computer-related crime. Global corporations themselves may be criminogenic in the sense that managers and workers alike may be operating in a diminished ethical space.

In a series of interviews with individuals who had been convicted of criminal acts involving computers, Parker (1975) constructed a profile of the typical "computer abuse perpetrator." The most striking features of the profile are 1) that the offenders were not professional criminals, 2) that their offenses involved small deviations from accepted practices, and 3) that "they were accepted as reliable, honest, bright, highly motivated in their work and most desirable people for a manager to hire." (Parker, 1975, p. 8)[2] This profile clearly does not describe pathological behavior. Criminal acts that deviate only slightly from accepted practices suggest a warped organizational ethos rather than morally defective individuals. It also appears that their organizations failed to win the allegiance of these offenders. This is apparent from what Parker terms the "Robin Hood Syndrome": several offenders asserted that harming individuals is immoral, but injuring organizations is permissible.

"Parker's observations suggest that the computer abuse perpetrators acted in a diminished ethical space. Insufficient opportunity to exercise consequential ethical judgment reduced their ability to make moral discriminations. This group of young, highly-skilled individuals worked in organizations that sanctioned practices only marginally different from criminal acts. The organizations failed to win their allegiance, and failed to provide an environment in which moral rectitude could be cultivated through the practice of making ethical judgments." (Mowshowitz, 1978, p. 680)

Ethical Conduct and The Culture of Global Business

Virtual organization has reached its most advanced stage of development in global businesses. The size, complexity, and objectives of multinational companies make them ideally suited to this kind of organization. As the culmination of an evolutionary process, virtual organization represents the ultimate achievement of management by the balance sheet.

One very important ethical implication of this orientation is the tendency of global enterprises to treat problems -- especially human problems -- as externalities, i.e., as extrinsic to business operation. In virtual organization, the consequences of corporate decisions and actions for suppliers, contracter, employees, consumers, and the residents of host countries are accounted for only as footnotes to figures on costs, sales, and net income.

The road from abstraction to cynicism and then to unethical conduct and criminality is not a long one. One is reminded daily of the first steps on this journey. Here is a random sample of newspaper headlines on the actions of some American-based multinationals: "Atari to Idle 1,700 at California Site, Move Jobs to Asia" (Wall Street Journal, 1983); "Ford to Cut Workers by 10,000" (New York Times, 1985b); "24,000 A.T.&T. Jobs to be Eliminated at Major Division"(Stevenson, 1985); "A.T.&.T. Moving Output of Some Phones to Asia" (New York Times, 1985a); "1,877 Jobs Go from Shreveport, La., to Singapore" (Reinhold, 1985).

Multinationals can still make these moves with impunity because they are under no legal compulsion to deal with the consequences of unemployment. When a division is shut down and managers move to a new location, they are spared the unpleasantness of witnessing the plight of the unemployed and the community. Sensitivity is the first casualty of abstraction. Fragmentation of production, work, and decision making make it difficult to accept -- or easy to evade -- responsibility for actions taken in the name of a giant corporation.

The long-term, and often devastating, effects of actions

such as plant closures are left to government authorities unwilling or unable to cope with them. What is more, there can be little doubt about the destructiveness of protracted unemployment. The disruption of the black American family is the result of "permanent joblessness and the devaluation of working-class black men." (Norton, 1985) If unemployment becomes more generalized, the problem of the black family will become the problem of the American family.

In a recent New York Times opinion-editorial, Charles Ansell, a psychologist, asks "What's happened to conscience?" (Ansell, 1985) Several well-publicized cases of unethical conduct are cited as evidence of the "adulteration of our view of conscience." Three of the cases involved American-based multinationals, namely, E. F. Hutton, General Dynamics, and General Electric. E. F. Hutton has admitted to an elaborate check-kiting scheme; General Dynamics and General Electric were both accused by the Pentagon of improper billing in their contract work for the Federal Government.

These cases are not anomalies. Choose a daily newspaper at random and with high probability there will be an article on some kind of white-collar crime. Williams (1985) in an article entitled "White-Collar Crime: Booming Again" argues that "Economic pressures, a new permissiveness and simple greed are eroding corporate morality." This explanation -- and countless others like it -- are valid as far as they go, but they overlook the more fundamental problem of systemic change resulting from virtual organization and abstractification.

Ansell's groping question "What's happened to conscience?" is the right starting point; but the answers will not be found by focusing on the failure of individuals -- who just happen to be executives or employees of large corporations -- to act ethically. Ultimately, responsibility must rest with individuals, but ethical norms are socially defined, the acquisition of values is a social process, and the application of normative principles is a social act.

Something is amiss in the corporate world, but hortatory moral appeals will be as potent a palliative as were former President Ford's WIN buttons in the war against inflation. To internalize organizational norms and to act in accordance with them, individuals need to be rewarded for good conduct and to have good role models to emulate. Above all, individuals need to feel part of a community perceived to be legitimate and caring. Virtual organization, because it treats individuals as abstract resources, prevents the formation of stable communities within organizations. Without these communities, there is not social base either for reinforcement of ethical conduct or for the legitimation of role models.

The ethical dilemmas faced by multinational enterprises stem from the way the firms are organized and managed. To prescribe remedies designed to correct or punish wayward individuals is to treat symptoms rather than causes. Displacement of labor and disruptions of local communities, certainly among the most important consequences of multinational actions, may be perceived by some managers as posing ethical dilemmas. However, virtual organization prevents such sensitivity from altering corporate policy. The same goes for issues of product safety, plant operations, cultural sovereignty, investment in developing countries, and all the rest.

The hold of virtual organization on multinational corporations is indicated by the way these issues surface. International product safety is an issue because of questionable marketing practices such as the peddling of infant formula in developing countries. Plant operations receive attention after such disasters as the leak of toxic gas in Bhopal, India. Cultural sovereignty is an issue because global enterprises sell education and cultural programs that bypass the institutions of host countries. Investment in developing countries is controversial because multinationals absorb local investment capital to the disadvantage of local enterprises.

Virtual organization militates against sensitivity to human problems and the needs of local communities. Without adjustments to organization and management, designed to compensate for the abstract treatment of human relationships and regional identification, the ethical dilemmas will persist and the controversies will intensify. Global enterprise is the sociopolitical organization of the future, and its constituency embraces more than the stockholders and executives of the traditional corporation. Indeed, that constituency reaches beyond those directly involoved in company activities to the many individuals and communities dependent on the company. This broad constituency will eventually have to be acknowledged by the multinational corporation, and not relegated -- as externalities -- to the footnotes of the balance sheet.

REFERENCES

American Bar Association (1984). Report on Computer Crime. ABA, Section of Criminal Justice. Washington, D.C.

Ansell, C. (1985). "What's Happened to Conscience?" New York Times, July 3, 1985.

Barnet, R. J., and Muller, R. E. (1974). Global Reach. New York: Simon and Schuster.

Business International (1983). "Transborder Data Flow: Issues, Barriers and Corporate Responses." Report, Business International, New York.

Crozier, M. (1964). The Bureaucratic Phenomenon. Chicago: University of Chicago Press.

Forbes (1984a). "Better Late than Never." Forbes 134 (1). pp. 129-133.

Forbes (1984b). "The Ever-Rising Sun." Forbes 134 (1). pp. 134-140.

Fromm, E. (1955). The Sane Society. New York: Rinehart & Company.

Hiltz, R. S., and Turoff, M. (1978). The Network Nation: Human Communication via Computer. Reading, MA: Addison-Wesley.

Mowshowitz, A. (1978). "Computers and Ethical Judgment in Organizations." In: ACM 78: Proceedings of the 1978 Annual Conference, pp. 675-683. New York: Association for Computing Machinery.

Mowshowitz, A. (1986). "Social Aspect of Office Automation." In: Advances in Computers, Volume 25 (M. Yovits, ed.), in press.

New York Times (1985a). "AT&T Moving Output of Some Phones to Asia." New York Times, July 6, 1985.

New York Times (1985b). "Ford to Cut Workers by 10,000." New York Times, August 23, 1985.

Norton, E. H. (1985). "Restoring the Traditional Black Family." New York Times Magazine, June 2, 1985.

Parker, D. B. (1975). "Computer Abuse Perpetrators and Vulnerabilities of Computer Systems." Report, SRI, Menlo Park, California.

Perlmutter, H. V. (1965). "L'entreprise internationale -- trois conceptions." Revue Economique et Sociale 23 (2), pp. 151-165.

Peters, T. J., and Waterman, R. H., Jr. (1982). In Search of Excellence. New York: Harper & Row.

Pipe, R. (1984). IBI survey on TNCs and TFD. In: The CTC Reporter, No. 17 (United Nations Centre on Transnational Corporations), pp. 42-43. New York: United Nations.

Reich, R. B. (1983). The Next American Frontier. New York: Times Books.

Reinhold, R. (1985). "1,877 Jobs Go from Shreveport, LA, to Singapore." New York Times, September 2, 1985.

Robinson, R. D. (1967). International Management. New York: Holt, Rinehart & Winston.

Stevenson, R. W. (1985). "24,000 AT&T Jobs to Be Eliminated at Major Division." New York Times, August 22, 1985.

Turner, L. (1970). Invisible Empires: Multinational Companies and the Modern World. New York: Harcourt Brace Jovanovich.

United Nations Centre on Transnational Corporations. The CTC Reporter, No. 17. New York: United Nations.

United States Congress, Senate Committee on Commerce, Science, and Transportation (1983). "Long-Range Goals in International Telecommunications and Information: An Outline for United States Policy." Washington, DC: United States Government Printing Office.

Vernon, R. (1977). Storm Over the Multinationals: the Real Issues. Cambridge, MA: Harvard University Press.

Wall Street Journal (1983). "Atari to Idle 1700 at California Site, Move Jobs to Asia." Wall Street Journal, February 23, 1983.

Williams, W. (1985). "White-Collar Crime: Booming Again." New York Times, June 9, 1985.

Zuboff, S. (1982). "New Worlds of Computer-Mediated Work." *Harvard Business Review* 60 (5), pp. 142-152.